[SPECIAL EDITION

USING
Microsoft®
Office Project 2007

CONTENTS AT A GLANCE

SPECIAL EDITION USING MICROSOFT® OFFICE PROJECT 2007

ISBN-13: 978-0-7897-3652-9

ISBN-10: 0-7897-3652-7

Library of Congress Cataloging-in-Publication Data

Special edition using Microsoft Office Project 2007 / QuantumPM.
   p. cm.
  ISBN 0-7897-3652-7
 1. Project management—Computer programs. 2. Microsoft Project. I. QuantumPM (Firm)
II. Title.

  HD69.P75S674 2007
  658.4'04028553—dc22   *658.404*

                    2007010927

Printed in the United States of America

First Printing: May 2007

Trademarks

Warning and Disclaimer

Bulk Sales

Que Publishing offers excellent discounts on this book when ordered in quantity for bulk purchases or special sales. For more information, please contact

   U.S. Corporate and Government Sales
   1-800-382-3419
   corpsales@pearsontechgroup.com

For sales outside of the U.S., please contact

   International Sales
   international@pearsoned.com

This Book Is Safari Enabled

The Safari® Enabled icon on the cover of your favorite technology book means the book is available through Safari Bookshelf. When you buy this book, you get free access to the online edition for 45 days.

Safari Bookshelf is an electronic reference library that lets you easily search thousands of technical books, find code samples, download chapters, and access technical information whenever and wherever you need it.

To gain 45-day Safari Enabled access to this book:

* Go to http://www.quepublishing.com/safarienabled
* Complete the brief registration form
* Enter the coupon code VTJ5-X81K-NS6F-HRLL-BL69

If you have difficulty registering on Safari Bookshelf or accessing the online edition, please e-mail customer-service@safaribooksonline.com.

Associate Publisher
Greg Wiegand

Acquisitions Editor
Loretta Yates

Development Editor
Kevin Howard

Managing Editor
Gina Kanouse

Project Editor
Andy Beaster

Copy Editor
Bart Reed

Indexers
Erika Millen
Larry Sweazy

Proofreader
Water Crest
Publishing

Technical Editor
Brian Kennemer

Publishing Coordinator
Cindy Teeters

Book Designer
Ann Jones

Compositor
Gloria Schurick

CONTENTS

III Project Execution Through Completion

13 Tracking Your Project Progress

ABOUT THE AUTHORS

Unlike most books, *Special Edition Using Microsoft Office Project 2007* was not written by an individual, but rather a group of experts from QuantumPM, LLC (QPM). The authors are undeniable experts; they have used Microsoft Project within their organization and have helped hundreds of customers understand and use this software. In addition, the QPM team works closely with the Microsoft team to support the rollout of the product and to provide input for future versions.

QuantumPM, LLC is a project, program, and portfolio management product and services firm that helps its clients create pragmatic and valuable solutions to address real-world problems. QuantumPM services include management consulting, technical consulting, training, hosting services, earned value management, and business intelligence solutions. To this end, QPM works closely with Microsoft, Inc., as a Gold Certified Partner, and with the Project Management Institute, as a Registered Education Provider and active participant in standards development and various local chapter activities. These partnerships allow QuantumPM, LLC to provide state-of-the-art products and services to its customers.

This book was written using a different approach than a lot of other books. In addition to the authoring team, several subject matter experts (SMEs) provided their expertise and guidance on the various aspects of the content. Contributing writers from the QPM team then composed chapters based on the author's and SME's input. Each participating member of the QuantumPM team has brought his or her unique perspective to this effort. Following are the QuantumPM team members who worked many long hours to develop the contents of this book:

- **Project manager and internal editor**—Genie Peshkova

- **Subject matter experts**—Kris Athey, Julie Batista, Rose Blackburn, Michelle Dalco, Steve Drevon, Mark Everett, Scott Footlik, Patti Jansen, Bruce Johnson, Yvonne Lett, Genie Peshkova, Jamie Wyant, and Russ Young

- **Authors**—Kris Athey, Rose Blackburn, Patti Jansen, Chris Newton, Genie Peshkova, and Russ Young

- **Contributing writers**—Chris Newton and Brian McCabe

ABOUT THE TECHNICAL EDITOR

Brian Kennemer has worked with Microsoft Office Project 2007 and its predecessor products for over 10 years. He was recognized by Microsoft as one of a select group of Most Valued Professionals (MVPs) for knowledge and contribution to the user community and was an MVP until last year when he joined Microsoft as a Project Server consultant. Prior to Microsoft, Brian was honored to work at QuantumPM as a consultant with some of the finest minds in the Microsoft Project partner community. Brian is an active member of the Microsoft Project Server community as a columnist for the MPUG newsletter and an active blogger about Project and Project Server. Brian lives near Bellingham, Washington, with his wife, Alicia, his daughter, Alivia, and his two sons, Riley and Jesse.

DEDICATION

This book is dedicated to two very important groups of people: our families and our customers.

Our families have been tremendously supportive and patient during the creation of this book. They supported us through empty periods of writer's block and anxious days when customer work took precedence over writing.

Our customers are the best. They challenge us daily with real-world problems that must be solved as efficiently as possible. They have helped us come up with creative solutions that combine practical business processes and best practices in project management with state-of-the-art tools such as Microsoft Project. We are much better consultants because of them.

In addition, we would like to dedicate this book to all project managers out there. Project management is an acquired skill as well as an art. Dedicated project managers make a difficult job look easy. They use the skills of communication and leadership, knowledge of the domain, and practical tools such as Microsoft Project to lead a team through a complex project to a successful conclusion. We applaud their efforts and hope that this book makes the journey a little bit easier.

ACKNOWLEDGMENTS

Over the past several years, we have worked closely with the Microsoft Office Project team. This group of people has helped us understand their plans for the product and the inner workings of the software. They continually seek advice on the future direction of Microsoft Project and have listened carefully to our input and that of their customers to design a product that provides project management capabilities to individual project managers as well as organizations.

QPM would also like to acknowledge the hard-working staff at Que Publishing who have helped make this book what it is today. We would especially like to thank Loretta Yates (acquisitions editor), Kevin Howard (development editor), Andy Beaster (project editor), and Bart Reed (copy editor) for their patience, collaboration, and efforts. It has been our pleasure working with them on a project of such a large scale.

WE WANT TO HEAR FROM YOU!

As the reader of this book, you are our most important critic and commentator. We value your opinion and want to know what we're doing right, what we could do better, what areas you'd like to see us publish in, and any other words of wisdom you're willing to pass our way.

As an associate publisher for Que Publishing, I welcome your comments. You can email or write me directly to let me know what you did or didn't like about this book—as well as what we can do to make our books better.

Please note that I cannot help you with technical problems related to the topic of this book. We do have a User Services group, however, where I will forward specific technical questions related to the book.

When you write, please be sure to include this book's title and author as well as your name, email address, and phone number. I will carefully review your comments and share them with the author and editors who worked on the book.

Email: feedback@quepublishing.com

Mail: Greg Wiegand
           Associate Publisher
           Que Publishing
           800 East 96th Street
           Indianapolis, IN 46240 USA

READER SERVICES

Visit our website and register this book at www.quepublishing.com/register for convenient access to any updates, downloads, or errata that might be available for this book.

INTRODUCTION

INTRODUCTION TO PROJECT MANAGEMENT AND MICROSOFT PROJECT

Throughout this book, you will see that project management is made up of two components: philosophy and tools. Although this book is primarily technical in nature, it is impossible to separate the technology from the environment in which it works. Microsoft Project is not a "silver bullet" that will solve all process problems. Although it is great software, it has limitations, and the primary one is that it is only as good as the processes and people that surround it.

WHY WE WROTE THIS BOOK

The Que Publishing *Special Edition Using* series is intended for both beginner and intermediate audiences. The primary purpose of this book is to provide you with knowledge about Microsoft Office Project 2007, a robust project management software application. This book is not meant to be a cradle-to-grave guide about Microsoft Office Project 2007, but rather provides guidance on using it in your everyday work. Although this book is procedural and referential in nature, it also includes theoretical information to get you familiar with the concepts applicable to project management.

The material covered in this book is simple enough for a beginner to understand, but also allows the reader to grow with the book as more advanced topics are covered as well.

Intermediate users will find that the material is new and interesting and provides practical tips, tricks, and guidelines based on the QuantumPM team's experience.

The team is excited to offer you the opportunity to look into their heads and get some practical, real-world examples on how to initiate, plan, execute, and close projects.

WHY YOU SHOULD USE MICROSOFT PROJECT

Microsoft technology solutions are accepted as the most user-friendly software tools in the world. They are easy-to-use and are also recognized as feature-rich tools that offer great flexibility. Microsoft Project 2007 is no exception to this rule. It automates the process of organizing, scheduling, recording, calculating, tracking, reporting, and analyzing schedule data for any project. The tool will help you achieve your project goals on time and within budget. The strength of the tool continues to grow because millions of users provide input to Microsoft regarding their use of the tool. This input is compiled along with industry best practices in regular releases of the software. You can use this software with the knowledge that it includes solid technology that is backed by the leader in the industry.

WHAT'S NEW IN MICROSOFT PROJECT 2007

Users of previous versions of Microsoft Project will be happy to see several new features in Microsoft Project 2007 that have been requested for a long time. The features identified in this section are explained in more detail in Chapter 1 and where appropriate throughout the book. The features are available in the desktop tools, Microsoft Project Standard and Professional 2007.

- **Multiple Undo**—The Multiple Undo feature is one of the most exciting additions to Microsoft Project 2007. It allows you to backtrack through recent changes or undo the most recent series of changes at once.

- **Change Highlighting**—When you make a change to a project, the Change Highlighting feature calls your attention to all fields affected by the change. Project managers can now see the impact of a change as it ripples through the tasks in the project.

- **Visual Reports**—Reports have always been an excellent way to examine and share data in Project. New to 2007 are visual reports, which display project information in visual charts, tables, or diagrams.

- **Task Drivers**—The Task Drivers feature opens a pane on the left side of the screen that displays information that impacts or *drives* the selected task.

- **Cost Resource Type**—The cost resource type enables users to identify specific fixed costs on a task, such as travel expenses or delivery charges for materials.

- **Budget Resource**—The budget resource feature allows the project manager to define budget at the summary-level task to represent capital budget or overall approved budget for the project.

- **3-D Gantt Chart Display**—Three-dimensional display of the taskbars in the Gantt Chart view makes the Gantt Chart view more visually appealing and eye-catching, especially when printed to show as a report.

NOTE

There are many additional features in the server components of Microsoft Project 2007 that will not be discussed in this book. For details on those features, refer to Sams Publishing book *Microsoft Office Project Server 2007 Unleashed*.

How This Book Is Organized

This book is divided into five parts, designed to be of interest to a wide variety of readers. Some of the chapters focus on planning and organization, whereas others are focused on technology details. The following information should help you decide which chapters are of most interest to you.

Part I: Getting Started with Microsoft Office Project 2007

Part I is an introduction to the software application and to the concepts within the project management domain. It is intended for all audiences to provide a context for the successful planning and managing of projects.

Chapter 1, "Power of Microsoft Project 2007," contains a general introduction to project management, explores the new features of the Project 2007 version, and introduces the tool.

Chapter 2, "Microsoft Project 2007 Quick Start," covers just the basics of using Microsoft Project 2007 and explains the minimum set of steps you have to take to create, manage, track, and close your project.

Chapter 3, "Microsoft Project and the Project Management Domain," explores the different project management standards, introduces commonly used terms, and helps to define how Microsoft Project fits into the various definitions.

Part II: Organizing for Success—Project Initiation and Planning

Part II starts with background on the best practices of the project management domain and walks you through all necessary steps that have to be performed during the initiation and planning of a project. In addition to the conceptual information, this part explores the features of Microsoft Project 2007 that help you accomplish this goal.

Chapter 4, "Getting Started After the Business Initiative Is Approved," discusses the concept of establishing the project scope, building the Work Breakdown Structure and creating the initial framework that you will need for a successful project.

Chapter 5, "Setting Up Project for Your Use," focuses on defining initial properties of your project as well as environment options and preparing the tool for planning your project.

Chapter 6, "Creating Your Project Schedule," explores the steps for defining and manipulating tasks.

Chapter 7, "Defining Task Logic," concentrates on defining relationships between tasks and creating task constraints.

Chapter 8, "Defining Project Resources," provides information about various resource types available in Microsoft Project 2007 and includes steps for creating the resource list for your project.

Chapter 9, "Understanding Work Formula Basics," helps you understand the subtleties of the Microsoft Project 2007 scheduling engine. You will learn about various factors that affect the way your tasks are scheduled. This chapter is key to understanding the logic behind the schedule created by Microsoft Project.

Chapter 10, "Scheduling Single and Multiple Resource Assignments," describes the process of assigning resources to tasks and discusses the complexities that occur when you use more than one resource on an task.

Chapter 11, "Using Standard Views, Tables, Filters, and Groups to Review Your Schedule," covers various strategies you can use to review different aspects of your project schedule.

Chapter 12, "Performing a Schedule Reality Check," discusses strategies you can use to ensure that your schedule is complete and realistic prior to moving into project execution.

PART III: PROJECT EXECUTION THROUGH COMPLETION

Part III guides you through the activities performed during project execution to maintain the accuracy of the project schedule. In addition, you will learn the actions you have to perform in order to successfully close the project.

Chapter 13, "Tracking Your Project Progress," focuses on the activities you perform for project tracking and explores various factors that affect tracking.

Chapter 14, "Analyzing Performance," covers the features of Microsoft Project 2007 that are available to determine how well the project schedule is tracking the project's performance.

Chapter 15, "Using Reports for Tracking and Control," describes the standard basic and visual reports and how they can be used for tracking your project progress.

Chapter 16, "Revising the Schedule," discusses actions you can take when things don't go according to plan. In addition, it explores the various strategies you can use to help when your scope, cost, and timeline do not meet expectations.

Chapter 17, "Closing the Project," covers the work required to properly close a project, report on its conclusion, and finalize the schedule.

PART IV: TAILORING MICROSOFT OFFICE PROJECT 2007 TO YOUR NEEDS

Once you master all of the standard features of Microsoft Office Project 2007, or if you want to explore the customization options Microsoft Project 2007 has to offer, this part will help you learn tips and tricks to achieve the exact results you need.

Chapter 18, "Managing Project Files," discusses how Microsoft Project 2007 stores, organizes, and uses various types of files. It provides background on the file that determines global settings and methods to save preferred settings.

Chapter 19, "Formatting Views," provides various options you can use to customize how information is displayed in various views.

Chapter 20, "Creating and Customizing the Basic Reports," explores options for customizing existing basic reports and provides instructions for creating new reports.

Chapter 21, "Creating and Customizing Visual Reports," discusses the many options you have when working with visual reports and what you can do to customize your project reports with information that is not available in a standard report.

Chapter 22, "Customizing Views, Tables, Filters, Groups, and Fields," describes the options you have to customize the look and feel of views, tables, filters, groups, and fields to streamline and optimize your daily management of the schedule.

Chapter 23, "Customizing Toolbars, Menus, and Forms," discusses what you can do to adjust and personalize the menus, toolbars, and forms within Microsoft Project 2007 that can help you increase productivity and efficiency.

PART V: MICROSOFT OFFICE PROJECT 2007 KNOWLEDGE IN DEPTH

Part V is designed for advanced users of Microsoft Office Project 2007. It explores advanced features for managing resources across projects and working with other applications.

Chapter 24, "Working with Multiple Projects," explores the complexities and benefits of working with multiple projects as well as options for creating a shared resource pool without using Microsoft Office Project Server 2007.

Chapter 25, "Resolving Resource Allocation Problems," discusses strategies you can use when resources are allocated to more work than they can manage. In addition, it explores many techniques for resolving resource conflicts as well as factors that create these types of scenarios.

Chapter 26, "Exporting and Importing Project Data," includes version compatibility options and ways to exchange selected parts of the information with other applications.

Chapter 27, "Manipulating Data Using Other Applications," explores ways to manipulate Project data by importing and exporting information with other applications.

WHO SHOULD READ THIS BOOK

This book is intended to be a comprehensive guide to the use of Microsoft Office Project 2007 for managing projects. This book is a great resource for project managers who are just starting out as well as ones who are experienced project managers.

This book is organized to follow the standard *PMBOK* process groups and discusses not only the features and functions of the tool, but also the practical application of project management concepts, best practices, and advice from consultants in the field.

SPECIAL FEATURES OF THIS BOOK

TIP

> Tips describe techniques and methods that the author has found to be very useful in streamlining or simplifying the use of a feature.

NOTE

> Notes offer advice to help you understand complex ideas or provide alternative explanations of concepts.

CAUTION

> Cautions are provided when the use of specific features may result in complex results that are not always necessary or useful in the situation described.

The Consultants' Tips section at the end of each chapter provides some additional advice from the project management consultants.

GETTING STARTED WITH MICROSOFT PROJECT 2007

CHAPTER **1**

POWER OF MICROSOFT PROJECT 2007

In this chapter

EXPLORING PROJECT MANAGEMENT

Welcome to *Special Edition Using Microsoft Office Project 2007*! This book will aid tremendously in using the tool to optimize your success. Unlike previous editions of this book, this one focuses exclusively on the two desktop software products: Project Standard and Project Professional. It describes the capabilities of the scheduling engine, which is used by project managers to plan and manage their projects, and does not include any of the Project Server capabilities. This was done to minimize confusion and focus solely on the product that supports the project manager.

The capabilities of the server product, Microsoft Office Project Server, and the associated desktop functions required to interface with it are described in detail in the Sams Publishing book *Microsoft Office Project Server Unleashed 2007*.

NOTE

> Microsoft has released several tools for project and portfolio management that have been designed to work together. They include two desktop tools—Microsoft Office Project 2007 Standard and Professional—and two server tools—Microsoft Office Project Server and Microsoft Office Project Portfolio Server. Only the desktop tools are addressed in this book.

If you are familiar with the other Microsoft Office tools, such as Word and Excel, you will quickly discover that many aspects of Project appear and function quite differently. Much of the menu setup and navigation is similar, but many of the screens and terms used throughout Microsoft Project 2007 may be unfamiliar to you. This book focuses on the differences and unique features of Microsoft Project. Familiarize yourself with the table of contents to get a feel for the flow and content of this book.

This chapter provides an overview of new features and how Project 2007 should be used to improve the role of the project manager. Upcoming chapters will drill into specific areas of the tool.

→ For more of a quick-start guide to using Microsoft Project 2007, which includes a walkthrough overview of how to use the tool, **see** Chapter 2, "Microsoft Project 2007 Quick Start," **p. 29**.

Before getting started using the tool itself, it is important that you take the time to understand the essentials of project management so that the tool can be used in its proper context. Microsoft Project 2007 is one of several tools that should be used to help project managers bring in their projects on time, on budget, and with the expected quality and functions. Microsoft Project 2007 is a scheduling engine. It does an excellent job of helping you keep track of what work needs to be done and the status of that work. It does have limits, however, and it cannot control the scope of your project or be used as a substitute for effective communication. So before you begin to enter tasks into the tool, take the time to organize your project for success. Use the information provided throughout Part I of this book to help you set up the project properly. The remainder of the book explores specific features and functions that will be much more useful if your project schedule is organized correctly.

Managing a project is different from operational management roles such as managing a business or department. Projects focus on change; they have specific goals and defined beginning and endpoints. Operational management tends to focus on a steady-state set of processes. There is no defined endpoint, and the work continues in a similar, repetitive nature. Because projects are designed to change the ways things are and they have definitive endpoints, the approach to project management is different.

NOTE

> Microsoft Project 2007 will help you organize your project data, create your project schedule, and manage your project overall. It will also aid in giving you the project management experience that is necessary to improve as a project manager. However, just as Microsoft Word will not make you a better writer, Microsoft Project will not automatically make you a better project manager. Your ability in this field will improve as you increase your knowledge and experience, and Project will contribute to that growth. You can leverage the features of Microsoft Project 2007 to help you, but you cannot rely solely on the tool itself.

Project management includes creating an overall plan (including a project schedule), leading a team to execute the plan, monitoring and adapting the schedule to changes, communicating progress to the project stakeholders, keeping the team focused on the project scope (the work that needs to be done to reach the objective), managing risks, and much, much more.

NOTE

> There is a difference between a project plan and a project schedule. A project *schedule* is the course of actions you intend to follow over time in order to reach the endpoint of your project. A project *plan* includes the project schedule, but is much larger overall. A project plan also involves defining the objective of the project, the team that will work to reach the objective, the budget, and so on. Microsoft Project is primarily a scheduling engine; it will create a project schedule based on the information you enter into the project file. It will also aid in tracking the progress on your project and organizing all of your project data.

The upcoming sections discuss the concept of managing a project, as well as provide a basic understanding of Project 2007. The chapters throughout this book describe implementing successful project management ideas using Microsoft Project 2007.

→ For more information on project management, **see** Chapter 3, "Microsoft Project and the Project Management Domain," **p. 69**.

PROJECTS ARE TEMPORARY

As stated previously, projects have a definitive start and finish. A project is a temporary endeavor that is finished when the project objective is reached. Each project is unique and should have a clear goal. Projects can be similar, but no project is ever duplicated exactly. Even if the plan and objective are the same on two separate projects, the project team and/or time period will be different. Thus, each project is unique.

Projects are temporary. However, *temporary* is a relative term. Some projects can take one week, whereas others can last for decades. A project is temporary in that its lifespan is less than that of the organization working on the project. It is temporary because it ends, and the end is intentional.

PROJECT OBJECTIVES ARE SPECIFIC AND MEASURABLE

In order for a project to be successful, the project objective(s) must be specific and measurable. That is, a project must have a specific goal that clearly can be labeled "complete" when reached. Vague generalizations do not provide a focus for the project to be successful. Projects like this result in a lot of work completed and resources expended but an endpoint that's never reached. For example, perhaps your organization takes on a project to design a new kind of car. You cannot simply say that the objective is to design a new car. You must develop a specific, measurable set of criteria as the goal, so you have an idea of exactly what to work for. Maybe the car must be a certain size, fall under a specific price range for the consumer, be a certain percentage more efficient than previous models, and so on. These are the kinds of things to identify before a project begins.

As a project manager, it is your responsibility to reach a clear goal with your stakeholders and then focus on executing the details of task management to reach the goal. Without defining this focus upfront, it is easy to lose direction of the individual task work that must be done to reach the end.

→ For more information about the scope statement of a project, **see** Chapter 4, "Getting Started After the Business Initiative Is Approved," **p. 87**.

PROJECTS ARE CONSTRAINED BY TIME, COST, SCOPE, AND QUALITY

Besides being temporary, with defined, unique sets of measurable objectives (scope and quality), projects are bounded by time and cost. In other words, all projects have limitations on the amount of time that can be allotted to work on them, the amount of money that can be spent, and the satisfactory quality level of the objective delivered at the end of the project.

Well-designed and managed projects balance three things: delivery of the desired *result* in as little *time* and for as little *cost* as possible. However, a tradeoff always needs to be made to determine which of the three is the most important. Individual task activities of the project also may be subject to constraints. Discussion of the tradeoffs with the stakeholders will help you prioritize so you can develop your plan and schedule.

Consider the following scenarios:

- The deliverable is required to be high quality, which likely will increase the cost and/or time spent working on the project to produce the high-quality deliverable. Projects in biotechnology or aerospace tend to fit in this scenario because the product produced by the project must protect human life.

- The project may be required to finish quickly, which may cost more to have more people working to finish on time and/or lower the quality to finish in time. Competitive situations such as a desire to be the "first to market" will prioritize time ahead of budget and quality.

1

- The cost is reduced, which may in turn reduce the quality of the deliverable and/or increase the time spent working, as less expensive resources may require more time to finish their work. "Do-it-yourself" projects tend to fit in this category.

As you can see, the project constraints are all related to each other. They form a type of push-pull relationship within the project; when one constraint is put into effect, the others are affected as well. This relationship is often illustrated by the triple constraint diagram, or the constraint triangle, as shown in Figure 1.1.

Figure 1.1
As a project manager, you must operate within the constraints of time (schedule), cost (budget), and scope or quality.

→ For more information about the domain of project management as it relates to Microsoft Project, **see** Chapter 3, "Microsoft Project and the Project Management Domain," **p. 69**.

WHAT MICROSOFT PROJECT 2007 CAN DO FOR YOU

Microsoft Project 2007 is extremely helpful for organizing, scheduling, recording, calculating, tracking, reporting, and analyzing schedule data for any project. The tool will help you achieve your project goals on time and within budget. However, using Microsoft Project 2007 does not guarantee you a successful project plan or project execution. When you take the time to learn how to organize your schedule and optimize the features of the tool, you will find that Project can help you in a number of ways:

- **Microsoft Project 2007 helps you create a better project plan and schedule**— Project forces you to think carefully about the details of your project because you must accurately enter all tasks necessary for successfully completing the project as defined in the scope statement. Thus, you create a better schedule and overall project plan because you can easily monitor activity and communicate information.

- **Microsoft Project 2007 helps you organize your project**—Dozens of screen views, tables, and reports are contained within Project that organize your project data in various ways. This makes it easy for you to visualize, organize, and adjust the project plan and schedule as work progresses. All of these screens are customizable, and you have the ability to create your own if none of the existing ones fully meets your requirements.

→ For more information about the screens in Microsoft Project 2007, **see** Chapter 11, "Using the Standard Views, Tables, Filters, and Groups to Review Your Schedule," **p. 369**.

→ For more information about creating and customizing views and tables, **see** Chapter 22, "Customizing Views, Tables, Filters, Groups, and Fields," **p. 755**.

→ For more information about creating and customizing reports, **see** Chapter 20, "Creating and Customizing the Basic Reports," **p. 657**, and Chapter 21, "Creating and Customizing Visual Reports," **p. 707**.

- **Microsoft Project 2007 accurately performs calculations**—Project will calculate a precise schedule based on the data you enter that illustrates when each task should begin and end. Additionally, if you enter cost data, Microsoft Project 2007 makes budget calculations and provides schedule data for a variety of reporting needs.

- **Microsoft Project 2007 makes it easy to search for the best possible project schedule and plan**—You can experiment with different scenarios by creating mock schedules for all possible circumstantial data for your project, and choose to work with whatever scenario produces the most desirable outcome.

- **Microsoft Project 2007 helps detect problems or inconsistencies in the schedule**—Project identifies when resources are overallocated (assigned more work than their schedule allows). Resources include the people, equipment, and facilities used to work on the project. Project also detects when deadlines are impossible to meet according to any constraints you have included in the schedule. The tool will help you resolve resource overallocation and deadline issues.

→ For more information about resolving resource overallocation, **see** Chapter 25, "Resolving Resource Allocation Problems," **p. 885**.

→ For more information about working with constraints and revolving deadline issues caused by constraints, **see** "Defining Constraints," **p. 223** (Chapter 7).

- **Microsoft Project 2007 helps communicate project data and the schedule to stakeholders and team members**—Poor communication is one of the primary causes for project failure. Use Project to help you communicate better. You can produce textual and visual reports with ease to illustrate any aspect of your project to clients, stakeholders, partners, team members, or anyone else who may be interested in project information of any kind. This makes it easier for you to obtain approval from supervisors and keep clients satisfied and informed with accurate, professional reporting data.

→ For more information about working with reports, **see** Chapter 15, "Using Reports for Tracking and Control," **p. 519**.

- **Microsoft Project 2007 helps you track progress and detect deviations from the plan**—After the schedule is created and approved and work begins on a project, you should enter actual data into the project file based on the progress. Project will compare this data to what was planned, and calculate any difference, or variance. You can then adjust accordingly to compensate for any deviation from the plan. Project also reschedules any remaining tasks and revises the finish date for the project based on the actual data.

→ For more information about tracking progress on your project, **see** Chapter 13, "Tracking Your Project Progress," **p. 443**.

- **Microsoft Project 2007 helps adjust the schedule when the situation changes—**
  Very rarely, if ever, is a project executed exactly as it is planned. Situations will arise
  when you need to adjust what was planned, sometimes quickly, and adapt to the new
  circumstances. Team members may leave the organization, work takes longer than
  expected, the scope of work changes, costs increase, and so on. Project helps to adjust
  and adapt to the changes.

→ For more information about adjusting and adapting to changes, **see** Chapter 16, "Revising the Schedule," **p. 557**.

The preceding list is just an overview of some of the things Microsoft Project 2007 can do
for you. As you examine this book further, apply its concepts, and become more familiar
with using Microsoft Project 2007, you will find it to be an extremely helpful tool for project
management. However, keep in mind that Project only works as well as the data you provide; if your data is inaccurate or incomplete, then your project file in Microsoft Project
2007 will be as well. Plan on taking the necessary time to accurately and carefully enter all
project data into the project file and establish a regular update cycle to keep it accurate.

ENTERPRISE VS. STANDARD THINKING

Project scheduling is an important function on its own, but many organizations also need
enterprise project management capabilities. They need to monitor an entire portfolio of
projects, share resources across the organization, store project artifacts, and collaborate more
effectively. Microsoft Office Project Server was designed to perform these functions and also
integrate with the desktop scheduling engine. The combination of tools provides a powerful
software system that supports the needs of many users, including leadership, the
Portfolio/Project/Program Management Offices, project managers, resource/staff managers,
and project team members.

A few additional features in Project Professional enable it to work with Project Server. The
Project Server features will be discussed only briefly in this book. For details on how the
Project Server software works, refer to the book *Microsoft Office Project Server 2007
Unleashed*, by Sams Publishing.

THE DESKTOP TOOLS: PROJECT STANDARD AND PROJECT PROFESSIONAL

As mentioned earlier in this chapter, Project Standard and Project Professional are desktop
scheduling tools. With the exception of collaboration and a few items discussed later in
this chapter, the features in both tools support the functions of creating and executing a
schedule.

Project scheduling, as described in this book, focuses on managing one project at a time.
With few exceptions, the features of the desktop tools are designed to affect only one project
schedule at a time.

→ Features that impact more than one project include master projects and resource pools. For more information on multiple project capabilities, **see** Chapter 24, "Working with Multiple Projects," **p. 853**.

1

COLLABORATION USING PROJECT PROFESSIONAL

Project Professional users have the ability to store their projects in Project Server, choose resources from an enterprise pool, and share information with stakeholders and team members using an Internet (Project Web Access) interface. Many of the capabilities can be performed from the Internet or via the Collaborate drop-down menu. If you are a Project Standard user, the Collaborate menu will not appear.

Figure 1.2 shows the Collaborate drop-down menu, located on the main menu in Project Professional.

Figure 1.2
The Collaborate drop-down menu in Project Professional allows you to perform many functions that work with Project Server, Microsoft's enterprise project management software.

The features available on the Collaborate menu provide an enterprise user with the ability to obtain updates from team members on task status, work with resources, perform enterprise analysis, and work with many project artifacts. As with many features in Project, users can customize the options to fit their needs.

WHAT'S NEW IN MICROSOFT OFFICE PROJECT 2007

Users of previous versions of Project will find several new features in Microsoft Project 2007. Take a moment to familiarize yourself with these new features, as they all improve the functionality of Project. All of the new features are discussed elsewhere throughout this book, so this section only provides an overview.

MULTIPLE UNDO

The Multiple Undo feature is one of the most exciting additions to Microsoft Project 2007. It allows you to backtrack through recent changes or undo the most recent series of changes at once. In previous versions of Project, you could only remove the last change made. Now, with the Multiple Undo feature, you can scroll down the list to the change you want to undo, and Project will undo that change and every change you made after it simultaneously.

The Undo button is located on the Standard toolbar. Previous versions of Project displayed this command as a curved arrow. In Microsoft Project 2007, a drop-down list has been added to the command button. To undo the most recent change, click the Undo button once without opening the drop-down list. To undo multiple changes at once, open the drop-down list by clicking the drop-down arrow located on the right side of the Undo command button. The drop-down list will display the most recent series of changes made. Select the change you want to undo, and Project will undo that change along with all the other changes listed above it. Each change that Project will undo is highlighted (see Figure 1.3).

Figure 1.3
The Multiple Undo feature allows you to undo the most recent series of changes simultaneously.

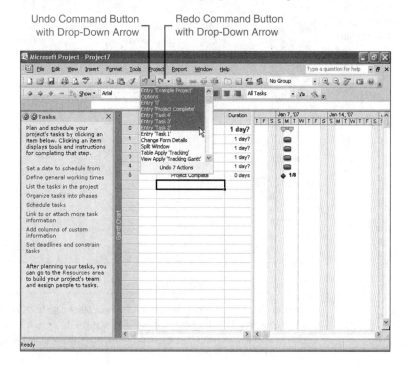

Undo Command Button with Drop-Down Arrow

Redo Command Button with Drop-Down Arrow

There is also a Multiple Redo feature, which functions in the same fashion as the Multiple Undo feature, only redoing the changes rather than undoing them.

CAUTION

As with many Microsoft tools, certain actions, such as Save, will purge the stack of changes, so make sure you have the file looking the way you want it before you save.

CHANGE HIGHLIGHTING

When you make a change to a project, the Change Highlighting feature calls your attention to all fields affected by the change. After you make the change, all affected task and resource fields are highlighted. This allows you to easily see how your change affects the other project data fields. The Change Highlighting feature is a great timesaver when you need to see how a change in one task ripples through the rest of your project.

You can opt to enable or disable the Change Highlighting feature. Select View from the main menu, and select either Hide Change Highlighting to disable the feature or Show Change highlighting to enable it. Figure 1.4 shows an example of fields affected by the most recent change.

Figure 1.4
The Change Highlighting feature highlights data fields that are affected by changes you make in the project.

Fields Affected by the Most Recent Change

TIP

> Use the Change Highlighting feature to view how other data fields are affected by changes you make to the project. If the Change Highlighting feature alerts you to changes in the data fields that are undesirable, undo the original change with the Undo (or Multiple Undo) feature.

VISUAL REPORTS

Reports have always been an excellent way to examine and share data in Project. Previous versions of Project always displayed reporting data in a text format. New to 2007 are visual reports, which display project information in visual charts, tables, or diagrams.

NOTE

> All of the basic text reports found in previous versions of Project still exist in Microsoft Project 2007.

Visual reports use either Microsoft Office Excel 2007 or Microsoft Office Visio 2007. The reports themselves can be modified in both their data content and their appearance.

To access the existing visual reports, select Report, Visual Reports. This will open the Visual Reports – Create Report dialog box, as shown in Figure 1.5. Select which report you wish to display, and click View to display it.

Figure 1.5
The Visual Reports –
Create Report dialog
box houses all of the
existing visual reports,
displayed using either
Excel or Visio.

Figure 1.6 displays a Cash Flow report, created in Excel. The report has been modified to appear three-dimensional. The color and background have also been altered.

Figure 1.6
The Cash Flow report
is an example of an
Excel visual report.

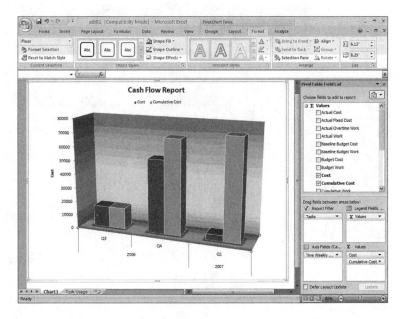

→ For more information about visual reports, including how to customize them, **see** Chapter 21, "Creating and Customizing Visual Reports," **p. 707**.

TASK DRIVERS

The Task Drivers feature opens a pane on the left side of the screen that displays information that impacts or *drives* the selected task. In other words, the Task Drivers pane displays the task's scheduled start date, predecessor dependency relationship information, calendar used to schedule work on the task, resource(s) assigned to work on the task, and other important information that influences the start date of the selected task.

NOTE

> A *predecessor* task is a task whose start or finish determines the start or finish of another task. Therefore, in the Task Drivers pane, all predecessor tasks—those tasks whose start or finish date determines the start or finish date for the selected task—are listed.

→ For more information about predecessor tasks and task dependency relationships, **see** "Linking Tasks," **p. 201**.

To view the Task Drivers pane, select Project from the main menu, and select Task Drivers. The Task Drivers pane will appear on the left side of the screen, as shown in Figure 1.7. With the Task Drivers pane displayed, you can click on any task in your task list to show its Task Drivers information. In Figure 1.7, "Task 2" is selected, and the Task Drivers pane shows the appropriate information for what drives Task 2.

Figure 1.7
The Task Drivers pane shows information for items that influence the start date of the selected task.

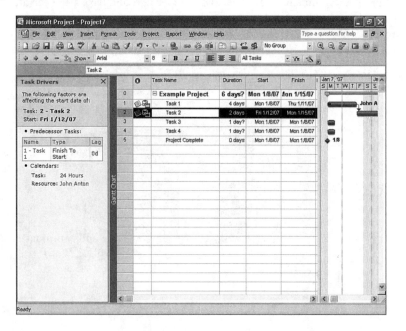

Furthermore, you can click on any hyperlink in the Task Drivers pane to view additional information about that particular item. In Figure 1.7, you could click on the name "John Anton," the resource assigned to work on Task 2, to view his resource calendar information.

COST RESOURCE TYPE

A new resource type has been added to Microsoft Project 2007 in addition to the existing resource types (work and material): the cost resource type. The cost resource type enables users to identify specific fixed costs on a task, such as travel expenses or delivery charges for materials. Cost resources will help the project manager improve the accuracy of the project budget; you can now more accurately model a type of project cost that was not easy to do in previous versions.

→ For more information about the resource types in Project 2007, **see** "Defining Resources and Resource Information," **p. 252**.

BUDGET RESOURCE

In addition to cost resources, Microsoft Project 2007 includes a special type of resource—budget. Any resource defined within your project can be designated as a budget resource. The budget resource feature allows the project manager to define budget only at the summary-level task to represent capital budget or overall approved budget for the project. This resource does not get updated automatically by Project; it is used more by the project manager to compare the baseline or actual project costs to the overall allotment for the project. To set a resource to be a budget resource, open the Resource Information dialog box and select the Budget check box on the General toolbar.

→ For more information about the resource types in Microsoft Project 2007, **see** "Defining Resources and Resource Information," **p. 252**.

3-D GANTT CHART DISPLAY

Also new to Microsoft Project 2007 is the three-dimensional display of the taskbars in the Gantt Chart view. As you may know, taskbars are time-phased visual displays of each task's duration, located on the timescale side of the Gantt Chart view. In previous versions of Project, the taskbars appeared as flat, square bars. In Microsoft Project 2007, the taskbars appear in 3-D and cast a small shadow. This makes the Gantt Chart view more visually appealing and eye-catching, especially when printed to show as a report.

INTRODUCTION TO THE MICROSOFT PROJECT 2007 INTERFACE

It is important to familiarize yourself with the interface and appearance of the Microsoft Project 2007 screen before really beginning to use this tool. Open it up and experiment with all the options using your mouse and keyboard. Once you become comfortable with navigating around the screen, you will be more comfortable with using the tool in general. If you are new to Microsoft Project, Chapter 2, "Microsoft Project 2007 Quick Start," will be a great aid in helping you learn how to get around.

NOTE

Users of previous versions of Project will not find very many changes in the Project 2007 interface. Some of the main menu options have changed, and some toolbars contain new or different command buttons, but in general, the screen appearance is similar to Project 2003.

→ For more information about navigating the Project interface, **see** "Navigating Microsoft Office Project 2007," **p. 32**.

The Gantt Chart view is the default view that is displayed when your first open Project. You can choose to display other views by selecting them from the View option on the main menu. Each view is advantageous for various reasons and is customizable.

→ For more information about using the standard views in Project, **see** "Understanding Standard Views," **p. 378**.

→ For more information about customizing views, **see** "Creating and Customizing Views," **p. 764** .

The following sections discuss some of the basic elements of the Microsoft Project 2007 interface and reference other areas of this book where more information can be found.

MICROSOFT PROJECT 2007 MENUS

The main menu area of Microsoft Project 2007 contains dozens of options you can use for formatting, saving, printing, displaying, editing, reporting, and just about anything else you can think to do to your project file. The main menu options have changed between Project 2003 and Project 2007.

Users of Microsoft Office tools will likely be familiar with the functionality of the main menu in Microsoft Project 2007. Different options are divided into categories. These categories are listed across the top of your screen in the main menu area (see Figure 1.8). Click on any of the menu categories, and a drop-down list will appear. Make your selection from the drop-down list by clicking on the selection, and Project will make the appropriate action based on your selection.

Project Guide Sidepane　　　　　　Main Menu Area

Figure 1.8
Select a main menu category, then make your selection from the drop-down list under that particular category.

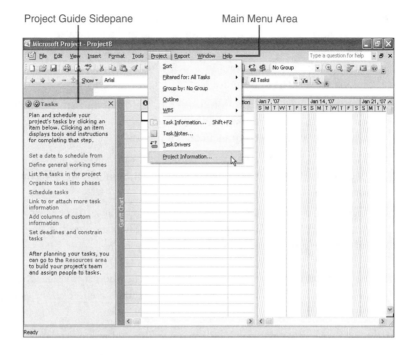

The following is a list of the main menu categories in Project 2007 and a brief description of their functionality. Many of these actions will be described in greater detail throughout this book:

- **File**—Perform general project file functions, such as open a new or existing project file, save, print, and so on.

- **Edit**—Edit the data using actions such as undo/redo, cut/copy/paste, fill cells, link/unlink tasks, and so on.

- **View**—Select different views to display from the drop-down list or by selecting More Views to open the More Views dialog box. Also, turn the Change Highlighting feature or the Project Guide on and off, select which toolbars to display or hide, and use the Zoom command to zoom in or out on your screen.

- **Insert**—Insert items such as a new task, recurring task, new project, column, drawing, object, hyperlink, and so on. Generally, you must select the location where you want to insert the item first, then make your selection from the Insert drop-down list.

- **Format**—Format different items on your screen. Select an item and format it specifically, or format the entire screen in general. You can format items such as text font, bar styles, gridlines, screen layout, and so on.

- **Tools**—The Tools category contains helpful devices such as spelling and grammar check, resource leveling, tracking options, and so on. Two important dialog boxes are accessed from the Tools menu: the Change Working Time dialog box (select Tools, Change Working Time) and the Options dialog box (select Tools, Options).

- **Project**—Perform project file-specific actions, such as sort, group, or filter your data, as well as view specific task information, enable the Task Drivers pane, and attach notes to tasks. The Project Information dialog box is accessed from the Project menu (select Project, Project Information), in which you set the project attributes. The Project menu options are displayed in Figure 1.8.

- **Report**—The Report menu displays your reporting options. Select Reports to view the basic reports, Visual Reports to view the visual reports, and Copy Picture to copy images from your screen to include in a report.

- **Window**—The Window menu category performs specific actions to your screen or window. The most used command is Window, Split, which splits the screen vertically to display two separate views.

- **Help**—Use the Help menu option to get help on any aspect of Project you are confused about. Select Help, Microsoft Office Project Help to open the Project Help dialog box, and you can type in an item to search for help.

The preceding list items are the categories found in Microsoft Project Standard 2007. Project Professional 2007 contains all of the same main menu options as Project Standard 2007, plus some Enterprise options.

Microsoft Project Professional 2007 has one additional menu category:

- **Collaborate**—The Collaborate menu option in Project Professional 2007 allows you to collaborate with the server. You can request updates or progress information from your team members, who are notified of your request through Project Web Access. You can also update your project status to the server, and access all the risks and issues associated with your project. You have access to the Project Center, which displays all projects published to the server, and Resource Center, which displays the enterprise resource pool. You can assign resources from the Resource Center to work on your project without having to reenter all their resource information. The Collaborate menu options are displayed in Figure 1.2.

Besides the Collaborate menu category, Project Professional 2007 also contains additional options in some of the other main menu categories:

- **File**—In addition to all Project Standard options, the File menu in Project Professional allows you to publish your project to the server and save your project file for sharing.

- **View**—The View menu contains one additional view option in Project Professional: the Enterprise Gantt Chart view. This view is one that includes fields defined in a standard manner for the entire enterprise. The fields are customizable, so they will vary by organization.

- **Tools**—The Tools menu in Project Professional allows you to build your resource team from the Enterprise resource pool on your server, substitute resources, and access a version of your project from the local project cache. There is also a selection for Enterprise Options, which allows you to open Enterprise Global, open the Enterprise resource pool, and import your project file or resources to Enterprise.

MICROSOFT PROJECT TOOLBARS

As in other Microsoft Office tools, Microsoft Project 2007 contains several toolbars, each of which contains command buttons for performing various actions to your project file or project data. To display or hide any toolbar, right-click on the toolbar area and select the toolbar you wish to display or hide. By default, the Standard and the Formatting toolbars are displayed when you open Microsoft Project 2007. Toolbars are also customizable.

→ For more information about using and customizing the toolbars in Project, **see** "Customizing Toolbars," **p. 817**.

MICROSOFT PROJECT GUIDE AND HOW IT CAN HELP YOU

The Project Guide is a built-in tool in Project that walks you through many of the common actions you perform on your project file. The Project Guide is especially useful for novice Project users. It appears as a pane on the left side of the screen when enabled (refer back to Figure 1.8). By default, the Project Guide is displayed when you open a new project file. You can click the X in the upper-right corner of the Project Guide pane to hide it.

You can also display the Project Guide toolbar by selecting Show or Hide the Project Guide from the View menu drop-down list. Alternatively, right-click in the toolbar area and select Project Guide. If Project Guide is not available as one of the options, follow these steps:

1. Open the Options dialog box by selecting Tools, Options.
2. On the Interface tab, select Display Project Guide by checking the box. Click OK to close the Options dialog box.
3. Right-click in the toolbar area. The Project Guide option will now be displayed. Select it to display the Project Guide toolbar.

The Project Guide can be extremely helpful in getting started with creating your project file and schedule, managing and tracking your project, managing your resources, and reporting.

→ For more information about using the Project Guide, **see** "Using Learning Aids," **p. 38**.

MICROSOFT PROJECT 2007 VIEW BAR

You can opt to display the View Bar in Project 2007, which is a vertical bar that houses several of the popular views in Project. With the View Bar displayed, you can simply click on the view in the View Bar that you wish to display, rather than selecting the view from the View menu.

The View Bar is not displayed by default when you first open Project. To display it, select View, View Bar. The View Bar will appear vertically on the left side of your screen, as shown in Figure 1.9.

Figure 1.9
Select View, View Bar to show the View Bar, which you can use as a shortcut to display the most popular views in Project 2007.

View Bar

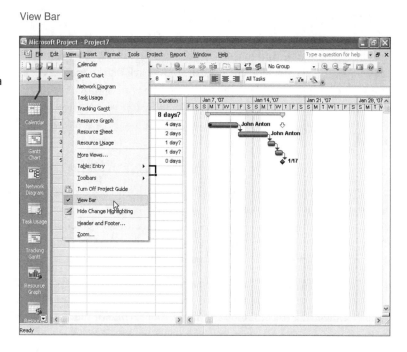

CONSULTANTS' TIPS

Microsoft Project 2007 is an excellent tool that can help a project manager be successful if it is used in the right way. There is much more to success than scheduling, however, so it is extremely important that you understand what the tool can do and what it cannot. The following set of recommendations are intended to help you put Microsoft Project in context as a tool that can support you but cannot be used as a substitute for leadership. Microsoft Project is a key component of project success but it does not stand alone.

COMMUNICATE

People skills and the ability to communicate in a healthy, understandable way are perhaps the most important part of project management. You can have all the greatest ideas in the world, but without being able to communicate those ideas to your team members, you are on your own. Use the data in Project to help you, but do not depend on it to be your only communication tool.

DEFINE PROJECT ROLES

Obtain clarity regarding the roles of everyone on your project team. Do not assume that your role as the project manager is clear just because you put a schedule together. There are many things that can complicate project roles. For example, in matrix-managed organizations, the team members may be assigned tasks by many other project managers on many other projects, so you will need to make sure they are as engaged in and committed to your project as you are.

Define Project Deliverables Prior to Building the Schedule

Involve your team in the planning stage of the project. Build the schedule interactively by first defining what deliverables need to be created and only then determine how the work will be done and who will do it. You will have a more complete schedule and a team that understands what they need to do.

→ For more information about defining a project's scope deliverables, and creating a Work Breakdown Structure (WBS), **see** Chapter 4, "Getting Started After the Business Initiative Is Approved" **p. 87**.

Define the Project Goal

State the goal of the project as concisely and as clearly as possible. Everyone associated with the project should be able to understand the project goal, including your supervisors who approve the project, other project managers involved with the project, and team members who perform the work on the project. Document the project goal in a summary statement, with language that is easy to understand. The goal should be realistic and measurable. You can only measure your success if you can measure your goal. "Design a new car" is not an acceptable goal, but "Design a new car that is 20% more efficient than last year's model" gives you a specific direction. There is more to it than this, of course; refer to Chapter 4 for details.

Create the Work Breakdown Structure

Avoid the tendency to create a schedule with chronological phases and tasks when you first open Project. Instead, first complete a Work Breakdown Structure (WBS) to define the deliverables at the level of work packages. This is probably the most important thing you can do to fully define and manage the scope of your project successfully. Again, Chapter 4 has more information on this.

Communicate the Schedule to Your Project Team

Document and distribute the planned project schedule to all people involved with supervising or working on the tasks. Be sure you answer any questions they have, and ensure that they fully understand and agree with their role in the schedule. Address their disagreements and revise the schedule as necessary based on their comments, and redistribute the revised schedule, complete with charts and tables that clearly identify the work flow and scope of the project. Be sure that everyone understands their responsibilities for successfully completing the project.

Acquire Commitment from the Project Team

Secure a firm commitment from all project team members and outside resources (such as subcontractors and so on) to do the work assigned to them as outlined in the project plan, with no deviation unless otherwise approved by you.

1

TRACK YOUR PROJECT PERFORMANCE DURING EXECUTION

When work on the project begins, monitor carefully the progress by tracking actual performance, and enter that data into the project file regularly. When variances arise, adjust the plan accordingly.

Tracking accurate performance information also helps document the history of the project, which will be useful for future similar projects. This is especially useful if unforeseen problem areas arise, and will be valuable in explaining why project goals were not met. Also, if problems arise that are significant enough to delay the project's completion, you can give ample warning to stakeholders who are expecting the project to finish on time, so they can prepare for the adjustments on their end.

CLOSE YOUR PROJECT AND RETAIN HISTORY

When work on a project is finished, document the entire process. This serves not only as a summary and closure on the project, but also as a history of what lessons were learned to improve performance on the next project.

CHAPTER **2**

MICROSOFT PROJECT 2007 QUICK START

In this chapter

INTRODUCTION TO PROJECT MANAGEMENT

Okay, so you have acquired Microsoft Office Project Standard 2007, you have installed it on your computer, and you are ready to go. Now, only one small obstacle is standing in the way of your rise to Supreme Project Manager: How does this thing work?

While this entire book encompasses the various concepts and methods behind fully utilizing Microsoft Project 2007, this chapter will provide an overview that will help you to get started immediately without having to read over a thousand pages first. Think back to when you were younger: Did you ever receive a present you just wanted to dive into and figure out its intricacies later? That is what this chapter is for—to help you dive into using Microsoft Project 2007 without going into too much detail. Maybe Microsoft Project is the present you have been asking for all year, or maybe it is something that was simply installed by your company for you to use (perhaps even against your will). Whatever the case may be, this chapter will aid you tremendously in getting started with the tool and introduce you to many of the concepts discussed in greater detail throughout this book.

NOTE

This chapter is a "quick start" to Microsoft Office Project 2007; it will walk you through the entire life cycle of a project from beginning to close (in this case, a kitchen remodeling project). However, it is only an overview. There are many cross-references to other areas throughout this book that discuss in much greater detail the concepts and methodology introduced in this chapter.

There are five main functions (referred to as process groups) for any project: Initiating, Planning, Executing, Monitoring and Controlling, and Closing.

→ For more information about the five process groups, **see** "Project Management Body of Knowledge (PMBOK)," **p. 71**.

The process groups have a logical, iterative flow (you begin with Initiating, cycle through Planning, Executing, and Monitoring and Control, and then end with Closing), with a recommended set of components to consider in each group. They do not imply the life cycle to be used for running your project but rather should be used to help you consider all of the components that may be required during your project's life.

During Initiation, the purpose and goals of the project are clarified with the stakeholders. It is here that a project manager should be assigned to the project, and the first scope statement is created. The *scope* will include the agreed-upon objective and set of project deliverables that must be completed to reach the end goal. The upcoming section "Define Project Scope" will discuss this concept further.

Microsoft Project probably will not come into play for you during Initiation. Its use typically begins during Planning. Microsoft Project desktop's primary purpose as a scheduling engine is to help you create a project schedule based on the deliverables and objectives you enter when setting up a project. In other words, Microsoft Project will help you plan your course of action before you begin work on a project.

To accomplish this, the scope is decomposed into a set of deliverables (*what* the project will deliver) and then further decomposed into activities and assignments (*how* work will be done). In Project, you break up work into *tasks* as defined by the scope's deliverables. The work on these tasks is performed by different types of *resources*, which can be anything from people and machinery to ink and camera film. A resource is anything you might use to complete a task. Therefore, resources you define within the project are assigned to different tasks throughout the project during the Planning process group. This quick start will focus on how you assign people resources.

Project calculates the start and finish dates for each task (and thus the entire project) based on the amount of work hours or duration you estimate for the task, and its relationship to other tasks in the project. The upcoming section "Create a Project Schedule Using Microsoft Project" will provide more information on the Planning process group.

People sometimes use Project in the planning process to create a schedule for the project, but do not maintain it for execution of the project. This happens because the schedule has become too difficult to maintain. If it was not organized in a logical decomposition from scope to deliverables to tasks, the schedule can become a disjointed set of activities that may or may not be focused on completion of deliverables. If the project is organized correctly, you should have a detailed understanding of what needs to happen, and when, in order to successfully execute the work on your project.

However, there has never been a project that was executed exactly as it was planned, and there likely never will be. Situations arise where resources cannot work on a task at the time they are scheduled to, additional work needs to be added as tasks in the schedule, one task is delayed, which in turn delays additional tasks that are dependent on its completion, and so on. You need to continue to review the schedule to see if it is executing according to plan.

The fourth process group, Monitoring and Controlling, occurs in conjunction with the Executing process group. While most of the activities of execution fall on your resources and project team, as a project manager you are essentially responsible for tracking the progress as compared to the plan. Project provides many helpful features that allow you to accurately track your progress, compare it to your original plan, and calculate the variance between what is actually happening and what was supposed to happen. Then, with that information, you can adjust your plan of action and the schedule itself to make sure you can accomplish the project goals. The upcoming section "Track Your Project" will discuss in greater detail how Project can aid in executing, monitoring, and controlling your project.

NOTE

> The Planning, Executing, and Monitoring and Controlling process groups are cyclical. Changes will occur as work is performed in the Executing process group based on tracking data you analyze in the Monitoring and Controlling process groups, and you may have to go back and adjust the plan. Expect to repeat this cycle throughout your project. It is normal to revert back to Planning as you track your project because you need to add a new task or reduce the scope of an activity. In fact, it would be considered bad practice if you did not readjust the plan based on the actual progress of the project.

Finally, when all work on a project is complete and all deliverables are accounted for, it is time to close the project, which is discussed near the end of this chapter in the section "Close Your Project."

This chapter demonstrates the use of the process groups using a real-life example to give you a feel for how to manage a successful project using Microsoft Office Project 2007. For this discussion, the example of remodeling the kitchen in your house will be used.

NAVIGATING MICROSOFT OFFICE PROJECT 2007

Before you start to create your project schedule using Microsoft Project 2007, it is important that you understand the functionality of the tool itself. Users of Microsoft Office tools may be familiar with many standard navigating aspects, but some features are unique to Project.

Figure 2.1 illustrates the appearance of your screen when you first open Microsoft Project 2007 based on the default settings. Notice the main menu and toolbar areas, the task entry grid, the time-phased Gantt Chart, and the Project Guide.

Figure 2.1
When you first open Project, your screen will look similar to this illustration.

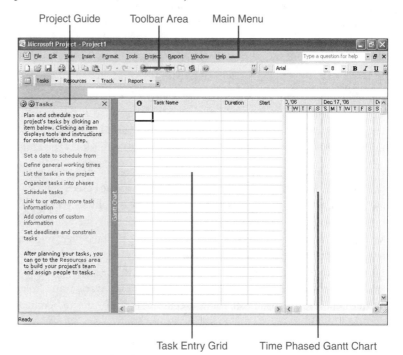

Project Guide   Toolbar Area   Main Menu

Task Entry Grid   Time Phased Gantt Chart

The following list briefly describes the five areas called out in Figure 2.1:

- **Main menu**—The main menu bar functions the same as other Microsoft tools. Options appear via drop-down lists when you click on one of the menu items.

→ For more information about the main menu options, **see** "Microsoft Project 2007 Menus," **p. 22**.

- **Toolbar area**—Like in other Microsoft tools, the toolbar area in Project houses the toolbars you wish to display. By default, the Standard and Formatting toolbars are displayed, along with the Project Guide toolbar if you are displaying the Project Guide (as in Figure 2.1). If you are unsure of a function of a particular button on any of the toolbars, hover your mouse pointer over the button, and a ScreenTip will appear. To display or hide any of the toolbars, right-click in the toolbar area and select the toolbar from the resulting list.

→ For more information about the toolbars and the buttons they contain, **see** "Reviewing the Built-in Toolbars," **p. 817**.

- **Task entry table**—The task entry table on the left is one half of the Gantt Chart view, which is the default view (and is discussed in the next section). It displays task information. Type a name directly into the Task Name column to create a new task, and define its information using this or other tables you can display. You can also opt to enter information by selecting the cell and typing into the Edit field above the table. This area functions similarly to an Excel spreadsheet.

→ For more information and helpful tricks for creating and manipulating the task list, **see** "Manipulating the Task List," **p. 161**.

- **Gantt Chart**—The right half of the Gantt Chart view is the time-phased display of the tasks. This area displays task bars that correspond to the tasks listed to the left in the task entry table. The separator bar between the timescale and the task entry table can be moved left or right to display more of either area, or you can use the scroll bars as with other Microsoft tools. The next section discusses in greater detail the Gantt Chart view.

- **Project Guide**—The Project Guide is a handy feature, especially for novice Project users. It walks you through various procedures within Project, such as creating schedules, managing resources, tracking, and reporting on your project.

N O T E

> The Project Guide pane and Project Guide toolbar are displayed by default when you create a new project file. To hide the Project Guide pane, click the X in the upper-right corner of the pane. To hide the Project Guide toolbar, right-click on the toolbar area and deselect Project Guide. To display the Project Guide, select Tools, Options, and on the Interface tab, check the box next to Display Project Guide.
>
> Many experienced Project users do not display the Project Guide to save screen space. For the same reason, the Project Guide does not appear in many of the figure illustrations throughout this book.

Like other Microsoft tools, Microsoft Project 2007 is navigated by using the various drop-down lists and command buttons found on the main menu and toolbars. Use the File option from the main menu to open, save, or print new or existing project files. To change the view or table displayed, select View from the main menu and then make your choice. More navigating options are discussed throughout this chapter and throughout this book in general. The following sections describe specific navigation options you should familiarize yourself with before creating your project schedule.

2

TIP

> The right-click function can also be a very helpful navigating shortcut. You can right-click almost anywhere on your screen to display various options for formatting, viewing, editing, and so on.

INTRODUCING THE GANTT CHART VIEW

As previously mentioned, the Gantt Chart view is the default view when you open Project. It has two main areas: the task table and the timescale. The task table lists the tasks and their accompanying information in a text or entry table, whereas the timescale is the visual aspect of the schedule showing task bars for each task listed in the table. The task bars show the duration of each task, from their planned start date to their planned finish date, over time.

NOTE

> The timescale side of the Gantt Chart view is unique to the Gantt Chart view and the Tracking Gantt Chart view only. It is a popular way of examining the overall timeline of a project, task by task, and is therefore the default view in Project because of its effectiveness.

Figure 2.2 shows a simple example of a Gantt Chart view. Notice that the task bars on the timescale side are displayed on the same row as the tasks they represent.

Figure 2.2
In the Gantt Chart view, tasks are listed on the table and visually represented on the timescale.

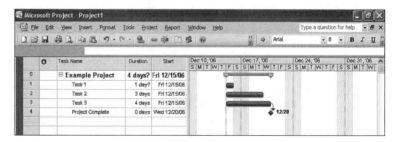

The timescale side of the Gantt Chart view displays time-phased information. You can choose to zoom in or out to show more or less of the task bars over time. For longer projects, it may be advantageous to zoom out on the timescale, allowing you to see more of your projects' task bars. Or, you can zoom in to specific time periods across your project. To zoom in or out of the timescale, select View, Zoom. This will open the Zoom dialog box, as shown in Figure 2.3.

As an alternative, you can also right-click on the timescale headings and select Zoom. Both methods will display the Zoom dialog box.

TIP

> The Standard toolbar contains Zoom In and Zoom Out buttons, which can also be used to zoom in or out on the timescale.

Figure 2.3
Zoom in or out of the
timescale using the
Zoom dialog box.

Choose from the list of zoom options in the Zoom dialog box. You can also choose to display the entire project or customize the zoom value. The smaller the time unit you select, the less will be displayed on your screen. In other words, zooming into one week will show less information than one month, but will also allow you to see more time-phased detail on the task bars. When you make your selection, click OK.

The vertical divider bar between the timescale side and the task table on the Gantt Chart can be moved left or right to show more of either side. To do so, follow these steps:

1. Hover your mouse pointer over the divider bar. The mouse pointer will become a double-sided arrow pointing left and right.
2. Press and hold the mouse button, and drag the bar either left or right.
3. When you have reached the desired location, let go of the mouse button.

You can display many tables in the task grid. In Project, views display tables of project information. By default, the task entry table is displayed in the Gantt Chart view, which displays the task ID field, Indicator, Task Name, Duration, Start date, Finish date, Predecessors, and Resource Names. To display another table, follow these steps:

1. Select View, Table. A list of the more popular tables appears, as well as an option for more tables.
2. Choose from any of the tables in the list, or choose More Tables to open the More Tables dialog box. The More Tables dialog box contains additional tables to choose from.

→ For more information about using tables in Project, **see** "Understanding Standard Tables," **p. 395**.

You can display many different tables on the left-hand side; however, the timescale side of the Gantt Chart view will still be displayed. The task list will remain, but different information about those tasks will be shown depending on which table you chose to display.

You can also opt to insert other data columns into any table. Perhaps you do not want to display a different table entirely, but just want to add a few additional columns. For example, the Work field is not displayed in the task entry table on the default Gantt Chart view. It may be useful to see the Work field, especially if your estimates for tasks are provided via hours of work rather than duration. To add another column into a table, follow these steps:

1. Select the place you wish to insert the new column by clicking the header of the column that is currently there. When you insert the new column, the selected column, and all columns to the right of it, will shift to the right to make room for the newly inserted column.

2. Select Insert from the main menu, and choose Column. This will open the Column Definition dialog box.

3. In the Column Definition dialog box, choose the column you wish to insert by selecting it from the drop-down list in the Field Name field. You can give it a different name by typing it into the Title field. The title will be the field name if nothing is entered into the Title field. If you do rename the column, you can hover your mouse over the column title, and you will see Project's original name of the column.

4. Define the alignment of the column heading and the data it holds. You can also define the width of the column. Both of these items are optional; if you do not define the alignment and width specifically, Project will format the column automatically.

5. Click OK when you are finished, closing the Column Definition dialog box and inserting the column based on your definitions. You will have to perform the same operation for each column you want to insert; you cannot insert multiple columns at the same time.

→ For detailed information on customizing views, **see** Chapter 22, "Customizing Views, Tables, Filters, Groups, and Fields," **p. 755**.

SCROLLING, SELECTING, AND ENTERING DATA FIELDS

Most of the views you can display in Microsoft Project 2007 are interactive, allowing you to use your mouse and keyboard to navigate and modify the data. As with other Microsoft Office products, Microsoft Project 2007 contains scroll bars when information is available beyond the current screen size. You can use the arrows to scroll vertically or horizontally, or you can drag the mouse through the scroll bar to your desired destination. If your mouse has a scrolling wheel, you can scroll up or down using that wheel.

To select or work with data in any field in a task table, click the mouse in the field. You can also use the arrow keys on your keyboard to navigate through the fields. If you double-click on any field in a task table, the Task Information dialog box will appear. It will provide more details about the selected task and can be used to update information.

→ For more information about using the Task Information dialog box, **see** "Editing Tasks Using the Task Information Dialog Box," **p. 159**.

When entering data in a table, you can either type directly into the cell, or select the cell and type into the Edit field located above the table, as in Excel. Sometimes, a cell will be grayed out, meaning that data cannot be entered into the cell. Generally that data is calculated automatically using other project information.

EXPLORING THE LOOK AND FEEL OF MICROSOFT PROJECT

Microsoft Office Project 2007 contains dozens of views to display and enter data in your project. To display any of them, select View from the main menu, and choose the view from the drop-down list or by selecting More Views. Selecting More Views will open the More Views dialog box, which contains all of the standard views available in Microsoft Project 2007. Each view has its advantages; some views will show task information, some will show resource information, some will show tracking information, and so on.

➔ For more information about using the standard views for specific situations, **see** Chapter 11, "Using Standard Views, Tables, Filters, and Groups to Review Your Schedule," **p. 369**.

Two views to mention are the Resource Sheet view and the Resource Usage view. These views will be helpful when you are entering and assigning your resources to tasks or reviewing existing assignments. They will be discussed in the upcoming section "Create Your Team and Assign Resources." To display either of these, select View and choose either Resource Sheet or Resource Usage.

While each view will display different kinds of project information, they all function similarly and can be navigated by using the methods described thus far in this chapter.

It is also worth noting that each view is customizable to varying degrees, and you have the ability to create a new view from scratch if none of the standard views meets your needs.

➔ For more information about creating and customizing views, **see** "Creating and Customizing Views," **p. 764**.

EXPLORING MICROSOFT PROJECT WINDOW

This chapter has already discussed the menu and toolbars located at the top of your Microsoft Project 2007 screen, as well as the task table and timescale sides of the Gantt Chart view. Each view is also able to be split, which displays a second view on the bottom half of the screen. Whereas the Gantt Chart view contains two parts divided by a vertical bar, a split view is divided horizontally.

To split the window in any view, select Window, Split. Unlike a lot of other Microsoft applications that provide a duplicate display of the content in the new window, the split window in Project provides a totally different display of the content to help you analyze or review your data. To remove the split and return to the original view (the one displayed in the top pane of a split window), select Window, Remove Split.

Figure 2.4 displays the Gantt Chart view after the Window, Split command is applied.

By default, the Task Form view is displayed on the bottom half of the screen when you split the window in a task view (such as the Gantt Chart view). The Resource Form view is displayed when you split the window in a resource view (such as the Resource Sheet view). You can display any view you want by selecting the bottom pane (click anywhere below the divider bar) and choosing View from the main menu. Select the view from the drop-down list or from the More Views dialog box.

Figure 2.4
Splitting the window in any view displays a second view in the bottom pane, which shows more detailed information.

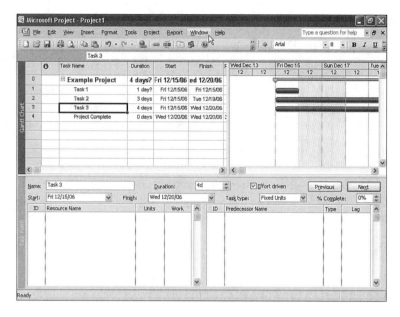

The Task Form view (or Resource Form view) shows specific information in the bottom pane for the task (or resource) that is selected in the top pane. In Figure 2.4, the task "Task 3" is selected in the top pane, and the Task Form in the bottom pane shows its detailed information. If the task had any resources assigned to it, they would appear in the left column under the Resource Name heading. Similarly, if the task had any predecessor task relationships, they would appear in the right column under the Predecessor Name heading. Task dependency relationships will be discussed in the upcoming section "Create Task Dependency Relationships."

Splitting the window is advantageous to view more detailed information for the items in the top pane, or to display two different views at once to compare the information contained in both views simultaneously.

Additionally, you can choose to display or hide any of the toolbars in Microsoft Project 2007 by right-clicking in the toolbar area and selecting or deselecting any of them. Each toolbar is built for changing specific areas of the Project window, from working with the data itself to formatting the display. Furthermore, each toolbar is customizable, so you can modify the toolbar commands to better meet your needs or preferences.

→ For more information about customizing toolbars, **see** "Customizing Toolbars," **p. 817**.

USING LEARNING AIDS

Project comes equipped with two primary aids for you to use when you are unsure how to do something or what function any feature in Microsoft Project 2007 serves. They are the Project Guide and the Help feature.

THE PROJECT GUIDE

The Project Guide can be enabled, as previously described, by displaying the Project Guide toolbar. Right-click in the toolbar area and choose Project Guide. If it is not an option, it is disabled. To enable it, follow these steps:

1. Open the Options dialog box by selecting Tools, Options.
2. Select the Interface tab.
3. Check the box next to Display Project Guide, and click OK.

To display the Project Guide, click the icon on the far left side of the Project Guide toolbar. As an alternative, you can select View, Turn On Project Guide from the main menu to display the Project Guide toolbar and open the Project Guide automatically. The Project Guide appears on the left side of the screen, as shown previously in Figure 2.1.

The Project Guide has four main categories: Tasks, Resources, Track, and Report. Click on any of these four categories on the Project Guide toolbar, and the options related to that particular category will be listed on the Project Guide pane. Alternatively, you can click the arrow next to each category's name on the Project Guide toolbar, and the options will be displayed in a drop-down list.

The options found in the Tasks category guide you through the process of planning and scheduling the tasks in your project. The Resources category aids in building your resource list and assigning your resources to tasks. The Track category helps you track and manage the progress on your project. And the Report category walks you through the process of reporting on the data in your project.

Many relatively inexperienced Microsoft Project users find the Project Guide helpful because it walks them through various processes that are integral to managing a successful project. However, people with more experience tend not to use the Project Guide as much because it takes up screen space and they are generally familiar with most of the concepts it holds.

TIP

In addition to walking you through various processes in Microsoft Project 2007, the Project Guide can also serve as a checklist. When you are finished creating your task list and schedule, open the Project Guide and verify that you have done everything it has listed under the Tasks category. Similarly, when you have finished creating and assigning your resource list, double-check the Project Guide to see if there is anything you may have missed.

PROJECT'S HELP FEATURE

The Help feature in Microsoft Project is also quite handy when you are stuck in a situation you are unsure how to resolve. Many dialog boxes in Microsoft Project 2007 have a Help button that will open the Help feature to information regarding that specific area or dialog box you are working in. In addition, the main menu has a Help option, located on the right side of the list (next to Window). Select Help, then select the first option, Microsoft Office

Project Help, to open the Project Help box. Choose from the categories listed in the box, or type in the area you wish to find help for in the Search box at the top of the Project Help box. For example, you could type in a question, or the key words of your question, and Project will search helpful information related to your entry. Figure 2.5 shows the context-sensitive help that is available within Microsoft Project 2007.

Figure 2.5
Choose Help, Microsoft Office Project Help to open the Project Help box. Type in the key-words to search for, or select from the categories listed in the box.

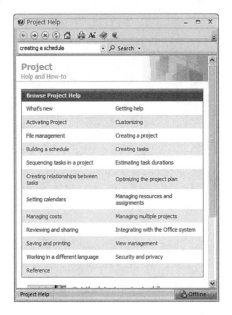

DEFINE PROJECT SCOPE

Before you begin to create the schedule for your project, you must first define and document the project's scope.

The stakeholder and fulfiller build a joint vision of the end result of the project. This joint vision sets the framework for the *scope* of the project. Therefore, to create your project's scope, you must identify exactly what the goals and limitations of the project are, define how you will measure the project's success, and what specific deliverables will be required to declare that the project is complete. In other words, defining a project's scope is defining exactly what you are trying to achieve, how you will achieve it, and how you will know you have achieved it.

It is very important to work through the scope and deliverables before you create a schedule. This seems like common sense, but that concept can be easy to forget when you factor in all other elements of beginning a project.

Determining and documenting your projects' objectives is an important part of your scope statement. Discuss with all project stakeholders exactly what the objectives of the project are, what is expected to be delivered at the end of the project, and what limitations will be enforced when working on the projects' tasks.

As mentioned previously, every project has to have a defined end goal. This is generally broken down into two parts: the Measure of Success (MOS) and the Final Deliverables. The Measure of Success is the framework for what is and is not included in the project. The MOS focuses on the desired result, and not the process of reaching it.

The Final Deliverables are a measurable set of components that must be met in order for the project to be considered successful and complete. Unless the criteria is specifically defined and documented up front, it is difficult to decide when a project is "good enough," because the stakeholders have different expectations.

For example, the reason for remodeling the kitchen could be to increase its efficiency, make it wheelchair friendly, or simply modernize an outdated look. Whatever the case may be, the MOS and Final Deliverables have to be measurable. In this example, there are hundreds of possible interpretations of what is meant by "efficient" or "modern." Until the reasons and measurements for the remodel are clear and the deliverables are defined, you cannot create a schedule that the stakeholders will agree meets their expectations.

The MOS sets the direction for the remodel and should drive all decisions behind what is included in the scope and what is out. Once that is clear, the final deliverables can be determined. There can be a difference in defining *a* remodeled kitchen and *this* remodeled kitchen. The more clarity you can achieve here, the easier it will be to measure success.

→ For more information about defining a project's scope, **see** Chapter 4, "Getting Started After the Business Initiative Is Approved," **p. 87**.

BUILD AND DECOMPOSE THE WBS

Building your Work Breakdown Structure (WBS), as part of defining your project's scope, is an important step between defining your scope statement and creating your schedule. It is imperative to build and decompose your WBS to give you an idea of the breakdown of work. With a WBS, it will be easier to construct your project schedule by breaking the work into logical deliverable components that further break down into tasks.

Think of your WBS as an outline of the work, designed in a tree diagram. The lowest level of the WBS contains the work packages—that is, the tasks and actions to complete the work. This diagram can be created using Microsoft Office Word, Visio, and a variety of other tools, or it can be drawn on a whiteboard. It can even be created within Microsoft Project with the use of an add-on tool called WBS *Director*. For more information on WBS Director, review Microsoft Project tools at www.quantumpm.com. No matter how you choose to build it, creating a WBS is a project management best practice and an opportunity to brainstorm and organize before creating the actual schedule.

NOTE

Building a WBS is a step that often gets overlooked. However, it is an important step because it allows you to lay all the work elements out in front of you, and gives you a foundation for creating your task list. Similar to constructing an outline before writing a research paper or drawing up blueprints for a new house, building a WBS organizes the work on your project.

→ For more information about building a WBS, **see** "Work Breakdown Structure," **p. 92**.

Generally, your WBS will have at least three levels. The first level is the project itself. From this top level, you *decompose* the work on your project. The next level lists all the major products, services, or common components in the project, and the third level and below decomposes the components from the second level. Decomposition below the third level will vary with the complexity of the project and the specific deliverable.

As you are drilling into each level, you are decomposing your work. Avoid the initial tendency to break the work into process groups because this tends to limit your thinking and you may miss some pieces of the scope. Use nouns when building the WBS, as opposed to an action verb–noun combination.

In the example of the Kitchen Remodel project, the first level of the WBS is "Kitchen Remodel." The next level is organized by major deliverable categories and includes Management, Preparation, Vendors, Surfaces, Storage, and Appliances. The third level, partially decomposed in Figure 2.6, lists further decomposition of each item in the second level.

When it is time to create your project schedule, you can build a task list by using the organization through the lowest level in your WBS (the work package level). This process is discussed in the upcoming section "Build Your Project Schedule Using the WBS."

Figure 2.6 shows an example of a WBS, created using Microsoft Office Visio. Notice the three levels and the tree diagram format. This is a very basic example; not all items of the Kitchen Remodel project have been listed, but this example gives you an idea of the look and feel of the WBS and its content.

Figure 2.6
Typically, a WBS is built in a tree diagram, decomposing the major components of a project. The task list is built using the WBS.

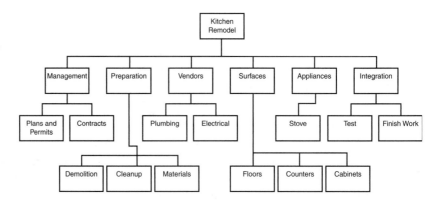

CREATE A PROJECT SCHEDULE USING MICROSOFT PROJECT

Once you have created your scope statement, have documented and distributed it to all project stakeholders, and have the approval to move forward, it is time to create your project schedule.

As mentioned previously, Microsoft Project 2007 is a scheduling tool. You will use Microsoft Project 2007 to create a project schedule based on task information you define. It is best to avoid entering start or finish dates for any tasks when you begin. Entering start or finish dates for tasks creates date constraints for those tasks. Instead, enter educated estimates of the tasks' durations or work hours, and be sure to accurately define all task dependency links, and Project will schedule them to start and finish accordingly. Upcoming sections will discuss entering task information and dependency links more thoroughly.

Table 2.1 is a quick checklist of how you would create a project schedule. It may be helpful for you to use this checklist as a quick reference when you create a schedule for your project. The items in the left column (the "Step" column) will be discussed in the upcoming sections. The kitchen remodel example will be used to maintain consistency in illustrating the steps involved with properly creating a project schedule in Microsoft Project.

TABLE 2.1 CHECKLIST FOR CREATING YOUR PROJECT SCHEDULE

Step	Complete? (Y/N)
Use project schedule templates or create a new project	
Set project attributes	
Set the project start date	
Select a project calendar	
Set the project summary task	
Build your project schedule using the WBS: 　　Enter or adjust summary tasks and subtasks 　　Create milestones 　　Set deadlines	
Create task dependency relationships	
Create your team and assign resources in Microsoft Project	
Enter estimates in Microsoft Project	
Adjust schedule based on estimates and resources	
Baseline your schedule	
Track your project: 　　Obtain project status 　　Enter your tracking data 　　Analyze your status 　　Adjust the schedule based on status	
Close your project	

USE PROJECT SCHEDULE TEMPLATES OR CREATE A NEW PROJECT

There are two primary ways to begin to create your project schedule: use one of the templates or create a new project from scratch. To view the project templates that come with Project, follow these steps:

1. Open Project and select File, New. A New Project pane will appear.

2. Under the Templates heading, select On Computer, which will open the Templates dialog box.

3. In the Templates dialog box, select the Project Templates tab, and a list of available project templates will be displayed, as shown in Figure 2.7.

4. Scroll through this list to see if any of the template titles relate to your project. You can click them once to see a preview in the Templates dialog box, or double-click them to open the templates.

→ For more information about creating a project template in Project, **see** Chapter 18, "Managing Project Files," **p. 581**.

Figure 2.7
Select a template to use for your new project from the Project Templates tab in the Templates dialog box.

You or your organization may have your own templates for similar projects that you can also use. Although using a template can be advantageous, creating a new project from scratch may be more beneficial for you in terms of familiarizing yourself with the overall functionality of Project.

To create a new project, select File, New and then select Blank Project. Alternatively, just click on the New Project icon on the Standard toolbar. For the example of a kitchen remodel, a blank project will be used.

If you choose to create your project schedule from an existing template, you will have to modify the data that is stored in the template to tailor it to your specific project. To do so, use the same methods described in the upcoming sections.

SET PROJECT ATTRIBUTES

The first step in creating your project schedule is to set your overall project attributes. To do so, open the Project Information dialog box by selecting Project, Project Information from the main menu. The Project Information dialog box will appear, as shown in Figure 2.8.

Figure 2.8
Define your general project attributes in the Project Information dialog box.

SET THE PROJECT START DATE

In the Start Date field of the Project Information dialog box, choose the date you want to begin the actual work on your project. When you begin entering tasks, Microsoft Project 2007 will automatically plan to have the first task start on this date, and continue scheduling forward from there. The first task will be assigned to begin at the time your working day starts on the date you enter in the Start Date field. The working time will be discussed in the upcoming section "Select a Project Calendar."

When you have entered the start date for your project, you cannot enter a finish date. Microsoft Project 2007 will automatically define the project's finish date based on the task information. In other words, if you enter a start date of January 8, 2007, Project will schedule the first task to begin on January 8, 2007. Microsoft Project 2007 will then schedule the rest of the tasks based on the durations and dependency links you define, and the finish date will be automatically defined as the day the last task is scheduled to finish. If you are entering dates other than the project start date, you are not utilizing Microsoft Project as a scheduling engine.

→ For more information about project start and finish dates, **see** "Understanding the Project Information Dialog Box," **p. 108**.

> TIP
>
> Be sure that the Current Date field in the Project Information dialog box is accurate. The Status Date field is used for tracking, controlling, and reporting on your project; leave it "NA" for now.

SELECT A PROJECT CALENDAR

The project calendar is defined in the Calendar field in the Project Information dialog box and is very important to the schedule of your project. The project calendar defines the working time for your project: which days are working days, which hours are considered working time in a typical workday, which days are nonworking time (such as holidays and so on). For the Kitchen Remodel project, the Standard calendar will be used.

Three default project calendars already exist for you to select in the Calendar field drop-down list:

- **24 Hour**—Continuous time from midnight to midnight, 24 hours a day
- **Night Shift**—Used for overnight work that begins at the end of one night and finishes the following morning
- **Standard**—The standard workweek in the United States: 40 hours, 5 days (M–F), 8:00 a.m. to 5:00 p.m., with an hour lunch break from 12:00 p.m. to 1:00 p.m.

If none of these three calendars match your typical working time, you will need to create a new project calendar and assign the newly created calendar in the Project Information dialog box.

→ For more information about creating a new project calendar, **see** "Defining Calendars," **p. 118**.

TIP

> You can define working time exceptions, such as holidays, vacation, and so on, in the Exceptions tab of the Change Working Time dialog box. This process is discussed in detail in the "Defining Calendars" section of Chapter 5, "Creating a New Project."
>
> Figure 2.9 provides an illustration of the Change Working Time dialog box. Notice the Exceptions tab. Select Tools, Change Working Time to open this dialog box.

Figure 2.9
Create new project calendars in the Change Working Time dialog box.

CAUTION

> If you do not specify a project calendar, Project will use the default (Standard) calendar. This is acceptable if you are working on the remodel during normal U.S. business hours. However, if you plan on working on the remodel during different hours, such as evenings and weekends, you will need to create and define those working hours on a new calendar and apply it to your project as described in this section. If not, Project will schedule your tasks based on incorrect working time, and your project will likely get off track quickly in terms of schedule.

TIP

> The preceding explanation on project calendars is more of an overview to help get you started. It is recommended that you take the time to read more about calendars in Chapter 5.

SET THE PROJECT SUMMARY TASK

Set up the project summary task (task ID number "0") on your project so you can see rolled up information that summarizes your entire project at a glance. Also, the name of your project shows as the task name in the project summary task. To set the project summary task, follow these steps:

1. Open the Options dialog box (Tools, Options).
2. Select the View tab (if it is not already selected).
3. Check the box next to Show Project Summary Task in the lower-right corner.

→ For more information about the project summary task, **see** "Selecting the Display Options for Outlining," **p. 173**.

BUILD YOUR PROJECT SCHEDULE USING THE WBS

When you have defined your project calendar, it is time to start building your task list in the project schedule. As mentioned previously, work on a project is broken down into tasks. While the WBS lists your work breakdown, the task list is the breakdown of the WBS into actions. The WBS is discussed in the previous section "Build and Decompose the WBS."

To enter a task into the project, simply type the task name into the Task Name field on the Task Entry table (the task grid) in the Gantt Chart view. Be sure to use an action verb and a noun, and be as specific as possible. A person should be able to read your task name knowing nothing about your project, and know exactly what the task is trying to accomplish.

Once you type the task name into the Task Name field, you can press Enter or use your arrow keys to move out of the cell. The task will be entered into the list. Some of the other fields will be filled in automatically (such as Duration, Start, and Finish). Do not worry for now about entering any other data into these fields; they will be discussed throughout this chapter. For now, enter the task names only.

Use your WBS to enter each major component, followed by each task within that component. List the major components ahead of the corresponding tasks. It is not required to list the tasks in chronological order, but it is recommended. You can always go back and move tasks, or insert new ones you may have forgotten.

For example, the WBS for the Kitchen Remodel project has "Surfaces" listed, with items such as "Cabinets" and "Floors" listed underneath it. You would likely create one or more tasks below "Floors," such as "Install Flooring," based on the items in the WBS. Underneath that task, you would enter more detailed tasks, such as "Install Underlayment" and "Install Tile," to provide more specific activities. The task names contain a comprehensive, descriptive action verb–noun format, and are organized as specific activities within a project process group.

TIP

> If you use the convention recommended for the WBS, it will be easy to see the difference between the WBS components and the tasks. WBS components are expressed as nouns (for example, "Cabinets") and tasks are expressed as actions with a verb and a noun ("Install Lower Cabinets").

Therefore, to build your project schedule using your WBS, do the following:

1. Enter a task by typing it directly into the Task Name field, and press Enter. Use the WBS to guide you in your task entries, and name your tasks using an action verb–noun format.

2. Determine whether the task is at the lowest level of detail needed for the work to be assigned to one or more resources. If it is not, enter more detailed tasks related to the original task directly underneath it. Later, you will indent these specific tasks, making the original task a summary task in the project (more about that later).

3. Double-check that all items from your WBS have been entered as tasks and that all work is accounted for.

To insert a new task in between two existing tasks, right-click on the row ID number where you wish to insert the new task and choose New Task. A blank task row will be inserted above the row you selected, and you can enter its task name as described previously. To delete a task from the list, right-click in its row ID number and choose Delete Task. The row ID number is located on the left side of the task entry table; clicking in it highlights the entire task row.

NOTE

> It is unlikely that you will get your entire task list right the first time; you may have to enter new tasks, remove tasks, or move tasks around as you continue to build your project schedule. Do not get discouraged if you find yourself constantly adjusting your task list; this should be expected as you learn more details about your project.

→ For more information about creating and manipulating the task list, **see** "Entering Project Tasks," **p. 144**, and "Manipulating the Task List," **p. 161**.

ENTER OR ADJUST SUMMARY TASKS AND SUBTASKS

The next step in creating your project schedule is to adjust your task list. Be sure that the Gantt Chart view is displayed. If it is not, select View, Gantt Chart to display it.

There are two types of tasks: summary tasks and subtasks. Summary tasks are larger, more general tasks, whereas subtasks are more detailed tasks that specify the actual work. Summary tasks are composed of subtasks; you do not actually work on a summary task. A summary task is complete when all of its subtasks are complete. Therefore, a summary task's duration is the total sum of all of its subtasks' durations. A summary task is scheduled to begin when its first subtask begins, and end when its last subtasks ends. For this reason, you cannot enter duration or start and finish date data for a summary task.

Summary tasks and subtasks are organized in an outline format, divided into task levels. For example, if a summary task is at outline level 1, then its subtasks are at outline level 2. Those subtasks can then have subtasks of their own, displayed at level 3. Therefore, a task can function both as summary task and a subtask simultaneously. Figure 2.10 shows a quick illustration of task levels.

Figure 2.10
This illustration demonstrates how some of the tasks in outline level 2 function as both summary tasks for outline level 3 as well as subtasks for outline level 1.

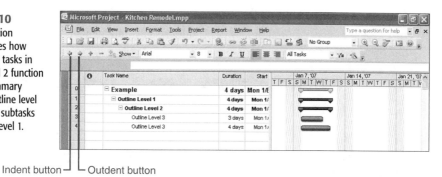

Indent button ⌐ └ Outdent button

To adjust the outline levels of your tasks, select the task(s) to adjust and then use the Indent and Outdent buttons located on the Standard toolbar (refer to Figure 2.10). The right arrow is the Indent button, and the left arrow is the Outdent button. Outdenting a task moves it to a higher outline level (a lower number), whereas indenting a task moves it to a lower outline level (a higher number). Therefore, to make a task or group of tasks subtasks, select them and click the Indent button. They will become subtasks of the tasks directly above them.

NOTE

> Hold down the Ctrl button and click on multiple tasks to select them simultaneously and indent or outdent them. They must be directly located underneath their prospective summary task.

You can choose to display or hide a summary tasks' subtasks. Sometimes it may be beneficial to hide the subtasks to save screen space, especially when all the subtasks for a particular summary task are complete. Next to each summary task is a box to hide the subtasks or display them (refer to Figure 2.10). If the subtasks are displayed, then a minus sign (–) is shown. Click on the minus sign to hide the subtasks. If the subtasks are already hidden, then a plus sign (+) is shown. Click the plus sign to display the hidden subtasks. You can also use the Show Subtasks or Hide Subtasks buttons, located directly next to the Indent and Outdent buttons on the Standard toolbar.

→ For more information about manipulating and adjusting the task list, including more information about summary and subtasks, **see** "Manipulating the Task List," **p. 161.**

2

CREATE MILESTONES

A *milestone* is a significant turning point, landmark, or decision in your project. You should create a milestone attached to the last task in each section in your project, at the end of the project itself, and anywhere else you feel is a place of significance in your project.

Milestones are created as tasks with zero duration. Therefore, to create a milestone, enter it as a task, with a specific name (such as "Phase 1 Complete"), and enter zero (0) in the duration field. Project will automatically create the task as a milestone.

Figure 2.11 shows the task list for the Kitchen Remodel project. Notice the milestones at the end of each process group in italics. Also, notice the components from the WBS in Figure 2.6 are now decomposed into tasks.

Figure 2.11
Task numbers 4, 8, 14, 18, and 22 are milestones. Notice the diamond shape that appears in the timescale side as opposed to a task bar.

TIP

> Always place a milestone at the end of your project, attached to the last task. Call it "Project Complete," or something to that effect. This adds a final, official close to your project, and avoids the all-too-often scenario of a project fizzling out after work is complete.

In Figure 2.11, the milestones are linked to the last task in each process group. The upcoming section "Create Task Dependency Relationships" discusses the concept of linking tasks in greater detail.

→ For more information about using and creating milestones, **see** "Defining Milestones," **p. 177**.

SET DEADLINES

Sometimes, you may need to clearly identify a task that must finish by a certain date. The recommended best practice is to use the feature of setting a task deadline. For example, perhaps you are remodeling your kitchen around the busy season for the distributor, and you must order the materials by a certain date in order to receive them in time. Rather than assign a finish date, which would put a constraint on that task, you could set a deadline.

To set a task deadline, do the following:

1. Double-click on the task to open its Task Information dialog box.
2. On the Advanced tab of the Task Information dialog box, select the deadline date in the Deadline field (see Figure 2.12).
3. Click OK to close the Task Information dialog box, applying the deadline.

Figure 2.12
Set a deadline date for a task on the Advanced tab of the Task Information dialog box.

If the project schedule changes in any way that would push the completion of the task past its deadline, the task will be highlighted to alert you of the potential missed deadline and you can make the appropriate adjustments.

→ For more information about using the Task Information dialog box, **see** "Editing Tasks Using the Task Information Dialog Box," **p. 159**.

CREATE TASK DEPENDENCY RELATIONSHIPS

Oftentimes in your project, you will find that certain tasks rely on the start or completion of other tasks for their own start or finish dates. For example, in the Demolition phase, you cannot remove the old appliances without first emptying the kitchen compartments. The start of the task "Remove Old Appliances" depends on the finish of the task "Empty Cabinets, Shelves, and Countertops." Project allows you to link these tasks so it can schedule the start date of the Remove Old Appliances task to coincide with the finish date of the Empty Cabinets, Shelves, and Countertops task.

Linking tasks is where the schedule really starts to be built by Project. You have created your task list, but the planned start and finished dates for tasks are determined by two primary items: the dependency relationships and the planned duration for each task. Entering task duration is discussed in the upcoming section "Enter Estimates."

This type of relationship between tasks is called a *task dependency relationship*. There are two types of tasks in dependency relationships: the predecessor and the successor. Successor tasks are dependent on predecessor tasks. In this case, Remove Old Appliances is the successor and Empty Cabinets, Shelves, and Countertops is the predecessor, because the removal of the old appliances is dependent on the emptying of kitchen compartments. This is called a Finish-to-Start relationship, because the finish of the predecessor determines the start of the successor. This is the most common type of dependency relationship. The four types of dependency links are as follows:

- **Finish-to-Start (FS)**—Predecessor's finish determines successor's start.
- **Start-to-Start (SS)**—Predecessor's start determines successor's start.
- **Finish-to-Finish (FF)**—Predecessor's finish determines successor's finish.
- **Start-to-Finish (SF)**—Predecessor's start determines successor's finish. This is a rarely used task dependency relationship.

To link tasks, select the two tasks by holding down Ctrl and clicking on them. Then click the Link Tasks button on the Standard toolbar. The task you select first is the predecessor, and the task you select second is the successor. By default, Project places a Finish-to-Start dependency link on the two tasks (see Figure 2.13).

NOTE

There are several methods to link tasks besides using the Link Tasks button on the Standard toolbar. These alternate methods are discussed in Chapter 7, "Defining Task Logic," in the section titled "Linking Tasks."

Figure 2.13
Link predecessor and successor tasks using the Link Tasks button on the Standard toolbar.

When tasks are linked, an arrow is drawn on the timescale side of the Gant Chart from the predecessor to the successor.

To remove a task dependency link, select the two tasks and click the Unlink Tasks button, located next to the Link Tasks button on the Standard toolbar.

NOTE

> Tasks do not have to be adjacent to each other to be linked. You can link a task on row 2 with a task on row 13.

You can change the dependency link type in the Task Information dialog box. Double-click on the successor task to open its Task Information dialog box. On the Predecessors tab, you will see the predecessor task(s) listed. Choose from the four task dependency relationship types in the drop-down list in the Type column and then click OK. The relationship type will be changed accordingly.

You will notice on the Predecessors tab of the Task Information dialog box that there is a Lag field for the dependency relationship. This is used in situations where the tasks have a dependency relationship, but need to allow for some time in between the predecessor and successor start or finish dates. For example, if the tasks can follow each other without delay, Microsoft Project 2007 would schedule the Remove Old Appliances task to start immediately after the Empty Cabinets, Shelves, and Countertops task finishes. However, for other tasks, you may need to wait some time before the next task can begin. For example, Install Grout cannot begin until the task Install Tile has been completed for at least a day so that the tile adhesive has time to cure. In that case, you would enter a 1-day (or more) lag (type **1d**) in the Lag field, and Microsoft Project 2007 would link the two tasks and schedule the grout installation to begin 1 day after the tile is installed.

Some tasks have a dependency relationship but can overlap a bit; that is, the successor task can start before the predecessor task is completely finished. An example of this in the Kitchen Remodel project would be during the preparation stage. Cleanup of one area of the kitchen can begin before demolition of the entire kitchen is complete. In this case, you can enter a lead time, which starts the successor task early. There is no Lead field; leads are entered in the Lag field using negative numbers. Therefore, to enter a lead of 1 day for Cleanup Kitchen, you would enter **-1d** in the Lag field, and Project would schedule the Cleanup Kitchen task to begin 1 day before the Demolish Cabinets task was scheduled to finish.

→ For more information about task dependency relationships and linking tasks, **see** "Linking Tasks," **p. 201**.

As you are creating dependency links, you are also beginning to create what is called the *critical path*. The critical path is composed of those tasks whose finish dates affect the finish date of the overall project. In other words, if a critical task finishes late, then the project will likely finish late also, unless you are able to adjust to the delay and make up time elsewhere. Some tasks can finish late and the project's finish date will be unaffected, but those tasks that will push the finish date are a part of the critical path.

→ For more information about the critical path, **see** Reviewing the Big Picture (Critical Path Analysis)," **p. 427**.

CREATE YOUR TEAM AND ASSIGN RESOURCES

When you have defined your dependency links, the next logical step in creating your project schedule is to enter your planned estimates for each task (such as duration, cost, and so on). However, before you do that, it is wise to create your project team and assign resources to work on the tasks. That way, you can gather input from your team to better assist in entering more accurate estimates. A plumber may be able to give you a better idea of how long it will take to install a new sink; therefore, it is important to build your team first before entering estimates so the team members can contribute to the process.

As you are creating your resource team, bear in mind that the members will have crucial roles in the successful completion of your project. You are the project manager, but your team will be performing most of the actual work on the tasks. Just like a quarterback in football depends on his teammates, you rely on the individual success of your project team members for the overall success of your project.

To enter your resource information in Project, display the Resource Sheet view by selecting View, Resource Sheet. Enter all resources you will use: people, facilities, equipment, and so on. Note that there are three types of resources in the Type field: work, material, and cost. Work resources are resources that work on tasks, such as people. Material resources are resources that are consumed while working on tasks, such as camera film, ink, or in the case of the Kitchen Remodel project, wood stain. A cost resource identifies specific project costs, such as travel expenses or delivery charges for appliances.

A fourth type of resource exists—the budget resource. A budget resource allows you to allocate the budget for the entire project. However, this is not an option in the Type field of the Resource Sheet view because a budget resource is assigned at the top (project summary) level, and not at the individual task level.

→ For more information about the four resource types, **see** "Defining Resources and Resource Information," **p. 252**.

This quick start focuses on entering people resources for building your schedule. After you enter the resource name, you define its type in the Type field. Work is the default resource type (people are work resources).

The following list describes the remaining major fields you might need to complete on the Resource Sheet to set resource attributes:

- **Max. Units (Maximum Units)**—The maximum amount of units the work resource is available to work on the project. If a resource works 8 hours a day, and can only devote 4 hours a day to your project, that resource's Max. Units is 50%.

- **Std. Rate (Standard Rate)**—The amount of money the resource costs, such as $20/hour or $32,000/year. Project calculates the total cost of a task by multiplying the rate by the work on the task for the resource.

- **Cost/Use**—For work resources, the amount of money the resource costs per use. You can use this instead of the standard rate when you want to indicate a one-time use cost for a resource.

■ **Base Calendar**—Which calendar the resource follows for workdays. By default, the project calendar is used (defined in the Project Information dialog box).

Figure 2.14 shows what a Resource Sheet view may look like for the Kitchen Remodel project.

Figure 2.14
Enter all your resources and resource information on the Resource Sheet view. Due to screen space, not all fields are shown in this example.

→ For more information about entering resource information, **see** "Using the Resource Fields to Define Resource Details," **p. 256.**

NOTE

> Sometimes you do not know the specific resources that will be available to work on your project. If this is the case, use the Resource Sheet view to create generic resources, and go back later to replace the generic resources with actual resources. That way, you have an idea of what kind of resources you will need and can assign generic resources to tasks to give you an idea.

When you have created your resource list using the Resource Sheet, it is time to assign resources to tasks. To do so, follow these steps:

1. Return to the Gantt Chart view (View, Gantt Chart).

2. Double-click on a task to open the Task Information dialog box.

3. On the Resources tab in the Task Information dialog box, assign resources to the task by choosing the resource from the drop-down list in the Resource Name field. The drop-down list contains all the resources you have listed on the Resource Sheet view. You can also enter different values for Units and Cost if those values are different from what is defined on the Resource Sheet view (see Figure 2.15).

4. Click OK to close the Task Information dialog box, assigning the resources as you defined.

NOTE

> You can assign multiple resources to one task.

Figure 2.15
On the Resource tab of
the Task Information
dialog box, you can
assign resources to
work on the task.

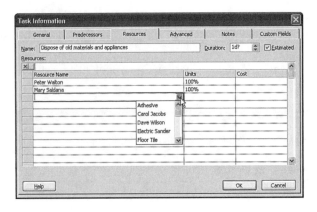

→ For more information about assigning resources to tasks, **see** Chapter 10,
"Scheduling Single and Multiple Resource Assignments," **p. 313**.

HOW DURATION, WORK, AND RESOURCE UNITS AFFECT YOUR PROJECT SCHEDULE

Before discussing estimates, it's important to take a moment to discuss the Work Formula.
Project uses a Work Formula to calculate either Work, Duration, or Resource Units. The
Work Formula is Work = Duration * Units. Therefore, you can only enter two of these
three fields (usually Units and Duration or Units and Work); Project will calculate the third.

These three data fields are very important to your project schedule. They affect the amount
of time scheduled to work on each task. For example, if you receive an estimate of 10 days
(Duration) and the resource can work at 100% of an 8-hour work day (Resource Units),
then the assignment will be completed in 80 hours (Work). In other words, 10 days * (100%
of 8 hrs/day) = 80 hours of effort, or work. However, if you obtain a work estimate of 20
hours, and your resource can only work at 50% of capacity because of other projects, then
the Duration will be calculated as 5 days (20 hours / 4 hours per day = 5 days). It is wise to
remember that resources are rarely able to work at 100% efficiency, so it's important to be
realistic regarding resource units so that either the work or duration is calculated by Project.

→ For more information about using Project's Work Formula, **see** Chapter 9, "Understanding Work Formula
Basics," **p. 283**.

ENTER ESTIMATES

Together with task dependency links, planned estimates will help Project shape your schedule. Enter your estimates—with the help and guidance of your project team—directly into
the entry fields in the Gantt Chart view. Obtain from them how much they can work (units)
and either the duration or work estimate for the task.

The five fields that exist to the right of the task names on the default Gantt Chart view are
Duration, Start, Finish, Predecessors, and Resource Names. It is often most accurate to get
your estimates for tasks in hours, so you will need to insert the Work field into this table and

enter the hours in that field. The table, called the task entry table, is the default table displayed with a timescale in the Gantt Chart view.

You should only concern yourself with entering the durations of tasks in the Duration field or the work effort for the tasks in the Work field. The Start and Finish fields will be calculated automatically based on the Project start (or finish) date, which you defined in the Project Information dialog box, as well as the task dependency links and duration or work estimates. The predecessors have already been determined when you created your task links, and the resources have already been assigned.

Duration is the amount of time scheduled to work on a task, usually shown in days. By default, when you create a new task, the duration of "1d?" is entered in its Duration field, meaning it is scheduled for 1 day, and the question mark indicates that this is a tentative estimate. You can specify a more solid estimate by entering a specific number and time unit in the Duration field. Or you can enter a work estimate (usually hours for the task to be completed) in the Work field and let the Duration be calculated by the Work Formula. It is best to first consult your team members who have expertise in particular areas of your project, and make duration or work estimate entries in all of your subtasks.

Some organizations consider work hours the best way to obtain estimates. For instance, it will take 10 hours to complete the task. Other organizations consider duration the best way to provide estimates, such as 2 days. Generally, work hours are more accurate, but many organizations are quite successful creating schedules using duration. In this example, duration has been used.

NOTE

You can enter other time units in the Duration field, such as hours. However, "days" is the default time unit. Similarly, you can enter alternate time units in the Work field, but "hours" is the default time unit.

TIP

Make your estimates as accurate as possible. Do not overcompensate to buy yourself more time, and do not underestimate to give the impression that you will get the project done sooner than expected. Enter realistic estimates, and try to ensure that the project stays consistent with those estimates, and things will run much more smoothly.

Figure 2.16 shows a portion of the Kitchen Remodel project with all task links defined and all durations entered. Notice now how the task bars on the timescale side create a chronological timeline for the project. Also, the assigned resources appear next to the task bars.

Figure 2.16
With the task dependency links defined and the estimates entered, your Gantt Chart displays the planned timeline for the project schedule.

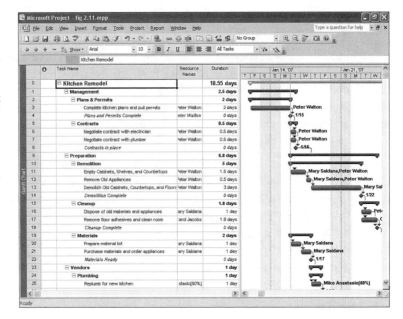

REVIEW THE SCHEDULE FOR OVERALLOCATION OR OTHER POTENTIAL ISSUES

At this point, you have created your initial project schedule, using Project as a scheduling engine. However, there are two more things you need to do before moving to the next process group of your project. The first is to double-check everything to make sure it looks correct, and the second is to fix any issues or complications.

Check for resource overallocation by displaying the Resource Usage view. Resource overallocation is when a resource is assigned to more work than can be completed in the default 8-hour day (or whatever capacity has been set to work in a day).

Figure 2.17 shows the Resource Usage view for the Kitchen Remodel project. You can see that Peter Walton and Mary Saldana are both overallocated; their names appear in red and there is an Overallocation indicator next to each name.

If you have any resources that are overallocated, you may want to go back and reassign other resources to take some of the work from the overallocated resources, or rearrange the schedule to spread the overallocated resources' workload out across time. In this case, Peter and Mary are the owners of the kitchen, and will be doing most of the work themselves. They can hire other workers to take some of the workload, but that would cost more money. So in this case, they will remain overallocated in order to save money.

Figure 2.17
The Resource Usage view shows whether or not any resources are overallocated.

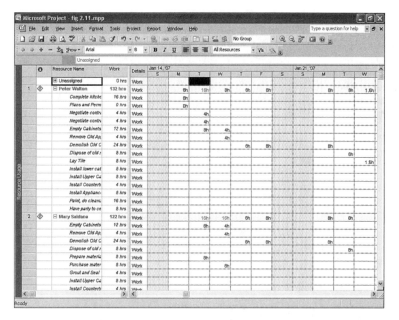

→ For more information about resolving resource overallocation, **see** Chapter 25, "Resolving Resource Allocations Problems," **p. 885**.

Besides checking for resource overallocation, review the timeline of your schedule to make sure no work is scheduled during any nonworking time you may have forgotten to define. Also check for any missing tasks or tasks without resource assignments, and make sure your dependency links are correct.

In short, double-check everything, because the next step is the last step in creating your project schedule!

→ For more information about reviewing your schedule for other potential issues, **see** Chapter 12, "Performing a Schedule Reality Check," **p. 419**.

BASELINE YOUR SCHEDULE

When you have verified that everything is in order, it is time to baseline your schedule. A baseline is essentially a snapshot of your project at a given time. Therefore, when you baseline your project after you have created the schedule, it is a snapshot of the planned schedule, with no actual work tracked or recorded yet. This baseline will be very important later in the project as you compare actual data with planned data; the baseline will allow you to compare what is happening with what was planned to happen according to the schedule you have just created. This is important because the Work and Duration fields are actually planned fields that will start to change as actual work is entered. Your original estimates that you entered into those fields will perhaps be changed if you do not capture the baseline.

To baseline your project schedule, select Tools, Tracking, Set Baseline. The Set Baseline dialog box will appear. Be sure Set Baseline is selected, as well as Entire Project, as illustrated in Figure 2.18. Then click OK to set your baseline.

Figure 2.18
In the Set Baseline dialog box, set the baseline for your project schedule, which will be very useful for future tracking and reporting processes.

→ For more information about capturing the baseline, **see** "Working with Project Baselines," **p. 445**.

TRACK YOUR PROJECT

When you have created your schedule and set your baseline, you are ready to begin the Executing and the Monitoring and Controlling process groups of your project. As mentioned previously, these two process groups overlap and will recur cyclically during the project life cycle. Work on a project begins (Execution), and you must track and analyze the actual work as compared to the baseline and make adjustments based on actual data (Monitoring and Controlling).

In order to accurately analyze your project's progress, two things must happen. First, you must set your baseline when your schedule is complete before any work begins, as discussed in the previous section. Then, you must accurately track the actual progress on your project. It is important to be consistent in your tracking habits. Develop a routine that works best for you, and stick with it. For example, you can hold a meeting every few days or every week with your project team members to get their latest progress updates and then enter that data into your project. Communication with your team is very important for gathering tracking information, so once you find what works best, stick with it consistently.

After you enter actual progress data into your project file, it is necessary to review the schedule to see the affect of the actual data. It may be necessary to modify the schedule to account for the changes and reset the baseline. Use the Tracking Gantt Chart view to help you review the changes caused by entering the actual data. Select View, Tracking Gantt to display the Tracking Gantt Chart view.

The following sections will discuss tracking and controlling your project data.

OBTAIN PROJECT STATUS

Regular meetings with your project team are essential for collecting actual data for the tasks they are working on. Keep the lines of communication open. Discuss any problems your team members are experiencing, and whether or not any solutions are available to resolve these issues. Team meetings are also a great place to discuss future tasks and prepare the team members for the work that lies ahead.

Get actual work or duration based on the kind of estimate you used. For instance, if you entered duration estimates, ask for how much the resource has completed in duration. If you had work estimates, ask how much work has been completed. You can also ask for % Complete to enter progress. However, no matter which way you get the progress status, you need to ask one more question: How much duration or work is left to complete the task? A common tendency is for team members to report that a task is 85% or 90% complete because they believe that most of their work is done, but in reality, they have quite a bit more work to finish. If you talk with them about how many more hours remain or what date they believe they will finish, you can get a better idea of the actual work that remains.

NOTE

> Project has fields for both Remaining Work and Remaining Duration, and it is important to track these fields as well as the actual data. A task may have 16 hours of planned work, and a resource may have worked 5 hours on it, so Project would assume there are 9 hours left. However, the actual Remaining Work may be only 3 hours, because the Work estimate was too much. That is why it is important to gather not only actual work but remaining work as well.

As you get progress information from your team, you will need to enter that data into Project, which is discussed in the next section.

ENTER YOUR TRACKING DATA

When you have obtained project data from your team, you must enter it into Project. A good way to display and enter tracking data is by using a split view. In the top pane, use the Tracking Gantt view with the Tracking table displayed. Select View, Tracking Gantt, then display the Tracking table by selecting View, Table, Tracking. The Tracking table has entry fields for actual data, percentage complete, and Remaining Duration.

You can also see the Baseline Work and Remaining Work for each resource on the task. To do so, follow these steps:

1. On the Tracking Gantt view with the Tracking table displayed, split the window (Window, Split).

2. In the bottom pane, right-click in the gray area and select Resource Work. The bottom pane will now display Baseline, Actual, and Remaining Work for each resource assigned to the task selected in the top pane.

Splitting the window also makes it easier for you to enter Remaining Work for each resource. This split window is displayed in Figure 2.19.

Figure 2.19
Split the window to view each resource's Baseline, Actual, and Remaining Work for the task selected in the top pane, and for easy entry for Remaining Work.

Before you enter any tracking data, it is important to set the Status Date field to the date through which you have collected data. For example, you may have a team meeting on a Tuesday, where you gather actual progress data from your team through the previous Friday. You would need to set the Status Date field to the previous Friday, because the data you enter is current only through that Friday. Because an entire week has passed since the data was collected by the team and obtained by you, Project should use the status date instead of the current date for updating the project schedule. To set the status date, open the Project Information dialog box (Project, Project Information) and enter the status date in the Status Date field (refer back to Figure 2.8).

Enter data into the Actual Work and Actual Cost fields directly from the information you gather from your project team. You can enter Actual Work as hours they spent working on their tasks, or you can enter % Complete for how far they are percentage-wise to completing their tasks. If a task has an estimated duration of 1 day, and the resource has worked 4 hours as of the status date on the task, you could enter **4 hours** in the Actual Work field, and the % Complete field will automatically display 50%. Or, you could enter **50%** in the % Complete field, and the Actual Work field would display 4 hours automatically.

However, if the task has been worked on for 4 hours, but is not yet 50% complete, you would enter the remaining duration in the Remaining Duration or Remaining Work field. Therefore, you could enter **4 hours** in the Actual Work field to show that 4 hours have been worked on the task, and then enter **6 hours** in the Remaining Work or Remaining Duration field to show that 6 hours of work remain to be done to finish the task. The % Complete field would show 40% instead of 50% to account for the remaining time as well as the actual time spent working on the task.

Figure 2.20 shows the Tracking Gantt view with the Tracking table displayed. Notice how the task bars on the timescale side display the percentage complete on the right, and for those tasks that have started but have not completed, the task bars display progress in a darker shade.

Figure 2.20
When you enter tracking data into your project, the task bars on the Tracking Gantt Chart will display percentage complete.

When tasks are entirely complete, it is very important that you zero out Remaining Work or Duration rather than just entering **100%** in the % Complete field. This practice will allow you to capture data on the current project to use as the basis for future project estimates. If you enter **100%** in the % Complete field, Project always assumes that the remaining work should be added to what is in the Actual Work or Actual Duration field. If the remaining work was not accurate, your historical record will also be inaccurate. Entering the actual work or duration, then zeroing out the remaining work or duration field, will make the task 100% complete. If you are not trying to capture estimates for historical reasons, then entering **100%** in the % Complete field is fine.

It is especially important to enter **100%** in the % Complete field for milestones. The check marks next to tasks visually indicate all tasks are closed and you can have a clean project finish.

After each time you enter project data, you should update the changes to your project. To do so, follow these steps:

1. Select Tools, Tracking, Update Project.

2. In the Update Project dialog box, select Reschedule Uncompleted Work to Start After and then enter the status date used for the most recent tracking update.

3. Click OK to update the project and close the dialog box. Any uncompleted work will be scheduled to begin after the status date.

Once your project is updated, review the schedule impacts caused by the tracking updates on the Tracking Gantt view. If the actual values are less than your estimates (through the status date), your schedule dates may move out and show a later finish date than what was originally planned, because the project is taking longer than expected. If more work was accomplished than planned, the finish date may be scheduled sooner than originally planned, because you have completed more work through the status date than you had estimated.

You may need to make adjustments to help get the schedule back on track if your project update is undesirable, such as reducing the scope or adding resources to help finish tasks faster. Keep in mind this may increase your budget.

→ For more information about tracking your project, **see** Chapter 13, "Tracking Your Project Progress," **p. 443**.

ANALYZE YOUR STATUS

Reports are an excellent method of analyzing your progress as compared to your baseline plan. Project offers many basic and visual reports, covering all aspects of your project. These reports are all customizable. In addition, you can create your own reports from scratch to display exactly the data fields you want included in the report.

To access Project's existing reports, select Report from the main menu and choose either Reports or Visual Reports. Report, Reports opens the Reports dialog box, which contains six reporting categories: Overview, Current Activities, Costs, Assignments, Workload, and Custom. The first five categories contain multiple reports relating to different reporting areas of your project. The Custom category opens the Custom Reports dialog box, which contains all of Project's basic reports for you to open, edit, and customize—or you can create a new report from scratch.

If you select Report, Visual Reports from the main menu, the Visual Reports – Create Report dialog box appears. You can choose from six categories, displayed on the tabs in the dialog box: Task Usage, Resource Usage, Assignment Usage, Task Status, Resource Status, and Assignment Status. The All tab contains all the reports found on these six tabs.

Visual reports are created using either Microsoft Office Excel or Microsoft Office Visio. Each report contains different dimensions of data and is accompanied by a visual representation of that data. Visual reports are brand new to Project 2007, so users of previous versions may be unfamiliar with them.

→ For more information about using the basic and visual reports in Project, **see** Chapter 15, "Using Reports for Tracking and Control," **p. 519**.

→ For more information about creating and customizing the basic reports, **see** Chapter 20, "Creating and Customizing the Basic Reports," **p. 657**.

→ For more information about creating and customizing the visual reports, **see** Chapter 21, "Creating and Customizing Visual Reports," **p. 707**.

Because it is impossible to plan the perfect project, project analysis is very important while you're working on a project. Unforeseeable issues will arise that delay certain tasks, and possibly delay the project in general. In short, life happens. All you can do is prepare as best as possible, stay patient and calm when things do not go as planned, and communicate issues to the proper members of your organization so they are not surprised by the changes and have the opportunity to help the project get back on track. Track and analyze your progress, make adjustments, and use Project to help you communicate the alternatives for project adjustments when the issues arise.

→ For more information about analyzing your project's progress, **see** Chapter 14, "Analyzing Performance," **p. 473**.

CLOSE YOUR PROJECT

When you are at the end of the work on your project, you are not quite finished. All too often, work on a project finishes, and the project just kind of fizzles out with no official ending. Do not let this happen to you. Take the time to properly close your project, and you will benefit greatly.

Before you officially close the project, examine your task list to be sure all tasks are completed and their % Complete field is 100% (including milestones). If for some reason a task is not complete, be sure to specifically document the reason by attaching a note to the task (double-click on the task, and in the Task Information dialog box, select the Notes tab). Also, be sure all project deliverables are delivered as agreed upon in the scope statement.

Once all tasks are completed and accounted for, it is time to close the project. Save the project file in the appropriate location on your computer or network for future reference.

One of the most important steps in closing a project is conducting a Lessons Learned session. This is a chance to sit down with your team and other project stakeholders and discuss what worked well and why, as well as what did not work well and why. No matter what the outcome of the project was, you have learned something. It is important to focus on the positive and not the negative, and close the project on a good note, no matter how successful or unsuccessful it was. Even if you installed your cabinets upside-down in the Kitchen Remodel project, you are still better at remodeling a kitchen than you were before the project began. Document all the lessons learned, and give all persons involved with the project a chance to voice their opinions about how everything went. It will allow them to leave their opinions with the project, and move on without feeling like they had more to say.

NOTE

When conducting a Lessons Learned session, it is important to stay positive and light-hearted. Even if there was tension during the project, your team members will feel better about their performance if you leave things on a good note.

TIP

Document the lessons learned. If they involve specific tasks or phases of the project, attach them as notes to the task or phase for future reference. Above all else, projects are learning experiences, and it is important to welcome the lessons learned. You will only improve your ability as a project manager for the next project you work on.

After you have closed the project and conducted a Lessons Learned session, celebrate the completion and hard work by having a party with your team and stakeholders. Projects are hard work, and the people involved deserve to celebrate their efforts.

And, at the end of a kitchen remodel project, what better place to host the party than the new kitchen itself, the project deliverable!

→ For more information about closing your project, **see** Chapter 17, "Closing the Project," **p. 565**.

CONSULTANTS' TIPS

The intent of this chapter was to give you a quick overview of the power of Microsoft Project so that you can begin to benefit immediately. Hundreds of great features are available in the tool that were not even mentioned in this chapter, so keep reading and discover many capabilities that will help you become a better project manager.

FORMULAS THAT AFFECT YOUR SCHEDULE

The primary complaint that people have about using a scheduling tool such as Project is that the tool "changed my data." In reality, that is exactly what it is supposed to be doing, and it does this in a very predictable manner. The trick is that you must learn how Project uses formulas to help you predict the future of your project. When things do not go according to plan, the scheduling engine will help you figure out what the ripple effect will be. Learn these formulas and rules so that it is not a surprise to you.

DURATION = ACTUAL DURATION + REMAINING DURATION

The total duration of a task includes all that has happened before today and all that is scheduled to happen in the future. You cannot reduce duration without considering both the past and the future.

WORK = ACTUAL WORK + REMAINING WORK

The same rule applies to Work. It is made up of whatever work has happened before (Actual Work) and all work yet to be completed (Remaining Work).

WORK FORMULA (WORK = DURATION × UNITS)

This is the basic formula that drives most of the behavior of the scheduling engine. You can only change two of the three items; the remaining item will be calculated by the software. Memorize this formula and practice changing two of the three items until you become comfortable with its properties.

CREATE WBS

The vast majority of projects that fail do so because the scope and requirements were not clear. The use of the WBS is the single most important thing you can do to ensure a project comes in on time, within budget, and with the quality and functions that were expected. It can be created on paper, or you can use a tool such as WBS *Director* to help you. Do not skip this step.

80/20 RULE

When you start a project, there are always some things that are unknown. Focus on the big picture and make progress on what you do know. Clearly identify the things that are not yet resolved, but do not let them keep you from making progress.

PROJECT IS A TRACKING TOOL

Microsoft Project is a scheduling and tracking tool. Use it to help you keep your project on target. If you only use it to create the initial schedule, you have left most of its value unused.

ALWAYS BASELINE!

A baseline is like a map. If you don't know where you planned to go or how long it would take you to get there, it is difficult to know when you have arrived. You cannot learn from your mistakes or celebrate your accuracy if you don't keep track of your original plan. It is an excellent tool for helping you keep your project's scope on target.

SPLIT WINDOW AND VIEWS

Get comfortable with the use of the split window and with these four important views: Gantt Chart, Tracking Gantt, Resource Sheet, and Resource Usage. Between them, they display most of the data that tells you what is happening in your project. If you get comfortable with them, you can quickly make Microsoft Project the most powerful tool on your desktop.

MICROSOFT PROJECT AND THE PROJECT MANAGEMENT DOMAIN

In this chapter

Chapter 3 provides the context for the use of Microsoft Project within the domain of project management. It identifies accepted standards and methodologies that are in use within the field and provides some examples of how they are used with Project.

HISTORY OF PROJECT MANAGEMENT

When Patrick Henry said, "I know of no way of judging the future but by the past," he could have been talking about project management. When faced with projects that have never been done before, all project managers can do is look at what has come before them.

While project management has been practiced for thousands of years, evidenced by the Egyptian and Roman dynasties, modern project management can be traced back to the late nineteenth century and the rise in large-scale government projects and growing technological advancements. Fredrick Taylor, the Father of Scientific Management, applied scientific reasoning to analyzing and improving labor, and Henry Gantt studied management of Navy ship construction during World War I. Gantt's use of charts, task bars, and milestone markers is still practiced today, and they bear his name. One of the major projects that brought detailed project planning, controlling, and coordination to the forefront was the Hoover Dam project, which involved $175 million dollars, six different companies, a major worksite with no existing infrastructure, and approximately 5,200 workers. The project was brought in under budget and ahead of schedule.

After developments in project management during two World Wars and the growing Cold War, major changes to project management were brought about with the launch of Sputnik. Fearful that the United States was falling behind in the race to space, the USA introduced several major programs to focus on science and exploration. Several agencies, including the Advanced Research Project Agency, a high-level research and development program that later became DARPA and NASA were founded. These agencies led the way in the development of project management.

Two other major developments for project management to grow out of this period were the Critical Path Method (CPM) and the Program Evaluation and Review Technique (PERT). CPM was devised by Du Pont and Remington Ran for use with the UNIVAC-1 computer mainframe. PERT was invented by the Program Evaluation Branch of the Special Projects office of the U.S. Navy, for use with the POLARIS missile program, and was also used on the Apollo program for NASA. CPM/PERT gave managers more control over extremely large and complex projects, but could only be calculated within large mainframe computer systems and were used mainly for government sector projects.

With the computer revolution of the 1980s and the move from mainframe computers to personal computers with the ability to multitask, project management software became more accessible to other companies. The Internet and networked systems only made project managers more efficient at controlling and managing the different aspects of their projects. More information on previously completed projects is available today than ever before, making the project manager's job of estimating the future by looking at the past easier than ever.

EXPLORING PROJECT MANAGEMENT INDUSTRY STANDARDS

Anyone can create a file using Microsoft Project. Organizing that file into a logical flow of work, however, requires a solid understanding of how projects should be managed and decomposed into logical units. To understand project management, one must understand the standards and methodology behind it. While Gantt Charts and other similar resources are used in almost all project management schedules, there are several different ways of using those resources. This chapter will discuss prominent industry standards that are often used to set a framework for building schedules. A variety of methodologies, team styles, and life cycles will also be explored. The approach and techniques will vary but the software can still be used to support virtually any approach to scheduling that an individual or organization chooses to use.

PROJECT MANAGEMENT BODY OF KNOWLEDGE (PMBOK)

The Project Management Institute, or PMI, is an internationally recognized organization that has developed standards for the domain of project management including standards for portfolio management, program management, project management, and work breakdown structures. PMI has several hundred thousand members in over 65 countries. It is widely recognized for its certification programs and continues to grow through a combination of volunteer efforts, certification programs, local chapter events, international seminars, and special interest groups.

The standards created by PMI are authored by a vast network of project management professionals who volunteer their time to create and update these standards on a regular basis. The standards groups are from many different countries across the globe; they research topics and collaborate to bring together the latest thinking and techniques from their collective experience.

The PMI standard that is of primary importance for this chapter of the book is in its third edition and is known as: "A Guide to the Project Management Body of Knowledge," also known as the PMBOK Guide. It will be discussed in some detail in this chapter to help in understanding all of the components that should be considered when creating a schedule. Because PMI is a standards and certification organization, it does not prescribe methodologies or "how to" approaches, rather it defines specific standards and offers certifications in the field of project management. The PMBOK provides a context for a way to do things, rather than the process that should be followed. Inexperienced project managers often try to make their schedules follow PMBOK as if it were a recipe for success. This can lead them into traps and complexity that is not useful in completion of their projects. Instead, they should look to the PMBOK for support of the methodology and life cycle that they choose to follow.

TIP

> PMI makes a clear distinction between a *project plan* and a *project schedule*. The *plan* is a formal document that includes narrative on communication approaches, assumptions, deliverables, and execution of the project. The *schedule* is one component of the plan that focuses on the timeline for the activities to be performed. As scheduling tools become more sophisticated, they are gradually including more elements that used to reside only in the plan. Microsoft Project Desktop still focuses on scheduling functions, but the server components have added capabilities to support more of the plan functions.

The PMBOK Guide has established five process groups to define the project management process. These processes are as follows:

- **Initiating Process Group**—Defines and authorizes the project or a project phase
- **Planning Process Group**—Defines and refines objectives, and plans the course of action required to attain the objectives and scope that the project is to address
- **Executing Process Group**—Integrates people and other resources to carry out the project management plan
- **Monitoring and Controlling Process Group**—Regularly measures and monitors progress to identify variances from the project management plan so that corrective action can be taken when necessary to meet project objectives
- **Closing Process Group**—Formalizes acceptance of the product, service, or result and brings the project or a project phase to an orderly end

Projects are created and implemented in environments that are larger in scope than the projects themselves. All projects must have a beginning and an end, as shown by the Initiating and Closing Process Groups. In between, a project will be engaged continually with the other three process groups, as shown in Figure 3.1.

The PMBOK identifies nine knowledge areas that a project manager should consider throughout the entire life cycle of a project. Knowledge areas focus on a specific aspect of the overall domain and identify the elements that need to be considered to properly manage a project.

- **Project Integration Management**—This knowledge area looks at the processes and activities that are needed to identify, define, combine, unify, and coordinate the different actions within a Project Management Process Group.
- **Project Scope Management**—This knowledge area handles scope planning, scope definition, creating a WBS (decomposition of the scope into smaller components), scope verification, and scope control.
- **Project Time Management**—This knowledge area concerns five different steps: activity definition, activity sequencing, activity resource estimating, activity duration estimating, and schedule development.
- **Project Cost Management**—This knowledge area involves planning, estimating, budgeting, and controlling costs so a project can be finished within budget.
- **Project Quality Management**—This knowledge area determines policies, objectives, and responsibilities to meet a project's quality standards.

- **Project Human Resource Management**—This knowledge area helps organize and manage a project's team, the people necessary for the completion of the project.

- **Project Communications Management**—This knowledge area involves the processes that ensure timely generation, collection, distribution, storage, retrieval, and disposition of information.

- **Project Risk Management**—This knowledge area envelopes risk management planning, identification, analysis, responses, monitoring, and controlling of a project.

- **Project Procurement Management**—This knowledge area involves the processes necessary to purchase products, services, or results from outside the project team.

Figure 3.1
The relationship among the PMBOK process groups (taken from Figure 3-4, *PMBOK Guide, Third Edition*).

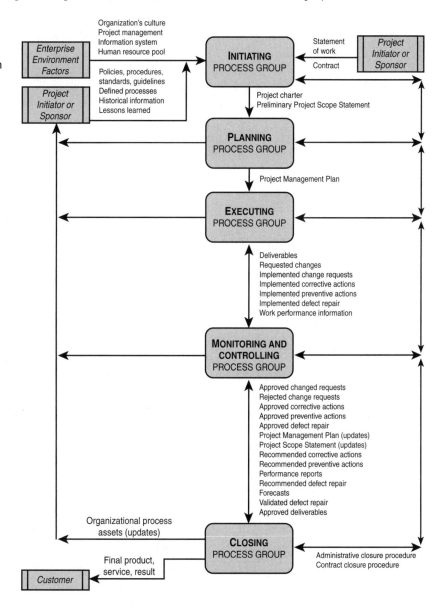

NOTE

> Do not confuse the PMBOK process groups with life-cycle phases of projects (more on phases later in this chapter). This is a common tendency when a project manager tries to decompose a project into logical components. Process groups pertain to all projects; life cycles vary by the type of project, the domain of the work, the complexity and time frame, and many other factors.

The nine knowledge areas are specifically designed to work with the five process groups to identify possible areas for management within the scope of the project. They are referred to here as the "5×9 checklist." When the two components are combined, they provide guidance for what elements should be considered at what time in a project. In the context of MSP desktop, the key knowledge areas are scope, time, and cost. These components will help you build the initial project schedule framework. All of the other knowledge areas will play a part in building the working baseline schedule, and it is recommended that each be considered in the context of the framework. For example, the resources to be applied to a project may involve both the Project Human Resource Management and the Project Procurement Management knowledge areas. Until you have a general idea of the scope, expected time-frames, and budget for that work, however, you will not be able to identify which area is most appropriate. The emphasis for each knowledge areas varies by phase of project; some will be more important in one phase than another, but all of the nine are used throughout the project.

PRINCE2

PRINCE2, which stands for *Projects in Controlled Environments*, is a project management methodology developed by the United Kingdom government. It is in its second release and was originally known as the PRINCE technique. The first release was established in 1989 by the Central Computer and Telecommunications Agency (CCTA) as a standard for information technology project management. Because of its success in IT, the methodology was republished about seven years later in a version that could be applied across many other disciplines. PRINCE2 was again updated in 2005 by the Office of Government Commerce (OGC) and has become the standard for project management in the UK, and is now used in 50 other countries. You can become certified in the use of PRINCE2 at either one of two levels: Foundation and Practitioner.

PRINCE2 uses a simple four-step process to explain what each project will need, as shown in Figure 3.2. This process is explained in more detail using the following eight different processes, sometimes known as the Validation, Quality, Verification, and Approval steps:

- **Start-up**—This is when a project manager is chosen. Then the need for the project is defined and outlined as to how it will be executed.
- **Direction**—The project manager, who reports to the Project Board, is responsible for managing the details. The Project Board is responsible for the overall success of the current project and defines the direction in which the project will be heading.
- **Initiation**—The Project Initiation Document is prepared and submitted to the Project Board for approval and possible revision.

- **Stage Control**—During this stage, the project is broken down into several different manageable stages. The number of stages will depend on the size and risk level of the project, and each stage must also plan for the succeeding stage. Before any new stage can begin, the current stage must be fully finished.

- **Stage Boundary Management**—At this stage, the Project Board must review the current stage and then develop the process for the next stage. It is only after the approval for the execution of the current stage and the planning of the next stage that the project can continue.

- **Planning**—This stage is used for deciding what products will be produced and what is required for their production. Then estimates are made for cost, time, and any other resources, plus any risk analysis, activity scheduling, and process streamlining that is necessary for the project.

- **Product Delivery Management**—This is the production stage, where the project manager confirms that the right goods are being produced correctly and on schedule.

- **Closing**—Once everything is finished, the project manager must perform a Post Project Review, which evaluates the outcome of the project. When this review is approved by the Project Board, the project is complete.

Figure 3.2
PRINCE2 four-step process.

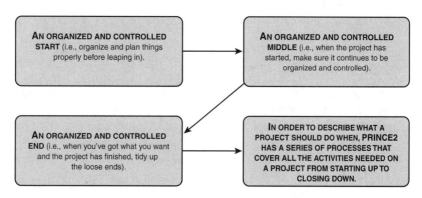

> **NOTE**
>
> There is no conflict between PMBOK and PRINCE2. They can be used together if a project manager chooses to use both. PRINCE2 is a methodology and focuses more on deliverables, whereas PMBOK is a standard and focuses on the process and knowledge areas. PRINCE2 establishes a Validation of Process (through a very specific focus on deliverables and the activities around them), whereas PMBOK focuses on the processes used to manage the deliverables.

In addition to consideration of these standards and methods, project managers need to understand the environment in which they will be working before they create a schedule. They need to be aware of the various methodologies and approaches that can be used to help them (or confuse them, if they do not understand how and when the methodologies and approaches should be applied). The following section provides an introduction to this information.

WBS, PHASES AND CONTROL POINTS, METHODOLOGIES, AND LIFE CYCLES

Many of the preceding terms are used by project managers to describe the approach that is used to define and execute a project. Each of these has been explained in many other texts and references. Since the focus of this book is using Microsoft Project, the topics are brought up here to provide context only; there is no attempt to provide the definitive use of any of the terms. Rather, the hope is that the reader can apply the concepts and techniques as appropriate when building a schedule. The work that needs to happen during a project's life does not automatically conform to a particular methodology.

Before building any schedule, the project manager must consider two key components: work decomposition (what work needs to be done, the Work Breakdown Structure or WBS) and managerial control (stages, phases, and life cycle requirements). The discipline used for either will depend on the environment in which the project is executed, so the formality will vary but both components must be considered. The tasks or activities and milestones (how the work will be accomplished) should not be defined in a project schedule until the WBS and control framework are determined. WBS will help the project manager set parameters around the scope of work to be done; the life cycle sets the controls in place for decisions during project execution. If these two components are kept in control, the project will have a much higher opportunity for success.

WORK BREAKDOWN STRUCTURE (WBS)

Step one in building a schedule is to begin with a Work Breakdown Structure (WBS) that allows decomposition of the scope of the project from major components to the smallest set of deliverables, called *work packages*. As a best practice, this process is completed before a true schedule is built. It can be done using Microsoft Project as long as ongoing "use" rules are defined and followed to keep the WBS components intact after the project is approved and baselined.

As mentioned earlier in this chapter, PMI has developed a standard for the WBS. It is a primary component of good project management practices because it forces the discipline of scope definition and control.

→ For detailed information of how to build a WBS, **see** Chapter 4, "Getting Started After the Business Initiative Is Approved," **p. 87**.

If the scope of your project is managed through a WBS, all of the tasks and milestones will be created in support of specific work packages and can be rolled up through the structure for tracking progress using Earned Value Management techniques. This practice eliminates some of the common failure points in project management, such as scope creep and fuzzy requirements. All work is clearly linked to the production of a deliverable, and progress against that deliverable can be monitored.

Managerial Control

So many terms are used in the context of managerial control that a few definitions are in order. Hundreds of resources are available to provide detailed explanations; the purpose here is context only. The hope is that these simple descriptions will help the user's understanding when building a project schedule, as discussed in the following sections.

Phases and Gates

Many organizations have established processes for deciding what projects will be approved and for overseeing the projects once they have been launched. In some organizations, the processes are rigorous and robust; in others, the processes may be simple guidelines that have been put in place to help project managers. In either case, a defined set of standard phases and control points (often called *gates*) simplify the decisions that need to be made when running a project. In most cases, templates can be created that standardize the phases and the required control points for different types of projects.

Phases and gates can allow more management control of the project, as they break the project down into smaller components. This helps to keep executive and team focus aligned on the same set of activities. A change between phases is usually defined by some kind of transfer. In many cases, the transfer requires a formal review before the project is allowed to move into the next phase. It is not unusual, however, for phases to begin before the completion of the previous phase, especially when the risks are judged as acceptable. Each organization will make its own determination of the level of control required.

Building the phases and control points into templates is an excellent way to minimize the amount of work that needs to be done when building a new schedule. Many examples are already available in Microsoft Project, and the organization can build additional ones as needed.

➔ For additional information on building and using templates, **see** Chapter 18, "Managing Project Files," on **p. 581**.

Methodologies

As organizations mature in the project management discipline, they very often adopt more formal management control systems. These systems are typically described as methodologies that include processes, rules, standards, and methods for how work will be done. In this section, we will identify a few of the ones used in specific industry segments. Each industry has its own set of methodologies, and this chapter will not attempt to identify all of them. The purpose here is to show how managing projects using Microsoft Project can be included in the methodology to assist in the enforcement and usability of the tools.

Life Cycles

Like methodologies, project life cycles are unique to the industries and disciplines in which they are used. Although all projects have a beginning and an end, they will vary greatly in how the work is accomplished. It is nearly impossible to define an ideal life cycle. Some companies and organizations use a single, standardized life cycle for every project, whereas others permit the project manager to choose the best life cycle for the project. In others, a variety of life cycles exists to accommodate different levels of complexity and different styles or types of work.

Regardless of the organization's choices regarding methodologies and life cycles, all choices can use a scheduling tool to help with project execution. The key to success in every case is that the schedule must be focused on the deliverables to be produced rather than the process. The process must be set up to assist with producing deliverables. The next section of this chapter provides several examples of methodologies and life cycles in the field of software development to illustrate how Microsoft Project can be used to enable management of a wide variety of projects.

USING MICROSOFT PROJECT WITH METHODOLOGIES AND LIFE CYCLES

Almost all organizations have at least a small number of technology projects underway, so software development is an excellent example of the wide variety of project-scheduling approaches available to organizations. The types of projects range from simple to complex, short duration to multiyear, and projects that have clear goals to those that are open-ended research. The following examples discuss the associated software development life cycle (SDLC) and how Microsoft Project can be set up to support the life cycle. As you review the examples, you should also keep in mind that these projects should be planned and executed using the principles described in the previous sections on project standards (the PMBOK Guide and PRINCE2). While strict adherence to the standards is not required or necessary on every project, it is useful to remember that there are five major process groups to be managed on each project and that there are nine knowledge areas that should be considered throughout the project's life cycle.

WATERFALL DEVELOPMENT PROCESS

Traditional software development is often described as a waterfall model because it is sequential in nature. The assumption with this model is that phases can be completed in order with little or no need to repeat the previous activities. Development is described as a waterfall, steadily falling down through traditional phases such as definition, preliminary design, detailed design, coding, testing, implementation, and transition to operations.

This method of development is used in many organizations today, especially those involved in multiyear programs. The phases can be lengthy and the work can be very exacting. Although the name suggests that all work from one phase is completed before moving into the next phase, these types of projects are often set up with overlapping phases so that design can begin on certain deliverables as soon as the definition of the work for those deliverables is completed. In addition, there is typically some level of iterative development involved in almost all projects but the term "waterfall" is still in common use today.

In this type of project, the tendency is to set up the project schedule in the same order as the major phase names. Instead, the project can be set up so that it is broken up into logical work packages that can be monitored and measured separately.

ITERATIVE DEVELOPMENT

Iterative development provides a strong framework for planning purposes and also flexibility for successive iterations of software development. The Rational Unified Process (RUP) and the Dynamic Systems Development Methods are two frameworks for this type of project life cycle. RUP is not only a methodology for software engineering project management, it also has a set of software tools for using the specific methodology that is the Rational Unified Process. Figure 3.3 depicts the RUP workflow.

Figure 3.3
RUP workflow.

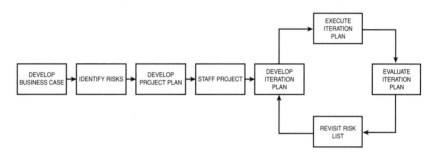

The goal for this type of software development life cycle (SDLC) is to allow the developers to learn through incremental development and the use of prototypes instead of trying to complete detailed requirements before the development work begins. Agile and XP can also be considered to be iterative methods.

AGILE DEVELOPMENT PROCESS

Agile is a philosophy of project management that moves away from the classic project management methods and focuses less on planning and more on execution. In Agile, crucial decisions are made during the project execution phase, instead of the planning phase. As business and project environments become more fluid and dynamic, the amount of time for effective planning becomes less and less. This does not mean that planning will be ignored; rather the focus will shift to supporting decisions during project execution instead of finalizing all decisions during the planning stage.

Agile is not an all-or-nothing methodology either; it is possible to combine Agile with more classic project management ideas. While classic project management is comprehensive and will work in diverse situations, Agile can add various ideas for facing new and unique situations that can be found in creative, knowledge-based industries.

Here are some of the attributes of an Agile SDLC:

- Short development cycles are used to produce working software in weeks rather than months.
- Communication between the business users and the developers occurs daily.
- Documentation of working functionality is captured after the software is completed; there is limited documentation of the requirements or design.
- Timeboxing is used to force tough decisions early in the project.

- Changes to requirements are expected; they are a result of early working prototypes and are a goal of the process.
- The project manager for an Agile team is focused on ensuring excellent communication as the primary mechanism to maintain progress.

Agile development can be difficult for large organizations to embrace because it does not require a focus on formal planning of an entire project. The use of Agile should not be used as an excuse to avoid planning or managing a budget. The approach is meant to provide a lighter and faster method to reach a goal, but the goal is still required. The major difference is that the primary measurement of progress is frequent delivery of small amounts of working software. With a focus on feature delivery, it can sometimes be difficult to understand the overall picture, so strong project management must provide this clarity.

In this type of environment, a project team can still use Microsoft Project to support its goals. In an Agile environment, the tool is not used to develop a robust schedule with a beginning-to-end flow of tasks and resources. Its use in this case supports communication to management and ensures that changes are captured and the backlog of work is moved through each successive iteration of the project schedule. In the following example, the project manager has established a budget summary task to provide rollup of budget for management purposes. Successive sets of work are defined in small iterations while the overall timeframe and budget are obvious for all (see Figure 3.4). This approach allows the team to perform iterative planning while still meeting the business requirements of not exceeding a specific timeframe and budget. By establishing a project schedule with an overall goal, the needs of the team and their management can be met. Refer to Figure 3.4 for an example of a short project that is expected to complete within a target effort of 340 hours. The work is not fully defined at the beginning so that the team has the flexibility to decide what work will happen in what order. Management is still able to see overall metrics of planned work, actual work, and the current estimate of work remaining.

Figure 3.4
An Agile project showing overall budget, work, and timeframe with iterative development.

Agile is an extremely successful method of software development that is very well suited to an environment with self-motivated teams, open communications, and leadership that is comfortable with a prototyping approach to work. It does not fit all projects, but when it works, it works very well. The schedule created in Microsoft Project for this type of approach becomes a tool for communication, overall budget and time goals, and historical tracking purposes.

NOTE

> For organizations that use the Project Server tool, this method will allow them use an Agile approach and yet have oversight of the entire project portfolio. Agile projects coexist with standard iterative projects in their Project Server environment; the projects have planned timeframes, resources, and budgets but are not required to have all of the work scoped out at the beginning of the project.

EXTREME PROGRAMMING

Extreme Programming, or XP, is another method within the Agile family that has become a simple and flexible way for developing software through the writing of tests. It is designed to be used by a group of two to ten programmers who are able to execute tests in a fraction of a day. It uses short cycles of phases, with early and continuing feedback during each cycle. This flexibility allows it to respond to changing business demands through the implementation of functionality. XP's use of automated tests, written by the programmers to scrutinize development, helps early detection of defects and also allows the cycle of phases to evolve as the project continues. These automated tests depend both on the short-term instincts of programmers and also on the long-term interests of the project. It also relies heavily on a system of oral communication, tests, and source code to help communicate the system structure and intent. These processes allow for the day-to-day programming of a feature, and then moving on to testing, implementation, design, and integration, all packed into each cycle.

The scheduling methods used in the preceding Agile example can again be adapted for XP.

SPIRAL DEVELOPMENT PROJECT

Spiral development was defined by Barry Boehm in 1985 and is often used in fairly large projects that take months to two years or more to complete. The initial focus may be on core functionality, and then the "bells and whistles" such as graphical user interfaces and reporting are added at a later time. This is sometimes considered to be another form of iterative development, but the structure of the plans and schedule focus on a robust core design in the early stages.

RESEARCH PROJECT

A research project may be the most difficult type of project to tackle when it comes to identifying a project schedule. Often, there is no clear goal in mind and there may not even be an expectation of a specific end date or budget. On the other side, however, even research projects must be funded by someone and they must have a working staff, so there is typically some expectation of a result. In most cases, there is also an expectation that the funding is used responsibly, so there must be a process in place to track how the money has been spent.

Microsoft Project can once again be used to support this type of project as a tracking mechanism and a place to bring together the set of work that will be performed. The schedule will not require all of the advanced features of critical path analysis, resource-leveling, and predecessor/successor relationships, but it can be used as an easy method of historical support and a loose prediction of the work that is to be accomplished.

ACCOMMODATING TEAMING STYLES

High-performance teams, self-managed teams, and other nontraditional structures began to emerge over 50 years ago in Great Britain and gained acceptance across the globe as several large corporations began to adopt the concepts. The general idea behind these teaming styles was to loosen managerial constraints in an effort to increase worker performance and make quantum leaps in accomplishment of organizational goals.

When framed correctly, the teams need little direction and excel in accomplishing the goals of their projects. If the dynamics are not understood, however, little is accomplished. From a project management perspective, Agile or XP projects can be a bit intimidating because the team dynamics can overwhelm the designated leader. In reality, successful self-managed teams are not leaderless. They have simply figured out a mechanism to allow many people within the team to play a leadership role.

Even in a team where a project management role has not been defined, someone must take on the job of setting a direction to accomplish a goal. The goal may only be one week in the future, but the team must coalesce around that goals, and the person who makes that happen is a leader. If the project manager understands the dynamics of the team, he or she can use these dynamics to improve the team's focus and increase its performance. The PM must be comfortable with sharing decision making and will need to focus heavily on communication of information within the team and with the stakeholders of the project. Things change quickly in this environment, so communication of status becomes a driving force for the project.

Microsoft Project is an excellent tool to aid the PM in communication. Two components need to be established to make this successful. The overall goal of the project needs to be clear to the team, and the boundaries of the project (overall timeframe, scope, resources, and budget) must be understood. If these components are established within the tool as a baseline, the remainder of the schedule can be flexible or rigid, as dictated by the project structure and the teaming style.

CONSULTANTS' TIPS

DETERMINE THE APPROACH TO USE IN MANAGING YOUR PROJECT

Microsoft Project 2007 has a rich set of features that enable the project manager and team to track projects at a very detailed level. It also has enough flexibility to allow high-level tracking without a demand for the detail. It can be and has been used to support all industries and all domains within those industries.

Because the software has so many capabilities, it must be well-understood to be used correctly. The scheduling engine will anticipate your needs and move the dates or adjust the amount of work that is to be accomplished based on the parameters that you set. Because it will do this, project managers must have a clear understanding of the approach that they wish to use on their projects before they begin entering tasks.

Use WBS as a First Step in Project Definition

Always start with a WBS to help you be clear on the goals of the project. Wait to add the task-level details until you are sure that you have decomposed the WBS to the work package level that is right for the type of project you are leading. Do not confuse the listing of activities with the completion of deliverables.

Use the 5×9 Checklist for Planning

Remember the 5×9 checklist and consider it when planning and executing each project. As you move through the phases of your project's life cycle, spend a moment to consider which of the five process groups is most dominant at the moment and which of the nine knowledge areas plays the most important part in the project's evolution.

3

PART II

ORGANIZING FOR SUCCESS—PROJECT INITIATION AND PLANNING

GETTING STARTED AFTER THE BUSINESS INITIATIVE IS APPROVED

In this chapter

The purpose of this chapter is to help you understand how to get your project started in the most optimal way so that you have positioned your project for success. Planning a successful project requires the skills of leadership and management and includes the following tasks:

- **Setting the direction**—Establish a goal that your stakeholders and team members can understand and work to achieve.

- **Sharing the vision**—Provide a framework and sufficient detail so that each member of the team knows what to do and when to do it.

- **Establishing the rules**—Establish methods for work to be accomplished, communication to occur, and methods to track status and manage the changes that will inevitably come your way.

Once you set the stage for success, you can use Microsoft Project 2007 to do what it does best: help you organize and track the work of your team. If you start with these basics, you can optimize all of the features that are available to assist you.

INTRODUCTION

A project has been approved and you have been assigned as the project manager. Now what? Before you reach for the keyboard to open Microsoft Project 2007, you need to do a variety of things to set your project up for success.

You can draw upon many resources to help you with this process. Several are used in this chapter as the foundation for the author's approach to running successful projects. Dr. William Casey, principal in the Executive Leadership Group, has provided the foundation for the work on Measure of Success in the next section. The information regarding Work Breakdown Structures is based on two primary sources: *Practice Standard for Work Breakdown Structures, Second Edition* (PMI, 2006) and *Effective Work Breakdown Structures* (Haugen, 2002).

ORGANIZING FOR SUCCESS

Much of your work will ultimately be reflected in a Microsoft Project 2007 schedule, but if you start that process before you are ready, you can end up with a project that is out of control. This is because Microsoft Project 2007 was designed to help you manage the *details* of your project schedule—the activities, the calendars, the resources, and many other details can be captured and managed in the tool. Before you dive into the details, however, you need to frame the big picture with the following:

- Where you are going (your goal and objectives).

- What you must provide as results of your project (end products or outcomes, deliverables).

- What boundaries and constraints you must work within (regulatory requirements, budgets, time frames, quality levels, and more).

- How you will manage change when it happens (and it will happen).

The details that will reside within your Microsoft Project 2007 schedule will become important, but it is much more important for you to start with a well-designed approach that is easy to explain to your team and to your stakeholders. Once that is in place, working out the details and controlling the scope of the project will be much more manageable.

DEFINE A MEASURE OF SUCCESS

Projects are most successful when they are focused on the achievement of *one* clear goal. The goal should be measurable and achievable. Project goals can range from very lofty (putting a man on the moon) to very simple (reduce errors in a report); if the team can rally behind the goal and understand the purpose, your chances of success are much improved. There can be many additional objectives involved in reaching the project goal that will also need to be defined, so it is extremely important to reach clarity among the team members and the stakeholders of the primary driver of the project. Once this goal is documented, all lower-level objectives can be reviewed against this goal to determine whether they should be included in the scope or should be defined as out of scope.

The illustration in Figure 4.1 explains the point. Jigsaw puzzles come in all sizes and shapes but the point of each is to complete a puzzle. If two puzzles are mixed together or pieces of one puzzle are missing, you cannot complete the goal of finishing the puzzle. All of the puzzle pieces (objectives) must be focused on the same picture and none of them should be missing.

Figure 4.1
If the parts of the puzzle (or deliverables you define for the project) are mixed with another puzzle, are in the wrong place, or are completely left out, the outcome will not be as you expected.

It is very important that the project has one—and only one—driving goal. Problems most often occur when stakeholders do not agree on the purpose of the project or have competing needs and objectives. Rather than try to accommodate all of the needs, the project must have one driver. All additional objectives should support that goal in some way or should be defined as "out of scope." A project with multiple goals can result in a lot of churn when things do not go according to plan, because the team cannot easily make a decision on which components are the most critical for project success.

In addition, clear boundaries and rules of fair play must be defined to ensure that reaching the goal is done in a manner that does not have a negative impact. The next section develops this idea further.

Clarify the Constraints and Boundaries

This section addresses two topics that are essential to building a good project schedule. It will help the team understand what is in scope and what is out of scope. It will also help you and your team define the work that must be accomplished and the manner in which it will be done.

Define the Boundaries—Rules of Fair Play

Reaching a goal should never be planned at the expense of everything else. Projects exist in an overall mission context that they must support and not negatively impact. A set of rules helps define and guard project boundaries while building a proper framework that enables flexibility within the project while also ensuring the overall corporate mission context is protected. For example, a company that produces playground equipment for schools may need to reduce the costs of its manufacturing process. If the company launches a project that has a primary driving goal to reduce costs for the manufacturing process, there are hundreds of ways that this could be accomplished. Some of the methods could cause safety issues with the playground equipment. To prevent this concern, the project team could set a boundary that states that the injury statistics for the equipment must not be increased. When the framework is initially set in this way, both the method in which the project is planned and the way that the project is measured will be impacted.

A similar, very obvious example is the project that put a man on the moon. Getting the man on the moon was the easy part; getting him back to earth, alive and well, was a bit more difficult! Not all projects have boundaries that are this critical or visible, but it is easy to see how they impacted the project's budget, schedule, and quality planning. The same is true for even the simplest of projects; the team must determine the rules within which the project will operate. Those decisions will help you decide what is truly in scope, what is out of scope, as well as how and when the project will be completed.

Identify Time, Budget, and Quality Constraints

Clarification of the goal and the scope is critical to obtaining some flexibility in time and budget. In many cases, only one of the factors (time, budget, or quality) is extremely important, and it may become a part of the driving goal. For example, it may be important to be the "first to market" with a particular product concept. In this case, being first is more critical than being the best, so the project manager must focus on timely delivery and limit the number of features or the quality of the product.

Often a project is chartered with preset expectations on not only what the project will provide but also when it will be delivered and how much it will cost. If this is the case, the project manager's job has little to do with managing a project and much more to do with managing expectations. Often, when one of the factors changes, it directly affects the other two. Similarly, if you were to lengthen or shorten one side of the triangle, one of the other two sides, or both, have to be adjusted in order to maintain the shape, as shown in Figure 4.2.

Figure 4.2
Time, budget, and quality are the key variables in a project. You can change the shape of the triangle by increasing or decreasing the variables but you can only change two of the three.

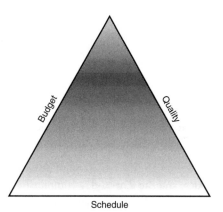

Regardless of the situation, the project team should still work with the stakeholders to clarify the goals and the boundaries before launching into creating a schedule. Even though the tendency is to get resources engaged in activities as soon as you can, it is more critical in this situation to have all resources working on meeting one clear goal.

DEFINE THE FINAL DELIVERABLES

If you have ever worked on a project that never seemed to end, it was probably because there was no clear definition of when the project was done. The goal that is set for a project must be measurable, and there must be a list of deliverables that, once completed, bring the project to a close.

For a home construction project, the deliverables would include a completed house, landscaping, and a certificate of occupancy (CO). Each deliverable must also include a quality component that can be measured. Because many details must be considered, homebuilders typically list them in a walkthrough document for the buyer's approval. The CO may take some time to achieve, but the final result is very clear and measurable.

For a software project, some of the final deliverables would include software, documentation, operational processes, and training. The quality measures can include things such as response times, number/severity of errors in the system test, user acceptance surveys, or other similar measures. The deliverables and the measures should all relate to the driving goal of the project or at least support one of the subordinate goals or objectives.

Without clear, measurable deliverables, there is no way to be sure that all of the stakeholders are in agreement regarding the project's goals. The project team may not even have identified some of the work that the stakeholders are expecting or the quality expectations may not be achievable within the time and cost constraints of the project. It is much better to clarify these points during the planning cycle than to reach the end of the project's budget and time and not be able to deliver work that was never defined.

The process of defining end deliverables will very likely require you to go back and reexamine both the goal and the constraints and boundaries of the project. This is an iterative process and it is time well spent. Without this process working through to completion, you will be creating a list of tasks that may or may not be useful in reaching your goal. The project will certainly expend a large amount of effort but may not earn any true value for the stakeholders.

ESTABLISH A CHANGE CONTROL PROCESS

The final component of organizing for success is planning for change. Change is inevitable, no matter how perfectly your plan. The only thing that you can do is prepare and have a process ready so that when it happens, your team knows how to respond.

Change control provides the discipline to identify and communicate the impact of scope changes, quality demands, risks, issues, and the day-to-day complexities of resource management. Microsoft Project 2007 will help you identify, manage, and report on project changes, so it is a good practice to determine the features that you will use during the planning cycle. For example, establish an expectation for when you will baseline your project, how often you will capture a snapshot of the current schedule, and what criteria you will use to determine if you need to reset the baseline because of scope changes. You should also set up guidelines for how you will track progress and status and what features you will use for reporting.

→ For more information about capturing the baseline and tracking your progress, **see** Chapter 13, "Tracking Your Project Progress," **p. 443**.

WORK BREAKDOWN STRUCTURE

Once you have clarity on the goal, boundaries, and constraints for your project, it is time to begin the process of identifying all of the work by decomposing the goal into manageable pieces. Of all the projects that fail, most are due to a failure to identify all of the changes to scope or to manage these changes. The *PMBOK Guide* recommends the use of the Work Breakdown Structure (WBS) as the best practice for identifying and managing packages of work in a project schedule. The identification and management of these packages of work are critical to understanding and maintaining project scope.

This section covers key principles of building and using a WBS with a focus on creation of the WBS for accurate and effective management of Microsoft Project 2007 schedules. It is important that your schedule is an accurate reflection of the work required to reach a successful conclusion of your project. Using a WBS will help you reach that goal by ensuring you cover 100% of the scope of your project without adding activities that are not related. This book does not attempt to cover all of the details; there are much more thorough reference materials for that as identified at the beginning of this chapter.

WORK BREAKDOWN STRUCTURE (WBS) CONCEPTS

You can create a WBS using Microsoft Project 2007, but it is often more useful to create the first iteration on a whiteboard because it will change multiple times before you are ready to finalize it. The iterative process typically begins with a top-down decomposition of deliverables through successive levels of detail until you reach a level where the work can be planned and controlled. This level is called a *work package*. All levels of decomposition from Level 1 (the project) through the lowest level (work package) are noun-based and focus on the deliverable, not how the deliverable is achieved. Many levels may be required, depending on the complexity of the project, and not all branches of the WBS will require the same number of sublevels of breakdown. The lowest-level WBS element (the work package) will eventually contain the set of activities or tasks that need to be performed to accomplish the achievement identified by the work package. A work package should be able to be assigned to one work group or an individual for performance. If that cannot be done, it may not be broken out as far as it should be.

The example in Figure 4.3 shows the levels of decomposition that are used in a WBS to break a project into the appropriate work packages.

Figure 4.3
Work is decomposed to the lowest level needed for effective management and tracking (work package).

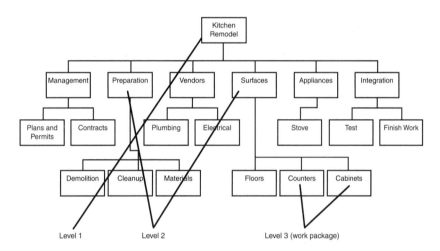

Decomposition of work into appropriate work packages and the associated activities for those packages can be reflected in Microsoft Project 2007 as well. The lowest level of the WBS—the work package—will be represented by a summary task. All activities within that work package should be kept together and linked with a starting and an ending milestone.

Figure 4.4 shows an example of a task activity list in Microsoft Project 2007 that is derived from the WBS example in Figure 4.3.

Figure 4.4
Work packages within Microsoft Project 2007 should have a starting and an ending milestone.

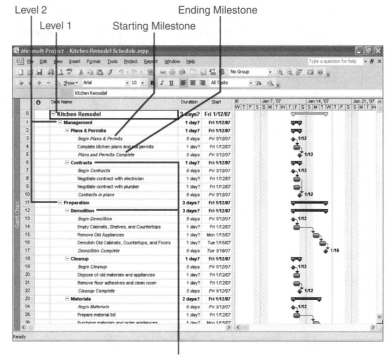

There are a few rules regarding building a WBS that should be kept in mind when developing a schedule in Microsoft Project 2007:

- **Number of levels**—The number of levels in a WBS will vary with the complexity of the project. Some elements may have more levels of detail than others. Elements are described with nouns and adjectives.

- **Level 2 elements**—This level includes project management and at least one other element, depending on the type of deliverables to be produced by the project: product, service, or result. There may also be additional elements at Level 2 and below that support neighboring elements (cross-cutting elements) or represent the next step in a process. See Figure 4.5 for an example.

- **Level 3 and below (work package elements)**—Decomposition continues as needed until the work package, the lowest element of a WBS, is reached. It must be at a level of decomposition sufficient to be controlled and performed by one individual or one organizational entity. A work package is broken into activities and tasks that are described with a verb (see Figure 4.5).

- **WBS dictionary**—Each element of a WBS may be described in more detail in a WBS dictionary. Additional information about the element, including budget, cost, and earned value data may also be included there.

■ **100% rule**—Each lower level of decomposition must represent all of the work of the higher-level element; conversely, all higher-level scope must be reflected in one of the lower-level elements. This is called the 100% rule, which ensures that all of the scope has been captured and that nothing extraneous is included.

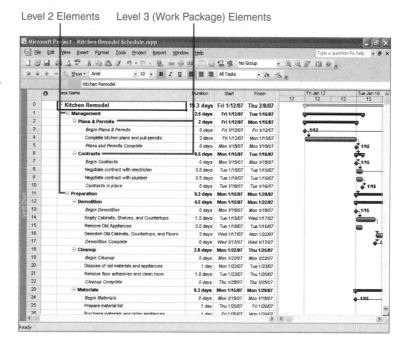

Figure 4.5
Level 2 elements include Management and at least one other element based on the type of deliverables that the project will produce.

As you can see from these examples, the WBS can be created in Microsoft Project 2007 or as a whiteboard exercise prior to opening a schedule. The *Practice Standard for Work Breakdown Structures, Second Edition* (PMI, 2006) recommends that the team be involved in the creation of the WBS. The focus for this process should be on the outputs to be produced so that the team uses nouns to describe what will be produced and can identify all of the cross-cutting elements that are required.

WBS AND SCHEDULING

Regardless of the methods that are chosen to create the schedule, the process will be iterative. Some groups will choose to begin the process using top-down decomposition. Others may choose to identify all of the work they can using brain-storming techniques and then organize the work into logical packages. Either method is effective as a starting point as there will be several iterations combining both completed before the team will be satisfied that all work has been identified. It is important to remember that certain types of work, such as integration of elements, are often only recognized from the bottom-up view. Examples of this would include assembly of components in a manufacturing project or quality testing in a software project.

The iterative nature of building a WBS, and subsequently a schedule, requires a great deal of realignment and reordering of elements. When developing and maintaining the WBS structure, it is important that you remember the 100% rule mentioned previously. You should maintain work packages as units and move them as units within the schedule rather than moving individual tasks below the work package. Once the work packages have been identified, they can be rearranged, but you should have the same set of lowest-level work packages regardless of the realignment. Use the 100% rule to validate the process and always focus on the outputs of the packages rather than the resources required to do the work.

TIP

> Remember that the work package is the lowest component of a WBS; once you are sure that you have captured all of them, organize them in a way that is meaningful to the team. Tasks are defined at the level below the work package.

Figures 4.6 and 4.7 show examples of how work packages can exist in different locations in the project schedule. In this case, the work package called "Cabinets" exists under the Level 2 task "Surfaces" in Figure 4.6, and under the Level 2 task "Storage" in Figure 4.7. Remember, a work package is defined as the lowest level of the WBS; the tasks (activities to be performed) are broken out below the work package level.

Figure 4.6
Work packages can be aligned in different ways; use the 100% rule to verify the scope.

Figure 4.7
The "Cabinets" work package has been moved. If "Storage" existed as a Level 2 component in your WBS, this may be a more appropriate place for the "Cabinets" work package.

Avoid the tendency to define the work according to the groups that may be performing the work during initial decomposition because this will limit your thinking and make it easier to violate the 100% rule. Instead, focus on the work to be delivered and then assign it to a group as appropriate.

Once the team is satisfied that all work has been captured and decomposed to the appropriate level, the WBS work packages are set to be the basis for adding precedence and resources and creating a schedule. The work packages should have starting and ending milestones to aid with work flow and to ensure that the focus remains on the production of deliverables. Refer back to Figure 4.4 for examples of these milestones.

USE OF TEMPLATES

Most organizations repeatedly deliver similar projects. Templates can be extremely useful for capturing the best practices developed into repeatable standards and reporting, giving new projects a jumpstart to success. The top two levels of the WBS can often be used consistently across an organization. The project management elements can be standardized, as can many other cross-cutting elements. Standard templates will minimize the amount of startup work required to determine process use for each project and will also improve the organization's ability to control scope on the elements that are consistent across projects.

WBS NUMBERING

Microsoft Project 2007 has a field called WBS that can be customized to fit the organization's WBS numbering schema. The default WBS code is identical to the outline numbers that Microsoft Project 2007 generates and stores in the Outline Number field. You can display both of these fields in a table by inserting the columns, as shown in Figure 4.8.

Figure 4.8
The Outline Number field and the default WBS code are identical.

To insert these fields onto your screen, follow these steps:

1. Right-click on the column header where you wish to insert the column (field), and choose Insert Column. This will open the Column Definition dialog box. All columns to the right, including the column you right-clicked in, will shift to the right to make room for the new column insertion.

2. In the Column Definition dialog box, choose either Outline Number or WBS from the drop-down list in the Field Name field.

3. Click OK to close the Column Definition dialog box and insert the column.

Repeat these steps to insert the other column (the one you did not just insert), either Outline Number or WBS.

If your team chooses to use these fields, you must be aware that the Outline Number field and WBS field are identical in Microsoft Project's default mode and the number associated with a work package will change if the package is moved within the project schedule. If the WBS numbering schema must remain the same throughout the life of the project, use a custom field that you must then maintain instead of the automatic WBS field provided by Microsoft Project 2007.

> By default, the value in the Microsoft Project 2007 WBS field will automatically change if a work package is moved from one location to another within the schedule.

CREATING CUSTOM WBS CODES

To customize the WBS code format in the Microsoft Project 2007 WBS field, you can generate custom codes using a *WBS code mask*. The mask contains numbers or characters for each outline level, with separators between the levels. There is a total limit of 255 characters, which is sufficient to handle even the most complex WBS structure. For projects that are part of a larger program, you can also include a project-level code that will be a prefix for all tasks within the project.

To create a custom WBS code, follow these steps:

1. Choose Project, WBS, Define Code to display the WBS Code Definition dialog box, as shown in Figure 4.9.

2. Enter a code prefix for the project, if needed, in the Project Code Prefix box. Identify a separator, such as a colon or period, to make it easier for the reader to identify the levels.

3. Click the first blank row under the Sequence column in the Code Mask table and select the appropriate option from the drop-down menu for numbers or letters, as appropriate for your organization. You can display your options with the pull-down arrow, which are:

   - **Numbers (ordered)**—Microsoft Project 2007 will insert sequential numbers for this part of the code. You can edit these numbers later.

   - **Uppercase Letters (ordered)**—Microsoft Project 2007 will insert sequential uppercase letters.

   - **Lowercase Letters (ordered)**—Microsoft Project 2007 will insert sequential lowercase letters.

   - **Characters (unordered)**—Microsoft Project 2007 will insert an asterisk (*). You can go back and change it to any character later.

4. Specify the length of the field or choose Any to allow flexibility in the number of characters. Use the pull-down arrow in the Length column to show the options for the number of characters you can use for this part of the formatting:

   - Select Any when you want to later edit this part of the code, using a variety of number of characters.

   - Select 1 though 10 when you want to set a fixed number of characters for this section of formatting.

5. Identify a separator from the choices in the drop-down menu or type another symbol directly on the keyboard.

4

6. Repeat steps 3, 4, and 5 for each additional level of the WBS. The Code Preview field at the top of the dialog box will show you what the custom WBS code will look like as you are creating the mask.

7. If you want Microsoft Project 2007 to automatically generate the WBS codes for you, select the box Generate WBS Code for New Task. If this box is cleared, you will need to enter the codes manually but will be required to follow the format defined in this process.

8. If you want Microsoft Project 2007 to check for duplicate codes, select the box Verify Uniqueness of New WBS Codes. The check will only occur when you edit the codes, and you will need to modify the codes manually to make them unique. It is generally a good idea to have this box selected to avoid confusion with the WBS codes.

9. Click OK to save the mask. Microsoft Project 2007 will automatically replace the default WBS code with the new codes you have designed. If your project is complex and has many levels, you may need to widen the column to see the entire code. Double-click the column header and click Best Fit in the Column Definition dialog box.

Initial codes
supplied by Project

WBS code mask

Edit bar

Figure 4.9
Microsoft Project 2007
will create custom WBS
codes through your
formatted mask.

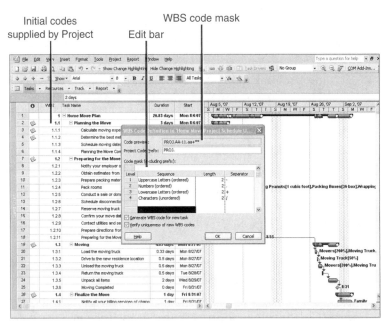

NOTE

If you have not defined enough levels in the mask for all of your WBS, Microsoft Project 2007 will use the default numbering system for the lower levels.

You can force Microsoft Project 2007 to renumber all of the codes in your WBS, but you will lose any special coding that you have done manually. (See the section "Renumbering the Custom WBS Codes," later in this chapter.)

If you use the check box to verify the uniqueness for new codes, Microsoft Project 2007 will only check the code when it is created or edited. If your project file has custom WBS codes that were set up when this feature was disabled, and you then decide to enable unique codes, Microsoft Project 2007 will not check the existing codes for uniqueness. If necessary, you can force Microsoft Project 2007 to renumber all of the codes, which is to say generate new codes for the task, to correct your non-unique ones. This will also cause you to lose any codes you have typed in manually.

If you want to reduce the number of defined levels in the mask, you can only delete the bottom-most level of the Sequence table. Start with the bottom-most level and use the Delete key to clear your mask, then work your way up the list, deleting from the bottom up.

TIP

> If necessary, you can edit every task's code, forcing Microsoft Project 2007 to check each task's uniqueness. You can do this quickly and easily by choosing the WBS column, so all of the cells are selected, and pressing F2 to edit the first cell. Then press Enter to force Microsoft Project 2007 to make a uniqueness check. If your code is unique, Microsoft Project 2007 will move onto the next cell in the selection. Press F2 and Enter again to process the next cell. It is easy to move down the column this way quite quickly, provided the codes are unique. If not, you will have to stop and change the code before you finish.

4

INSERTING, DELETING, AND MOVING TASKS WITH CUSTOM WBS CODES

It is a best practice to stabilize your WBS and your schedule before adding the custom WBS codes so that you do not have to spend too much time making changes to them. On occasion, however, you will find that you need to add or delete tasks and perhaps move entire work packages to different areas of your WBS. Microsoft Project 2007 makes some automatic numbering changes, and you will need to be aware of how these changes work if you use custom WBS codes.

When you insert a new task into a work package (summary task group), Microsoft Project 2007 will automatically give it the next highest codes for the level. If you delete a task, Microsoft Project 2007 will renumber the tasks that follow. If these are not the behaviors that you want, you will need to manage the addition and deletion carefully.

If you move a task to another row within a work package, it will keep its original code even though it will no longer be in sequence. If you move a task from one work package to another (not a recommended practice), it will acquire the correct prefix code for the new work package. The final part of the code may change if it would be a duplicate of an existing task within the package.

EDITING CUSTOM WBS CODES

You can only edit the last segment of any of the custom codes; all of the higher-level segments are derived from the higher levels (summary task levels). The segment codes can be changed at the summary task level if the assignment made by Microsoft Project 2007 does not fit with what your organization would like to see.

For instance, in Figure 4.10, the major phases have been edited as abbreviations or acronyms for the name of the phase. AA was the default WBS code for the Planning the Move phase, but it has been changed to PLAN. It makes it easier to realize a task's place within the WBS code.

Figure 4.10
Editing the default letters assigned by Microsoft Project 2007 in the custom WBS codes lets you describe how a task fits into the task list.

When your WBS column is not displayed in the table, you can edit the code in the Summary Task Information dialog box. You can see the custom fields on the Custom Fields tab, as shown in Figure 4.11. Simply choose the Value cell for the field you want to change and then enter the change in the Entry bar.

Entry bar   Value cell

Figure 4.11
You can use the Custom Fields tab of the Summary Task Information dialog box to edit the WBS code.

If you want to show the tasks in their WBS code order, select Project, Sort, Sort By, and then select the WBS field in the Sort By box.

You will lose your edited codes if you edit custom codes for summary tasks and then tell Microsoft Project 2007 to renumber the tasks. Use the following steps to prevent that from happening:

1. Open the Options dialog box by selecting Tools, Options, View tab.
2. Clear the Show Summary Tasks check box and then click OK. Only the normal and milestone tasks should be displayed.
3. Choose one of the column headings to select all displayed tasks.
4. Select Project, WBS, Renumber to bring up the WBS Renumbering dialog box.
5. Click the Selected Tasks button instead of the Entire Project button.
6. Click OK to begin renumbering.
7. You can then restore the display of summary tasks by selecting Tools, Options and selecting the Show Summary check box in the View tab. Close the dialog box by clicking OK, and then click any cell to unselect all tasks.

Your entire task list will be displayed again. Your summary tasks have not lost their edited codes, but all of your other tasks have been renumbered to the current order of the outline.

RENUMBERING THE CUSTOM WBS CODES

As you are designing your project, you are likely to revise the task list somewhere along the line. If you have already defined the custom WBS codes by this time, they might not be in sequence after the editing. Microsoft Project 2007 will recalculate the WBS codes for the whole project, putting them into sequence for you. Follow these steps to renumber the WBS codes:

1. If you are only renumbering a small, selected set of tasks, choose those tasks first (they must be adjacent to one other). The first selected task will not be renumbered, but will be the starting point for renumbering the rest of the selection.
2. Go to Project, WBS, Renumber to pull up the WBS Renumbering dialog box, shown in Figure 4.12.
3. Pick either Selected tasks or Entire project.
4. Click OK to begin renumbering.
5. If you decide to renumber the whole task list, Microsoft Project 2007 will ask you to confirm your decision. Click Yes or No as necessary.

Figure 4.12
You can renumber the entire project, or just a small select set of tasks, using the WBS Renumbering dialog box.

If, even with a warning to confirm your decision, you still end up realizing that you did not want to renumber, you can go back and use the Undo feature to restore your original codes.

SCOPE CONTROL AND CHANGE CONTROL

If you use the WBS approach to building your schedule, it is much easier to control the scope of the project. The 100% rule defeats the "as long as you are there" phenomenon: the tendency to add features that are not within scope because they would be nice to have.

Using the 100% rule allows you to perform top-down planning and budgeting and also enables tracking and reporting at the work package level. This is essential if you will be using any type of the earned value reporting in your project. You will be able to baseline the project and keep track of history at a work package level rather than trying to manage at the individual activity level.

Change control should also be viewed at the work package level. Budget and schedule impacts are easier to control in logical units, and it is also much easier to see the ripple effect of a requested change at the work package level.

CONSULTANTS' TIPS

UNDERSTANDING A WORK BREAKDOWN STRUCTURE

Microsoft Project 2007 uses the term "Work Breakdown Structure (WBS)" to mean a hierarchical list of working activities. The tasks you create in a Microsoft Project 2007 schedule are really an Activity Breakdown Structure (ABS) showing the relationship of tasks throughout the schedule.

The term WBS has a formal definition and United States government MIL-HDBK-881A standard. That standard describes how a WBS is used to define the cost and management control structures that define the official scope of your project. Even though this is a government military standard, project management discipline has adopted this standard as the basis for defining a Work Breakdown Structure. You should review this standard to better understand the distinction between Activity Breakdown Structure and Work Breakdown Structure.

You should also consider reviewing ANSI/EIA Standard 748 that defines Earned Value Management (EVM) and specifically refers to the formal WBS definitions. EVM is a well-defined strategy to clearly determine how your project is performing against defined Work Breakdown Structure scope.

Use your favorite internet search engine to learn more about Work Breakdown Structure and Earned Value Management.

TIP

> You can also learn more about these subjects from the QuantumPM website that has reference to a Microsoft Project add-in tool for creating a Work Breakdown Structures and using EVM methods. Visit www.quantumpm.com to learn more about WBS and EVM.

4

DEFINE THE FULL SCOPE OF YOUR PROJECT

When building a schedule, it is always easier to add more detail later than to take it out. If you keep your schedule focused on deliverables, it will be much easier to identify deliverables that have not been fully defined. This allows much greater flexibility in setting the scope for a project. (This is accomplished naturally if you follow the best practice of creating a WBS prior to creating a schedule! It is extremely difficult to keep WBS principles in mind when you jump to creation of a schedule without having gone through prior creation of a WBS.)

BUILD WBS USING DELIVERABLES

Avoid the tendency to structure your schedule according to workgroup during initial decomposition because it will limit your thinking and make it much easier to violate the 100% rule. Focus on the work to be delivered, describe it completely in a WBS and WBS dictionary, and then assign the logical flow of precedence and the resources.

DEFINE PROJECT WORK PACKAGES

Understand the work package level of your project as the most important component for providing scope management and control. This will keep you "out of the weeds," and you can make decisions based on the impact to the work package rather than trying to deal with many activities. You can rearrange work packages in a variety of ways and still be assured that the scope of the project is accurate. There is no single correct structure for WBS; work packages can be arranged in a variety of ways.

Make sure that all of the work packages within your project support the Measure of Success and that you have an objective method to measure both progress and accomplishment of the project goal. Most project failures are due to not understanding or managing scope; project success requires a clear goal and a scope of work that supports the goal.

BUILD THE WBS FIRST, THEN DEFINE THE PROJECT SCHEDULE FROM IT

Many project managers skip the process of building a WBS before they build a schedule because the demands of business tend to push for decisions on resources and dates. Microsoft Project was created to answer the scheduling need and does an excellent job of scheduling, but it does not help the project manager control scope unless the WBS rigor is applied at the beginning. QuantumPM, LLC has created some tools to make it easier for project managers to apply the WBS rigor and still get the scheduling components in place as quickly as possible. Review the products **WBS *Director*** and **Earned Value *Manager*** for more information. See the QuantumPM website for more product information (www.quantumpm.com).

4

CHAPTER **5**

SETTING UP PROJECT FOR YOUR USE

In this chapter

DEFINING PROJECT INFORMATION

When you sit down to plan the scope of a new project, it is important to ask yourself exactly what your objectives are, and to take your time and be thorough when defining your project information. Planning a project can be daunting, especially to the novice project planner, but taking the time to plan and organize your project at its beginning will provide for much smoother and more efficient execution during the project stages. Project 2007 will aid tremendously in the process of planning, creating, and maintaining a schedule that is appropriate for the project you will manage.

There is no such thing as perfect project planning. It is inevitable that situations will arise during your project that require modifying your plan in one way or another. The best defense is a comprehensive, realistic project schedule that anticipates setbacks and provides the foundation for your success as a project manager.

Microsoft Project 2007 supplies several settings that will affect how you schedule and manage your project. It is a good idea to examine these settings when first creating a project and make any necessary changes to them that will work to your benefit. You can change many of these settings after tasks and resources have been entered into the project, but by addressing these issues up front, you are guaranteed to create a schedule that is based on logic and calculated reason.

TIP

> You should enter all known information about the project at the beginning. The more information you know about any aspect of the project, the more consistent and organized your project will be.

Microsoft Project is an excellent tool to help you manage the three main areas of information of any project schedule (scope, schedule, and cost), but before you enter any tasks, you should ask yourself the following questions:

- What makes up my entire project? What is agreed upon work scope and what should be considered out of scope?
- What expectations have already been set for start and completion dates? Do I have any set constraints on the schedule of this project? If so, the scope of the project must be very tightly managed.
- How much is the project going to cost? Do I have any set constraints on the budget of this project? Again, if expectations have been set, the project scope must be closely managed.

These questions will help you establish the correct parameters for creating the schedule.

UNDERSTANDING THE PROJECT INFORMATION DIALOG BOX

A limited set of project information can be defined, viewed, and edited in Project using the Project Information dialog box. To view the Project Information dialog box, click Project, Project Information. The Project Information dialog box will appear (see Figure 5.1).

Figure 5.1
The Project
Information dialog box
allows you to set high-
level parameters for
your schedule dates,
scheduling approach,
and calendar choices.

The Project Information dialog box is used for entering basic information about a project. It includes project start and finish dates, as well as the base calendar to use for scheduling. The following sections describe in greater detail the fields represented in the Project Information dialog box.

NOTE

The Project Information dialog box in Project Professional 2007 also includes additional, enterprise fields that are not part of the Project Standard 2007. These fields include Priority and any project-level enterprise custom fields. Note that the Priority field also exists in Project Standard 2007, but the only place where you can specify it is if you display the zero-level project summary task in the Gantt Chart view.

START DATE, FINISH DATE, AND SCHEDULE FROM

One of the key decisions to make in the Project Information dialog box is whether you are going to schedule your project from the start date or from the finish date. By default, Project uses the start date. This is the preferred method of scheduling because it provides the most flexibility in determining when work must begin. Tasks within the schedule are set to begin as soon as possible so there are no artificial time delays in the plan. The finish date will also be as soon as possible, based on the relationships established between tasks. Most project managers use this default option if they can because it is intuitive and the logic is easy to follow.

In some cases, a project may be required to complete on a specific date and the project manager will choose to use Project Finish Date. If there is plenty of time available to complete the project, this will put the start date in the future and so the method can be useful in determining the last possible date for launching the project. In most cases, however, project managers find themselves in the situation where the project has more work to be done than there is time to complete and so the Start Date will be calculated in the past. You haven't even started the work and you are already behind schedule. Deciphering how to pull the start date forward to a current date is much more problematic because all of the tasks are starting as late as possible. This method is time-consuming and difficult to manage so be aware of the consequences if you choose to use it.

In Figure 5.1, the project is scheduled to begin on Tuesday, August 1st, 2006. You can change the start date by typing the date in the Start Date field, or by clicking the drop-down arrow and choosing the date from the calendar. When you enter a start date, Project schedules the first task to begin on that date, and calculates the project's schedule based on that date and the sequence of tasks that follow.

5

If you want to schedule your project from the finish date, click the drop-down arrow in the Schedule from field and choose Project Finish Date. Then you can enter the date in the Finish date field by typing it in or choosing from the calendar with the drop-down arrow. Project schedules the final task to finish on the finish date, and schedules the task before it to finish in time for the final task to start, and so on, until the first task is scheduled and the project now has a defined start date.

NOTE

> You cannot choose both a start date and a finish date for your project. If you schedule from the start date, Project automatically calculates the finish date based on the duration of the project's tasks. If you schedule from a finish date, Project schedules the project's final task to finish on that date, and its start date is determined by the duration of the tasks.

If you choose Project Start Date in the Schedule from field, Project will only allow you to enter the start date. If you choose Project Finish Date, then you can only enter the finish date. You can change this setting as often as you like. This setting can helpful for anticipating a schedule. For example, if you would like to know when you would need to start a project based on its finish date, enter the finish date and the task details of the project, and Project will calculate the start date to give you an idea of when you would need to begin work. The same concept applies if you are trying to get an idea of when a project will be finished if it starts on a certain date. Be aware that the logic at the task level does not automatically change, however, so the logic for the task constraint type will remain as it was.

→ For additional information on constraints and logic applied when scheduling tasks, **see** Chapter 7, "Defining Task Logic," **p. 197**.

TIP

> Although Project provides the ability to schedule the project from a finish date, it is not recommended. Most common practice is to schedule the project from the start date, which is also easier to manage because if the schedule slips, it is more natural to perform actions that bring it back to the planned finish. If you do decide to schedule the project from the finish date and the project slips, Project will push the start date further into the past. Unless you are experienced with Project and project management concepts, it will be difficult for you to manage the situation and figure out the appropriate actions to repair the schedule. It is also a lot more natural for most people to schedule forward instead of backwards.

CURRENT DATE AND STATUS

Project 2007 uses the Current Date and Status Date fields to perform several date-related calculations. The Current Date is supplied automatically from your computer's internal clock. When viewing the Gantt Chart, the dashed date line represents the current date, defined by this field. Because it can lead to unnecessary confusion, it is not recommended that you change the Current Date field, unless your computer's internal clock is incorrect. If you leave the Status Date box as NA, Project uses the Current Date as the Status Date.

You can use the Current Date as a point of reference when tracking progress. However, if you want to track progress using a date other than the Current Date, you enter that date in the Status Date field. The status date is what Project uses for calculating Earned Value and other tracking purposes.

For example, it is typical that project managers will track a week's progress after the end of that week. If on Monday a project manager wanted to track the progress from the previous week, then he or she would enter the previous Friday's date (or whatever date the workweek ended on) in the Status Date box. That information is then processed back to the project schedule and to the project manager, and he or she would use a status date that reflects the latest information.

→ For more information about tracking progress, **see** "Tracking Your Project Progress," **p. 443**.

To change the Current Date field or enter a Status Date setting, select the box and either type in the date or choose it from the calendar via the drop-down arrow.

CALENDAR

When scheduling tasks within projects, Microsoft Project 2007 uses base calendars to define the default working and nonworking days. In the Project Information dialog box, click the Calendar drop-down field to view all available base calendars, including the ones you have defined yourself. Out-of-the-box Project contains three base calendars:

- **24 Hour**—Continuous time from midnight to midnight, 24 hours a day
- **Night Shift**—Used for overnight work that begins at the end of one night and finishes the following morning
- **Standard**—The standard workweek in the United States: 40 hours, 5 days, 8:00 a.m. to 5:00 p.m., with an hour lunch break

The default base calendar is the Standard calendar. This calendar assumes 5 days of work each week (Monday through Friday), from 8:00 a.m. to 12:00 p.m., an hour for lunch, and then 1:00 p.m. to 5:00 p.m. This Standard calendar does not designate set holidays; you have to do that yourself. To define the base calendar best suited for your project, you can edit the Standard calendar, use one of the other built-in base calendars, or create your own base calendar.

The calendar is critical to a major schedule assumption. Anytime you are planning, you are basing your estimates and basing your schedule on the information you know when you are creating your project. For example, you might know that a particular resource, such as a contractor, is available to work part time at 4 hours per day, Monday through Friday. However, if you schedule the resource as someone who works 8 hours a day, you can imagine that your schedule will soon be off because that employee will fall behind. Creating and editing base calendars will be covered later in this chapter.

→ For detailed information on task durations and creating subtasks, **see** Chapter 6, "Creating Your Project Schedule," **p. 143**.

STATISTICS

Next to the Help button is the Statistics button. Click this button to view the Project Statistics dialog box. This box contains brief summary information about the project. You can also view it by clicking the Project Statistics icon on the Tracking toolbar. To display the Tracking toolbar, right-click anywhere in the toolbar and select Tracking. Figure 5.2 shows the Project Statistics dialog box.

Figure 5.2
The Project Statistics dialog box provides a quick summary of a project's status.

Project Statistics for 'Home Move Project Schedule.mpp'				[X]
		Start		Finish
Current		Tue 8/1/06		Fri 9/1/06
Baseline		Tue 8/1/06		Tue 8/29/06
Actual		Tue 8/1/06		NA
Variance		0d		3.17d
	Duration	Work		Cost
Current	24d	58h		$551.12
Baseline	20.83d	56h		$525.12
Actual	12.25d	50h		$408.31
Remaining	11.75d	8h		$142.80

Percent complete:
Duration: 51%   Work: 86%   [Close]

Data in the Project Statistics dialog box cannot be modified. It is simply a quick reference to view or print.

The Project Statistics box shows the currently scheduled values for five project factors: Start Date, Finish Date, Duration, Work, and Cost. If you have saved the baseline copy of the schedule, the baseline values are also displayed for comparison.

When work is performed on the project and the progress is recorded, the information in the Actual row is updated to reflect the recorded progress. Also, at the bottom-left corner, the percent complete of the duration and work of the project are shown. The Project Statistics dialog box in Figure 5.2 displays statistics mid-way through the project's duration; out of the scheduled 20.3 days, 12.25 days have been completed, or 51% overall. The Project Statistics box also includes Start and Finish variance values that allow you to easily see how many days the Start or the Finish dates vary from those that you planned.

Click Close to exit the Project Statistics dialog box.

PRIORITY

The Priority field allows you to set the priority of the project. Although it is visible within the Project Information dialog box only if you are using Project Professional 2007, you can still set it within Project Standard.

The Priority field is helpful when you are sharing a group of resources with other projects. When the leveling feature in Microsoft Project is used, if a resource is assigned to work on tasks from different projects at the same time, the project with the higher priority level is what the resource will be leveled to work on first.

→ For more information about Project's leveling feature, **see** Chapter 25, "Resolving Resource Allocation Problems," **p. 885**.

All projects have the same priority level until you change it. The priority starts at a mid-point, 500. 1000 is the highest priority, 0 is the lowest. Refer to Figure 5.3 for an illustration of the Project Information dialog box in Project Professional 2007, which contains the Priority field.

In order to set the Priority field within Project Standard 2007, expose the project summary task by selecting Tools, Options, View tab, and then check the box called Show project summary task. In the Gantt Chart view, add the Priority column by right-clicking on one of the columns in the view, selecting Insert Column, and then selecting Priority from the drop-down list.

TIP

> The Priority field is not as useful within Project Standard as it is within Project Professional because you cannot easily compare the project to other projects you have created within the system. One of the ways to compare the project priorities is to create a master project or combine projects into one Project view using the Window command. For example, if you want to review project priorities within a program.

→ For more information about creating master projects and combining projects into a single Project window, **see** Chapter 24, "Working with Multiple Projects," **p. 853**.

CUSTOM FIELDS

In Project Professional, you are able to view the Custom Fields Table in the Project Information dialog box. The custom fields shown in the Project Information dialog box are Enterprise Custom Fields set within the server environment and do not exist in Project Standard.

→ For more information about local custom fields, **see** "Defining Custom Fields," **p. 127**.

5

Figure 5.3
The Project Information dialog box in Project Professional has two additional fields: Priority and the Custom Fields.

DEFINING PROJECT PROPERTIES

The other area to find and define information about your project is the Properties dialog box. Here, you can view and edit a number of options that describe the project. To open the Properties dialog box, select File, Properties.

Figure 5.4 shows the Properties dialog box opened to the Summary tab. You can see there are five tabs: General, Summary (the default selected tab), Statistics, Contents, and Custom. The following sections will discuss the options available within these tabs.

Figure 5.4
The Properties dialog box provides another area to define and edit aspects of your project.

SUMMARY TAB

The Summary tab is the default selected tab when you open the Properties dialog box (see Figure 5.4). It is an area to define the summary information about a project. The first five fields (Title, Subject, Author, Manager, and Company) are general information about the project and who is associated with it. As the project manager, you may already know this information; but for someone who is viewing this project for the first time, the Summary tab is a useful reference point to the basic project information.

You have the ability to use any information from the Properties dialog box as headers or footers of printed views or reports for the project. The information from the Summary tab is especially functional for this purpose. For example, each printed report could have the project's name (Title), the project manager (Manager), and the company associated with the project at the top of the page. This can help keep documents organized and make your project reports appear much more professional.

→ For a discussion about including information from the Properties dialog box as headers or footers on printed documents, **see** Chapter 20, "Creating and Customizing the Basic Reports," **p. 657**.

The remaining fields—Category, Keywords, and Comments—are useful when searching for the project on your computer. If you have several projects in various stages, it may be difficult to keep track of all of them. Filling in these fields helps keep all of your projects organized into categories, then narrowed down by keywords that will quickly identify the specific project you are looking for. You can keep notes on the project in the Comments field, which for example may help you remember where you left off when last working on the project. The Properties box is a great way to document metadata (information about data) for your project. If in the future you have trouble locating project files, you can search for words entered in the Summary tab in the Open dialog box. Some of the fields in the Properties dialog box are also utilized when using Windows SharePoint Services to share your project with others.

The Hyperlink Base field is where you would enter the main addresses to the hyperlinks associated with the project, whether it is a link to a file on your computer, your server, or a web address.

By default, the Save Preview Picture check box is not selected. To select it, click inside the box. By selecting it, you are telling Project to save a thumbnail sketch of the current view when you save the file. You can browse these pictures when you search for files using the File, Open command.

To enter information in any of the fields in the Properties dialog box, simply select the field and type in the information. Pressing Tab on your keyboard will select the next field below the one you were just in. When you are finished entering the information you want, click OK or press Enter. Click Cancel to exit the box without making any changes. Clicking OK and Cancel have the same function for all five tabs in the Properties dialog box.

NOTE

Pressing Enter will select the OK button everywhere except when the Comments field is selected. Pressing Enter in the Comments box moves you to the next line of text, like in a Word document.

TIP

It is good practice to enter all the information you can in the Summary tab and everywhere else in the Properties dialog box. This is an excellent place to put the metadata of a project. If the information is not entered, a person viewing the project will have to figure out what the project is and who is managing it by sifting through the project itself and deducing. With this information entered, it is clearly defined all in one location in an organized manner. In addition, many file storage systems use metadata in their searches, so this increases the chances of your document being returned in the search results.

GENERAL TAB

The General tab provides information about the project file: the filename, type, location where it is saved, and size. It also displays the dates when the file was created, last modified, and last opened. This tab is blank until the project file is saved for the first time.

The Attributes section of the tab displays the current file permission setting. They get set using the File Properties dialog box. By default, the Archive setting is checked when the file is saved, but access settings can be set by the file owner.

STATISTICS TAB

The Statistics tab provides helpful information about the work on the file. Included are dates when the file was created, last modified, last accessed, and last printed. The other section of the Statistics tab shows who the file was saved by last, how many revisions have been made, and how much total time has been spent editing the file. The information in the Statistics tab is especially useful if there are multiple people accessing, editing, and saving the project. It helps you to keep track of who did what to the file.

CONTENTS TAB

The Contents tab displays the most commonly reviewed information about the project schedule. Included are the project start and finish dates, the scheduled duration, work and cost amounts, and the percentage complete for both duration and work. This is a handy reference point for a quick project schedule review.

CUSTOM TAB

The concept of custom properties is to give project managers the ability to add project attributes to a project file. In the Custom tab, you can add more properties to a file (or delete them). You can then search for files by the values of these properties. This can bring more meaning to your project file. The properties are listed in the Properties list in the bottom of the Custom tab. Figure 5.5 shows the Custom tab in the Properties dialog box.

Figure 5.5
The Custom tab allows you to customize the fields in the Properties dialog box.

To create a custom property for a project, follow these steps:

1. Open the Properties dialog box (File, Properties) and choose the Custom tab.
2. Type a property name in the Name box, or choose from the list. The list includes commonly used properties.
3. In the Type box, use the drop-down list to define the type of data to place in the field. You should use this option only when you will type the value of the property instead of linking it to a field in the project file. When you link the property value to a field, the Type drop-down list is unavailable. The allowable data types are Text, Date, Number, and Yes or No.
4. If you chose Text, Date, or Number in the Text box (step 3), type a value in the Value text box. If you chose the Yes or No option in the Type box, you see Yes and No buttons in the Value box. Select either Yes or No.
5. Click the Add button to add the property to the list in the Properties dialog box. The newly created property appears in the Properties list box at the bottom.

If you want to link a property value to a project field, follow these steps:

1. Open the Properties dialog box (File, Properties) and select the Custom tab.
2. Type a property name in the Name box.
3. Select the Link to Content check box. The Type box is grayed out, and the Value text box becomes a drop-down list. The name of the Value box changes to Source.
4. In the Source drop-down list box, choose the field that has the value you want the property to reflect.
5. Click the Add button to add the property to the list in the Properties dialog box.

If you want to modify the value for a property, follow these steps:

1. Select the property name in the Properties list. This places the current name and value in the text boxes at the top of the dialog box.
2. Change the Type or Value field as needed, and the Add button automatically changes to Modify.
3. If you change the Name field, you have to use the Add button to include it as a new property.
4. You can then use the Delete button to remove the original, leaving the newly named version.
5. Click Modify to complete the change.

To delete a custom property, select it in the Properties list and click Delete.

When you are finished with the custom properties list, click OK, or select another tab to work in. When you are finished with all the tabs, click OK.

DEFINING CALENDARS

Calendar functionality has improved significantly for Project 2007, primarily when entering exceptions and recurrence patterns, which is discussed later in this section.

One of the first major assumptions you have to make in any schedule is how much time you are going to assume is available to complete tasks. You want to make sure that you plan enough time and that you account for all nonworking time as you plan. If, for example, your resources do not work weekends, you will need a schedule that excludes weekends as working days. You will also need to account for all holidays, vacation time, and all other foreseeable nonworking time.

As previously mentioned, all projects are assigned to base calendars, and the Standard calendar (the default) is 40 hours a week, Monday through Friday, 8:00 a.m. to 5:00 p.m., with an hour off for lunch. However, even if this base calendar matches your working schedule, you still may need to make modifications and define exceptions to the working time. Project will allow you to do this, as well as create other calendars for your project.

TIP

> It is important to keep your organization's working environment in mind when constructing base calendars for projects. Choose a calendar so that you can plan for success. If you simply accept the Standard base calendar, you automatically run into an issue: your people cannot spend 8 hours a day working only on your project. Your project schedule ought to reflect reality.
>
> A resource may typically spend 6 out of the 8 hours in a day working on your project, and the other 2 hours on administrative tasks or miscellaneous activity. You could change your base calendar to reflect 6 hours of working time in a day. However, it may be better to simply keep in mind when you are creating your task list that an 8-hour task may take a little more than an 8-hour day.
>
> For most organizations, it is recommended that you keep your 8 hour a day calendar or another calendar that reflects the general start and finish working times of an average day/week, and instead adjust the percentage of time that resources have available each day. This is accomplished by adjusting the resource Max Units which is explained in more detail in Chapter 8. For example, you can use 75% for the Max Units if your resources spend on average 2 hours a day for every day of the week for miscellaneous activities and only 6 hours per day for work on your project.

→ For additional information on Max Units and their use, **see** Chapter 8, "Defining Project Resources," **p. 249**.

MODIFYING AND DEFINING BASE CALENDARS

Much of your calendar modifications will occur on the Change Working Time dialog box. To access it, click Tools, Change Working Time. Figure 5.6 shows the Change Working Time dialog box. The Change Working Time dialog box contains a For Calendar field to define which calendar you are viewing, a legend, a calendar, and two tab options (Exceptions and Work Week) to modify the calendar. When you open the Change Working Time dialog box, the current date is highlighted in bold on the calendar.

Figure 5.6
The Change Working Time dialog box is where you can modify and create base calendars.

DEFINING EXCEPTIONS

The Change Working Time dialog box has improved significantly between Project 2003 and Project 2007. Before, you had to define exceptions to working time (such as holidays and vacation time) one at a time, wherever they occurred each month. Now, you can define a recurrence exception along with its recurrence pattern, so each exception only has to be defined once and you can define a recurrence pattern that you want to apply throughout your project.

For example, if Labor Day is always a nonworking day at your company, you can tell Project to define every Labor Day as an exception. To do this, follow these steps:

1. Open the Change Working Time dialog box (Tools, Change Working Time).
2. Scroll to the month of September using the arrows on the right side of the calendar.
3. Click on Labor Day, the first Monday of every September. In 2007, Labor Day is September 3rd.
4. Under the Exceptions tab, type **Labor Day** in the Name column, and click Enter, or press the directional arrow to the right. The Start and Finish columns will display the date of the highlighted day in the calendar (in this case, 9-3-07).
5. Select the cell in the Start column next to the exception name (in this case, select the 9-3-07 cell in the Start column next to Labor Day) and click the Details button.

5

6. The Details dialog box will appear, as shown in Figure 5.7. If Labor Day is a nonworking holiday, leave the Nonworking option selected. If you want to define working hours (such as a half day), select Working Times and enter the hours of working times for Labor Day.

7. Under Recurrence Pattern, select Yearly, because Labor Day happens once a year. Figure 5.7 shows this selection.

Figure 5.7
The Details dialog box allows you to define the details of your exception, including its recurrence pattern and range.

TIP

The Recurrence Pattern options are Daily, Weekly, Monthly, and Yearly. Click each option to familiarize yourself with defining in detail the recurrence pattern information for all four options. Information appears at the right of the options and varies depending on which one you choose.

8. Since the date for Labor Day changes annually, select the The... option, and then the First Monday of September is filled in automatically. Since this is the appropriate description for Labor Day, you do not have to change anything else.

NOTE

If you were defining a nonworking day that occurs each year on the same date, such as Christmas Eve, you would select the On option and type in the date.

9. The Range of Recurrence automatically fills the selected date from the calendar in the Start field. Since this is the first Labor Day in your project, you do not have to change this field. If you wanted the exception to start on a different date, you can type in the date or use the drop-down list to choose from a calendar.

10. The final step is defining the end of the range of the exception. You can select End By and fill in a date (type it in or use the drop-down), or you could select End After and fill in the number of occurrences you want the exception to end after. Project 2007 supports information up until 12-31-2049, so the maximum number of occurrences you could enter is 43, because there are 43 Labor Days between 9-3-07 and 12-31-2049.

11. Click OK. The date is now highlighted as an Exception Day (as defined in the legend), and if you scroll through every month of September, you will notice the same for every first Monday. Click OK again to close the Change Working Time dialog box, or continue modifying your calendar.

Similarly, if you have a long meeting every Friday, you can simply click on the Friday of the first meeting and repeat the process. Define working hours around the meeting, select a Weekly recurrence pattern on Friday, and define the end of the exception.

You can also define longer exceptions, such as office closures for an extended period. For example, if your company shuts down starting on Christmas until the end of the year, you can define that entire time period as non-working time. To set this up so that it occurs each year, the changes must be made one day at a time,

1. Open the Change Working Time dialog box by selecting Tools, Change Working Time.

2. Scroll to the month of December using the arrows on the right side of the calendar.

3. Click on December 26th.

4. Under the Exceptions tab, type **Holiday** in the Name column, and click Enter, or press the directional arrow to the right. The Start and Finish columns will display the date range of the highlighted period in the calendar.

5. To set up the recurrence pattern for this date click the Details button. Under Recurrence Pattern select Yearly and the On (December 26 in this case) option is automatically selected.

6. Under Range of recurrence you can either specify the number of years by selecting the End after option and then entering the number (of years, in this case) that this exception will apply to. Or you can also select the End by option and select the specific date (in this case 12/26/2009) until which the exceptions will apply. The date you provide here is inclusive, so in this example the last year the exception will be applied is 2009. Click OK.

Repeat this process for each day in the closure period, even if it falls on a weekend in the first year. This will allow you to make sure that all days between 12/26 and 12/31 are non-working days, regardless of where they fall in the week. You can verify that the change is correct by reviewing the number of occurrences shown in the dialog box in Figure 5.8. In this example, the number is "3" because the recurrence time period was established as 3 years.

5

Figure 5.8
The Details dialog box allows you to define the details of your exception period and set up the exact period as well as the recurrence pattern in which it occurs.

If you have successfully made an exception, the numbers on the dates of the exception will appear as defined in the legend.

CREATING NEW BASE CALENDARS

It is helpful to make exceptions to your base calendar to account for small changes in working time. However, sometimes it is more efficient to simply create a new base calendar completely and apply that to your project. For example, assume your resources work 40 hours a week, but only 4 days a week. Rather than going through and changing every Monday through Thursday to 10 hour days and making Friday a nonworking day, it is easier to just create a new base calendar that more accurately depicts your standard working time.

To do this, follow these steps:

1. Open the Change Working Time dialog box by selecting Tools, Change Working Time.

2. Click the Create New Calendar button at the top, which opens the Create New Base Calendar box.

3. Type in a distinctive name in the Name field.

4. Select the Create New Base Calendar option if you want to start from scratch on the standard 40-hour workweek, or select the Make a Copy Of option if you want to use an existing base calendar as your template. Click OK.

NOTE

> Selecting Make a Copy Of changes your calendar name from what you named it to "Copy of [name of calendar you are making a copy of]." If you still want to call it your original name, change it back.

Notice that the For Calendar field at the top of the Change Working Time dialog box has defined the new base calendar with the name you gave it. Also, when you are finished creating the calendar, if you open your Project Information dialog box (Project, Project Information), you will see the new base calendar listed as an option for the project base calendar in the Calendar drop-down list.

5. Once you have defined your new base calendar, it is time to define your workweek. Click the Work Weeks tab, and click the Details button or double-click on Default in the Name column. The Details dialog box will appear, in which you define your workweek (see Figure 5.9).

Figure 5.9
Define your workweek when creating a base calendar in the Details dialog box.

6. To define a 40-hour, 4-day workweek (Monday–Thursday, 10 hours a day), go through each day in the Details dialog box. Sunday is selected first. Since this is a nonworking day, you can select either Set Days to Nonworking Time or Use Project Default Times for These Days.

7. Next, highlight Monday. Select Set Day(s) to These Specific Times. In the From and To columns, set the appropriate working hours. Be sure to press Enter after each cell entry to save the information. For example, you could type **8:00 a.m.** in the From column, press Enter, and type **12:00 p.m.** in the To column and press Enter. Then for afternoon hours, type **1:00 p.m.** in the From column, press Enter, and type **7:00 p.m.** in the To column and press Enter. This will give you a 10-hour day with an hour off for lunch. If you are satisfied with this schedule, repeat the process for Tuesday, Wednesday, and Thursday.

> **TIP**
>
> To enter time for multiple days simultaneously, hold down Shift and drag your mouse over the multiple days you want to change. Alternatively, hold down Ctrl and click each day individually.

NOTE

> You can enter time in 12-hour clock format or 24-hour clock format (military time). If you're using the 12-hour format, noon is 12:00 p.m. and midnight is 12:00 a.m. If the time is on the hour, you only have to enter the single number (5 p.m. for 5:00 p.m.). Be sure to define a.m. and p.m. Otherwise, Project may misinterpret your times.

NOTE

> Generally, only the first four working hours boxes are defined: the top two for morning hours and the bottom two for afternoon hours. Sometimes you will use the remaining boxes to account for multiple breaks or meals, or for other unusual work schedules. You must define the To and From fields as pairs, and the From field must come later than the To field.

8. Finally, highlight Friday and select Set Days to Nonworking Times. Do the same for Saturday, and press OK.

Notice how the new calendar is created, with all Fridays set as nonworking days, and the working times for Monday through Thursday reflect what you defined.

When you have finished, click OK to close the Change Working Time dialog box, or click Cancel to exit without saving.

SETTING PROJECT AND RESOURCES CALENDAR

Start dates for tasks are generally determined by resource calendars, unless you create a task calendar, in which case the resource will operate based on the task calendar. Resource and task calendars begin as the base calendar for the project. You can modify the resource and task calendars without changing the base calendar. The previous sections talked about the base calendar; the next few sections will discuss resource and task calendars.

Project uses the following order to calculate when a resource and task are scheduled to work by using the calendars:

1. Project (base) calendar
2. Resource calendar
3. Task calendar

A task is scheduled according to the project calendar if it has no resources and no specific task calendar assigned. A task is scheduled according to the resource calendar if it has resources assigned and no specific task calendar.

RESOURCE CALENDARS

Resources are the people and materials that work on tasks within the projects. This section will focus specifically on resource calendars.

→ For information about resources, **see** Chapter 8, "Defining Project Resources," **p. 249**.

TIP

Work resources are the only ones that include resource calendars. The other three resource types, material, budget, and cost, do not have calendars associated with them as they are assumed to always be available.

By default, when you create a resource, the resource calendar is the same as the project calendar. You can modify the resource calendar specifically for the resource without changing the base calendar to the project. To modify the working time of a resource, follow these steps:

1. Open the Resource Sheet view by selecting View, Resource Sheet.

2. In the Resource Name field, click the name of the resource that needs a resource calendar. Click the Resource Information icon on the Standard toolbar, or select Project, Resource Information, or right-click the resource name and select Resource Information. This opens the Resource Information dialog box (see Figure 5.10).

Figure 5.10
Click the Change Working Time button under the General tab of the Resource Information dialog box to make changes to a resource's schedule. In this case, the resource has a week-long vacation scheduled for the third week of September 2007.

3. In the Resource Information dialog box, under the General tab, click the Change Working Time button.

4. The Change Working Time dialog box will appear. To change the resource's base calendar, choose from the Base Calendar drop-down list at the top.

5. To make additional modifications, use the same methodology discussed in the section "Defining Exceptions," earlier in this chapter.

6. When you are finished modifying the resource calendar, click OK to save the changes or Cancel to exit without making any changes.

The resource will now operate based on the base calendar plus the exceptions that are defined in his or her resource calendar. Referring back to the example of a 4-day workweek, if a resource normally works those hours, but had a 3-day vacation coming up, you could define that vacation and Project would schedule work for that resource around the vacation dates. Similarly, if a resource had a standing obligation every week outside of your project, you could define that exception and the appropriate recurrence range, and Project would not assign task work to the resource during that time. (See the section "Defining Exceptions" earlier in this chapter for instructions for defining exceptions to schedules.)

TIP

> The Project Guide can walk you step by step through this process. The Project Guide contains the Calendar Wizard, another helpful tool when working with calendars. To access the Project Guide, click the icon on the Project Guide toolbar. Right-click in any toolbar to turn the Project Guide toolbar on or off.

TASK CALENDARS

As mentioned previously, if you assign a resource to a task, the work on the task will follow the resource calendar. If the resource has no specific resource calendar, or if there are no resources assigned to the task, the task will follow the project (base) calendar.

However, you can create a calendar specifically for a task. To do this, create a base calendar specifically for the task by following the process described in the earlier section "Creating New Base Calendars."

Once you create the base calendar, assign it to the task by following these steps:

1. In any view where you can see your tasks, such as the Gantt Chart view, select the task you want to assign the newly created base calendar to.

2. With the task (or tasks) selected, select Project, Task Information to open the Task Information dialog box. Alternatively, right-click on the task and select Task Information to open the Task Information dialog box.

3. Under the Advanced tab is a Calendar field (see Figure 5.11). Click the arrow to open the drop-down menu with the base calendars listed. If you successfully created a new calendar, it will be on this list. Select it.

Figure 5.11
Assign calendars to tasks under the Advanced tab of the Task Information dialog box. In this case, the New Base Calendar is being assigned the "Drive the moving truck to the new location" task.

4. Next to the Calendar field is a check box labeled Scheduling Ignores Resource Calendars. If you want your task calendar to override the resource calendar for the resource assigned to the task, then select this box. If you want Project to schedule based on the resource calendar, leave it blank.

5. Click OK to close the Task Information dialog box with the changes made, or click Cancel to close it without making any changes.

As the project manager, you must decide if assigning task calendars will be beneficial for your project. If you have multiple resources working on a task from different locations, it may be easier to schedule with the task calendar rather than the various resource calendars.

For example, if you run a newspaper printing facility, you will have tasks that do the actual printing. Often this happens overnight, so the task may cover multiple shifts. In addition to your human resources, you would include the machines used to print the newspaper as resources. Since these machines and people all operate under different schedules, it would be advantageous to schedule the task based on its own calendar, not the project's base calendar or the resource calendar. Likely you would use a version of the 24 Hour calendar, because the task is constantly being worked on by various resources at all hours of the day. However, your project of compiling the entire newspaper may have a standard base calendar, which would not be a good calendar to schedule this task by because there would be too many exceptions to enter. It is easier to simply customize a calendar for this specific task and schedule from that. Regardless of which resources work on the task, the task is completed on schedule.

DEFINING CUSTOM FIELDS

While Microsoft Project 2007 is a very thorough and valuable tool to use for project management, it is designed to aid in managing every type of project imaginable. Therefore, some areas may be general, and you may want to customize certain aspects of the tool specifically for your project because, like the people who manage them, every project is unique.

The following sections will discuss the tactics and logic behind customizing fields.

THE CUSTOM FIELDS CONCEPT

Project has dedicated predefined fields for the user to customize in a variety of ways. All the fields are accessible through the Tools menu: Tools, Customize, Fields. This command opens the Custom Fields dialog box shown in Figure 5.12.

Figure 5.12
Define custom fields in the Custom Fields dialog box.

There are two categories of customizable fields: task fields and resource fields.

In each of these categories, you can:

- Rename the custom fields permanently so that the new name appears wherever the field name appears.
- Add a value list to a custom field.
- Add a formula to a custom field.
- Designate graphic indicators to appear in a custom field in place of the data.

There are nine types of custom fields, as shown in the Type drop-down list: Cost, Date, Duration, Finish, Flag, Number, Start, Text, and Outline Codes. Within these types, there are designated numbers of fields. These are detailed in Table 5.1.

TABLE 5.1   THE CUSTOM FIELDS TYPES

Type	Number of Available Fields	Description
Cost	10	Can contain currency data you want to enter in your project.
Date	10	Can contain dates you want to enter in your project.
Duration	10	Can contain duration or work values you want to enter in your project.
Finish	10	Can contain finish dates you want to enter in your project.
Flag	20	Can contain yes/no flags you want to enter in your project.
Number	20	Can contain numeric (positive or negative) values you want to enter in your project.
Start	10	Can contain start dates you want to enter in your project.
Text	30	Can contain textual information you want to enter in your project alphanumerically, up to 255 characters.
Outline Code	10	Create an alternate structure for your project that you can use to sort, filter, or group tasks or resources (in other words, alphanumeric outline structures).

Custom fields can be beneficial for an infinite number of reasons. Perhaps you need to identify the status of a task as something other than percentage complete, such as approved/not approved. Perhaps you want to create a stop-light style status field to show whether the project is on schedule and on budget. The following section will explain how to define custom fields for your project.

DEFINING CUSTOM FIELDS

All changes to a custom field are done in the Custom Fields dialog box (Tools, Customize, Fields). To work with a particular field, select the general type (Task or Resource) first. Then select a particular category of custom field (such as Cost or Duration) from the Type drop-down list. The list of available fields for that particular category will appear in the box; click on the one you want to customize.

TIP

> The Project Guide and the Help button are both quite useful when defining custom fields at the intermediate level. To perform advanced actions, such as constructing and applying formulas, use the Help button in the appropriate dialog box.

RENAMING, DELETING, AND IMPORTING CUSTOM FIELDS

To avoid having to change the name label every time you open a new table or display a custom field, you can give the generic name provided in Project an alias that is a more accurate description for your purpose. Once you have selected your general type and custom field category, highlight the custom field you want to rename. If you have not renamed any of them yet, their names all appear as the category type and a number after (such as Duration1).

When you have the custom field highlighted, click the Rename button, which opens the Rename Field dialog box. Type in the name you want, and click OK. Notice that the new name appears in the box with the old name in parentheses. The new name will now appear any place the custom field is used instead of the generic custom field name.

If you want to delete a custom field alias, click the Rename button, highlight the alias, and click the Delete button.

You can also import a custom field from your project, another project, or from a template. The imported custom field is imported with all its attributes, such as formulas or indicators, associated with it.

Click the Import Custom Field button to open the Import Custom Field dialog box. From there you can import the custom field using the drop-down list in the Project field as your source, selecting the field type and the field. All open projects will appear in the Project field drop-down list. The Field drop-down list displays all available custom fields from the source you selected. Click OK to import the custom field, or click Cancel to cancel.

NOTE

> The information relating to custom fields in this chapter is more of an overview. More detailed information, as well as advanced actions when working with custom fields, can be found later in this book.

→ For more advanced actions and information about custom fields, **see** Chapter 22, "Customizing Views, Tables, Filters, Groups, and Fields," **p. 755**.

DEFINING ENVIRONMENT OPTIONS

The Options dialog box is the area in Microsoft Project to view, modify, and define assumptions about your project. There are two types of options: global (which affect all your projects) and file-specific (which affect only the specific project file you are working with when you open the Options dialog box). To display the Options dialog box, select Tools, Options (see Figure 5.13).

Figure 5.13

The Options dialog box contains 10 tabs to define elements of your project.

In the Options dialog box, you use 10 categories divided into tabs to define the environment options of your project (or projects, as global options affect all your projects). Most of the settings are global options, affecting all of your projects, including previously created projects. If you change these settings, they stay that way until you change them again. For example, Figure 5.14 shows the Options dialog box open to the Schedule tab. If you change the top section, Schedule Options for Microsoft Office Project, it will affect all your projects.

There are also option settings that affect only the project you are currently working with (have the project files open). These settings have the filename included in the option heading. For example, in Figure 5.14, near the middle, there is a section called Scheduling Options for Simple Moving Plan. This tells you that changes you make in this particular section will only affect the project you are currently working on, which in this case is the Simple Moving Plan.

Project allows you to make a file-specific change and update the Global template to reflect the option settings. To do this, click the Set as Default button, if it is available. This does not make the option setting global, because it will affect the project you are working on and future projects but will not affect projects previously created (present and future, not past). If you see a Set as Default button in the project-specific section you are modifying, you can click the button to set these option settings as defaults from then on until you change them again. In Figure 5.14, you could click the Set as Default button in the Scheduling Options for the Home Move Project Schedule section to apply the option settings to the Simple Moving Plan and all other projects you create down the road.

5

Figure 5.14
In the Schedule tab, some settings will affect all projects, and some will affect only the project you are working on. This is true throughout all tabs in the Options dialog box.

DEFINING PROJECT STANDARDS

As previously mentioned, there are 10 tabs in the Options dialog box. Option settings are file-specific if they have the filename in their title; otherwise, they are global and affect all your projects. The following sections discuss the 10 tabs of the options dialog box.

> **TIP**
> Each tab contains a Help button. Use this feature as an alternate resource for any questions or confusion you have relating to the particular tab you have open.

VIEW TAB

By default, the View tab is selected when you open the options dialog box (refer to Figure 5.13). Here, you can decide what view you want to see when you open Project. The Gantt Chart view is the default. In the date format field, you can choose how you view dates: Month/Day/Year, Month/Day/Year with time, month written out as a word, month written out as a word with time, or abbreviations.

> **TIP**
> It may be helpful to change the date format to include the time. It is easier to keep track of project details such as task start and finish times that way. This depends on your project (if your project or task list is time sensitive) and your personal preference.

> **NOTE**
> Use the Control Panel to set regional international-style time settings. Open the Start menu and choose Settings, Control Panel. In the Control Panel folder, choose Regional Settings. In the Regional Settings dialog box, choose the Date and Time tabs and make your changes.

In addition to selecting any of the predefined views as a default, it can be especially useful to define your own custom view and set it as the default instead. For example, you may have added special text formatting for Summary, Critical, and Milestone tasks to the Gantt Chart view.

→ For additional information on customizing views, **see** Chapter 22, "Customizing Views, Tables, Filters, Groups, and Fields," **p. 755**.

You can choose which options you want to see on the screen in the Show section, and how you want your links to appear visually in the Cross Project Linking Options section (this is file-specific).

In the Currency section, you can define how you want your currency displayed. The default is standard U.S. (for example, $10.50).

The last section is the file-specific Outline options.

When you are finished, select another tab to work in, click OK to exit and save your changes, or click Cancel to exit without saving your changes.

GENERAL TAB

Like the name suggests, the General tab deals with general information (see Figure 5.15). In the User Name field, be sure your user name is correct. Project uses this user name for the Author and Last Saved By properties. You can dictate whether or not you want the Planning Wizard's advice. Planning Wizard means well, and novice users of Project would do well while listening to its advice. You can also set default standard and overtime rates for resources, and if Set As Default is selected, Project sets those rates as defaults for all your projects.

Figure 5.15
The General tab of the Options window provides general information about your project configuration.

EDIT TAB

The Edit tab is where select editing options such as whether or not you will allow cell drag and drop (see Figure 5.16). Also, you can set time labels and what abbreviation you want Project to use (minutes = m, min, or minute, etc.). You also set the hyperlink color in the Edit tab.

Figure 5.16
Use the Edit tab of the Options window to set Project's editing standards and automated options.

CALENDAR TAB

The Calendar tab is one of the more critical tabs in the Options dialog box (see Figure 5.17). All fields in the Calendar tab are file-specific; click the Set as Default button at the bottom if you want to use the information on all future projects as well as the one you are working on. This tab is discussed in greater detail in the section, "Reviewing Critical Calendar Options," later in this chapter.

Figure 5.17
Use the Calendar tab of the Options window to set Project's calendar options, which include the default calendar used for all of your projects.

SCHEDULE TAB

In the Schedule tab, you can decide whether you want assignment units shown as a percentage or a decimal format (refer to Figure 5.14). This is a matter of personal preference. Also, in the New Tasks field, choose whether you want new tasks to begin on the project start date or on the current date.

The next two fields allow you to enter the unit of duration and work: minutes, hours, days, weeks, or months. Again, this is a personal preference, depending on what is best for you and your project. Be sure your working time and Calendar tab entries coincide; if you enter duration in days, be sure you have defined the correct number of hours in a day, and so on. Also, these fields will determine the default units when entering tasks. For example, if you assign a duration to a task, and have Days entered in the Duration in Entered In field, you could simply type **2** for 2 days. However, if you wanted to assign a different time unit, you would have to enter the unit, such as **2 w** for 2 weeks.

Choose the task type: Fixed Duration, Fixed Units, or Fixed Work. The task type defines how Project will calculate the schedule, work, and units. Then there are six check boxes, which are all checked by default. Decide which option is the best for you. If you are unsure, it is a good idea to leave them checked until you decide otherwise. When you are finished with the Schedule tab, you can click the Set as Default button to apply these options to your current project and all future projects.

CAUTION

It is unwise to use months as a duration unit because of the inconsistency of the length of months throughout the year. Use hours, days, or weeks as the duration unit.

CALCULATION TAB

Under the Calculation tab, you define how you want Project to make calculations—automatically or manually—and which projects this applies to—All Open Projects or Active Project (see Figure 5.18). Typically, it is most convenient to select the Automatically option, which is the default. However, if you choose Manual, you can click the Calculate Now button to run the calculations. This applies not only to the scheduling of your project, but also to the status as compared to the planned estimates (like how much you are behind or ahead of schedule). The Manual option can be useful on large projects when you are making updates to the status and want to prevent calculations from occurring until you have entered all of the data. This will speed up your entry process and prevent pop-up warnings from showing until you are ready to review the changes. In addition, the Manual option is effective when you are working on multiple projects that have links established between them and you are making a lot of changes in one of them. It will speed up your editing process, but keep in mind that links will not be updated between the projects until you manually calculate.

Checking the box next to Updating Task Status Updates Resource Status will automatically update the task and resource status together when either is updated. For example, if you update a task's percent complete to 50%, the % Work Complete field is automatically calculated to reflect that task's percent effort complete (50%). The same methodology applies if you update the resource status; Project will automatically update the task status.

The next two check boxes have to do with tasks that were scheduled to start before or after the status date but started early or late. Leaving them unchecked will not change your schedule and allow the tasks to finish according to their modified start dates.

The Earned Value button opens the Earned Value dialog box, where you can specify whether the % Complete (duration percent complete) or the Physical % Complete (your own independent assessment of what is complete) will be used for earned value analysis, and which baseline (up to 11) it should be compared to.

Figure 5.18
Use the Calculation tab of the Options window to set Project's calculation settings, such as whether Project should use automatic calculation or allow you to do it manually.

SPELLING TAB

Under the Spelling tab, you designate which fields you want Project to spell-check automatically (see Figure 5.19). By default, everything is selected to spell-check. Exceptions are defined with the check boxes on the right.

Figure 5.19
Use the Spelling tab of the Options window to set which fields you want Project to spell-check automatically.

5

SAVE TAB

The Save tab is where you define what kind of file you want your project to save as and where you want to save it (see Figure 5.20). You can also turn on the Auto Save feature to automatically save your project as you are working. We all know how a power outage can cause you to lose all your unsaved data; this feature is a great option to avoid that situation.

Figure 5.20
Use the Save tab of the Options window to define the default file type and location for saving your project files.

→ For additional information on manipulating Project files, **see** Chapter 18 "Managing Project Files," **p. 581**.

INTERFACE TAB

Under the Interface tab you can decide to show Indicators and Option buttons (see Figure 5.21). You can also decide whether to display the Project Guide and define its functionality: you can use Project's default Project Guide or a custom Project Guide you or your company have developed.

TIP

It is a good idea to leave all indicators, option buttons, and the Project Guide on if you are a novice project user. The indicators and option buttons are helpful hints as to what is going on with your project. The Project Guide walks you through various Project procedures and assists in acclimating you to the tool. Most experienced Project users turn the Project Guide off to save screen space.

Figure 5.21
Use the Interface tab
of the Options window
to define Indicators,
Interface, and Project
Guide options.

SECURITY TAB

The first check box in the Security tab allows you the option of removing the file properties (Author, Manager, Company, and Last Saved By) when you save the file (see Figure 5.22). This is a privacy option that is not selected by default. You can also adjust the security level and edit the trusted publishers by clicking the Macro Security button.

NOTE

> The second option, Require Project Server and Workspace Sites to Be Added to the IE Trusted Sites list, is a security option that applies to Project Professional 2007. This option requires the Project Server and Windows SharePoint Services project site URLs to be added to the trusted sites in Tools, Internet Options, Security Tab, Trusted Sites.

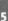

Figure 5.22
Use the Security tab of the Options window to define the project privacy options.

REVIEWING CRITICAL CALENDAR OPTIONS

From the Options dialog box (Tools, Options), you can select the Calendar tab. On this tab, you define some very important information regarding your projects' schedules. It is critical that this information is consistent with the information in the Base calendar you decide to use for your project calendar, as well as consistent with your organization's working habits.

On the Calendar tab in the Options dialog box, the Hours Per Day, Hours Per Week, and Days Per Month fields are crucial to the interpretation and display of your estimates of task duration. Days, weeks, and months are the basic task duration units. However, minutes are the fundamental time unit in Project 2007. Thus, all durations are converted into minutes, and the conversion is based on the information you enter on the Calendar tab. If this information is inaccurate, your schedule will be inaccurate. For example, if you define a day as 8 hours, then Project calculates that there are 480 minutes of working time in a day. If you define a day as 10 hours, Project calculates that there are 600 minutes of working time in a day. Even though they are both one day, there is a big difference in the amount of working time in that day.

To avoid confusion, make your estimates of the amount of work in hours rather than in days and then validate that the duration of the work matches what you expected it to be. This topic will be covered in great detail in the rest of the Part II chapters.

The Week Starts On field at the top of the Calendar tab can be used to change the way that a week is displayed in timescales and dialogs. It does not change any calculations for the project. Similarly, the Fiscal Year Starts In field affects reports and displays that show annual and quarterly information. The default setting is the same as a calendar year so this field should be changed if your fiscal year does not begin in January.

The Default Start Time and Default End Time fields define the start and end times of the normal working days. Again, it is very important that these times match the times defined in your base calendar, discussed earlier in this chapter.

While you may assign tasks to begin on a certain day, Project does not actually schedule the task until the start time of that day. So, if your workday starts at 6:00 a.m., but you have not changed the Default Start Time from 8:00 a.m., Project will schedule that task to start 2 hours late. This will also affect how you track a task. If a task took a full 8-hour day from 6:00 a.m. to 3 p.m. (accounting for an hour lunch break), and you mark the task as 100% complete but still have 8:00 a.m. in the Default Start Time field, Project will show the task as finishing later than it actually did.

If the information you defined in the Calendar tab is the standard calendar information for your organization, click the Set as Default button to make these values the default for future projects.

In short, be sure to define your calendar options accurately and realistically, and be sure that the Calendar tab on the Options dialog box matches the information defined in the base calendar you use for your project, created in the Change Working Time dialog box.

CONSULTANTS' TIPS

PROJECT INFORMATION CONSULTANT TIP

It is always a best practice to include as much information about the project with the schedule. Take advantage of Projects' capabilities to store project information with the new project when you create it. The project properties, Project Information dialog box, and the custom fields give project managers the ability to include project, task, and resource information within the project schedule. This allows the project manager to use this "metadata" for reporting, filtering, and organizing schedule information for the various audiences that will need it. Project properties settings are very useful when searching project archives for specific types of information.

Custom fields are especially helpful in extending basic schedule information to include your organization's unique information. All companies categorize task, resource, and project information with unique labels that they will use to report projects from. There is virtually no limit on the amount of "extra" information you can add to the project schedule by using custom fields.

Project calendars are an effective way to define the basic expectations you have for planning project work. They allow you to consider other distractions in your workday so you can plan project tasks in a realistic manner, planning for success instead of assuming 100% of your time can be devoted to project tasks. Good project planning and execution begins with the best assumptions you have available when you create your project plan. Considering available work time is a key part of that process. The calendar features in Microsoft Office Project 2007 give you the ability to clearly define how you expect time to be allocated to project tasks.

CALENDAR CONSULTANT TIP

Developing a good schedule can be difficult so do not make it any more complicated than it needs to be. Establish a calendar for your project that works for the majority of the requirements you have and then handle exceptions on a case-by-case basis. Do not attempt to account for all possible conditions. Getting in the weeds to account for resource efficiency is not justified in most cases.

Establishing an accurate calendar is an excellent way to minimize the number of surprises you will have in your project and improve the accuracy of your estimates. Pay close attention to holidays, vacations, and resource availability so that you do not have a schedule that is too optimistic. People are seldom capable of delivering at 100% efficiency so you need to account for some loss of productivity. The easiest way to do this is to make sure the calendar captures the correct daily working time for the organization (whether that is 7 hours, 8 hours, 10 hours, or something else) and that you predict the effective time that people apply to the project by setting their true availability at less than 100%.

This approach will minimize the amount of corrections you will need to make as your project evolves. Optimism is not a good thing when estimating project schedules; be at least a little pessimistic!

5

CHAPTER **6**

CREATING YOUR PROJECT SCHEDULE

In this chapter

ENTERING PROJECT TASKS

Once you have created your new project (define its propeties, calendars, and so on, as discussed in Chapter 5, "Setting Up Project for Your Use"), it is time to create the project's schedule. This chapter focuses on doing just that.

As you know, work on a project is broken up into tasks. These tasks are the building blocks of a project's schedule, so it is important that you take the time to enter all of the tasks within your project and provide realistic estimates of each task's duration. Often, tasks are dependent on each other; their start or finish dates may rely on the start or finish of another task. Also, a task may be part of a larger task. Thus, organizing your tasks properly is a vital element in successfully creating your schedule and managing your project. This chapter will show you how to properly organize your tasks into ,a task list.

→ For additional information on task dependency relationships, **see** "Linking Tasks," **p. 201**.

ENTERING TASKS USING THE GANTT CHART VIEW

When you are ready to create, the schedule for your new project, the default view you begin in is the Gantt Chart view. The Gantt Chart view is a great example of combining table (linear) and graphical (time-phased) information on one screen.

The Task table has several columns that relate to each task. Figure 6.1 shows the standard Gantt Chart view: the Task Entry table on the left and the Gantt Chart timescale on the right. In addition to the displayed columns, you can insert new ones by right-clicking on any column and selecting Insert Column. You can then select a field name in the Column Definition dialog box and the column will be inserted before the column you clicked on. If not all of the columns are visible in the view, scroll to the right using the arrow at the bottom of the Task table, or use the mouse to drag the vertical divider bar.

You may take two approaches to creating a task list. The most common approach is to start by listing the major phases of the project and then listing the detailed tasks under each major phase. This approach is called the *top-down* approach.

The other approach is the *bottom-up* approach. In this approach, you list all of the detail tasks first. When using this approach, it may be helpful to list these tasks in chronological order. Once they are all listed, you can come up with the major phases of the project. This approach may be more useful for smaller projects, but for complex projects that have hundreds of detailed tasks, this approach is not ideal because you will likely forget to list some of the tasks. In the bottom-up approach, you list the entire scope of tasks for the project, whereas in the top-down approach, you concentrate on each phase, one at a time, thus allowing less room for error. The top-down approach also supports the concept of scope breakdown, where you start with the project scope statement and decompose it into smaller and smaller parts. The top-down approach is also often associated with the Work Breakdown Structure (WBS) concept. Using WBS, the work and scope of that work is broken down layer by layer, starting at the top project scope statement.

Figure 6.1
The Gantt Chart view displays the Task Entry table on the left and the timescale on the right, separated by the vertical divider bar.

Subtask   Task Entry table   Gantt Chart timescale

Summary Task

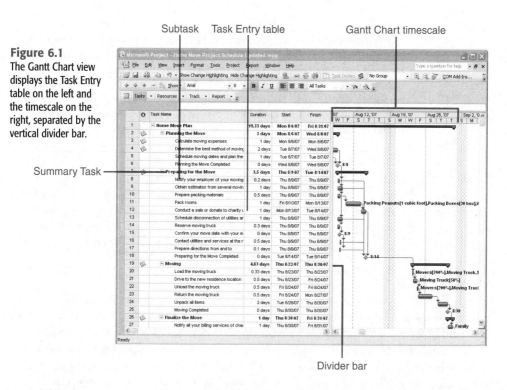

Divider bar

This chapter uses a project example of moving into a new home. The top-down approach is used to determine the major phases of a home move, such as Planning the Move and Move Preparation. There are more major phases to a move than this, but they should suffice for illustrating creating a task list.

Under the Planning the Move task, you would create separate tasks for events such as Calculate Moving Expenses, Determine the Best Method of Moving, and Schedule the Moving Dates. The Move Preparation task can have detailed tasks, such as Notify Your Employer of Your Moving Dates, Obtain Estimates from Several Moving Services, Prepare Packing Materials, and so on (see Figure 6.1). You can see how each major task breaks down into detailed tasks, sometimes on several levels, but they all relate back to the original major phase. The major phases are called *summary* tasks, and the detailed tasks are called *subtasks*. Subtasks are displayed as indented under the summary tasks. Summary tasks and subtasks are discussed in greater detail later in this chapter. As described in Chapter 4, "Getting Started After the Business Initiative Is Approved," you should consider building the work breakdown structure (WBS) first, and then build your task list from it. It will help you organize your thoughts and understand the scope of the work of the project, prior to entering tasks into Microsoft Project 2007.

6

TIP

> Your first task should be the project summary task. That way, your first task encompasses the entire project, and everything under it are details of the overall project scope. Microsoft Project 2007 automatically creates the project-level summary task, but it is not displayed by default. To display it, select Tools, Options, View tab, and then select the Show project summary task option. The project summary task is shown in Figure 6.1 at the top of the task list. For more information on the project summary task, see the section "Selecting the Display Options for Outlining," later in this chapter.

Creating a task begins by entering the task's name into the project. The most common way of doing this is by typing the name of the task directly into the Task Name field in the Task Entry table. Once you have typed in the name, press Enter or use the arrow keys to exit the cell. Microsoft Project 2007 automatically supplies values in the ID, Duration, Start, and Finish fields. The following sections describe the default Gantt Chart view entry fields.

THE ID FIELD

The ID field is the column all the way on the left. Although you cannot see the label on the field, if you were to insert a column, you would see the column identified as "ID" at the top. This field is defined automatically when you type in a task and cannot be manually edited. The ID numbers refer to a task's position in the Task table, beginning with 1 and continuing in ascending numeric order (1, 2, 3, and so on). The ID field is also used to reference a task in the task outline. These numbers are not permanently associated with the task; if you move a task from row 5 to row 2, for example, the task's ID field changes according to the move (from 5 to 2 in this case).

NOTE

> Although the ID number is not permanent, Microsoft Project 2007 does create some permanent numbers it associates with each task. Unique ID associates the original ID number permanently with the task for review within the project itself and the GUID (generated unique identifier) creates a 32-character number that may be used for integrating custom programs or programming macros.

6

THE INDICATORS FIELD

The Indicators field is the column to the right of the ID field. At the top of the column is an icon with a small *i* in white surrounded by a blue circle. If a task has additional information that is not revealed in the other columns, an indicator icon will often appear in this field next to the task. Hover your mouse pointer over the indicator to view a tip about what the icon indicates. For example, a check mark will appear in this field when the task is complete. Not all tasks will have an indicator.

Table 6.1 shows all the Project indicators and their meaning.

TABLE 6.1   INDICATOR ICONS AND THEIR DESCRIPTION

Indicator Icon	Description
	Indicates that a note is attached.
	Indicates that a hyperlink is attached.
	Indicates that the resource needs leveling.
	Indicates that the task will finish later than its Deadline date.
	Indicates that the task has an inflexible constraint; that the task is tied to a specific date (such as Must Finish On, Must Start On, and so on).
	Indicates that the task has a moderately flexible constraint; the task is constrained but not to a specific date (such as As Soon As Possible, As Late As Possible, and so on).
	Indicates that the task has missed its constraint deadline; it has not been scheduled or completed within the constraint's timeframe.
	Indicates that the task is recurring.
	Indicates that the task is complete.
	Indicates that the task is a subproject, or inserted project (a project file consolidated as a summary task in another project).
	Indicates that the task is a read-only inserted project.
	Indicates that the task has a calendar related to it (a task calendar).
	Indicates that the task calendar and a resource calendar conflict for accomplishing the work on the task.
	Indicates that the task is assigned to a resource, but the resource has not accepted or confirmed. Note that this indicator appears only if you are using Microsoft Office Project Professional in conjunction with Microsoft Office Project Server.

6

continues

TABLE 6.1   CONTINUED

Indicator Icon	Description
	Indicates that some part of the task has changed and the resource should be notified of the change. Note that this indicator appears only if you are using Microsoft Office Project Professional in conjunction with Microsoft Office Project Server.
	Indicates that a resource has not yet responded to the task's status inquiry. Note that this indicator appears only if you are using Microsoft Office Project Professional in conjunction with Microsoft Office Project Server.
	A contour indicator that means scheduled work is back-loaded (the work assigned is heaviest toward the end of the task).
	A bell contour indicator that means assigned work is heaviest in the middle and lighter at the beginning and end of the task.
	A double-peak contour indicator that means scheduled work is distributed over time in peaks and valleys.
	An early-peak contour indicator that means scheduled work peaks shortly after it starts and becomes increasingly lighter.
	An edited contour indicator that means scheduled work has been manually entered.
	A front-loaded contour indicator that means scheduled work is heaviest at the beginning of the task and decreases over time.
	A late-peak contour indicator that means scheduled work starts light, increases over time, and peaks near the end of the assignment, but not the very end.
	A turtle contour indicator that means scheduled work starts and ends the same but becomes heaviest in the middle.

THE TASK NAME FIELD

The Task Name field contains the text you defined as the name of the task. Task names should not be vague; they should make sense out of context. See the section "Creating Task Names," later in this chapter, for more information about task names.

THE DURATION FIELD

The Duration field is extremely important for scheduling tasks. When you first enter a task, Microsoft Project 2007 automatically enters the default duration of **1 day?** with a question mark next to it. The question mark signifies that the duration in this field is tentative, and you should enter the actual estimated duration for the task later as you confirm and enter more confident estimates. For more information about the Duration field, see the section "Entering Task Durations," later in this chapter.

THE START AND FINISH DATE FIELDS

The Start field displays the date the task is scheduled to begin, and the Finish field shows the date it is scheduled to finish (based on the duration).

Although you can enter dates in the Start and Finish fields, it is best to let Microsoft Project 2007 calculate these dates based on the durations you enter. If you enter the dates on your own, Microsoft Project 2007 places a date constraint on the task. You should only enter Start and Finish dates for tasks if in fact they must start or finish on a certain date and time. For example, you may not be able to get into your new house until a certain date, so you would have to schedule your tasks that involve moving in to start no earlier than that specific date.

> **TIP**
>
> You should not enter start or finish dates when you are initially building your schedule. Microsoft Project 2007 is an excellent project management tool that builds a schedule based on estimated durations, logical dependencies, resource assignments, and calendars. If you find yourself consistently entering specific start and finish times for tasks, you are not utilizing the full benefits and potential of Microsoft Project 2007. After you have built your schedule using Microsoft Project's scheduling engine, you may then want to consider entering constraints for those tasks that are date-constrained, like your set move-in date, or a specific date and time your new refrigerator is being delivered.

> **NOTE**
>
>
>
> As you build your task list and the Gantt Chart expands based on the start and end dates of your tasks, you might have problems finding the task's Gantt bar on the Gantt Chart. You can select the task and then use the Scroll to Task button on the Standard toolbar. This will show you the beginning of the selected task's Gantt bar.

6

THE DEFAULT START AND FINISH DATES

When you set up your project, you will need to decide if you want to set a fixed start date (a *forward-scheduled project*) or set a finish date (*backward-scheduled project*). You should be aware that scheduling from the project's finish date can complicate building the schedule. You may find that as you build your backward-scheduled project, your schedule shows you should have started the project two months prior to the current date.

If you have scheduled your project from a fixed start date, Microsoft Project 2007 automatically enters the project's start date as the task's start date. Similarly, if you scheduled your project from a fixed finish date, Microsoft Project 2007 sets the tasks to finish on the project's finish date and calculates the start date by subtracting the duration from the finish date. Microsoft Project 2007 automatically recalculates and changes this date as you link and assign dependency relationships to tasks and make other modifications.

You can tell Microsoft Project 2007 to schedule tasks from the current date (if it is different from the project's start date). This is especially helpful when scheduling tasks after the project has already begun, because the project start date has already occurred.

To do this, perform the following steps:

1. Open the Options dialog box by selecting Tools, Options.

2. On the Schedule tab, select Start on Current Date from the drop-down list in the New Tasks field. However, if you are planning for a future project, it is best to leave the default as the project start date, and let Microsoft Project 2007 recalculate the start date for the task for you. The project start and finish dates and the current date are defined in the Project Information dialog box (select Project, Project Information).

THE DEFAULT TIME OF DAY   Microsoft Project 2007 automatically includes both the time of day and the date in the date field, even if it has not been formatted to show the time. If you do not enter a time of day when you enter a task with a start date, Microsoft Project 2007 will use the default start time, usually 8:00 a.m. The same is true when you enter a finish date for a task with no time of day; Microsoft Project 2007 will set it at 5:00 p.m. You can, however, change the default start and end times in the Options dialog box (see Figure 6.2).

You can also enter the time of day manually, even if the date field does not show it. For instance, if you wanted a task to start at noon on October 13, 2007, you would enter **10/13/2007 12:00 PM**.

Figure 6.2
You can change the start and end times for a workday using the Options dialog box.

TIP

Use capital letters to define morning or afternoon. For example, to schedule a task to start at 2:00 p.m., enter **2:00 PM** next to the date in the Start field. However, enter time sparingly in your project schedules, unless you truly need to control a project task so discretely.

You can also enter time in the 24-hour clock format (14:00), but Microsoft Project 2007 will display it as 2:00 p.m. To display time in the 24-hour format, you must change the format in the Windows Control Panel. If you decide you want to change to 24-hour time, open the Windows Control Panel and access the Date, Time, Language and Regional Options. You will want to change the time format, not the time itself, so click the time format button to open the Regional and Language Options. Then, click the Customize button, which will open up the Customize Regional Options dialog box, and select the Time tab. You will need to change the time format, which is probably set to h:mm:ss tt. You can also select this from the drop-down menu. The setting for the 24-hour clock is HH:mm:ss.

Perform these steps to set the default time of day:

1. Open the Options dialog box by selecting Tools, Options, and then choose the Calendar tab.

2. Enter the time you want Microsoft Project 2007 to use if you do not include the time of date with a start date, using the Default Start Time field.

3. Enter the time you want Microsoft Project 2007 to use if you do not include the time of date with a finish date, using the Default End Time field.

4. You can click the Set as Default button if you want to make your changes apply to all of the new projects you create from now. This will not affect any existing project files, only the new ones.

DISPLAYING THE TIME OF DAY WITH DATES   You can turn on the time display in the Start and Finish fields by using Tools, Options to open the Options dialog box. Then, go to the Date Format list box on the View tab. From the drop-down list of different date formats, you can choose the one that works best for you. The first one on the list has both the time and the date; however, there are others in the list that have both the time and date, simply in different formats.

NOTE

You may experience difficulties with the Start and Finish fields when you add time to the date format. If you see a column displaying pound signs, it is an indicator that the column is not wide enough to display the new format. You can double-click the column header and then select the Best Fit button to expand it.

THE PREDECESSORS FIELD

The Predecessors field displays the ID numbers for any tasks linked to the selected task. As previously mentioned, tasks often are dependently linked to each other, so one task often cannot start or finish until another task has started or finished. For example, you cannot install new carpeting until you have measured the square footage of each room that is getting new carpet. Therefore, the task ID number for Measure Room Square Footage for New Carpeting would be in the Predecessors field for the Install New Carpeting task. As a note, each task should have a task that starts after the previous task which is called a successor task. The Install New Carpeting task is a successor task for Measure Room Square Footage for New Carpeting. The Successor field does not show by default.

→ For details about task predecessor/successor relationships, **see** "Linking Tasks," **p. 201**.

THE RESOURCE NAMES FIELD

The Resource Names field displays the names of any resources assigned to work on the task. When multiple resources are assigned to the task, their names are separated using a comma. If a resource is assigned at less or more than 100% units, you will see the number of units assigned in brackets next to each resource name.

→ For additional information about assigning resources to tasks, **see** "Assigning a Resource to a Task," **p. 288**.

CREATING TASK NAMES

As previously mentioned, when you enter a name into the Task Name field, you create a task. Several critical pieces of information must be included when creating a task, all of which will be discussed in this chapter, but the first step is choosing the name itself.

CAUTION

> A task is created when you make an entry in any of the Task Entry table fields, not just the Task Name field. If you create a task by accident and want to remove it, simply click the ID number for the accidentally created task and click the Delete key on your keyboard. You can also select any field in the task row, click the Delete key and then select "Delete the entire task" from the smart tag that appears.

Task names can contain any combination of characters and spaces, up to 255 characters long. Most project managers advocate using a verb-noun format when creating task names, such as Assemble Boxes or Load Truck. This is because action verbs provide more information to you and your resources on what action is supposed to be performed and remove any possible confusion. As another example, if you have a task named System Test Plan, it can be confusing as to what needs to be done—whether the system test plan is being created, reviewed, approved, and so on. However, if you specify Create System Test Plan as the task name, there is no question about what exactly the task entails.

Nevertheless, it is important that you take the time to ensure the task name is clear and comprehendible when taken out of context. Ask yourself, if someone reads this task name who does not know much about the project, will he or she be able to understand the gist of the task?

This is important because there are possible scenarios when people will see the task name out of the context of your project schedule. For example, if you are using Microsoft Project

Professional in conjunction with Microsoft Office Project Server, when resources are assigned tasks, and they go to update their work schedule to include the tasks you have assigned them, the task name appears on its own. If the task name is vague, they will come to you asking for further explanation. You can avoid this by making sure your task names are specific and make sense outside the project schedule.

If you create very descriptive, long task names, it makes them harder to fit in their cells and they will most likely get cut off in your Gantt Chart view. The section "Displaying Long Task Names," later in this chapter, explains how to resolve this problem so that the task name can be read and understood with ease, no matter what its length is.

When you have completed entering a new task and click Enter on your keyboard, the selection will automatically change to the next row so you can enter another task. However, if you do not want the selection to change when you press Enter, you can turn off this feature by choosing Tools, Options, Edit tab. You need to clear the Move selection after enter check box and then click OK.

CAUTION

Although you can create tasks using the mouse by drawing bars in the timescale side of the Gantt Chart view, this is not a good method of doing so. You still have to name the tasks and enter their information. Also, you usually have to adjust your duration unless you are very accurate with the mouse, and you automatically create a date constraint on the task. Either the task is constrained to start no earlier than the date you clicked on if you dragged the mouse to the right, or it is constrained to finish no earlier than the date you clicked on if you dragged the mouse to the left.

COPYING TASK NAMES FROM ANOTHER APPLICATION

Besides typing task names into the Task Name field directly, an alternative option for entering task names is to copy them from another application and paste them into your task list in Microsoft Project 2007. Perhaps these names already exist in another document, spreadsheet, or database. You may save yourself some time by copying and pasting them rather than retyping them all.

NOTE

This section describes the process for copying and pasting task names only. There is a way to copy and paste additional task information, such as dates and duration, but it is a more complicated process.

→ For details about copying additional task information from another application, **see** "Copying Data from Other Applications into Microsoft Project 2007," **p. 962**.

Follow these steps to copy a task name or list of task names from another application:

1. Open Microsoft Project 2007 and the application to copy the task names from.

2. Select the names you want to copy in the other application, keeping these requirements in mind:

- Each task name must be on a separate row of text if the other application is a word processing document, such as Microsoft Word or Microsoft PowerPoint.
- Each task name must be in a separate cell in a column of entries, and all the names you want to copy must be adjoining, if the other application is a spreadsheet, such as Microsoft Excel.
- The task names must be in a single field of the database if the other application is a database, such as Microsoft Access. Select the cells in that field only. Do not select the records because that would select other fields as well, and Microsoft Project 2007 would not know what to do with the other fields.

3. Use the Copy command (generally located under Edit, Copy) or use the Ctrl+C keyboard combination, which copies the list of names to the Clipboard.

4. In Microsoft Project 2007, select the cell in the Task Name field where you want to place the first name in the list, and use the Paste command (select Edit, Paste from the Standard toolbar or use the Ctrl+V keyboard combination).

ENTERING TASK DURATIONS

Although it is best to create the entire task list prior to entering durations, the Duration field is extremely important for creating your project schedule. *Duration* is defined in Microsoft Project as the amount of time scheduled on the project calendar to work on a task. In other words, duration is the amount of working time between a task's start and finish dates.

Duration is not the amount of work needed to complete a task; rather, it is the amount of time units that are scheduled to work on a task. The time units are defined in the project calendar, such as 8 hours for 1 day of duration. The Duration field is governed by the scheduling algorithm as soon as you enter Work or Resource Names on a task. What makes Microsoft Project confusing for novices is that it will shorten or lengthen the Duration you enter based on how many resources you add to a task, on the default Task Type, and if it is effort-driven or not. Before you get too frustrated about entering estimates into the Duration field and seeing the Duration change when you add resources, see Chapter 9, "Understanding Work Formula Basics."

Some key things to keep in mind when estimating by duration of a task:

- Working hours do not have to be continuous, but duration usually is. Microsoft Project 2007 assumes that work should be assigned to the first available hours on the calendar, starting with the default of 8 a.m. and continuing to the default of 5 p.m. on the start date. For instance, Microsoft Project 2007 will initially schedule the work of 8 hours for one day, but you can go back later and change the schedule to fit your needs, even assigning work for 1 hour a day for the 8 hours if necessary. If you do, then each hour will occur on one day at a time, and the duration for the task will be 8 days.

- Duration does not measure total work or effort, it only measures the number of units of time on your calendar that are scheduled. So, a 1-day task that has two people working on it for 4 hours may be the same as one person working for 8 hours, or four people working for 2 hours. Again, the actual duration may be predicated on how you have set up task types, effort, and the number of resources on the task.

- When you are estimating duration, always ask experts, leads, work managers, or the resources themselves to help increase the accuracy of the estimate. Consider past experiences, the skills and experience of your resources, and how many resources you plan to use. If possible, talk to other project managers or look at past projects.

→ For additional information about task types and effort-driven and non-effort-driven scenarios, **see** Chapter 10, "Scheduling Single and Multiple Resource Assignments," **p. 313**.

As indicated previously, when you first enter a value in the Duration field on the Task Entry table, Microsoft Project 2007 schedules that task to occur as soon as possible. That is, if you define a task's duration as 5 days, Microsoft Project 2007 schedules that task for the first 5 working days after the start of the task (at 8 a.m. of the start date if that has been defined in the calendar). You can also choose to reschedule the task so it is not continuous (such as 1 day a week for 5 weeks). See "Defining Recurring Tasks" later in this chapter for more information.

CREATING TENTATIVE DURATION ESTIMATES

If you have previous experiences with tasks similar to the one you are working with currently, take those experiences into account when estimating the duration for the current task. How long did it take last time? How many resources worked on it? Was their skill level comparable to the skill level of the resources you have now?

Gather whatever information you can to postulate the most educated, realistic duration estimate for your task. Keep in mind the number and skill level of resources you may assign to the task and the amount of effort per day they could actually work on the task. For instance, a resource may be available for only 4 hours of each day (more or less) to work on your task, so the duration may be twice as long as the hours in a day. A task taking 40 hours could take 2 weeks based on resource availability. This duration estimate will determine the start and finish dates for the task, unless you have already defined those (which is not advised unless those dates are definite).

> **TIP**
>
> The Notes field can aid you in remembering your thought process as you are creating your duration estimates. If you assign resources to tasks days or weeks after you have entered the duration estimates, it may be difficult to remember how many resources you were thinking about, and who those resources are. Keep track of that kind of information in the Notes field. See the section "Attaching Notes to Tasks," later in this chapter, for more information on the Notes field.

6

As you have seen already, when you create a new task, Microsoft Project 2007 gives it the default duration of 1 day, followed by a question mark (1 day?). The question mark signifies that the duration estimate is tentative and serves as a good reminder to go back later when you have a more informed idea of the duration to correct it. Once you have determined your best estimate for the duration of the task, replace the default duration value with your own, and the question mark will disappear. You can also remove the question mark by double-clicking on the task, and clearing the Estimated field check box in any tab within the Task Information dialog box.

TIP

> If you want to display all the tasks with tentative duration estimates together, to see which tasks you need more confident estimates on, use the Tasks with Estimated Durations filter (Project, Filtered for:). Microsoft Project 2007 displays only those tasks with a question mark in the Duration field.

→ For details about using the Tasks with Tentative Duration filter, or any other filters, **see** "Understanding Filtering and Grouping," **p. 399**.

UNDERSTANDING THE DURATION TIME UNITS

For the time units of durations, you can use minutes, hours, days (the default), weeks, or months. Microsoft Project 2007 automatically applies the default duration time unit even if your organization uses a different unit for duration. To change the default duration time unit from days to something else, open the Schedule tab in the Options dialog box (Tools, Options) and choose from the drop-down list in the Duration Is Entered In field. The new default time unit will also appear in the Duration field every time you create a new task.

CAUTION

> Because months are inconsistent from each other in their length, it is not advised to choose months as your default time unit.

No matter what your default time unit is, Microsoft Project internally converts it into minutes, because all calculations in Microsoft Project are performed in minutes. These conversions are based on the calculation that 1 hour is always 60 minutes. Other time unit assumptions are defined in the Calendar tab of the Options dialog box (Tools, Options).

The default time unit assumptions are:

- 1 day equals 8 hours
- 1 week equals 40 hours (five 8-hour days if you are using the default)
- 1 month equals 20 days

If your organization works five 7.5-hour days a week, you would want to adjust the definition of a day to be 7.5 hours, and a week to be 35 hours. The same is true for a company that works four 10-hour days a week. You will not need to change the definition of a week, because the total number of hours is the same as the default 40 hours, but you will need to change a day from 8 to 10 hours. If your organization works under different time units, you want to define those assumptions in your project. To do so, follow these steps:

1. Open the Options dialog box by selecting Tools, Options, and select the Calendar tab.

2. In the Hours per Day field, enter the number of work hours in a day (the default is 8).

3. Enter the number of weekly work hours in the Hours per Week field (Hours per Week = Hours per Day × Days per Week). The default is 40 hours per week.

4. Enter the number of days you want to define in each month in the Days per Month field. The default is 20 days per month.

5. If you would like the change to be applied to all subsequent project schedules, click Set as Default and click OK to save and apply these definitions. If you would like the change to be applied only to the current schedule, just click OK.

CAUTION

> You should make sure project and resource calendars match these daily and weekly work settings as well. For details about setting up calendars to reflect different hours for work during the week, **see** "Defining Calendars," **p. 118**.

USING TIME UNIT ABBREVIATION

If you prefer, you can enter time units as abbreviations instead of the complete word. You can also abbreviate in the plural form. Refer to the following list for acceptable abbreviations:

- **Minute**—m, min, mins, minute, minutes
- **Hour**—h, hr, hrs, hour, hours
- **Day**—d, dy, dys, day, days
- **Week**—w, wk, wks, week, weeks
- **Month**—mo, mon, mons, month, months

CAUTION

> Minutes and months are easy to confuse because they both start with *m*. It may be helpful to avoid abbreviating "months" so you do not accidentally define the time unit as "minutes."

Therefore, to enter "2 weeks," you could type **2w**, **2wk**, **2wks**, **2 week**, or **2 weeks**. No matter which one you choose, Microsoft Project displays it as "2 wks." You can change the default display to a different spelling of the time unit in the Options dialog box (Tools, Options). In the Edit tab, under the View options for time units section, use the drop-down lists to change the default spellings.

NOTE

> Years can be abbreviated as y, yr, and yrs. However, years is not a duration time unit; it is used for resource pay rates.

DEFINING ELAPSED DURATION

The previous sections discussed time units for working time. Additionally, you can schedule an *elapsed* duration amount for a task. Elapsed duration means uninterrupted work on a task.

In other words, an elapsed duration entry includes all time, both working and nonworking, continuously.

This is helpful in situations where the task can or must run after working hours. For example, if you are painting a bathroom in your new house, you may include the time the paint needs to dry as a task. If the paint takes 10 hours to dry, you would not want to enter **10 h** in the Duration field, because Microsoft Project 2007 would schedule the paint to finish drying well after it was actually done. If you were working with the Standard base calendar (8 hours = 1 day), and you assigned a duration of 10 hours, Microsoft Project would calculate its finish date to be a day or two later, depending on the task's calculated start time. This is because it would take up an entire 8-hour day, and the remaining 2 hours would be scheduled the following day to finish the task.

However, you can define the task's duration as 10 elapsed hours, so it would be scheduled to finish exactly 10 hours later.

To do this, enter the letter *e* before the time unit in the Duration field. In this case, you would enter **10 eh**, which stands for 10 elapsed hours. Microsoft Project would then schedule the task accordingly.

Figure 6.3 displays the task (Task A) that has elapsed duration. The first row (ID number 1) is the task with assigned a duration of 7 elapsed days, and the second row (ID number 2) is the task assigned a regular duration of 7 days. Notice how the first row is scheduled to finish much sooner than the first row. Because it is assigned an elapsed duration, row number 1 does not have to wait until working time resumes; it is scheduled continuously.

Figure 6.3
Use elapsed duration to define tasks that work on continuous time.

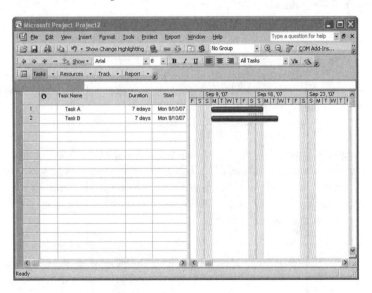

NOTE

Elapsed days are defined as 24 hours, as opposed to the default working day, which is 8 hours. Elapsed weeks are 168 hours (seven 24-hour days), and the elapsed month is 720 hours (thirty 24-hour days). The elapsed month amounts will vary, depending on the month. Microsoft Project will adjust appropriately if your Current System Date is accurate.

CAUTION

The resource calendar governs when a resource can work. Therefore, if a resource is assigned to a task with elapsed duration, the calendar will not let the resource work outside of the defined working time. You must either assign overtime to the resource or modify the resource calendar to complete the task.

Alternatively, you can assign a task calendar to the task and define the working time on the task calendar to coincide with the extended working time for the particular task. Microsoft Project will give you an option to schedule from the task calendar and ignore the resource calendar on this task, and you should select that option.

EDITING TASKS USING THE TASK INFORMATION DIALOG BOX

The Task Information dialog box allows you to view more fields of task-related information than any view in Microsoft Project. There are several ways to open the Task Information dialog box: double-click any cell in the task row, right-click any cell in the task row and choose Task Information, select any cell in the task row and click Project, Task Information, or click the Task Information icon on the Standard toolbar (see Figure 6.4).

Figure 6.4
You can define and edit all task details in the Task Information dialog box.

The Task Information dialog box is the only single place to edit task information. Most of the fields in the Task Information dialog box are displayed in other views, but no single view contains all the fields found in the Task Information dialog box.

The Task Information dialog box contains six tabs. The following list briefly describes these tabs:

NOTE

The Task Name and Duration fields are displayed on every tab in the Task Information dialog box. Also, next to the Duration field is a check box for estimates. Select it if the duration you entered is estimated, or tentative. Microsoft Project puts a question mark next to your entry to signify it is tentative.

- **The General tab**—Define and edit general task information under the General tab, such as Start and Finish dates. Also, adjust the priority (0 is the lowest, 1000 is the highest, and 500 is the default). If a resource is scheduled to work on multiple tasks in a project at once, you can use the Leveling feature in Microsoft Project 2007. Microsoft Project will then schedule the resource to work first on the task with a higher priority. You can also define the progress of a task in the Percent complete field. Select the Hide task bar option to hide the task bar in the timescale, and select Roll up Gantt bar to summary to hide the subtasks. This is further explained later in this chapter in the section "Using Rollup Taskbars."

→ For more details about leveling task, **see** Chapter 25, "Resolving Resource Allocation Problems," **p. 885**.

- **The Predecessors tab**—Define the task's predecessor tasks in this tab, including the predecessor task's ID number, task name, dependency relationship type, and lead/lag. Predecessor tasks are tasks whose finish or start date determines the finish or start date of another task.

→ For more details about predecessor/successor dependency relationships, **see** "Linking Tasks," **p. 201**.

- **The Resources tab**—Display and assign resources to the tasks in this tab.

→ For more details about assigning resources to tasks, **see** Chapter 10, "Scheduling Single and Multiple Resource Assignments," **p. 313**.

- **The Advanced tab**—Create deadlines and date constraints for the task in this tab. Also, choose the task type, assign calendars and WBS codes, and choose the Earned Value method, all of which are discussed in greater detail throughout this book. If a resource is assigned to the task, you can choose to ignore the resource calendar. Finally, you can mark the task as a milestone (milestones are explained later in this chapter in the section "Defining Milestones").

- **The Notes tab**—Attach a note to the task in this tab. This concept is explained later in this chapter in the section "Attaching Notes to Tasks."

- **The Custom Fields tab**—Create and define custom fields for the task in this tab.

→ For more details about custom fields, **see** "Creating and Customizing Fields" **p. 801**.

TIP

All six tabs in the Task Information dialog box contain the Help button. This feature comes in handy if you are unsure about the use of a field in that particular tab.

USING THE MULTIPLE TASK INFORMATION DIALOG BOX

You also have the ability to make the same changes to several tasks at once. From your task list, choose the tasks you want to make the same change to by holding down Ctrl and selecting the tasks. Then, select Project, Task Information. The Multiple Task Information dialog box appears, as shown in Figure 6.5.

Figure 6.5
Make the same changes to multiple tasks using the Multiple Task Information dialog box.

Any change you make is applied to all selected tasks. For example, the Multiple Task Information box is helpful when you want to give multiple tasks the same duration value.

Some tabs or fields will be restricted because you cannot apply certain values to multiple tasks. Those tabs are grayed out, as shown in Figure 6.5.

MANIPULATING THE TASK LIST

No matter how hard you try to avoid it, you will almost always have to make changes to your task list after you have started creating it. Many of these edits can be made by selecting the cell and typing directly into it, or typing in the Edit bar above the Task Entry table. If you use the Edit bar, click the check mark to the left of the bar to apply the change, or click the red X to cancel it.

You can perform other commands to edit or manipulate your task list to be more accommodating to your project, or to account for changes that will inevitably arise. These commands apply to all views, not just the Gantt Chart view, and are discussed in the following sections.

DISPLAYING LONG TASK NAMES

Earlier in this chapter, the section "Creating Task Names" discussed the concepts behind constructing task names so they make sense when taken out of the context of the project schedule. This can make for a longer task name than the original cell space provides for, and you may want to adjust the width of the column to display the entire name.

You can do this with the mouse. At the top of the column, in the cell that contains the column header (in this case, Task Name), place your mouse on the right-side border of the cell (the left border moves the column to the left of it). Your mouse pointer becomes a

6

double-headed left and right arrow with a vertical line down the middle. When you see this arrow, double-click on the column's border. Microsoft Project 2007 will automatically adjust the width to fit the column's longest entry.

Alternatively, when you see the double-headed arrow, you can click and drag the border while holding down the mouse button, and adjust it as much or as little as you want.

Double-clicking in the middle of the column header cell (when you do not see the double-headed arrow) will open up the Column Definition dialog box, as shown in Figure 6.6. In this box, you can define the width numerically, or click the Best Fit button, which adjusts the width to the longest entry in the column.

NOTE

This process works not just in the Task Name column, but in any column in the Task Entry table.

Figure 6.6
Adjust the width of a column in the Column Definition dialog box.

ADJUSTING THE HEIGHT OF TASK ROWS

Another option for displaying long entries such as task names is adjusting the height of the rows. Like adjusting column width, adjusting row height enables you to display longer entries into the fields. By default, each row is one line of text in height. If you have already adjusted the row height, you can always lower it again to a more suitable height.

Adjusting row height is similar to adjusting column width. Highlight the row you want to adjust by clicking the ID field. Move your mouse to the bottom border of the cell (the top border moves the row above it; see Figure 6.7). A double-headed arrow will appear, only this one has arrows pointing up and down and a horizontal bar going though the middle. In the highlighted cell, drag the bottom border down or up until you reach your desired height. The maximum number of lines of text you can define for a row is 20.

You can also adjust the heights of multiple rows simultaneously. Highlight the multiple rows by holding down Ctrl as you click the ID numbers, or select all the rows by clicking in the upper-left cell, above the row numbers and next to the column headings. Then drag the bottom of any of the ID number cells of any of the selected rows to your desired height. All selected rows will become the same height, regardless of their previous height.

Select All button

Figure 6.7
When you have long task names, it is easy to change the height of a row so the text will wrap around.

Row of height 2 with wrapped text

Row of height 1

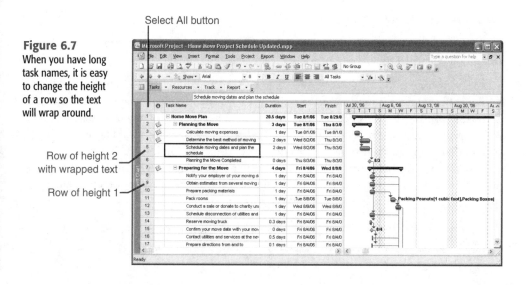

UNDOING CHANGES IN THE TASK LIST

Undoing changes has been significantly improved for Microsoft Project 2007. You used to only be able to undo the most recent change and perform each undo one at a time.

NEW Microsoft Project 2007 has a new feature—the Multiple Undo. The Multiple Undo feature can be accessed by clicking the down arrow in the Undo icon on the Standard toolbar. From the drop-down list you can then see all the recent changes you have made, as shown in Figure 6.8. Select any of those, and Microsoft Project undoes that change, and everything that came before it. In addition, the Multiple Undo feature allows you to undo multiple changes at once, as many as you select.

Figure 6.8
Click the arrow in the Undo icon on the Standard toolbar to display the multiple undo drop-down list.

6

You can also select Edit, Undo to undo the most recent change.

The same concept applies for multiple redos. The Redo icon is just to the right of the Undo icon on the Standard toolbar.

NEW Another new feature for Microsoft Project 2007 is Change Highlighting. This feature highlights all affected fields when you make a change. For instance, if you change the duration of the task, Microsoft Project will highlight the start and finish dates of any tasks that are its predecessors or successors, or its summary tasks, because those fields would be affected by the duration change, as shown in Figure 6.9. The Change Highlighting will also be activated if you undo any previously made changes. By default the Change Highlighting feature is enabled; to disable it, click its icon on the Standard toolbar, or select View, Hide Change Highlighting.

Figure 6.9
The areas are highlighted because a change in another field affected the highlighted fields. Enable or disable this feature on the Standard toolbar, or select View, Hide/Show Change Highlighting.

Affected areas are highlighted

INSERTING, DELETING, AND CLEARING

As your project develops, there will be a need to insert, delete, or clear tasks. These are simple revisions made on your task list.

When inserting a new task, keep in mind that new rows are always inserted above the selected row. Therefore, select the row that you want directly under the new task by clicking its ID number. Once that row is selected, press the Insert button on your keyboard, or select Insert, New Task. You can also insert a new task by right-clicking the row where you want to insert a task and then selecting New Task. The blank new row will appear above the task, and you can enter the task information.

If you want to insert multiple new tasks in the same location, highlight the number of rows you want to insert and follow the same process. For example, to insert three rows, highlight three existing adjacent rows. The top row will be directly below the newly inserted rows. Click the Insert key, or select Insert, New Task, and three blank new rows will appear above the tasks you had selected.

NOTE

> Microsoft Project 2007 will not let you insert multiple rows unless the rows you selected to insert and the new rows above are adjacent to each other. To insert three rows, you must select three adjacent rows. You cannot select two rows, skip one, and select the next row.

If you select the Task Name cell and press the Delete key, only the contents of that cell are deleted. Furthermore, a delete smart tag appears (see Table 6.1 and Figure 6.10). Click the smart tag, and you can choose to delete the entire task or only the Task Name field.

Figure 6.10
When you delete a task name, click the delete smart tag to select to delete the task name only or the entire task.

To delete an entire task altogether, select the row header (the task's ID number in many views) to highlight the task and then press the Delete key on your keyboard. You can also delete an entire task by clicking in any cell in the task you want to delete and selecting Edit, Delete Task.

If you accidentally delete anything, just use the Undo command to restore it (Edit, Undo, or the Undo icon on the Standard toolbar).

Besides pressing the Delete key, you can delete or clear a task or the contents of a cell by highlighting the cell, selecting Edit, Clear, and then choosing which Clear option you want to apply. You can clear multiple cells in the same column at once by holding down Ctrl and clicking any number of cells, or you can select the entire row by clicking the task ID number. The Clear options are as follows:

6

- **All**—Choosing All clears all contents of the cell(s). If you have selected the task ID number, and thus the entire row, choosing Clear, All clears all the fields but leaves the task row intact. Automatically, the default duration and start and finish dates are entered.

- **Formats**—Clear, Formats leaves all of the content intact, but clears any formatting for the cell(s) you have selected.

- **Contents**—As the name suggests, this command clears the contents of the selected cell(s). If you select the entire task row, this command will clear all task fields, including those that are not displayed in the view you are working in. Like the Clear All command, the Clear Contents command automatically reapplies the default duration and start and finish dates. The shortcut for this command is Ctrl+Del, or you can right-click in a cell and choose Clear Contents as another option.

- **Notes**—No matter which cell you have selected, choosing the Clear Notes command clears only the notes for that particular task. The Notes field is usually not displayed.

- **Hyperlinks**—Like the Notes field, the Hyperlinks field is not always displayed. To clear the Hyperlinks field, select the task ID number and choose Edit, Clear, Hyperlinks.

- **Entire Task**—This command clears the entire task. Select any cell in the task row and apply this command to clear the entire task. Unlike the Clear Contents and Clear All commands, the default duration and start and finish fields are not refilled; the entire row is left blank.

> **NOTE**
>
> You cannot restore formats that have been cleared. All other cleared items can be restored with the Undo command, unless the Undo queue has been purged. There are several actions in Microsoft Project 2007 that will purge the undo, after which you cannot restore to the previous action. One of the purging operations is a save.

COPYING, CUTTING, AND MOVING TASKS

In Microsoft Project 2007 you can cut, copy, and move entire tasks or cells within task rows. You may decide to move tasks on your task list so they are listed in a more appropriate order. Or, you may want to copy a task or several tasks and paste them in another project file.

> **NOTE**
>
> No matter if you are cutting, copying, or moving, your selections must contain only adjacent cells or rows. If you want to cut, copy, or move cells or rows that are not adjoining, you must cut, copy, or move those cells or rows separately.

Follow these steps to move a task field, entire task, or group of tasks with the Cut/Copy and Paste method:

1. Decide what you want to cut or copy. To select an entire task, click its ID number, or select any cell in the task row and press Shift+spacebar. To select multiple adjacent

tasks, click the first task, hold down Shift, and click the last task. All tasks in between, including the tasks you clicked, will be selected. You can also select single cells, or multiple adjacent cells, using the same method.

2. Decide whether you want to cut your selection (removing it entirely) or copy it (leaving the original task[s] or cell[s] intact). To cut, you can use any of the following methods: Right-click and select Cut Task (or Cut Cell); choose Edit, Cut Task (or Cut Cell); use the Cut command on the Standard toolbar; or press Ctrl+X. To copy, you can right-click and select Copy Task (or Copy Cell); choose Edit, Copy Task (or Copy Cell); use the Copy command on the Standard toolbar; or press Ctrl+C.

3. Select the task row or cell where you want to put your copied or cut selection(s). If you are relocating multiple tasks or cells, you still only select one row or cell.

4. To paste, use one of the following methods: Right-click and choose Paste; choose Edit, Paste; use the Paste command on the Standard toolbar; or press Ctrl+V. Pasting whole rows inserts new rows and shifts the existing ones in the targeted area down to make room for the new ones. Pasting cells replaces the existing data in the targeted cells, or creates new tasks if the targeted area is blank.

CAUTION

If you want to cut, copy, or move an entire task, be sure you either click its ID number or use the Shift+spacebar command when you have a cell highlighted. This will ensure that you are selecting all task fields, including those that are not displayed. Otherwise, you may only be moving part of the task fields, because none of the views originally display all task fields.

Once you have cut or copied data, you can paste it as often as you like as long as it remains on your Clipboard.

Additionally, you can move a task or multiple tasks using the drag-and-drop method. To do this, follow these steps:

1. Click the Task ID number for the task you want to move. To move multiple tasks, click the ID number of the first one, hold down Shift, and click the ID number of the last one. Remember that in order for you to move multiple tasks, they must be adjacent.

2. Hover the mouse over the ID number of any of the selected tasks. The mouse pointer becomes a four-headed arrow.

3. Holding down the mouse button, drag the pointer in the direction you want to move it. A shadowed I-beam will appear. Release the mouse button when this I-beam is located across the top of the row you want to move the selected task(s) to.

You can also use this procedure to copy and paste the task(s). As you drag the selected task(s), as described in step 3, hold down the Ctrl key.

6

CAUTION

> When you move a task using the cut-and-paste method, the old task is being deleted from the list, and a new task is being created. This means that the new task will now have its own unique ID number. This will not effect the task list if you are inserting or deleting other tasks, or moving the task around, but might be important if you compare versions of the project files and cannot understand why there are two different unique ID numbers for what is essentially the same task.

USING THE FILL COMMAND

Sometimes, you may have several fields that contain the same value. For example, you may have multiple tasks with the same duration, such as tasks relating to appliance deliveries and installations in your new house. Microsoft Project's Fill command makes it easy to enter these values without having to type in each one.

To use the Fill command, first select the cell that you wish to copy, and while holding the mouse button, drag the mouse pointer up or down through all the cells you want to insert the copied value into. The original cell (the one with the value to fill into the other cells) should be at the very top or very bottom of the highlighted list. When you have the cells selected, choose Edit, Fill, Down to copy the value if the original cell is at the top, or choose Edit, Fill, Up if it is at the bottom. You can also press Ctrl+D to use the Fill Down command; Fill Up has no shortcut command.

If the cells are not adjacent, you can still perform this command. Select the nonadjacent cells by holding down Ctrl and clicking in the cells. In this case, the original cell (the one with the value to be copied) must be the top cell in the entry table (you cannot "Fill Up" when working with nonadjacent cells). When you have them all selected, choose Edit, Fill, Down. All the selected cells will now share the value of the original cell.

Another method to fill cells with a copied value is by using the cell's *fill handle*. The fill handle is the small black square in the lower-right corner of the cell. When you hover the mouse pointer over the fill handle, it becomes a plus sign (+). Click the fill handle, and while holding down the mouse button, drag the mouse pointer to other adjacent cells to enter the identical value. You can use Fill Up or Fill Down, but the cells must be adjacent.

DEFINING SUMMARY TASKS AND SUBTASKS

In Microsoft Project 2007, there are three kinds of tasks: summary tasks, subtasks, and milestones. Milestones will be discussed later in this chapter in the section "Defining Milestones."

A *summary* task is a major topic or phase in the project. A summary task summarizes the duration, cost, and amount of work that is spent on a major phase in the project. Summary tasks are broken into *subtasks*, which are detail tasks that make up the total work for the summary task. Most tasks in a project are subtasks. Think of summary tasks as the end goal, and subtasks as the steps you must achieve to reach it.

On the timescale side of the Gantt Chart view, summary tasks are displayed as black bars with upside-down triangles on the ends, and subtasks are the rounder, blue bars (see Figure 6.11).

When you have created your task list, you can then outline the lists to reflect summary tasks and subtasks (and milestones). Outlining organizes the tasks into functional groups, and is visually quite helpful. Subtasks are indented under summary tasks. When you indent a task, it is called *demoting* the task. Likewise, outdenting a task is called *promoting* it. The theory is, the more a task is outdented, the more significance it holds to the overall project scope, and the more general it is. The more a task is indented, the more detailed it is. These concepts are described in more detail in the following sections.

After you have transformed a task into a summary task, you cannot define its start or finish dates. The summary task's start date is the earliest start date of its subtasks, and its finish date is the latest finish date of its subtasks. Similarly, the total cost and amount of work for a group of subtasks are rolled up and summarized in the Cost and Work fields of their summary task.

CAUTION

> Following project management best practices, do not assign resources or work to the summary-level tasks. Instead, create another subtask underneath your summary task and provide the work and resource information there. Summary tasks are there to organize and summarize information. Furthermore, if you do add work and resources to a summary-level task, your work totals for higher summary tasks may not add up properly, so it is best to avoid this.

Figure 6.11
Summary tasks and subtasks are displayed in an outline form in the Gantt Chart view. Notice the difference in their placement (indented vs. outdented) in the Task Name column on the Task Entry table side, as well as the taskbars on the timescale side (summary taskbars are black). The arrows on the timescale side represent dependency links.

→ For more details about the critical path, **see** Chapter 12, "Performing a Schedule Reality Check," on **p. 419**.

UNDERSTANDING DURATION OF SUMMARY TASKS

Just as you cannot modify a summary task's start or finish dates, you cannot modify its duration. A summary task's duration is the amount of working time between its subtasks' earliest start date and latest finish date.

No matter how its subtasks' durations are displayed, a summary task's duration is always displayed in the default setting for the time units. To change this setting, go to the Schedule tab of the Options dialog box and choose the time unit you want in the Duration Is Entered In field. For example, if most subtasks are entered in hours, but the default time unit setting is days, the summary task's Duration field will show the value in days.

INDENTING AND OUTDENTING TASKS

Summary tasks can contain subtasks that are also summary tasks to another series of tasks. For example, Planning the Move is the summary task of Calculate Moving Expenses, but Calculate Moving Expenses is the summary task of Calculate Moving Company Fees. As tasks become more and more indented, they become more detailed. Outdented tasks are more general, and rely on the completion of their indented subtasks for their own completion.

Microsoft Project 2007 offers several methods of indenting (demoting) and outdenting (promoting) tasks to define them as summary tasks or subtasks. All of the following methods produce the same result.

TIP

> If you are new to the concept of outlining in Microsoft Project, you may want to use the Project Guide to walk you through the process. On the Project Guide toolbar, choose Tasks, Organize Tasks. Select one or more tasks on the Task Entry table to be indented or outdented, and click the Indent or Outdent tool in the side pane.

First, select the task or tasks you want to indent or outdent, and then do one of the following:

- On the Formatting toolbar, use the Indent or Outdent button to change the outline level of the task(s). The Indent button is an arrow pointing to the right, and the Outdent button is an arrow pointing to the left (refer to Figure 6.11).
- Drag the task name to the right or left using the mouse. In the Task Name field, place the mouse over the first few letters of the task name. The mouse pointer will become a double-headed arrow pointing left and right. Drag the pointer to the right to indent or to the left to outdent. If you have selected multiple tasks, they are indented or outdented together.
- Select Project, Outline, and then either Indent or Outdent.
- Select the Task ID number(s) for the task or tasks. Right-click the ID number and choose Indent or Outdent.
- Press the key combination Alt+Shift+right arrow to indent, or Atl+Shift+left arrow to outdent.

CAUTION

> All outlining actions you apply to summary tasks are in turn applied to their subtasks. If you indent a summary task, all its subtasks are indented (demoted) even further. Furthermore, if you delete, copy, move, promote, or demote a summary task, all of its subtasks follow the same action. This includes other summary tasks that are subtasks to the summary task you are changing.

If a task is indented and you promote it (outdent it to the left), the tasks below it are affected in one of three ways:

- If the tasks immediately below the newly promoted task are at its same level of indentation, they become subtasks of the newly promoted task. If you want them to remain at the same level, select them all and promote them simultaneously.

- If the tasks immediately below the newly promoted task are already subtasks, then they remain subtasks, but shift to the left as well, following their summary task (remember, an action done to a summary task is in turn done to its subtasks). If a subtask is indented one level more than the newly promoted task, it remains indented one level more by moving with it.

- If the tasks below the newly promoted task are at a higher level of indentation (already further left than the promoted task), these tasks are unaffected by the promotion.

Alternatively, if a subtask is indented one level to the right of its summary task, and if you promote it, it is no longer a subtask because you promoted it to the same level of indentation as its summary task. The tasks then become equal in terms of their outline level.

If you want to add a new task into the task list as a summary task, you must enter it just above the task(s) you want it to summarize. If the subtasks are already indented, you can simply outdent the newly inserted task to define it as their summary task. If the subtasks are not indented at all, you must indent all the tasks you want to be subtasks of the newly inserted summary task.

For example, if you have a summary task called Pack Rooms, its subtasks would be all the tasks for packing all the rooms in your old house. After you list them all, you probably would realize that there are many subtasks for packing the rooms of an entire house, and you would want to organize them further by creating summary tasks for each room, such as Pack Kitchen, and so on. These new summary tasks would be subtasks of Pack Rooms, but summary tasks to the original subtasks. You can insert these new summary tasks above the appropriate tasks for packing that particular room, and indent all of the applicable subtasks for the newly inserted summary task. If they are not in order, you can move them accordingly using the methods described in the section "Copying, Cutting, and Moving Tasks," earlier in this chapter.

COLLAPSING AND EXPANDING THE OUTLINE

When you want to look at the general progress of your project without viewing all the subtask details, Microsoft Project 2007 allows you to collapse the outline by hiding all the subtasks and viewing only the summary tasks. Since the progress of a summary task is determined solely by the progress of its subtasks, you can quickly examine the overall status of each summary task.

When the tasks are collapsed, they are not deleted, but just hidden. When a summary task is collapsed, nothing about its subtasks is displayed, including the row ID numbers (see Figure 6.12).

Figure 6.12
Collapse or expand the outline or part of the outline using the Show button on the Formatting toolbar.

Show Use the Show command to display or hide various outline levels. The Show button is located on the Formatting toolbar. Click it to display the Show submenu. Or, choose Project, Outline, Show. On the Show submenu, select the outline level you want to display. Selecting All Subtasks displays all levels of the outline. Outline Level 1 displays only the top-level tasks (regardless of subtasks), Outline Level 2 displays top-level tasks plus the first level of subtasks, and so on, down to the ninth level.

You can also expand or collapse subtasks for individual summary tasks. Double-click on the summary task's ID number. If the outline is collapsed, it will expand to show all its subtasks, and their subtasks. If it is expanded at all, it will collapse entirely.

If outline symbols are displayed, summary tasks contain a Hide Subtasks button, which is a minus sign (–), or a Show Subtasks button, which is a plus sign (+), to the left of their name in the Task Name field. If the subtasks are already shown, the Hide Subtasks button is in the field (refer to Figure 6.10). Click it to hide the subtasks. If the subtasks are hidden, the Show Subtasks button is in the field. Click it to show the subtasks. For more information about displaying outline symbols, see the section "Selecting the Display Options for Outlining," later in this chapter.

If these symbols are not displayed in the Task Name field of a summary task, you can use the Hide Subtasks and Show Subtasks buttons, located next to the Indent and Outdent buttons on the Formatting toolbar. Alternatively, follow these steps to hide or show subtasks:

1. Select the summary task(s) whose subtasks you want to hide or show.
2. Choose Project, Outline, Hide Subtasks to hide them, or Project, Outline, Show Subtasks to show them.

> **TIP**
>
> It is good practice to have a minimum of three outline levels within a project: project level (a project summary task over the entire project; the entire level is only one task row), phase level (summary tasks of the projects' phases), and work level (subtasks). You can, of course, have more levels than this. No matter how many levels you have, the lowest is the work level. It is here, on the work level, that the tasks should be linked and the resources assigned. Linking tasks and assigning resources are discussed later in this book.

EDITING OUTLINED PROJECTS

When you have created outline levels in your project, you still edit tasks in the same way described earlier in this chapter. However, some fields cannot be edited, such as the Duration fields for summary tasks (because summary task durations are defined by the start and finish dates of their summary tasks, as described previously in this chapter).

Double-click any task to display the Task Information dialog box to make any edits, or use any of the other task-editing options previously discussed in this chapter.

Keep in mind that changes you make to a summary task are also done to its subtasks (such as deleting, copying, cutting, pasting, moving, promoting, or demoting). However, summary tasks have their own Notes field, which you can and should use for notes about the summary task itself. The section "Attaching Notes to Tasks," later in this chapter, describes that process.

SELECTING THE DISPLAY OPTIONS FOR OUTLINING

Microsoft Project 2007 automatically indents subtasks under their summary tasks as a means of organizing the task list by outline levels. This is the default feature, but it can be disabled, along with several other display options that can be modified to best suit your needs.

Make these changes at the bottom of the View tab in the Options dialog box (Tools, Options), as shown in Figure 6.13.

6

Figure 6.13
Define display options for outlining in the View tab of the Options dialog box, under the bottom section Outline Options for *"Project Name."*

Outlining options

There are several display options for formatting your outline structure, all located at the bottom of the View tab. Refer to Figure 6.13 while reading the following list of display options:

- If you prefer, you can disable the indenting of subtasks, so all tasks are lined up evenly on the left. This may be helpful to save room on your screen, or if you simply do not favor indenting the tasks. To disable indentation of subtasks, clear the Indent Name check box.

- If you do disable task indenting, you can choose to display the task outline number next to the name to help distinguish summary tasks from subtasks. Unlike task ID numbers, outline numbers cannot be edited. If the outline number of a summary task is 4, then its first subtask is 4.1, its second subtask is 4.2, and so on. If subtask 4.2 has its own subtasks, they would begin with 4.2.1, 4.2.2, and so forth. To display outline numbers, select the Show Outline Number check box.

- As mentioned previously in this chapter, Microsoft Project 2007 by default places Hide Subtasks (–) or Show Subtasks (+) to the left of the summary task name, depending on whether the subtasks are displayed or not. These symbols not only make it easy to expand or collapse a summary task with one mouse click, they also serve as an indicator that a task is a summary task, and that if the Show Subtasks symbol is showing, then that task has subtasks hidden. If you prefer not to display these symbols, clear the Show Outline Symbol check box.

- You can hide summary tasks, displaying only milestones and subtasks. This may be useful for sorting tasks for reports by start date, duration, or alphabetically. Since the summary tasks are not actually assigned resources to work on, they may get in the way and take up space in the reports. To hide summary tasks, clear the Show Summary Tasks check box.

- As advised earlier, it is good practice to display an overall summary task for the entire project, called the Project Summary task. Its duration spans from the start of the very first subtask to the finish of the very last one. When this task is displayed, all other tasks are indented at least one level. The task name is the name of the project, which is taken from the Summary tab of the Properties dialog box (File, Properties); editing the task name changes the project name as well, so the Project Summary task name and project name are always the same. To display the Project Summary task, select the Show project summary task check box.

To change the outline formatting feature, the active view has to be a task view that must be the only pane, or top pane, in the window. You can select the outline options by following these steps:

1. Select Tools, Options to open the Options dialog box, and then choose the View tab, as shown in Figure 6.13.
2. Select or clear the check boxes as described above.
3. Click OK to apply the changes to your new setting.

You can regulate the display of outline projects with the Options dialog box.

USING ROLLUP TASKBARS

By default, in the timescale side of the Gantt Chart view, summary taskbars are displayed spanning the entire summary task as black bars with upside-down triangles at the start and finish dates, and subtask taskbars are blue, rounded-edge bars spanning the duration of the particular subtask. Each task bar is located to the right of its row in the Task Entry table.

However, you can roll up the subtask taskbars to the summary taskbar, which will mark each subtask's start and finish on the summary taskbar. This produces a segmented bar that shows the duration of each subtask within the summary taskbar (see Figure 6.14).

Figure 6.14
A subtask's taskbars are displayed within their summary tasks to show duration within the summary task when you roll up the subtask taskbars.

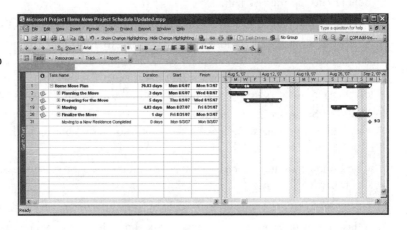

You can roll up all of the subtask taskbars, or roll up some and leave the others alone.

To roll up all taskbars, choose Format, Layout, which displays the Layout dialog box (see Figure 6.15). Or you can right-click in the bar chart (timescale) area and select Layout. In the Layout dialog box, select the Always Roll Up Gantt Bars box. The rollup bars will then appear in front of the summary taskbar.

Also in the Layout dialog box, you can choose to display the rollup taskbars only when their subtasks are hidden by checking the Hide Rollup Bars When Summary Expanded box. That way, when the summary task is expanded, you will not see the rollup bars.

Figure 6.15
Roll up taskbars by using the Layout dialog box.

To roll up particular subtask taskbars and leave others alone, clear the Always Roll Up Gantt Bars check box in the Layout dialog box. You must also mark each subtask you want rolled up. To do this, follow these steps:

1. Select the subtask you want to roll up, and open the Task Information dialog box by double-clicking the task name.

2. On the General tab, select Roll up Gantt bar to summary and click OK.

3. Select the summary task whose taskbar you want to display the rollup in. If the summary task is a subtask of another summary task, the higher-level summary task can show the rollup as well, whether you show it on the lower-level summary task or not. Each summary task must be selected separately to control the display of rollup bars.

4. Open the Summary Task Information dialog box for the summary task by either double-clicking the summary task, clicking the Task Information button in the Standard toolbar, or selecting Project, Task Information.

5. If you want the summary task to display rolled up taskbars, select the Show rolled up Gantt bars check box.

6. Click OK to save the settings and close the Task Information dialog box.

7. Repeat this process for every summary task above the subtask you want to display the rollup bar.

TIP

> If you want the rolled-up toolbars to show milestone markers at their finish date instead of showing the whole bar, go to Tools, Macro, Macros, and select Rollup_Formatting and then click Run. To reverse the changes, just run the macro again. Remember, though, that this macro will discard any custom bar styles you might have created. If you have custom bar styles, you will need to edit them directly to change the display of rolled-up tasks.

DEFINING MILESTONES

As in real life, a *milestone* in Microsoft Project 2007 represents a critical landmark, turning point, or decision within your project. In the project Move to New House, a milestone would be the time you signed the papers and got the new house keys, moved completely out of your old house, or any successful completion of a major phase of the move. Milestones come in handy for marking major phases in the project, and you can filter the task list to display only the milestones in order to quickly see all the important dates a milestone represents.

You can and should create a milestone at a point in a project you want to monitor closely. If, for example, you are re-carpeting your new house before you move in, you may want to enter a milestone when all tasks of that phase are complete. The milestone could be called Re-Carpeting Completed. The duration would be zero, because, similar to a summary task, no actual work is done on a milestone. (Remember, though, summary tasks do have durations; their durations are defined by the total duration of their subtasks.)

The end of each phase of the project, as well as the end of the entire project itself, should be marked with a milestone.

To create a milestone, enter **0** in the Duration field. Microsoft Project 2007 will automatically classify the task as a milestone.

The following list contains examples of when you would want to add a milestone in your project:

- It is beneficial to add a milestone for every crucial deliverable.

- Perhaps you have a client or a project sponsor who wants to see project milestones. If you do, then it is recommended that you create two separate types of milestones—ones that are internal to the team, and ones your client or project sponsor would like to see. Separating the two will help both you and the client or sponsor. Your client probably does not want to see every single one of your milestones, just the driving ones that either make or break the project. Similarly, you do not want to limit yourself to only a handful of milestones that do not include intermediate deliverables that you will need to consider.

- There may be specific milestones associated with the billing. If there are, it may be beneficial to include those specific milestones to remind yourself which of your deliverables influence the invoicing.

6

Your project should also have a final milestone to close the entire project. This milestone connects your entire schedule together and defines the formal completion of a project. All too often, work on a project finishes, but the project just fizzles out because there is no formal completion to it. A final project milestone prevents this from happening and adds a final element of organization to your project.

Alternatively, you can use the Project Guide to create a milestone. On the Project Guide toolbar, choose Tasks, then select List the tasks in the project. Select the task you want to define as a milestone from the list, and select the Mark selected task a milestone check box. On the other hand, if it is already a milestone and you do not want it to be, clear that box.

Another way to define a milestone is in the Task Information dialog box. Open the Task Information dialog box by double-clicking on the task name, or by any other method described earlier in this chapter. On the Advanced tab, select the Mark task as milestone box (or clear it to remove its milestone status) and then click OK.

By default, a milestone is displayed as a diamond on the timescale side of the Gantt Chart view. There is no taskbar to show duration. To change the display of a milestone to something other than the black diamond, select Format, Bar Styles. The Bar Styles dialog box will appear (see Figure 6.16). In the Bar Styles dialog box, select Milestone and change its appearance using the drop-down lists at the bottom of the dialog box.

→ For more details about using the Bar Styles dialog box to change how items are displayed in the Gantt Chart view, **see** "Formatting the Gantt Chart Views," **p. 616**.

Figure 6.16
Change the display of a milestone in the Bar Styles dialog box. In this example, the milestones have been changed to be displayed as solid red diamonds.

While it is possible to mark a task as a milestone that has a duration greater than zero, this is not a good practice because it can be misleading. Instead, apply the duration to the tasks that coincides with the milestone, and leave the milestone's duration set at zero.

ATTACHING NOTES TO TASKS

When managing a project, it is always good practice to stay as organized as possible. As you get deep into the work of a project, you as the project manager are often juggling several things at once every day. It is easy to say you are going to remember a little detail, and quickly forget it in minutes due to another issue that inevitably arises.

Therefore, you should attach notes to tasks in your project to give you the peace of mind of staying on top of things without having to remember every little detail about a task. A note can be a reason why you made a specific decision about a task, the scope of particular item, a reminder of a situation involving the task, an informational message to other users (other project managers or resources) of the project file, any assumptions you have made, or anything else relating to the task.

These notes can be included on printed reports if you desire by choosing File, Page Setup, and in the View tab, selecting the Print notes check box.

Tasks with notes attached display the Task Notes icon in the Indicator field (refer to Table 6.1). If you hover the mouse pointer over the Task Notes icon, it will display the beginning of the note's text.

> **TIP**
>
> Notes are a great way to capture the scope of a task and explain in greater detail the goal of the task. This is also relevant for summary tasks, which have their own notes field.
>
> Furthermore, you can document the changes made to the scope of a task, its result on the task's duration, and its effect on the overall project.

TYPING AND FORMATTING NOTES

You can attach notes to tasks in a variety of ways:

- On the Project Guide toolbar, select Tasks, then select Link to or attach more task information. Next, select Add a note, which takes you to the Notes tab of the Task Information dialog box.
- Double-click on the task to open the Task Information dialog box (or use any of the other methods described earlier in this chapter). Then open the Notes tab.
- Click the Task Notes button on the Standard toolbar. This button looks identical to the Task Notes icon that appears in the Indicators field (refer to Table 6.1).

At the top of the Notes text box in the Task Information dialog box is a formatting toolbar that provides options to format the note (see Figure 6.17). Hover the mouse over the buttons for a description of what they do.

6

TIP

You can perform a search of the Notes field to find specific text for a task note in your project. However, Microsoft Project stops the search as soon as it encounters most non-printable characters, such as the Enter key. To avoid the problem where the Find command stops searching a note when it encounters the Enter key, use Shift+Enter when you want to start a new paragraph when typing your note.

Figure 6.17
Type your note in the Notes text box in the Task Information dialog box, and format the text using the toolbar at the top of the text box.

TIP

You can type hundreds of thousands of characters in the Notes text box. However, if your note is large, it may be easier to insert a link to an external document rather than type it all out (see Figure 6.17). This process is discussed in the next section.

The Notes text box contains many of the text formatting capabilities of Microsoft Word. Edit your notes as you would a Word document as it supports rich text format.

TIP

While notes can hold thousands of characters, Microsoft Project can will only search the Notes field for the first 255 characters. It will also stop when it runs up against a non-printable character, such as Enter. If you need to make long notes, see "Inserting Objects in Notes," later in this chapter.

When you are finished entering your note, click OK.

Several keys are useful when moving through the Notes text box:

Key	Effect
Home	Moves the cursor to the beginning of the line
End	Moves the cursor to the end of the line
Ctrl+Home	Moves to the beginning of the note
Ctrl+End	Moves to the end of the note
Ctrl+left arrow	Moves one word to the left
Ctrl+right arrow	Moves one word to the right

INSERTING HYPERLINKS IN NOTES

You can insert a hyperlink in the Notes text box to link to a website. To do so, type the website address in its full format (for example, http://www.website.com). Alternatively, you can copy and paste the address into the Notes text box. The hyperlink will be displayed underlined and in the color used for hyperlinks on your computer (the default is blue). When you click the hyperlink, the browser is opened to the web page. See the section "Attaching Hyperlinks to Tasks," later in this chapter, for more information on hyperlinks and tasks.

INSERTING OBJECTS IN NOTES

Another option when adding notes to tasks is inserting data objects from other applications into notes. An *object* is defined as a data file in a format maintained by another application, such as a picture, reference document, spreadsheet, word processing document, presentation, sound and video clip, and so on. You could, for example, insert an Excel spreadsheet and edit that spreadsheet within the note to apply it more directly to the task or project.

You have a choice of inserting the actual object into the note, or inserting just a link to the area where the object resides outside of the project. If you insert the actual object, rather than just a link, the size of the project file increases by the size of the object. If you are trying to keep your project file size as small as possible, you should insert the link to the object instead of the object itself.

Inserting the link rather than the object is also beneficial if the object is something that needs to be seen by other people. When you click on the link, Microsoft Project opens the object, and any edits you make are saved to the object outside of Microsoft Project. The link will open the object with the saved changes next time you click the link (if you saved your edits properly). This includes changes made by other people. If you insert the actual object, only the edits made within Microsoft Project will be seen when you open the object in Microsoft Project; if you or other people edit the object outside of Microsoft Project, those changes will not be saved in the note.

Most objects will be larger than the actual Notes text box can be expanded to display. Therefore, you should insert an icon that, when double-clicked, will open up the actual object.

Follow these steps to insert a data object into a note:

1. Open the Task Information dialog box (double-click the task) for the task and open the Notes tab. Click the Insert Object button on the formatting toolbar at the top of the Notes text box, or right-click in the Notes text box and select Object. This will open up the Insert Object dialog box (see Figure 6.18).

2. To insert a blank object that you can design and edit only from within Microsoft Project, choose Create New. Then choose the application to create the object from in the Object Type list (see Figure 6.18).

6

Figure 6.18
Insert objects into notes in the Insert Object dialog box. This example is what the box looks like if you are creating a new object.

3. To insert an object from an outside application that is already saved as a file, choose Create from File. The Object Type fields changes to a File field. Type the path and filename in the box, or use the Browse feature to select the file from the directory structure (see Figure 6.19).

   Alternatively, you can create a new file and insert it as an object here. Browse to the folder where the new object is to be stored, right-click over a blank space in the file list, select New, and select the application that will create the file. Replace the default name for the new file with the filename you want to use, and click Insert. When you finish step 6, double-click the object to create its data.

4. If you want to insert only a link, select the Link check box. If you want to insert the actual object, clear this box. Refer to the beginning of this section for explanations of the two options.

5. Select Display As Icon to display an icon for the object instead of the object itself. Most of the time, it is best to insert the icon, due to lack of space in the Notes text box. Then you can double-click the icon to open the object.

6. Click OK to finish and insert the object in the note.

CAUTION

> While you can set up the Notes field as a column in a table, if you edit the note in the field, be warned that you will lose all of your inserted objects. A warning message will remind you of this if you forget the warning here.

Figure 6.19
Insert objects into notes by using the Insert Object dialog box. This example displays the dialog box when inserting the object from an existing file.

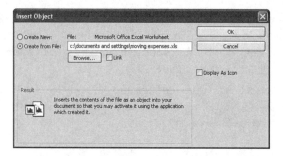

→ For more details about inserting objects in Microsoft Project, **see** "Placing Objects into Microsoft Project 2007," **p. 974**.

ATTACHING NOTES TO THE OVERALL PROJECT

Instead of attaching a note to a particular task, you can attach it to the entire project. Use the File, Properties command to display a short and simple note. In the Summary tab, enter the note in the Comments field. You cannot insert objects here.

For longer, more extensive notes, you should display the project summary task. As described earlier in this chapter, display the project summary task by choosing Tools, Options, and on the View tab select the Show project summary task check box. The project summary task will be listed at the top of the task list.

Once the project summary task is displayed, open its Task Information dialog box (double-click the task name, which is also the name of the project). Then, attach a note as you would to any other task (see the previous sections for further explanation).

CAUTION

If you insert an object in the project summary task, it will be lost if you later attach or edit a note in the Comments field in the Properties dialog box. A warning will appear if you make edits in the Comments field and click OK. You can cancel the changes to save your inserted object, or keep the changes and lose the object. You can avoid this problem by creating a milestone task at the top or bottom of the task list strictly for attaching a note with links to important documents or other data objects.

ATTACHING HYPERLINKS TO TASKS

Hyperlinks can be a useful tool to gather information not directly contained in your project. Perhaps it is to another project file, another task or resource, or a website. In the moving example, you could link to a moving company website or to a public storage website.

As previously discussed, you can insert a hyperlink to websites in the Notes text box of a task. In addition, you can store hyperlinks for tasks in the Hyperlink field. There are several reasons why using the Hyperlink field is more versatile than using the Notes text box:

- If there is a link in the Hyperlink field, an icon appears in the Indicator field, and you can simply click the icon to open the hyperlink. If it is attached in the Notes text box, you have to open the Task Information dialog box or the Task Form view to access the note that contains the hyperlink. It is more convenient to just click the icon.

- Whereas the hyperlink in the Notes text box can only link to Internet or intranet sites, a link in the Hyperlink field has much more flexibility. You can link to other files on your computer, network, other locations within those files (such as a specific task in another project file or a specific cell in an Excel spreadsheet), file folders, other tasks or resources within your current project, or an email message to a specific person.

- You can browse to find the location you want as a hyperlink when you define it in the Hyperlink field. If it is attached to a note, you must know the URL for the site; you cannot browse.

6

However, there is one advantage to storing a hyperlink in a note: you can store multiple hyperlinks in a note. You can only define one hyperlink in the Hyperlink field.

As with attaching notes to tasks, there are several ways to attach a hyperlink. You already know about inserting it in the Notes field. To attach a hyperlink directly to a task (without using the Notes field), do one of the following:

- On the Project Guide toolbar, choose Tasks, and then select Link to or attach more task information. Then, select a task and click Add a hyperlink in the Project Guide pane.
- Select the task, and on the Standard toolbar, select the Insert Hyperlink tool.
- Select the task and select Insert, Hyperlink.
- Right-click the task and choose the Hyperlink option.
- Select the task and press Ctrl+K.

Any of these options open the Insert Hyperlink dialog box (see Figure 6.20). The remaining steps are detailed in the next few sections, depending on what you want to do.

Besides these options, there is a more direct route if you want to link to a specific location in another file. Open the file, select the location you want to link to, and copy it (using any copy method discussed previously). Then, select the task you want to attach it to and choose Edit, Paste as Hyperlink.

ATTACHING HYPERLINKS TO EXISTING FILES OR WEB PAGES

To attach a hyperlink to an existing file or web page, follow these steps:

1. Select the task you want to attach the hyperlink to, and open the Insert Hyperlink dialog box by any of the methods described in the previous section. The Insert Hyperlink dialog box is displayed as in Figure 6.20.

Figure 6.20
Locate files or websites to attach to tasks as hyperlinks in the Insert Hyperlink dialog box.

2. On the left of the Insert Hyperlinks dialog box, click the Existing File or Web Page option.

3. If you know the full path and filename, enter it in the Address box at the bottom. If not, you can browse for the address of the existing filename or website. The following is a list of ways the Insert Hyperlink dialog box helps you browse for the address:

- In the Address box, click the arrow to open the drop-down list to choose from the list of recently accessed folders and websites.

- Click Current Folder to browse folders on your computer, starting in the folder listed in the Look In box.

- Click the Browse for File button (icon on the right) to browse for the file using Windows Explorer, starting in the folder listed in the Look In box.

- Click Browsed Pages to choose from the list of recently viewed web pages.

- Click Recent Files to choose from the list of recently opened files.

- Click the Browse the Web button (icon to the left of Browse for File) to search for a website using the Internet.

- If you have chosen a file that supports bookmarks, click the Bookmark button to see a list of bookmarks defined in that file. This causes the hyperlink to go directly to that part of the document when you open the hyperlink.

4. If you want to display the link using custom text (such as a description of the hyperlink rather than its address), change the text in the Text to display box.

5. If you want to customize the ScreenTip that appears when you hover the mouse pointer over the hyperlink indicator, click the ScreenTip button.

6. Click OK to save the hyperlink.

You can also create a hyperlink by using the Paste as Hyperlink command:

1. Open your document and select the location you want to link to.

2. Choose some part of the document in that location and select the Copy command. Specific applications require different selections:

- Microsoft Project requires choosing a cell in a task row.

- Excel requires choosing a cell or group of cells.

- Word requires choosing a word or section title.

- PowerPoint requires choosing a word or title in a slide or the outline.

3. Go back to Microsoft Project 2007 and choose a cell in the row for the task you want to hold the link.

4. Select Edit, Paste as Hyperlink, and your link is set.

ATTACHING HYPERLINKS TO NEW FILES

You can insert a hyperlink to a file that does not yet exist and create that file simultaneously.

If you want to insert a hyperlink into a document that does not yet exist, follow these steps:

1. Click the Create New Document button in the Insert Hyperlink dialog box.

6

2. Enter a name in the Name of New Document box and remember to include the file extension, so Microsoft Project 2007 will know which application to open when it creates the file. It will default to the path of the active project file, but you can use Change to pick a different folder.

3. Choose either Edit the New Document Later or Edit the New Document Now.

ATTACHING HYPERLINKS TO TASKS OR RESOURCES IN THE SAME PROJECT

Perhaps you want to attach a hyperlink to a task to jump to a resource or another task in your project. This can be a helpful shortcut to a related task or resource. You can also specify the view to display when you link to that task or resource. To create this kind of hyperlink, follow these steps:

1. While attaching the hyperlink, you cannot browse for the task or resource. Therefore, find the task or resource and note its ID number.

2. Select the task you want to attach the hyperlink to and open the Insert Hyperlink dialog box (right-click the task, choose Hyperlink, or use any of the other methods previously described).

3. Choose Place in This Document.

4. In the Enter the task or resource ID box, enter the ID number for the task or resource to link to.

5. Select the view you want displayed when you open the hyperlink in the Select a view in this project field. Select a resource view if you are linking to a resource. Otherwise, Microsoft Project 2007 just keeps the current task view.

USING HYPERLINKS TO CREATE EMAIL MESSAGES

You can use a hyperlink to open Outlook or other email programs to compose an email message. That way, when you open the hyperlink, the email message is addressed and ready to go; you just have to write the content.

To set up an email hyperlink, follow these steps:

1. From the Insert menu, select Hyperlink and then select the E-Mail Address option on the left.

2. Enter the address for your recipient in the E-mail address box. You are required to enter an address; however, there is no link to your address book or contacts folder. Recently used address can be found in the Recently used e-mail addresses box. If you enter something into the Subject box, Microsoft Project will use this text to fill the Subject field every time you open the hyperlink to send a message.

3. Click the OK button to save your changes.

EDITING AND DELETING HYPERLINKS

To edit a hyperlink, select the task and open the Insert Hyperlink dialog box (right-click the task and choose Hyperlink, Edit Hyperlink, or use any of the other method described earlier). Make your edits in the Insert Hyperlink dialog box.

To delete a hyperlink, click the Remove Link button in the Insert Hyperlink dialog box.

You an also use the Clear command: Select the task and choose Edit, Clear, Hyperlinks.

PLACING HYPERLINKS IN THE CUSTOM TEXT FIELDS

As mentioned before, there is only one Hyperlink field for each task. However, there are 30 custom text fields available to store additional hyperlinks in. To use these custom fields, you must first display the text field as a column in the Task Entry table.

Use the Project Guide to insert a custom text field with these steps:

1. On the Project Guide toolbar, choose Tasks. In the Tasks pane, choose Add columns of custom information.
2. Select Show me custom fields.
3. Choose Text as the field type.
4. Choose one of the text custom fields (Text1 through Text30) and click Insert.
5. You may need to scroll to the far right to find your inserted field. You can then use the field to insert a hyperlink by either directly entering a URL, typing a document path, or using the Ctrl+K option.

To see the new custom field displayed as a column, scroll to the far right of the Task Entry table.

Alternatively, you can click on any column heading and select Insert, Column. The Column Definition dialog box appears. In the drop-down list in the Field Name box, scroll down to one of the text fields and click OK. The new column is inserted to the left of the column you originally selected.

Like attaching hyperlinks in the Notes field, there are limitations to storing hyperlinks in text fields. The hyperlink must be the only thing typed in the text field. Also, like attaching to notes, there is no browse feature to help define the hyperlink. You can copy the site and paste it into the text field, however. Also, you must enter the complete URL. For example, www.*website*.com would not work, but http://www.*website*.com would. Be sure to enter the entire address.

DEFINING RECURRING TASKS

Sometimes in your project you will have *recurring* tasks—tasks that repeat regularly throughout the project. For example, perhaps you have a weekly or monthly meeting scheduled with your lawyer or Home Owner's Association, or perhaps you have regular inspections on the progress of your home. You could set up a recurring task to make your monthly house or utility payments that occur during the life of the project. You may also schedule a weekly project team status meeting using recurring tasks.

Instead of entering the task every week or every month, you only have to enter it once as a recurring task, and Microsoft Project 2007 will apply it to the entire project schedule.

CREATING RECURRING TASKS

To create a recurring task, follow these steps:

1. Find the row where you want to insert the recurring task, and click the Task Name field. If the row is blank, the recurring task will be housed in the row when you finish creating it. If the row is occupied, that task will be pushed down to make room for the new recurring task.

2. Choose Insert, Recurring Task. This will open the Recurring Task Information dialog box (see Figure 6.21).

Figure 6.21
Create recurring tasks in the Recurring Task Information dialog box. This example shows a weekly status meeting with your project team every Monday for 1 hour.

3. Enter the task name and duration information in the Task Name and Duration fields at the top of the Recurring Task dialog box.

4. Choose the recurrence pattern for the recurring task: Daily, Weekly, Monthly, or Yearly. If the task happens every week, choose Weekly. If it happens every day, choose Daily. If a task happen twice a week, you would choose Weekly.

5. Define the frequency of the recurring task within the recurrence pattern. The frequency options vary depending on the recurrence pattern you defined in step 4:

   • If you have selected Daily, choose whether the task occurs every day, every other day, and so on, up to every 12th day from the drop-down list. Then, select whether you mean every day or every workday. You will define the calendar (which will in turn define what workdays are) shortly.

   • If you have selected Weekly, choose whether the task occurs every week, every other week, and so on, up to every 12th week from the drop-down list. Then, select the day or days of the week the task occurs.

- If you have selected Monthly, you have two options. Either the task occurs on the same date of every month (such as the 21st of every month) or on the same day of every month (such as the third Monday of every month). If it occurs more than once in a month, you want to define your recurrence pattern as Weekly, and specify the recurring task using a Weekly frequency pattern.

- If you have selected Yearly, you have a similar option to Monthly. Either the task is the same date every year (such as August 21st) or it is the same day every year (such as the third Monday of August).

6. Next, define the date range. Choose when you want the recurring task to start its recurrence pattern in the Start field. Then, define its end. You can enter a specific number of times the task occurs before it ends in the End After field, or enter a specific date it should end by in the End By field. If you choose a specific date in the End By field, Microsoft Project shows the projected number of occurrences in the End After field. However, you cannot edit this number unless you select End After.

By default, the Start and End By fields show the project start and finish dates. If the task is to start occurring sometime after the project starts, enter that date in the Start field. Also, if the task occurs at a specific time, such as a meeting that is always at 2:00 p.m., enter the time in the Start field. To display the time, change the Date Format field to include time, which can be found on the View tab in the Options dialog box (Tools, Options, View tab, Date Format field).

CAUTION

> If you enter a finish date for the recurring task that is past the finish date of the project, the duration for the project is extended to the finish date of the recurring task.

7. Choose the calendar to use when scheduling the recurring task in the Calendar field. If you have created base calendars or task calendars, they will be in the drop-down list along with the default base calendars. Selecting None automatically uses the project base calendar.

→ For more details about creating and using calendars, **see** "Defining Calendars," **p. 118**.

8. Resources have their own calendars to define their working and nonworking times. If you assign a resource to the recurring task and want Microsoft Project 2007 to ignore their availability defined in their resource calendar, select the Scheduling ignores resource calendars check box. The resource will be assigned to the task regardless of his or her resource calendar.

6

9. Click OK or press Enter to complete the creation of the recurring task, or click Cancel to exit without creating it.

CAUTION

> When you are setting up recurring tasks and you enter a number larger than the calculated default, Microsoft Project 2007 will automatically set up the number of occurrences you enter. However, these later occurrences are beyond the original finish date, and they will extend the duration of your project.

If the newly created recurring task falls on any nonworking days, Microsoft Project 2007 warns you and gives you the following options: Reschedule the affected tasks to the earliest available working time, skip the dates that are affected and not schedule those recurring tasks that fall on nonworking time, or cancel the creation of the recurring task altogether.

When the recurring task is created, it appears on the Task Entry table as a summary task. Its duration begins on the first occurrence and ends on the last occurrence. Rather than a solid taskbar on the timescale, it is displayed as short segments representing the time the task occurs throughout the project (see Figure 6.22).

Figure 6.22
Once a recurring task is created, it is displayed as a summary task, and all the recurrences are rolled up to one row on the Task Entry table. Here, the Project Team Meeting2 recurring task is expanded to show all occurrences.

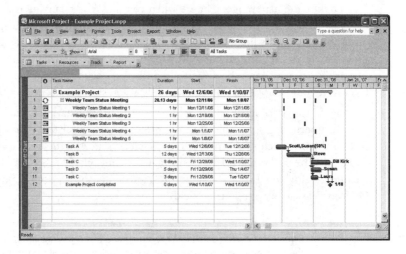

An icon is displayed in the Indicators column that signifies the recurring task (see Figure 6.22 and Table 6.1). Hover the mouse pointer over the indicator, and the Screen Tip displays the number of occurrences and the date range for the recurring task.

If the Project Team Status Meeting were collapsed, the task ID numbers would jump several numbers between the recurring task and the task under it (Task ID numbers 2–11 would be missing). This is because each recurrence of the task is assigned its own ID number, but the tasks are rolled up as a summary task and thus not displayed. To display all the recurring tasks on the task entry table, expand the summary task by clicking on the plus sign (+) in the Task Name column (see Figure 6.22) or by using any of the Show Subtasks command methods described earlier in this chapter. Click the minus sign (–) to hide them again, or use any of the Hide Subtasks command methods.

It is possible when setting up a recurring task that Microsoft Project 2007 might place the task on a non-workday. If this happens, Microsoft Project 2007 will warn you, as shown in Figure 6.23, and then will ask you what you want to do:

■ Select Yes if you want Microsoft Project 2007 to reschedule the task to the earliest possible working time.

- Select No if you want Microsoft Project 2007 to skip those days and leave the tasks out of the series of recurring tasks.

- Select Cancel to stop creating recurring tasks altogether.

Figure 6.23
When you run into a problem while setting up recurring tasks, Microsoft Project will display a message.

NOTE

You can link other tasks in the project to individual occurrences of the recurring task without linking all occurrences of the recurring task. To do so, you must display, or show, all the recurring tasks as described in the preceding paragraph.

→ For more details about linking tasks, **see** "Linking Tasks," **p. 201**.

EDITING RECURRING TASKS

You can edit recurring tasks by double-clicking the task, thus opening the Recurring Task Information dialog box. Make your changes and click OK. A warning box appears, informing you of the consequences of making your edits (see Figure 6.24). All scheduled occurrences will be deleted, and the recurring task will be rescheduled based on your edits. Click OK if this is okay, or Cancel if it is not, which will not apply your edits.

Figure 6.24
Microsoft Project 2007 will automatically warn you when it has to delete existing tasks, after you change the frequency of your recurring task.

6

You can delete a recurring task as you would any other task (click the row ID number, which selects the entire task, and click Delete, or follow any of the other task-deletion methods described earlier in this chapter). You can also delete or edit individual occurrences of the recurring task. Display all the recurring tasks in the Task Entry table and delete or edit as you would any other task.

CREATING WBS CODES

When you add a task, Microsoft Project 2007 will create a default WBS code in the WBS field for each task, automatically. These default codes are the same as the outline numbers that Microsoft Projects 2007 creates and stores in the Outline Number field.

If you want to show the WBS field, you will need to insert the WBS column. You can also see the WBS field using the Task Information dialog box by selecting the Advanced tab. If your client or company requires a specific format for the WBS codes, you can easily edit them in either of these locations, changing the project outline number to your own WBS code. Changing the WBS field, however, will not change the entry in the Outline Number field.

You can easily define the customized format to match your specific WBS code scheme. Microsoft Project 2007 will then use the custom format to set up new default codes for the WBS field, instead of the value in the Outline Number field. Your custom format can include numbers, letters, and symbols, plus ASCII characters.

If you have a custom WBS format defined for another project file, you can copy it right into your current project without having to create it anew. Open the Organizer, then use the Fields tab to copy your custom WBS format from one project file to another. If you want to use it in all files, you can copy it to the Global template.

→ For more details about building the WBS, **see** "Work Breakdown Structure," **p. 92**.

The WBS code can be customized to fit organization's WBS numbering schema or to simplify the display of your project tasks.

→ For detailed information and steps on creating WBS codes; inserting, deleting, and moving tasks with custom WBS codes; editing and renumbering custom WBS codes, **see** "WBS Numbering," **p. 98**.

USING OTHER VIEWS TO CREATE TASKS

The Gantt Chart view is the most commonly used view to create task lists. It displays the Task Entry table and the timescale containing the task's duration bar side by side. However, some people prefer to use different views. The following sections discuss two other popular views for creating a task list: the Task Entry view and the Task Sheet view.

6

NOTE

Views are just different ways to display the same information in a project. If you change the data in one view, it will be reflected in all the other views.

→ For additional information about views, **see** Chapter 11, "Using Standard Views, Tables, Filters, and Groups to Review Your Schedule," **p. 369**.

USING THE TASK ENTRY VIEW

The Task Entry view is a slightly more advanced version of the Gantt Chart view. In the Task Entry view, the Gantt Chart view is displayed in the top pane and a Task Form view is displayed in the bottom pane. The Task Form view in the bottom pane shows details for whatever task is selected in the top pane (see Figure 6.25).

Figure 6.25
The Task Entry view combines the Gantt Chart view in the top pane with a task form, displaying additional details for the selected task, in the bottom pane.

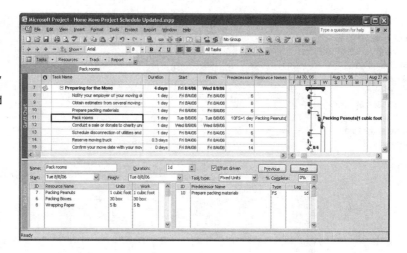

The task form in the bottom pane is very effective for assigning resources and linking tasks as you are creating a task list, because it is all done on the same screen. It may not be very helpful to have open if you are simply defining basic task information such as task names and durations.

To change from the Gantt Chart view to the Task Entry view, choose Window, Split. Whenever you split the screen when you have a task view displayed, Microsoft Project displays the task form in the bottom pane. To take the task form off the screen, select Window, Remove Split.

You can also right-click over the timescale area and choose Split to display the task form, or double-click the split box located just below the vertical scroll bar to the right of the timescale in the bottom-right corner of the screen.

If more details are available but are not displayed, you can select Format, Details to display them in the task form.

USING THE TASK SHEET VIEW

The Task Sheet view is the Task Entry table. Basically, it is the Gantt Chart view without the timescale side (see Figure 6.26). This view is advantageous because there is more room on your screen to display the columns that might otherwise be hidden by the timescale. It is also a good view to print if you want to show just the task outline and not the timescale graphics. In addition, Task Sheet view may be especially helpful when initially entering tasks. It allows you to concentrate on creating the list of tasks and breaking down the scope

6

of your project and work more efficiently, without additional elements that could be a distraction.

To display the Task Sheet view, choose View, More Views, and select Task Sheet from the list. Click Apply to display the view. You can also split the window to display the task form in the bottom pane (choose Window, Split).

Figure 6.26
The Task Sheet view is the Task Entry table of the Gantt Chart view, and is helpful in displaying additional columns that may have been hidden by the timescale in the Gantt Chart view.

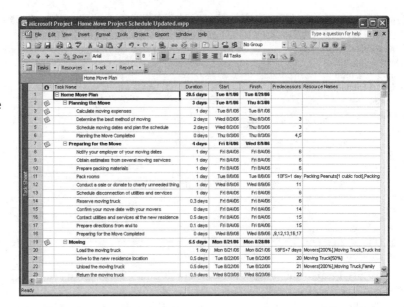

CONSULTANTS' TIPS

For the seasoned project management veteran, this chapter seems underwhelming. A great caution is offered if you believe your experience exempts you from the "basics." Let's use baking a cake as an example. Go to your pantry or the local grocery store, and take out your favorite cake mix. Look at the instructions on the side of the box. Now get a competitor's cake mix and look at their instructions for the same type of cake. See any difference? Chances are, there is little to no difference.

Creating an award-winning cake and an award-winning project schedule are pretty much the same; both start with the instructions, or task list. Are you specifying the right things to do? Can you be successful with the cake by following the instructions? How about the project? Are the instructions clear, crisp, concise, yet achievable? How about your project schedule tasks?

What about the order? Must you perform cake step 2 after step 1? Order is important in cake mixes and in project schedules. Can the resource be successful in performing the cake steps? How about your project schedule sequence? The analogy goes on and on.

Not to endorse any particular product, but Betty Crocker is one of the best project managers in the history of the profession. She can give you a clear, crisp, concise project schedule that's highly successful, highly repeatable, and a hit at the office pot luck. Following the advice in this chapter may not get your name on a baking product box, but it can win you recognition as one of the desirable project managers in your business. Do not shun the basics because you have done this many times before.

6

CHAPTER

7

DEFINING TASK LOGIC

In this chapter

UNDERSTANDING THE TASK SCHEDULING PROCESS

After you enter project tasks and estimate durations, you must focus on developing the schedule of start and finish dates for project tasks. This chapter focuses on logic: how to link tasks to define the logical sequence of activity, thus giving Microsoft Project 2007 specific information for calculating a schedule. Besides linking tasks, this chapter task constraints, and performing advanced actions on tasks.

In short, if tasks are not worked on in a logical order, then schedules will not make sense and the project will turn into chaos. This chapter will help you avoid that, and show you how to logically link and schedule tasks.

A project schedule depends on a number of factors, including the following:

- The project schedule either begins on a fixed start date or is calculated to end on a fixed finish date. You control this factor in the Project Information dialog box.

→ For more information on defining the start or finish of a project, **see** "Understanding the Project Information Dialog Box," **p. 108**.

- Microsoft Project 2007 normally schedules tasks only during the working times defined by the base calendar that you select for the project. Exceptions can occur when you assign resources or attach task calendars to tasks. The resource or task calendars define working time that is different from the project's base calendar.

→ For guidelines on defining the project base calendar, **see** "Defining Calendars," **p. 118**.

- The schedule depends heavily on the duration estimates for the individual tasks. The duration of the tasks is one of the driving forces of the schedule. The longer the task duration for any given start date, the later the scheduled finish date for that task.

- The schedule also depends on the logical order, or scheduling sequence, for the tasks. Typically, most tasks have start or finish dates that depend on the start or finish date of some other task. These are called *dependency links*, and this chapter is largely devoted to defining them.

- The schedule accommodates any arbitrary limits, or *constraints*, that you might impose on the start or finish dates for individual tasks. Imposing date constraints is covered later in this chapter.

- You can modify the schedule for an individual task by assigning a *task calendar*. Assigning calendars to tasks is covered in the section "Creating and Using Task Calendars" at the end of this chapter.

- By default, a task is scheduled without interruption for its duration, based on the Task, Resource, or Project calendar's defined working time. Non-working time will also interrupt a task. You can insert one or more interruptions in the work on a task by splitting the task schedule. See the section "Splitting Tasks," later in this chapter.

- The task schedule also depends on the availability of resources that are assigned to work on the tasks when you level resources to prevent overallocation.

- The schedule is affected if you delay a resource assignment to start after other resources have started or if you contour the daily work assignment for a resource.

→ For additional information on contouring and delaying resource assignments and the effects they have on the task schedule, **see** Chapter 10, "Scheduling Single and Multiple Resource Assignments," **p. 313**.

In practice, after you learn to use Microsoft Project 2007, you will probably outline, link, and impose constraints on the task list as you enter the tasks. The process is divided into separate chapters in this book to focus on all the options and techniques possible for each activity. Once you learn it, the process will become second nature.

By far the most important topic in this chapter for you to understand is linking tasks. The sequencing or linking of tasks makes it possible for Microsoft Project 2007 to calculate a schedule—and that is one of the main reasons for using it. This is also what makes it possible for Microsoft Project 2007 to identify the critical tasks—those that must finish on time or may be worthwhile attempting to finish faster when you need to compress the overall duration of the project. Critical tasks are tasks with little to no slack and that directly influence the completion of the project on time. Critical tasks are discussed in more detail throughout this chapter.

MANIPULATING YOUR SCHEDULE

NEW Microsoft Office Project 2007 is equipped with two new features for manipulating your schedule: the Multiple Undo/Redo feature and the Change Highlighting feature. They are described in the next two sections.

USING THE MULTIPLE UNDO AND REDO FEATURE

NEW New in Microsoft Project 2007, the Multiple Undo and Redo feature allows you to view all changes you have made and to select any number of them to undo or redo simultaneously. The Multiple Undo and Redo features are located in the Standard toolbar, as shown in Figure 7.1.

To use the Multiple Undo feature, click on the arrow directly to the right of the Undo button, which will open a drop-down list of your recent actions. When you hover up and down the list of the Multiple Undo button, the changes are highlighted, and if you click on an item, your selection and all of those above it will be undone at once. The undo items are also now shown by "name." For example, if you have switched to the Gantt Chart view, this item will appear labeled as "View apply 'Gantt Chart'." If you have changed the duration of a task to 2 days, for example, it is labeled "Entry '2'." The button directly to the right of Multiple Undo is Multiple Redo, and it provides the same options—you can redo any number of changes you removed from the schedule.

Combined with Change Highlighting (discussed in the next section), this is a very powerful feature because you have never had an opportunity before to see what happens to your schedule when you make modifications. The combination of these features can also be used for light modeling because you can make a lot of changes and undo them all if the result is unsatisfactory. You are able to observe what happens to your project schedule if those changes were to occur.

7

Redo button

Undo button

Multiple Undo drop-down list

Figure 7.1
Use the Multiple Undo and Redo features to undo or redo several items at once.

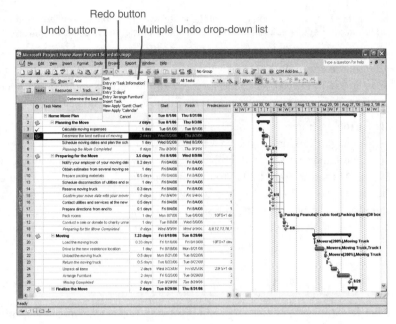

USING CHANGE HIGHLIGHTING TO VIEW CHANGES

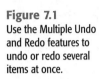 Another new feature of Microsoft Project 2007 is Change Highlighting. This feature auto-matically highlights all tasks affected by a change to another task. For example, if you change the finish date on a task, all its dependent tasks will be highlighted, alerting you that they are affected by the finish date change. Similarly, if you add a task dependency to a task, all tasks that are linked to it will be highlighted to note the change. Figure 7.2 shows the schedule with change highlighting feature turned on, where changing Task 7 duration affects Task 7, Task 4 (Task 7 summary task), and Task 0 (project level summary task).

Figure 7.2
Use the Change Highlighting feature to analyze the effects of your changes on your project schedule.

To enable or disable the Change Highlighting feature, choose View and select Hide Change Highlighting or Show Change Highlighting from the list.

LINKING TASKS

As you know, projects are made up of tasks. Together, these tasks should represent the entire scope of work that needs to be completed in order to successfully finish the project. In that sense, all tasks of a project are connected; they all contribute to the successful completion of the project.

However, some tasks are linked to each other in greater detail. There are two types of tasks when working on a project: *summary tasks* and *subtasks*. Summary tasks provide summary information about the tasks that are subordinate to the summary within a project, and the subtasks are the detailed tasks that must be accomplished to complete the summary tasks. For example, if you had a project called Home Move Plan, a summary task would be Packing, and subtasks would be Inventory and Organize All Possessions, Clean Closets and Storage Areas, Conduct a Sale or Make Donations, and so on. The subtasks are detailed tasks of the summary task, and they can (and should) be logically linked to each other. The total span of time, from the earliest start date to the latest finish date, for all of the subtasks is the duration of the summary task. These types of relationships between tasks, and how they apply to Microsoft Project 2007, will be discussed in the following sections.

UNDERSTANDING TASK RELATIONSHIPS

Some tasks in a project often cannot start until one or more other tasks have finished. Usually this is because a task might need to use the output generated by another task. In the example of moving to a new house, you must calculate your expenses before you can determine the best method of moving. Therefore, the start of the task Determine the Best Method of Moving is determined by, and should be linked to, the finish of the task Calculate Moving Expenses. The link expresses that the schedule for determining the best moving method is dependent on the schedule for calculating your expenses, because you cannot make the decision until you know your moving budget.

A novice scheduler in this moving project might just list the tasks and type in start and finish dates for all the tasks. But if the scheduler later finds out that for some reason the Calculate Moving Expenses task will be delayed, he or she will then have to go through the entire project, typing in later start and finish dates for all the tasks that will be affected by the initial delay; an inefficient and error prone process. When project schedule tasks start or finish dates are manually entered, a Constrained Task symbol is added to the Indicator column.

However, if the tasks are typed into Microsoft Project 2007 and dependency links are defined, the scheduler can simply enter a delayed start date for Calculate Moving Expenses, and Microsoft Project 2007 will calculate the new start and finish dates for all the tasks that are dependent, directly or indirectly, on that task. To correct the schedule due to a delay all the scheduler has to do is modify the task (the start date or the duration) and all the other tasks will be recalculated and those changes highlighted. The reason you take the time to define links between tasks is so that Microsoft Project 2007 can recalculate the schedule for you quickly when there is a schedule change that affects other tasks.

7

DEFINING DEPENDENCY LINKS

Tasks are linked to show a dependency relationship as *predecessor* and *successor* tasks. The predecessor task determines the schedule of the successor, or dependent task. The terms predecessor and successor are used to refer to the direction of the link and not the position of the tasks. You will see that more sophisticated linking can create a situation where successor tasks begin before predecessor tasks are accomplished, even though the successor tasks depend on the predecessor tasks for completion. See the section "Choosing the Dependent Tasks," later in this chapter, for an example.

To illustrate usage of the terms *successor* and *predecessor*, suppose you need to schedule the painting of a room. Four tasks are involved: Put on the Protective Tape, Apply the Primer, Apply Paint, and Clean Up. The start of Apply Paint depends on the finish of Apply Primer; therefore, Apply Primer is the predecessor to Apply Paint. Similarly, Apply Paint is the predecessor to Clean Up (because you cannot clean up until you have applied the paint). In theory, Clean Up is the successor to Apply Paint, because you want to clean up after all the painting is done, but realistically you can begin to clean up before completing the Apply Paint task. This variation is discussed in the section "Allowing for Delays and Overlaps," later in this chapter.

The start date for the successor task should be linked to the finish date for the predecessor. As illustrated in Figure 7.3, Microsoft Project 2007 draws a small arrow from the finish of each predecessor task to the start of its successor task.

Figure 7.3
Predecessor and successor task relationships are indicated by arrows drawn from the predecessor taskbar's start to the successor taskbar's start.

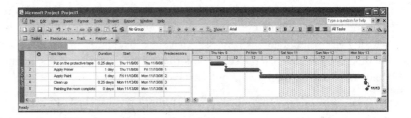

When you refer to a dependency link, the linked date of the predecessor task (either its start or its finish) is named first, and the linked date of the successor task is named last. In the painting example in Figure 7.3, the dependency relationships for the first three tasks are called *Finish-to-Start links* because the predecessor's finish determines the successor's start. Finish-to-Start is the most common type of link, but there are three other types you can use: Finish-to-Finish, Start-to-Start, and Start-to-Finish. The section "Defining the Types of Dependency Link Relationships," later in this chapter, describes the use of all four types of links.

By establishing the link in the painting example, you instruct Microsoft Project 2007 to set the start date for Apply Paint based on the scheduled finish date for Apply Primer. Any change that alters the calculated finish date for the predecessor causes Microsoft Project 2007 to also reschedule the start date for the dependent or successor task. If you define task links, Microsoft Project 2007 automatically reschedules dependent tasks when the schedule for the predecessor changes.

CAUTION

> Do not link two unrelated tasks just to level out the workload for a resource who is assigned to work on both tasks. It is true that the link forces Microsoft Project 2007 to schedule the tasks one after the other, thus allowing the worker to complete one task before starting the next. But if the worker is later removed from working on one of the tasks, there is no way to tell that the link no longer serves a purpose and can be removed (unless you just happen to remember it or create a note on the task), and you will be left with an unnecessary delay that could prolong the finish of your project. The preferred way to deal with this problem is to *delay* one of the tasks by using the Leveling Delay Field.

→ For steps to follow in using leveling delays, **see** "Leveling Delay Effects," **p. 307**.

DEFINING THE TYPES OF DEPENDENCY LINK RELATIONSHIPS

You can create four types of dependency relationships, depending on whether you use the start dates or finish dates when linking tasks. The name for each dependency type includes a reference to the linked date for the predecessor (either its start date or its finish date), followed by a reference to the linked date for the dependent task (either its start or finish date). Therefore, a Finish-to-Start relationship signifies that the finish date of the predecessor task is used to schedule the start date of the dependent task. The predecessor is referenced first, and then the dependent or successor task is referenced.

Microsoft Project 2007 usually uses two-letter code abbreviations for the four dependency types, as shown in Table 7.1. The first letter in the code refers to the predecessor's start or finish, and the second letter refers to the dependent task. Thus, the code for Finish-to-Start is "FS." The following subsections describe the different dependency types.

TABLE 7.1   THE LINKING RELATIONSHIPS IN MICROSOFT PROJECT

Code	Dependency Type	Meaning
FS	Finish-to-Start	Predecessor's finish determines successor's start.
SS	Start-to-Start	Predecessor's start determines successor's start.
FF	Finish-to-Finish	Predecessor's finish determines successor's finish.
SF	Start-to-Finish	Predecessor's start determines successor's finish.

By default, when you link tasks, they are defined as a Finish-to-Start relationship. You can change this dependency relationship type in the Task Information dialog box. After you have established the link, open the Task Information dialog box for the successor task by right-clicking on the task and selecting Task Information. Then, on the Predecessors tab, you can change the dependency relationship from the drop-down list in the Type column. Be sure you choose correctly; remember that the predecessor comes before the successor in the name (Start-to-Finish means the predecessor's start determines the successor's finish).

This concept is examined further in the upcoming section "Creating Links by Using the Task Information Dialog Box."

→ For more details about the Task Information dialog box, **see** "Editing Tasks Using the Task Information Dialog Box," **p. 159**.

USING THE FINISH-TO-START RELATIONSHIP

The Finish-to-Start relationship is the most common of the four types of dependency relationships. The finish date of the predecessor determines the start date of the successor task. For example, framing the walls of a new house should be scheduled to start after the foundation is prepared, with the foundation pouring task acting as the predecessor to the framing task. Referring back to the painting example, the links between Tasks 1 and 2 and Tasks 2 and 3 in Figure 7.3 are all Finish-to-Start links. The linking arrow in the Gantt Chart is drawn from the finish of the predecessor task to the start of the dependent task. The Finish-to-Start dependency relationship is the default relationship created via the Edit, Link Tasks command, or by highlighting the tasks and clicking the Link Tasks button on the Standard toolbar. You must select the predecessor task first and then the successor when highlighting the tasks.

USING THE START-TO-START RELATIONSHIP

In the Start-to-Start relationship, the start date of the predecessor task determines the start date of the successor task. You can schedule the two tasks to start at or near the same time by using this type of relationship.

NOTE

> A lag is often associated with Start-to-Start links. The start of the dependent task is delayed until some time after the predecessor task is underway. Lags and leads are discussed later in this chapter.

For example, suppose a company leases new office space and plans to move to the new space when remodeling is completed. As part of the move from one office to the other, several tasks need to be accomplished, such as packing boxes, disconnecting desktop computers, disassembling furniture, and loading the boxes and furniture into the moving truck. Because the movers can start loading the vans shortly after the packing starts (after the first load is ready to move), the start of the Load Trucks task can be linked to the start of the Pack Boxes and Disassemble Furniture task, with a small amount of delay or lag time (see the tasks in Figure 7.4). The arrow is drawn from the start of the Pack Boxes and Disassemble Furniture task (predecessor) to the start of the Load Trucks task (successor/dependent) with a day of lag time.

Figure 7.4
You can use the Edit, Link Tasks command to link the tasks and change the dependency type to Start-to-Start in the Task Information dialog box.

USING THE FINISH-TO-FINISH RELATIONSHIP

In the Finish-to-Finish relationship, the finish date of the predecessor determines the scheduled finish date of the successor task. In other words, you schedule two tasks to finish at or about the same time. For example, when remodeling a kitchen, the delivery of the new kitchen appliances should be completed by the time the cabinets and countertops are installed, so that the new appliances can be installed as soon as the cabinets and countertops are completed (see Figure 7.5).

Figure 7.5
Finish-to-Finish relationships entail the predecessor's finish scheduling the successor's finish.

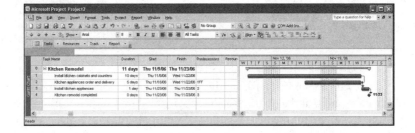

> **NOTE**
>
> The link types Start-to-Start and Finish-to-Finish with leads and lags can be used to schedule tasks to overlap and are commonly used when *fast-tracking* a project—that is, compressing the overall duration of the project by overlapping tasks that are normally scheduled to be completed sequentially. For additional information on fast-tracking, see Chapter 12, "Performing a Schedule Reality Check."

USING THE START-TO-FINISH RELATIONSHIP

In the Start-to-Finish relationship, the start date of the predecessor task determines the scheduled finish date of the successor. With this type of relationship, you schedule a task to finish just in time to start a more important task that it supports. This type is most helpful when scheduling from the finish date rather than form the start date.

Here are some examples that illustrate the Start-to-Finish relationship:

- When scheduling the delivery of merchandise to a new store, the grand opening date determines when the deliveries must be scheduled. A delay in construction that pushes back the grand opening leads to having the merchandise suppliers to delay their deliveries.

7

- *Just-in-time scheduling* in manufacturing is a policy that strives to stock raw materials just in time for the manufacturing process to begin. This policy saves money by not tying up cash in materials' inventories any longer than necessary.

Figure 7.6 illustrates a project where the framing materials (lumber) are to be purchased just in time for framing the walls. The Purchase Lumber task is scheduled to finish just as the Frame Walls task begins. Lumber Purchase and Delivery is dependent on Frame Walls, because you are scheduling the purchasing to be finished just in time for the framing, making Frame Walls its predecessor. If the framing is delayed (for weather, availability of workers, or another reason), the delivery of lumber will be delayed too. The link is a Start-to-Finish link, and the arrow is drawn from the start of the predecessor to the finish of the dependent task. In actual practice, it is very rare to see the Start-to-Finish link type used in anything but a project that is scheduled from the end date.

Figure 7.6
Use a Start-to-Finish dependency link for circumstances where you want the successor task to finish just in time for the predecessor to start.

Now, say for example, preparing the foundation has a longer duration than in the original schedule, and that delays the scheduled start for Frame Walls. Automatically, Microsoft Project 2007 delays the dependent task Lumber Purchase and Delivery just enough so that it will still be finished just in time for the new start date of Frame Walls. That is the difference between setting up the dependency link like the illustration in Figure 7.6 and using a Finish-to-Start dependency relationship. If the predecessor is delayed, then the successor is delayed. Otherwise, the Lumber Purchase and Delivery task would have occurred as planned, and you would have a huge pile of lumber sitting around your work site, waiting for the Frame Walls task to begin, rather than have the lumber purchased just in time for the walls to be framed.

CHOOSING THE DEPENDENT TASKS

Deciding which of two tasks is the dependent task (the successor) and which is the predecessor is often obvious. In many cases, as with the building example used earlier, the dependent task requires the output of another task. In such a case, you make the other task its predecessor. Other times, however, it is not so simple.

Consider the following case, in which a person, not a computer, is doing the scheduling.

Katy is an on-the-job trainee for a residential construction project. She is responsible for making sure that lumber and materials are on hand when the foundation is finished and it is time to frame the walls of the new house. Katy must watch the progress on finishing the foundation and call the lumberyard 4 days before the foundation is finished to schedule the delivery of the lumber. Katy's instructions are to avoid ordering the lumber any earlier than necessary because that would mean paying interest on borrowed money for a longer period of time.

When it is just about time to call the lumberyard, Katy learns that the carpenters are being diverted to another project that has a higher priority, and the framing has been put on hold for a week. Katy's common sense tells her that the lumber order is really linked to the start of the framing, not to the finish of the foundation, and she delays placing the delivery order until 2 days before the new start date for the framing. Although her instructions were to order the lumber 4 days before the foundation is finished, these instructions assumed that there would be no gap between working on the foundation and the framing. Since there was a gap, Katy was correct to link her task (ordering lumber) with the framing task.

If you were scheduling this example, you would want to give Microsoft Project 2007 enough information to be able to do what Katy did—delay the start of the lumber order task if the framing task is delayed. To do that, you need to treat the lumber order as a task that is dependent on the start of the framing task.

The decision about which task should be the predecessor and which task should be the dependent, or successor, might depend on which task you have more control over. If you have equal scheduling control over both tasks, make the task that must come first the predecessor and let the later task be the dependent successor. In cases for which the schedule for one task is out of your control, you might want to arbitrarily make the more flexible scheduled task the dependent task—regardless of which task actually must come first in time (like Katy did in the previous example).

ALLOWING FOR DELAYS AND OVERLAPS

Sometimes you might need to schedule a delay between the predecessor and the successor tasks. For instance, in the painting example, you need to allow time for the first coat of paint to dry before you apply the final coat. This kind of delay is known as a *lag* or *lag time* in a task scheduling, and you could add a 1-day lag to the Finish-to-Start link between the Apply the Primer and Apply Paint tasks. The successor task's start would lag behind the predecessor's finish in the manner you define.

Other times you might want to allow the dependent task to overlap or start before the predecessor task is finished. You add *lead time* to a link when you want the linked date for the successor task to anticipate the linked date of its predecessor. For example, the Clean Up crew can begin the Clean Up task when the painters are close to finishing the Apply Paint task. The successor task's start would lead to the predecessor's finish.

Figure 7.7 shows the painting example again. The first set of tasks has no lead or lag defined, whereas the revised schedule has lead and lag time added to the links. There is a lag added to the link between the primer and paint, because you have to wait for the primer to dry. But there is a lead time between the Apply Paint and the Clean Up task, because you can begin cleaning up before the paint is dry. The lag adds to the overall duration of the painting project, but the lead allows the project to finish faster than it would otherwise.

7

Figure 7.7
Lag and lead times allow you to create a more realistic schedule, and often allow you to finish faster than expected.

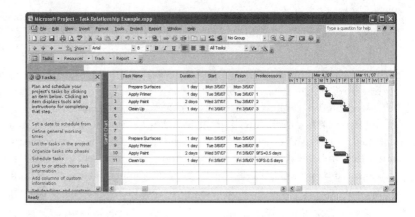

TIP

> Identifying task relationships where overlaps such as lead time are possible is one of the best ways to shorten the overall time it takes to finish a project.

→ For more information on compressing (or crashing) a schedule, **see** Chapter 12, "Performing a Schedule Reality Check," **p. 419**.

Lags and leads can be defined in ordinary duration units or in elapsed duration units. If you want Microsoft Project 2007 to schedule the lag during working time on the calendar, you use ordinary duration units. If Microsoft Project 2007 can use nonworking time also for scheduling the lag, you use elapsed duration units. For example, assume the Apply Primer task finishes on a Friday, the last day of the working week. If the 1-day lag for the Apply Paint task was defined as one ordinary day (typically 8 hours of working time on a standard calendar), Microsoft Project 2007 would let 1 day of working time pass before scheduling the start of the Apply Paint task. Since the next working day after Friday is Monday, the successor task would be scheduled for Tuesday. But if the lag was defined as 1 elapsed day (that is, 24 hours of continuous time), Microsoft Project 2007 would use the weekend days for the lag and the paint would be scheduled for Monday.

→ For more information about using elapsed duration, **see** "Defining Elapsed Duration," on **p. 157**.

Although you usually define lags and leads in fixed time units (such as 9 hours or 4 elapsed days), Microsoft Project 2007 also allows you to define lags and leads as a percentage. With the percentage format, Microsoft Project 2007 makes the length of the lag or the lead a multiple of the length of the predecessor task. For instance, if a predecessor task is scheduled for 1 day (8 hours), and you define a lag time of 50%, the lag time will be 4 hours. Using the different methods of entering leads and lags is discussed in the following section.

ENTERING LEADS AND LAGS

Entering leads and lags is done the same way whether you use the Task Information dialog box mentioned previously or other dialog boxes or forms. When entering lags and leads, bear in mind that both are entered in the same Lag box; there is no separate Lead box. Use positive numbers to represent lag time and negative numbers to represent lead time.

You can enter a lag or lead as a number followed by one of the regular or elapsed time code letters you use for entering duration time: minutes=m or em, hours=h or eh, days=d or ed, weeks=w or ew, and months=mo or emo. Lead time is entered as a negative lag. For example, you enter **4d** to define a 4-day lag and **-8h** to define an 8-hour lead. You type **4ed** to schedule a lag of 4 elapsed days (4 full, real-time days, as opposed to 4 working days, which would not include weekends or holidays). If you type a number without a time unit, Microsoft Project 2007 attaches the default duration unit (which is days by default).

You can also express lag or lead time as a percentage of the predecessor's duration. If you want a task to start when its predecessor is within 20% of being finished, you can enter a Finish-to-Start link with a 20% lead, entered as **FS-20%**. Microsoft Project 2007 schedules the task to start so that it overlaps the last 20% of the predecessor task duration. Using percentage lags and leads enables the amount of lag or lead to vary with changes in the duration of the predecessor. Thus, the longer the duration of the predecessor, the more time a percentage lag or lead would entail.

When you use percentage lags and leads, Microsoft Project 2007 uses the start or finish of the predecessor (as specified in the link type) for the starting point, and offsets the start or finish of the successor from that point by the lag percentage multiplied by the duration of the predecessor. For example, if the predecessor has a duration of 8 days, a Start-to-Start lag of 25% causes the successor's start to be scheduled 2 days after the predecessor starts. A Finish-to-Start lead of 75% produces the same start for the successor—as long as the duration of the predecessor remains unchanged. Changes in the duration of the predecessor, however, cause these two links to result in a different start date for the successor.

> **TIP**
>
> If changes in the schedule occur as the project develops, a percentage would likely give you a more preferred successor start date than a time duration, because the time duration may not accurately reflect that changed schedule. Creating this relationship works well in outlining company methods and templates in which the scaling of the project is dependent on the relationship delay or overlap, not a specified duration.

LINKING SUMMARY TASKS

As discussed earlier in this chapter, summary tasks roll up the information from the working tasks that are executed to complete the summary tasks. Standard practice is to link subtasks and not to link summary tasks. However, summary tasks can be linked to each other, or to subtasks under other summary tasks. Microsoft Project 2007 will not let you establish an explicit link between a subtask and its summary task because summary tasks are implicitly linked to their own subtasks.

Subtasks are bound to many of the same attributes as their summary tasks. If the summary task is linked to a predecessor, the predecessor relationship dictates when the summary

7

task—and therefore its subtasks—can begin. Likewise, as you will see later in this chapter, if the summary task has a date constraint, its subtasks are effectively constrained to that date also. If the summary task has no link or date constraints, its start date is derived from the earliest start date of any of its subtasks, and its finish date is derived from the latest finish date of its subtasks.

TIP

> Linking summary tasks is not considered to be good practice. This is because summary tasks do not define the activities where work gets done; they summarize data from the component tasks that are subordinate to the summary. For example, the summary start date is the earliest start date in the summary's subordinate tasks. "Planning the Move" is a summary task, and "Calculate Moving Expenses" is one of its subtasks. Links should generally reflect the scheduling requirements of the tasks where work is done.
>
> However, linking summary tasks can be an accepted scheduling practice in some circumstances. Linking summary tasks may be useful if a summary task represents a self-contained group of tasks that have a logical relationship to subtasks under another summary task. In that case, linking the summary tasks has the advantage of allowing you to change the subtasks within each group without worrying about redefining the link between the summary tasks.

NOTE

> If you select all tasks and let Microsoft Project 2007 link the tasks in an outlined project, Microsoft Project 2007 links all tasks at the first outline level to each other, whether they are summary tasks or not. It then links the next level of subtasks within any summary task to each other, and so forth, until all outline levels in all summary tasks are linked at their own levels. All links are the default Finish-to-Start link type. Linking tasks in this manner is not recommended.

If you create a task link that involves a summary task as the dependent (or successor) task, you can only use the link types Finish-to-Start and Start-to-Start. Microsoft Project 2007 does not let you establish the other link types; it does not allow you to link the summary task's finish date as a dependent task. However, if the link involves a summary task as the predecessor to a subtask, you can use any of the four possible link types. These rules apply the same in both fixed start-date and fixed finish-date projects.

The following sections describe the various methods of linking tasks. Some processes are more complicated than others, but may provide greater compatibility. It is recommended that you try all the following methods as you read about them, and decide which method you prefer.

CREATING LINKS BY USING THE MENU OR TOOLBAR

There are several ways to link tasks. One option is to select the tasks and then click the Link Tasks button on the Standard toolbar. Another way is to select the tasks and choose Edit, Link Tasks from the menu, or press Ctrl+F2. These links are always the default

Finish-to-Start links, without lag or lead. You have to edit the links if you want a different link type or if you want to add lag or lead. In Figure 7.8, four tasks are selected and have been linked in series with the Link Tasks button on the Standard toolbar.

Figure 7.8
There are multiple ways to link tasks, and you can link more than two tasks at a time.

There is no limit to the number of tasks you can select for linking with the menu or Link Tasks tool. You can link just one predecessor and one successor at a time, or you can link all the tasks in the project with the same operation.

If you select adjacent tasks by dragging the mouse pointer or by using the Shift+down arrow or Shift+up arrow key combination, Microsoft Project 2007 links the selected tasks from the top down. In other words, tasks higher on the list (that have lower ID numbers) are predecessors for the tasks below them (that have higher ID numbers). The same concept applies if you select all tasks by clicking one of the column headings, such as Task Name.

If you build the selection by using Ctrl+click (holding down Ctrl and clicking on the tasks you want to link) to add tasks, Microsoft Project 2007 links the tasks in the order in which you added them to the selection. The first selected task is the predecessor to the second, and so forth.

> **TIP**
>
> You have the same options to remove a task link as you have to create links. To remove a link, select the linked tasks and either click the Unlink Tasks tool, use the Edit, Unlink Tasks command, or press Ctrl+Shift+F2. To remove all links to a task, including all of the task's predecessors and successors, select just the task itself and use the Unlink Tasks toolbar button or command.

CREATING LINKS BY USING THE TASK INFORMATION DIALOG BOX

You can use the Predecessors tab of the Task Information dialog box to create and edit a selected task's predecessor links, no matter what view is active (see Figure 7.9). Unlike the Edit, Link Tasks command, the Task Information dialog box enables you to choose the type of link and to enter the lag or lead time.

To create a dependency relationship by using the Task Information dialog box, follow these steps:

1. Select the dependent (the successor) task.
2. Open the Task Information dialog box by selecting the Task Information tool on the Standard toolbar, or by double-clicking the task.

7

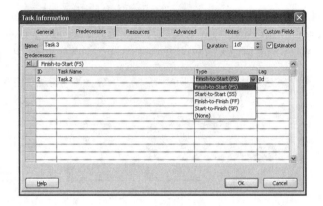

Figure 7.9
The Predecessors tab in the Task Information dialog box allows you to create dependency relationships.

3. Click the Predecessors tab. The Predecessors tab features a table in which you can define predecessors, including the type of link and any lead or lag time (refer to Figure 7.9).

4. Activate the first blank cell under the Task Name field. Choose the name of the task to be the predecessor task from the drop-down list in the field. The drop-down lists the names of all tasks in the project. Project automatically supplies the ID number and the default Finish-to-Start link type, with no lag, unless you choose otherwise.

   Alternatively, if you remember the ID number for the predecessor task, you can enter it in the cell in the ID column. Press Enter to finish the cell entry or select the green check button on the Entry bar. Project automatically supplies the task name for that ID number and supplies the default Finish-to-Start link type, with no lag.

5. Use the drop-down list in the Type column to change the dependency type, if needed.

6. To create lag or lead time, click in the Lag field and type the amount of lag or lead time, followed by a time unit (unless you want to use the default time unit). Use a negative number to specify a lead time.

7. If additional predecessors exist for the task, repeat steps 4 through 6 as needed for each predecessor.

8. To delete a predecessor, select any cell in its row and press the Delete key.

9. Click OK or press Enter to accept the changes.

CREATING LINKS BY USING THE TASK FORM VIEW

With a task view such as the Gantt Chart view in the top pane, you can split the window and use the Task Form view in the bottom pane to define the predecessor and successor relationships (see Figure 7.10). To split the window, choose Window, Split. This is an easy way to define or edit complex dependency relationships. Select a task in the top pane and define its predecessor or successor link in the predecessor or successor details in the bottom pane.

The default display of task details in the Task Form view is to show resources and predecessors. If you want to display both predecessor and successor details, right-click over the Task

Form and choose Predecessors & Successors, as shown in Figure 7.10. Or you can activate the Task Form view and choose Format, Details, Predecessors & Successors.

Figure 7.10
Split the window (Window, Split), which opens the Task Form view in the bottom pane, allowing you to define predecessor and successor relationships.

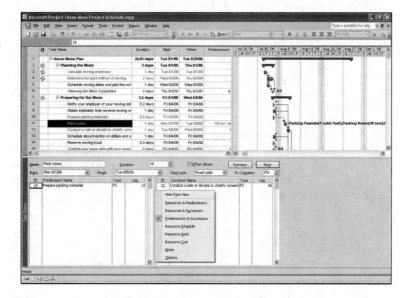

If you display the predecessor details, you can define a predecessor for the dependent task by following these steps:

1. Select the dependent task in the top pane or use the Previous and Next buttons in the lower pane to move to the desired task.

> **NOTE**
>
> If you want to enter the successor details in the Task Form view, select the predecessor task in the top pane and use the successor detail fields in the steps that follow instead of the predecessor fields. The link is defined exactly the same in either detail area.

2. In the bottom pane, activate the first cell in either the ID or Predecessor Name column.

3. If you selected the Predecessor Name field, use the drop-down list of task names to select the name of the task to be the predecessor. The Task Form view still shows the OK button because selecting the task name completes only the cell entry.

   You can also type the predecessor's ID number in the ID field and press Enter to complete the cell entry. Project automatically fills in the predecessor name when you click the OK button to complete the linking definition.

   If you do not know the ID number of the predecessor, you can use the vertical scroll bar in the top pane to view the predecessor task. The ID field remains selected while you scroll the task list. Do not select the predecessor; just view its ID number. Type this

7

number into the ID field. You can then press Enter or click the green check button on the Entry bar to complete the cell entry for the ID number.

4. Select the predecessor's Type field if you want to define a link type other than Finish-to-Start. If you leave the Type field blank, Project supplies the default Finish-to-Start type when you click the OK button. Type in the two-letter code (FF, FS, SF, or SS) or use the drop-down list to select the code. Press Enter to complete the cell entry in the Type field.

NOTE

> The Type field only accepts the two-letter abbreviations for the link types. If you have an AutoCorrect entry for the link type you want to use, Project converts it to the AutoCorrect text when you click OK—and it then rejects the result because it only accepts the abbreviations. There is nothing to do but click Cancel at this point, and then either delete the AutoCorrect definition or edit the link elsewhere (for example, in the Task Information dialog box).

5. Select the Lag field if you want to define a lag or lead time. The default, 0d (zero days, meaning no lag or lead time), is supplied automatically when you click the OK button if you leave this field blank. You can move the spinner control up to display lags (positive values) or down to display leads (negative values) in the default duration time units or by using a percentage amount.

6. If necessary, add more predecessors on the following rows in the Predecessors table by repeating steps 2–5.

7. To delete a predecessor, click any cell in its row and press the Delete key.

8. Click the OK button to execute the changes you entered in the Task Form view.

CREATING LINKS BY USING THE ENTRY TABLE

You can create or edit dependency relationships in the Predecessors field on the Entry table (see Figure 7.11). The Entry table is the default table displayed in the Gantt Chart view. To see the Predecessors fields on the table, either move the vertical split bar to the right, or click the right arrow on the horizontal scroll bar at the bottom-left side of the Gantt Chart view.

TIP

> Using the Entry table for creating predecessor/successor link relationships is one of the most commonly used methods. Furthermore, you can add the Predecessor/Successor column to any table view by selecting a column in the table, clicking Insert Column, and then selecting either Successors or Predecessors.

7

NOTE

You can add the Successors field to the table and edit both predecessors and successors for tasks in the table.

Figure 7.11
You can also use the Predecessors field in the Entry table to add dependency relationships.

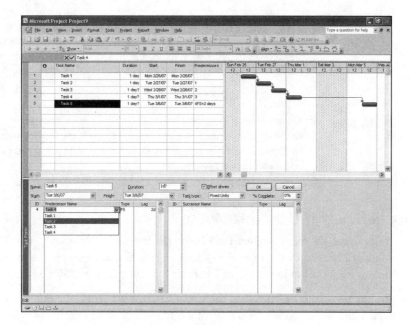

You can enter the simplest relationship, Finish-to-Start, by just entering the task ID number for the predecessor task in the Predecessors field (or the ID for the successor in the Successors field). The other dependency relationships require a very specific pattern of coding.

Assume that you want to make the Pack Rooms task a predecessor with a Start-to-Start link and a 1-day lead. The code in the Predecessors column would be 10SS-1d. The explanation for the code is as follows:

- Enter the ID number for the predecessor first (in this case, 10).

- Follow the ID number without any spaces by the abbreviation for the type of link (in this case, SS). If the link is the default FS, you usually do not have to include the abbreviation, except when you want to add a lag or lead. You must add the abbreviation in order to add a lag or lead.

- Optionally, you can follow the link type with a plus sign (+) for a lag or a minus sign (–) for a lead. You cannot omit the plus sign with a lag.

- Follow the plus or minus sign with the length of the lag or lead, using duration units (that is, m, h, d, w, mo), elapsed duration units (that is, em, eh, ed, ew, emo), or a percentage sign (%). If the current example had a 2-day lag, the code would be 10SS+2d. If the lag were 2 elapsed days, the code would be 10SS+2ed. If a lead were 10%, the code would be 10SS-10%.

7

If a task has more than one predecessor, you separate the predecessor definitions with commas without any spaces. For example, the code 5SS-2d,6,3FS+1d would link the current task to tasks 5, 6, and 3.

TIP

If you do not remember the ID number of the predecessor, leave the cell you are editing selected while you scroll through the task list to find the predecessor task. Do not select the predecessor; just view its ID number. As you start typing, the row for the cell you are editing returns to the screen, and you can finish the link definition.

NOTE

You form codes for the Successors field identically to the way you form codes for the Predecessors field. The only difference is that you begin with the ID number for the successor instead of the predecessor.

CREATING LINKS BY USING THE MOUSE

You can use the mouse to link taskbars on the timescale side of the Gantt Chart view, in the Network Diagram view, or in the Calendar view. You can also use the mouse to edit the linking relationship in the Gantt Chart view or the Network Diagram view.

To link tasks with the mouse in the Gantt Chart view, center the mouse over the predecessor task until the pointer changes into a four-arrow icon. Then click and drag the pointer (which should then turn into a linked-chain icon) over the center of the successor task. Hold the mouse button until Microsoft Office Project 2007 interprets your action as creating a link. The pointer changes into a linked-chain icon, and displays the Finish-to-Start Link information box (see Figure 7.12).

Using the mouse for linking is the most convenient when you can see both tasks you are trying to link onscreen at the same time. If only one taskbar is visible, you have to drag offscreen, and Project begins rapidly scrolling the tasks. You can probably do better with one of the other methods of linking the tasks, as described earlier in this chapter, such as selecting the two tasks (select the predecessor first) and using the Link Tasks tool.

Figure 7.12
Drag the mouse pointer from the predecessor to the successor in the timescale side of the Gantt Chart view to create a dependency link.

CAUTION

The mouse pointer is designed to perform a number of actions on tasks, so be careful when creating links by using the mouse. It is easy to accidentally move the task or mark the task as being partially complete. You must watch the shape of the mouse pointer carefully to ensure that you are doing exactly what you intend to do.

TIP

If you start using the mouse to link tasks and then want to cancel the linking procedure, simply drag the mouse up to the menu or toolbar area of the Gantt Chart view or the Calendar view and release the button. In the Network Diagram view, you must return the mouse to the task you started with before releasing the mouse button, or you will create a new successor task.

NOTE

In the Network Diagram and Calendar views, you must drag from the *center* of the predecessor task's box or taskbar, and the pointer is the plain white cross, not the four-arrow shape you look for in the Gantt Chart view. In those views, the four-arrow shape appears when the pointer is over the border of the task box or taskbar, and means that you will move the task if you drag the border. In all cases, make sure that the mouse pointer is the linked-chain shape when you are over the successor task before you release the mouse button.

The dependency type created with the mouse is always a Finish-to-Start relationship. You can change the link type, add a lag or lead, or delete the link by displaying the Task Dependency dialog box with the mouse in the Gantt Chart or Network Diagram view.

To display the Task Dependency dialog box, scroll to display any portion of the linking line between the predecessor and successor tasks. Position the tip of the mouse pointer on the line connecting the tasks whose links you want to edit. A ScreenTip should appear, with the details of the link. Double-click the linking line, and the Task Dependency dialog box appears, as shown in Figure 7.13. The From task in the dialog box is the predecessor, and the To task is the successor. You can change the dependency type with the drop-down list in the Type field. Choosing None removes the link, as does clicking the Delete button. You can redefine the lag or lead in the Lag field. Click the OK button to complete the change.

Figure 7.13
Edit the dependency link in the Task Dependency dialog box.

7

NOTE

You cannot change the names of the linked tasks in the Task Dependency dialog box, nor can you change which task is the predecessor and which is the successor.

WORKING WITH AUTOMATIC LINKING OPTIONS

If you use only simple Finish-to-Start links in a project, Project's Autolink feature (which is enabled by default) can help you maintain the dependency link sequences when you move, delete, or insert tasks within a linked sequence of tasks. However, Autolink works only if the affected links are Finish-to-Start links, and are in the middle of the linked sequence (Autolink does not apply to the first or last task in a linked sequence).

When you change the order of tasks, and thus their ID numbers, in a task table (such as the one in the Gantt Chart view), you create a break in the link sequence chain. Autolink repairs the break in the following ways:

■ If you cut or delete a task from within a chain of Finish-to-Start linked tasks, Autolink repairs the break in the chain by linking together the former predecessor and successor of the deleted task. In essence, it mends the gap created in the chain by the deletion.

■ If you insert a task in a chain of Finish-to-Start linked tasks, Autolink breaks the former link between the tasks. The new task is inserted between the existing tasks, and then the newly inserted task is linked to the task above and below it to keep the linked sequence intact.

■ If you move a task from one Finish-to-Start sequence to another, Autolink repairs the chain at the task's old site and inserts the new task into the chain at the new site.

In the Network Diagram and Calendar views, Autolink behaves this way only when you delete a task or insert a new task, because you cannot cut, copy, or move tasks to a different ID order in those views.

NOTE

If you insert or remove a task from the beginning or end of a linked chain, instead of in the middle of the chain, Autolink does not include the new task in the chain. Inserting a task at the beginning of a series of linked tasks, or after the last task in a linked sequence, does not cause Autolink to extend the chain to include the new task.

To include a task in a sequence, when the task has been added either to the beginning or end of the sequence, you must link the tasks yourself, using one of the previously discussed methods.

By default, Autolink is enabled, but you can disable it by changing the status of the Autolink option. Choose Tools, Options, and display the Schedule tab in the Options dialog box. Clear the Autolink inserted or moved tasks check box. To set the option status as a default for all new projects, choose the Set as Default button. Otherwise, the change you make affects only the active project document.

TIP

If you have disabled Autolink and need to insert or paste tasks into a Finish-to-Start sequence, you can quickly reestablish the sequence to include new tasks. Select the tasks, starting with the row above the insertion and including the row below the insertion, and use the Unlink Tasks tool to break the original link. Then, with the tasks still selected, use the Link Tasks tool to include the new tasks in the sequence. If there was a lead or lag included in the old link, you need to decide which of the new links should include it.

If you delete or cut tasks from a Finish-to-Start sequence, select the rows above and below the deleted rows and click the Link Tasks tool.

CAUTION

As convenient as Autolink can be when editing a simple task list, it can cause problems in large or complex projects by creating unintended task links when tasks are inserted. You should double-check the links to ensure that they are as you intended for the project. Unintended task links can become a troublesome problem in a project schedule.

If automatic linking is enabled and you rearrange an outline, you should carefully review the links that result each time you move a task or group of tasks in the outline. You might have to edit the links to reflect exactly the relationship you want defined.

TIP

Many project managers leave Autolink disabled because it makes changes without asking for approval. Sometimes they do not notice an unintended change in the linking for their task lists—a problem you should take care to avoid.

MODIFYING, REVIEWING, AND REMOVING DEPENDENCY LINKS

As you develop a project plan, you will inevitably make changes in the task list, and when you do you will have to adjust the sequence of links you have established. You might want to modify the type of links between tasks, insert lag or lead time, or remove a link entirely. You can modify existing links in the following locations, all of which are described in previous sections of this chapter:

- Select the successor task and modify its predecessor links in the Predecessors tab of the Task Information dialog box.
- Split the window and display the Task Form view in the bottom pane, beneath a task view. With the predecessor and successor details displayed in the Task Form view, select a linked task and modify its links in either the Predecessors or Successors table.
- Double-click a linking line in the Gantt Chart view or Network Diagram view to display the Task Dependency dialog box, where you can modify the link.

If you find that a link between tasks is no longer necessary, or if you prefer to change a link to another task, you have to remove the existing link. Just as you have several ways to create links, you can use many different methods to remove links. You can use the following techniques to remove links:

- You can easily unlink tasks in any of the task views by using the menu or toolbar. Either select the tasks you want to unlink and click the Unlink Tasks button on the Standard toolbar; choose Edit, Unlink Tasks; or press Shift+Ctrl+F2. The result depends on the task(s) selected:

  - If you select a single task and then choose Unlink Tasks, Project removes all predecessors and successors for that task.

  - If you select multiple tasks, Project removes all links between any pair of the selected tasks.

  - To remove all links from the project, display any view with a task table and select all tasks by clicking a field name, such as a Task Name, before using Unlink Tasks.

- You can select a successor task and remove its predecessor links by using the Task Information dialog box. For each predecessor listed on the Predecessors tab that you want to remove, click the row for the predecessor and press the Delete key. Clicking OK closes the dialog box and removes those links.

- With a task view in the top pane and the Task Form in the bottom pane, you can display the resource and predecessor—or predecessor and successor—details in the bottom pane. Select the task in the top pane. For each predecessor link you want to remove, click its row in the details area and press the Delete key. Click OK to finish the deletion. If you display one of the detail's choices that includes successors, you can select the predecessor task in the top pane and delete the link in the Successors table in the bottom pane.

- In a view that includes a task table, such as the Gantt Chart view, click on the row for the successor task and clear the entry in its Predecessors field by pressing Ctrl+Delete. Remember not to press the Delete key alone because that deletes the entire task!

- You can double-click a linking line in the Gantt Chart or Network Diagram view to display the Task Dependency dialog box and choose Delete to remove the link.

AUDITING TASK LINKS

The project schedule is heavily influenced by the linking relationships you establish among tasks. It is very easy to accidentally link tasks or break task links, and if you work with Autolink enabled, some changes you have not noticed might have been made. Therefore, you should always review the link relationships carefully before committing to the project schedule. Accidental links can easily distort the finish date of the project.

The Network Diagram view concentrates on the linking relationships by representing each task as a box or node with arrows from predecessor to successor tasks. It is helpful to print the views when using them to review all task links because you see so few tasks on the screen.

→ For information about using the Network Diagram view, **see** Chapter 11, "Using Standard Views, Tables, Filters, and Groups to Review Your Schedule," **p. 369**.

The Gantt Chart view shows the task links as arrows connecting the taskbars, with the arrow always pointing from the predecessor to the successor task. The Gantt Chart view shown earlier in this chapter, with the predecessor and successor details in the Task Form view in the bottom pane, provides a good review of the task links. For the task you have active, the predecessor and successor tasks are listed in the bottom pane, along with any lag or lead associated with the link. Use the Previous and Next buttons in the bottom pane to review the links.

The Relationship Diagram view is perhaps the most useful view for auditing task links (see Figure 7.14). It shows the predecessors and the successors for just the selected task as task nodes, like the Network Diagram view, and is useful for confirming that you have defined the task relationships as you intended. You can display the Relationship Diagram view by itself, but it is most useful when displayed in the bottom pane, beneath another task view in the top pane, such as the Gantt Chart or Network Diagram view.

Figure 7.14
The Relationship Diagram view displays the dependency relationships for the task selected. In this case, the window is split, and the task selected in the top pane is displayed in the Relationship Diagram view in the bottom pane.

The task you have selected in the top pane is represented by a box or node in the center of the relationship diagram in the bottom pane, with links to nodes for its predecessors on the left and successors on right. The type of relationship and any lag or lead is shown next to the linked task nodes. In Figure 7.14, the relationship diagram in the bottom pane makes it clear that Pack Rooms has one successor and one predecessor, and it defines those dependency relationship types.

NOTE

> The Relationship Diagram view is a display-only view. You cannot make changes in this view, nor can you print it. You can, however, display the Task Information dialog box for the selected task and make changes there.

7

To display the Relationship Diagram view below the Gantt Chart view, split the window (Window, Split) and activate the bottom pane by clicking in it. Choose View, More Views, and select Relationship Diagram in the More Views box. Then click the Apply button to display the view.

You can select tasks in the top pane to see their predecessors and successors displayed in the bottom pane.

TIP

> If you select multiple tasks in the top pane, you will see only one of the selected tasks in the center of the bottom pane at a time. You can use the horizontal scroll bar in the Relationship Diagram pane to scroll through all the selected tasks. Pressing the Home key displays the view for the first of the selected tasks, and pressing the End key displays the view for the last of the selected tasks. You can use these same techniques to scroll through the tasks if you display the Relationship Diagram view as a full-screen view.

USING TASK DRIVERS TO REVIEW TASK DEPENDENCIES

NEW Task Drivers is a new feature in Microsoft Office Project 2007 that enables you to view details of task dependencies. To open the Task Driver box, click Project, Task Drivers. This will display the Task Drivers options in the Project Guide on the left. The Task Drivers feature displays tasks that are linked to the selected task, as well as their relationship. Once the Task Drivers option is displayed in the Project Guide, you can select any task, and its attributes will be displayed in the Task Drivers box (see Figure 7.15).

Figure 7.15
Task Drivers allow you to easily trace relationships and dependencies between tasks in your project schedule.

TIP

> The Task Drivers feature is most useful when working on projects with complex calendars and/or a large number of tasks. It is a quick and effective method of reviewing a tasks' links and progress. In addition, task drivers help you determine what tasks will be affected if you make any changes to the selected task.

DEFINING CONSTRAINTS

If a project has a fixed start date, you probably want Microsoft Office Project 2007 to schedule tasks as soon as possible after the start of the project in order to minimize the overall duration of the project. For the same reason, if a project is scheduled from a fixed finish date, you want Microsoft Project 2007 to schedule tasks as late as possible so that they are close to the fixed finish date and keep the duration of the project as short as possible.

However, there are many circumstances in which a task must be scheduled to start or finish by a specific date. These fixed-date requirements are called *task constraints* in Microsoft Project 2007. The constraint types are classified as *inflexible* if they present a barrier to an expanding project schedule, and *flexible* if they do not. The As Soon As Possible (ASAP) and As Late As Possible (ALAP) constraints present no barriers in any situation and are always classified as flexible. Inflexible constraints might be due to requirements from outside the project, or they might be the result of temporary deadlines imposed by the project manager. Constraints that are internal to the project might be such things as progress reviews and reevaluations of the schedule as each major phase of the project nears completion. External constraints might be the deadlines specified by customers, contractors, the government, or policies within the organization that are external to the project. The following are some specific examples of task constraints:

- You are planning a Fourth of July fireworks display, and the fireworks need to be delivered a day in advance to have enough set-up time. The fireworks delivery task must completed by July 3rd.

- An alteration facility needs 2 weeks to alter a bride's dress, so the dress-fitting task must be completed at least 2 weeks before the wedding date.

- An environmental agency is examining erosion over a specific period of time. The tests must begin on a specific date, so the test preparation task must be completed before the test date.

- Progress reports are due at specific intervals throughout the project. The person in charge of compiling the reports must have them ready on specific dates.

In all cases, either the start or finish date of a task is linked to a specific date in the schedule, and you want Microsoft Project 2007 to take this constraint into consideration when scheduling the task.

7

UNDERSTANDING THE TYPES OF CONSTRAINTS

Constraints are defined by entries in the Constraint Type and Constraint Date task fields on the Advanced tab in the Task Information dialog box (see Figure 7.16). By default, a new task you create has no constraint date. When you add a task to a project that is scheduled from a fixed start date, Microsoft Project 2007 supplies the default entry As Soon As Possible in the Constraint Type field. This entry means that there are no fixed-date requirements—no constraints—and the task will be scheduled as soon as possible after its predecessor requirements are met. The Constraints Date field for the task is given the default entry NA (the Constraint Date field is not applicable because there are no constraints).

Figure 7.16
On the Advanced tab of the Task Information dialog box, you can set constraint types and constraint dates in the appropriate fields.

If the project is scheduled from a fixed finished date, Microsoft Project 2007 supplies new tasks with the default entry As Late As Possible in the Constraint Type field. This entry also means that there is no constraint, and the task will be scheduled as close to the finish date of the project as possible. Microsoft Project 2007 considers the schedule for successor tasks, which must also finish before the project's finish date, when scheduling the task. Again, the Constraint Date field has the default entry NA.

Besides using the Task Information dialog box, you can insert the Constraint Type and Constraint Date fields as columns in a task table. The Constraint Type field provides a drop-down list of the eight possible constraint types that you can use to define any possible date constraint. These types are described in Table 7.2. Constraint types are usually referred to by the acronym shown in the first column in the table.

TABLE 7.2   THE CONSTRAINT TYPES

Acronym	Constraint Type	Description
ASAP	As Soon As Possible	Marks a task as not constrained and not requiring a constraint date. The task will be scheduled as soon as its predecessor requirements are met.

Acronym	Constraint Type	Description
ALAP	As Late As Possible	Delays the task as long as possible, considering the scheduling requirements of its successor task, all of which must finish before the project finish date. This constraint type does not require a constraint date.
SNET	Start No Earlier Than	Means the task must start on or after the defined constraint date.
SNLT	Start No Later Than	Means the task must start on or before the defined constraint date.
FNET	Finish No Earlier Than	Means the task must finish on or after the defined constraint date.
FNLT	Finish No Later Than	Means the task must finish on or before the defined constraint date.
MSO	Must Start On	Means the task must start exactly on the defined constraint date.
MFO	Must Finish On	Means the task must finish exactly on the defined constraint date.

The first two constraint types in Table 7.2, ASAP and ALAP, have no associated constraint date. In fact, they are really non-constraints.

The duration of a sequence of tasks can expand for a variety of reasons. For instance, new tasks might be inserted in the sequence, or existing tasks might experience *duration inflation*—an increase in duration values. In a project with a fixed start date, the expansion of duration pushes tasks to later dates. If the tasks in the sequence have the constraint type ASAP, they can be rescheduled to later dates without limit as the sequence expands. In a project with a fixed finish date, the expansion pushes tasks back to earlier dates. If the tasks in a sequence have the constraint type ALAP, they can be rescheduled to earlier dates without limit as the sequence expands.

The constraint types are classified as in*flexible* if they present a barrier to an expanding project schedule, and *flexible* if they do not. The ASAP and ALAP constraints present no barriers in any situation and are always classified as flexible.

The last two constraints in Table 7.2, MSO and MFO, are considered inflexible in all circumstances because they can block the expansion of a task sequence. If the linked sequence expands so much that it requires a task with one of these constraints to move beyond an MSO or MFO constraint date, Microsoft Project 2007 cannot honor both the defined links and the defined constraints at the same time because they contradict one another. By default, Microsoft Project 2007 honors the constraint and ignores the dependency link, forcing the constrained task to overlap its linked task in a way that is contrary to the intent of the link. See the section "Deciding to Honor Links or Honor Constraints," later in this chapter, for information about changing this default.

7

Figure 7.17 illustrates the conflict between a task link and an inflexible constraint. The milestone Product Ready for Delivery must be completed by March 5th, 2007. It has a Finish-to-Start link to its predecessor, Prepare for Shipping. The predecessor finishes in time for the milestone to meet its deadline in Scenario A. In Scenario B, however, the predecessor has been delayed because of duration inflation in an earlier task, and now it is impossible to honor both the link and the constraint. Microsoft Project 2007 allows you to choose to honor the constraint or the link. Honoring the link would push the milestone to a later date. In this example, the milestone has been chosen over the link, and Microsoft Project 2007 schedules the milestone on its constraint date, which requires that it ignore the intent of the link. The predecessor finishes after the milestone's date, causing the linking line to wrap back around as though the link were defined with lead time.

While not a constraint, the Deadline feature discussed later in this section provides a visual indication of a deadline on a task and will alert you to missed deadlines.

Figure 7.17
Sometimes, you will have to choose to honor a constraint or a link, as the two will conflict each other. In this example, in Scenario B, the constraint was chosen over the link.

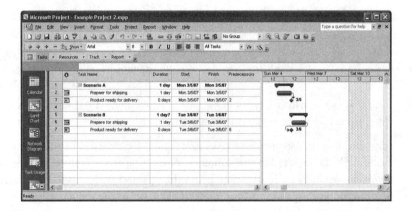

In a fixed start-date project, duration inflation in predecessor tasks tends to push successor tasks to later dates. Constraints that prohibit successor tasks from being rescheduled to later dates are therefore inflexible constraints. Thus, SNLT and FNLT constraint types are called inflexible in fixed start-date projects.

In a fixed finish-date project, duration inflation in successor tasks tends to push predecessor tasks to earlier dates. Constraints that prohibit predecessor tasks from being rescheduled to earlier dates are inflexible constraints. Consequently, the SNET and FNET constraint types are called inflexible in fixed finish-date projects. But the SNLT and FNLT constraints are flexible in fixed finish-date projects.

7

NOTE

Although the SNET and FNET constraints are flexible for the expansion of the fixed start-date schedule, they nevertheless create a barrier if you are attempting to compress the project's duration. To shorten the overall project, you must shorten the critical path, and if a task with one of these constraints is on the critical path, it can block your efforts. Although you might shorten the duration of its predecessors, a SNET or FNET task will not move to an earlier date, and the critical path will not be shortened.

Similarly, in fixed finish-date projects, the SNLT and FNLT constraints are called flexible because they do not inhibit the natural expansion of the project. However, they can block compression of the project duration.

CAUTION

If you change a project from a fixed start date to a fixed finish date, the ASAP constraint type for existing tasks is replaced with ALAP constraints. However, all new tasks are given the new default ALAP constraint type. Likewise, changing a fixed finish-date project to a fixed start-date project leaves the ALAP constraints unchanged, but the new tasks are set to ASAP. Neither of these results affects the duration of the project, but some tasks are scheduled earlier or later than they could possibly be without affecting the start or finish of the project.

If you change a fixed start-date project to a fixed finish-date project, SNET and FNET constraints change from flexible to inflexible. Similarly, the flexible SNLT and FNLT constraints in a fixed finish-date project become inflexible if you switch to fixed start-date scheduling. If you change the project scheduling type, you should look for constraints that switched from flexible to inflexible and consider modifying them to avoid potential conflicts as the schedule changes.

TIP

If you decide to permanently change a project from fixed start date to fixed finish date (or vice versa) and want to change all the old default constraints to the new default (such as replacing ASAP with ALAP), you can use Project's Replace command. For example, type **As Soon As Possible** in the Find What box, type **As Late As Possible** in the Replace With box, and select Equals in the Test box.

One of the most common mistakes made by novice users of Microsoft Project 2007 is unintentionally creating a constraint. Any time you type a date into the Start or Finish field for a task, or drag the taskbar to a new date in the Gantt Chart view, Microsoft Project 2007 creates a constraint to honor that date. When you create a recurring task, Microsoft Project 2007 also creates a constraint for each occurrence.

Fortunately, Microsoft Project 2007 always makes these flexible constraints. Therefore, if you type in the start date for a task in a fixed start-date project, Microsoft Project 2007

7

changes the constraint type to SNET and places the date in the Constraint Date field. The task is then scheduled to start on the date you typed (even if its predecessors would allow it to be scheduled earlier), but it can be freely moved to later dates if its predecessors experience duration inflation. Similarly, in a fixed finish-date project, the flexible constraints SNLT and FNLT are supplied when you specify start or finish dates for tasks.

NOTE

Some constraints also affect the critical path. If you apply a Must Start On or Must Finish On constraint, Project automatically makes the task a critical task. If you are scheduling from a fixed start date, an ALAP constraint makes the task critical. If you are scheduling from a fixed finish date, an ASAP constraint makes the task critical.

When a task has a constraint type other than ASAP or ALAP, Microsoft Project 2007 displays an icon in the Indicators field of the Gantt Chart view. The icon looks like a calendar with either a blue or a red dot in the middle. A blue dot signifies a flexible constraint, and a red dot signifies an inflexible constraint. Table 7.3 summarizes the flexible/inflexible status for the eight constraint types in both fixed start-date and fixed finish-date projects, and describes the indicators you see for them.

TABLE 7.3   FLEXIBLE AND INFLEXIBLE CONSTRAINTS AND THEIR INDICATORS

Constraint Type	Fixed Start Date	Fixed Finish Date
ASAP	Flexible (no indicator)	Flexible (no indicator)
ALAP	Flexible (no indicator)	Flexible (no indicator)
SNET	Flexible (blue dot)	Inflexible (red dot)
FNET	Flexible (blue dot)	Inflexible (red dot)
SNLT	Inflexible (red dot)	Flexible (blue dot)
FNLT	Inflexible (red dot)	Flexible (blue dot)
MFO	Inflexible (red dot)	Inflexible (red dot)
MSO	Inflexible (red dot)	Inflexible (red dot)

ENTERING TASK CONSTRAINTS

As mentioned previously, if you enter a date in a task's start or finish field or drag the taskbar in the Gantt Chart view, you create a flexible constraint for the task. You can also create task constraints by using the Schedule Tasks Project Guide or by filling in the Constraint Type and Constraint Date fields in the Task Information dialog box. If you want to create or modify many task constraints, you might want to enter the constraint fields to the Entry table or display the Task Details Form view, which makes the constraint fields available for editing.

TIP

Because creating inflexible constraints can affect a schedule so significantly, it is very important that you document why a constraint has been defined. You should always add an explanation to the Notes field to explain the purpose of the constraint. This is especially important information if you are sharing the project file with colleagues or if someone else takes over the project. It is also a valuable reminder if there is a later conflict that you must resolve.

TIP

When you type a constraint date, you can also include the time of day with the date. If you do not include the time of day, Project supplies one for you. Using the default values from the Calendar tab of the Options dialog box, Project includes the default start time for all constraint types that restrict the start of a task and the default end time for all constraints that restrict the finish of a task.

NOTE

No matter which method you use for creating constraints, if you create an inflexible constraint, the Planning Wizard displays a warning. More detailed information about the Project Wizard's warning is covered at the end of this section.

CREATING CONSTRAINTS WITH THE SCHEDULE TASKS PROJECT GUIDE

To add a constraint to a single task by using the Project Guide, click Task on the Project Guide toolbar, and choose Set Deadlines and Constrain Tasks from the bottom of the list in the Project Guide pane to display the deadline and constraint definition controls (see Figure 7.18). Select the task to be constrained, select the constraint type, and enter the constraint date under the Constrain a Task section.

NOTE

If the Project Guide is not displayed once you select the Set Deadlines and Constrain Tasks option, then it is not set to be visible. To display the Project Guide, select Tools, Options, Interface tab, and then select the Display Project Guide option.

Remember to click the Task Notes tool on the Standard toolbar to document the purpose for the constraint in the Notes field.

7

Figure 7.18
The Project Guide
provides another
method for creating
constraints.

CREATING CONSTRAINTS IN THE TASK INFORMATION DIALOG BOX

To enter task constraints in the Task Information dialog box, follow these steps:

1. Display the Task Information dialog box by double-clicking the task you want to modify.

2. Select the Advanced tab (see Figure 7.19).

Figure 7.19
The Advanced tab of
the Task Information
dialog box provides
fields to create
constraints.

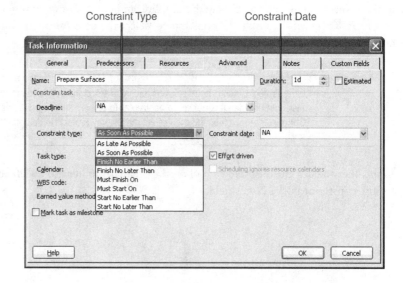

3. In the Constraint Type field, select the constraint type from the drop-down list.

4. For constraints that require a date, which are all the constraints except ASAP and ALAP, enter the constraint date in the Constraint Date box. Enter the time of day if you want a time other than the default start time or default end time.

    If you do not enter a date, Project uses the task's current start or finish date as the constraint date—the start date and time for start date constraints, and the finish date and time for finish date constraints.

5. Select the Notes tab and add a note explaining the reason for the constraint.

6. Click OK to complete the constraint definition.

CREATING CONSTRAINTS IN A TASK TABLE

If you need to create or edit a number of constraints, you can display the Constraint Dates table in the Gantt Chart view (see Figure 7.20). This is also a good view to use when reviewing the constraints in a project. To display the Constraint Dates table and create a constraint, follow these steps:

1. Display a task view that includes a table, such as a Gantt Chart.

2. Right-click the Select All cell (upper-left corner of the table) and choose More Tables. Or, choose View, Table, More Tables to open the More Tables dialog box. In the More Tables dialog box, select Constraint Dates and click Apply.

Figure 7.20
The Constraint Dates table allows you to set task constraints in the Constraint Type and Constraint Date fields.

3. On the row for a task you want to constrain, use the drop-down list in the Constraint Type column to choose the type. Press Enter to assign the constraint. As mentioned previously, if you have defined an inflexible constraint, the Planning Wizard makes you confirm that you want to keep the constraint (see Figure 7.21). Project supplies a default date in the Constraint Date column, unless the constraint type is ASAP or ALAP. To do so, Project uses the task's start date and time if the task's start is constrained and the finish date and time if its finish is constrained. For additional details on the Planning Wizard warning, see "Responding to Warnings from the Planning Wizard," later in this chapter.

4. If appropriate, type a different date or use the drop-down calendar to select one. Enter the time of day if you do not want Project to supply the default time.

7

NOTE

> To return to the Entry table with its task fields, repeat step 2, but select Entry.

NOTE

> You can add the constrained fields to any task table. See "Creating a Modified Constraint Dates Table," later in this chapter.

CREATING CONSTRAINTS IN THE TASK DETAILS FORM

The Task Details form provides easy access to the constraint fields. It is best used in the bottom pane with the Gantt Chart view or another task view in the top pane (see Figure 7.21). To enter task constraints in the Task Details form, follow these steps:

1. Display the Gantt Chart view or other task view in the top pane and split the window (select Window, Split).

2. When the window is split, activate the bottom pane and choose View, More Views to display the More Views dialog box.

3. Select Task Details Form from the Views list and click Apply.

4. Right-click over the Task Details form and choose the Notes details for display so that you can document the reasons for the constraint.

You can select the task to be constrained in the top pane, or use the Previous and Next buttons in the bottom pane to scroll to the task. Then in the bottom pane, select the constraint type from the drop-down list in the Constraint box, and enter the constraint date and time in the Date field.

RESPONDING TO WARNINGS FROM THE PLANNING WIZARD

As mentioned previously, if you define an inflexible constraint for a task that has dependency links, you create a potential conflict between the requirements of the constraint and the requirements of the links. When you create an inflexible constraint, the Planning Wizard warns you that your action could create a problem either now or in the future and makes you confirm the action. The Planning Wizard displays the dialog box in Figure 7.22 to warn you and give you three options. You must select the third option to create an inflexible constraint.

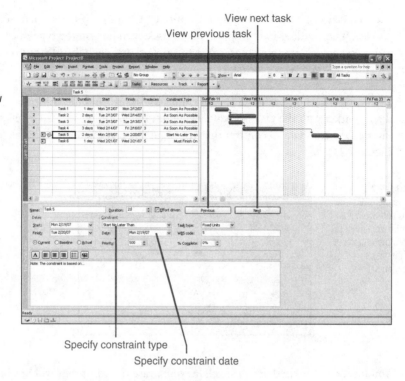

Figure 7.21
The Task Detail Form view in the bottom pane of a split window provides a means for you to define task constraints, as well as attach notes as to the reason for the constraint.

View next task

View previous task

Specify constraint type

Specify constraint date

Figure 7.22
Whenever you create a conflict by placing a date constraint on a task, Project displays a warning, confirming further actions.

The three options include:

- You can select Cancel, which is the default. If you leave the default option selected, you can click either the OK button or the Cancel button to cancel the action. Either way, no constraint will be set.

- You can select the second option: Continue but avoid the conflict by using a Finish No Earlier Than constraint instead. Depending on the type of the constraint originally set, the wording in this option may vary. If you select this option and click OK, Project substitutes the flexible version of the same constraint. For example, if you define an FNLT constraint in a project that is scheduled from a fixed start date, Project offers to change it to an FNET constraint.

7

- You can select the third option: Continue. A Finish No Later Than constraint will be set. The wording in this option may vary, depending on the type of constraint you tried to schedule. You must both select this option and click the OK button to actually create the constraint you specified.

If you confirm the creation of the inflexible constraint, and the constraint creates and immediate conflict with the task's dependency links, the Planning Wizard displays another warning that requests you to confirm that you want to go ahead and create the conflict (see Figure 7.23).

Figure 7.23
The Planning Wizard warns you again if an inflexible constraint is created that interferes with the task's dependency links.

You must choose whether to cancel, in which case the constraint will not be created, or to continue, in which case the constraint will be created and the scheduling conflict will exist. Again, you must choose the Continue option before you click OK to actually create the constraint.

NOTE

> Project does not display the second warning if you have deselected the Tasks Will Always Honor Their Constraint Dates check box in the Schedule tab of the Options dialog box. More information is discussed in the next section, "Deciding to Honor Links or Honor Constraints."

The Planning Wizard warning in Figure 7.23 is also displayed by another action that causes a constraint date to be in conflict with a dependency link—for example, if you create new links or increase the duration of a predecessor task so much that the constraint date becomes a barrier.

The Planning Wizard warning that a constraint conflict had been identified includes a task ID number to help you troubleshoot the conflict (refer to Figure 7.23). The ID number is usually the ID of the predecessor for the task that has an inflexible constraint. In a fixed finish-date project, it would be the successor task's ID. However, in some instances the ID number is for the constrained task itself, as in Figure 7.23. Thus, in Figure 7.23, the message identifies Task 4, the task that is being given an inflexible constraint.

If you see this warning from the Planning Wizard and choose to continue and allow the conflict to be created, you should make a note of the task ID number because you will not see this message again and you need to do something to resolve the conflict.

For ways to find and resolve constraint conflicts, see the sections "Finding and Reviewing Tasks That Have Constraints" and "Resolving Conflicts Caused by Constraints," later in this chapter.

DECIDING TO HONOR LINKS OR HONOR CONSTRAINTS

As mentioned earlier in this chapter, in the section "Understanding the Types of Constraints," when you define an inflexible constraint for a task, it might be impossible for Microsoft Project 2007 to honor both the constraint and one or more links that you have defined for the task. When this type of conflict arises, Project's default scheduling method is to honor the constraint definition and ignore the link definition, as shown in Scenario B in Figure 7.17, earlier in this chapter.

When Microsoft Project 2007 honors inflexible constraint dates, the inflexible constraints are called *hard constraints*. You can change Project's default behavior and force it to honor a task's links instead of its constraint. Choose Tools, Options, and then click the Schedule tab and clear the check box labeled Tasks Will Always Honor Their Constraint Dates (see Figure 7.24).

Figure 7.24
Clear the Tasks Will Always Honor Their Constraint Dates box, which tells Project to honor tasks' links instead of constraints.

In Figure 7.25, another set of tasks, Scenario C, is added to those from Figure 7.17 to show how Microsoft Project 2007 schedules soft constraints to honor their links instead of their constraint dates.

Figure 7.25
In Scenario C, a soft constraint is applied, so Project honors the link rather than the milestone's constraint, and the milestone is scheduled later than its constraint date.

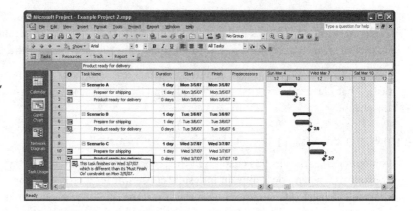

In Scenario A, there is no constraint conflict. In Scenario B, the Product ready for delivery milestone is a hard constraint and is scheduled to honor its constraint date. In Scenario C, a soft constraint is scheduled to honor its link. Therefore, it falls 2 days after the constraint date (in this case, on Wednesday, March 7th, 2007).

If you go back into the Options dialog box and select the Tasks Will Always Honor Their Constraint Dates check box again (in other words, turn soft constraints into hard constraints again), the presence of any existing constraint conflicts in the project causes Microsoft Project 2007 to display the warning shown in Figure 7.26. You should make a note of the task identified at the start of the warning message so that you can find the tasks involved in the conflict and resolve the issue.

Figure 7.26
The Planning Wizard warning box appears if you turn soft constraints into hard constraints.

If all the links and constraint definitions are both appropriate and necessary to the project, it is best to use soft constraints (in other words, to have tasks honor their links) for the following reasons:

- **Honoring links is usually most realistic**—The project manager needs to revise the schedule so that the constraints can be met while honoring the links. This requires shortening the duration of the linked sequence of predecessors (or successors, in a fixed finish-date project) that have caused the conflict.

- **Honoring links causes the Missed Constraint indicator to appear in the Indicators column**—This is the only reliable way to find constraint conflicts in a schedule. You can scan the Indicators column to see if you find tasks that have the indicator and then do something to the schedule to remove the indicator. Honoring constraints, on the other hand, merely causes the linking line to curve around the task that has a conflict, which is visually no different than a link with a lead time. These missed links are very difficult to find in the schedule; you have to carefully scan all linking lines in the entire timeline, and often the need for corrective action is overlooked until it's too late.

→ For additional information on techniques and tools you can use to find problem areas in your schedule, **see** Chapter 12, "Performing a Schedule Reality Check," **p. 419**.

TIP

> Based on these two points, it is recommended that you clear the Tasks Will Always Honor Their Constraint Dates check box as described previously and make it the default for all your new projects by clicking the Set as Default button. However, be aware that clearing the check box means that you no longer get the warning shown in Figure 7.23 when you create a conflict between links and constraints. In this case, you have to diligently search for them, as described in the next section.

FINDING AND REVIEWING TASKS THAT HAVE CONSTRAINTS

Just as it is important to double-check the task sequencing links before committing to a project schedule, you should also review all the task constraints to be sure they are warranted and correctly defined. At the very least, you should attempt to identify any constraint conflicts and resolve them, or your project schedule will be unrealistic.

To review the constraint conflicts, disable the Tasks Will Always Honor Their Constraint Dates option on the Schedule tab of the Options dialog box, as described in the previous section. Then, scroll down to the list of tasks in the Gantt Chart view while you watch for the Missed Constraint indicator in the Indicators column. If your project is large, it will be easier if you also filter the task list for constrained tasks, as described next. When you find a task with the Missed Constraint indicator, follow the guidelines outlined in the section "Resolving Conflicts Caused by Constraints," later in this chapter.

If your project is scheduled from a fixed start date, you can use the Tasks with Fixed Dates filter to display the tasks that have a constraint other than ASAP, for both flexible and inflexible constraint types. This filter also selects tasks that have an actual start date entered; so, if you apply this filter after you start tracking work on the project, it also selects the tasks that have started. However, if you use it during the planning stage of a fixed start-date project, it selects just the tasks that have a non-default constraint.

To apply the Tasks with Fixed Dates filter, choose Project, Filtered For, More Filters, and select Tasks with Fixed Dates from the list of filters. Click Highlight to highlight the

7

selected tasks, or click Apply to hide all but the selected tasks. You can also click the drop-down list arrow in the Filter tool on the Formatting toolbar and choose the Tasks with Fixed Dates filter, but you cannot apply a highlight filter if you use that tool.

Microsoft Project 2007 selects all tasks that do not have the constraint type ASAP, as well as those that have a start date entered. Microsoft Project 2007 also displays the summary tasks for the selected tasks, which is helpful for remembering where the task falls in the outline in a large project. You can scroll through the filtered task list to easily review the constrained tasks.

TIP

> A convenient view for reviewing constraints is the Gantt Chart view, with the Task Details Form view and the Notes field in the bottom pane, as described in the section "Entering Task Constraints," earlier in this chapter.

When you are finished using the filter, press the function key F3 to clear the filter, or select All Tasks from the drop-down list on the Filter tool.

TIP

> A practical way to review tasks that have constraints is to display the Constraint Dates table in the Gantt Chart view, as described earlier in the section "Entering Task Constraints." Even better, you can create a customized version of this table that is more useful (see the section "Creating a Modified Constraint Dates Table," later in this chapter). Click the AutoFilter tool on the Formatting toolbar. In the title cell of the Constraint Type column, click the AutoFilter drop-down list arrow. The drop-down list includes the names of all constraint types that appear at least once in that column. Click one of the constraint type names in the list, and Project displays all tasks that have that constraint type, along with their summary tasks.

TIP

> You can create much more useful filters for finding inflexible constraints, for both fixed start-date and fixed finish-date projects. If you often work with fixed finish-date projects or want to be able to isolate constrained tasks after tracking has begun, or if you want to find scheduling conflicts, these filters are well worth adding to your Global template.

REMOVING TASK CONSTRAINTS

To remove a task constraint, simply change the constraint type to ASAP (or ALAP in a fixed finish-date project) using one of the methods discussed earlier in this chapter for creating constraints.

To return several tasks to an unconstrained state, follow these steps:

1. Select all the tasks you want to change.
2. Display the Multiple Task Information dialog box by clicking the Task Information tool.

3. Choose the Advanced tab and select As Soon As Possible or As Late As Possible from the Constraint Type drop-down list.

4. Click OK to make the changes in all the selected tasks.

To remove all constraints in the project, select a column heading in the task list table and choose the As Soon As Possible or As Late As Possible constraint type in the Task Information dialog box.

RESOLVING CONFLICTS CAUSED BY CONSTRAINTS

As previously discussed, when you add an inflexible constraint to a linked task or link a task that has an inflexible constraint, the Planning Wizard displays the potential conflict warning shown in Figure 7.22. If Microsoft Project 2007 is honoring task constraints (the default) and the potential conflict becomes a reality, the Planning Wizard gives you the warning shown in Figure 7.23. This can happen when you complete the constraint definition, or the link definition, or it can happen later, as a result of changes in the schedule that push the linked task past its constraint. If Microsoft Project 2007 is not honoring task constraints, you do not get the warning shown in Figure 7.23, but you see the Missed Constraint indicator in the Indicator column.

CAUTION

You can discontinue the display of Planning Wizard warnings by selecting the Don't Tell Me About This Again check box. However, you might then be unaware of the conflict. You should leave the Planning Wizard active to warn you about scheduling conflicts.

If you see the Planning Wizard warning and choose to create the constraint conflict, you should make a note of the task ID number in the message because you will not see this warning again. You need to examine that task and the task to which it is linked to find a way to resolve the conflict.

TIP

When you first open a project document, you can press F9 (the Calculate key) to force Project to display its most recent scheduling error message. The message you see should be similar to the one displayed in Figure 7.26. However, you only see one warning message like Figure 7.26, even if there are several constraint conflicts.

The three fundamental ways to resolve a constraint date scheduling conflict are as follows:

- Reassess the need for the constraint and the conditions that make the constraint necessary. Substitute a flexible constraint, if possible.
- Reevaluate the dependency relationships in the sequence of tasks that are linked to the constrained task. Be certain that all links are necessary and defined in order to allow maximum overlapping of tasks, using Start-to-Start, Finish-to-Finish, and lead time, where reasonable.

7

■ Change the duration of individual tasks that are in the linked sequence. You can change the duration by entering a number and time unit directly into the Duration field on the Task Value table.

→ For more information about how to change the duration of individual tasks, **see** "Entering Task Durations," **p. 154**.

You must choose the course of action that makes the most sense in your project. Frequently, a careful review of the tasks, constraints, and task relationships reveals that new definitions are called for. Conditions might have changed since the original definitions were entered and the definitions might now be more restrictive than they need to be.

TIP

Check to see whether a task note exists that might explain the need for the constraint. This might give you some guidance about how to resolve the conflict.

CREATING A MODIFIED CONSTRAINT DATES TABLE

It is easier to analyze constraint conflicts if you modify the standard Constraints Dates table to include the Indicators, Predecessors, and Successors fields. The Indicators field allows you to see the Constraint Conflict indicators (if Microsoft Project 2007 is honoring task links instead of constraint dates). The Predecessors field allows you to identify the links that conflict with the constraints in a fixed start-date project, and the Successors field serves the same function in a fixed finish-date project.

To customize the table, follow these steps:

1. In a task view such as the Gantt Chart view, right-click over the Select All cell (the table's upper-left cell over the ID number column) and choose More Tables from the shortcut menu (or choose View, Table, More Tables).

2. In the Tables list in the More Tables dialog box, select Constraint Dates and click the Copy button.

3. In the Name box, change the name for the new table if desired.

4. To insert the Indicators field, click on the row below ID in the Field Name column and click the Insert Row tool to insert a blank row.

5. Select Indicators in the Name column. Press Enter to add the field.

6. Repeat step 5 in the blank rows at the bottom of the list of field names to add the fields Predecessors and Successors. You should change the Align Data entry to Left for both of these fields.

7. Select the Show in Menu check box if you want this table to appear on the menu of table names.

8. Click OK to create the table, and click Apply to display it.

PERFORMING ADVANCED ACTIONS ON TASKS

You can perform several advanced actions on tasks, such as entering task deadlines, filtering for missed deadlines, splitting tasks, and creating task calendars. These actions, and the methodology behind them, are discussed in the following sections.

ENTERING DEADLINE DATES

You saw earlier in the chapter that you can define a constraint date for a task when the task must be finished by a certain date. You can also use the Deadline Date field to record a task's finish deadline. The Gantt Chart view shows a deadline marker next to the taskbar, and if the task finish is scheduled after the deadline date, a special icon appears in the Indicators column to alert you that the task finish is scheduled after the deadline date (see Figure 7.27).

Figure 7.27
Notice the downward pointing arrow to the right of Task 10's taskbar, representing the deadline, and the indicator in the Indicators column, signifying that that deadline is scheduled to be missed.

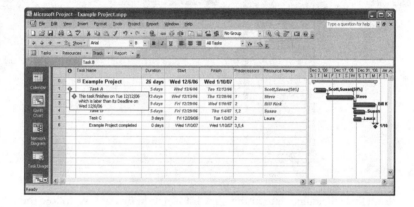

NOTE

If you are highlighting critical tasks, a missed deadline also turns the task into a critical task.

Unlike an inflexible constraint date, there are no conflict error messages or warnings when a deadline is missed. However, you can apply the Tasks with Deadlines filter to select all the tasks that have deadlines defined, and you can check the Indicators column for the Missed Deadline icon. To create a custom filter to select missed deadlines, see the "Filtering for Missed Deadline Dates" section later in this chapter.

An especially useful application of the Deadline Date field is for tasks that have a constraint date defined for the task start, and also a deadline for the task finish. Because you can have only one constraint date per task, the deadline date allows you to define requirements for both the start and finish of a task.

You can define deadline dates in the Project Guide, in the Task Information dialog box, or in the Deadline column if you add that field to a table. When you enter a deadline date, you can also enter the time of day. If you fail to enter the time of day, Microsoft Project 2007

7

supplies the default End Time, as defined on the Calendar tab of the Options dialog box (5:00 p.m., by default).

To create a deadline with the Project Guide, choose Task on the Project Guide toolbar, and select Set Deadlines and Constrain Tasks. Select the task to receive the deadline, and then type in a date or use the deadline date control in the Project Guide to select the date (see Figure 7.28). You can append the time of day after the date is entered. To remove a deadline, enter NA in the Deadline field.

Figure 7.28
The Project Guide can be used to set deadlines by selecting the task and entering the deadline date.

To define a deadline date in the Task Information dialog box, follow these steps:

1. Select the task and activate the Task Information dialog box by either double-clicking the task or using the Task Information tool.

2. Select the Advanced tab (see Figure 7.29).

3. Type a date, including the time of day if appropriate, in the Deadline field, or activate the drop-down box and choose the date in the Calendar control. To remove a deadline, type NA instead of a date. You can enter a time of day after the date is entered.

4. Click OK to complete the definition.

If you want to enter many deadlines, or if you want to review all the deadlines, you might want to add the Deadline field to a task table (refer to Figure 7.27). Click the column heading where you want to insert the field and press the Insert key. Select Deadline in the Field Name box on the Column Definition dialog box and choose Best Fit to display the column. You can then enter deadline dates in this column for any task.

Figure 7.29
Deadlines can also be set in the Task Information dialog box.

Microsoft Project 2007 includes a built-in filter that lets you select the task for which deadlines are defined. You might want to insert the Deadline field in a table to review the deadlines. Otherwise, you have to use the Task Information form for each selected task to see the deadline date.

To apply the filter, click the Filter tool on the Formatting toolbar and choose the filter named Tasks with Deadlines to hide all but the tasks that have deadlines in the display. If you want to merely highlight the tasks that have deadlines, choose Project, Filtered For, More Filters, select Tasks with Deadlines in the More filters dialog box, and click the Highlight button to display the full task list with tasks that have deadlines highlighted.

> **NOTE**
>
> Project does not provide a filter for *missed deadlines*. See the following section, "Filtering for Missed Deadline Dates."

FILTERING FOR MISSED DEADLINE DATES

The standard Tasks with Deadlines filter selects all tasks with deadline dates, whether the deadlines are missed or not. The deadline is missed when the task's Finish date is later than the date in the task's Deadline field.

To create a filter that selects only missed deadline dates, follow these steps:

1. Choose Project, Filtered For and select More Filters.
2. Select the Tasks with Deadlines filter name and choose the Copy button.
3. Type Missed Deadline Dates or another suitable name in the Name text box.
4. In the table of criteria, select the first blank cell on the second row (under the column named And/Or) and type and.
5. In the Field Name column, type Finish.
6. In the Test column, type is greater than.
7. In the Value(s) column, type [Deadline].

7

8. Select the Show in Menu check box if you want this filter on the Filtered For menu.

9. Click OK to complete the filter, and click Apply if you want to apply it immediately.

SPLITTING TASKS

Normally Microsoft Project 2007 schedules work on a task to continue uninterrupted until the task is complete. If you know that there will be interruptions or periods of inactivity on a task, or if after starting work on the task you find that you must interrupt the work and resume at a later date, you can split the task into two or more scheduled segments.

Several examples of tasks that would be good candidates for task splitting include the following:

- Suppose someone is scheduled to work on a task, but a week-long vacation is planned during the time he or she is scheduled to work on this task. The work on the task is going to stop during the week the person is gone and will resume when the person returns. You can incorporate the interruption in the planning stage of the project by splitting the task around the vacation.

- Suppose that a specialized employee is working on a low-priority task when a task with a higher priority requires his or her attention. You can slip the low-priority task and reschedule the remainder of its work after the higher-priority task is complete.

- Suppose work on a task has already begun but nothing has recently been done on the task. The remaining work needs to be rescheduled to start now or in the future. You can split the task at the point where work is completed and reschedule the remaining work to a later date.

NOTE

> A task can have an unlimited number of splits. When you link to a task that is split, the link is to the task. You cannot create a link to a split segment of a task.

The easiest way to split a task is in the Gantt Chart view, where you use the mouse to split a taskbar and drag the right-hand segment to the right to resume at a later date. To split a task in the Gantt Chart view, follow these steps:

1. Activate the Gantt Chart view, and select the task you wish to split.

TIP

> When using your mouse to create a split task, it is recommended that you modify the Timescale of the Gantt Chart to make the action more accurate and easier to perform.
>
> To modify the timescale, right-click on the current timescale in the Gantt Chart and select Timescale…. Use the Top Tier, Middle Tier, and Bottom Tier tabs to decrease the default units. For example, you may want to modify the timescale to include only two tiers, Middle and Bottom, where the Middle tier displays days and the Bottom one displays hours. This is a very detailed timescale and may not work for longer tasks. In this case, you may want to increase the timescale to be able to see the task in its entirety.

2. Select the Split Task tool on the Standard toolbar or right-click the taskbar and select Split Task from the shortcut menu. You can also choose Edit, Split Task from the menu. The Split Task information box appears (see Figure 7.30).

Figure 7.30
The Split Task information box appears when you choose to split a task.

3. Position the mouse pointer over the taskbar where you want to split, but do not click yet. As you hover the pointer right and left over the taskbar, the Start date in the Split Task information box tells you the date where the split will occur once you click the mouse.

4. When you locate the correct Start date, you can either click the taskbar or click and drag. The different results are as follows:

   • If you click the taskbar, Project inserts a split in the schedule, starting on the date in the Split Task information box, at the default start time of day (normally 8:00 a.m.). The length of the split or interruption is one unit of the time unit used in the minor scale of the timescale. If the minor scale is days, even if it displays every third day, the split is one day.

   • If you click and drag, you insert the split as you would by clicking the taskbar, but you also drag the remainder of the task on the right to begin on another date, thus modifying the length of the split. As soon as you start dragging, the Split Task information box is replaced by the Task Information dialog box, which tells you the start date of the new segment (that is, that date when the task will resume) and the finish date for the task. Release the mouse when your reach the date on which you want the new segment to start.

CAUTION

If calculation is set on manual, a task split does not appear graphically on the Gantt Chart until you press F9 to recalculate and refresh the screen. To check the calculation setting, go to Tools, Options, Calculation, Calculation Options for Microsoft Project. The default setting is Automatic.

TIP

Watch the start and finish dates in the Split Task information box carefully to determine when this segment of the split task resumes.

7

NOTE

> You can also split tasks in the Task Usage view, and if resources are assigned to a task, you can split the resource assignments to the task in the Resource Usage view. If all assignments are split at the same point, the task itself is effectively split.

→ For additional information on creating splits in tasks and assignments, **see** "Splitting Tasks," **p. 900**.

After you have split a task, resting the pointer over a split segment displays the Task information box for just that segment, telling you the start date, the finish date, and duration for that segment.

Dragging the first segment of a split task moves all segments of the task together. Holding down the Shift key as you drag a later segment also moves all segments together.

You can drag any but the first segment to the right or left to change the start and finish of that segment of the task, as long as you don't touch another segment of the task.

You can remove a split (that is, rejoin segments of a split task) by dragging the segment on the right toward the left until it touches the next segment.

CAUTION

> Do not drag a middle segment to the right to touch a later segment. Project often loses track of part of the task duration.

To change the duration of a segment, and thus the duration of the task, drag the right end of the segment to the right or left. The Task information box appears and shows the effect of the current position of the cursor to the finish and duration. If you are adjusting the final segment of the split task, the finish and duration are those for the entire task. If you are adjusting any other segment, the finish and duration are those for that segment.

CONSULTANTS' TIPS

THE DEADLINE FEATURE

The Deadline feature is often overlooked because people do not understand the difference between a milestone and deadline. But think about how the milestone is used—it sits there, either standing alone with some kind of task constraint or linked as a successor to the final task in a phase. In the latter case, if your schedule is slipping, then the milestone will march right along with the tasks. If you have not baselined, it becomes difficult to use the milestone as a reliable indicator of the project's progress.

Deadlines, especially when used in conjunction with a milestone, provide a great visual indicator, because you set the deadline date, and when the task or milestone associated with the deadline passes that date, you get a visual reminder in the Indicator column. Of course, you do not want to set the Deadline feature on the actual deadline, because if you are late, it is almost too late to do much about it. So for really critical events in your project, use milestones and the Deadline feature to provide a checkpoint.

SCHEDULING LOGIC

With all the help from PMI and Microsoft to get your schedule defined and ordered quickly, consider that you are taking the "road less traveled." First, sit down by yourself with just an old pad of paper and an antique pencil (#2 or mechanical, your choice). Using these tools, compose the right things to do in the right order to define the high-level network diagram of work necessary to meet the scope of the project. If you do not know the scope, then before you try to solve the problem or create a new product, get the scope recorded and agreed upon.

Once you have the "big box" work defined on paper, share this information with your team. Did you miss anything big? Is the task list accurate? Is the order logical? Will the scope be achieved if you do what is on the paper? Let your team of experts help you refine the high-level network diagram.

The result of using pencil and paper tools is that you slow down and use all your senses to start the project planning. Going slowly in planning often means you can move more quickly in execution with greater certainty of delivery and success. Just because a tool as sophisticated as Microsoft Office Project 2007 is available doesn't mean that you have to or even should start from a blank project. (Get the schedule logic right, and the schedule will be so much more understood and manageable.)

DEADLINES VS. SPONSOR SCHIZOPHRENIA

Many project-driven organizations believe that they must schedule using constraints because they face manic and schizophrenic sponsors. The sponsor says, "We have to have it on June 30," so they apply Must Finish On constraints in order to reinforce the volume managed demands of red-faced sponsors. There are two problems with this seemingly standard project management behavior.

As one who understands scheduling, you should first take the requests and demands and all other information at your disposal and plug it all into the Microsoft Project scheduling engine and let the real expert crunch the numbers, values, and assumptions and tell both you and the sponsor what is doable. Trust the tool and your expertise to explain to the sponsor that the original values applied to the Triple Constraint are unrealistic, but you have a solution! Trust the tool and your ability!

Also, why use scheduling methods that only cause you pain? Scheduling with constraints out of fear is both uninformed and unwise. This does not mean that you have to schedule without using constraints, but understand that judicious application is prudent and often warranted. The use of constraints needs wise counsel.

7

Here is an alternative. Use the Deadlines feature. It will capture the request from the sponsor whether sane or not, allowing for the visual representation of the captured promise, but will not upset the scheduling engine from producing the best possible answer, given the planning assumption. Using deadlines is a pain-free way to attempt to appease the sponsor without breaking your schedule against unrealistic constraints. Try diplomacy, but trust in your tools. You just may hear an improvement in the volume of your project meetings.

USING THE MOUSE TO CONNECT TASKS IS DIFFICULT ON SHORT DURATION TASKS OR ON TASKS THAT ARE NOT ON THE SAME SCREEN. HOW DO I FIX THAT?

It can be difficult to precisely control the mouse pointer on very short duration tasks, so use the Zoom In feature to change the timescale and make the Gantt bars longer and easier to manipulate.

For tasks that are not on the same screen, you have several choices. You can use the Zoom Out tool to see more tasks on the screen, you can roll up subtasks between the two tasks, or you can select the first task, hold the Ctrl down, and then select the second task. As you have probably learned already, the scroll can become very fast.

I HAVE SOME VERY COMPLEX LOGIC IN MY PROJECT PLAN AND THE LINK LINES MAKE IT DIFFICULT FOR SOME PEOPLE TO SEE DETAIL ON THE GANTT CHART. HOW CAN I FIX THIS?

In the Format menu, click on the Layout link. At the top of that dialog box, you can choose to show no link lines (it just hides the line, it doesn't remove the link), or you can choose to have the link connector to the successor task come in at the end of the Gantt bar, instead of at the top, which is the default. Choosing the second option can make the view more complex.

Of course, you can also use the Zoom controls to manage the display, so you can see the link lines as separate lines.

7

CHAPTER 8

DEFINING PROJECT RESOURCES

In this chapter

UNDERSTANDING HOW PROJECT USES RESOURCES AND COSTS

This chapter focuses on resources: understanding what resources are, how to organize them, and how resource costs are defined and calculated in Microsoft Project. With this foundation, you will then be prepared to assign resources and costs to tasks, modify those assignments, and resolve conflicts that arise with overallocated resources, which will all be discussed in the later chapters.

Resources are the people, facilities, materials, and equipment that are assigned to work on a task of a project. Although it is possible to create a schedule in Microsoft Project without assigning resources to the tasks, it is not recommended. By not assigning resources to tasks, you are assuming that you will have all the necessary resources on hand whenever you need them, and that assumption is dangerously unrealistic. People get sick, go on vacation, or have unique work schedules. Machinery and equipment fail and require downtime for maintenance. Employees who play a crucial role in your project will leave the company and new ones will arrive in need of training. New facilities are sometimes not ready for occupancy until mid-way through a project. All these are realistic examples of situations in which a resource that is necessary to complete a task might not be available when Project schedules the task. You can avoid these problems and make a project schedule more realistic by defining and assigning resources to tasks (someone has to do the work!). At the very least, you should assign a person's name to each task he or she is responsible for seeing through to completion.

There are several benefits of including resources in a project schedule:

- By including resources in your project schedule, you can create a more valid timeline of activities and support your schedule finish date. Without using resources, you have a checklist of activities to be accomplished and a unsupported timeline.

- You can communicate assignments to the resources and other project managers through MS Project reports

→ For additional information about reports, **see** Chapter 15, "Using Reports for Tracking and Control," **p. 519**.

  - The working time information for each resource, (Resource Calendar) is used by Project to automatically schedule tasks during those times only, creating a more realistic schedule.

  - After you assign resources to all the tasks, Project can help you model your schedule to see the staffing levels required to meet a specified completion date.

  - Every project manager needs to know how much the project will cost, not necessarily in dollars but at least in effort (work). Exempt personnel (salaried) will get paid whether they work on a specific project or not. The cost incurred is opportunity cost of doing another project. If financial cost of a project is required, you can include the cost information for each resource. Project automatically calculates the cost of each resource assignment to individual tasks and sums those costs to show the total cost of each task and the overall cost of the project. These cost calculations can be very helpful in estimating the budget for the project and in capitalizing labor costs on a capital project.

You can define a comprehensive list of resources at the beginning, including resource cost rates and availability information. Later, you will assign these resources to tasks. Alternatively, you can define the resources as you create the tasks, while you are thinking about how the work will be performed. When you assign new resource names to a task, Project adds these names to the list of resources (see Figure 8.1). As you create new resources, you must remember to at some point modify the resource cost rates, availability information, and other fields as necessary.

Figure 8.1
Splitting the Gantt Chart and Resource Sheet views allows you to enter the additional resource information as you create resources by assigning them to the tasks in the Gantt Chart view.

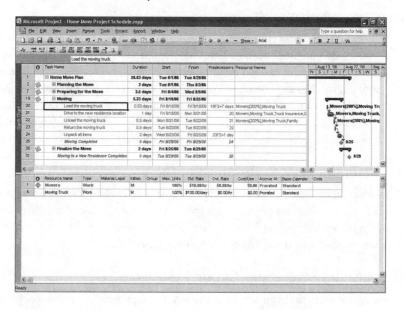

In addition to commonly known resource types (Work and Material), Project 2007 now includes cost resources. Cost resources allow you to identify specific project costs across multiple tasks, such as travel expenses, per diem costs, and so on. In addition to being able to identify these resources, cost resources can be used for integration with the accounting systems. Cost resources add another dimension to the cost model of Project 2007, allowing for additional flexibility and traceability of costs.

Work and Cost resources can also be defined as budget resources. Budget resources are assigned on the project summary task and allow you to allocate the budget on a time-phased basis. The planned cost/actual cost/Estimate at Completion (EAC) can then be compared to the budget on the project.

DEFINING RESOURCES AND RESOURCE INFORMATION

Resources are the backbone of a project. Without resources to complete assigned tasks, those tasks would not be completed. Essentially, the cost of a project is a reflection of the sum of all project resources' costs needed to complete each task within the project.

Examples of resources are workers, supervisors, managers, facilities, factories, equipment, travel costs, supplies, and materials.

→ For detailed information on assigning resources, **see** Chapter 10, "Scheduling Single and Multiple Resource Assignments," **p. 313**.

UNDERSTANDING RESOURCE TYPES

Project 2007 includes three types of resources: work, material, and cost. Work resources are resources that are not consumed at the completion of their assigned task and are available to be assigned to future tasks. The ultimate example of a work resource is people. Material resources, on the other hand, are consumed or used up as a task progresses. Ink, gasoline, concrete, and camera film are examples of material resources. Cost resources represent additional costs incurred on a task that used to be hard to track prior to the addition of the Cost resource type in Project. The most common example of a cost resource is travel expenses.

UNDERSTANDING BUDGET RESOURCES

In addition to the three resource types, Project 2007 includes an option to define the cost or work type as a Budget resource. Budget resources are assigned on the project summary task. Budget Cost and Budget Work are included in baselines and can be used as a reference point when creating and tracking your schedule costs/work.

DISTINGUISHING SINGLE AND GROUP RESOURCES

Some resources that you add to a resource list represent individual people or assets. A resource name could be a person's name, for example. Also, you can name a single piece of equipment, a facility, or a raw material as a resource. If you contract out a task to a vendor who is totally responsible for the task, you could simply name the vendor as a resource, even though there might be many individuals on the vendor's team who actually work on the task.

You can also define a resource to represent multiple resources. These could be a group of individual people with similar skills, or multiple pieces of identical equipment. The max units for the resource should be set to the total number of resources available as part of the set. For example, Moving Truck's Max Units of 500% mean you have 5 trucks included within the resource defined. With this type of resource, you are not concerned with assigning individual resources by name to a given task. For example, you might define a group of seven engineers as the "Engineers" resource, and the manager of those engineers would dictate which of the seven engineers would work on the task. Similarly, you could define a group of five work trucks as the "Trucks" resource, and assign at 500% to a single task. This would represent in the schedule that the task needs 5 trucks to accomplish the work within the duration of the task. Or assign at 100% and the person in charge of the work trucks would decide which one would be used to complete the task.

CAUTION

> Individual members of a group resource cannot be assigned a unique cost rate and you cannot recognize separate vacation days or other nonworking times for the individuals. All the individuals in a group resource must share a common cost rate and must be scheduled by a single resource calendar that is defined for the group.

USING GENERIC RESOURCES FOR COMMON SKILLS

In many cases the project manager does not know the capabilities and skills of many individual resources and/or does not have the authority to assign individuals by name to a task. Generic resources can be defined as a common skill or capability. For example, you are starting a project that will require carpenters to work on multiple tasks. If you are staffed with three carpenters but are unsure of which one will be the best for a certain task, you could create a generic resource called "Carpenters" and assign it to all the individual tasks. Later, you can substitute the names of the specific carpenters in the appropriate task assignments.

This process gives you the advantage of deducing the total number of carpenters needed to complete the project without assigning individuals to the specific tasks. This is especially relevant when many project managers share the same resources in a shared resource pool. Once you have figured out how many carpenters you need, you can see which specific individuals are available and best fitted for the specific tasks.

NOTE

> Project Professional 2007 in conjunction with Project Server 2007 allows organizations to define an enterprise level, shared resource pool. The resources in the organization are added to the resource pool and when a project manager creates a schedule, he or she can add resources to their project directly from the pool. This level of resource sharing also allows to more accurately track resource availability across the organization. If you are using Project Standard 2007, the resource sharing becomes more difficult and does not include the flexibility available in the enterprise environment.

USING THE RESOURCE SHEET VIEW

One of the most effective and commonly used views for manually entering basic resource information is the Resource Sheet view. The Resource Sheet allows you to see many resources on the screen at once. It also shows you a number of important fields for each resource. Indicators notify you when there is critical information in other fields (see Figure 8.2). To display the Resource Sheet view, choose View, Resource Sheet.

TIP

> The resources defined within the Resource Sheet view detail what resources are available to the specific project you are working on (or to all the projects in the case of shared resources). This view does not specifically define which resources are assigned to tasks, but rather which ones are available to be assigned.

Figure 8.2
The information column includes additional information available about a resource, such as external hyperlink, note, and so on.

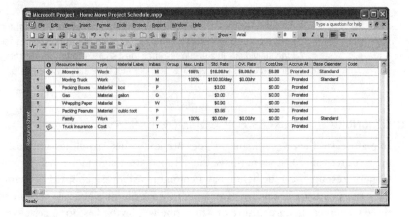

If your video resolution is 800×600 pixels or less, you will have to scroll to the right to see all the columns of the Resource Sheet. Use the Window, Split command to display the Resource Sheet view in the bottom pane. You can see all the fields for the resource that is selected in the top pane (refer to Figure 8.1).

You can also use the Resource Form view to display and edit the Notes field. To display the notes, follow these steps:

1. Activate the Resource Form view by choosing Window, Split from the top navigation menu.

2. In the top navigation menu, select Format, Details, Notes. Figure 8.3 shows the Notes field in the details section of the Resource Form view.

Figure 8.3
In addition to Notes, you can select many other details, such as Cost, Schedule, and Work.

To add a resource in the Resource Sheet view, simply select an empty cell in the Resource Name column and type in a descriptive name for the resource. Project will automatically provide default values for a number of fields to the right. Replace the default values or fill in the blanks for the rest of the fields, using the definitions and instructions from the "Using the Resource Fields to Define Resource Details" section later this chapter.

→ For detailed information on resource views, **see** Chapter 11, "Using Standard Views, Tables, Filters, and Groups to Review Your Schedule," **p. 369**.

DEFINING RESOURCE INFORMATION USING THE RESOURCE INFORMATION DIALOG BOX

The Resource Information dialog box contains almost all of the imperative resource definition fields, including several important resource fields that are not available on the Resource Sheet view or the Resource Form view (see Figure 8.4). The additional fields on the Resource Information dialog box supply the following information:

- When the resource is normally available for work (General tab).

- When the normal working times are changed for vacations, illnesses, or other exceptions (Change Working Time option on the General tab).

- Alternative cost rates to use for different types of work and when different cost rates become effective (Costs tab).

- How to communicate electronically with the resource (General tab and Details button).

- Notes about the resource (Notes tab).

- Custom fields defined for the resource such as department, division, skills, and so on (Custom Fields tab).

Figure 8.4
The Resource Information box contains the most comprehensive and important details about each resource.

8

You can complete the definition of the resource by using the Resource Information dialog box with the Resource Sheet. Enter the resource name in the Resource Sheet. Then use the Resource Information button on the Standard toolbar (or double-click the resource name) to display the Resource Information dialog box for that resource. Fill in the rest of the fields, and then click OK to return to the Resource Sheet view.

USING THE RESOURCE FIELDS TO DEFINE RESOURCE DETAILS

The Resource Sheet view is the simplest, most convenient view for entering and reviewing resource information because it resembles an Excel sheet. To access the Resource Sheet view, click View, Resource Sheet. You can use this view in combination with the Resource Information dialog box to enter all the important fields of information that define a resource. Double-click on the resource name to bring up the Resource Information dialog box, as shown in Figure 8.4.

When defining a resource, you should provide a resource name and information about the availability and cost of the resource. The following sections list the fields that are commonly used in defining resources. Their order in this chapter coincides with the order of the columns in the Resource Sheet view and the related fields in the Resource Information dialog box.

USING THE RESOURCE ID FIELD

The ID numbers for the resources are the row numbers listed all the way to the left side of the screen in the Resource Sheet view. The ID number does not appear in the Resource Information dialog box. These numbers are fixed; if you move a resource on the list, it automatically acquires the ID number for the row that you moved it to. Like the task ID numbers, you cannot edit this field.

INTERPRETING THE INDICATOR FIELD

Indicator icons are helpful in pointing your attention to additional information about the resource. The Indicator field displays icons that show the status of critical fields that might not normally be displayed. For example, the Hyperlink indicator in Figure 8.3 signifies a hyperlink associating the resource with a website or a document file. The Overallocation indicators mean that those resources have been overallocated at some point in the project; they may have been assigned to work on two different tasks at the same time, violating the amount of time they were available to work. The Note indicators show that there is text in the Notes field for those resources. Resource Indicators only appear on resource table views such as the Resource Sheet view.

SPECIFYING RESOURCE NAMES USING THE NAME FIELD

You can define a descriptive name for a resource in the Resource Name field. The name can contain any characters except for the square brackets ([ ]) and the Windows separator character, which is, by default, the comma (,) in the United States. Resource names can be up to 255 characters in length. The resource name can be a specific name, such as John Smith, or it can describe a group of resources, such as Movers.

CAUTION

> Be cautious when entering resource names to avoid duplicate ones. If you add a resource name that is a duplicate of another name on the list, Project accepts it and does not warn you that you have duplicate names. Additionally, if you assign a nonunique resource name to a task, Project uses the first resource it finds with that name from the resource list.

TIP

> It is helpful to come up with a standard naming convention for resources. Two approaches are commonly used: full first name space full last name (John Smith), and full last name space full first name (Smith John). The format last name comma first name (Smith, John) is not allowed in many language versions because Project uses the comma to separate the resource names when assigning multiple resources to a task. Also with cost or budget resources, it is helpful to prefix or Suffix the resource name, i.e Budget Expense, Travel Costs.

USING RESOURCE TYPE TO CATEGORIZE RESOURCES

As stated previously, Project distinguishes between work resources (resources that are not consumed after contributing their work to tasks), material resources (resources that are consumed by their assignments), and cost resources (resources that represent additional costs on a project). The cost of work resources is based on the number of hours the resource works on a task and the hourly cost for the resource. The cost of material resources is based on the cost of a unit of the resource and how many units are consumed. The cost of cost resources is an assigned one-time charge. The default resource type is Work, but you can select either Work, Material, or Cost with the drop-down arrow in the Type field.

Work resources units can be formatted as a percentage (the default) or decimal values. Material resources are formatted only as decimal values.

CAUTION

> Be cautious about changing resource types after they are assigned to tasks. When you assign a resource to a task, its type determines how the assignment affects the schedule for the task. For instance, if it is a work resource, the resource calendar determines when the work can take place. If it is a material or cost resource, there is no resource calendar to consider. Project warns you with a dialog box that the schedule will be affected and that the changes cannot be undone if you try to change the type of resource after it has been assigned.

8

A material resource is said to have a fixed consumption if the amount of the material that is consumed does not depend on the duration of the task. For example, the amount of metal used to build a car's body does not depend on the duration of the task.

A material resource is said to have a variable consumption rate if the amount of the resource consumed varies with the duration of the task. For example, the amount of film consumed when shooting a movie depends on the number of takes a director chooses to shoot the scenes. Project factors the duration of the task when calculating the cost of using a variable-consumption-rate resource. In order to tell Project that it should factor duration into the calculated cost for a material resource, you have to attach a time unit abbreviation when you enter the assignment units. For example, to assign five reels of film per hour to a task, you would enter the units as **5/h**.

→ For details on assigning various resources types to tasks, **see** Chapter 10, "Scheduling Single and Multiple Resource Assignments," **p. 313**.

USING THE MATERIAL LABEL TO SPECIFY UNITS OF RESOURCE MEASURE

You use the Material Label field to define the unit of measure for material resources. For example, lbs for pounds, ea for each, bx for box, and gals for gallons are all measuring units. You define the unit cost of the resource using the measuring unit. This field is not available for work or cost resources.

USING THE INITIALS COLUMN TO SHORTEN RESOURCE NAMES

Sometimes using full names creates clutter and takes up unnecessary space. The Initials field provides a place for a shortened form of the resource name. The abbreviated name can be used in views such as the Gantt Chart and Network Diagram views. After you enter the resource name in a new row, Project automatically provides the first character of the name as the default initial but makes no attempt to keep it unique. If you intend to use the initial to identify resources in any view, be sure to edit the initial to make it uniquely identify the resource and be meaningful to you.

USING THE GROUP FIELD TO CATEGORIZE RESOURCES

The Group field allows you to enter an identifying label or keyword that you can use for organizing (sorting, grouping, or filtering) resources. For example, you could identify all packing materials, such as boxes, tape, wrapping paper, and so on, by entering Packing Materials, all moving personnel by entering Movers, or all pieces of equipment by entering Equipment. You can then use the Resource Group filter to view only the resources that have one of those values in this field.

TIP

Some users of Project find it helpful to put the name of the department that manages a resource in the Group field.

NOTE

When applying a filter to locate one keyword in a list in the Group field, you should use the logical test "contains" rather than "equals." See the section "Filtering Resources" later in this chapter for an example of using filters.

Many users put skills in a custom text field so they can filter the resource list for resources that have comparable skills. It is also useful to identify the skill level. The most effective method is to combine the skill category with the skill level.

For example, if you adopt the scale 1=Trainee, 2=Semi-Skilled, 3=Skilled, and 4=Expert, then any semi-skilled technician could be identified with Technician2. Use commas to separate entries for people who have multiple skills.

TIP

In Project Server, skills are defined using enterprise custom fields. Even when you are not using Project Server, you can use resource custom fields to define skill sets. Figure 8.5 illustrates a skill implemented in a custom field. Note that each level of the outline gets more specific about the skill of the resource. This allows you to find an engineer, a mechanical engineer, or specifically an advanced mechanical engineer based on the level of specificity you request when searching the Skill field.

Figure 8.5
Resource skill sets can be defined using the Custom Fields Lookup Table option.

→ For additional information on customizing custom fields, **see** Chapter 22, "Customizing Views, Tables, Filters, Groups, and Fields," **p. 755**.

8

USING THE MAX UNITS AND RESOURCE AVAILABILITY TABLE TO SPECIFY RESOURCE AVAILABILITY

Use the Max Units field to enter the maximum number of units that can currently be assigned to tasks at any one time. Project uses the Max Units field to determine when the resource is overallocated (when more units of the resource have been assigned than are available) and when leveling resources.

For instance, suppose that Greg's Max Units field shows 80%. That means that Greg is available to spend up to 80% of his working time on tasks in your project. If you assign Greg to spend 30% of his time on one task and 60% of his time on another task, and if the scheduled dates for those two tasks overlap, you will have assigned 90% of Greg's time during the period of the overlap. Since this is more than the Max Units of 80%, Project calculates that the resource is overallocated; the resource name turns red in the Resource Sheet view and displays a symbol in the Indicator field to flag the overallocated resource.

You can format the Max Units field as a percentage or as a decimal. The default is the percentage format. You can change the format for the Max Units field in the Options dialog box by following these steps:

1. In the Tools menu, select Options.
2. In the Options dialog box, select the Schedule tab.
3. Use the drop-down list in the "Show assignment units as a" box and select either Percentage or Decimal.

Project applies a default Max Units of 100% (or 1 in decimal format) when you create a resource. However, you can change the value to anything between 0% and 6,000,000,000% (between 0 and 60,000,000 in decimal format). For a single-unit resource, the default value of 100% means that this resource is available to work 100% of the hours on its calendar on this project. It can also signify that the resource is fully dedicated (100%) to complete the assigned task during the defined period. If you are grouping resources into a group resource, you enter a greater value than 100%. Thus, if you have two full-time movers in a Movers resource, you can enter 200% (or 2 in decimal format).

> **NOTE**
>
> There is no Max Units value for material or cost resources. Project assumes that you will acquire as many units as you have assigned.

A resource may have some variability concerning its actual availability. For instance, sometimes a resource is not hired until after the project starts, so up until that date its Max Units remains 0%. On the reverse side, a resource might leave the company before the project is completed, so after his/her last day with the company, the Max Units field will be 0%. At all other times, the resource availability may vary from 0 to 100% for very specific reasons during very specific times.

You might also intend to add more units of the resource over the duration of the project. In this case, you need to record the dates when the additional units would come on board using the Resource Availability table.

You can find the Resource Availability table on the General tab of the Resource Information dialog box. Use this table to define the time periods and the max units for each time period (refer to Figure 8.4). The default values for both the Available From and Available To columns in the Resource Availability table are NA (not applicable), and the default value in the Units (Max Units) field is 100%. The NA value means from the earliest possible date (Jan 1, 1984) and latest available date (Dec 31, 2049) respectively. Figure 8.6 shows that the Movers resource will not start work until 8/18/2006, even though the project starts earlier, and will be available until 8/22/2006 per the contract agreement, even though the project still continues after 8/22.

Figure 8.6
The Resource Information dialog box's Resource Availability table is used to track the changes in resource availability down to specific date ranges and units.

The Max Units field on the Resource Sheet view and on the Resource Form view displays the Units value from the Resource Availability table for the current date. The current date is normally the computer's current date, but it can be any date you choose to enter into the Current Date field in the Project Information dialog box. If you look at the Max Units field for Movers on the Resource Sheet view on any date prior to 8/18/2006, the value will be 0%, because the movers are unavailable to work on the project before 8/18/2006 according to the Available From column. After 8/18/2007, it will be 200%.

When Project examines this schedule to see if the Movers resource is overallocated, it shows the overallocated indicator if the total assignments for the Movers resource exceed 200% on any date outside the date range of 8/18/2006 - 08/22/2006.

To change the Resource Availability table for a resource, follow these steps:

1. In a view that shows resource names, such as the Resource Sheet view, select the resource and click the Resource Information button on the Standard toolbar. You can also simply double-click the resource name.

2. Click the General tab, if it is not displayed.

3. Click the cell for the date you want to change under the Available From or Available To

8

column. You can either type in the date or use the drop-down arrow to select the date.

4. Enter the max units for that row's date range in the Units column.

5. After all entries are completed, click OK to save the changes. Or you can click Cancel to close the dialog box without saving any changes.

TIP

Be sure that the dates in the Resource Availability table are in sequential order and that you leave no gaps in the dates from one row to the next. If you have an Available From date that is more than one day later than the Available To date on the previous row, Project assumes the resource is unavailable between those dates and uses 0% as the Max Units value for the dates in the gap.

CAUTION

When entering dates in the Available From and Available To columns, be aware that those dates are fixed unless you change them. If a resource's availability dates change, be sure to correct the changes in the Resource Availability table.

NOTE

The Resource Availability table is not available for material resources, which are assumed to be always available to the project.

SELECTING RESOURCE CALENDAR TO SPECIFY RESOURCE BASE AVAILABILITY

In addition to Max Units and the Resource Availability table, Project 2007 uses resource base calendars to specify resource availability. One of the project's base calendars is designated to define the normal working days and hours for the resource.

To select a specific resource calendar, use the drop-down arrows to display a list of all the base calendars that have been defined and select the one that most closely fits the resource. The resource calendar inherits all of the chosen base calendars' values: the working days and hours as well as the individually marked nonworking days and hours that are defined in the base calendar. The default base calendar is Standard.

TIP

You may want to create a special base calendar if you have more than one named resource with the same set of exceptions to one of the standard base calendars. Otherwise, you will have to mark the same exceptions in each of the resource calendars. For example, if several resources will be assigned to work on a project on a night shift and they all have the same basic schedule on night work hours, you can save time by creating a base calendar for night shift work and then using that base calendar for all resources with these hours. Instead of customizing each night shift worker's resource calendar, you can define the hours only once and apply the base calendar wherever necessary.

> **TIP**
>
> If you create additional base calendars in your project that resources or tasks are linked to, remember to make company-wide changes in working days and hours to all base calendars. For example, if your company decides to make the day after Thanksgiving a holiday, you need to edit each base calendar used by resources or tasks in order to apply the holiday to all schedules.

→ For details on creating the base calendar, **see** Chapter 5, "Setting Up Project for Your Use," **p. 107**.

SPECIFYING THE RESOURCE WORKING TIME

As previously mentioned, a resource calendar is based on one of the base calendars, and it inherits the base calendar's normal working times per week, as well as all the holidays or other exceptions to the normal working times. You can enter exceptions to working time on the base calendar for a resource by using the resource calendar. In order to modify the working time for the resource on a particular day, follow these steps:

1. In the Resource Information dialog box, select the General tab if not already selected.
2. On the General tab, click the Change Working Time button.
3. Ensure that the Work Weeks tab is selected and then select a date on the calendar.
4. Click the Details button and enter the working time hours for the resource in the resulting dialog box, as shown in Figure 8.7.

Figure 8.7
You can use the Details dialog box to specify any working hours deviations from the standard resource calendar.

In order to create an exception, follow these steps:

1. In the Resource Information dialog box, select the General tab if not already selected.

2. On the General tab, click the Change Working Time button.

3. On the Exceptions tab, enter the name of the exception and then enter the exception start and end dates.

4. Click the Details button and ensure that the Nonworking option is selected.

For example, in Figure 8.8, the resource calendar for Brian Smith shows that he will not be available to work August 10–17 because he has scheduled vacation during that time.

Figure 8.8
Use the Exceptions tab and the Details button to specify exceptions to the standard calendar and the specific times resource will not be available.

Follow these additional steps to edit a resource calendar:

1. Select the resource in a resource view or on the Assign Resources dialog box and double-click the resource name to display the Resource Information dialog box. Click the Change Working Time button to display the resource calendar and time fields.

2. Use the Base Calendar drop-down list to select the base calendar for the resource.

3. To give the resource time off on dates that are normal working dates on the base calendar, select the dates on the calendar and click the Details button. Select the Set Days to Nonworking Time option.

4. Similarly, to schedule a resource for work on dates that are normally nonworking dates, select the dates (they are shaded before you select them), click the Details button, and select the Set Day(s) to These Specific Working Times option. In the Working Times table, specify the From and To hours the resource will be available to work on that day.

5. Modify the hours of work on any date as needed. The date appears with a diagonal shading pattern to indicate that the hours are nonstandard for that day of the week, and the date is underlined to show that it is an exception to the base calendar.

6. Click the OK button to save your changes in the resource calendar, or click the Cancel button to abandon the changes without saving them.

DEFINING RESOURCE COSTS

There are three cost measures you can associate with a resource. The Standard Rate is used for work completed during normal working hours. The Overtime Rate is used for work completed during overtime hours. Cost Per Use is a special, one-time cost per assignment that is independent from the number of hours worked. Each of these cost measures has a default rate that you can define in the Resource Sheet view or in the Resource Information dialog box.

You can create four additional sets of the three rates in the Resource Information dialog box if you want to charge different rates for different kinds of work. You can also define time periods when the rates will change. These features are covered in the section "Understanding the Cost Rate Tables" later in this chapter.

APPLYING THE STANDARD RATE TO A RESOURCE

You use the Standard Rate field to show the current default cost of each unit of the resource assigned to a task:

- For work resources, the standard rate is the amount to charge per time unit of normal working time for the resource. Enter the rate as a number, followed by a forward slash (/) and one of the following units or its abbreviation: minute (m), hour (h), day (d) , week (w), month (mo), or year (y). Project assumes an hourly rate if you type just a number without a time unit. For example, you can type **900/w** for $900 per week, **46000/y** for $46,000 per year, or just **18.7** for $18.70 per hour. Suppose you were to rent a moving truck for $100 per day. You could create a resource named Moving Truck and enter the standard rate **100/d**.

- For material resources, the standard rate is the amount to charge tasks per unit of the resource consumed. The unit is defined in the Material Label field. There is no time unit attached to the dollar amount. Enter the standard rate as an amount, with no time unit, and it is understood to be the amount per unit of the resource. For example, if you include gas as a material resource for the moving truck, its material label might be gallons (which is already defined in the Material Label field) and the standard rate might be 3.00, which means $3.00 per gallon.

8

- Cost resources use a flat charge amount assigned to it and do not have either units or standard rate.

If the standard rate is entered with a time unit, the rate is converted to an hourly rate and is applied to the number of hours of work it takes to complete the task. For annual rates, the hourly rate is calculated by assuming there are 52 weeks in a year, and the number of hours per week is that which is defined on the Calendar tab of the Options dialog box. For the standard workweek of 40 hours, the annual rate is divided by 2,080 (52 weeks × 40 hours) to get an hourly rate. For monthly rates, the hourly rate is calculated using the Calendar tabs' definitions for days in a month and hours in a day (Hourly Rate in a Month = Monthly Rate / (Days in Month × Hours in Day).

When you want to charge more or less than the default rate, you can define four more rates in addition to the default standard rate that can be used for assignments. See the section "Understanding the Cost Rate Tables" later in this chapter for details.

TIP

Although the standard rate is frequently the hourly or salaried rate for a resource, organizations often define the standard rate as the billed-at rate. When the standard rate is defined as the billed-at rate, a project plan serves as a budget estimate for the work to be performed under contract.

Oftentimes, a project plan demonstrates to the client early in the proposal stage that client requirements are understood and acknowledged and gives the client important confidence. Expectations are set for the project in the early stages of planning, as opposed to being unpleasantly discovered during project execution. Estimates of cost and work are based on defined work rather than ballpark estimates.

APPLYING THE OVERTIME RATE TO A RESOURCE

Project uses the entry in the Overtime Rate field when calculating the cost and actual cost of overtime hours that you schedule for a work resource. There is no overtime rate for material and cost resources. The default overtime rate is zero (0.00), so for salaried employees you can leave the zero value if these resources are not paid extra for their overtime hours. If the rate for overtime work is the same as the regular rate and you intend to collect actual overtime work, you must enter that amount again in the Overtime Rate field, or overtime hours will be charged at the zero default rate.

NOTE

Overtime work can be scheduled using the resource or task usage views by displaying the overtime work column. Overtime work can only be scheduled and actual overtime collected at the assignment level.

Resources that are paid by the hour often receive a higher wage when working overtime. Be sure to enter this amount in the Overtime Rate field.

As with the standard rate, you can define four additional overtime rates for each resource and use them for special tasks. See the section "Understanding the Cost Rate Tables" later in this chapter.

NOTE

You can set the default values for the standard and overtime rates for all new resources in the Options dialog box. Choose Tools, Options, and then click the General tab. Enter an amount per time unit in both the Default Standard Rate and the Default Overtime Rate fields. All resources added from that point on initially show these default rates.

APPLYING THE COST PER USE TO A RESOURCE

The Cost Per Use field is titled "Cost/Use" in the Resource Sheet view and "Per Use Cost" in the Resource Information dialog box. This field contains any cost that is to be charged once for each 100% of a unit of a resource that is assigned to a task, regardless of the duration of the assignment. In other words, the amount entered in the Cost Per Use field will be charged every time the resource is assigned to a task.

For example, if you rent a piece of equipment by the hour but also have to pay a flat charge of $400 for having it delivered to the work site, you could enter the delivery charge as a Cost Per Use cost. Keep in mind, however, that if you assign the equipment to more than one task, the $400 will be charged for each assignment. Therefore, you should always be careful when using the Cost Per Use field with work resources, because the amount entered in that field will be charged once for each 100% of the resource that is assigned to any task.

TIP

Be sure to take advantage of the Cost Per Use field when you are laying out your project plans. One example of this would be a required trip charge for deploying a resource. Perhaps a plumber charges $50 to examine a plumbing problem, regardless of the number of hours spent and the materials necessary to fix the problem. The Cost Per Use field allows you to assign flat-rate costs to various tasks.

UNDERSTANDING THE COST RATE TABLES

The Costs tab of the Resource Information dialog box contains five Cost Rate tables—Tables A through E—which show the default cost rates (Table A) plus four other levels of cost that you can define for different types of assignments. For example, a Plumber resource's Table A would contain its default rates, which might be for new commercial plumbing assignments. Table B might contain the rates for new residential plumbing assignments, Table C might show rates for modifying commercial plumbing, and Table D might contain the rates for modifying residential plumbing. You can select the rate to apply to an assignment in the Assignment Information dialog box.

TIP

> You cannot change the labels on the five cost tabs to something more descriptive than A–E, so you should use the resource Notes field (in the Resource Information dialog box) to document what each rate is to be used for.

Figure 8.9 shows Cost Rate Table A for Brian Smith. This table defines the default cost rates to use for Brian's assignments.

Figure 8.9
Use the Cost Tables to specify various cost rates for each resource.

Project Start Date (if no date set)

20% calculated raise

20% raise starts

The entry in the first cell in the Effective Date column is always two dashes, signifying that there is no set start date for that level of rates. To enter additional levels for subsequent dates, enter the change date in the Effective Date column and then enter the values for the Standard Rate, Overtime Rate, and Per Use Cost columns. Brian Smith will receive a raise of 20% to both his standard and overtime rates on 8/21/2006 (see Figure 8.9). You can enter up to 25 dated rate changes in each of the five tabs.

You can also allow for changes over time in these rates. For example, if you assume that inflation will cause your costs to increase by 5% per year, you could show different rates for each of the years during which the project lasts.

If you want Project to calculate a percentage increase or decrease in one of the rates, enter the plus or minus percentage with a percent sign (%), and when you leave the cell, Project applies that increase to the value in the cell just above it, displaying the calculated result instead of the percentage you entered (see Figure 8.10).

Figure 8.10
Enter the 5% raise increase in a new row of the Cost Table A Standard Rate field and click the Tab button on your keyboard to have project automatically calculate the dollar value.

> **TIP**
> The various cost tables allow for the use of a resource that might be billed at different rates for various services and functions within the project. For example, suppose one of your resources is a bilingual writer who is billed at one rate for writing in English but charges a different rate for writing in Russian. By factoring in the resource's competency in using each language, a different rate can be charged for utilizing the same resource with various skill sets within the same project.

SELECTING THE COST ACCRUAL TYPE

The Cost Accrual field determines when costs are recognized for standard and overtime costs. You can choose one of three options: Start, End, or Prorated.

The default accrual method is Prorated, which means that planned cost is distributed equally across the duration and if you mark a task at 15% complete, the actual costs for all assigned resources would be estimated to be 15% of the scheduled or estimated cost of those assignments. This method is the most widely used because it keeps up with the pace of the project, allowing the cost to coincide with task progress.

If you choose Start as the accrual method, total planned costs are shown on the task start date then as soon as you indicate that work on a task has started, Project considers the entire standard and overtime costs of the assignment as the actual cost. In other words, once a task has begun, the entire cost is incurred and recognized as if the task were complete.

If you choose End, Project postpones recognition of the actual cost until you enter a finish date and the assignment is 100% complete.

The Cost Accrual setting only matters when you are printing interim reports and when work on a task assignment has started but is not finished.

> **NOTE**
> Only the standard and overtime rates are affected by the accrual method you choose. The Cost Per Use value is always accrued at the start of an assignment, no matter which accrual method you choose for the resource.

8

USING THE TASK FORM VIEW TO ADD ADDITIONAL RESOURCES

One of the most popular views for assigning resources is the Gantt Chart view with the Task Form view in the bottom pane. You can also add resources in that view by using the resource details in the lower pane. To add resources in the Task Form view, follow these steps:

1. Display the Gantt Chart view. Choose Window, Split to display the Task Form view in the lower pane.

2. If the resource details are not displayed in the Task Form view, click anywhere in the lower pane to activate it and then choose Format, Details from the menu. Select Resources and Predecessors (see Figure 8.11).

3. In the top pane, select a task.

4. Click in the Resource Names column in the Task Form view, where you can select an existing resource to assign to the task, or you can type in the name of a new resource to assign to the task. In Figure 8.11, Gas is being typed in as an additional resource. If you type in a new name and click the OK button, Project will provide the default values for the Assignment Units and Work, since you did not.

5. Double-click the resource name to display the Resource Information dialog box, where you can fill in the rest of the fields that define the resource.

Figure 8.11
The split-screen Gantt Chart and Task Information view is one of the most convenient views for assigning resources to a task.

→ For additional details on using views, **see** Chapter 11, "Using Standard Views, Tables, Groups, and Filters to Review Your Schedule," **p. 369**.

UNDERSTANDING RESOURCE CONSTRAINTS

In order to complete the resource definition process, resource constraints need to be completed. There are few definable resource constraints, but there are many different constraining factors on a resource. Human resources may be constrained due to scheduling conflicts, overallocation, availability, physical location, or controlled budgets. Other resources such as machinery may be constrained due to condition, compatibility, or failure. These and other resource constraining factors can create serious headaches for project managers and are often the root cause for task or project failures. Using Project can help avoid these headaches and manage resource constraining factors with more control.

By using Project 2007, you can create a profile for a resource that will help you manage your project from start to finish. You have, at your fingertips, all the attributes of a resource that could potentially lead to problems or constraints. For example, Mary Powell is a resource you need for a specific task, but when assigning her to a task, you realize there is a conflict. Perhaps she is on vacation, or lives in another city, or only works part time, or has already been assigned to tasks and is unavailable during the time you have allotted for completing the task.

As a project manager, you have to analyze the risks involved with changing your plan and predict all the various outcomes. Maybe there is another resource that can perform the task you wish to assign to Mary Powell, or maybe you can move the task to a later date when she is available to work on it. You need to weigh the risks and ask yourself, "If I wait until Mary is available to start this task, what will be the consequences? Is it worth the risk, or should I assign another resource to the task?" If you have another resource that is capable and available, chances are you should assign the task to the other resource. But if Mary Powell is the only qualified resource to complete the task, then it is worth the wait. Resource and risk management are significantly aided by Project.

WORKING WITH RESOURCES

As you are undoubtedly aware by now, Project offers several options when categorizing, organizing, and working with resources. Depending on your project, some methods will be of more use to you than others. The following pages discuss these different methods and will give you a greater understanding of working with resources in Project.

SETTING THE AUTOMATICALLY ADD NEW RESOURCES AND TASKS OPTION

Setting the Automatically Add New Resources and Tasks option determines how Project reacts when you assign a resource to a task that is not currently in your resource list.

When you assign a resource name to a task, Project checks the resource list for the name you have entered. By default, if Project does not find the resource, it adds it to the resource list without asking your permission. This causes problems if you did not intend to add a new resource, but rather typed in the wrong or misspelled resource name accidentally.

8

CAUTION

> All resource fields for the new name receive default values, and you must remember to update those fields later. You can end up with miscalculations in your costs if you neglect to go back and fill in the data for the new resource, because the default cost rates are usually zero (and by now you must know that is inaccurate!).

This feature can be dangerous because it allows you to accidentally create multiple resource names for the same resource. For example, suppose you have created a list of resources that includes Matt, Maria, and Charles. As you are assigning resources to tasks, you type in Marie instead of Maria as a typo. A new resource, Marie, is added to the list of resources, so you then have Matt, Maria, Charles, and Marie. You end up not having a comprehensive list of the assignments for Maria, because they are split between the Maria and Marie resources.

However, if the Automatically Add New Resources and Tasks option (in the Tools, Options, General tab) is disabled, Project prompts you to choose whether it should add the new resource to the resource list. If you did in fact type in a wrong or misspelled resource name, disabling this feature allows you to double-check your possible error.

In Figure 8.12, the resource name Bill Kirkk was accidentally typed in an assignment, and Project prompts you to decide whether this is a new resource you want added to the list. If you confirm that you want to add the resource, the resource is added, and you must remember to define the rest of the resource fields. In this example, you would choose the No button to avoid adding a misspelled version of Bill Kirk's name to the resource list.

Figure 8.12
Disabling the Automatically Add New Resources and Tasks option allows you to avoid accidentally creating erroneous resources.

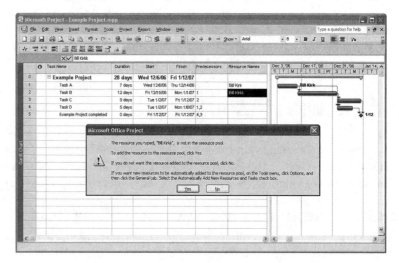

→ For detailed information on how resource assignments work, **see** Chapter 9, "Understanding Work Formula Basics," **p. 283**.

8

TIP

It is a good idea to disable the Automatically Add New Resources and Tasks option to avoid the possibility of creating new resources unintentionally. If you are going to leave the option enabled, you should avoid typographical errors by always using the pick list of resource names that is available when you assign a resource to a task.

To disable or enable the Automatically Add New Resources and Tasks option, choose Tools, Options, and then click the General tab. Clear the check box Automatically Add New Resources and Tasks to disable the feature, or check the box to enable the feature.

SORTING RESOURCES

The resource names in the Resource Sheet view are normally listed according to ID number, which initially reflects the order in which you enter the resources. Project allows you to temporarily sort the resource list for analysis purposes. Also, after you sort the resource list, you can permanently change the row ID numbers to match the new order.

NOTE

Permanently changing the ID numbers does not change the unique ID that is assigned when you add a resource.

CAUTION

Never cut and paste to change the order of the resource rows if you have already assigned resources to tasks. Cutting deletes the original resource and its assignments are deleted also. Therefore, the new resource you paste in will have a new unique ID and will have no assignments.

For instance, after entering all the resources, you could permanently sort the list so that all the work resources are listed first in alphabetical order by name and the material resources are listed below in order by name (see Figure 8.13). Or, if you have used generic resource names, you might sort the list to show the generic names first and then the actual names.

Figure 8.13

By using Sort By, you can sort the list of resources by up to three columns at once.

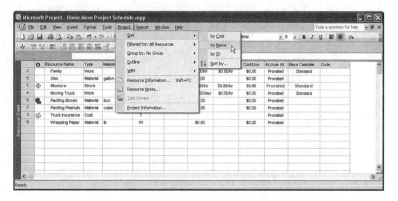

Another useful application of sorting is to see which resources add the most cost to the project. In this case, you apply the Cost table to the Resource Sheet view, to show the cost of all the task assignments for each resource. Then you could sort the resource list by the Total Cost field, in descending order (see Figure 8.14).

Figure 8.14
Applying the cost sort allows you to view the most cost-impactive resources in your project.

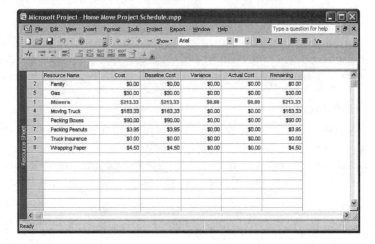

You can sort a table by up to three fields at a time. Each of those fields can be sorted in ascending or descending order. For example, to produce the sort of order in Figure 8.13, you would sort first on the resource's Type field, in descending order, to put work resources before material resources alphabetically. Next you would sort by the Resource Name field in ascending order to list the names in alphabetical order.

NOTE

If you sort the resource table by the Standard Rate field, Project sorts the work resources that have been defined with annual cost rates using the hourly equivalent of the annual amount, based on 52 weeks of 40 hours each.

To sort resources, choose Project, Sort to display the Sort submenu. Sorting by cost, name, or ID is done so often that these options appear on the submenu. Cost sorts in descending order, but both Name and ID sort in ascending order by default. These three choices use the current settings at the bottom of the Sort dialog box.

If you choose Sort By at the bottom of the Sort submenu, Project displays the Sort dialog box, where you can define up to three fields to use for sorting, and each can be sorted in either ascending or descending order, as shown in Figure 8.15.

Figure 8.15
Use the Sort dialog box to customize the current view.

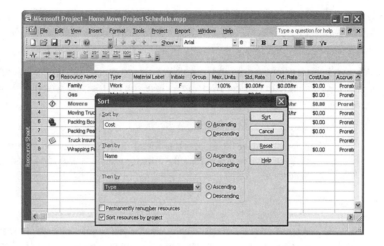

8

To produce the sort order by Type and then by Name, as illustrated in Figure 8.13, follow these steps:

1. Display the Resource Sheet view, by choosing View, Resource Sheet.

2. Choose Project, Sort, Sort By to display the Sort dialog box.

3. You can sort a maximum of three fields, using the Sort By, Then By, and Then By fields. Enter the first sort fields in the Sort By box. In the example shown in Figure 8.15, the field is the Type field. Use the drop-down arrow to display the list of fields. Type the first letter of the field name (in this case, *T*), and Project highlights the first field that begins with that letter. Scroll down and select the Type field.

4. Click the Ascending button if you want the field sorted in normal order. In this example, you click the Descending button to list work before material resources.

5. In the first Then By box, select the Name field.

6. Select Ascending to sort the names in normal order.

7. Select the Permanently Renumber Resources check box if you want Project to change all ID numbers to match the new sort order. See the following Caution box if you elect to fill this check box.

CAUTION

If you fill the Permanently Renumber Resources check box in a sort operation, then as soon as the sort is completed, you should immediately open the Sort dialog box again, click the Reset button, and then click Sort. The Reset button disables the Permanently Renumber Resources option and sets the sort key to ID, and does not interfere with the initial sort you just completed. If you do not take this extra step, the Permanently Renumber check box remains filled, and every future sorting using the Sort submenu renumbers your resources until you clear the box. Also, future sorting of tasks permanently renumbers the tasks.

If you decide to cancel a sort operation and you have already filled the Permanently Renumber Resources check box, be sure to clear the check box (or click the Reset button, which also clears it) before clicking the Cancel button.

8

8. If you have combined several project files into a consolidated display, you can select the Sort Resources By Project box to keep the resources for each project together and sort them within that grouping.

9. When all settings are ready, click the Sort button to execute the sort and close the dialog box. Or, click the Cancel button to close the dialog box without sorting the resources.

TIP

> If you have done a custom sort previously in the same session and used three sort keys, click the Reset button to clear the extra (second and third) sort keys if you no longer need them.

NOTE

> You can undo a sort operation, even after you permanently renumber the resources. However, you must undo the sort operation before you make any other changes. Just as a precaution, it is wise to save a copy of the file before permanently renumbering the resources, just in case you want to undo it later.
>
> You can put the rows back into the order in which they were originally entered by sorting the Unique ID field. This action puts the rows back in their original order.

To return the list to the ID order, you can either press Shift+F3 (which cancels the current sort order) or choose Project, Sort, ID from the menu.

TIP

> Press Ctrl+Shift+F3 to reapply the last sort instructions. This is in case you have sorted the resource list in a special order and have made changes that might make the order of the resources no longer fit the sort order you defined. For example, if you sorted by resource type and cost and then you make task assignments or change some resource cost rates, the list might no longer be in descending cost order within each type. You can press Ctrl+Shift+F3 to sort by type and cost again.

NOTE

> If you frequently use a custom sort order and would like to place it on the Sort submenu, you can create a macro and customize the Sort menu to include that sort order.

→ For information on customizing the menus, **see** Chapter 22, "Customizing Views, Tables, Filters, Groups, and Fields," **p. 755**.

GROUPING RESOURCES

You can sort tasks or resources into groups, based on the entries in one or more of the fields, by using the Group By command. For example, you could group resources by resource types (see Figure 8.16) or by entries in the Group field.

→ For detailed information on the Group By command, **see** "Creating Custom Groups," **p. 797**.

Figure 8.16
Use the Group By command to sort the resources and organize them into logical groups to simplify the resource views.

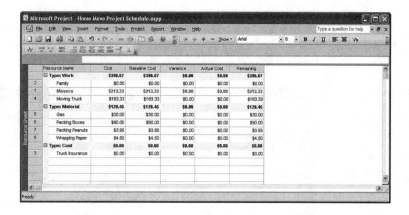

NOTE

Project displays the resource list in outline format by outline code number if you define a custom outline code for resources and use that field for the Group By order.

A difference between sorting and grouping is that in grouping, a Group By record is inserted at the start of each group. Project calculates totals for any numeric fields in this record for the records grouped beneath it. In Figure 8.16, the cost table has been applied and the fields show various measurements of the cost of assignments for the resources. You can see that the total cost of assignments for work resources is $396.67, whereas the total cost of assignments for material resources is only $128.45. The inserted grouping rows have no resource ID or row number and they disappear when you remove the grouping.

TIP

If you create a custom outline code for resources—perhaps outlining them geographically by divisions, cities, departments, and job codes—you will find that grouping on that outline field produces a hierarchical outline with rolled-up costs that can be very useful.

If you use a custom text field to identify resource skills, you can insert the Work column in the table and then group by the skills and by start dates to see the total amount of work needed for each skill per week or month. If you insert the Peak column (which shows the maximum number of units assigned for a resource at any moment during a given time period), you could forecast the number of units of a skill that are needed per time period.

To group resource records on the resource type as in Figure 8.16, choose Project, Group By, Work vs. Material Resources. To remove the grouping, choose Project, Group By, No Group, or press Shift+F3.

You can change the sort order while the resources are grouped. The sort settings are applied within each group. In other words, resources do not move to a different group as a result of the new sort order. The resource list in Figure 8.15 is sorted by cost, in descending order. You can also apply filters while the resources are grouped, which is discussed in the next section.

FILTERING RESOURCES

Use filters to select all the resources that meet some condition that you specify. For example, you might want to select all your material resources. This condition—that the resource type must be Material—is called the filter criterion. Project has a built-in filter named the "Resources – Material" filter that implements this criterion for you, as shown in Figure 8.17.

Figure 8.17
When the filter is applied, the resources that do not satisfy the selected criteria are hidden from the current view.

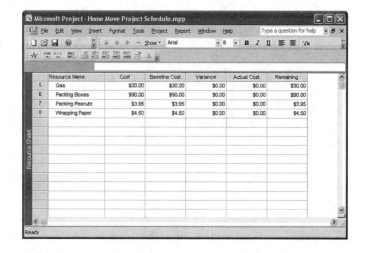

TIP

> Filtering for specific resources is a great way to isolate only the resources that meet specific criteria that you have defined and to temporarily omit the other ones. By doing so, you can save a lot of time by applying a single change that affects an entire group of resources instead of having to change each one independently.

After Project selects the resources that meet the criteria, it normally changes the display to show only the selected resources, temporarily hiding all those that do not meet the criteria. However, you can also choose to filter as a highlight filter, and Project simply highlights the selected resources, without hiding all the others. In Figure 8.18, the Resources – Material filter is applied as a highlight filter, formatted with blue font.

Figure 8.18
A highlighting filter allows you to continue to display all available resources, but highlighting the ones that meet the filter criteria.

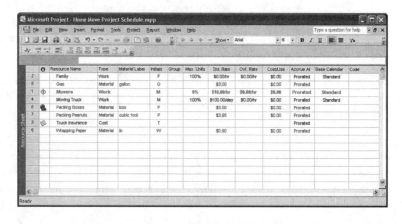

→ For information on how to customize the highlight filter, **see** Chapter 22, "Customizing Views, Tables, Filters, Groups, and Fields," **p. 755**.

When you finish using the filtered display, you must apply the "All Resources" filter to return to the normal display, or simply press the F3 key.

Another useful filter for reviewing how you categorized your resources is the Group filter. You can quickly filter the list to show all the resources that have a specific keyword if you have entered keywords in the Group field. For example, if you entered department names in the Group field, you could filter the list for "Design" to identify all the resources that are managed by the Design department. If you used job titles, you could use the filter to isolate resources who might qualify for a certain resource assignment.

Project 2007 lets you filter the list of resources to be displayed in the Assign Resources dialog box. This dialog box is especially useful for substituting one resource for another. Usually, you want to substitute resources that have the same skill set. If you use a custom text field to enter skill keywords, you can filter the resource list to see all resources that might be appropriate substitutes. If you include a comma-separated list of multiple skills, you need to define a special filter for this purpose.

TIP

> Project 2007 also lets you use the Assign Resources dialog box to do availability-based scheduling. Highlight a task and check the Available to Work check box, and Project will only show you resources that have a specified amount of availability during the time a task is scheduled. This technique is extremely helpful when trying to find the right people to work on a schedule that has inflexible dates.

You can use filters to quickly check the status of resources after work on the project has begun to see at a glance where problems might lie. The following partial filter listing illustrates how useful filters can be in managing a project and allows you to identify specific categories of resources:

- Use the Overallocated Resource filter to focus on resources that are assigned to more work than they can possibly finish in the scheduled time period.

- Use the Cost Overbudget filter to find resources whose scheduled costs are more than you had budgeted.

- Use the Work Complete filter to find resources that have finished all their work.

- Use the Slipping Assignments filter to see which resources are taking longer than planned to finish their assignments.

- Use the Resource/Assignments with Overtime filter to see which resources have been assigned overtime work.

→ For a complete list of the built-in filters and how to use them, **see** Chapter 11, "Using Standard Views, Tables, Filters, and Groups to Review Your Schedule," **p. 369**.

→ For instruction on creating your own custom filters, **see** Chapter 22, "Customizing Views, Tables, Filters, Groups, and Fields," **p. 755**.

NOTE

> You can apply filters only to full-screen views or views that are in the top pane of a combination view. The bottom pane views are already filtered for the task or resource that is selected in the top pane. Thus, you cannot apply filters to views in the bottom pane.

You can apply a filter with the menu or by using the Filter button on the Formatting toolbar. If you want to apply the filter as a highlight filter, you must use the menu. For example, if you want to display only material resources in a resource view, you would follow these steps:

1. Display one of the resource views that has a table of resources in the top pane.
2. Click the Filter tool to display the drop-down list of resource filters, and then click Resources – Material.

Alternatively, you can choose Project, Filtered For to display the Filter menu, and then click Resources – Material.

No matter which method you use, Project hides everything but the resources that have Material in the resource's Type field.

TIP

> To use a filter that is on the menu as a highlight filter, simply hold down the Shift key as you select the menu choices, and Project highlights the filtered (selected) records without hiding the other records.

TIP

> If you have applied a filter and then made changes that might alter which resources are selected by the filter, use Ctrl+F3 to reapply the filter.

CONSULTANTS' TIPS

Make sure you have a solid understanding of resource types and apply those accordingly in your project schedule. The new cost resource adds another dimension to the capabilities of Project 2007 and improves your ability to model an accurate project. You should become very comfortable with it and the other resource types. Learn how to use them in the right context to improve your accuracy in predicting time and cost.

Use the new feature of Budget resource type to include your capital project budget, if you have one that you must maintain and meet. Even though you will baseline your project to capture your planned values, the Budget resource can help you maintain a comparison value to compare to your baseline, ensuring that you did not exceed it in your planning. This feature also becomes important if your planned budget is less than your capital budget, in which case you may have a budget reserve that you can use later in the tracking phase if the project begins to slip.

Keep the resource calendars and availability contouring simple. As you have seen, Microsoft Project 2007 has tremendous capability to model resources. Only use the data fields required, remember any data included needs to be maintained. For example, if you create a separate resource calendar for a resource, you will need to maintain it throughout the life of the project so make sure that it is going to be worthwhile to do that. Contouring is an effective way to model and predict resource usage but it can be difficult to maintain the precision and accuracy in a real-world project. Keep the level of detail appropriate to the accuracy required for your project.

Use the resource availability from date to indicate when the resource became available to your project. This can give you time-phased staffing levels and eliminate confusion when looking back at how resources were applied to your project.

8

UNDERSTANDING WORK FORMULA BASICS

In this chapter

MICROSOFT PROJECT AS A SCHEDULE MODELING TOOL

Welcome to the most critical chapter in this book. If you read nothing else in this book, you should read this chapter and at the very least, this introduction.

Microsoft Project is a scheduling engine. A scheduling engine is a tool that helps you "model" the actions you need to perform to achieve a goal. This "model" allows you to plan actions prior to making them. Planning is important for understanding ALL of what must be done and WHEN it must be done, but once you begin the process of fulfilling the plan, the "model" underneath must be able to adjust when real life collides with the beautiful vision of 'what will happen'; otherwise, the plan will be useless immediately.

Project models the actions you need to perform (i.e. 'tasks', sometimes called 'activities'). Each 'task' can be performed by one person or many. One person's contribution to the fulfillment of a 'task' is called an 'assignment.' Microsoft Project must correctly model the different kinds of 'assignments' a person may be asked to do AND how a set of 'assignments' contributes to the achievement of a 'task.'

This is the foundation of Microsoft Project. On the foundation is built layer upon layer of further logic to handle additional needs. Think of it as an inverted pyramid. Knowledge of the bottom-most level is a key component to understanding all of the higher levels. The pyramid has the following levels and each higher level requires another layer of 'modeling' logic to be provided by Project (see Figure 9.1):

- Program: The impact of projects on each other.
- Project: The impact of tasks upon each other.
- Task: How the set of individual resource contributions (assignments) interplay to achieve an activity (or action) to be performed.
- Assignment: How one person fulfills on their portion or contribution to the achievement of a task. For purposes of this discussion, assignments will be performed only by people and no other resource type (material, cost, or budget).

This is the simple list… Real life supplies other things that impact this pure pyramid. Things like individual resource work calendars, the impact of a person working on multiple tasks at the same time, the impact of changing resources mid-stream and the loss of productivity while the new person gains familiarity with the 'task,' the delays that are part of the 'task' itself (observing the moon can only happen at night), and many other things.

Microsoft Project models all these things, but the first thing that must be understood, the base of the inverted pyramid upon which all else is built, is the 'assignment'—a single person's contribution to the completion of a task. In everyday real life, many things impact how the performed assignments are achieved. Modeling this is the real purpose of the 'Work Formula' and it is not as simple as one might at first think.

Figure 9.1
The inverted pyramid represents the levels of modeling logic involved in achieving a realistic output, your project schedule.

The formula itself is Work = Duration * Units. If a resource works for 5 days at 100% of their 8 work hours per day, then they have an assignment that will be completed in 40 hours. 5 days * (100% of 8 hrs/day) = 40 hours of effort. Simple. The formula also reflects that if a resource works 125% of their workday (or 10 hours), then they would work 50 hours. But remember, Project at this level is modeling the activity that must be completed (the result of the effort), not the effort to achieve it. The result of the effort is the Work to be performed where 'Work' is used as a noun; or call it the 'job.' So if it would take a resource 40 hours to complete the assignment and the resource chooses to work 10 hrs per day, those two values (units and work) are held constant and the third one (duration) is solved for by the formula. Used this way, the 'activity' is correctly modeled as having a duration of 4 days instead of 5 days. This is an example of how the formula is used. Two of the 3 variables are held constant and the formula is used to 'solve' for the third.

The next level up in the pyramid is about how multiple assignments (multiple resources) work together to achieve the task, which again comes down to the type of work the task is intended to model. It could be that the task is 'eat a 100 foot long hotdog,' the more people you add to the task, the faster the hotdog is eaten. Or it could be that the task is like a meeting, no matter how many people you put on it, they are all still there for the hour-long duration of the meeting, so the work effort grows with each person added. All of this is modeled in project. Real life continues to impact this scenario through the scheduling of the work produced over time. The meeting lasts longer if you break for lunch in the middle. The hotdog takes longer to eat if you only have the people available on lunch hour or if some of the people can only stay for 10 minutes, but others can stay for an hour.

The next level up in the inverted pyramid represents the modeling of the impact tasks have on each other. The hotdog must be cooked before it can be eaten. The meeting attendees must read the document that is the topic of the meeting prior to having the meeting, and so on.

The program level adds additional modeling complexity in regards to rollups, prioritization, external links, program phases, cross program leveling, and so on.

For the purposes of this chapter, the levels are referred to as the 'assignment level,' 'task level,' and 'project level.' Duration, Units, and Work are the three key 'variables' in the formula. The results of the formula are used by higher modeling layers in the inverted pyramid and when all of this is applied to a schedule, additional Real Life impacts come into play as well (resource calendars and availability, learning curves, and so on). These Real Life impacts here are called 'schedule modifiers,' as they modify how the result of the formula is applied to a calendar.

This is an introduction to the complexity that Microsoft Project must model. The rest of this chapter will drill into each of these areas again and provide more depth.

UNDERSTANDING RESOURCE AND TASK ASSIGNMENTS

This chapter and Chapter 10, "Scheduling Single and Multiple Resource Assignments," are the key components in the Microsoft Project scheduling engine, or as one consultant put it, "This is where the rubber hits the road." This chapter will help you will gain an understanding of the background behind resource scheduling and the calculations that Project makes when you assign one or more resources to a task. You will also look at the Work Formula and the behavior that the combination of task types (from Chapter 8, "Defining Project Resources") and the Work Formula drive. Microsoft Project will be making calculations while you are editing resource assignments. Not understanding why it is making the changes that it makes may cause frustration as even minor changes may have a much larger impact than you ever expected. This chapter will help you understand why Microsoft Project makes those changes and how to interpret and even predict those changes, thus preventing frustration and getting the outcome you expect.

TIP

> The majority of this chapter will discuss the Work Formula. It is made up of three basic variables: the *duration* of a task (D), the amount of effort or *work* (W) that will be required, and the amount of resources or *units* (U) that will perform the work. It is important to understand that you can control *two* of the three variables; the remaining variable will be calculated by the Work Formula. Understanding this fundamental principle will make the rest of this chapter much easier to understand and your scheduling efforts much less frustrating.

In Chapter 10, you will see how the basic formula adapts for single-resource or multiple-resource assignments, complex calendar requirements, and the specific scheduling requirements of your project.

You will also learn how the task types affect the Work Formula. To understand the Work Formula, you must have a strong grasp of the different task types and understand their relationship and how they work together.

→ For information on task relationships, **see** Chapter 7, "Defining Task Logic," **p. 197**.

REVIEWING THE ESSENTIAL COMPONENTS OF WORK RESOURCE ASSIGNMENTS

A work resource is anyone or anything that does "work," such as an employee or the backhoe that the employee is using. When a work resource is assigned to a task, Project will complete the work formula and schedule the resource for a specific time period, based on the dates that were established when the task was entered into the schedule. The time period is determined by a variety of factors, including calendars, task types, preset start and finish dates, duration, work, and links to other tasks.

When you are assigning resources to tasks, you must keep several key factors in mind. Each of these factors is discussed in more detail in other sections of the book. See the "Schedule Modifiers That Affect the Complexity of the Scheduling Engine" section for the list of schedule modifiers that influence the behavior of the Work Formula.

After work resources have been assigned to tasks, Project will calculate the schedule assignment, taking into consideration the schedule modifiers listed in the section, "Schedule Modifiers That Affect the Complexity of the Scheduling Engine." This schedule can then be modified to suit any specific requirements or needs you might have. You can adjust it in a variety of ways, as will be discussed in more detail in Chapter 10.

UNDERSTANDING THE RESOURCE ASSIGNMENT FIELDS

When a resource is assigned to a task, you must, at the very least, identify the resource; Project will provide default values for the other essential assignment fields. You can also assign the number of resource units to the task and the amount of work that the assignment will require. Figure 9.2 shows where the fields are to enter this information.

Figure 9.2

The bottom pane of the combination Gantt Chart view allows you to enter multiple resources and various resource assignment attributes.

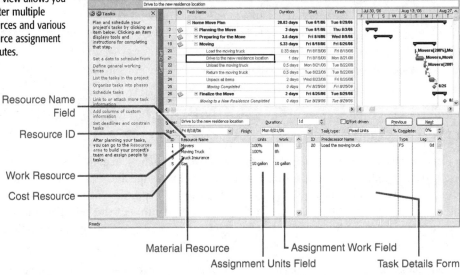

Resource Name Field

Resource ID

Work Resource

Cost Resource

Material Resource

Assignment Units Field

Assignment Work Field

Task Details Form

ASSIGNING A RESOURCE TO A TASK

In order to assign a resource to a task, you have to identify the resource by either its name or its ID number. In most cases, the Resource Name field has a drop-down list of the names that have already been defined in the resource sheet. You can also add a new resource name, and Project will add that name to the resource sheet as it assigns the name to the task.

CAUTION

As mentioned in Chapter 8, you should have Project alert you before a new name is added to the resource sheet. This will prevent the name from being mistyped. If you do enter a resource that is mistyped, Project will create a new variation of the same resource in the sheet, but with a different spelling. This can cause the workload of the correctly spelled resource to be misrepresented because it does not include the assignments incorrectly given to the misspelled resource.

→ For details on how to change the option for Project to automatically add new resources, **see** "Setting the Automatically Add New Resources and Tasks Option," **p. 271**.

UNDERSTANDING THE ASSIGNMENT UNITS FIELD

Assignment units, often simply labeled *Units*, define how much of a resource is assigned to an individual task. The Assignment Units field can be seen in Figure 9.2.

Project will show units for work resources in both the Max Units and Assignment Units fields as percentages, but these can be changed to a decimal format. While the percentage format can be advantageous when assigning individual people resources, it becomes very confusing when you are working with group resources.

→ For additional information on group resources, **see** Chapter 8, "Defining Project Resources," **p. 249**.

To select the format for the resource Units field, perform the following actions:

1. In the main menu, choose Tools, Options, and then the Schedule tab.
2. In the Show Assignment Units as A field, select Decimal or Percentage.
3. This setting will affect the display for all work resources.

The easiest way to understand how to assign work resources is to think about the way you spend your day. If Jenny, the graphic artist, is needed all day working on one project, you need to set her Assignment Units field at 100%, so Project will schedule her for 100% of her time. If Dan, the attorney, is only needed for part of the day, to review the contracts, then set his Assignment Units field at 10%, since he will probably spend the rest of his day working on other assignments. When using named resources such as people, it is easy to think in percentages of their days.

If, however, you are working with several named resources, such as a group of computer programmers or a fleet of delivery trucks, then it is often more intuitive and logical to use the decimal point format in the Assignment Units field. Instead of using 500% to represent the five computer programmers you have working on a project, it makes more sense to use 5.0 in the decimal format, or instead of having 1600% of your truck fleet working, you have 16.0 trucks on the road. The flip side to this is that it does not make sense to have Dan the attorney working .25 units, while instead it is much more intuitive for him to be working 25% of his day on something. Just use your logical judgment when deciding whether to use the decimal or the percentage format.

Using the percentage format, however, helps to explain the way that Project uses the Assignment Units field. Project uses this field to calculate how many hours of work it will schedule for the resource per hour of working time on the calendar. For instance, if you have two mechanics, Scott and Mike, but they are set up as one work resource, you expect 1 hour of effort from each of them during every hour of time they spend on the project. And that is what happens if you assign units equal to 200%; Project will assign 2 hours of effort for every hour of working time on the calendar until the task is complete.

NOTE
You can also contour the work to assign a resource to exact expectations of actual work in a given day or work period. Resource contours are discussed in more detail later in this chapter.

NOTE
Percent Allocation is a time-phased field and can be viewed in the task or resource usage views.

When using a work resource that is actually a team of individuals—such as a group of computer programmers or several drivers for your fleet of trucks—you must remember that a 100% entry into the Assignment Units field will not represent all of your individuals. Project will only schedule 1 hour of effort for every hour of working time on the calendar until the task is complete. If there are five individuals on your team, you must enter 500% into the Assignment Units field to represent all five of them. A 500% entry will tell Project to schedule 5 hours of effort for every 1 hour of working time on the calendar, until the task is complete.

NOTE

For the purpose of this chapter, it is important to remember that units can be assigned in percentages of any amount.

→ For additional details on assigning multiple resources, **see** Chapter 10, "Scheduling Single and Multiple Resource Assignments," **p. 313**.

NOTE

Remember that Project will take any entry into the Assignment Units field and schedule it down to the minute across the specified or calculated duration. If you were to enter 25%, it would in fact represent 2 hours out of an 8-hour workday. However, Project will schedule 15 minutes for work for each hour in the 8 hour day, which will total 2 hours. In most cases, the resource, or employee, will realistically sit down and complete all the work in 2 hours, in one sitting, rather then working for just 15 minutes an hour every hour on the project. If you are only concerned about the overall time (in this case, 2 hours and not the exact amount of time the resource is actually spending during each hour), you can just ignore the difference between the way that Project schedules time and the way the work is actually performed. If you want the schedule to reflect that the resource worked full time for 2 hours continuously and then was idle for the rest of the task, you can enter the Assignment Units field at 100% and then change the duration to .25 days.

The default Units value for work resources is usually 100% (or 1.0 in the decimal format). However, if the Max Units value is set at less then 100%, the default Units value will reflect that change. You can set the Max Units number at anything between 0% and 6,000,000,000% (or 0.0 to 60,000,000 in the decimal format).

NOTE

When assigning a resource to a task, Project sets the assignment units to the lesser of the value of the Max Units for the resource or 100% unless you set the units value. Project does not enforce a maximum number of available units when you make resource assignments. You can assign more units than the Max Units value when you are planning a project. When the maximum units for any resource is exceeded within any duration unit, you will get an overallocated special indicator for those resource names in the Resource Sheet or the Resource Usage view.

> **NOTE**
>
> You can enter fractions of a percentage into the Assignment Units field, but they will automatically be rounded up to the nearest whole number. Project will use fractional percents in the calculations, but it will not display them.

Material resources are always formatted as a decimal. If you miss entering the assigned units, it will default to 1, followed by the material label defined for the resource. If you defined the material resource of dirt with the Yd label (for cubic yard), then the default units supplied by Project will be 1 Yd, which means the task will consume 1 cubic yard of dirt.

When you enter a numeral into the Units column for a material resource, it is called a *fixed consumption rate*. The amount is considered to be fixed and independent of the task duration. Using our current example, Project figures 1 yard of material for the task, and if the task duration changes, the consumption rate will not.

> **NOTE**
>
> If you enter something that Project does not understand, such as **yards** instead of **Yd**, it will show you the warning (see Figure 9.3). This warning is to let you know that what you entered is not a valid Units value. Simply enter a numeric value and let Project provide the correct label.

Figure 9.3
Click OK in the warning window and let Project figure out the units for the selected resource.

If you want to assign material resource units that have a variable consumption rate, where the amount of material resource depends on the duration of the task, then you simply enter the units, followed by a forward slash (/). For instance, if you have a backhoe that uses 10 gallons of gas an hour, you can enter either **10/h** or **10 gal/h**. Project will then calculate the consumption of 10 gallons of fuel per hour for every hour of working time on the calendar until the task is complete.

ASSIGNING THE WORK

Work resources spend hours of time working on a task, and you can measure their contribution in hours, days, or some other kind of time unit. It is this unit of the work resources that gives a task duration in the first place as well as the time it takes to finish the work on a task. In fact, when you estimate the duration of a task, you should be thinking about how long it will take the work resource to complete the work, or how long it takes an employee to do a task. Material resources do not expend effort, however; they are simply used up by a task.

That is why you measure them as units consumed. While both work and material resources are displayed in the Work field, Project ignores values for material resources and just calculates the hours for the work resources when figuring total work.

In the case of work resources, the term *work*, sometimes called *effort*, measures the time required by a resource on a task. Project displays work in hours, by default, but you can change the default to any standard time unit, such as minutes, days, weeks, or months. To change the time unit used to display work, follow these steps:

1. In the top navigation menu, choose Tools, Options.
2. Click the Schedule tab and select the time unit in the Work is entered in list box.

Work can be entered by the user, but Project will complete it automatically when a resource is assigned if nothing is entered. You can also enter work by using any time unit, regardless of the unit used to display work, as long as you follow your entry with the time unit label.

If a work resource is scheduled for full time on a task that has a duration of 1 week, then that resource is assigned for 40 hours of work. However, if the resource is assigned to the task only half time (that is, Units is equal to 50%), then it is assigned to 20 hours of work during the week. If two resource units work full time all week (or 200%), then there are 80 hours of work or effort. Other things being equal, the following will hold true:

- The longer the duration of the task, the more work is scheduled.
- The larger the resource units assigned, the more work is scheduled.

The amount of work that Project schedules for the resource is tied to the duration of the task and the number of units assigned to the task. This relationship is defined more precisely in the next section, "Understanding the Work Formula."

In the case of material resources, the Work field shows the total number of physical units consumed in completing the task. If you enter the units, Project will complete the work units for you. For fixed-rate consumption assignments, the Work field acts the same as the Units field. If you assign 10 gallons (10 gal) of fuel, the Work field will show 10 gallons. If you assign 10 gallons per day (10 gal/d), however, Project will calculate 50 gallons in the Work field for a week-long task.

ASSIGNING THE DURATION

The Duration field that Project uses in the scheduling engine refers to the duration of an assignment as the number of days covered by spreading the Work from the Start date forward across the available work hours *as determined by the combined Project, Resource, and Task calendars.*

NOTE

> Note that this calculation does NOT include the Finish date!

The Finish date is calculated on an assignment basis by spreading the work from the Start date forward across the available work hours *as determined by the Hours per day setting* (select Tools, Options, Calendar tab). The Gantt bar always displays Start date to Finish Date.

Task level Duration and Finish fields are calculated from merging the assignment day coverage (using Start and Duration fields) and the latest assignment Finish date.

The Duration calculation at the Task level is based on the set of assignments for the Task. If there are no assignments, then, for the purpose of calculating duration field only, a single assignment will be assumed (using 100% units and the Project and Task Calendars).

The fact that Finish date is calculated using a different duration calculation can lead to confusion, see the section, "Difference Between Calendar Duration and the Actual Assignment Duration" under the "Consultants' Tips."

UNDERSTANDING THE WORK FORMULA

The work formula consists of three variables: Work, Duration, and Units. One variable is fixed based on the task type, one variable is a fixed constant based on user input, the free ranging variable (remaining variable) will be calculated by Project using the work formula.

The calculating formula works as follows:

Duration × Units = Work

In symbols, it is represented like this:

$D \times U = W$

You multiply the task duration (D) by the assigned units (U) to calculate work (W).

> **NOTE**
>
> These formulas do not apply to material resources that have fixed consumption rates. For those resources, the value in the Work field is identical to the value in the Units field. The formulas do apply, however, to resources with variable consumption rates. These formulas were developed and implemented before the material resource type was introduced, and so the following makes more sense if you think in terms of work resources.

Simple algebra can be used to reformulate this equation to calculate values for Duration when Work and Units are given:

Duration = Work / Units *or* D = W / U

The same applies to when Duration and Work are given, and you need to calculate Units:

Units = Work / Duration *or* U = W / D

> **NOTE**
>
> Even though duration can be displayed in minutes, hours, days, weeks, or months, Project will convert the duration to minutes when calculating work and then display it in the default units for work, which is usually the hour.

Project uses assignment units as a multiplier to calculate how work must be scheduled, and understanding this formula is very important and can save you a headache down the road.

An example of this formula works like this: If you assign two movers (200%) to work on a task with a duration of 4 hours, Project will schedule 2 hours of work for each of the four hours duration; total work equals 8 hours.

APPLYING THE WORK FORMULA IN NEW ASSIGNMENTS

Before you assign resources to a task, the task has duration (1 day by default or entered value) but usually does not have a work value unless entered, because in the Work Formula, Units = 0, and therefore Work = 0. When you create the resource assignments, Project calculates the work and sums that value into the task's Work field. In some cases, the work called for in an assignment cannot be completed within the initial duration estimate for the task, and Project might have to change the task duration to accommodate the needs of the assignments. If the task has multiple resources assigned and some of those assignments take longer to complete than others, the task duration is calculated to be at least as long as the longest assignment. However, if the task is a fixed-duration task, Project cannot recalculate the duration. See "Setting the Task Type," later in this chapter, for more information on this topic.

To help you understand how Project calculates the changes brought about by assigning resources, the simplest case will be examined first, where you assign a single resource in an initial task. Subsequently, Project's response to changes in existing assignments will be explored.

It is best to experiment with each of the three different cases in order to have a better understanding of how the Work Formula operates. Remember, the better grasp you have of this information, the easier it will be later on.

1. In the top navigation menu, select View and then select Gantt Chart view.
2. In the top navigation menu, select the Window, Split command to display the Task Form view in the bottom pane.
3. Right-click the Task Form view and choose Resources and Predecessors from the Detail list.
4. The Assignment Units and Work fields appear next to the resource name in the resource details (see Figure 9.4).
5. Enter different values for units and work until you feel comfortable predicting the outcome when you create an assignment.

In order for the Work Formula to operate properly, Project defaults all new task durations to 1 day. The duration for a task is already defined before you assign the first resource to the task. Thus, task duration is already established. Project handles your entries when assigning the initial resource slightly differently for work and material resources, so they need to be considered separately.

Figure 9.4
Customizing and combining views allows you to maximize the use of the screen and see exactly the fields you need.

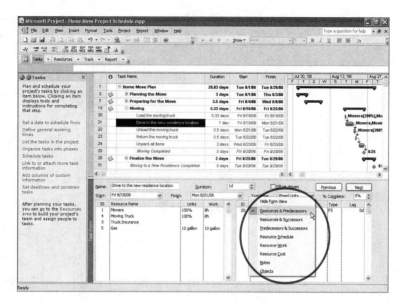

9

The following examples show what happens for an initial assignment of a work resource. The distinctions are based on task type and which fields you fill in: Units only, Work only, or both Units and Work. Each example assumes that the task has a duration of 1 day and that days and weeks are defined to be 8 hours and 40 hours, respectively. It is also assumed that the task type used is fixed units. To verify your settings and ensure that they meet the assumptions described here, follow these steps:

1. View the calendar options by selecting Tools, Options, Calendar tab.

2. In the Calendar tab, verify the Hours per day, Hours per week, Days per month settings.

3. Click OK to close the Options dialog box.

There is more information on other task types later in the chapter.

Project will respond to entries when creating a work resource assignment as follows:

If you enter the resource name when creating the assignment and do not provide the values for Units or Work, Project will assume that you want the default units (the lesser of Max Units or 100%) and will calculate the work from the duration and units. For example, if you assign a work resource to a 1-day task without specifying the units, Project supplies 100% to the Units field and calculates 8 hours for the Work field (see Figure 9.5).

Figure 9.5
Duration × Units =
Work. Therefore,
8h × 100% = 8 hours.

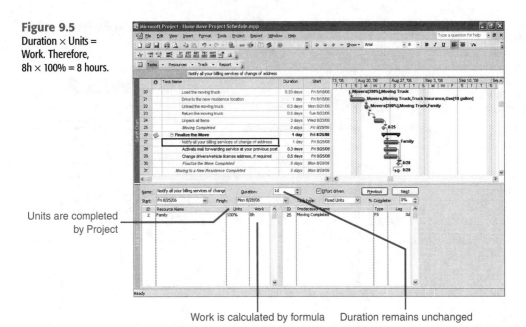

Units are completed by Project

Work is calculated by formula   Duration remains unchanged

If you enter the Units value, Project uses that value with the duration to calculate the work. For example, if you assign a resource to a 1-day task and enter **50%** in the Units field, Project calculates the work (see Figure 9.6).

Figure 9.6
Duration × Units =
Work. Therefore,
8h × 50% = 4 hours.

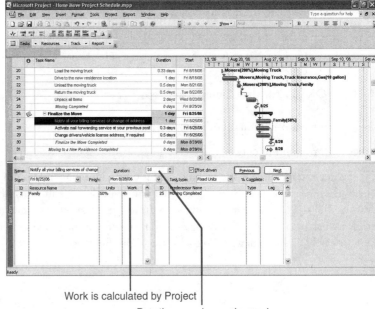

Work is calculated by Project
Duration remains unchanged

The task duration, however, is still 1 day.

If you enter the Work value but do not supply the units, Project assumes that you want the default units (the lesser of Max Units or 100%) and will calculate a new value for the duration, based on the specified work and the assumed value for units. For example, if you assign a resource to a 1-day task and enter **16h** in the Work field but leave the Units field blank, Project will calculate a new Duration value (see Figure 9.7) because it takes more than 1 day for a single resource unit to complete 16 hours of work.

Figure 9.7
Duration × Units = Work. Duration × 100% = 16 hours. Therefore, Duration = 16h / 100% = 16 hours (that is, 2 days).

Units are completed by Project

Duration is recalculated based on the formula

If you enter both the Units and Work values, Project recalculates the existing task duration, using the new entries. For example, if you assign Units the value **200%** and Work the value **32h**, Project calculates a new task duration by using this variation of the Work Formula (see Figure 9.8).

Figure 9.8
Duration × Units =
Work. Duration ×
200% = 32 hours.
Therefore, Duration =
32h / 200% = 16 hours
(that is, 2 days).

Duration is recalculated based on Units and Work entered

When the resource is a material resource, there are fewer alternatives to consider than with work resources. Similarly, assume that the task is a 1-day task. This time, however, the resource is the material resource Packing Peanuts, and its label is cubic feet. As you might remember for material resources, the Units field is always displayed in decimal format. Project's response to your entries when creating a material resource assignment are as follows:

- If you just enter the material resource name but do not provide either the Units value or the Work value of the assignment, Project will assume that the Units value is 1 and calculate all the work to be 1 cubic foot. For example, if you assign the Packing Peanuts resource to a 1-day task without specifying the units, Project supplies 1 cubic foot to both the Units and Work fields (see Figure 9.9).

- If you enter the Units value as a number (in other words, as a fixed consumption rate), Project enters that value into both the Units and the Work fields. For example, if you assign the Packing Boxes resource to a 1-day task and enter 30 in the Units field, Project supplies 30 boxes to both the Units and Work fields (see Figure 9.10).

Figure 9.9
Duration × Units = Work. Therefore, 1 × 1 cubic foot = 1.

Figure 9.10
Duration × Units = Work. 1 day × 30 boxes = Work. Therefore, Work = 30 boxes.

- If you enter the Units value as a variable consumption rate, Project uses that rate with the task duration to calculate the Work field. For example, if you enter **5 / h** in the Units field for gasoline, Project converts that to 5 / hour and multiplies that value by the duration (1 day, 8 hours) to calculate the Work field entry of 40 (see Figure 9.11).

Figure 9.11
Duration × Units =
Work. 1 day (8 hours)
× (5 gallons/hour) =
Work. Therefore,
Work = 8 × 5 = 40.

Work is calculated based on the consumption rate and Duration

■ If you enter the Work value of **5 lbs** for Wrapping Paper but do not supply the units, Project assumes that the amount you entered has a fixed consumption rate and puts that amount in both the Units and Work fields (see Figure 9.12).

Figure 9.12
Work / Duration =
Units. 5 lbs / 1 day =
Units. Therefore,
Units = 5 / 1 = 5 lbs.

Units are completed by Project based on the Work Formula

■ If you enter a variable consumption rate of **5/h** (5gal per hour) for gasoline in the Units field and also enter **200** in the Work field, Project recalculates the duration so that the consumption rate yields the total units in the Work field (see Figure 9.13).

Figure 9.13
Duration × Units = Work. Duration × (5gal/h) = 200. Therefore, Duration = 200 / 5 = 40 hours, which is 5 days.

Duration is recalculated based on the Units and Work provided

An advantage of using the Task Form view to create assignments is that the initial assignment can include all resources that are to be assigned to the task, and you can specify units and/or work for each assignment. Other methods of assigning resources require you to complete each assignment individually or do not let you regulate both units and work, so the Task Form view may become your preferred entry method. As you will see in Chapter 10, individually assigning multiple resources to a task creates additional variations on how Project calculates the task work and duration.

To create multiple assignments with the initial assignment, you can simply enter multiple rows in the Resource Details table before you click the OK button. Project then calculates each of the assignments individually, using the principles outlined previously and using the exiting task duration in each calculation.

For example, in Figure 9.14, two task forms are shown (select View, More Views, Task Form). The top form shows the initial assignment being created, and the bottom form shows the results after the OK button has been clicked. The task is a 0.5-day task; 2 movers assigned and 1 moving truck. The task will also consume 5 gallons per hour for gasoline.

Figure 9.14
List all your resources
first and then click the
OK button.

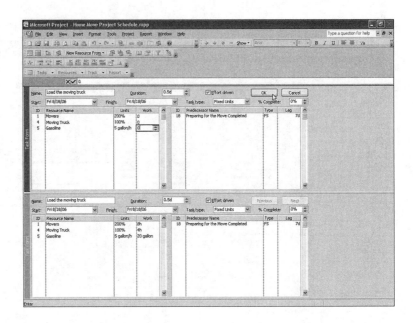

Applying the Work Formula in Changes to Existing Assignments

In the examples so far in this chapter, it may seem as though Project is free to recalculate any of the three variables in the Work Formula. However, in the next section, you will see that one of the three variables in the equation is always fixed for a task, which also means it is fixed for any assignments to that task. Project chooses not to allow you to change the fixed value when it has to recalculate the work equation for an assignment.

For example, by default, tasks are created as Fixed Units tasks, as indicated by the underline in the following formula:

$$D \times \underline{U} = W$$

If you change the duration, Project has to leave the units unchanged and must recalculate the work, or if you change the work, Project must recalculate the duration. You can define which variable is fixed for a task and is therefore fixed for all of that task's assignment calculations. This is how you control how Project responds when you make changes in assignments.

Selecting Task Settings

Now that you have a grasp of the Work Formula, this section will discuss the three types of tasks, as defined in the Task Type field: Fixed Units, Fixed Work, and Fixed Duration. Sometimes the task will fall easily into one of the three categories. Perhaps the task duration is set by the client and you must work within that timeframe. You could define the task as a Fixed Duration task to keep Project from changing the duration. Or perhaps you have a contract to provide a fixed amount of work for the client, in which case you could define the task as a Fixed Work task so Project will not change the amount of work scheduled.

NOTE

> When using the task types, remember that Fixed Units will always be Project's default type. You can change the default type in the schedule options so that any new task created uses the specified task type. To do so, select Tools, Options, Schedule Tab, and select the Default task type that you want Project to apply to all tasks.

You can make changes to the Task Type field to control how Project responds to an assignment change. If you wanted to increase the duration of a task, but keep the amount of work constant, you can make a Fixed Work task and then change the duration. Figure 9.15 provides a model for illustrating how the work formula is affected by the Task Type. The Work Formula can be thought of as a triangle with three sides: duration, units, and work. In the work formula, one variable is always fixed by the Task Type and the user has two remaining variables to modify. When a user modifies one variable by decreasing or increasing its value (lengthening or shortening one side of the triangle), Project will recalculate the free range variable that is not fixed (the free side of the triangle is resized to ensure that the triangle remains geometrically intact). This model provides an easy way to visualize the work formula as you cannot resize one side of a triangle and expect the other two sides to remain unchanged, the triangle shape will not be maintained. For example, in Figure 9.15, when you have a Fixed Duration task, the Duration side of the triangle remains unchanged and true to the original size. If the user increases the Units by lengthening the Units side of the triangle, the Work side will automatically resize to maintain the triangle shape. Similarly, when the user increases Units on a Fixed Duration type task, the Work is recalculated by Project to maintain the mathematical proportion.

Figure 9.15
Using the different task types, one variable is always fixed by the specified Task Type, the second one is specified by the user, and the third one is a free range variable that is calculated by Project based on the changes user made to the second variable.

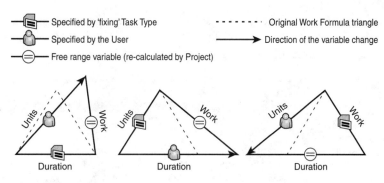

Table 9.1 helps to summarize which variable Project will recalculate when a value changes in an existing assignment. The table assumes that your initial change is an increase in the respective variables, indicated by the plus signs in the column. If your initial change is a decrease, simply reverse the plus and minus signs for the columns to the right.

The first column lists the variable that you might change, while the three columns to the right show which variable Project recalculates as a result. The plus or minus sign indicates the direction of the resulting change. An underline in the formula is used to indicate which is the fixed variable (set by the Task Type applied). This allows you to follow the logic of the changes. In the first row, an increase in Duration for a Fixed Units task leads to an increase in Work, but for a Fixed Work task, it leads to a decrease in Units.

Table 9.1 Task Type and Work Formula Calculations

Variables You Change	Variable Calculated if the Task Is Fixed Units	Variable Calculated if the Task Is Fixed Work	Variable Calculated if the Task Is Fixed Duration
+ Work	+ Duration	+ Duration	+ Units
+ Duration	+ Work	- Units	- Units
+ Units	- Duration	- Duration	+ Work
Formula:	$D \times U = W$	$D \times U = W$	$D \times U = W$

If the initial change is to the fixed variable itself, the rule is a little more complicated. Those results are underlined in the table. Remember that duration is a task variable and that units and work are assignment variables. When you change one of the assignment variables, such as Units or Work, and it is a fixed variable, then Project will leave the other assignment variables alone and change task duration. When Duration is fixed and you change it, Project leaves the assignment work unchanged and adjusts the units.

Suppose you want to force Project to calculate the number of resource units you need to assign when you know the duration of the task and the amount of work you want done. As an example, you can make the task a Fixed Duration and enter the amount of work. Project has to calculate the necessary units in order to keep the Work Formula in balance.

Setting the Task Type

You can define the task's type in the Task Information dialog box and in the Task Form view, or you can add the Task Type field to any task table. Figure 9.16 shows the Task Type field in the Task Information dialog box and on the Task Form view.

Figure 9.16
Both the Task Form view and Task Information dialog box allow you to set the task type one task at a time.

As mentioned earlier in this chapter, the default task type in Project is Fixed Units, Effort Driven. You can change the default type for new tasks in a project by selecting Tools, Options. In the Options dialog box, select the Schedule tab and set the Default Task Type field value (see Figure 9.17).

Figure 9.17
Use Default Task Type to set the task type for all tasks in your project.

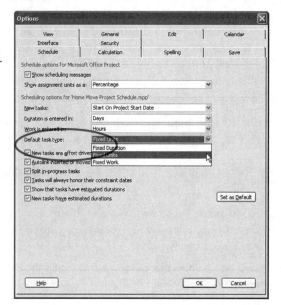

It is helpful to add the "Type" column in the Gantt Chart view for recognition of task types to understand the rules about how the Work Formula is calculated. Project will respond in the following ways when you create a new assignment for a task:

- If you enter a value in Units and leave the Work field blank, Project calculates the unknown Work, because both Units and Duration have been given values. This is true no matter what the task type.

- If you enter the value in Work and leave the Units blank, Project's calculation depends on the task type:

  If the task is not a Fixed Duration task, Project adjusts the Duration value. It assumes that the Units value is the default and calculates the Duration value that is necessary for the resource to complete the amount of work you assigned.

  However, if the task is a Fixed Duration task, Project cannot change the Duration entry and it calculates the Units needed to complete the Work value you entered and places that value in the Units Field.

- If you entered values in both the Units and Work fields, Project again bases its calculations on the task type:

  If the task is not a Fixed Duration task, Project adjusts the Duration to accommodate the Work and Units values you entered.

  If the task is a Fixed Duration task, Project keeps the Work amount you entered and calculates a new Units value that can do the specific work in a given (fixed) duration.

9

Schedule Modifiers That Affect the Complexity of the Scheduling Engine

In addition to the work formula itself, there are several schedule modifiers that affect the calculations of the scheduling engine and, therefore, the result shown in your project schedule. Schedule modifiers are additional Project functions that when used, can change the way Project schedules the tasks and assignments within your project. In addition to the function-related schedule modifiers described in this section, behavioral schedule modifiers can influence the scheduling as well. The behavioral schedule modifiers include learning curves, change of project teams, increase of the scope of work, and many others.

It is important to recognize that scheduling is driven not only by the formula, but by other constraints you define within the assignments, tasks, and project.

Project Scheduling the Resource Assignment to Start When the Task Starts

When a resource is assigned to a task, Project will always schedule that resource's work to start on the same date as the task and to continue working at a constant and uninterrupted assignment rate until all of the work is scheduled.

→ For details on advanced scheduling techniques that can be used to modify this default approach, **see** Chapter 10, "Scheduling Single and Multiple Resource Assignments," **p. 313**.

Splitting Task Assignments

A task can be interrupted by splitting the assignment; setting a no-work period for the resource in the middle of the task. For instance, if you had a construction crew digging up and fixing a section of drainage pipe, you might only need the backhoe and operator during the digging and burying parts of the task, but not while the pipe is being fixed. You could therefore split the assignment for the backhoe operator.

The splitting of task assignments affects the second tier of the inverted pyramid, the Task level, which represents the interplay of assignments within the task (refer to Figure 9.1).

→ For additional information on splitting task assignments, **see** Chapter 10, "Scheduling Single and Multiple Resource Assignments," **p. 313**.

Scheduled Delay Effects

A scheduled delay can be introduced at the start of the work for one specific resource, which will allow the other resources to start the task as scheduled. So, if a human resource is needed to inspect a product, but only toward the end of its development phase, you can schedule a delay into that human resource's schedule, so that he or she will only be assigned hours as the task reaches its end.

→ For additional information on scheduled delays, **see** Chapter 10, "Scheduling Single and Multiple Resource Assignments," **p. 313**.

LEVELING DELAY EFFECTS

Leveling Delay is a Project field that allows you to specify the amount of delay for the assignment of a resource. This field can be found in several views and windows in Project. For example, you can see it within the Task Entry view (select Views, More Views, Task Entry, right click in the bottom part of the split view, the Task Form, and select Resource Schedule).

If the schedule has an *overallocated* resource, meaning that there are more units of the resource assigned to the task than the maximum units of resources available, you can add a *leveling delay*. This is a delay similar to the scheduled delay mentioned previously, but serves a different purpose. A scheduled delay will likely remain indefinitely; that's the way the task should normally be scheduled. A leveling delay might become unnecessary if there are other ways to eliminate the overallocation—for example, if another resource is substituted for the overallocated resource to reduce the workload and eliminate the overallocation.

Leveling delay is a way for you to postpone the start of the assignment for a particular resource on a task and to create a model that is closer to the real-life scenarios that fit into this model. For example, if you have Task A and you assign Jim and Karen to it, Task A is scheduled to start on 12/4/2006 and to last for 5 days. You know that Jim will be unavailable to begin working on it until 12/5/2006 because he is tied up on another project. In this case, you can schedule a leveling delay of 1 day for Jim, allowing him to begin his assignment on 12/5 when he is available, instead of overallocating him by double-booking his time on 12/4.

NOTE

> The Leveling Delay field is used by Project when the automatic leveling function is run by the user (select Tools, Level Resources). In this case, if you have manually entered a value in the Leveling Delay field, it will get overwritten by Project. However, if you do not use the built-in Project leveling feature and level your resources manually instead, the Leveling Delay field can be used with no problems.

The consequences of scheduling a leveling delay are that the assignment will not begin when originally planned and that duration may increase if the resource with the leveling delay is the driver resource. In this case, it will cause the task to slip.

The leveling delay schedule modifier affects the scheduling engine at the second level of the inverted pyramid, the Task level, that represents the interplay of assignments within the task (refer to Figure 9.1).

It is important to remember the effects the leveling delay has on scheduling when you add it to resources within your project.

→ For additional information on resource overallocation and leveling delays, **see** Chapter 25, "Resolving Resource Allocaton Problems," **p. 885**.

Work Contour Effects

Work contours are pre-defined patterns for scheduling work that is spread over the duration of the assignment. Work contours allow you to distribute the work based on the pattern in which the work will be done. You can contour the work assigned to each period of the task manually, overwriting the default flat distribution of the work that is normally scheduled. This will create a period of high activity and another period of low activity for the task during the assignment. If you needed someone to work on a task, for instance, but only need him or her to work part time during the first 2 weeks and full time during the second 2 weeks, you could use this option.

You can also use Project's predefined work contours (distribution of work on a task), which will automatically change the amount of work assigned to different times of the task. For instance, you could use the *front-loaded* contour to schedule full-time work at the beginning of the task, which will then contour down to part time as the task wraps up.

Work contours help accommodate scenarios where the amount of work done on a task is not constant throughout the duration of the task. For example, if you have resources transitioning from one task to another, the transition may not be as clean as finishing the first task and then beginning to work on the second one. In many real-life cases, the resource will start on the second task, coming up to speed and getting familiar with the task, while still finishing the last touches on the first task. Another scenario may be that you have tasks that are more labor intensive in the beginning than at the end. For example, you may have a developer working on a piece of code, so he or she will spend a lot of time in the beginning designing the code architecture and writing the code, and less time at the end, which involves fixing some minor bugs and other code maintenance.

Work contours affect the scheduling engine at the first level of the inverted pyramid, at the individual task assignment (refer to Figure 9.1).

It is important to remember the effects work contours have on the resource assignments within your schedule to ensure that the scheduling model you are trying to portray is indeed the correct one.

→ For additional information about work contours, **see** Chapter 10, "Scheduling Single and Multiple Resource Assignments," **p. 313**.

Resource Availability Effects

Resource availability is defined by the percentage of time (or units) a resource is available to be scheduled for work. Resource availability is impacted by the calendars (project, task, and resource). The remaining resource availability is influenced by the interplay of projects within the organization, where the remaining availability is equal to total availability minus the work already assigned to that resource on other projects or tasks.

A resource may be unavailable because he or she has requested vacation during the week that you want to assign them to your project for work. Or a resource may be unavailable because he or she is working full time on another project in your organization. If you do not take into consideration this schedule modifier, you may schedule a resource to work on a task when he or she is unavailable, therefore, delaying the planned start of the task, and potentially, your entire project.

You must be aware of this schedule modifier when scheduling the work in your project as it will affect the scheduling level starting at the Task level and up, all the way to the Program (refer to Figure 9.1).

→ For additional information about the resource availability and how it affects the scheduling within your project, **see** Chapter 10, "Scheduling Single and Multiple Resource Assignments," on **p. 313**.

CALENDARS EFFECTS

Project contains three types of calendars: Project, Task, and Resource. Each of these calendars is used to define the standard working times specific to the project, a task, or a resource. Calendars are also used to define any exceptions that may influence how the work is scheduled within your project. For example, if resources will work four 10-hour days (Monday through Thursday) on your project each week, you must modify the Project calendar to reflect the change. Otherwise, Project will schedule the tasks to get executed Monday through Friday, which are the default working times. This can in turn affect the duration of tasks and the completion date for your assignments, tasks, and your project.

Project will only schedule work during the dates and times that are identified as working time according to the project's and resource's calendar. In other words, it will not schedule work during weekends, vacations, or any other time that has been marked as nonworking on the project or resource calendar. This means that the assignment will change to show the available working times according to the schedule.

When a task calendar is attached to the task, Project will, by default, only schedule work during times that are working times for both the task calendar and the resource calendar. You can, however, disregard the resource calendar and simply schedule work for the resource whenever the task is scheduled. Be cautious when you choose to ignore the resource calendar and schedule the work based on the task calendar, as you may be ignoring important exceptions to the availability of the resource.

The amount of work scheduled for any given day is the number of working hours as defined for that day by the relevant calendar, multiplied by the number of resource units assigned to the task. Therefore, if you have two resources scheduled for 8 hours that day, the total amount of work is 16 hours.

Calendars affect the scheduling engine at each level of the inverted pyramid and it is important to keep them in mind when creating your project schedule.

→ For additional information about calendars, **see** Chapter 5, "Setting Up Project for Your Use," on **p. 107**.

EFFORT-DRIVEN TASKS EFFECTS

An effort-driven task is a special type of task that allows you to have fixed work on a task, when you assign additional resources to it, so the work on the task becomes shared (distributed) between the resources. As a matter of fact, effort-driven means that the task is fixed work type. For instance, if you have two movers unloading a moving truck, the original assignment is for 200% units (two people); however, if you changed that to 400% (add two more movers), then because the work is fixed, Project will cut the duration in half.

The effort-driven option for tasks also modifies the work formula because in addition to having one variable fixed by the Task Type, work is now fixed because the task is effort-driven.

The effort-driven option affects the scheduling engine at the Task level, represented by the interplay of assignments within that task.

→ For additional information about effort-driven tasks, **see** Chapter 10, "Scheduling Single and Multiple Resource Assignments," on **p. 313**.

EFFECTS OF USING DRIVER RESOURCES

Driver resources are the resources whose assignment(s) drive the task end date. In some cases, you may have multiple resources assigned to a task, which do not begin the work on the task at the same time. The resources whose assignments last until the end of the task, determining the task end date, are referred to as the driver resources. Because driver resources have direct impact on the task end date, it is important to take them into consideration when creating your project schedule.

Driver resources affect the scheduling engine at the Task level of the inverted pyramid (refer to Figure 9.1).

→ For additional information about driver resources, **see** Chapter 10, "Scheduling Single and Multiple Resource Assignments," on **p. 313**.

CONSULTANTS' TIPS

WORK FORMULA FACTORS

The Work Formula consists of three variables: the duration of a task (D), the amount of effort or work (W) that will be required, and the amount of resources or units (U) that will perform the work. It is important to remember that you can control two out of the three variables; the remaining, free range variable, gets calculated by the Work Formula. Remember that in addition to the Work Formula, Project's scheduling engine contains many different schedule modifiers that also affect the way your project is scheduled. The modifiers include: work contours, leveling delays, scheduled delays, resource availability, calendars, task types, effort-driven assignments, and many others.

80/20: USING TASK TYPES

Remember to change the Project default task type of Fixed Units, Effort Driven when scheduling tasks within your project, if you have different constraints. If the amount of work you schedule on a task cannot be changed, then you may want to set the task type to be Fixed Work. Similarly, if your duration cannot be changed due to the project requirements, then using the Fixed Duration task type will work best for you.

Determine and set the default options for your project before creating tasks.

Use standard naming conventions for task names to make it easier to set/check task types. You can use "Meeting" in tasks and ensure the task type is set to Fixed Duration and NOT effort driven. Or use "SS" as a suffix for "Steady State" tasks.

Use Fixed Units NOT effort driven for "Steady State" type tasks. Those tasks that you want to retain a fixed assignment level for the duration of the task. You may want a "Project Management" task and assign a Project Manager at 25%. Based on the actual work rate the duration will expand or contract and will need to be adjusted.

Analyze the real-life constraints that have the affect on your schedule and configure your Project schedule accordingly to closer mimic the real-life work scenarios. When getting used to working with the Work Formula, it is a good idea to use the split screen option that was described earlier in this chapter. Apply one change at a time (to work, unit, or duration as appropriate) and watch how it changes your schedule until you have mastered the formula.

80/20: USING EFFORT-DRIVEN TASK TYPE

Remember that effort-driven means that the work you assign to the task is shared (or distributed) between the resources on that task. Set this option for tasks where resources truly share the work and the task gets completed faster if more resources are assigned. Also remember that the effort-driven setting changes the operation of the work formula, but only when you change the task's assigned units by adding or removing a resource.

DIFFERENCE BETWEEN CALENDAR DURATION AND THE ACTUAL ASSIGNMENT DURATION

You may run into a scenario where the task duration in the Duration field of the Gantt Chart view may not match the duration of the Gantt bar for that task. This situation is possible if your Project or Task calendar working times do not match your default Hours per day (set under Tools, Options, Calendar tab, Hours per day). If you make a change in the Project calendar, remember to make the change in the Hours per day option under Tools, Options, Calendar tab, and visa versa.

For example, in a project using the Standard Project Calendar (working times of Monday through Friday, 8 hours per day) and the default Hours per day option (8 hours per day) do the following:

1. Create a task (Fixed Units type is the default), do not assign a resource to it, and enter 10 days in the Duration field.
2. Modify the Hours per day to 20 (select Tools, Options, Calendar tab) and make no changes to the Project Calendar.

The Duration field changes to show 4 days because that is how long it would take to complete the assignment using the 20 hours per day now set in the Hours per day field on the options dialog box.

The Gantt bar duration still shows 10 days because it uses work settings from the Project calendar which have not changed and are still based on 8 hours per work day. Also note that the Finish field will show the same finish date as the Gantt bar because it uses the same calculation as the Gantt bar. This means that when you are dealing with task or assignment duration you should focus on Task Start + Duration, rather than involving the Finish field.

Summary tasks will maintain the inconsistency with the Gantt bar length being calculated from the earliest start to the latest finish while the Duration field on the Summary line reflects the merged durations as calculated from Task Start + Duration.

9

SCHEDULING SINGLE AND MULTIPLE RESOURCE ASSIGNMENTS

In this chapter

In Chapter 7, you learned how to create tasks. In Chapter 8, you learned how to create resources. In Chapter 9, the Work Formula was introduced. In this chapter, you will learn how to combine resources and tasks using the work formula to create assignments that make sense for your project.

In essence, you have no real "work" to model until you have something that needs to be done (a task) assigned to one or more people who will do the work (resources). Work just does not exist without this mapping. In other words, the basic Work Formula that you learned in Chapter 9 does not apply until you have created an Assignment. This chapter is all about creating those Assignments and mapping the tasks and/or activities (that you need to complete) with the resources (that will accomplish them).

The chapter itself is organized in four broad groupings:

- First you will be introduced to the screens and views that allow you to map resources to tasks. The different areas/mechanisms through which Assignments are created and maintained are highlighted.

- The second grouping focuses on initial creation of the Assignments, first looking at the simplest case (one resource to one task) and then looking at the differences when mapping multiple resources to a task.

- The third grouping in this chapter is on Assignment maintenance and the details of updating existing Assignments that you have already created.

- The last grouping in this chapter goes into more specific information on how to achieve the modeling you want through a series of "how-to" descriptions.

MECHANISMS: METHODS FOR ADDING RESOURCES

This section focuses on the mechanisms (views, screens, dialog boxes, tables, and so on) that you have available to you to add resources to tasks, thereby creating assignments. Step guidance is provided for simple assignment creation techniques. The in-depth details around what you are actually accomplishing will be provided in the next section.

The primary mechanisms discussed are:

- Assign Resources Dialog Box
- Task Entry View
- Task Information Dialog Box
- Task Table
- Assignment Information Dialog Box
- Task and Resource Usage Views

NOTE

Some of the mechanisms focus on tables that are available in multiple views.

NOTE

> The Task and Resource Usage Views are covered in the third grouping in this chapter regarding the updating and maintenance of existing Assignments.

ADDING RESOURCES USING THE ASSIGN RESOURCE DIALOG

The Assign Resources dialog box is the most common and the preferred way to assign resources. It is easy to remember because of the friendly People-in-Profile icon that opens the dialog box.

Follow these steps to change assignments using the Task Information dialog box:

1. In a Task view (use the Gantt Chart View for simplicity), select the task to which you would like to add a resource.
2. Click the Assign Resources icon on the Standard toolbar (the People-in-Profile icon).
3. The Assign Resources dialog opens with the name of the task selected and a list of possible resources. Filter the list as needed to find the resources you want. If you do not see any resources in the list then it is likely that you have a filter specified in the filter section of the dialog or you have not created any resources. In the latter case, go ahead and type the resource name directly into the list. This is a fast way to create the resource (See the Consultants' Tip: "Config: Turn off Automatic Resource Creation").
4. Select a resource by clicking (or ctrl-clicking to select multiple resources) the resource Name field and click the Assign button.
5. The resource(s) are assigned to the task at the default Unit value (see the Consultants' Tip at the end of the chapter) and moved to the top of the dialog list with a checkmark to the left to indicate they are assigned.
6. Remove resources mistakenly assigned to the task by clicking the Remove button (which is un-grayed out and available when an already assigned resource is selected).
7. Modify the Units and Cost fields as appropriate.

TIP

> Creating resources in anything other than the Resource Sheet View or the Assign Resources dialog is generally not a good practice (it is too easy to add the same person twice because you cannot easily see the full list of resources to keep from creating multiple entries for the same resource). See the Consultants' Tip, "Config: Turn off Automatic Resource Creation."

ADDING RESOURCES BY USING DRAG-AND-DROP

NOTE

> The initially released version of Microsoft Project Standard 2007 has a bug in the Assign Resources dialog box's drag-and-drop functionality. The bug assigns all resources even though only one may be selected. Use the "Assign" button until a fix is released.

With the Assign Resources dialog box, you can create an assignment by dragging a resource name to a task. The advantage to using the drag-and-drop method is that you do not have to preselect the task for which a resource should be assigned. Microsoft Project 2007 will, however, automatically assign the default units (usually 100%).

To assign resources to the task by using the drag-and-drop method, follow these steps:

1. Display the Assign Resources dialog box by clicking the Assign Resources button on the Standard toolbar.

2. Select the resource by clicking the Name field.

3. Position the mouse pointer over the gray button just to the left of the resource name. The Assign Resources graphic appears just below the mouse pointer. You can see the pointer and graphic in Figure 10.1, where Movers is being assigned to a task.

Figure 10.1
Assign resources to tasks by using the drag-and-drop method in the Assign Resources dialog box.

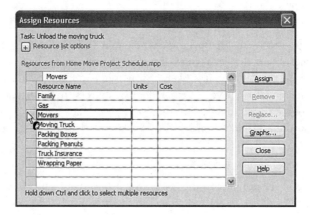

4. Hold down the mouse button and a plus sign will appear next to the pointer graphic. Now drag the mouse pointer to the task for which the resource should be assigned.

5. When the task is highlighted, release the mouse button and assign the resource.

TIP

> To assign multiple resources to a task by using the drag-and-drop method, hold down the Ctrl key while selecting the resource names in the Assign Resources dialog box. When you click on one of the gray buttons and drag the mouse pointer to the task, all selected resources are assigned at once.

ASSIGNING RESOURCES WITH THE TASK ENTRY VIEW

The Task Entry view, with the Gantt Chart view in the top pane and the Task Form view in the bottom pane, is one of the best combination views for assigning resources. The default (and most commonly used) form in the bottom pane is the "Resources and Predecessors" form. To see a list of other forms, just right-click in the background color of the form for a list and choose the one you want. (The "Resources Schedule" form is particularly good for understanding scheduling lags in assignments within tasks.) The "Resources and

Predecessors" form is a convenient place for assigning resources because it allows you to enter resource units, work, or both, for each resource assignment.

> **TIP**
>
> If you are using the Task Entry View (or any method other than the Assign Resources dialog methods), you can use the Assign Resources dialog box (at the same time) to review and find the best resources and make the initial assignment. The Task Form can then be used to easily modify the assignment.

The Task Entry view is not one of the default views shown in the View Bar or immediately visible on the View menu. Display the Task Entry view by clicking the View menu and selecting More Views.... You will have to scroll down to find the view. The Gantt Chart view will then be displayed in the top pane and the Task Form view in the bottom pane with eight possible sets of details. You can right-click over the form, and select the detail forms you want to use. For assigning resources, you should either use the default "Resources and Predecessors," or you should use the "Resource Work" as shown in Figure 10.2

Figure 10.2
Right-click in the bottom pane of the Task Entry view to choose from the list of detail forms to display in the bottom pane.

→ For additional information on using views and tables, **see** Chapter 11, "Using Standard Views, Tables, Filters, and Groups to Review Your Schedule," **p. 369**.

ASSIGNING RESOURCES USING THE TASK INFORMATION DIALOG BOX

You can use the Resources tab on the Task Information dialog box to add, change, or delete the resource assignment information for a selected task. As with the Assign Resources dialog box, you can use the Units field of the Task Information dialog box to enter a work value rather than a unit value by using a numeral followed by a time unit. Be careful, entering work in this way preserves the duration of the task. Microsoft Project 2007 calculates (and then displays) the units that would produce that much work while keeping the duration of the task the same. This is NOT the same behavior as entering Work in a Work field (which, in the default task type of Fixed Units will hold 100% Units constant and extend the duration of the task).

Follow these steps to change assignments using the Task Information dialog box:

1. Select the task for which you want to add or change a resource assignment.

2. Display the Task Information dialog box by doing one of the following:
   - Clicking the Task Information icon on the Standard toolbar (the one that looks like a file folder)
   - Double-clicking the task line you selected
   - Right-clicking the task line you selected and choosing Task Information from the pop-up shortcut (see Figure 10.3)
   - Typing Shift-F2

3. Select the Advanced tab and review the selections for the Task Type and Effort Driven fields. Be sure these are appropriate for the change you intended to implement.

4. Select the Resources tab to assign or view the resource information for the selected task.

Figure 10.3
Change assignment information on the Resources tab of the Task Information dialog box.

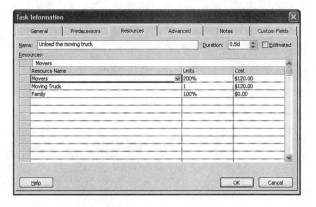

5. In the Resource Name box, edit an existing entry or choose a blank row to add a new resource. To add or change the resource, select a resource from the drop-down list in the field. You can create non-existent resources by typing the name in directly unless the default option "Automatically add new resources and tasks" has been cleared on the General tab of the Options dialog (Tools>Options>General).

6. Type the unit assignment for the resource in the Units field. If you leave the Units field empty, Microsoft Project 2007 will supply the default value, the lesser of 100% or the Max Units value for the resource. You can modify an existing assignment by entering a work amount followed by a time unit in the Units field. If you enter a work amount, Microsoft Project 2007 adjusts the assigned units, not the duration of the task.

7. To add more resources to the selected task, click the next Resource Name field and repeat the preceding steps.

8. After you have completed all of the resource assignments for the task, click OK.

If you use the Ctrl key or drag across multiple rows to select more than one task before opening the Task Information dialog box, Microsoft Project 2007 displays the Multiple Task Information dialog box so that any resource you select is automatically assigned to all selected tasks. The dialog box will not display any existing assignments on the tasks (you cannot edit these using the Multiple Task Information dialog box). The resource assignment entries you make in the Multiple Task Information dialog box are added to existing resource assignments for the selected tasks.

NOTE
You cannot change existing resource assignments for multiple tasks by using the Multiple Task Information dialog box.

ASSIGNING RESOURCES WITH THE TASK TABLE

You can use the Resource Name field on the Task table to assign resources to a task but you should be aware of some potential problems before you use this method. The field can be edited in two ways, via direct typing and via a pulldown list function that displays all of the resources from the Resource Sheet View. Use of the pulldown is the recommended method because you will be selecting an existing resource from the resource sheet and will not be able to automatically create a new resource if you accidentally misspell the name. You can only enter one resource at a time using the pulldown list. If you choose to type directly, you can type ResourceName1, ResourceName2, etc. and each resource will be assigned to the task at 100% Units or their Max Unit setting from the Resource Sheet view (whichever is the lessor). Note that if a resource is assigned at 100% units, then the entry will revert to the name without square brackets. To enter varying unit values while you type requires the following syntax:

ResourceName1[Units],ResourceName2[Units],ResourceName3[Units]…

When you are entering data using this format, note that the Units value is placed in square brackets and follows immediately after the resource name, without an intervening space. Unit values of the lesser of 100% or the resource's Max Units value (from the Resource Sheet view) do not need to be specified. The Resource Name field entry for the "Unloading the moving truck" task might be:

Movers[200%],Moving Truck[1],Family

Figure 10.4 shows this assignment. Because of the width of the Resource Names column, other columns and the Gantt Chart view are hidden in the figure.

Figure 10.4
Using the Task table for resource assignment is most convenient when using the pulldown list to assign a single resource at their Max Units setting (as specified on the Resource Sheet view). If you choose to type the resource names, regularly change to the Resource Sheet view to visually make sure you have not accidentally created duplicate resources through misspelling!

NOTE

> If you want to import a list of tasks with resource assignments, you must have the Resource Name field format in the source data to identify the resource assignments. For information about importing date, see Chapter 26, "Exporting and Importing Project Data."

Follow these steps to assign resources to tasks in the Resource Names field:

1. View a Task table like the one in the Gantt Chart view.

2. If the Resource Names column is not displayed, after you scroll through the columns, right-click the column header before which you would like to insert the Resource Names column and choose "Insert Column..." Select the Resource Names column to add it to the current table. Alternatively, you can select Menu, View and then "Table:xxx" with the right arrow to select any table that includes a Resource Names column, such as the Entry table. The "Table:xxx" entry on the View menu will provide the name of the table you are currently viewing in place of the "xxx".

3. Select the "Resource Names" cell for the task to which you want to assign resources.

4. Enter the resource name. You can select the name from the drop-down resource list, which appears in the cell when the Resource Names column is active.

5. If the number of units required is not 100% (or the resource Max Units from the Resource Sheet, if lesser than 100%), enter the units, enclosed in square brackets, immediately after the name in the edit bar.

6. If you want to assign more resources to the same task, use the list separator (which is a comma in North America) to separate the resources, and then repeat steps 5 and 6 until all resources are complete.

7. Press Enter or select any other cell to complete the resource assignment.

CREATION: ASSIGNING A SINGLE RESOURCE

Now that you have seen methods for making resource assignments, it is time to review how Microsoft Project 2007 uses the information to schedule work. This section will focus on the initial creation of an Assignment accomplished the first time you map one Resource to a Task. It is very helpful to treat the mapping of a single Resource to a single Task separately from mapping multiple Resources to a Task because it teaches you what is going on without adding in the complexities of how multiple resources interplay within a task. This section will walk through the process to assign one resource to one task to build a framework for the more complex discussion following the following section.

ASSIGNING A RESOURCE (USING THE ASSIGN RESOURCES DIALOG BOX)

The previous section demonstrated many possible ways to add a resource to a task. Although any of the methods will work, this section will use only one: the Assign Resources dialog box.

When a resource is assigned to a task, Microsoft Project 2007 schedules that resource's work to start on the same date as the task and to continue working at a constant and uninterrupted assignment rate until all of the work is scheduled.

The creation of the first assignment on a task establishes an initial schedule for work to be done. Task Types, work values, and Calendars will have an impact on the assignment. Manipulations of load, inter-relationships with other assignments, and manipulations of a task to 'model' real work performance can be done after initial assignment creation. (See "Contouring Resource Usage" later in this chapter for details on advanced scheduling techniques that can be used to modify this default approach.)

To add a resource assignment to a selected task or group of tasks, follow these steps:

1. Select the task or tasks to which you want the resource assigned.
2. Display the Assign Resources dialog box by clicking the Assign Resources button on the Standard toolbar.
3. Select the resource name from the Resource Name list or type the name for a new resource.
4. Different resource types require different uses of the Units field when you are assigning them:
   - If the resource is a work resource, then the Units field determines the percent of a full work day to allocate for that resource. 100% would be full allocation of a single resource. (See the consultant notes for how to determine the default Units value used.) If you want to assign a different number of units, select the Units cell to the right of the resource name and enter the new value.
   - If the resource is a material resource, enter the number of units to be consumed by the task in the Units cell. If you just enter a numeral, Microsoft Project 2007 will schedule that total number of material units to be consumed by the task, no matter what the duration is. If you enter a number with a time period appended

10

(for example, 2/d), then Microsoft Project 2007 will schedule that number to be consumed per time period for the duration of the task.

• If the resource is a cost resource, do not bother with the units. Enter the Cost of the resource. The cost will accrue over the timeframe of the task using the accrual type defined on the Resource Sheet in the Accrual Type field (prorated, start, end).

TIP

> For work resources, the units should be no greater than the maximum units available for the resource at the time the task is scheduled. If you do not know the max units available, double-click the resource name to see the Resource Information dialog box. The Resource Availability table in that dialog box shows the maximum units for different time periods.

5. Click the Assign button or press Enter to assign the Resources and Unit or Cost information to the selected tasks.

6. If you are using Project Professional, select either Request or Demand in the R/D field. A resource that is *demanded* cannot be replaced using the Resource Substitution Wizard. A *requested* resource is free to be replaced. *Requested* is the default used if the field is left blank. This field is not of any particular value if Project Professional is used without Project Server or if the Resource Substitution Wizard is not used.

NOTE

> Project Professional carries an additional attribute (settable from the Resource Sheet) that allows you to mark each resource in a project as soft-booked or not. When soft-booked resources are assigned to a task, they are considered tentative placeholders and the assignment will not reduce the global (across all projects) availability of the resource.

When using the Assign Resources dialog box to change resource assignments, Microsoft Project 2007 will display a SmartTag to let you choose how it should calculate changes in the schedule (see Figure 10.5). The SmartTag feature compensates for the limited control you have over the variables when you modify an assignment in the Assign Resources dialog box. For example, if you change the units assigned, Microsoft Project 2007 immediately changes the task duration, unless it is a fixed-duration task. However, you can use the SmartTag to have Microsoft Project 2007 put duration back where it was, and change the work instead.

Figure 10.5
Increasing the Movers units from 2 to 3 creates a conflict, so Microsoft Project 2007 provides options for adjusting the schedule given the unit change.

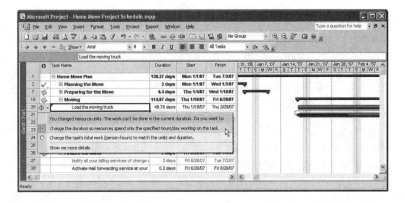

When you change the assignment, a small green triangle appears in the top-left corner of the Task Name cell. If you select the cell or even move the mouse over that cell, an active button appears, and you can click it to display the calculation options. SmartTags stay visible only as long as you can undo an action.

For example, if you change the units for an assignment, the SmartTag will let you choose to have either work or duration change as a result. If you assign an additional resource to a task or remove an existing resource, the SmartTag lets you choose to change duration (keeping work and units unchanged), change work (keeping duration and units constant), or change units (keeping work and duration constant).

NOTE

> SmartTags are triggered by assignment changes that are made in the Assign Resources dialog box and in cells in tables. They are not triggered when you make changes by using the Task Form view or the Task Information dialog box, because in those venues, you can control all the scheduling variables before you click OK.

CREATION: ASSIGNING MULTIPLE RESOURCES

The last section discussed how to create a single resource assignment within a task. When you add more than one resource to a task, there are many aspects of a task that can be intuitively treated as the aggregation of the information from each individual resource assignment. However, some impacts are less intuitive. This section will discuss the less intuitive complexities involved with multiple resources associated with a task.

The three task level impacts of multiple resources that are the least intuitive are:

- Impacts to overall task duration
- How total task work is impacted by the addition of multiple resources, and how work is distributed across resources (the Effort Driven flag)
- Understanding how multiple resources interact to impact the finish date of a task (the concept of Driver Resources)

CALCULATING TASK DURATION WITH MULTIPLE RESOURCES

The Microsoft Project 2007 definition of *task duration* is the number of active working time periods on the calendar required to complete a task. When multiple resources are assigned to a task, some of them might not be scheduled for the entire task duration. Individual schedules for some resources can be modified to delay an assignment or to split the assignment with a period of inactivity.

For example, Carrie and Nick are both assigned 5 days to prepare for an upcoming sales conference. The task duration is 5 days if both Carrie and Nick do their work during the same time periods. However, suppose that Nick is taking 2 vacation days when the task starts, so Carrie starts working on the task alone. Nick also has 1 more vacation day at the beginning of the following week. Nick starts working on the task 2 days later than Carrie does. Then, they work together for 3 days, and Carrie completes her part of the task. Nick still has 2 days of work to do, but he does not do those days until he returns from his second vacation.

The task duration is the number of time periods during which anyone is working on the task. Since Carrie has an earlier start date and Nick has a later finish date, the duration is extended. In this case, the task duration is actually 7 days—the 2 days when Carrie worked alone, 3 days when they worked together on the task, and 2 days when Nick returned to work alone, after Carrie had completed her part and after he returned from his second vacation (see Figure 10.6).

Figure 10.6
The Task Usage view is displayed, and the time-phased work details show the precise work schedule of both Carrie and Nick.

You can see in Figure 10.6 that Nick and Carrie work independently some days and together some days. If you count the number of days in the task row, where total work (across all assignments) is greater than 0, you can see that there are 7 such days. That is what determines the task duration of 7 days.

UNDERSTANDING EFFORT-DRIVEN TASKS

As mentioned previously, if a task is set as Fixed Work, you can increase the number of units assigned to the task and Microsoft Project 2007 will reduce the duration of the task, leaving the Work amount unchanged. The addition of named resources to a task is another way to change the duration of a task. For instance, if you have three movers unloading a moving truck, the original assignment is for 300% units (3 people). If you change the number of units to 600% on a Fixed Work task (that is, add three more movers), Microsoft Project 2007 will cut the duration in half.

The same is true when you increase named resources assigned to a task, since it is the same as adding units. Instead of a resource named Moving Truck Personnel, you might have Tim, Melissa, and Mike, and you want to add Gary, Chris, and Pam. Just as when you added units to the Moving Truck Personnel resource, you should expect Microsoft Project 2007 to cut the duration in half.

> **NOTE**
>
> There are two things to remember when using effort-driven tasks. First, adding resources to effort-driven tasks will never affect work. The task Work will be redistributed and either Duration or Units will change (depending on Task Type). Second, effort-driven tasks assume that the resources are interchangeable (no distinctions where one resource may be more efficient than another). If you add more people who are trained to load and unload moving trucks, then you can honestly expect the duration to be cut in half, just like the schedule says. However, if you added three people who are trained to be cashiers, and the task is Fixed Units, then the resulting reduction of duration may not be achieved in reality. (Subsequent sections of this chapter will provide you with techniques to change this default distribution model.)

This is an example of an *effort-driven* task calculation. When you want the amount of work for the whole task to be fixed and you add resources to the assignment list on a Fixed Unit task, Microsoft Project 2007 is allowed to reduce the workload for the resources already assigned to the task. This also works if you have to remove a resource from the assignment list, freeing up work that must be redistributed to the resources remaining on the task's assignment list.

When you add resources to an effort-driven task, Microsoft Project 2007 will guard the total work and the task type (Fixed Duration, Fixed Units) and reduce the remaining free variable (either Duration or Units). If a task is shown as effort-driven and the task type is Fixed Work, Units is held fixed and Duration will be used as the free variable. (In essence, you are holding the same variable constant, leaving two possible free variables.)

There are many different ways to model work and the work formula is sophisticated enough to adapt but it can be confusing. The order in which you choose to model the work will dictate how Microsoft Project 2007 works. For example, suppose you decide to add David to the task of unloading the truck at the grocery store. David is not there to help unload the truck; instead, he is there to track the inventory as it comes off the truck. This is not the same work, but rather a parallel task activity. You can create a new task for David or you can add David's work into the total work being done on the task. If you choose to use the later option, you must change the task to non-effort driven, add David as a resource and then change the task back to effort driven. This will allow you to assign him to the task without affecting the amount of work assigned to others on the task. The order of your manipulation will control the impact.

> **NOTE**
>
> When you set a task as a Fixed Work task, it automatically becomes an effort-driven task, since effort-driven means "fixed work." Microsoft Project 2007 will fill in the Effort Driven check box and then dim it so that it cannot be cleared.

10

Microsoft Project 2007 will, by default, make all new tasks effort driven, but not all tasks you add may be effort-driven tasks. Consider each resource to be sure that it is calculated properly by Microsoft Project 2007. The Effort Driven field is a check box found on the Task Information dialog box and on the Task Form view and can be cleared to turn it off.

NOTE

> Adding or removing material or cost resources will not effect effort-driven calculations because the work value for them is not effort hours but rather a consumption rate or a cost.

The effort-driven status of a task has no effect on calculations when you are first assigning resources (the initial assignment), because no work has been defined for the task until the first work assignment. So, if you are using the Task Form view and create a list of multiple resource names with assignments before clicking the OK button (in effect, creating all the assignments at once), Microsoft Project 2007 will treat them all as the initial assignment and calculate the hours of work for each of the work resources and the sum as the total work amount for the task. This works only if you enter them all before clicking OK. If you click OK for each, only the first assignment will count as the initial assignment and the effort driven state in combination with task type will drive the rest of the calculations.

You can change the default effort-driven status for new tasks by performing the following steps:

1. In the top navigation menu, select Tools, Options and then the Schedule tab.
2. You can change the default setting by clearing the New Tasks Are Effort Driven check box.

After the initial assignment of resources to a task, if you add or remove some of the work resources, Microsoft Project 2007 will automatically figure the effort-driven status of the task in its calculations. If Effort Driven is on, as it is by default, Microsoft Project 2007 will redistribute the work for the task across the revised work resource list, prorating the work for each resource, according to its share of the total number of work resource units assigned to the task.

When you increase resources for an effort-driven task, Microsoft Project 2007 will reapportion the work amount among the existing resources. It will do this in proportion to the resources' share of the total work units assigned. For example, Drew and Scott are assigned a 5-day (40-hour) effort-driven task. You can see in Figure 10.7 an example of the table portion of a Task Usage view, showing three numbered tasks and their resource assignments indented beneath them.

Task A shows the original assignment of Drew and Scott. The total work is 60 hours, and because it is an effort-driven task, the work will remain fixed if you add or subtract resources.

Figure 10.7
The original task assignment (effort-driven) shows both Drew and Scott performing 30 hours of work each, totaling 60 hours.

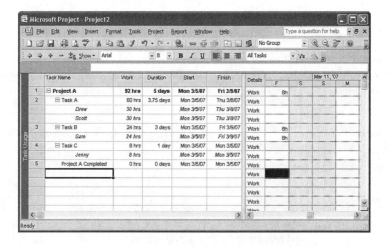

Figure 10.8 shows an example of what happens when Kim is assigned to the task at 50% units. Because Task A is effort-driven, total work remains unchanged, at 60 hours. In the Assignment Units column is the sum of the units assigned, 250%. The custom column Share of Units shows that Kim contributes 20% of the total units (50% / 250%), and Scott and Drew each contribute 40% of the total (100% / 250%). This shows how Microsoft Project 2007 calculates the work assignment for each resource. Microsoft Project 2007 assigns Kim 20% of the total work for the task, which is 12 hours, while Scott and Drew are each assigned 24 hours. Each of these new work assignments can be completed in 3 days, so the duration changes from 5 days to 3 days.

Figure 10.8
Kim's assignment to an effort-driven task has not changed the total amount of work, but has shortened the overall task duration to 3 days.

If Drew were removed from the assignment, the changes would be reversed. Without Drew's assignment, Kim would contribute one-third of the units and Scott would contribute two-thirds. Kim would be assigned one-third of the total 60 hours (20 hours), while Scott would be assigned two-thirds (40 hours).

If you disable the Effort Driven field, by clearing the check box in the Options dialog box, Microsoft Project 2007 will assume that the work of a newly assigned resource is *in addition* to the existing work of all other named resources. The assignments of the existing resources are not changed.

If you remove a named resource from a task, with the Effort Driven check box not selected, then Microsoft Project 2007 will reduce the total work for the task by the amount of that resource's work assignment, and will not recalculate other resource assignments.

NOTE

> The Effort Driven setting regulates calculations only when you add or subtract from the list of assigned resources on a task. If you change the duration of an effort-driven Fixed Unit task, Microsoft Project 2007 will not keep the work of the assigned resources the same, but will change their work to fit the new duration. If the effort-driven task is a Fixed Work task, Microsoft Project 2007 would change the Unit values of the assignments instead of the Durations.

When changing the number of assigned resources, you must consider whether you want the total work to change and then change the Effort Driven status for the task as appropriate. You will do this when you build a list of assigned resources one at a time. For example, suppose you create a task for 30 hours of work unloading a truck and you have already assigned shipping workers. Now you want to assign the pallet jacks they will be using. If the duration, work, and units for the workers' assignment are based on the assumption that they will have pallet jacks to work with, you need to clear the Effort Driven check box before adding the pallet jacks. After the pallet jacks are added, you can turn Effort Driven back on for future calculations.

UNDERSTANDING THE DRIVER RESOURCE CONCEPT

Chapter 9 explored how various changes in assignments will produce changes in both the assignments and the task duration. Understanding the concept of the driver resource will help you understand these changes even better.

The term *driver resource* is used to identify resources whose assignments determine the duration or finish date of the task. The driver resources and the time-phased Work as rolled up from the set of assignments associated with a task define how the task Work (for a Fixed Unit task) or Units (for a Fixed Work task) will be impacted when you edit the Duration of the task. For simplicity, only the Fixed Work task type will be used in the following discussions.

It is not uncommon to have a resource that only adds some minor finishing touches to a task—a small amount of work scheduled right at the end of a task. Unfortunately, you cannot schedule one assignment to start "as late as possible" while the other resource starts when the task begins in Microsoft Project 2007. You can, however, delay an individual resource assignment so that it finishes at the same time the task finishes, making that resource the *driver* for the task. Any increase in the amount of time scheduled for the driver resource delays the finish of the task, unless you offset the increase by reducing the amount of delay.

As mentioned earlier, the significance of the driver resource concept is that increasing the duration of a driver resource assignment affects the task duration, but modest increases in the duration of a non-driver resource have no effect. As we will see in more detail in the table to follow, increasing the duration of the task changes the Work by increasing the work assigned to the driver resources (Fixed Unit task). Decreasing the duration of the task reduces the Work and may include driver resources or non-driver resources. When duration is shortened, non-driver resources may become drivers.

Figure 10.9 shows the driver resource concept. Jenny, Brian, and Chris are assigned to Task A with differing work amounts, as shown in the Work column. The custom column, Assignment Duration, shows how long it will take each of them to complete the assigned work, given the assignment units. Brian and Chris will both require 4 days, but Jenny can finish in 1 day. The task duration is 4 days, and Brian and Chris are both driver resources.

10

Figure 10.9
Brian and Chris represent driver resources as their assignments are as long as the task duration, whereas Jenny is a non-driver resource with an assignment of only 1 day.

NOTE

Note that in Figure 10.9, Jenny is assigned full time for 1 day, but because she only has 8 hours of work, she finishes her assignment before the task finishes. If she were assigned 8 hours at 25% units, it would take her all 4 days to complete the task, putting in 2 hours each day. In that case, she would also be a driver resource.

In this example, a change in the assigned work or units for Brian and/or Chris, would affect the duration of the task. For example, if you increased Brian's workload to 50 hours, he would need a longer time to finish, and the task duration would also have to increase. However, an increase in Jenny's workload, up to a point, would not affect the duration of the task:

- You could increase the work assigned to Jenny from 8 hours to 32 hours, without needing to increase the task's duration.

- You could also change Jenny's units from 100% to as low as 25% before it would affect her ability to complete her assignment in the current duration.

- You could reduce the task duration from 4 days down to 1 day without affecting Jenny's assignment, if she worked 8 hours at 100% effort. Jenny would become a driver resource.

Figure 10.10 provides an example setup for use with Table 10.1 shown below. Two of the resources have a delayed start on the task. This is a planning scenario and so the Assignment Delay field is used to delay the assignments. An equivalent time-phased Work profile can occur naturally when you are maintaining an active project's status and you enter 0 actual hours for 2 of the resources on the first day and 8 actual hours for the third resource on the first day.

Figure 10.10
The Example Fixed Unit task whose work and duration will be manipulated using Table 10.1.

TABLE 10.1 MICROSOFT PROJECT 2007 DURATION AND DRIVER RESOURCES

A decrease in Task Work is distributed across the assignments by their commitment of Units (all 100% here).

O	Task Name	Type	Effort Driven	Duration	Work	Mar 11, '07 Day -1	Day 1	Day 2	Day 3	Day 4	Day 5
1	ExampleTask	Fixed Units	Yes	3.67 days	64 hrs					Amar,Jose,Sue	

	Task Name	Assignment Delay	% Complete	% Work Complete	Details	Mar 11, '07 Day -1	Day 1	Day 2	Day 3	Day 4	Day 5
1	ExampleTask		0%	0%	Work		8h	24h	21.33h	10.67h	
	Sue	1 day		0%	Work		0h	8h	8h	5.33h	
	Amar	0 days		0%	Work		8h	8h	5.33h		
	Jose	1 day		0%	Work		0h	8h	8h	5.33h	

An increase in Task Work is evenly distributed across the assignments by their commitment of Units (all 100% here).

O	Task Name	Type	Effort Driven	Duration	Work	Mar 11, '07 Day -1	Day 1	Day 2	Day 3	Day 4	Day 5
1	ExampleTask	Fixed Units	Yes	2 days	32 hrs				Amar,Jose,Sue		

	Task Name	Assignment Delay	% Complete	% Work Complete	Details	Mar 11, '07 Day -1	Day 1	Day 2	Day 3	Day 4	Day 5
1	ExampleTask		0%	0%	Work		8h	24h			
	Sue	1 day		0%	Work		0h	8h			
	Amar	0 days		0%	Work		8h	8h			
	Jose	1 day		0%	Work		0h	8h			

A decrease in Duration of 1 day reduces the Task Work by the sum of the hours trimmed off when the last working day is trimmed from the task. (Note: only 2 resources are affected.)

O	Task Name	Type	Effort Driven	Duration	Work	Mar 11, '07 Day -1	Day 1	Day 2	Day 3	Day 4	Day 5
1	ExampleTask	Fixed Units	Yes	1 day	8 hrs			Amar,Jose,Sue			

	Task Name	Assignment Delay	% Complete	% Work Complete	Details	Mar 11, '07 Day -1	Day 1	Day 2	Day 3	Day 4	Day 5
1	ExampleTask		0%	0%	Work		8h				
	Sue	1 day		0%	Work		0h				
	Amar	0 days		0%	Work		8h				
	Jose	1 day		0%	Work		0h				

A decrease in Duration of 2 days reduces the Task Work by the sum of hours trimmed off when the last 2 working days are removed from the task. (Note: all 3 resources are affected, disproportionately.)

O	Task Name	Type	Effort Driven	Duration	Work	Mar 11, '07 Day -1	Day 1	Day 2	Day 3	Day 4	Day 5
1	ExampleTask	Fixed Units	Yes	4 days	64 hrs						Amar,Jose,Su

	Task Name	Assignment Delay	% Complete	% Work Complete	Details	Mar 11, '07 Day -1	Day 1	Day 2	Day 3	Day 4	Day 5
1	ExampleTask		0%	0%	Work		8h	24h	16h	16h	
	Sue	1 day		0%	Work		0h	8h	8h	8h	
	Amar	0 days		0%	Work		8h	8h			
	Jose	1 day		0%	Work		0h	8h	8h	8h	

An increase in Duration of 1 day increases the Task Work only by the extended assignment Work from the "Driver Resources".

As you can see from Table 10.1, the Driver Resources primary impact is when the task Duration is extended. In all other cases, the profile of time-phased hours across the assignments composing the task and the change of duration (as associated with the current Finish of the task) determine the remaining impacts.

MAINTENANCE: MODIFYING EXISTING RESOURCE ASSIGNMENTS

The prior sections were really about Task/Assignment creation and introduced the impacts that modeled work has on a Task at the Assignment level.

This section takes everything a step further to the actual maintenance of existing resource Assignments. These are the tools you need to model the reality of Work on an ongoing basis.

The views most used here reflect the maintenance aspect of your job. Task Usage and Resource Usage views are key elements. This section will introduce these views and go through some of the maintenance concepts.

The section following this will focus even more on how to achieve some of the common modeling results you desire.

MODIFYING RESOURCE ASSIGNMENTS

Remember that Microsoft Project 2007 will take any entry into the Assignment Units field that is less than 100% and schedule it down to the minute. If you were to enter **25%** on a Fixed Units or Fixed Work task (the default is Fixed Units), it would in fact represent 2 hours out of an 8-hour workday. However, Microsoft Project 2007 will actually schedule 15 minutes of work for each hour in the 8-hour day, which will total 2 hours. In most cases, the resource or employee will realistically sit down and complete all the work in 2 hours, in one sitting, rather then work for just 15 minutes an hour, every hour, on the project. If you are only concerned about the overall time (in this case, 2 hours) and not the exact amount of time the resource is actually spending during each hour, you can just ignore the difference between the way Microsoft Project 2007 schedules time and the way the work is actually being done. If you want the schedule to reflect that the resource worked full time for 2 hours and then was idle for the rest of the task you can enter **100%** in the Assignment Units field and then change the work to only 2 hours or manually contour the work to be 2 hours.

A slight twist on this is when you are actually trying to schedule tasks WITHIN a day. In this case it is better to set the duration of the task to 2 hours BEFORE you assign the resource. Then it will be a task with 2 hours duration and 2 hours work (at 100% Units). You can even designate the Task Start Date down to the hour of the day. To do this, you must set the Date format on the View tab of the Options dialog box (on the Tools menu) to a format that allows entry of Date and Time.

NOTE

Microsoft Project 2007 does not enforce the maximum number of available units when you make resource assignments. You can assign more units than the Max Units value when you are planning a project, but when you exceed the maximum for any resource, in the Resource Sheet and Resource Usage views the Resource Name will turn red and a special warning indicator will be displayed in the Indicator Column.

In prior versions of Microsoft Project there were some instances where you wanted to set the Assignment Units field at zero. If this field is set at zero, then Microsoft Project 2007 will calculate work as zero, and accordingly, will set the cost of the work at zero also. This has been simplified in Microsoft Project 2007 by the addition of the Cost Resource. If you had a situation where a contractor would be working on a task and will complete it for a fixed fee, you would now create a Cost Resource representing the contractor, and enter the fixed fee into the Cost field on the Resources tab of the Task Information dialog box (see "Assigning Fixed Costs and Fixed Contract Fees" later in this chapter for additional discussion).

CAUTION

You can enter fractions of a percentage into the Assignment Units field, but they will automatically be rounded up to the nearest whole number. Microsoft Project 2007 will use fractional percents in the calculations, but it will not display them.

Material resources are always formatted as a decimal. If you miss entering the assigned units, it will default to 1, followed by the material label defined for the resource. If you define the material resource of dirt as Yd (for cubic yard), the default units supplied by Microsoft Project 2007 will be 1 Yd, which means the task will consume 1 cubic yard of dirt.

When you enter a numeral into the Units column for a material resource, it is called a *fixed consumption rate*. The amount is considered to be fixed and independent of the task duration. Using our current example, Microsoft Project 2007 figures 1 yard of material for the task, and if the task duration changes, the consumption rate will not.

NOTE

If you enter something that Microsoft Project 2007 does not understand, such as *yards* instead of *Yd*, project will show you a warning. This warning is to let you know that it is not a valid Units value. Simply enter a numeric value and let Microsoft Project 2007 provide the correct label.

If you want to assign material resource units that have a variable consumption rate, where the amount of material resources depends on the duration of the task, then you simply enter the units, followed by a forward slash (/). For instance, if you have a backhoe that uses 10 gallons of gas an hour, you can enter either **10/h** or **10 gal/h**. Microsoft Project 2007 will then calculate the consumption of 10 gallons of fuel per hour for every hour of working time on the calendar until the task is complete.

→ For details on assigning units to various resource types, **see** Chapter 9, "Understanding Work Formula Basics," **p. 283**.

ENTERING THE ASSIGNMENT VALUES

Assignment values for resources can be entered in a variety of ways; one of the most commonly used methods is the Task Form because it allows you to view all needed resource attributes and easily select as many resources as you need for a task. One of the easiest ways to display the form is to go to the Task Entry View (mentioned earlier). On the View menu, select More Views… and scroll down to click the Task Entry view. This form can also be displayed from any split screen view with tasks in the upper pane. Right-click on the background in the lower pane and select Resources & Predecessors.

Assuming you are using the Task Entry view, follow these steps to assign resources using the Task Form view in the bottom pane:

1. Select the task in the top pane of the Gantt Chart view.

2. In the bottom pane, select the Task Type field to be sure that it is set appropriately to manage the calculations for the assignments you are about to enter. If you are adding work resources and you want to make sure the duration does not change, then make the task "fixed-duration" for this assignment, and then return it to its prior setting after completing the assignment.

3. If you are adding new work resource names to an existing list of resource name assignments, select the Effort Driven field for its appropriateness. This also works when deleting existing resource names. If the changes you are about to enter alter the total work associated with the task, clear the Effort Driven check box. However, if changes simply redistribute the existing total work among the resources assigned to the task, leave the field selected.

4. Select the Resource Name field and identify the resource by selecting the name from the drop-down list. You can also type the name, but you must be careful to spell it correctly, so that Microsoft Project 2007 does not create a new resource for the misspelled name.

5. If you leave the Units field blank, Microsoft Project 2007 assigns the default (the lesser of 100% or Max Units for the resource). If you want to specify the units for the assignment, select the Units field and enter the units you want to assign, as follows:

   • For work resources, type a units value as a percentage (for example, 200%) unless you have chosen to use a decimal format for units (for example, 2).

   • For material resources that have a fixed consumption rate, type a decimal number that represents the total units to be consumed by the task. For example, if 20 gallons of fuel are to be assigned, enter **20**. Microsoft Project 2007 replaces this entry with 20 plus the material label.

   • For material resources that have a variable consumption rate, type the number of units as a decimal, followed by a slash and a time unit to indicate a rate of consumption. To assign 20 gallons of fuel per week, enter **20/wk**. Microsoft Project 2007 will replace this entry with 20 gallons/week.

   • Cost resources, such as insurance on a (rented) moving truck, are not measured in units. Their cost is not even specified on the resource sheet. Their cost is specified when you assign the resource to a task (in the Task Entry pane you change the form to the Resource Cost form in order to see the Resource Cost field). The cost is accrued across the duration of the assigned Tasks and is identified in the Resource Sheet by specifying the Accrual Type (Prorated, Start or End).

6. If you leave the Work field blank, Microsoft Project 2007 calculates the work based on the task duration and the assigned (or default) units. If you want to specify the amount

of work for the assignment, select the Work field and type the work amount. For work resources, work must be entered with a number plus the unit of measure: m (minute), h (hour), d (day), w (week), or mo (month). For material resources, enter a decimal value. Microsoft Project 2007 uses this value as the fixed consumption rate for the task.

TIP

> PMI suggests that tasks should be sized so that the work associated with them is esti-mated to take no more than 80 hours of effort and no fewer than 8 hours. This is for purposes of managing the activity. The larger the task, the more room for error on both the original estimate and the progress status gathered. The suggested maximum is also why it is suggested to have at least biweekly but preferably weekly project status meet-ings. At the other end of the spectrum, most project managers would not be interested in micromanaging activities that take less than 8 hours of work. The actual maximum/mini-mum effort ranges you should use for your task decomposition and how frequent your status meetings should be will be determined by the kind of work you are doing and how early you wish to be able to correct the impacts of flawed estimates or delays.

NOTE

> Remember that if you enter both units and work when you assign the first resource, Microsoft Project 2007 recalculates the duration. However, with fixed-duration tasks, Microsoft Project 2007 keeps the duration and work and recalculates the units.

If you are assigning multiple resources, follow these steps:

1. Enter additional resources in the next rows of the Resource Name column before you click the OK button. For instance, Figure 10.11 shows the resources to be assigned to the task *Unload the moving truck*.

2. After all resource assignments are made for the task, click the OK button and Microsoft Project 2007 calculates the fields that were left blank.

Figure 10.11
The movers are assigned at 200% to indicate 2 people per-forming the job, the moving truck has con-sumption rate of $50/hour, and the Family will get assigned the default units of 100% once the OK button is clicked.

When you click OK, Microsoft Project 2007 calculates the values for the fields that you did not fill in, in accordance with the principles discussed in Chapter 9, "Understanding Work Formula Basics" (see Figure 10.12).

Figure 10.12
In order to correctly calculate the consumption rate and have it not affect the Movers resource, that resource was added first with the Effort Driven box selected, and then the remaining resources (Family and Moving Truck) were added with the Effort Driven box cleared.

ASSIGNING RESOURCES WITH THE TASK USAGE VIEW

Everything you accomplished in the previous section with the Gantt Chart view in the top pane can be done with the Task Usage view in the top pane. In fact, you can do much more:

- You can display the Assignment Information dialog box, where you can apply work contours and different Cost Rate tables to an assignment and where you can write commentary notes about the assignment.

- You can view the *time-phased* work schedule. The time-phased view shows work broken down into specific time periods.

- You can display the number of time-phased work and cost measures.

- You can edit many of the time-phased values directly in the grid cells. You could, for instance, reapportion work among the time periods or create and fine-tune splits or delays in an individual assignment.

Figure 10.13 shows the Task Usage view in the top pane and the Task Form view in the bottom pane.

To display the Task Usage view, click the icon for the view on the View bar or choose View, Task Usage.

The table area of the Task Usage view displays all the tasks in the project, using by default the Usage table. Indented under each task are rows for that task's assignments. You can hide or show the assignments by using the outline icon on the left of the task name. The Work field for the task is the sum of the Work field values for the assigned resources.

The right side of the view is a timescale grid of cells that show time-phased assignment details. In Figure 10.13, the work details are displayed in the grid. This is the default assignment detail, but you can display other details if desired. Work detail is the most useful for creating and editing assignments. The value in the Work field for each resource in the table on the left is the sum of the time-phased values displayed in the cells on that row in the timescale.

Figure 10.13
Split the window to display the Task Usage view in the top pane and the Task Form view in the bottom pane.

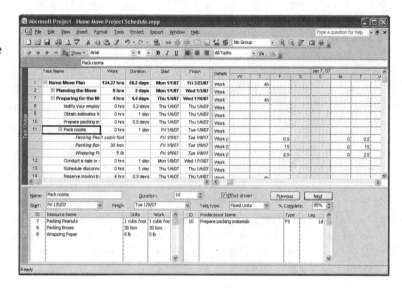

MODIFYING WORK SCHEDULES WITH THE TASK USAGE VIEW

As mentioned before, you can use the Task Usage view to customize the amount of work scheduled for each period and to slip and delay task assignments.

To change the amount of work scheduled for any given time period in the Task Usage view, simply select the time-phased cell, type a new value, and either press Enter or select another cell. When you type a value for a work resource, Microsoft Project 2007 assumes that the unit is hours unless you provide a different time measurement unit.

NOTE

If you type a value with a time unit that is not hours, Microsoft Project 2007 converts the value to hours in the display. For example, if the timescale unit is days (that is, each cell is 1 day) and you type 1 week, Microsoft Project 2007 displays 40h (40 hours) in that cell. If the assignment units is 100%, this is too many hours for that 1 day. This example also serves to warn you that you should not enter a work value that represents more hours than are available for that time period.

There are several different techniques for editing the cells in the time-phase grid:

- If you select a cell or group of consecutive cells in a row, you can use Ctrl+C to copy these values or Ctrl+X to cut those values from the grid. You can then select a cell at a new location and use Ctrl+V to paste the values into the cell at that location. If you choose to cut cells, the cells then display 0h.

- If you select a cell or group of consecutive cells in a row, you can drag the border around the selection to a new location and drop the cells into that new location. The original location cells display 0h.

- If you select a cell or group of consecutive cells in a row, you can drag a copy to a new location by holding down the Ctrl key as you drag the selection border to the new location. The caution about dropping cells on nonworking days applies here also.

- The bottom-right corner of the cell selection border displays a small black square, which is called the *fill handle*. You can drag this handle to bordering cells in the same row to copy the value in the selection into those cells.

- If you select a cell or group of consecutive cells in a row, you can press the Insert key to insert nonworking time (0h) in place of the selection, pushing the selected values to the right. Thus, you effectively introduce a split.

- If you select a cell or group of consecutive cells in a row, you can press the Delete key to remove that work from the assignment. After clearing the cells you had selected, Microsoft Project 2007 shifts to the left any cells on the right that contain work, to fill in the space you deleted.

For example, if you want to increase the work and duration of an assignment, you can select the last cell in the assignment and drag its fill handle to the right to fill as many additional work periods as you choose. If you want to introduce a split in an assignment, you can select the cells where the slip is to occur and press the Insert key. To remove the split, you can select the cells that display 0h and press the Delete key.

If you modify a time-phased cell on the task Work row, the new value is apportioned among all the work resource assignments that had work scheduled for that time period. The relative proportions of the total work for each resource are kept the same. If you modified a time-phased cell on an assignment row, the new values change the sum in the row for the task.

When you complete a cell modification, Microsoft Project 2007 immediately recalculates the task and assignments as follows:

- If you modified a cell on the task row, the changes are applied to all assignments that were scheduled during that time period.

- If you modified a cell on a row for a work resource, Microsoft Project 2007 updates the summary value for that time period on the task row.

- The Work column entries for assignments in the table on the left are updated. These are the totals for all time periods for each assignment.

- The Work column entry for the task in the table on the left is updated. This is the total for all assignments for all time periods.

■ The duration for the task is updated. If you have not changed the number of time periods in which work is scheduled, there is no change in the duration.

CAUTION

Be very careful when using these editing techniques when you have a project with a fixed finish date. The results are not the same as for a fixed-start-date project and therefore are likely to cause you to loose a lot of time trying to correct the changes.

Follow these steps to introduce a split in a task or in an individual assignment using the Task Usage view:

1. Display the Task Usage view in the top pane. You can type changes into time-phased cells in the bottom pane, but you cannot use drag-and-drop techniques in that pane.

2. Select the cell or cells that currently have work in them where you want to insert the split. If you select cells on the task row, the split is applied to all the resource assignments for the task. If you select cells on an assignment row, only that assignment is affected.

3. Press the Insert key. Microsoft Project 2007 shifts the work values to the right, leaving the selected cells with no scheduled work during that period.

To delay an assignment, you could select the cell for the beginning of the assignment and press the Insert key repeatedly until the work is moved to the date when you want it to start. You could, on the other hand, select all the work cells for the assignment and drag the selection to the period where you want the work to be scheduled.

In Figure 10.14, the usage of the material resource Drafting Paper is shown to be delayed until 8/29/07. Originally, Microsoft Project 2007 had distributed the one roll of paper evenly over the task duration (0.04 rolls per day). To create a delayed usage as in Figure 10.14, you would have to delete all the fractional units and type in the new usage, as shown in the figure (0.1 rolls per day beginning on 8/29/07). The quick way to remove all the fractional units is to type **0** in the Work column on the left. Then select the time-phased cell for the date where you want to schedule the usage (8/29/07) and type in the value.

Figure 10.14
The use of the Drafting Paper material resource is delayed until after the task has started.

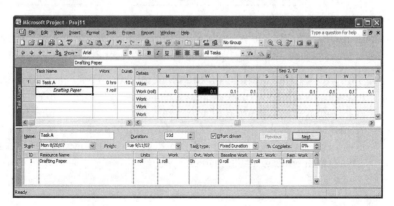

TIP

> Drag-and-drop can be difficult to use if the destination is off-screen, because when you drag past the last visible cells, the screen scrolls rapidly. In these instances, it is easier to cut the selection, scroll to the destination, and paste. Alternatively, you can make an entry in the last cell of the selection and drag back (to the left).

USING THE ASSIGNMENT INFORMATION DIALOG BOX

You can display the Assignment Information dialog box by selecting an assignment row in either the Task Usage view or the Resource Usage view and then clicking the Assignment Information button, or double-clicking the assignment row. You can also display the dialog box by choosing Project, Assignment Information.

Figure 10.15 shows the Assignment Information dialog box for the "Unload the moving truck" delayed assignment from the previous example. As you can see, the dialog box provides several fields that you have already worked with on forms and tables, including Work, Units, and Start and Finish. The Cost field is a read-only total cost for the assignment. You can also change the name of the assigned resource here, but there is no drop-down list to choose the resource, so you must know how to spell the name, or you may end up creating a new resource out of a typographical error.

Figure 10.15
The Assignment Information dialog box shows only one resource at a time for the resource you selected.

There are three fields in the Assignment Information dialog box you will not find on any other standard view or dialog box in Microsoft Project 2007:

- **The Work Contour field on the General tab**—This field enables you to choose from a set of predefined work contours. A *contour* is a planned pattern of scheduled work that is spread over the duration of an assignment, a distribution function in mathematical terms. For example, the Front Loaded contour schedules a lot of work per day at the start of the assignment and the daily work tapers off toward the end of the assignment. The default contour is Flat, which means the resource is scheduled to work the same number of hours each day, as called for by the assigned units and the hours available on the resource calendar. Thus, the workload is the same everyday unless the calendar has varying amounts of working time. If you have edited the assignment or applied one of the other contours, you can return the assignment to the standard schedule by applying the Flat contour. The only other way to access and select the predefined contours is to display the Work Contour field as a column in the table in the Task Usage or Resource Usage view.

- **The Cost Rate Table field on the General tab**—This field enables you to select one of the five different Cost Rate tables as the standard and overtime rates for the assignment. The default assignment is Table A. The Cost Rate Table field can also be displayed as a column in the table.

- **The Notes field on the Notes tab**—This field enables you to record notes about an assignment. For instance, you should record why you have delayed an assignment or chose a different Cost Rate table. You could also embed links to other documents such as job specifications, cost worksheets, or websites.

The Tracking tab has fields you can use to monitor work progress and record when work starts, how much work has been done so far, and when work is completed.

→ For additional information about using these fields, **see** Chapter 13, "Tracking Your Project Progress," **p. 443**.

SCHEDULING A LATE START FOR AN ASSIGNMENT

It is possible to assign a resource to a task whose work is not expected to be started until after some work on the task has been completed by others. Suppose that a team is assigned to design a new accessory to its main product and it needs to be able to consult with an expert concerning the design. The consultant's assignment to the design task can be delayed so that it starts after the task has been worked on long enough for the team to understand what it needs to ask the consultant. In addition, another member of the team is a draftsman whose only job is to prepare a drawing of the design, something that cannot be finished until after the design is finished. His assignment must also be delayed.

In Figure 10.16, Brent and Jim are assigned full time to a 5-day task, but the Consultant and Draftsman each have only 4 hours of work assigned. As explained later, Task 1 represents the way Microsoft Project 2007 will assign the work, while Task 2 shows how individual assignments can be delayed.

Figure 10.16
Task 2 schedules the consultant to perform his or her work 2 days after the team has begun its work. The draftsman is scheduled to begin 3 days after work has begun.

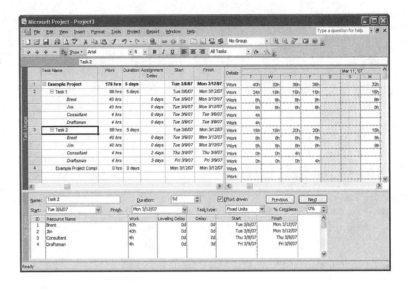

Figure 10.16 displays a Task Usage view, with the time-phased assignment details in the grid on the right, just like the Resource Usage views. The names of the assigned resources are indented under the task names, and the assignment values are rolled up or summed on the row for the task. The Work column in the table on the left shows, for each row, the total of the time-phased work details in the grid.

Task 1 shows how Microsoft Project 2007, by default, schedules the hours for all assignments at the start of the task (March 6th). Task 2 shows the delayed hours for the consultant (March 8th) and the draftsman (March 9th).

The bottom pane shows the Task Form view, with the Resource Schedule details table at the bottom. The column titled Delay shows the amount of an assignment delay. The Start and Finish fields show the scheduled dates for the assignment.

TIP

The Leveling Delay column in the Task Form is a different kind of delay, and is explained in Chapter 25, "Resolving Resource Allocation Problems."

You can create an assignment delay in several different ways:

■ You can enter the amount of the delay in the Delay column in the resource schedule details of the Task Form view (see Figure 10.16). The Delay field is also available in the schedule details on the Resource Form view. If you enter a value in the Delay field, Microsoft Project 2007 automatically calculates the delayed dates for the Start and Finish fields.

NOTE

> The default entry in the Delay field is 0d, which means no delay. The Delay field is never blank. You can remove the delay by entering zero into the Delay field. However, you cannot erase an entry and leave the field blank.

■ You can enter a delay start date in the Start field to the right of the Delay field. Microsoft Project 2007 automatically calculates the value for the Delay field as well as the new finish date.

NOTE

> If you enter a date into the Finish field to the right of the Delay field in the Task Form view, Microsoft Project 2007 does not calculate a delay for the start date. Instead, it recalculates the amount of work that is completed between the (unchanged) start of the assignment and the new finish date you just entered.

■ If you add the Assignment Delay column to the Task Usage view, you can enter the delay or the start date for the assignment on the row for the assignment.

■ You can also create a delay for an assignment by editing the time-phased work details in the grid in the Task Usage view or the Resource Usage view. You can simply select the cells that contain the hours of work you want to delay and drag them to a later date. You can use the mouse to drag the consultant's 4 hours of work from March 6th to March 8th. Microsoft Project 2007 will then calculate the values for the Assignment Delay, Start, and Finish fields.

■ If you double-click anywhere in an assignment row in either the Task Usage or the Resource Usage view, or if you select a cell on that row and click the Assignment Information tool in the Standard toolbar, Microsoft Project 2007 displays the Assignment Information dialog box for that assignment (see Figure 10.17). You can enter a delayed start date in the Start box or use the calendar control to the right of the field to select a start date. Although the Delay field does not appear on the Assignment Information dialog box, its value is recalculated if you enter a new date in the Start field.

Figure 10.17
The Assignment Information dialog box displays all information about the selected assignment.

10

> **NOTE**
>
> You can enter negative amounts in the assignment Delay field only if the project is scheduled from a fixed finish date. You can enter positive amounts only if the project is scheduled from a fixed start date. (See the "Forward-Scheduling vs. Backward-Scheduling" section in "Consultants' Tips" at the end of this chapter.)

SPLITTING A TASK ASSIGNMENT

Splitting an assignment means that you schedule an interruption in the work. There are many conditions that may require you to split an assignment, such as a timing conflict for a resource or a required delay after work has begun. There are two basic methods for splitting:

- You can split the task, and Microsoft Project 2007 automatically splits each resource assignment for the task, with zero work scheduled during the period of the split.
- You can split the individual resource assignment by introducing one or more periods of zero work in the middle of the assignment.

If you introduce a split in an individual resource assignment, Microsoft Project 2007 does not show the split in the task unless it is the only resource assignment for the task, or unless you introduce the same split in all the assigned resources.

You can see in Figure 10.18 the three tasks that both Kim and Dan are assigned. The view has the Gantt Chart view in the top pane and the Task Usage in the bottom. The work detail in the bottom pane for their assignments to Task A shows a split in the assignment on Monday. This split was the result of splitting the tasks, thus making the schedules of all the assigned tasks split.

Dan also has a 1-day split on the following Thursday, in his assignment to Task B. However, the Gantt bar for the task in the top pane of Figure 10.18 is not split, because Kim is assigned to the task and continues to work on those days, while Dan works on another task.

Figure 10.18
Note how Task B does not contain a split even though Dan's work for Thursday is set to 0, this is because Kim continues to work on the task without interruptions so there is never a period of inactivity on the task.

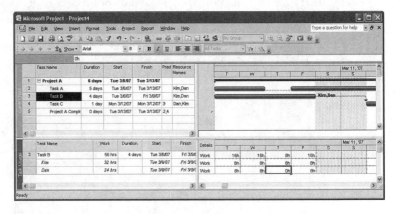

REMOVING RESOURCE ASSIGNMENTS FROM ONE OR MORE TASKS

As the work on a project moves forward, there will be times when the resources that were planned to be used on tasks are not going to be used. Follow these steps to remove a resource assignment from one or more selected tasks:

1. Select the task or tasks in the view that has the resource assignments you want to remove.

2. Display the Assign Resources dialog box, shown in Figure 10.19, by clicking the Assign Resources tool on the Standard toolbar.

Figure 10.19
Remove a resource assignment using the Remove button in the Assign Resources dialog box.

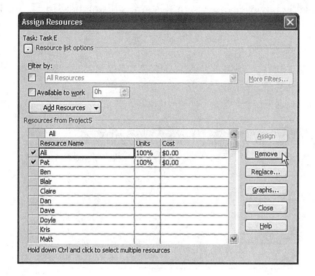

3. Select the resource you want to remove from the assignment by clicking the row for that resource. Use Ctrl+click to select multiple resources for removal.

> **NOTE**
>
> Resources assigned to the selected task are identified by check marks to the left of the resource name. If a check mark is gray instead of black, your task selection in the view includes some tasks that have that resource assigned and some that do not.

4. Click the Remove button. The resources that are selected in the Assign Resources dialog box are removed from any assignments they might have with the tasks that are selected in the underlying view.

REPLACING A RESOURCE ON AN ASSIGNMENT

You can use the Assign Resources dialog box to replace one resource with another, to change the assigned units for a resource, or to change the amount of work assigned to a resource. Each assignment should be modified individually, and different techniques can be used, depending on what you want to modify.

Follow these steps to replace an assigned resource with another resource name:

1. Select the task. You can select multiple tasks by using the Ctrl key if you want to make an identical assignment change in all of them. In Figure 10.20, Task D is selected, and Claire will replace Doyle in the resource assignments.

2. Display the Assign Resources dialog box by clicking the Assign Resources tool on the Standard toolbar.

3. Select the resource name to be replaced.

4. Click the Replace button. Microsoft Project 2007 will now display the Replace Resources dialog box over the Assign Resources dialog box. In Figure 10.20, only the Replace Resource dialog box is shown.

5. Select the new resource name.

6. Select the Units field for the selected resource and a new value if you do not want to use the same units value.

7. Click OK or press Enter.

Figure 10.20
Replace resources in the Replace Resource dialog box; access by pressing the Replace button in the Assign Resources dialog box.

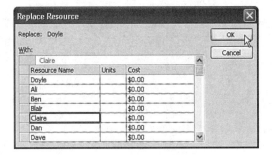

NOTE

If you have filtered the list of resource names, the list in the Replace Resource dialog box will be filtered also.

To replace the number of units in a resource assignment, you simply edit the entry in the Units field. You select a different cell or press Enter to complete the change. You can then use the SmartTag to override Microsoft Project's default calculation.

To replace the amount of work assigned to a resource, you should select the cells for the units and type a work amount (a number followed by a time unit abbreviation). Microsoft Project 2007 will divide the task duration by the work amount you entered, and assign the resulting units. You can use the SmartTag to override Microsoft Project's default calculation.

HOW-TO'S: MODIFYING RESOURCE ASSIGNMENTS

This section provides more individual scenario level guidance on how to achieve the work modeling results you want. The section is loosely ordered from the more general/common situation to the more esoteric.

Key parts to this section are:

- Graphing resource availability
- Scheduling resources for a specific amount of work
- Contouring resource usage
- Selecting a Predefined Contour Using the Assignment Information Dialog Box
- Using Overtime to shorten Duration
- Selecting a cost rate table for an Assignment
- Assigning fixed cost and fixed contract fees
- Scheduling with Task Calendars
- Adding delay to an Assignment

GRAPHING RESOURCE AVAILABILITY

Suppose that you want a specific resource to work on a task, but the resource does not have available work hours during the time the task is currently scheduled. One of the possible solutions could be to reschedule the task to a time when the resource has enough work time available. You can do this by selecting the resource in the Assign Resources dialog box and then clicking on the Graphs button to display timeline graphs and accompanying data tables. The timeline graphs and data tables show information about the selected resource's availability and currently assigned work. You can choose from three different graphs:

- **The Remaining Availability graph**—You can choose the Remaining Availability graph to see the remaining available working time along a timeline (see Figure 10.21). You can zoom in and out on the timeline to look at the data by hours, days, weeks, months, and so on. If you have selected multiple resources, the date for each is color-coded, and check boxes in the graph legend will let you temporarily remove and restore the individual resources in the display.

10

Figure 10.21
The Graphs window allows you to select one out of the three available graphs.

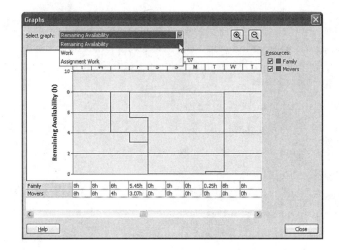

- **The Work graph**—The Work graph looks similar to the Remaining Availability graph, but it shows already assigned work. You can zoom the timeline, and multiple resources are color-coded and can be removed and restored from the graph.

- **The Assignment Work graph**—You can choose the Assignment Work graph (see Figure 10.22) to see both the work already assigned and the total availability. You can select a task in the underlying view to which the resource is assigned. This graph also distinguishes the work assignment on the selected task from assigned work on all other tasks. For example, if you select a task and assign the resources to it, this graph will show you the total available work for the resource, the amount of work assigned to the selected task, and the total work assigned to other tasks. You can easily see if the total of all the assignments exceeds the availability for the resources. If it does, you know you have overallocated the resource.

Figure 10.22
You can use the Assignment Work graph to review resource availability versus the amount of work the resource is assigned, not only for the selected task, but for other tasks in the project.

To view a graph, follow these steps:

1. Display a task view as the active view; it cannot be one of the task forms.

2. Display the Assign Resources dialog box by clicking the Assign Resources tools on the Standard toolbar.

3. Select one or more resources whose data you want included in the graph. Use Ctrl+click to add nonadjacent resources to the selection.

4. If you are going to view the Assignment Work graph and want currently assigned tasks to be included, select the tasks now. After the graph window opens, you cannot change your selection. The quickest way to include all tasks assigned to the selected resource(s) is to select all tasks by using the Select All button, the blank space above the ID column.

5. Click the Graphs button to display the Microsoft Graph window.

6. Choose the graph type in the Select Graph box.

7. If you select multiple resources, remove and restore individual resources by using the selected boxes next to their names in the legend.

8. Use the Zoom In and Zoom Out buttons to compress or expand the timeline.

9. When you are finished, do not forget to click the Close button.

> **NOTE**
>
> You cannot modify the formatting of the graph. All of the controls you have are listed here.

SCHEDULING RESOURCES FOR A SPECIFIC AMOUNT OF WORK

For work resources, you can also use the Assign Resources dialog box to calculate the number of units needed to complete a specific amount of work within the task's current duration. In the Assign Resources dialog box, enter a work amount in the Units column (a number followed by a time unit, such as **40h** for 40 hours). Microsoft Project 2007 will then calculate the number of units needed to do that much work, within the current duration for the task. *This procedure does not work if the task is effort driven and this is the first assignment of the resource to the task.* You can use this technique to recalculate an existing working resource assignment, even if the task is effort driven.

Follow these steps to assign resources by using the work amount:

1. Select the task or tasks to which you want the resource assigned.

2. Display the Assign Resources dialog box by clicking the Assign Resources tool on the Standard toolbar.

3. Select the resource name from the Name list.

4. Select the Units field and type the work amount followed by the unit it is measured in: m (minute), h (hour), d (day), w (week), or mo (month).

5. Select a different cell, click the Assign button, or press Enter to have Microsoft Project 2007 calculate the units and assign the resource to the selected tasks.

CONTOURING RESOURCE USAGE

The default resource work pattern is known as the *flat pattern*. In the flat pattern, Microsoft Project 2007 schedules a resource's work to begin when the task begins and to continue working at a constant and uninterrupted rate until either all of the remaining work from the Task is allocated on the assignment or until the Task finish date is reached. This means Microsoft Project 2007 will use the same (specified) units every day until the assigned work is complete. On some occasions, you might want a resource to put greater effort into a task at the outset, and then taper off the daily effort until the task is finished. If that's what you hope to accomplish, then you will want to assign more units and hours for the days at the beginning of the task and then use a reduced number of units and hours each day to complete the task. This is known as *front loading* the work on the task. Other times, you might want to *back load* the work, by starting with a small number of hours and assignment units up front and then increasing the work as the task nears completion. Different scheduling patterns like these are available in Microsoft Project 2007 as *work contours*. The default is a flat contour pattern, but you can have Microsoft Project 2007 change an assignment schedule by applying one of seven different predefined work contours. You can also create your own contour by editing the time-phased values in the Usage View grid.

To change the scheduling pattern, you can display either the Task Usage view or the Resource Usage view. The Resource Usage view is similar to the Task Usage view in that it displays all the resources with their assignments indented beneath them and provides assignment details for each period in the timescale in the grid of cells. You can use either of these views to apply contoured assignments, by either applying one of the built-in contours or by editing the work assigned in any given time period in the grid.

To illustrate contouring, suppose that Ben is assigned to Task A, which is estimated to take 40 hours to complete. In the beginning, he needs to concentrate completely on the task, but once it is underway, he can spend more time on other tasks. You could schedule his assignment like the "before and after" example in the Task Usage view in Figure 10.23. Task A shows the standard assignment schedule.

Figure 10.23
Because the front-loaded contour was applied to Task A After, the amount of hours Ben works each day gradually decreases.

Task A After shows Ben's assignment schedule after the front-loaded contour is applied. Note the icon in the Indicator column that flags this assignment as having a front-loaded contour. You can see the icon in the Indicator column that flags this assignment as having a front-loaded contour. Ben's assignment starts at 100% but soon drops to lower and lower levels, until all the work is finished. As a result of this lowering of levels, the hours of work scheduled for each day become less and less; Ben will still do 40 hours of work, but now it takes more days to complete the work. Notice that the duration for Task A After is 8.33 days, instead of 5 days.

In Figure 10.24, you can see the Resource Usage view of Ben's front-loaded task. The main record is now the resource Ben instead of the task, but indented under it is the same assignment record, now labeled with the associated task name. The details in the grid are the same as those for Task A After in Figure 10.23.

The bottom pane of Figure 10.24 shows the Resource Graph view. This view displays a histogram (a vertical bar chart) to give a graphical image of the resource assignment detail that you select. In this case, the peak units detail is graphed and illustrates very nicely the declining nature of the front-loaded work contour. This graph, in fact, is the source of the image that is used in the indicator for front-loaded contours.

Figure 10.24
Ben's decreasing work concept of the front-loaded contour is perfectly demonstrated in the Resource Graph view in the bottom pane.

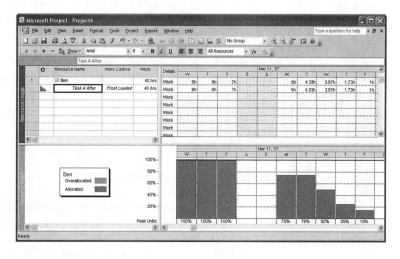

Microsoft Project 2007 has eight predefined work contour patterns that you can apply to a resource assignment. These are in addition to the Flat pattern, which is the default, and used when Microsoft Project 2007 first calculates an assignment. The contour patterns are described in Table 10.2.

TABLE 10.2   MICROSOFT PROJECT 2007 WORK CONTOURS

Contour Icon	Contour Name	Contour Description
	Flat	This is the pattern that Project uses in the initial assignment calculation. All work is assigned as soon as the task starts, and it continues until the assignment is complete. There is no indicator icon for this pattern.
	Back Loaded	The daily workload starts light and builds until the end of the task.
	Front Loaded	The heaviest daily load is the beginning of the task and tapers off continuously until the end of the task.
	Double Peak	The daily workload starts low, builds to an early peak, drops off, builds to another peak, and then tapers off to the end of the task.
	Early Peak	The daily workload starts light, builds rapidly to a peak, and then tapers off until the end of the task.
	Late Peak	The daily workload starts light, builds slowly to a peak near the end of the task, then drops off somewhat at the end.
	Bell	The daily workload starts light, builds to a peak in the middle of the assignment, and then tapers off until the end of the assignment.
	Turtle	The daily workload starts somewhat light, builds rapidly to a plateau, and remains there for most of the rest of the assignment, then drops back to a somewhat light level at the end.
	Contoured	This pattern does not illustrate a predefined contour; rather, it illustrates the fact that you can edit the work assignments to produce your own work pattern. The indicator, with a pencil in the bar chart, shows that the work assignment has been manually edited. Note that you can only edit the Work cells; you cannot edit the Peak Units values directly.

Figure 10.25 shows the different contour types in an actual calculation by Microsoft Project 2007. Task A, assigned to Claire, shows a Flat contour. The default assignment of 40 hours of work is scheduled evenly over 5 days for a resource with a unit assignment of 100%.

Figure 10.25
This illustration shows the different contour types for a 40 hour assignment.

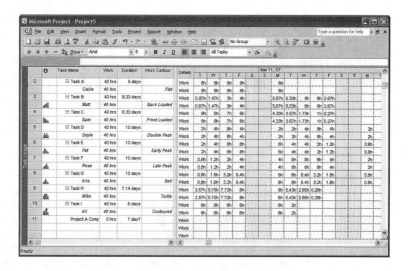

In the time-phase details on the right, you can see the work and peak units for each day. Claire is assigned 100% to the task for all 5 days; 100% of her time is allocated to the task.

Rows 2 through 8 show how Microsoft Project 2007 would schedule the work if one of the predefined contours were applied. The total work remains 40 hours in all cases, as shown in the Work column. The work assignments for each day vary, depending on the contour pattern, as do the peak units.

All the contours reduce the unit assignment during different days in the assignment. The choice of which days determines the pattern that is the source of the different contour names. Since there is less work scheduled on some of the days, the total assignment necessitates that it will take longer to complete. Notice that the duration of the task is extended when the contours are applied. Instead of the task being completed in 5 days, work must continue into additional days.

TIP

> Beware of scheduling back-loaded work effort on as task. This should be done only with careful consideration as you are also back-loading all the risk around the task. Back-loaded tasks have little chance of correction for underestimation. By the time you become aware that the effort estimate was flawed, you are at the end of the task and missing the targeted completion date is very likely. In addition, if the contour expectations are communicated to the resource, you also take the risk of being impacted by basic human nature—via procrastination.

The last row in Figure 10.25 is labeled Contoured and is not a predefined contour pattern. It is the name Microsoft Project 2007 applies when the user edits the work details for an assignment. In this case, the resource is scheduled to work only six hours on Friday (instead of the eight hours possible). Forcing Friday to six hours instead of eight is done in either the

Task Usage or Resource Usage view where you can edit the assigned hours in the work details cells. In either case, you are forcing a custom contour through the edit actions.

To apply a predefined contour to an assignment, see the steps in the next section.

> **NOTE**
>
> If overtime hours are assigned to a task when you apply a contour, Microsoft Project 2007 spreads out the overtime evenly, over the duration of the assignment, no matter which contour is applied.

> **TIP**
>
> If you want to add a resource with a contoured assignment to an existing task that has other resources already assigned and you do not want the task duration or the other resource schedules to change, make the task a Fixed Duration task and disable Effort Driven before assigning the contour. You can later return the task to its previous task type and effort-driven status. Microsoft Project 2007 applies the contour but has to stop scheduling hours when it reaches the end of the task duration. As a result, the new resource has a lower total amount of work than it initially did. You will undoubtedly have to manually edit the work assignment values to get the results you want.

SELECTING A PREDEFINED CONTOUR USING THE ASSIGNMENT INFORMATION DIALOG BOX

By default, the work that Microsoft Project 2007 schedules for an assignment is evenly distributed across available time periods of the assignment (that is, the Flat contour). As you have already seen, you can edit the assignments in individual time periods to customize the schedule. You can also choose one of eight predefined contour patterns for Microsoft Project 2007 to apply to an individual assignment.

For example, if a resource schedule needs to show lots of hours up front, with a tapering off toward the end, you could assign the Front Loaded contour to the assignment, and Microsoft Project 2007 will change the work in the individual periods to reflect that pattern.

> **TIP**
>
> If you change the work contour, it is a good idea to document why you made the choices you made in the assignment Notes field. You can click on the Notes tab in the Assignment Information dialog box and enter supporting documentation about an assignment, including links to external documents such as job specifications or standards.

Follow these steps to select a contour for an assignment:

1. Select the assignment in the Task Usage view or the Resource Usage view.
2. Display the assignment Information dialog box by clicking the Assignment Information tool or by double-clicking the assignment row.

3. On the General tab, use the drop-down list in the Work Contour field to select one of the predefined contours (see Figure 10.26).

4. Click OK to have Microsoft Project 2007 calculate the new assignment pattern.

Figure 10.26
You can change the Work Contour in the Assignment Information dialog box.

USING OVERTIME TO SHORTEN DURATION

Another way to reduce the duration of a task is by scheduling some of a resource's time as overtime. *Overtime work* means work that is scheduled outside the resource's normal working hours. For Microsoft Project 2007, that means work that is scheduled during nonworking time on the resource calendar. Assigning overtime does not reduce the total amount of work for an assignment; instead, the amount scheduled during regular working time is reduced by the amount of the overtime. Microsoft Project 2007 schedules the overtime work by spreading it out evenly over the duration of the assignment. Later, when you enter actual work completed, you can specify exactly how many hours of overtime were completed in any given time period.

Microsoft Project 2007 also charges the resource's overtime rate for overtime work, so costs might rise, depending on your entry in the Overtime Rate field. The cost of the overtime hours is calculated by using the overtime rate that you defined in the Resource Information dialog box for the period in which the work took place.

> **TIP**
>
> Planned overtime can come in handy when you have to plan a mid-project correction to get back on track but should be avoided in most other cases. It leaves little time for corrective action should an activity slip. Excessive consecutive overtime can take a heavy toll on productivity/performance and therefore quality. Remember, resources are people too.

> **TIP**
>
> Scheduled weekend tasks often carry high impact/risk as weekend activities typically consist of tasks that would interrupt or delay many other activities if performed during the week. So make sure you have a good backup plan or solid resources if you do schedule for a weekend.

Example 1, suppose that Eric has been assigned full time (100% units) to upgrade the office's computer system, a task scheduled to take 60 hours of work with a duration of 7.5 days to complete (see Task A in Figure 10.27). Eric is scheduled to start on a Monday and finish at midday on Wednesday the following week. The cost of the task is $1,500 (based on Eric's standard rate of $25/hour).

The assignment details in Figure 10.27 have been augmented to show not only work, which is the total work per time period, but also the regular work and overtime work components of total work, as well as the cost of the assignment. The Regular Work, Overtime Work, and Cost columns have been added. These columns and the work column show the task totals for the corresponding time-phased details in the grid.

For Task A (No Overtime), the total work is 60 hours, which is the sum of the work hours in the grid. You can see the total work for each day is made up of regular work only. The duration of Task A is 7.5 days, and that is due to the fact that there are 7 full days of work and 1 half-day of 4 hours. The total cost of the task is $1,500, which is the sum of the daily Cost values in the grid.

Figure 10.27
Eric will finish faster in Task A (With Overtime) but the task will cost more than if he worked regular hours with no overtime assigned.

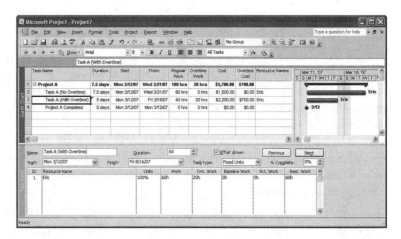

Task A (With Overtime) in Figure 10.27 shows what would happen if Eric's manager decided that she needed the task completed in no more then 5 days, and authorizes 20 hours of overtime work for Eric. Eric still spends a total of 60 hours on the task, but 20 hours are overtime hours and only 40 hours are regular working time. Eric now does 12 hours of work per day—8 hours of regular work plus 4 hours of overtime. All 60 hours of work are completed in just 5 days; thus, the task duration is 5 days. The cost for each day is $340. This is figured at $200 standard-rate hours (8 hours at $25/hour) plus $140 of overtime-rate hours (4 hours at $35/hour). Note that if Eric's overtime rate had been at the default zero, the daily cost for the task would have actually fallen to $200 (the cost of the regular work hours).

NOTE

> Overtime work that is scheduled by Microsoft Project 2007 cannot be adjusted manually, meaning you cannot edit the cells in the grid to change the number of overtime hours scheduled on a particular day. However, when you are tracking progress on a task, you can add Actual Overtime Work to the details in the grid, and enter the amount of actual overtime work in each time period to show exactly when the overtime work was performed.

The bottom pane in Figure 10.27 shows the Task Form view with the resource work details displayed at the bottom. Because Task A (With Overtime) is selected in the top pane, the details show the values with overtime assigned. Note that the Overtime Work field displays 20 hours. The Work field shows the total work, 60 hours, which includes overtime.

TIP

> Another way to schedule more work during a specific time is to change the resource calendar and increase the working time hours for that time period. You can edit the resource calendar and change nonworking days or hours into working time. Note that Microsoft Project 2007 charges the standard rate for work scheduled during the regular working time hours. This is not a good solution if you must actually pay the resource an overtime rate that differs from their standard rate. However, if pay difference is not an issue, editing the Calendar gives you the ability to state explicitly when the extra work time takes place. The drawback in this situation is that if you are to reassign the resource to different tasks, or if the task gets rescheduled to a different date range, you no longer need the extra working time. Microsoft Project 2007 uses the time for other assignments unless you remember to remove the extra working time from the calendar.

You can view scheduled overtime in the Task Usage and Resource Usage views, but you cannot enter overtime in those views unless you add a column to the table for the Overtime Work field. The Overtime Work field appears in three views for you to view and edit:

- The Task Form view, with the resource work details table displayed at the bottom of the form
- The Task Details Form view, with the resource work details table displayed at the bottom of the form
- The Resource Form view, with the work details table displayed at the bottom of the form

NOTE

> If you assign all the work to be done in overtime, Microsoft Project 2007 reduces the duration of the task to zero and automatically flags the task as a milestone. You can remove the Milestone flag by opening the Task Information dialog box and clearing the Mark Task as Milestone check box on the Advanced tab. The milestone symbol no longer appears in the Gantt Chart view for the task, although its duration is still zero.

10

TIP

> To remove overtime work, you must reset the Overtime Work field to zero; it cannot be cleared.

Follow these steps to enter overtime in the Task Form view:

1. Choose a task view such as the Gantt Chart view from the View menu for the top pane.
2. Select the task for which you want to schedule overtime.
3. Display the Task Form view in the bottom pane by choosing Window, Split.
4. Press F6 to activate the Task Form view in the bottom pane.
5. In the bottom pane, right-click the form and select Resource Work from the shortcut menu to display the Resource Work fields in the entry table (see Figure 10.28).
6. Select the Overtime Work field and enter the amount of work that you are scheduling in overtime. Enter a number followed by a time unit abbreviation (m, h, d, w, or mo) and then press Enter. Do not reduce the entry in the Work field. That field's entry must show the *total* amount of work to be done, including both the regular work and the overtime work.
7. Click OK.

Figure 10.28
In the first task, no overtime is assigned. 40 hours of overtime is assigned in the second task, which is identical to the first, but will finish one week faster.

NOTE

> If you want to eliminate overtime, you must enter 0 in the Overtime field. This field must contain a value, so it cannot be left empty.

Example 2, in Figure 10.28, overtime has been entered for Linda Elliot's assignment to the Create Advertising Plan task. The total workload for this assignment is 120 hours, which was originally scheduled to take 3 weeks, but after recording 40 hours of overtime, the regular hours are only 80 and the task duration is reduced to 2 weeks. Usually, overtime is scheduled for just this reason—to reduce the calendar time required to complete a task.

SELECTING A COST RATE TABLE FOR AN ASSIGNMENT

One of the important features in Microsoft Project 2007 is the ability to define and specify different sets of standard and overtime cost rates for a resource so that work on assignments can be charged at different rates for different types of work. For example, a consulting firm might assign a seasoned consultant to high technical cases at higher rates than it would use for the other more mundane tasks.

Setting which Cost Rate table to use for an assignment is done only in the Task Usage view or the Resource Usage view. In either of these views, you can either add the Cost Rate Table field directly to the view (for easy visibility/access on each assignment row) or use the Assignment Information dialog box. If you are using the Assignment Information dialog box (brought up by double-clicking an assignment), you will see the pulldown to specify the Cost Rate Table on the General tab. When you see the field (in either the view itself or the Assignment Information dialog box) choose one of the lettered cost tables in the drop-down list in the field to assign that cost table's standard, overtime, and per-use rates to the assignment.

The Cost Rate Table for a resource can have different rates for different time periods (to accommodate salary raises, etc.). If there are dated changes in the rates, Microsoft Project 2007 applies the rates that are defined in the table for the dates in which the task is also scheduled.

See Chapter 8 for how to define the Cost Rate Table entries for a resource.

> **NOTE**
>
> You can edit the Cost Rate table only in the Resource Information dialog box. First, display a view with fields for resources, and then either double-click a resource name or click the Information tool on the Standard toolbar to display the Resource Information dialog box. Click the Costs tab to display the five Cost Rate tables, A through E.

ASSIGNING FIXED COSTS AND FIXED CONTRACT FEES

Some tasks might have costs that are not linked to a particular resource that you have named and are not affected by the task duration. This type of cost is treated as a *fixed cost* in Microsoft Project 2007, and it is entered on the Task level (not the Assignment level) in the Fixed Cost column of the Cost table on a task view such as the Gantt Chart view. Microsoft Project 2007 adds the fixed cost amount to the total of the resource costs and displays the sum in the Cost (Total Cost) columns of various views.

> **NOTE**
>
> You can associate fixed cost with summary tasks as well as with normal tasks. Because the field might be used for summary task fixed costs, Microsoft Project 2007 does not roll up the Fixed Cost field to summary tasks. In other words, although the fixed cost is included in the Total Cost column, you cannot see a total for all fixed costs.

You can also have a cost that is associated with a resource but that is not affected by the task duration or any variations in work for the resource. For instance, the resource might be a contractor or vendor who is to deliver the completed task at a fixed cost. In these cases, the contractor or vendor should be listed as a resource and the cost should be entered as part of the assignment information on the Task Form view. If you were to simply add this cost to the task fixed cost, you would lose the relationship of the cost with that specific resource.

To display the Fixed Cost field, display a task view such as the Gantt Chart view in the top pane. To display the Cost table, right-click over the Select All button, the blank area just above the row numbers, and choose Cost (see Figure 10.29)

TIP

> You should document any fixed-cost amounts in the task's Notes field so that you and others will always know what the cost represents.

Figure 10.29
The Cost table displays the various costs for the project, such as Fixed, Total, Baseline, Accrual, and so on.

TIP

> You can also apply the Cost table to any task view by selecting View, Table, and then Cost.

In Figure 10.30, the resource cost details for Task A are displayed in the Task Form view in the bottom pane. The sum of those costs is $3,300. In the top pane, the $1,000 entry in the Fixed Cost column is added to the resource costs to create the value in the Total Cost column.

Figure 10.30
The total cost for the task is equal to resource cost ($1,300 + $2,000 = $3,300) plus the fixed cost ($1,000) for the final value of $4,300.

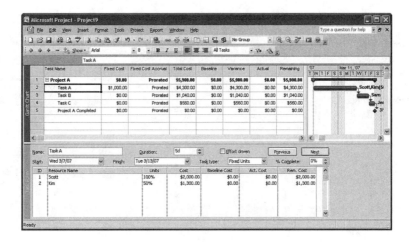

TIP

If you enter an amount in the Total Cost (Cost) field to overwrite the calculated value that is displayed there, Microsoft Project 2007 treats this as the sum of the calculated resource costs and a new fixed cost amount. It then changes the entry in the Fixed Cost column to support this interpretation.

If a resource that is assigned to a task is working for a fixed fee (say, a contractor or vendor on an outsourced task), you want that cost to remain fixed no matter what happens to the task duration. You do not need Microsoft Project 2007 to track the hours of work for the resource because those hours are important to the contractor or vendor, but not to you. Your cost is not affected if the job takes more work or money than estimated, as long as it is completed on time.

In prior versions of project, to accommodate this case, you had to make the task a fixed-duration task and assign the contractor or vendor as a resource to the task; then enter **0** in the Units field for the assignment. The work amount was then calculated as zero. Therefore, the hourly resource cost value for this resource is also zero. After creating this assignment, Microsoft Project let you enter the contract amount in the resource Cost field, and that entry was not overwritten by Microsoft Project's calculations.

In Microsoft Project 2007, life is much simpler. With the addition of the Cost Resource you can go to the Resource Sheet and create a new resource with the same name as the vendor. Select "Cost" as the Type for the resource and select "End" for the Accrue At field (specifying that you will not pay them until the task is complete). You now have a Cost Resource, representing the vendor. You can apply this resource to any task and provide a fixed fee contract cost for that specific task. You enter the cost value when you assign the resource, by entering a Cost value instead of a Units value. The contract cost will be scheduled to accrue on the last day of the task. If the task moves in time or extends in duration, the cost accrual date will change with it, always accruing on the last day of the task (see Figure 10.31).

10

Figure 10.31
By using a Cost Resource, you can create a Fixed-Fee Contract task. Create the task, assign the Cost Resource, and enter the contract fee.

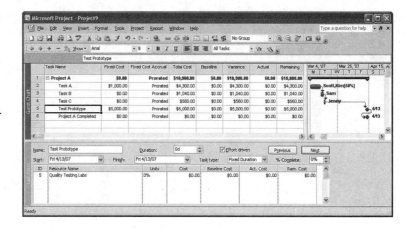

SCHEDULING WITH TASK CALENDARS

If a task has its own special calendar assigned to it, then by default Microsoft Project 2007 schedules work for the resources only when the working times for both the task calendar and the resource calendar intersect. Microsoft Project 2007 displays the Assigned Calendar indicator for the task (see Figure 10.32).

Figure 10.32
The Assigned Calendar indicator identifies tasks using Task Calendars.

This option is useful when there are special nonworking times associated with the task (therefore impacting ALL resources on the task). Adding these nonworking times to each resource calendar could cause errors with the scheduling of those resources on other tasks. For example, equipment maintenance might make the company's bulldozers unavailable for 2 hours every week. You could create an Equipment Maintenance base calendar to define those nonworking hours and assign it to a task. The alternative, adding the nonworking times for this resource to the calendars for all the other resources assigned to the task, would interfere with scheduling the other resources for other tasks.

Another use for task calendars is scheduling a task during normally nonworking time. For example, if you wanted to schedule the upgrade for a network server on a weekend to minimize user inconvenience, you could create a task calendar (and assign it to the task) that has working time only on the days and hours when you want the task scheduled. You would then tell project to ignore the resource calendars on the task (see below).

To assign a calendar to a task, you need to create the special base calendar first, using the Tools, Change Working Times command. Then select the task and display the Task Information dialog box. On the Advanced tab, you display the drop-down list of base calendars in the Calendar box and select the appropriate calendar (see Figure 10.33)

Figure 10.33
Assign a calendar to a task on the Advanced tab of the Task Information dialog box.

If you want Microsoft Project 2007 to ignore the resource calendar working times, then you need to select the Scheduling Ignores Resources Calendars check box. Once that box is selected, the number of hours of work scheduled for a resource on any given day will depend on the units assigned and the work hours defined on the task calendar, not on the resource calendar. You must verify that the resources can meet this schedule.

For example, Eric gets assigned to the network server task scheduled for a Saturday, using the task calendar that specifies only weekend days as working time. Eric's resource calendar is based on the standard calendar that specifies that weekend days are nonworking time. In this case, there is insufficient intersecting working time for both the task calendar and the resource calendar to be honored.

If the task and resource calendars do not intersect for enough hours to complete the task, then Microsoft Project 2007 will display a warning to alert you that there are insufficient intersecting working times (see Figure 10.34). You then need to modify one of the calendars to tell Microsoft Project 2007 to ignore the resource calendar.

Figure 10.34
Microsoft Project 2007 displays this warning when resource and task calendars do not share enough common working time to complete the task as scheduled.

ADDING DELAY TO AN ASSIGNMENT

When you assign a resource to a task, Microsoft Project 2007 schedules the work to start when the task starts. Sometimes, however, one or more of the resources assigned to a task might be allowed to delay starting until after the task is partly completed by other resources.

For example, if you assign a marketing manager, an engineer, and a draftsman to draw up a preliminary design for a product, the draftsman's work on the task does not really start until some design details have already been proposed. To accurately schedule the draftsman's work, Microsoft Project 2007 needs to delay the start of the draftsman's scheduled work to some time after the task starts.

Microsoft Project 2007 provides an Assignment Delay field, which you can use to force a delay in the scheduled work for a resource beyond the start of the task. If you want to enter a value in the Delay field on the Task Form, you need to display the resource schedule details, where the Delay field is available for editing.

> **NOTE**
>
> You can get the Delay field by replacing the Task Form view with the Resource Form view and displaying the schedule details, which is just like the resource schedule details on the Task Form view. You can also enter delays on the Task Usage and Resource Usage views. The Task Usage view is discussed in the section "Modifying Work Schedules with the Task Usage View" earlier in this chapter. The Resource Usage view is explored in greater detail in Chapter 25, "Resolving Resource Allocation Problems."

Figure 10.35 shows the Task Form view with the resource schedule details displayed. The Prototype Design task is selected, and the assigned resources are listed in the assignment details. The Draftsman resource is scheduled to work only 16 hours, which is less than the hours for the other work resource.

You can also see in Figure 10.35 that Microsoft Project 2007 has scheduled the Draftsman resource to begin thirteen days after the task's start, which is 8/13/07. Because of the task split, the difference between the start and finish dates is more than the task duration. In reality, the draftsman is expected to execute his assignment in the last 2 days of the task, 8/29/07 and 8/30/07, after the other resource has completed most of his or her work.

Figure 10.35
The Task Form view with the resource schedule details displayed.

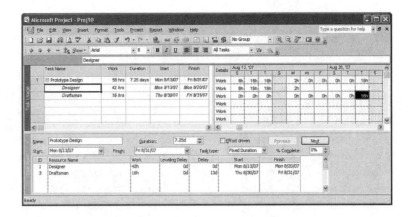

You can create a delay in the Task Form view by entering the amount of the delay in the Delay field or by entering the start date for the assignment. Because of the task split, it is easier to create this particular delay by entering the start date for the draftsmen assignment (8/29/07) than to try and calculate the amount of the delay.

In Figure 10.35, the date 8/29/07 was entered in the Assignment Start field for the Draftsmen resource, and Microsoft Project 2007 has calculated the delay and the assignment finish to be 8/30/07. Of course, if the delay causes the draftsman's assignment to finish after all the other assignments are finished, it also delays the finish of the task and increases the task's duration.

Follow these steps to enter a delay in an assignment:

1. Display the Task Form view or Task Details Form view in the bottom pane of the task view.

2. Activate the form in the bottom pane and display the schedule details by right-clicking and choosing Resource Schedule.

3. Select the task for the assignment in the top pane.

4. Select the cell in the Delay field for the resource name you want to delay, and then enter a delay value. Use a number followed by the measurement units for the delay (minutes, hours, days, weeks, or months). You could also enter a delayed start date for the assignment in the start field, as an alternative, and then Microsoft Project 2007 will calculate the amount of delay.

5. Click the OK button to complete the entry.

CAUTION

As noted earlier in the chapter, you can create a delay by either entering the Delay value or by entering a new date in the Start field. You should not, however, attempt to enter a delayed date in the Finish date column because Microsoft Project 2007 does not treat that as a delaying tactic. Instead, Microsoft Project 2007 treats it as extending the assignment, and it recalculates the Work value of the assignment.

To remove a delay for an assignment, you enter **0** in the Delay field in place of any existing value and click the OK button. Microsoft Project 2007 will remove the delay and the assignment start date will match the task start date.

CONSULTANTS' TIPS

This chapter provides only a portion of the possibilities that Microsoft Project 2007 provides for manipulating your project's resources. As you experiment, you may find many other methods that work well for you. Whatever choices you make, remember to use the Notes tab of the Resource Information dialog box to document an assignment or special contours that you choose. You can type and format the note's text just as you do the text of task notes and resource notes. You can insert documents into the notes or insert links to documents that are stored outside of the Microsoft Project 2007 file. You can also insert hyperlinks to websites.

80/20: USE THE TASK ENTRY VIEW FOR RESOURCE ENTRY AND MODIFYING ASSIGNMENTS

In addition, use the "Assign Resources" dialog to find resources to assign to the task (it has the best filtering capabilities and allows you to see all the resources). Use both the Task Entry view and the Assign Resource dialog box for the best results.

DEPTH: CALCULATION OF THE DEFAULT UNITS VALUE USED WHEN ASSIGNING A RESOURCE

When you assign a resource to a task an assignment is created. If you do not specify the Units value to the Resource when you create the assignment, a calculated default value is used. The rule behind this is simple but not necessarily intuitive. The value used is the lesser of 100% or the Max Units field set on the resource in the Resource Sheet. If Yvonne has her Max Units set to 125%, then when she is assigned to a task (without specifying her units), 100% will be the value used. If her Max Units had been set to 75%, then 75% would have been used.

CONFIG: TURN OFF AUTOMATIC RESOURCE CREATION

By default, resources are automatically created if you type the resource name into any of the fields/forms/views that allow you to specify a resource. This is a source of a serious potential problem. Typing errors can leave you with two or more resource entries all representing the same real person. Frequent checking of the Resource Sheet view is necessary to keep the subtle issues caused by this from creeping in. As an alternative, you can turn off the ability to automatically create resources when typing. Go to the Tools menu, select Options, and go to the "General" tab. Near the bottom, you will see "General Options" for your project. Clear the "Automatically add new resources and tasks" option.

FORWARD-SCHEDULING VS BACKWARD-SCHEDULING

The discussion in this chapter is presented in terms of forward-scheduled projects—projects with fixed start dates and dynamic, calculated finish dates. Microsoft Project 2007 can be set to backward-scheduling mode through the Project Information dialog box opened from the Project menu. Setting the "Schedule From:" pull-down to "Project Finish Date" effectively reverses all the scheduling logic in project to drive from the finish date backwards to calculate the start dates of assignments, tasks, and therefore of the whole project. If you see calculations behaving oddly in all areas of Microsoft Project 2007, check this setting!

As an example, instead of the value in the Assignment Delay field being added to the task start to calculate the assignment start, in fixed-finish-date projects, the Assignment Delay value is *subtracted* from the task finish to calculate an early assignment finish. That, in turn, leads to an earlier start for the assignment.

For fixed-finish-date projects, the Assignment Delay field accepts only negative numbers and the delay amount is subtracted from the task finish date to calculate an early finish for the assignment; then the start is calculated. You can also enter an earlier date in the Finish date field, and Microsoft Project 2007 calculates the negative delay and new start date for you. If you enter a new date in the Start Date column, Microsoft Project 2007 recalculates the Work value of the assignment instead of calculating a delay.

10

USING STANDARD VIEWS, TABLES, FILTERS, AND GROUPS TO REVIEW YOUR SCHEDULE

In this chapter

Views, tables, filters, and groups provide an efficient way to review your project information and display precisely the details you are looking for. The previous chapters of the book discussed some view and table basics in order to define your project's tasks and resources as well as to assign resources to tasks. This chapter explores in detail all other views you can utilize in order to efficiently review your project schedule and focus on the information you need.

WHAT CAN I VIEW USING MICROSOFT PROJECT 2007?

When discussing views, tables, filters, and groups, it is important to first understand the types of entities that can be viewed within Microsoft Project 2007.

Microsoft Project 2007 includes information about the following entities:

- **Tasks**—Project activities and their relationships with one another
- **Resources**—People and materials assigned to the tasks within a project schedule

In addition, each entity has three dimensions of project data that can be applied to it, as shown in Figure 11.1:

- **Cost**—Costs associated with tasks and resources in your project
- **Schedule (Duration)**—The length of a task and the time it tasks to complete
- **Effort (Work)**—The amount of work completed, number of effort hours remaining and worked, and general progress of your project's schedule

Figure 11.1
Cost, Duration, and Work represent the three main dimensions for tasks and resources and influence the formula used to calculate work in Microsoft Project 2007.

When using views and tables to display entity information, you will find that some views and tables are more appropriate for displaying information than others. Choosing the right view not only depends on the common usages of the view, but also knowing yourself and the best ways you absorb information. For example, if you are a person who works a lot with calendars, Calendar format may be more meaningful to you than something displayed in a spreadsheet. Similarly, if you are a visual person, the graphical representation of information may be the most useful. The "Viewing Strategies" section of this chapter discusses some general strategies for choosing the appropriate views based on the task at hand.

VIEWING STRATEGIES

This section provides a light high-level overview of strategies you need to consider when selecting the appropriate view to review your schedule.

STRATEGIES ON USING VIEWS

Views are logical organizations of data displayed on the screen. Microsoft Office Project Standard 2007 (Microsoft Project 2007) provides many built-in standard views that can be used "as is," or customized and combined with other views and tables to create more personalized and practical data displays.

Views can be organized by the entity type they display: either task or resource. They show information about one or the other, but never both at the same time.

Views can be accessed by selecting from the View menu, as shown in Figure 11.2, which displays the most commonly used views in Microsoft Project 2007. To display additional views, select View, More Views, as shown in Figure 11.3.

Figure 11.2
Accessing commonly used views in Microsoft Project 2007.

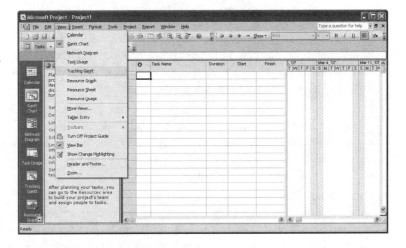

Figure 11.3
Accessing all Microsoft Project 2007 views.

Views can be organized into four main categories:

- **Graphical views**—As the name suggests, these views show a graphical representation of information. Most graphical views, except for the Network Diagram, are particularly good at displaying time-phased task and resource information. Graphical views can also help you visualize your project schedule information much better. This can be especially useful to more visually oriented people. Table 11.1 details the views included within this type.

  For example, reviewing the Gantt Chart provides a high-level view of all tasks and milestones within your project over time. That allows for two-dimensional data display, but lacks the amount of detail you could get if you were to combine it with something like a Task Sheet view, providing for a third dimension—the drilldown.

  > **NOTE**
  >
  > All Gantt Chart–type views are variations of the standard Gantt Chart view and differ by the formatting of the Gantt Chart itself and the table combination selected to complement it.

- **Sheet views**—These views are similar to an Excel presentation of data and allow for large amounts of information to be logically grouped and displayed on the screen. The Sheet views are especially useful when entering task- or resource-related information. Table 11.1 details the views included within this type.

  Sheet views may not be the best choice to view timeline data because they make it hard to view where all the tasks in your schedule fall relative to time, but they can be a great way to view multiline, large-volume data. Sheet views can also be customized to include helpful visual queues, such as graphical indicators to provide schedule and cost status of each individual task and of the entire project.

- **Form views**—These are views displayed in a two-pane format that allow you to easily see information about a particular item, such as a task or a resource, by showing you one item at a time. Isolating each item helps drill into its details and declutter your screen. However, Form views fail when comparison of data is needed. Table 11.1 details the views included within this type.

- **Combination views**—Combination views make use of several views in order to bring together types of information that usually are not contained in one view, but that complement each other. Table 11.1 details the views included within this type.

  Combination views are more complex and create multidimensional representation of entities. They allow you to mix time-phased, detail, and graphical information all on one screen. This can be a great tool when performing analysis or reviewing several aspects of your projects at once. As useful as combination views are, they can be too complex for simple jobs, such as entering task, resource, or cost information. They can also clutter the screen and distract you from concentrating on the details you need.

Table 11.1 summarizes the four view types and the predefined views by the entity they relate to—task or resource. Views marked with an asterisk are the most commonly used views and are displayed in the View menu. The rest of the views can be accessed by clicking More Views on the Views menu.

TABLE 11.1   STANDARD VIEWS BY TYPE AND ENTITY

View Category	Task View	Resource Views
Graphical views	Calendar*	Resource Graph*
	Gantt Chart*	
	Network Diagram*	
	Tracking Gantt*	
	Bar Rollup	
	Descriptive Network Diagram	
	Detail Gantt	
	Leveling Gantt	
	Milestone Rollup	
	Multiple Baseline Rollup	
	Relationship Diagram	
Sheet views	Task Usage*	Resource Sheet*
	Task Sheet	Resource Usage*
Form views	Task Details Form	Resource Form
	Task Form	Resource Name Form
	Task Name Form	
Combination views	Task Entry	Resource Allocation

In addition to the predefined Microsoft Project 2007 views, you can customize and/or create new views.

→ For detailed information on customizing views, **see** Chapter 22, "Customizing Views, Tables, Filters, Groups, and Fields," **p. 755**.

The detailed information about each view is provided later in this chapter.

STRATEGIES ON USING TABLES

Tables are the backbone of Microsoft Project 2007 and add another dimension to its viewing capabilities. They are logical combinations of data in the context of task and resource information. Tables consist of columns and, similarly to views, can be altered to display only the needed information. They are filtered based on and controlled by the type of view selected. For example, if a Gantt Chart view is selected, the tables displayed will all relate to the task entity. Tables can be accessed by selecting View, Table, which displays a list of tables that complement the views you can see in the View menu, as shown in Figure 11.4.

Figure 11.4
Accessing commonly used tables in Microsoft Project 2007.

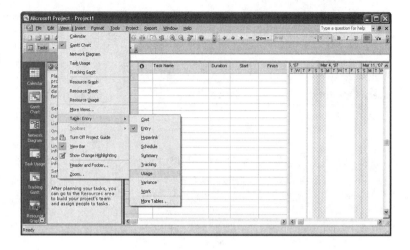

Additional views are available for both task and resource entities by clicking View, Table, More Tables. When you access the More Tables window, you can choose the entity to display by selecting the Task or Resource option button (see Figure 11.5). In addition to the predefined Microsoft Project 2007 tables, you can customize and/or create new ones.

Figure 11.5
Accessing all Microsoft Project 2007 views by entity.

→ For detailed information on customizing tables, **see** Chapter 22, "Customizing Views, Tables, Filters, Groups, and Fields," **p. 755**.

TASK TABLES

Task tables allow you to view various information about tasks (activities) in your schedule. Task tables have several dimensions, such as cost, work, and schedule, as shown in Figure 11.1. The combination of those three dimensions encapsulates all available standard views.

Table 11.2 details the task entity standard views available in Microsoft Project 2007.

TABLE 11.2 STANDARD TASK TABLES		
Table Name	**Commonly Used**	**Table Application**
Cost	Yes	This table shows the cost variation between the values you planned and the current ones. It contains the standard columns (such as Fixed Cost, Actual Cost, Total Cost, Baseline, Variance, and so on) for viewing various cost data and is a great tool for comparison.
Entry	Yes	As the name suggests, this table is particularly useful for entering task-related information in the planning project phase. This table is displayed by default with the Gantt Chart view.
Hyperlink	Yes	This table displays hyperlinks to other files that are not necessary project files. It provides an easy way to manage your external links.
Schedule	Yes	Including slack in your project can make the difference in meeting your deadline or performing a heroic effort to barely finish when needed. A Schedule table allows you to view the slack you have and adjust your schedule accordingly.
Summary	Yes	The Summary table is a great way to get a quick glance at high-level information about your project schedule, from basic task information to progress.
Tracking	Yes	One of the project management objectives is to consistently update the progress of your schedule and reevaluate the effect it has on your scope, schedule, and cost status. Use the Tracking table to update your project schedule progress.
Usage	Yes	The Usage table can be used to view progress information for each task in your schedule. Usage is the default table displayed with the Task Usage view.
Variance	Yes	In addition to tracking progress, it is important to regularly reevaluate your schedule and analyze any deviations from the original plan. Variance table allows you to compare your estimates with your actuals and includes precalculated variance fields.

continues

TABLE 11.2   CONTINUED

Table Name	Commonly Used	Table Application
Work	Yes	The Work table displays information about planned and actual work on a particular task. It is an efficient way to analyze your project schedule for tasks requiring additional effort than originally planned.
Baseline	No	The Baseline table provides a snapshot of project schedule information when it was frozen at the end of the planning phase. Baseline is used to compare your project progress to the plan for improvement and risk mitigation.
Constraint Dates	No	This table is an excellent tool for locating tasks with applied constraints, whether those were intentional or accidental.
Delay	No	The Delay table displays the leveling delay field, which can be used to see the delays that have been applied to your schedule either by you or by Microsoft Project 2007. This is the default table for the Detail and Leveling Gantt views.
Earned Value	No	This table is used for analyzing progress on your project based on the work planned and work performed by your resources. It is used to determine whether the task will meet its target budget or exceed it.
Earned Value Cost Indicators	No	This table is based on the Earned Value table and provides additional calculations of variances and factors that affect earned value on your project.
Earned Value Schedule Indicators	No	This table is related to the Earned Value table and provides details about schedule-related factors that affect earned value on your project.
Export	No	The Export table provides an easy and efficient way of exporting your project details to another application.
Rollup Table	No	The Rollup table allows you to control the placement of the task name text for the rollup bar. This is the default table for the Rollup views.

NOTE

Several task views within Microsoft Project 2007 do not utilize tables as their display mechanism; therefore, when they are selected, you cannot choose a table to apply to these views. These include Calendar, Network Diagram, Descriptive Network Diagram, Relationship Diagram, Resource Form, Resource Graph, Resource Name Form, Task Details Form, Task Form, and Task Name Form.

RESOURCE TABLES

Resource tables allow you to view various information about resources (people or materials) in your schedule. Resource tables have several dimensions, such as cost, work, and schedule, as shown in Figure 11.1. The combination of those three dimensions encapsulates all available standard resource views. Resource tables are available for selection when a resource view is selected. Table 11.3 details the predefined standard task tables in Microsoft Project 2007.

TABLE 11.3   STANDARD RESOURCE TABLES

Table Name	Commonly Used	Table Application
Cost	Yes	The Cost table displays cost information related to each resource. This view can be used to analyze which resources are the most expensive and which ones are over or under budget.
Entry	Yes	The Entry table displays the general resource information and is recommended to be used during the planning phase of the project to record your project resource data. This is the default table used in the Resource Sheet view.
Hyperlink	No	This table provides information about external links to the files linked to your project.
Summary	Yes	The Summary view contains high-level information about your project resources.
Usage	Yes	The Usage view displays data about the amount of resources used by your project. The Usage view is a great tool for analyzing which resources are over- or underutilized.
Work	Yes	The Work table is used for displaying resource progress on tasks they are assigned to and comparing the current information to the planned fields.

continues

TABLE 11.3   CONTINUED

Table Name	Commonly Used	Table Application
Earned Value	No	The Earned Value table compares budgeted work and cost to the planned work and cost. This is an analysis view and provides recalculated fields for how much the work performed by your resource is actually costing.
Export	No	The Export view is used to export resource information to another application for distribution, further analysis, or history-archiving purposes.
Entry – Material Resources	No	This view is commonly used during the planning phase of the project to enter information about material resources (instruments, machinery, hardware, and so on) needed for the project.
Entry – Work Resources	No	This view is commonly used during the planning phase of the project to enter information about work (people) resources needed for the project.

NOTE

Several resource views within Microsoft Project 2007 do not utilize tables as their display mechanism; therefore, when they are selected, you cannot choose a table to apply to these views. These include Resource Graph, Resource Form, and Resource Name Form.

UNDERSTANDING STANDARD VIEWS

In order to efficiently use views, it is important to gain a thorough understanding of the different view types and the details displayed in them.

THE CALENDAR VIEW

The Calendar view is just what it sounds like: a calendar representation of project schedule tasks. The Calendar view displays information by week or month, or allows for a custom selection of the period to display. The information shown by default in the Calendar view includes every task in the currently opened project schedule, displaying task name, task duration, and task type (milestones are displayed using a black bubble with white text), as shown in Figure 11.6.

Figure 11.6
Calendar view displays project schedule tasks in a familiar calendar format for reviewing and printing the project schedule.

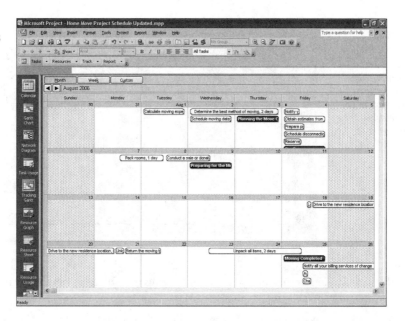

Calendar view is particularly friendly because it is probably the most familiar visualization of time-phased information everyone has used in the past. However, Calendar view can be limiting because it can only display up to a certain level of detail for each task before getting too cluttered and unusable.

The most common use of this view is to review your project schedule and to possibly print it to keep by your desk as another calendar to abide to.

CAUTION

> Even though it is possible, it is not recommended to use the Calendar view for editing information. Many details are hidden from the calendar and, therefore, can lead to the wrong adjustment decisions. In addition, creating new tasks using this view adds constraints to the task, which can be dangerous because you may not even be aware of them.

In order to simplify a complex Calendar view, it is also recommended that you use various filters to reduce the amount of data shown in the calendar. For example, if you are trying to get an idea of when the major deliverables for your project are, create milestone tasks for completion of each deliverable and then filter the Calendar view to display only milestone tasks. Another helpful filtering option would be to display only the critical path tasks.

From the Calendar view, you can double-click any particular task to view the Task Information box, which will provide you with all task-related information you would like to know, as shown in Figure 11.7.

Figure 11.7
Even though the Calendar view is not the best option for viewing task details, you can easily access the Task Information box by double-clicking any task within the calendar.

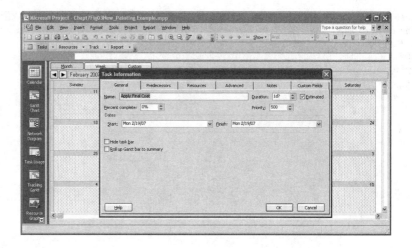

If you are trying to locate a particular task using the Calendar view, you can use the Go To option and search for the particular task.

→ For details on customizing and formatting the Calendar view, **see** Chapter 19, "Formatting Views," **p. 601**.

THE GANTT CHART VIEWS

The Gantt Chart view is, by default, the first view you will see when initially opening Microsoft Project 2007. This view consists of two main parts: the Task Sheet table and the Gantt Chart graphical view (see Figure 11.8). Gantt Chart is, and always has been, one of the most popular project management views.

Figure 11.8
The Gantt Chart view combines the time-phased summary-level information and the detailed drill down into project schedule details with the Task Sheet table to provide an informative display of your project schedule.

The chart part of the view contains several different types of bars. The solid black bar spanning a large portion of time represents a summary-level task. Microsoft Project 2007 also includes new 3-D effect Gantt Chart bars.

Milestone tasks are shown in the shape of a diamond and include the date in MM/DD format. The length of each bar is determined by the duration of the task. It is also possible for a task to be split, which is illustrated with a dotted line connecting the parts of the split task. Arrows are used to visualize the predecessor/successor relationships between tasks. The Gantt Chart also includes the names of the resources above the task they are assigned to. See Figure 11.9 for a visual representation of the various task information in the Gantt Chart.

Figure 11.9
In addition to the default types of information, you can customize the data and its visual representation on the Gantt Chart.

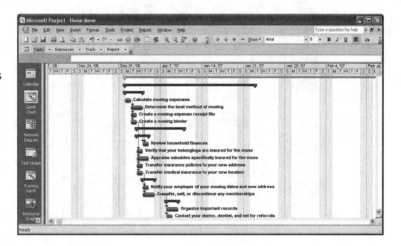

The Gantt Chart view is a multipurpose view and can be very useful at the different phases of the project. For example, you can use the Task Sheet view portion of the Gantt Chart view for task entry during the planning phase. The Gantt Chart will be automatically updated and will visually display the information you are adding to your project. The Gantt Chart is a great view to review your project schedule prior to moving into the execution and control phases by analyzing task dependencies, resource assignments, and milestone tasks in a view that adds the perspective of time.

The options and choices for formatting the Gantt Chart view are extensive.

→ For detailed information on formatting and customizing the Gantt Chart view, **see** Chapter 22, "Customizing Views, Tables, Filters, Groups, and Fields," **p. 755**.

The Gantt Chart view also has many predefined variations that are all customizations of the original Gantt Chart and were each designed for concentrating on a different views of project data. These variations are discussed in more detail in the following sections.

THE DETAIL GANTT VIEW

The Detail Gantt view shows the same information as the regular Gantt Chart, but in addition, it shows where delays have been created as a result of leveling, either by automatic Microsoft Project 2007 or manual leveling using the leveling delay field. The Detail Gantt View does not show the task history of scheduling prior to leveling, but it does include the slack amount at the right side of the slack bar (see Figure 11.10).

→ For detailed information on leveling your project schedule, **see** Chapter 25, "Resolving Resource Allocation Problems," **p. 885**.

Figure 11.10
The Detail Gantt chart highlights critical path tasks in red and also adds an additional column of Leveling Delay to the standard Gantt Chart view.

The Detail Gantt can be used for reviewing your project scheduling after it has been leveled to analyze the changes made to the project schedule.

THE LEVELING GANTT VIEW

The Leveling Gantt view is very similar to the Detail Gantt chart in that it displays delays. It can be used for both viewing the leveling effects on the project schedule and scheduling a delay on a task if resources or materials are not available for the task in time. The Gantt Chart part of the Leveling view remains nearly unchanged from the standard Gantt, but in addition, it displays a narrow line in front of the tasks, tracing from the initial task schedule date to the new start date based on the delay (see Figure 11.11).

To the right of each task bar is another narrow line that demonstrates free slack. Free slack represents an amount of time a task can be delayed without delaying its successor tasks.

Figure 11.11
The Leveling Gantt view visually shows slack, free slack, and schedule changes due to the leveling of the project schedule.

→ For detailed information on leveling your project schedule, **see** Chapter 25, "Resolving Resource Allocation Problems," **p. 885**.

THE MULTIPLE BASELINES GANTT VIEW

The Multiple Baselines Gantt view is generally a view used during the execution and control phases of the project. It is used to compare multiple baselines and evaluate the evolution of the project schedule. The baseline process generally directly relates to the changes in the project scope. Baseline view can be used to analyze the effect a new baseline has on the schedule and review the scope and contract information to ensure that the project does not contain scope creep (slow escalation of scope due to the changes from the client or project sponsors).

The Multiple Baselines Gantt view does not show any additional columns within the Task Sheet part of the view, but it does demonstrate, usually by using a different color, the migration of the project schedule (see Figure 11.12).

Figure 11.12
The Multiple Baselines Gantt view will display all saved baselines in a graphical format within the Gantt Chart itself.

THE NETWORK DIAGRAM VIEW

The Network Diagram view, also referred to as *Program Evaluation and Review Technique (PERT)*, is a logic diagram that graphically represents relationships between tasks. Network Diagram can be viewed as a type of flowchart, where the main objects are tasks (including milestones and summary tasks), and the lines between tasks represent predecessor/successor relationships. The Network Diagram view is also structured to show the critical path tasks, displayed in red, while regular tasks are blue, the project summary tasks are black with white text, and milestones are in the shape of hexagons (see Figure 11.13).

Figure 11.13
To navigate the Network Diagram view, use the scroll bars to move vertically and horizontally around the view and use Zoom In/Zoom Out features to increase/decrease the level of detail visible.

This view can be used for viewing all of your project tasks and detecting any tasks that are currently not linked within your project schedule. This application is particularly useful if your schedule is large and contains many tasks. Often it is hard to notice such detail in a list view.

Another common use for the view is to communicate project information to the project team by printing it out and displaying it on a wall. This provides an everyday visual queue and allows the project team to view the schedule as a whole, as well as the specific tasks within it.

Network Diagram, however, can be awkward for modifying a project schedule and moving tasks around. Even if the view is zoomed out, sometimes it is not feasible to display the entire project schedule in a Network Diagram format on a computer screen. Modifying and moving tasks in this view can cause potential problems.

If you are really looking to modify tasks in this view, you can double-click a particular task within the Network Diagram to view the Task Information box. This provides all of the task-related information, and you can safely change it.

Network Diagram also is not time-phased, so it is hard to picture the timeline of the project against a time window. However, you can modify the order of tasks according to time periods by selecting Format, Layout, and then choosing the option Top Down by Day, Week, or Month in the Arrangement box.

DESCRIPTIVE NETWORK DIAGRAM VIEWS

The Descriptive Network Diagram view is a variation of the Network Diagram view. Similarly, it concentrates on demonstrating tasks relationships. However, the boxes representing tasks contain more detailed information (see Figure 11.14).

Figure 11.14
Apply additional filters to the Descriptive Network Diagram view to simplify the view and sort out the unnecessary information.

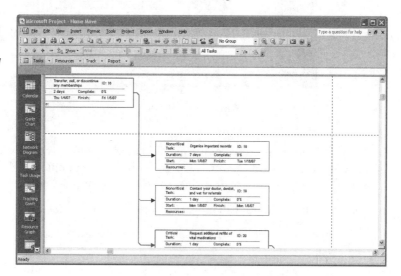

THE TASK USAGE VIEW

The Task Usage view is used during the execution and control phases of the project. It presents actual task information by showing the amount of work scheduled and performed on a particular task.

Task Usage view is time-phased and allows you to customize the frequency at which the data is displayed—daily, weekly, quarterly, and so on.

This view is especially helpful when checking resource assignments and the scheduled work for a particular task (see Figure 11.15).

Figure 11.15
Providing additional
information, such as
Resource Availability
and Actual Work, can
expand the use of the
Task Usage view.

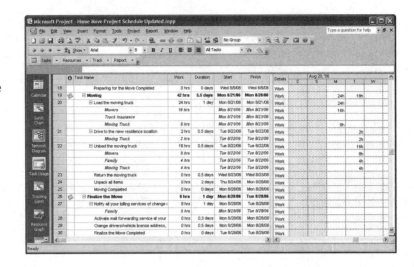

THE TRACKING GANTT VIEW

The Tracking Gantt view is used primarily during the Execution and Control phases of a project. It uses the standard Gantt Chart view for its bases, but differs in displaying baseline information in addition to the current project schedule view (see Figure 11.16).

The Tracking Gantt view displays progress information in two ways:

- By showing solid color on the scheduled taskbar, where the Gantt Chart shows a black progress line
- By showing the percent complete value on the right side of each bar

Figure 11.16
Tracking Gantt is one
of the most powerful
views used by project
managers because it
not only shows task
scheduled dates, but
also includes baseline
information.

THE RESOURCE GRAPH VIEW

The Resource Graph view is used to display resource allocation and overallocation time-phased information in a bar chart format. The Resource Graph view is often used in combination views, with the top pane showing the Gantt Chart or a similar detail view. The Resource Management toolbar provides quick access to the overallocated resources via the Go to Next Overallocation button. It not only shows which resources are overallocated and when, but it also specifies by how much, based on their availability during that period (see Figure 11.17).

Figure 11.17
The Resource Graph is sometimes referred to as *Resource Histogram* because it provides great historical and upcoming resource allocation information.

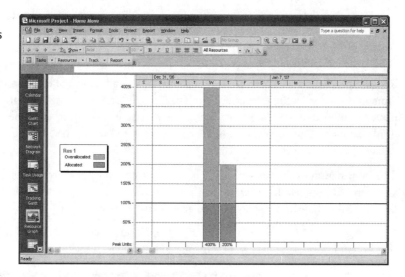

TIP

The Resource Graph can be used throughout the project life, but it is especially beneficial during planning because it can help detect and resolve resource allocations early.

THE RESOURCE SHEET VIEW

The Resource Sheet view is a list view that is used to display detailed resource information. Being a list view and providing a fair amount of detail, Resource Sheet view is beneficial to use during the planning phase of the project to enter project resource information. Each row of the view is dedicated to a resource (see Figure 11.18). It also contains visual queues, such as the Indicators column that alerts you to which resources are overallocated. The Resource Sheet view can be heavily modified by selecting one of many different tables that can be applied to it. In addition, you can customize the view even further by adding more columns.

→ For detailed information on customizing views, **see** Chapter 22, "Customizing Views, Tables, Filters, Groups, and Fields," **p. 755**.

Figure 11.18
The Resource Sheet view can be combined with other views, such as the Resource Graph, to add the time-phased dimension.

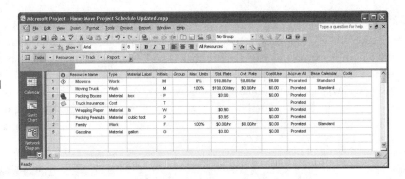

THE RESOURCE USAGE VIEW

Resource Usage view is a resource allocation and overallocation sheet view that displays the same information as the Resource Graph, using a different format. The information displayed in the Resource Usage view can be viewed based on a different timescale. Columns displayed include hours of work, hours of overallocated work, cost, available time, and other details.

The information in the Resource Usage view is grouped by resource, displaying all the tasks a resource is responsible for underneath its name. You can use the symbol similar to the outline symbol to hide and display particular tasks for a resource.

For example, tasks for Family have been hidden. The plus symbol next to the name indicates that not all information is currently displayed (see Figure 11.19).

Figure 11.19
The Resource Usage view is used to resolve resource overallocations and detect when resources require leveling.

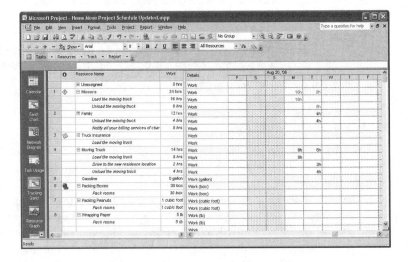

Resource Usage view also helps detect resources that need to be leveled. These resources contain a diamond with an exclamation point in the Indicators column.

Combining the Resource Usage view with a Gantt Chart creates a powerful combination with the task- and resource-level information and is useful for reviewing the schedule.

THE BAR ROLLUP VIEW

The Bar Rollup view is part of the collection of views that represent grouped information. This view displays the task information that has been rolled up onto collapsed summary views. The bar rollup view uses colored boxes on the summary taskbar for each rolled-up task. When any task other than the milestone is rolled up, the summary taskbar resembles more of a regular task than a summary task. The Bar Rollup is useful for highlighting certain tasks when task details are not displayed (see Figure 11.20).

Figure 11.20
The Bar Rollup view helps emphasize task details within the collapsed outline.

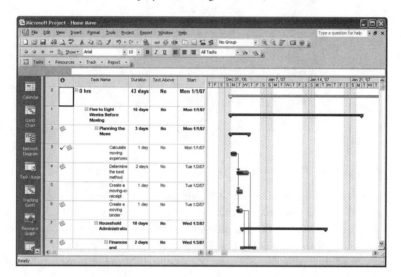

THE MILESTONE AND MILESTONE DATE ROLLUP VIEWS

The Milestone and Milestone Date Rollup views are part of the collection of views that represent grouped data. As the name suggests, these views roll up only the milestones within the project schedule.

The Milestone Rollup view is similar to the Bar Rollup because it rolls up only the milestones themselves and excludes the dates. The main purpose of this view is to provide a summary display with only specific types of tasks—milestones.

The Milestone Date Rollup view rolls up both the milestones and their dates to the summary-level tasks. The dates are displayed directly in the Gantt, eliminating the necessity to have to print the sheet view along with the Gantt in order to have complete information about a milestone. The milestone names appear above the summary taskbar, and the date is displayed below it (see Figure 11.21). The diamonds represent milestone tasks only in this view.

Figure 11.21
The Milestone Date Rollup view rolls up milestone name and date information within the Gantt.

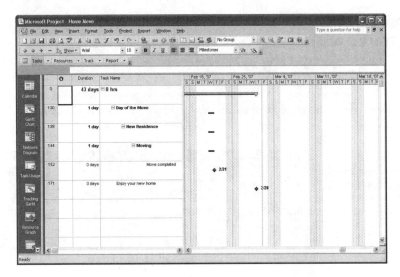

THE RELATIONSHIP DIAGRAM VIEW

The Relationship Diagram view is another view from the Graphical Views category that displays task-related information and is a special type of Network Diagram view. Similar to the Network Diagram, the Relationship Diagram view graphically displays task relationships within your project schedule. The Relationship Diagram is generally displayed in the bottom part of the task split view and shows immediate predecessors and successors for the task selected in the top frame.

NOTE

> You cannot apply any filters to the Relationship Diagram view because the view is already automatically filtered by Microsoft Project 2007 based on the task selected in the top part of the view.

This view is especially useful during the planning phase of a project to ensure that all tasks are properly linked within your project schedule. The Relationship Diagram also displays the type of relationships between the tasks to provide even more detail (see Figure 11.22).

Figure 11.22
The Relationship Diagram view helps you ensure that every task within your project schedule is linked and verify that a correct relationship type has been established.

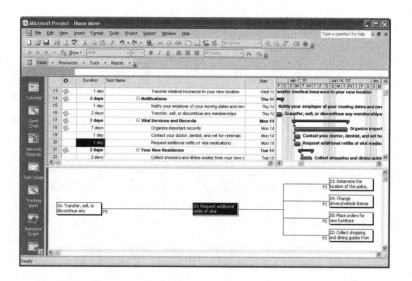

THE RESOURCE ALLOCATION VIEW

The Resource Allocation view is displayed for the Resource entity and is a combination view. Resource Allocation view combines the power of the detail in the Resource Usage view and the graphical, time-phased representation of a Leveling Gantt. As the name suggests, this view is intended for resolving resource overallocations. The Resource Usage part of the view helps you determine which resources are overallocated or require leveling, during what time frame, and to what extent. The Leveling Gantt can then be used to identify the tasks assigned to the overloaded resource. This combination creates a complete scenario of the current situation, which will help you then determine the appropriate plan of action to resolve the overallocation (see Figure 11.23).

Figure 11.23
The Resource Allocation view is a powerful tool in analyzing resource overallocation problems by looking at both resources and tasks assigned to the resources.

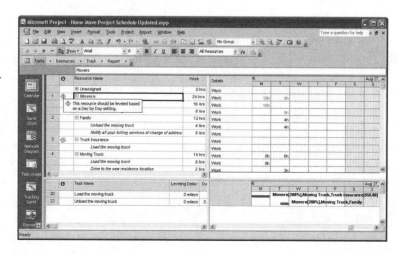

11

THE RESOURCE AND RESOURCE NAME FORM VIEWS

The Resource and Resource Name Form views are variations of one another and display information in a form. The only difference between these views is the amount of detail they include. Resource Form views are often used at the bottom of a combination view, such as the one in Figure 11.24, and allow you to view the detailed resource information based on one task at a time.

The Resource Form view is opened by default when a resource view with a split frame is displayed. It contains the same information as the Resource Sheet view. When you select a resource in the Resource Sheet view, the Resource Form view is automatically filtered to display the details about the selected resource. The bottom part of the Resource Form view can be formatted to display tasks assigned to the resource. To customize the bottom part of the Resource Form, select Format, Details or right-click within the form view itself.

Figure 11.24
The Resource Form view can be combined with any other resource view for an additional level of detail that provides a drill-down to the resource attributes.

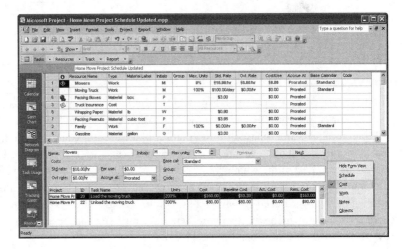

The Resource Name Form view acts identically to the Resource Form view, but displays only the resource name in the top portion of the view. You can customize the bottom part of the view similarly to the Resource Form view by selecting Format, Details.

THE TASK, TASK DETAIL, AND TASK NAME FORM VIEWS

Task Form views, similarly to the Resource Form views, present detailed information based only on one task at a time. The Task Form views are generally used at the bottom of a combination view to provide additional drill-down into selected tasks. In order to display the Task Form view at the bottom of another view, select Window, Split. Click in the bottom part of the screen and from the View menu, select the particular Task Form view to display (see Figure 11.25).

Figure 11.25

Task Form views help to easily and efficiently display task details for one particular task at a time.

You can customize the level of detail displayed in a Task Form view by selecting Format, Details or by right-clicking within the view itself. This will show all available fields that can be added to the view for more information.

In addition to adding the Task Form view to a combination view, you can also view it independently and navigate between the tasks by clicking the Previous and Next buttons in the top-right corner.

The Task Details view is a variation of a Task Form view that includes additional details about the task, such as Current, Baseline, and Actual dates. You can also use this view to display the constraints on tasks. If you are using a split view, the default Task Form view is probably displayed in the bottom pane. To switch to the Task Detail Form view, click in the bottom pane and then select View, More Views, and Task Detail Form.

The Task Name Form view displays only the name of the task in the top portion of the form. Similar to the Task Form and Task Details Form views, the Task Name Form provides formatting options and the ability to add more fields to be displayed in the view. This view is especially useful in a combination view and allows you to compress the amount of data displayed in it, thus decluttering the screen.

THE TASK ENTRY VIEW

The Task Entry view is a combination view that combines the power of the Task Sheet, Gantt Chart, and Task Form views. The Task Entry view provides the three dimensions to your project schedule: the Task Sheet view displays the high-level task details and is easy to read, the Gantt Chart view adds the time dimensions, displaying the time-phased data, and the Task Form view displays the drill-down into the task details (as shown in Figure 11.26). The Task Entry view is the most comprehensive task view you can display in Microsoft Project 2007 and is great for combining all task-related information on one screen.

11

Figure 11.26
The Task Entry view is a combination view that combines summary-level, graphical representation, and task detail information on one screen.

The Task Sheet View

The Task Sheet view is a list view that provides a linear display, reminiscent of the Excel sheet, and is great for entering task information during the planning phase of a project. The Task Entry does not provide time-phased information about the tasks, except for start and end dates.

The Task Sheet view can be used standalone or in a combination view to display all tasks in a project schedule as rows with columns of information details. The Task Sheet view uses tables to designate which columns are displayed in the view. You can modify the columns you see by relating them to specific information you are trying to view (see Figure 11.27). For example, if you are trying to review task-related costs within the Task Sheet view, then from the View menu select the Cost table. If you are interested in viewing task work information, then select the Work table, and so on.

When the Entry table is applied to the Task Sheet view, it actually becomes the Task Entry view used during planning to create the initial project schedule.

TIP

In addition to the columns displayed in the Task Sheet view, you can add more columns, such as Cost, Baseline, and so on. To do so, right-click on a column and select Insert Column Option. In the Column Definition window, select the column to add and click the OK button.

Figure 11.27
The Task Sheet view is a simple way to display task details in a list format, but you can customize it to include visual queues, such as Status Indicators and Information icons.

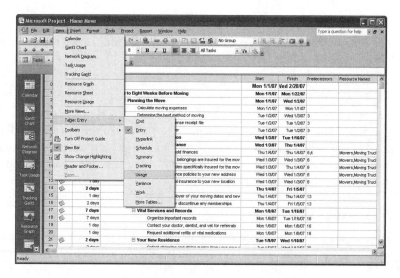

UNDERSTANDING STANDARD TABLES

Now that you have seen all the different views that can used to display data within Microsoft Project 2007, this section discusses the details of the standard tables. Tables are used to determine the fields of information that are displayed within views and are crucial to efficiently reviewing the information. As previously discussed, tables can be divided into task and resource information tables. The specific table types within these categories are discussed in the following sections.

TASK TABLES

Task tables are used to display task-specific information. Task tables use the three dimensions of project data (cost, schedule, and work; refer to Figure 11.1) to provide a complete picture of each task within your project schedule. The various types of task tables are discussed next.

THE COST TABLE

The purpose of the Cost table is to view task-specific cost information. The Cost table displays not only the actual and planned cost data for each task, but also includes the baseline cost and variance information.

The Cost table can be applied to a combination Gantt Chart and Resource Form view to display schedule, cost, and resource information on one screen, which can be beneficial for reviewing your schedule.

THE DELAY TABLE

The Delay table is intended to provide the leveling delay information. This table is used in the Leveling Gantt Chart view and allows viewing and easily modifying the task delay information.

THE ENTRY TABLE

The Entry table allows for viewing the general task information and is a great way to enter initial project schedule data.

THE SCHEDULE TABLE

The Schedule table provides schedule-related task details, such as start, finish, and slack. The Schedule table is a great way to perform analysis of the project schedule while updating the slack available on a task. You can easily see the effect the slack has on the start and finish dates. You can also combine the Schedule table with a Gantt Chart view to see the slack effect in a graphical view.

THE SUMMARY TABLE

The Summary table does just that—summarizes task data used for tracking task progress. It includes the start and end dates for each task, duration, percentage complete, cost, and work. This task table incorporates all three dimensions of project information and allows you to view it all on one page.

THE EXPORT TABLE

The Export table is used for exporting data to another application. It is a common practice to include all available column information in a view like this one. Following those practices, the Export view incorporates all task columns available in Project Standard 2007. This view contains the most comprehensive set of information about tasks, but can be hard to use to review it on a computer screen because the information area is too broad.

THE HYPERLINK TABLE

The Hyperlink table exposes all external hyperlinks linked to tasks. This table can be efficiently used for both entry and review of the task hyperlinks.

THE ROLLUP TABLE

The Rollup table is used in the Rollup Data view and rolls up task information to the summary level.

THE CONSTRAINT DATES TABLE

The Constraint Dates table displays the constraint details for each task within the project schedule. This table is especially useful for reviewing your schedule to ensure it does not contain any unnecessary constraints.

THE EARNED VALUE

The Earned Value table displays the standard precalculated fields used to calculate the value produced by executing the project. Even though Earned Value can be a great way to analyze how a project is performing and assess your budget, schedule, and scope problems, in order for this to be meaningful, the Earned Value table must contain the most up-to-date, accurate actual information.

→ For detailed information on using Earned Value and Work Breakdown Structure on your project, **see** Chapter 4, "Getting Started After Business Initiative Is Approved," **p. 87**.

THE EARNED VALUE COST INDICATORS TABLE

The Earned Value Cost Indicators table is a variation of the Earned Value table that displays only the cost fields of the Earned Value, excluding the Schedule Variance and other schedule-related fields.

THE BASELINE TABLE

The Baseline table concentrates on displaying all available baselines side by side, allowing you to compare and analyze the progress, effects, and the evolution of your schedule since the planning phase.

THE TRACKING TABLE

The Tracking table is used during the execution and control phases of the project and provides progress and status information related to each task.

THE USAGE TABLE

The Usage table is generally used in combination with other views and provides the standard task information, such as start and end dates, duration, and work.

RESOURCE TABLES

Resource tables are used to display resource-specific information. Resource tables use the three dimensions of project data (cost, schedule, and work; refer to Figure 11.1) to provide a complete picture of each resource within your project schedule.

THE ENTRY TABLE

The Entry table is a simple way to enter your resource information using a list during the planning phase of your project. The entry table provides many different columns of fields and allows for easy viewing, but it does not allow you to view time-phased resource information. Once the Entry Table is populated, you can utilize other views to see time-phased resource data.

THE ENTRY – MATERIAL RESOURCES TABLE

The Entry – Material Resources table is a filtered entry table that includes only resources of the Material type (hardware, tools, machinery, and so on). This entry table allows you to quickly and efficiently add all material resources to your project.

THE ENTRY – WORK RESOURCES TABLE

The Entry – Work Resources table is a filtered entry table that includes only resources of the Work type (that is, people). This entry table allows you to quickly and efficiently add work resources required for your project.

11

The Entry – Cost Resources Table

The Entry – Cost Resources table is a filtered entry table that includes only resources of the Cost type (airplane tickets, lodging, and so on). This entry table allows you to quickly and efficiently add cost resources required for your project schedule.

The Export Table

The Export table is used for exporting data to another application. It is a common practice to include all available column information in a view like this one. Following those practices, the Export view incorporates all resource columns available in Microsoft Project 2007. This view contains the most comprehensive set of information about resources, but can be hard to efficiently use for reviewing it on a computer screen because the information area is too broad.

The Hyperlink Table

The Hyperlink table exposes all external hyperlinks linked to resources within Project 2007. This table can be efficiently used for both entry and review of the resource hyperlinks.

The Summary Table

The Summary table does just that—summarizes resource data used for tracking task progress. It includes the start and end dates for each task, duration, percentage complete, cost, and work. This task view incorporates all three dimensions of project information and allows you to view it all on one page.

The Work Table

The Work table displays all the work dimension resource-related information, organized by resource. You can use the Work table to view the amount of work, overtime, baseline, remaining, and actual work performed by the resource. The Work table can be combined with several views, such as the Resource Overallocation, to determine which resources have scheduled overtime or are overallocated.

The Usage Table

The Usage table displays the use of a resource on your project. This table provides a one-to-one relationship between the resource and the work scheduled for the project.

The Cost Table

The Cost table displays all cost information about the resources in your schedule. You can use this view to analyze the scheduled and actual costs for a particular resource, the budget remaining to spend on that resource, the baseline cost, and the current variance. This table can be used to analyze and reevaluate your planning process and resource and budget allocation.

THE EARNED VALUE TABLE

The Earned Value table for resources allows you to tie the Earned Value variances and indicators to a specific resource. Even though Earned Value can be a great way to analyze how a project is performing and to assess your budget, schedule, and scope problems, in order for this to be meaningful, the Earned Value table must contain the most up-to-date, accurate actual information. It is especially hard to include such information about your resources, as an organization's financial system often contains the most up-to-date, valuable data. But, if you commit to attaining Earned Value and keeping your financial and project information synched up, this view can help you improve your projects in the future and prevent scope creep and other problems associated with scope from occurring.

→ For detailed information on using Earned Value and Work Breakdown Structure on your project, **see** Chapter 4, "Getting Started After Business Initiative Is Approved," **p. 87**.

UNDERSTANDING FILTERING AND GROUPING

In addition to views and tables, the information displayed in Microsoft Project 2007 can be broken down further using filters and logically combined using groups. When these features are properly utilized, they can add a lot of value to how effectively you can view your project data and locate the exact information you need.

EXPLORING FILTERS IN MICROSOFT PROJECT 2007

A filter is a mechanism to sort the information displayed, based on the criteria you provide. Filters, same as tables and views, are an important feature of Microsoft Project 2007.

You can apply filters to all views, except for the Relationship Diagram, which is limited to the information it displays and, therefore, does not require filtering.

Microsoft Project 2007 provides two different types of filters:

- **Standard filters**—These filters are available under Project, Filtered For, as shown in Figure 11.28. These filters are predefined and include the commonly used columns by which to filter the view or table. Microsoft Project 2007 provides different options for standard filters based on the entity to which the view or table relates, such as a task or resource.

11

Figure 11.28
Selecting a standard filter to apply to the current view.

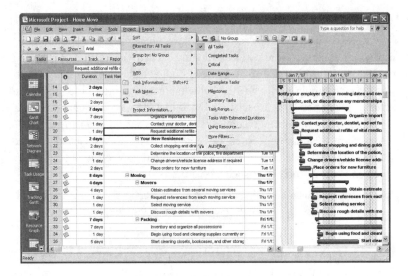

■ **AutoFilter**—This is the filter that, when applied, displays the filtering options above each column in the table, giving you the flexibility of choosing which column to filter by. AutoFilter has two positions: on and off. It can be accessed by selecting Project, Filtered For, AutoFilter, as shown in Figure 11.29.

> **NOTE**
> The AutoFilter can only be applied to tables because it requires the current view to contain columns to filter by.

Figure 11.29
Selecting an AutoFilter to apply to the current view with a table.

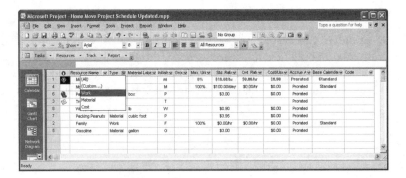

> **NOTE**
> When you are using combination views with a split screen, the view on the bottom part of the page cannot have any filters applied to it because it is automatically being filtered by Microsoft Project 2007 based on what is selected in the top part of the view.

When a filter is applied to the view, only tasks or resources that meet the specified criteria are displayed. All other tasks or resources are temporarily hidden and can be viewed again once the filter is removed.

TIP

Color highlighting may be used in cases where the filter does not suppress the items that do not meet the filter criteria. For detailed information on how to change the filter highlighting and customize filters, see Chapter 22.

Filters can also be subdivided into two categories:

- **Calculated**—These filters are used to compare a value you provide with values available for a particular field in the Microsoft Project 2007 database. Calculated filters can also be used to compare two values, such as baseline cost and actual cost. Calculated fields do not require you to use only values from the Microsoft Project 2007 database. You can, for example, compare the task start date to a value you provide and view only the tasks that start on that date.

- **Interactive**—These filters require user collaboration in the form of providing a comparison value to apply to the filter. For example, using the Resource Sheet view, you can filter only for resources that are part of a particular group (department), such as Marketing.

NOTE

Any filter provided in the list that includes ellipses (…) at the end of its name is an interactive filter.

In addition to simple filtering, Microsoft Project 2007 includes composite filters that use multiple conditions in combinations to filter for a task or resource. When using composite filters, you can either include or exclude particular criteria:

- **Inclusive**—This test uses the AND condition and requires that all tests must be true for it to return a value.

- **Exclusive**—This test uses the OR condition and requires at least one condition to be met in order to meet the filtering criteria.

In addition to the commonly used filters that are displayed directly under the Project, Filter For menu, Microsoft Project 2007 includes other filters that can be accessed by selecting More Filters from the menu. In the same way tables and views can be applied to the two main entities in Microsoft Project 2007, filters are grouped by tasks and resources as well.

USING STANDARD FILTERS

Standard filters are provided to define the commonly used and recommended filters for the user. When you use standard filters, several rules must be met:

- Filters can only be applied to the view of the same entity as the filter. For example, task filters can only be applied to task views and resource filters to resource views.

- The Highlight filter can only be applied to a list view because it requires column/row information in order to apply the highlighting. For example, you will not be able to apply a filter to any of the form views.

- When a filter is applied, it compares the provided criteria to all resources or tasks available in the Microsoft Project 2007 database. In order to apply more than one criteria at a time, you must use the AutoFilter, edit a standard filter, or create a new one.

Table 11.4 provides the list of standard task filters included in Microsoft Project 2007.

TABLE 11.4   STANDARD TASK FILTERS OF MICROSOFT PROJECT 2007

Task Filter Name	Commonly Used	Purpose
All Tasks	Yes	Displays all tasks within your project schedule.
Completed Tasks	Yes	Displays only the completed tasks (that is, tasks with the %Complete field equal to 110%).
Critical	Yes	Displays only tasks that are part of the critical path for the project.
Date Range…	Yes	Displays tasks that are planned to start or finish within the specified date range. This is an interactive filter and requires the user to enter the values to filter for.
Incomplete Tasks	Yes	Displays all tasks that have not been yet completed. It tests for the %Complete field to be less than 100%.
Milestones	Yes	Displays only tasks that are milestones.
Summary Tasks	Yes	Displays only summary-level tasks.
Task Range…	Yes	Displays all tasks whose ID is within the specified range. This is an interactive filter and requires the user to enter the values to filter for.
Tasks with Estimated Durations	Yes	Displays tasks whose duration has not been finalized and still contains a question mark (?) next to it.
Using Resource…	Yes	Displays tasks that have the specified resource assigned to them. This is an interactive filter and requires the user to enter the values to filter for.
Cost Greater Than…	No	Displays tasks whose cost exceeds the specified value. This is an interactive filter and requires the user to enter the values to filter for.

Task Filter Name	Commonly Used	Purpose
Cost Overbudget	No	Displays all tasks that are overbudget (that is, tasks whose actual cost is greater than the baseline cost).
Created After...	No	Displays all tasks that have been created after the specified date. This is an interactive filter and requires the user to enter the values to filter for.
In Progress Tasks	No	Displays all tasks that are currently being performed (that is, started, but not yet completed).
Late/Overbudget Tasks Assigned To...	No	Displays all tasks that are overbudget (whose actual cost exceeds the baseline cost) and are assigned the specified resource. This is an interactive filter and requires the user to enter the values to filter for.
Linked Fields	No	Displays all tasks that have a link to another application.
Resource Group...	No	Displays tasks that are being performed by a resource within the specified resource group. This is an interactive filter and requires the user to enter the values to filter for.
Should Start By...	No	Displays all tasks that should start by the specified date. This is an interactive filter and requires the user to enter the values to filter for.
Should Start/ Finish By...	No	Displays all tasks that should either start or end by the specified date. This is an interactive filter and requires the user to enter the values to filter for.
Slipped/Late Progress	No	Displays tasks whose actual finish date is later than the baseline date or whose budgeted cost of work scheduled is greater than the budgeted cost of work performed.
Slipping Tasks	No	Displays tasks that have not yet been completed and whose actual finish dates are later than the planned ones.
Tasks with a Task Calendar Assigned	No	Displays tasks that in addition to using a project calendar have their own task calendar assigned.
Tasks with Attachments	No	Displays all tasks that contain an attachment.

11

continues

TABLE 11.4   CONTINUED

Task Filter Name	Commonly Used	Purpose
Tasks with Deadlines	No	Displays tasks with a particular type of constraint assigned—deadline. These tasks must finish by the deadline date.
Tasks with Fixed Dates	No	Displays tasks that have been constrained by any constraint other than As Soon As Possible or that have already started.
Tasks/Assignments with Overtime	No	Displays tasks and assignments that include overtime work.
Top Level Tasks	No	Displays tasks that are at the highest summary level.
Unstarted Tasks	No	Displays tasks whose actual progress is zero.
Work Overbudget	No	Displays tasks that contain overbudget work, determined by comparing the actual work to planned work.

Table 11.5 provides the list of standard resource filters included in Microsoft Project 2007.

TABLE 11.5   STANDARD RESOURCE FILTERS OF MICROSOFT PROJECT 2007

Resource Filter Name	Commonly Used	Purpose
All Resources	Yes	Displays all resources in the Microsoft Project 2007 database.
Budget Resources	Yes	Displays only the budget type resources.
Cost Overbudget	Yes	Displays only resources whose actual cost is larger than the baseline.
Group...	Yes	Displays resources that belong to the specified group. This is an interactive filter and requires the user to enter the values to filter for.
Non-budget Resources	Yes	Displays all non-budget resources—that is, resources with the type material or work only.
Overallocated Resources	Yes	Displays resources who are assigned to a task for too many hours during any timeframe of the project.
Resource Range...	Yes	Displays a resource whose ID is in the specified range. This is an interactive filter and requires the user to enter the values to filter for.

Resource Filter Name	Commonly Used	Purpose
Resources-Cost	Yes	Displays only resources with type cost. These resources include additional costs on the project, such as airplane tickets and hotel room charges for travel required for execution of the project.
Resources-Material	Yes	Displays only resources whose type is material. These resources include hardware, machinery, instruments, and so on needed for the project execution.
Resources-Work	Yes	Displays only resources whose type is work. These resources are people who have been assigned to complete activities within the project.
Work Overbudget	Yes	Displays resources with overbudget work, calculated by comparing scheduled work to the baseline work.
Cost Greater Than...	No	Displays resources whose cost exceeds the specified value. This is an interactive filter and requires the user to enter the values to filter for.
Created After...	No	Displays resources that have been added to the project (created) after the specified date. This is an interactive filter and requires the user to enter the values to filter for.
Date Range...	No	Displays resources that are assigned to tasks occurring during the date range specified. This is an interactive filter and requires the user to enter the values to filter for.
In Progress Assignments	No	Displays resources that are currently in progress of completing a task. This is calculated by analyzing if the %Complete field is greater than 0 and less than 100%.
Linked Fields	No	Displays resources that contain links to other applications.
Resources with Attachments	No	Displays resources that have attachments.
Resource/Assignment with Overtime	No	Displays resources that are assigned tasks that contain overtime work.

11

continues

TABLE 11.5   CONTINUED

Resource Filter Name	Commonly Used	Purpose
Should Start By...	No	Displays resources that are assigned to a task who have not yet started, where the calculated start is after the date specified. This is an interactive filter and requires the user to enter the values to filter for.
Should Start/Finish By...	No	Displays resources that are assigned to a task, whose calculated start or finish date are before or after the specified date. This is an interactive filter and requires the user to enter the values to filter for.
Slipped/Late Progress	No	Displays resources whose tasks are marked as late, where the finish date is later than the one specified in the baseline or whose budgeted cost of work scheduled is greater than the budgeted cost of work performed.
Slipping Assignments	No	Displays resources that are assigned to a task that has not yet been completed and whose scheduled actual finish date is greater than the baseline.
Unstarted Assignments	No	Displays all resources assigned to tasks that have not yet started. This can be calculated by checking whether Actual Start has been set to a date or still remains N/A.
Work Complete	No	Displays resources assigned to tasks with percent complete equal to 100.
Work Incomplete	No	Displays resources assigned to tasks that have been started (Actual Start date has been given a date value) and whose percent complete is less than 100.

USING AUTOFILTERS

AutoFilters are a filter type that allows the user to select any columns to filter by. It also allows more than one selection simultaneously.

When AutoFilter is selected, a drop-down list appears above each column in the current view, allowing you to filter by a specific value selected in the drop-down, as shown earlier in Figure 11.29.

Depending on the view and the columns displayed in the view, some of them include special values within the AutoFilter. For example, the Gantt Chart view with the Task Entry table contains Today, Tomorrow, This Week, Next Week, This Month, and Next Month options for the Start and End Date columns.

You can customize the AutoFilter by selecting the Custom option from the drop-down list. This allows you to create two exclusive or inclusive conditions. You can also save the custom filter to use it in the future without having to re-create it. To save the custom filter, click the Save button, provide a meaningful name for your custom filter, and click the OK button, as shown in Figure 11.30.

Figure 11.30
Creating a custom filter from the AutoFilter.

Exploring Standard Groups

In addition to using filters, you can group information in views and tables into logical categories to perform further analysis or to organize large quantities of data for easier comprehension using groups. In addition to creating categories of data, grouping also allows you to calculate subtotals, which are numeric values based on the grouped information. Whenever a new grouping strategy is applied, the outline of tasks and/or resources in the view is temporarily rearranged, according to the criteria specified in the Group By condition.

To better control the subgrouping structure of your new outline, grouping also allows you to include value intervals for the Group By fields.

Groups can be accessed by selecting Project, Group By..., as shown in Figure 11.31.

11

Figure 11.31
Group By options change based on the view you have selected. For example, when Gantt Chart is selected, you can group by various task properties, such as whether the task is critical.

Like the rest of the viewing mechanisms within Microsoft Project 2007, Group By is divided into the entity types it can be applied to—either task or resource.

Table 11.6 provides a list of predefined and commonly used task Group By options.

TABLE 11.6 STANDARD TASK GROUP BY OPTIONS OF MICROSOFT PROJECT 2007

Group By Option Name	Commonly Used	Purpose
No Group	Yes	Displays all tasks without applying any grouping condition.
Complete and Incomplete Tasks	Yes	Groups tasks into two categories—first, completed tasks; second, incomplete tasks.
Constraint Type	Yes	Groups tasks into categories by the constraint type applied to the task. The groups are listed in alphabetical order.
Critical	Yes	Groups tasks into two categories—critical and non-critical tasks. The non-critical tasks group is displayed first.
Duration	Yes	Groups tasks into categories by their duration. The number of categories depends on the number of unique Duration field values.

Group By Option Name	Commonly Used	Purpose
Duration Then Priority	Yes	Groups tasks first by duration and then within each duration grouping by priority, with the lowest one first.
Milestones	Yes	Groups tasks into two categories—milestone and regular tasks. The regular tasks group is displayed first.
Priority	Yes	Groups tasks by their priority, using intervals of 100.
Priority Keeping Outline Structure	Yes	Groups tasks by their priority, using intervals of 100, while maintaining the outline structure.

Table 11.7 provides a list of predefined and commonly used resource Group By options.

TABLE 11.7   STANDARD RESOURCE GROUP BY OPTIONS OF MICROSOFT PROJECT 2007

Group By Option Name	Commonly Used	Purpose
No Group	Yes	Displays resources without applying any grouping conditions.
Assignments Keeping Outline Structure	Yes	Groups resources by resource assignments, while maintaining the original outline structure.
Complete and Incomplete Resources	Yes	Groups resources into two categories—the ones assigned to completed tasks and the others to the tasks that have not been completed yet. The incomplete tasks group is displayed first.
Resource Group	Yes	Groups resources by resource group and subtotals the values based on the Group field entries within the Resource Sheet view.
Resource Type	Yes	Groups resources by resource type, based on the number of resource types present. At maximum, there are three categories: Work, Material, and Cost, displayed in that order with Work always being first.
Standard Rate	Yes	Groups resources by resource pay scale.

COMBINING VIEWS, TABLES, FILTERS, AND GROUPS TO REVIEW PROJECT SCHEDULE DETAILS

This section of the chapter explores some specific examples and viewing strategies you can apply when reviewing your schedule during your project's planning phase. The examples provided here represent the common usage scenarios employed by project managers when reviewing their project schedule. This section is also intended to serve as an initial checklist for reviewing your project schedule, but you should consider other checks, specific to you and your project, because this list is not all-inclusive.

DOES MY SCHEDULE CONTAIN THE NEEDED MILESTONES?

When finalizing and reviewing your schedule, it can be crucial to a project's success whether or not it contains all required milestones. Milestones not only ensure that there is an expected deliverable at the end of each step of the project, but they also help ensure that your schedule is organized correctly. There are several things you should evaluate when deciding what types of milestones you need to include in your schedule:

- Do you have crucial deliverables in your project? If you do, then it is beneficial to add a milestone for each one of those deliverables.

- Do you have a client or a project sponsor who wants to see project milestones? If so, then it is recommended that you create two separate types of milestones—internal to the team and ones your client or project sponsor would like to see. Separating the two will help both you and the client/sponsor. Your client/sponsor probably does not want to see every single one of your milestones, just the crucial ones that either make or break the project. Similarly, you do not want to limit yourself to only a handful of milestones that do not include intermediate deliverables that you will need to consider.

- Does your project have a final project milestone that connects your entire schedule together and defines a formal completion?

- Are there specific milestones associated with the billing? If there are, it may be beneficial to include those specific milestones to remind yourself which of your deliverables influence the invoicing.

Once you have answered these questions for your project, there are some techniques and view combinations you can apply to your project schedule to ensure it contains the necessary milestones:

- **Formatting text styles**—You can format the text styles to highlight the milestones in order to make them more visible and noticeable. To do so, select Format, Text Styles, and then in Item to Change select Milestone Tasks. Modify the style options, such as font color, size, italics, bold, and so on. Figure 11.32 shows an example of using different text styles.

Figure 11.32
Milestone tasks stand out in the schedule and are easy to notice because they are in blue italics.

- **Creating a custom field to filter by**—Using the custom fields in Microsoft Project 2007, you can create a custom text field that provides various categories for milestones, which you can then use to filter or group by. Figure 11.33 shows an example of grouping by the custom field Milestone Type, where the Milestone Type column has been added to the Gantt Chart view and then a custom group is applied to group by it.

Figure 11.33
Grouping by the Milestone Type custom field allows you to easily assess whether your project contains the needed milestones.

11

TIP

One of the easiest ways to customize any of the views or tables is to provide additional columns by right-clicking on the column area and selecting Insert Column. This allows you to view not only other fields within Microsoft Project 2007, but also the custom ones you have added.

DO I KNOW MY CRITICAL PATH?

When reviewing your schedule, it is important to review your critical path tasks. These are the tasks that have no slack, and if they slip, they will dramatically affect your entire project schedule.

You can apply several techniques to your project schedule to ensure that you know your critical path tasks and that they are easy to see:

- **Formatting text styles**—You can format the text styles to highlight the critical path tasks in order to make them more visible and noticeable. To do so, select Format, Text Styles, and then in Item to Change select Critical Tasks. Modify the style options, such as font color, size, italics, bold, and so on. Figure 11.34 shows an example of using different text styles.

Figure 11.34
Highlighting critical path tasks within the Gantt Chart view in red helps you easily distinguish the tasks that drive your project schedule.

- **Displaying the Total Slack column**—By definition, critical path tasks are tasks whose total slack is equal to zero. By displaying the Total Slack column, you can easily locate the critical path tasks because their Total Slack value is zero, as shown in Figure 11.35.

> To view the Total Slack column, just apply the Tracking Gantt view.

- **Grouping critical and non-critical tasks**—You can apply the Group By, Critical predefined group to the Gantt Chart view, which clearly separates critical from non-critical tasks, as shown in Figure 11.35.

Figure 11.35
Grouping the tasks by type is one of the easiest views to visually separate them and ensure you know what your critical path is.

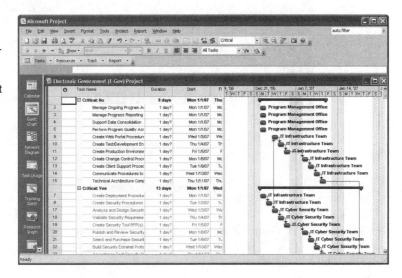

- **Filtering for critical path tasks**—You can apply the Filter By, Critical predefined filter to the Gantt Chart view to view only the critical path tasks.

ARE MY TASKS LINKED?

One of the easiest things to miss can be a task that gets added at the last minute and does not get linked with the rest of the schedule. If that happens, that can have really bad consequences when you cannot view its impact on your project. One of the most important aspects of the schedule to review is that all of your tasks are not only linked, but have the correct relationships with one another.

These are just several techniques and views you can use to ensure task relationships are properly defined within your project schedule:

- **Combining Gantt Chart and Relationship Diagram views**—This allows you to view the relationship of each task within your schedule. When you select the task in the Gantt Chart, the bottom part of the screen (the Relationship Diagram view) will filter to display the predecessors and successors of the selected task, as shown in Figure 11.36.

Figure 11.36
Combining the Gantt Chart and Relationship Diagram views allows you to easily see the relationships between tasks in your project schedule.

- **Displaying the Task Entry view**—This view is particularly helpful when ensuring that task relationships are correct and all tasks within your project are linked. The Task Entry view shows the Task Entry table with a Gantt Chart and the Task Form view at the bottom. The Gantt Chart can be of great help identifying which tasks have not been linked into the rest of the schedule. Similarly, the Task Form displays predecessors for each task, so if there are none, you need to make sure you intended that task to not have any.

TIP

To display predecessors and successors in the Task Form view, right-click in the view and select Predecessors & Successors. This will change the view and display predecessors in the right table and successors in the left one.

- **Displaying the Predecessor/Successor column**—This allows you to view both the predecessors and successors for each task. The non-summary-level tasks that have no predecessors or successors should be of concern to you and are a good idea to double-check. To add the Predecessors and Successors column, right-click and select Insert Column.

DOES MY SCHEDULE CONTAIN CONSTRAINTS?

Project schedules that contain constraints can be a little dangerous because a lot of the time those are constraints you are unaware of. Before finalizing and baselining your project schedule, it is a good idea to double-check that the constraints you do have in your schedule are intentional.

One of the easiest ways to find out what types of constraints are set on various tasks is by displaying the Constraint Type column within any of the task views, as shown in Figure 11.37.

> **N O T E**
>
> When task constraints are applied, special symbols appear in the Indicators column of the Gantt Chart. You can hover over each icon to see the name of the constraint applied.

Figure 11.37
Displaying the constraint column and grouping/filtering by Constraint Type is an easy way to verify task constraints.

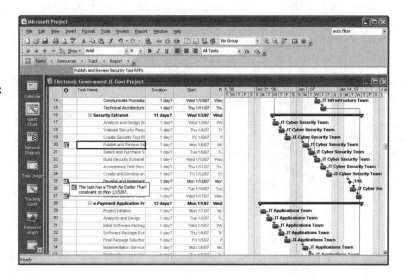

ARE ALL NEEDED TASK DETAILS INCLUDED?

Another detail to verify in your project schedule is that you have included the necessary attributes and details for each task.

To review the details of your tasks, use the Detail Gantt combination view and apply the Task Form view on the bottom (as shown in Figure 11.26). You can change the detail displayed in the Task Form view by right-clicking and selecting a different option to display.

MAKING SURE THERE IS FLEXIBILITY IN THE SCHEDULE

When scheduling your project tasks, it is important to include enough flexibility in your schedule so that if it were to slip, the final completion date would not change.

One of the task attributes that defines the schedule flexibility is how much slack each task in your project schedule has. It is also important to know which tasks have the most slack because those can be easily delayed, if needed, without affecting the final project completion date.

In addition to possibly affecting the project completion date, schedule flexibility influences project risks. For example, if you have a schedule delay risk associated with Task A, and Task A has a week lag time, then the risk severity and priority are minimized because of the extra time built into the schedule.

The Detail Gantt Chart view allows you to view the lag on each task. In addition, you can then filter or group your tasks by the amount of lag they have.

ARE MY RESOURCES OVERALLOCATED?

One of the most important things to review in your schedule prior to baselining is whether any of your resources are overallocated.

You can combine the Resource Usage view on the top and the Resource Graph on the bottom. This allows you to not only view which resources are overallocated and by how much, but also which days and which tasks contribute to the overallocation, as shown in Figure 11.38.

Figure 11.38
The Resource Graph and Resource Usage views allow you to view all your resource allocations and drill into the task level.

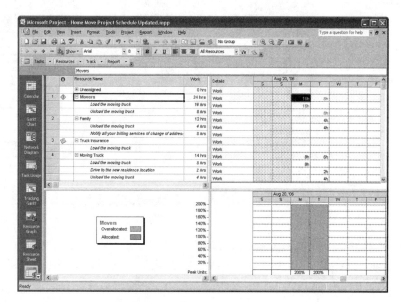

IS MY SCHEDULE BASELINED?

As an official completion of the planning phase, your project schedule must be baselined.

→ For details on baselining your schedule, **see** Chapter 12, "Performing a Schedule Reality Check," **p. 419**.

To view the current baseline information, you can apply the Multiple Baselines view. You can also modify the Gantt Chart view and display additional columns, such as any of the baseline columns. These include Budget Cost, Budget Work, Cost, Deliverable Finish, Deliverable Start, Duration, Finish, Start, and Work.

HOW DO I COMMUNICATE THE TASKS?

Microsoft Project 2007 provides some convenient ways to communicate your project schedule to your team:

- **Calendar view**—This is an easy-and-familiar-to-everyone way to display the project schedule. You can customize the Calendar view to display tasks for a specific resource and then print that view either to a printer or a PDF.

- **Network Diagram view**—This is one of the older, more common ways of presenting your project schedule to the rest of the team. The Network Diagram view can be more complex because it most often does not fit nicely on the page, so printing or exporting it can be a complicated task. The Network Diagram view, however, clearly and consecutively presents your project schedule and the needed information within it.

- **Resource Usage view**—This view is grouped by the resource, displaying all of the tasks assigned to the resource under the resources' name. Columns displayed include hours of work, hours of overallocated work, cost, availability and other details.

- **Gantt Chart view**—The old and reliable Gantt chart, with the appropriate filtering, sorting and grouping is a great way to show your team members their assigned tasks along with the time-phased data shown in the Gantt section.

TIP

> It is not considered a best practice to let other people (other project managers, team members, sponsors, and so on) access your project schedule directly. So it is recommended that you not just send the file as a method of sharing the information. Your project schedule file is a controlled environment, and any potential changes can jeopardize it.

HOW DO I PRESENT MY PROJECT SCHEDULE TO THE PROJECT SPONSORS?

As mentioned earlier, it is not recommended that you distribute your project schedule file to other parties, so in order to effectively communicate with your project sponsor, consider the following methods:

- **Export the project schedule to Excel**—To export your project schedule data to an Excel workbook, in the File menu select Save As and then under the file type select Excel Workbook.

→ For additional information on exporting to other file formats, such as Excel, XML, CSV, and so on, **see** Chapter 26, "Exporting and Importing Project Data," **p. 913**.

- **Format and print the Gantt Chart view**—You can display only the necessary tasks and columns by filtering, grouping, and hiding/displaying columns within the Gantt Chart view. This allows you to also format the printing options and print a clean, easy-to-read project schedule that communicates clearly to your project sponsors.

→ For additional information on printing views and reports, **see** Chapter 14, "Analyzing Performance," **p. 473**.

- **Create a Visual Report using Excel or Visio**—A new feature in Microsoft Project 2007 called Visual Reports allows you to create Excel- or Visio-based reports that display any type or detail level of data contained in the Microsoft Project 2007 database. Visual Reports can be an effective way to create custom information displays for communicating your project schedule information.

→ For additional information on creating and working with Visual Reports, **see** Chapter 21, "Creating and Customizing Visual Reports," **p. 707**.

- **Present a Calendar view showing only project milestones**—By customizing the Calendar view and the tasks displayed on it, you can provide an easy display of project information for sponsors. Although this view is useful and familiar, it might not be the best option for sponsors because they may be interested in seeing additional task and project information, such as cost.

- **Use the Copy Picture to Office Wizard**—This wizard takes a snapshot of the current view that can then be pasted into any other Office application, such as Word, Excel, Visio, and so on.

→ For additional information on using the Copy Picture to Office Wizard, **see** Chapter 27, "Manipulating Data Using Other Applications," **p. 959**.

CONSULTANTS' TIPS

KEEP IT SIMPLE

There is often a tendency for people to want to create views that contain a lot of information—so much information, as a matter of fact, that it becomes difficult to understand. Before you spend a lot of time designing a new Microsoft Project 2007 view, get a good understanding of the views that are available to you and how they might be easily modified. For example, in a Resource Usage or Task Usage view, right-clicking in the grid on the right side of the screen gives you a number of options to add more information to the view.

Remember that views are there to assist you in providing the most efficient, useful, and effective display of the information, so a minimalist approach is often the favorable one.

PROVIDING TASK ASSIGNMENTS TO YOUR TEAM USING THE GANTT CHART VIEW

There are a few ways to accomplish this. The easiest is to use the filter "Using Resource..." or "Using Resource In Date Range...." You could combine that with a grouping if you need to keep them focused on critical tasks. It's always a good idea to give them the full Gantt chart too, so they can see how their work fits into (and impacts) the big picture.

EASY WAY TO NOT ACCIDENTALLY TYPE IN ACTUALS WHEN USING RESOURCE OR TASK USAGE VIEWS

In either of those views, right click in the data grid and then select Detail Styles from the menu that pops up. On the right side of the Detail Styles dialog, in the Show these fields box, select All Assignment Rows and then click Hide. This will prevent entry of data in the default Work rows. To add actuals, select Actual Work from the Available fields section and click Show. You can configure each type of data with different colors to make it easier to manage the process of entering data.

CHAPTER 12

PERFORMING A SCHEDULE REALITY CHECK

In this chapter

Auditing the Schedule for Reasonableness

Before you are ready to call your project planning phase complete, it is important to review your project schedule and ensure it is ready for execution. This chapter provides some important questions that you need to ask yourself, as well as some good reality checks to ensure you are truly ready to execute what you planned.

During the planning phase, you have created your task schedule, defined the task relationships and dependencies, and assigned all necessary resources. This chapter provides guidance for reviewing your schedule and making the necessary adjustments. The more time you spend on making sure your project is complete and realistic while you plan, the more problems you can avoid during the execution.

Many organizations require that you capture a baseline of your schedule at the end of the planning phase. You should capture a baseline of the entire project after you are satisfied that your schedule is a realistic structure for work activities. The baseline allows you to later assess the performance of the project compared to the plan as you execute the details of the project. Make sure you check your organization's policies to determine when a baseline capture is required.

Looking for Logic Errors

Logic errors in a project occur when, for example, you forget a task or summary task while setting up your project, or schedule your tasks in the wrong order. It can be difficult to judge your own schedule as the errors may be harder to notice because of how familiar you are with it.

However, you can do some initial logic checks by answering the following questions:

- **Is all required work included in the schedule?** To answer this question, review your project scope statement and your Work Breakdown Structure (WBS) to ensure that your schedule captures the full scope of your project and all work has been included.

- **Does the organization of the schedule achieve the project's Measure of Success?** When starting up any project, you define the Measure of Success, which is your metric for what it really means for your project to have successfully achieved everything you planned for it to achieve. The tasks and milestones you have defined in your schedule must represent the Measure of Success you have defined.

- **Does the schedule include all and only necessary deliverables and tasks that achieve the work in the WBS?** It is important to recognize all of the project deliverables that support the Measure of Success you have defined. It is also important to remember that a successful project schedule should not include extraneous deliverables that may seem like they are needed, but are really not part of your project scope. For example, you have a house remodeling project in which you set out to replace the floors throughout the entire house. The tasks to purchase the materials, to hire the contractors, and to replace the flooring in each room of the house are all part of your scope. But the natural human thinking may lead you to consider that while you are replacing the floors, you might as well replace the doors on the interior of the house, even though it is not part of the original plan. Following this way of thinking, you can end up remodeling your entire house, even though your initial intent was to only replace the flooring. This is called *scope creep* and can be a dangerous scenario for any project, because scope creep is often responsible for projects finishing over budget and behind schedule. Even though the example described here may be an exaggerated one, situations similar to this occur and can lead to serious problems.

- **Are the tasks scheduled to occur in the correct order?** The order of tasks can be as essential as the tasks themselves. It is important to remember that not only should tasks occur in chronological order, but you should also allow for enough slack in tasks with the most risk. For example, adopting a new technology can be a risky task because you may encounter unforeseen problems, so scheduling those tasks earlier can be beneficial and can help you avoid delays later in the project. In addition, you must ensure that each task has all of its prerequisites met. For example, you would not schedule movers to come in and load the moving truck before you have packed your belongings. Similar logic should apply to all of the tasks in your project.

A good practice for determining logic errors is to have a trusted associate or your project team look at the project for you. Make sure the reviewers understand that he or she is just looking for your logic errors by reviewing your scope, tasks, task arrangement, and planning logic. It is possible your associates will want to change your schedule because they might have done things differently in another project. Everyone has his or her own way of doing things, and just like everything else in Microsoft Project, there is more than one way to accomplish the same result. In this case, ask the people reviewing your schedule to concentrate on your logic, not trying to improve your project using his or her own standards. But be open to the criticism too; that is one of the best ways to learn.

SCHEDULE ESTIMATION METHODS (PERT AND OTHER TECHNIQUES)

Schedule estimation errors are the second type of errors you need to check against when reviewing your project schedule. Estimation errors are caused by mistakes in setting your task durations, work, and budget. There are several ways to help you resolve estimation errors.

In order to discover estimation errors, you need to ask yourself the following questions:

- **Are tasks, work, and duration estimates viable?** Make sure that your work and duration estimates are realistic for all tasks. Many people underestimate, which leads to additional work, time, and in turn budget increases. Similarly, overestimating the work and duration is also undesirable because you may not be able to meet your project requirements. Ideally, your estimates should attempt to reflect the reality as closely as possible. For tips on achieving this, see the section "Are You a Pessimistic or an Optimistic Estimator?" at the end of the chapter.

- **Are budget estimates viable?** Budget estimates are also an important aspect of project planning. Ensuring that the budget you have allocated for your project is met and not exceeded can be the deciding point between success and failure. Ensure that the initial budget estimates you have are realistic and meet your project requirements.

12

In order to better understand estimation errors, it is important to review the three main estimation methods—analogous, expert judgment, and parametric.

ANALOGOUS ESTIMATION METHOD

Analogous duration estimates simply ask the question, What was the duration the last time we did this? If you have been following the project management best practice of recording lessons learned at the end of each project, you have proof, which increases in accuracy with every project you complete. You can use the past performance as an estimation comparison if your previous project is similar to your current scope.

The advantages to analogous estimates is that they focus on system-level activities, such as integration, documentation, configuration management, and others. They also require minimal project detail and are usually faster and easier to develop; plus your information is readily accessible in previous Microsoft Project schedules.

The downside to analogous duration estimates is that if you do not have any previous information, you have no detailed basis for justifying your estimates. Also, because it focuses on the system level, it can be hard to identify lower-level problems that can raise costs.

EXPERT JUDGMENT ESTIMATE METHOD (USING PERT)

Expert judgment is a great tool to use when hard data is scarce. Microsoft Project includes a Program Evaluation and Review Technique (PERT) analysis tool. PERT uses a network diagram analysis technique to create three estimates: Optimistic, Expected, and Pessimistic. These three estimates are then combined to estimate an activity's duration, using a weighted statistical average of the three values. The statistical technique considers: 1 part Optimistic, 4 parts Expected, and 1 part Pessimistic all divided by 6 parts. This method yields a weighted average duration for a given task.

To enter work/duration estimates, follow these steps:

1. Open the project schedule.
2. Display the PERT Analysis toolbar (see Figure 12.1) by right-clicking in the top menu area and selecting PERT Analysis or selecting View, Toolbars, PERT Analysis.

Figure 12.1
The PERT Analysis toolbar allows you to calculate each task's duration based on three types of estimates.

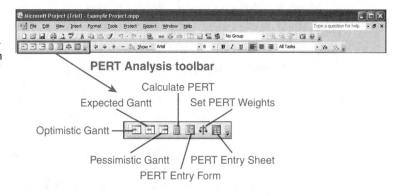

3. The PERT Analysis tool allows you to display and edit Optimistic, Expected, and Pessimistic durations for each task. You can enter your estimates for each task individually by using the PERT Entry form, as shown in Figure 12.2. You can also use the PERT entry sheet to view the three types of estimates for the entire project at once, as shown in Figure 12.3.

Figure 12.2
Use the PERT Entry window to define the estimates for each individual task.

Figure 12.3
The PERT entry sheet allows you to view all three estimates types on one screen and can be a quick way to enter your estimates.

You can also view the individual estimate types for the entire project by using the Optimistic Gantt, Expected Gantt, and Pessimistic Gantt views found on the PERT Analysis toolbar.

4. Use the PERT weights to specify the influence each estimate type has on your project schedule. The weight value should be based on the probability of that particular estimate scenario occurring. To do so, select Set PERT Weights in the PERT Analysis toolbar for each task.

5. Calculate the duration of every task in your project by selecting Calculate PERT in the PERT Analysis toolbar. As a result, Microsoft Project displays a warning that your duration fields will be recalculated based on the Optimistic, Expected, and Pessimistic estimates you have entered. Click Yes in the warning dialog box, and PERT will modify your task durations to the new values, as shown in Figure 12.4.

Figure 12.4
Using PERT, you can create a more accurate, probability-based estimates for your project.

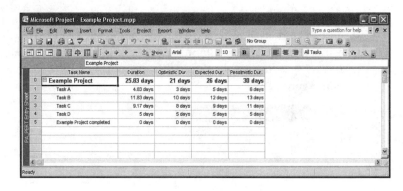

PARAMETRIC DURATION ESTIMATION METHOD

Finally, the parametric duration estimates are simply mathematical models used when estimating task durations. If you had a machine that produced a product at a rate of 10 units per hour and you needed to make 200 units, you are looking at 20 hours. This process produces exact estimates, but your estimate can change if you add another machine, increase the productivity, or decrease the duration of the task. Many different industries already have standard calculations, devised from years of experience, that can be used for this type of estimating.

LOOKING FOR TECHNIQUE ERRORS

Technique errors are problems such as data omissions or mistakes made while putting a schedule together. Here are some of the most common technique errors:

- Missing data
- Data where there should be blanks
- Misspellings
- Duplications
- Incorrect variables

In order to prevent or detect technique errors, audit your tasks, resources, schedule, and calendars.

AUDITING TASKS FOR TECHNIQUE ERRORS

When auditing your tasks for technique errors, check for the common problems related directly to the individual tasks:

- **Do all tasks have at least one predecessor and successor?** If you do not verify this, you may end up with "dangling" tasks. These are tasks that do not explicitly drive from the beginning or to the end (measurable definition of success) of your schedule. This can cause problems for the following reasons:
  - You may have tasks in your schedule that are extraneous or unnecessary. You may also have forgotten important relationships between tasks; this situation can cause your schedule to reflect incorrect dates.

- There are exceptions when it is acceptable to have tasks with no predecessors or successors—for example, recurring meetings and ongoing tasks, such as project management. It also may be okay for tasks to have no resources assigned, although this situation needs to be reviewed. For example, a task that is outside of the control of the project may be added to represent the elapsed time.

- **Do all tasks have resources assigned?** Milestones and summary tasks are exceptions. If tasks do not have resources assigned, then who is going to be completing those tasks? This can be a problem because if no one is assigned to complete a certain task, the work will not get accomplished and your project can be potentially delayed. In addition to this, you should ask yourself whether you have enough resources or too many resources.

- **Are there any unnecessary task constraints?** Task constraints are based on the logic of the workflow and natural deadlines, such as the start date of a trade show, the favorable season for climbing in Nepal, the availability of launch pads, and so on. However, if you incorrectly schedule your tasks, Microsoft Project 2007 can insert constraints, so make sure you are aware and agree with all constraints in your project.

- **Are the tasks the appropriate size?** This is a personal measure: How large or small do you want tasks to be? Is 2 days too small; is 4 weeks too large? Only you can decide. Typically, tasks that are under 40 hours of effort are the easiest to manage. The task size depends on the purpose of the project schedule. If the purpose is to calculate the overall duration of the project for a rough estimate based on the achievement network at the top level, task sizes of 2 weeks or more are acceptable. However, it may be more helpful to your team to have tasks broken down into smaller parts to create a well-defined list of deliverables and the actions that need to be performed to achieve them. Here are additional considerations for task sizes:

    - Is the schedule used for execution?
    - How often is progress monitored?
    - What is the experience level of the people doing the work?

AUDITING RESOURCES FOR TECHNIQUE ERRORS

Problems relating to resources are very important. If your resources are not available, are overallocated, or are assigned to incorrect tasks, you will have problems. To audit your project resources, review the following common problems:

- **Does your project contain duplicate resources?** Have you used two or more names for the same person? This can happen easily when multiple individual resources are assigned to multiple tasks in a schedule. If work is assigned to duplicate resources, you may have created overallocation for the actual individual resource.

- **Does your project schedule contain generic resources?** This scenario can occur if you, for example, have assigned a task to "System Engineer" because you are not sure about the specific individual resource available for this task assignment but you know the skill set required to complete the task. Until the individual resource is determined, uncertainty can exist in your schedule. What if this person is assigned to a higher priority task in another project in the meantime, then who will be responsible for the task in your schedule? As a final step in verifying your schedule, ensure that all generic resources have been replaced with the real ones.

■ **Are any of the resources in your project schedule overallocated (or underallocated)?** This is a situation where a resource is scheduled to perform more work during a workday than he or she can accomplish. As a result:

- The overallocated resource can fall behind on his or her work, affecting the schedule. If the resource is working on critical path tasks, this may cause the entire project finish date to slip.
- The overallocated resource may become very unhappy or burnt out.

■ **Are any resources scheduled for overtime?** How would you define overtime? When is it appropriate to use and not use overtime? When does overtime become a problem? Based on previous experience take into consideration the following:

- Extended periods of overtime for many weeks tend to burn people out.
- Scheduling overtime creates a more optimistic view of the project completion date than may be warranted.

AUDITING THE SCHEDULE FOR TECHNIQUE ERRORS

When auditing your project schedule for technique errors, concentrate on the following questions:

■ **Is your schedule up to date?** Verify that your project reflects the latest contract changes and that the scope of the project has not changed since the last time the schedule was updated.

■ **Is your schedule the appropriate size?** Does it include all of the necessary deliverables and milestones?

■ **Is your schedule baselined?** Baselining allows you to finalize the project estimates and designates the end of the planning phase. If you neglect to baseline your schedule, Microsoft Project 2007 will not have any base values to compare your actuals to, making reporting and analysis difficult.

■ **Are all milestones entered correctly?** Ensure that all tasks you intended to be milestones have a duration of 0. In addition, milestones represent the mark for starting or completing something, so ensure that your milestones are linked to the correct tasks.

■ **Are project costs specified in the schedule?** In order to effectively track your project budget, ensure that it reflects the most up-to-date cost rates for your resources. Having erroneous costs in your project can cause problems during analysis.

AUDITING CALENDARS FOR TECHNIQUE ERRORS

Correctly defined calendars are fundamental and a very important component of your project schedule. When auditing calendars, address the following common problem areas:

■ **Are corporate holidays defined in the project calendars?** If holidays are not defined in the resource calendars, then Microsoft Project 2007 will schedule work during those days. This can cause problems because work will be scheduled when resources are not available, which guarantees the tasks to slip. In addition, this creates a more optimistic view of the project completion date than may be warranted.

- **Are vacation days defined in the resource calendars?** If vacation days are not specified in the resource calendars, then work will be scheduled during those days. This can cause problems because work will be scheduled when resources are not available, which guarantees the tasks to slip. In addition, this creates a more optimistic view of the project completion date than may be warranted.

- **Is the working-day length set correctly?** Scheduling 8 working hours per day may be unrealistic. Very few days are that productive, especially over a long period of time because of other obligations, such as meetings, email, and so on. Take this fact into consideration when scheduling working time in your project calendar.

REVIEWING THE BIG PICTURE (CRITICAL PATH ANALYSIS)

Critical path can be defined as the longest path through your project and determines the finish date for the project as a whole. Tasks that are on the critical path contain no slack, so if these tasks slip, a delay will result in the chain of tasks within your project. It is important to review your project's critical path because it determines whether your project can be completed on schedule.

Not knowing your critical path and what you can do to reduce it can cause problems, such as the following:

- The overall project schedule may be extended unnecessarily.

- As the project manager, you need to monitor the schedule to guard against slippage. If tasks are not on the critical path, improving the speed of delivering them will not change the project end date.

- The critical path can and does change very quickly during the life of a project. As the project manager, you must continuously monitor the amount of slack available for tasks so that unexpected problems you are not prepared for do not arise.

- Your sponsor or client may be willing to shorten the schedule by using different task scheduling techniques or spending more money. You need to be able to identify these opportunities to your sponsor or client.

WHAT IS MY CURRENT CRITICAL PATH?

The critical path is the longest path of linked tasks in the project and includes all tasks that will impact the overall project end date if any of them are delayed. Some tasks have slack and, therefore, are not considered critical. Free slack is the amount of time a task can be delayed without delaying any successor tasks. Total slack is the amount of time a task can be delayed without delaying the finish date of the project. In addition to critical tasks, your project contains the near-critical tasks, tasks that are considered high risk and can potentially become critical. If a near-critical task slips and it is close to critical, it can jeopardize your critical path. This scenario is often overlooked, but when reviewing your critical path, pay attention to the tasks that can become critical if project conditions change.

You can use Microsoft Project 2007 to help you distinguish your critical path by applying a different text style to these tasks using the Text Styles tool. To do so, select Format, Text Styles from the top menu. In the Text Styles dialog box under Item to Change, select Critical Tasks. Select a distinct font style, color, background color, and so on to help you visually distinguish critical tasks, as shown in Figure 12.5.

Figure 12.5
The critical-path tasks are styled in red, bold, italic font to help easily distinguish them from the rest of the schedule.

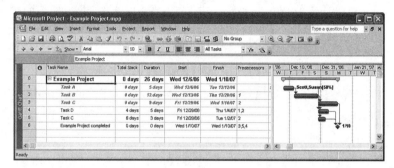

By default, Microsoft Project 2007 critical tasks are tasks with total slack less than or equal to 0. You can change the tolerance level and set the total slack to a different number you feel more comfortable with. To do so, open the Options dialog box by selecting Tools, Options. In the Options dialog box, select the Calculation tab and change the number displayed in the Tasks are critical if slack is less than or equal to option to, say, 4 days. As a result, additional tasks that are near-critical are then added and become part of the critical path, as shown in Figure 12.6.

Figure 12.6
Task D is a near-critical task because its Total Slack is greater than 0, but it is part of the critical path because the tolerance has been changed to 4 days.

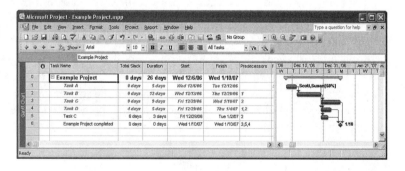

You can display the Total Slack column in your current view to help you distinguish between the true critical tasks and the near-critical ones. To do so, click the column header, right-click, and then select Insert Column. In the Column Definition window, select Total Slack under Field Name and then click OK. Tasks whose Total Slack is less than or equal to 0 are your critical tasks, and tasks with slack greater than 0 that are still marked as part of your critical path are the near-critical ones.

HOW CAN I REDUCE THE DURATION OF MY CRITICAL PATH?

You will encounter situations when you need to reduce your project's total duration. Here are two established methods for reducing your schedule duration and therefore the critical path:

- **Crashing**—This common project management term refers to a method used to decrease the duration of an activity by assigning more resources. The distinguishing point of crashing when compared to the second method (fast tracking) is that crashing employs changes to resources to reduce the critical path. Be cautious because when you add more resources you also add more cost, so be aware of the tradeoff conditions when using this method.

- **Fast tracking**—This common method is used to reduce your project's critical path duration by shortening a sequence or path of activities via overlapping or accomplishing activities in parallel. The fast tracking method takes advantage of changes made to the activities schedule to reduce the critical path. This method may increase the quality risks to your project because activities are started before the original intended sequence.

Both of these methods achieve the same result but have different effects on your project.

When decreasing the critical path duration, you do have to be aware of the effects this has on the rest of your project attributes, such as scope, cost, and quality. All these variables are interdependent, so when you change one variable, one of the other variables has to change in order for the project to maintain balance. For example, if you crash your project schedule by adding additional resources to the project, your project cost will increase to accommodate for the pay of the added resources. Similarly, if you use the fast tracking method and break a critical task into smaller tasks worked on by different resources, then the quality of the project may suffer because the work is being divided between a lot of different people.

STRATEGIES FOR CRASHING THE SCHEDULE

As it was mentioned in the previous section, crashing the schedule is a technique used to help you reduce your critical path by making changes to the way the resources are scheduled in your project. This section discusses methods you can use to crash your project schedule.

ASSIGNING ADDITIONAL RESOURCES

The first method for crashing your project schedule is to assign additional resources to the critical path tasks. Adding resources will in turn decrease the duration, thus shortening the critical path. When using this method, be aware of the effects it has on the rest of your project. If you have unlimited use of resources, then this method can be a great way to reduce the critical path without it having any effects on your overall project. However, if you have to pay for the additional resources you add, you are increasing the overall cost of your project, which can put your project over budget. Carefully weigh your options to make sure that the tradeoffs you are making are worth it.

12

SCHEDULING OVERTIME

Another way to crash your schedule is to arrange overtime for the resources already assigned to the critical path tasks. This option can work well, but you must ensure that the resources are available to work overtime and that the amount of overtime is reasonable and not going to burn out your resources. You can schedule overtime by modifying the task's calendar to schedule resources to work, for example, on Saturdays. Besides having negative effects on your resources, this method can also influence other aspects of your project, such as budget, if your resources are contracted to be paid overtime.

STRATEGIES FOR FAST TRACKING THE SCHEDULE

As mentioned previously, fast tracking is a technique used to reduce your project's critical path duration by making changes to the way tasks are scheduled within your project. This section discusses methods you can use to fast track your schedule.

PARALLEL SCHEDULING

The first option is to revise the task dependencies to allow more parallel scheduling. This overlaps the activities within your schedule to shorten the overall critical path duration. There are times when this option is not feasible because the critical path tasks have Start-to-Finish relationships, and one cannot be started until the previous one is fully completed. In addition, this can have an effect on your project resources. For example, if you have the same resource working on the two tasks that you schedule to be performed in parallel, either the resource will be unable to complete his or her assignments or he or she will have to work overtime. This, in turn, can have an effect on your budget, if this resource gets paid an additional rate for the overtime hours. Make sure you evaluate the consequences of parallel scheduling and ensure that this will not cause further problems within your project.

DECOMPOSING TASKS

The second option for fast tracking is to break critical task into smaller tasks that can be worked on simultaneously by different resources. The tradeoff of using this method is that it can potentially decrease the quality of work being performed on the tasks because you have many different people performing separate parts of the task. This can cause inconsistencies in the final product. In addition, ensure that the resources are available to perform the work that you schedule to prevent having resource-overallocation problems in the future.

CHANGING THE SCOPE OF YOUR PROJECT

Changing the scope of your project is really a third technique that does not fit under either crashing or fast tracking the schedule, but it does allow you to reduce the length of your critical path. This option, however, generally requires the involvement of your project sponsors in that you must receive their approval. This option is commonly used on product development projects. For example, if the goal of a project is to release software as soon as possible, you may need to remove some of the features from the original design in order to have the project finish on time. The removed features can then be released as a patch later in the product life cycle or moved to a consecutive phase of the product release.

REVIEWING THE PROJECT-LEVEL STATISTICS

As part of your schedule reality check, it is important to review the project-level statistics so you can see high-level metrics about the schedule. To do so, follow these steps:

1. Open the Project Information dialog box by selecting Project, Project Information in the top menu.

2. Open the Statistics dialog box by clicking the Statistics button. The Project Statistics dialog box is displayed, as shown in Figure 12.7. Project Statistics displays the baseline, actual, and variance values for your project.

Figure 12.7
Use the Project Statistics dialog box to review high-level summary information about your project.

METHODS OF EXAMINING YOUR SCHEDULE

Take advantage of the tools included in Microsoft Project 2007 to help you examine various aspects of your project. You can use groups, filters, and views to review the parts of your project, as follows:

- **Groups**—A very useful feature for organizing items in your schedule based on predefined criteria. To apply groups, select the menu Project, Group By.

- **Filters**—Allows you to limit what information is displayed in the current view based on the criteria you select. To view all available filters for the selected view, go to the menu Project, Filter For, More Filters.

- **Views**—Collections of data that are used to present a certain type of information in a particular way. In addition to the Gantt Chart view, the Resource Usage and Task Usage views are very useful views for analyzing and finding potential problems with your schedule.

  - Task Usage view shows you each task you have entered into the schedule, with resource assignment information grouped directly under each task. You can review the assignments, when they are scheduled for work, and, if necessary (although not recommended), edit the time-phased resource work data cells. Once you edit the work, you may restrict Microsoft Project's 2007 capability of leveling and moving the resource assignment work.

  - Resource Usage view displays resource's scheduled work for your project. This can be useful to get an overall picture of which tasks are assigned to each resource, as they are grouped by resource name. This can be an easy way to determine which tasks have no resources assigned to them. In addition, this view is helpful in reviewing the resource allocations where overloaded resources are highlighted in the color red. You may want to change the timescale to view the alloca-tion on a week-by-week or month-by-month view. To do so, use the menu Format, Timescale to change the formatting settings for the timescale or use the Zoom buttons on the Standard toolbar.

→ For additional information about using groups, filters, and views to review your schedule, **see** Chapter 11, "Using Standard Views, Tables, Filters, and Groups to Review Your Schedule," **p. 369**.

STRATEGIES FOR ANALYZING COSTS

In addition to schedule and resources, cost plays a significant role in each project. Often when reviewing your final project schedule, it is important to review the project costs and attempt to reduce them as much as possible. Reducing costs can provide you with more leverage during the project execution because if your original estimate is lower than the cap-ital budget you have for the project, you can use the difference to correct problems that arise throughout execution.

Microsoft Project 2007 includes a new feature—budget resources, that allows you to add another resource to the project summary-level task, also known as task number zero, within your project to capture the capital budget. This is a placeholder field that does not get changed by Microsoft Project 2007, and you can use it to compare your baseline and actual total project budget to.

→ For additional information about budget resources, **see** Chapter 8, "Defining Project Resources," **p. 249**.

You can use two techniques to reduce the cost in your project schedule:

- Reduce resource costs
- Decrease project scope

These options are discussed in detail in the later sections.

REVIEWING THE COST TABLE

Microsoft Project 2007 provides many different ways to review your project costs. One of the ways is to display the Resource Sheet view (select View, Resource sheet) and apply the Cost table (select View, Table, Cost). This view displays all resources in your project and their costs. To make this view even more useful, you can use sorting, filtering, and grouping to help you identify various cost categories.

For example, you can group your resources by type and then sort the list in descending order, so that the most expensive resources in each category are displayed at the top of the list. To do so, follow these steps:

1. Select Project, Group By, Resource Type.
2. Select Project, Sort By, Cost. This will sort the list of resources in descending order, with the most expensive resource at the top, as shown in Figure 12.8.

Figure 12.8
Use the Resource Sheet Cost table, grouped by resource type and sorted by cost, to review your most expensive resources in each resource category.

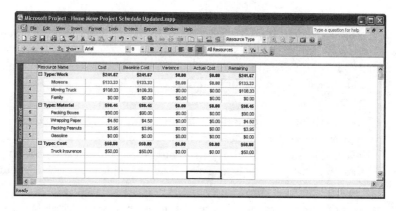

→ For additional information about using groups, filters, and views to review your project costs, **see** Chapter 11, "Using Standard Views, Tables, Filters, and Groups to Review Your Schedule," **p. 369**.

REDUCING THE COST OF WORK

One way to reduce the cost of your project is reduce the cost of work. This can be accomplished by using less expensive resources, for example. Here are some points to keep in mind:

- If you have contractors assigned to perform some of the tasks in your project, you can replace them with employees, which are generally cheaper to use. If you decide to do this, ensure that internal resources are available for work and that you will not cause any resource overallocations.

- If you have material resources in your project, you can try to find a better deal or a cheaper source for purchasing them. Similarly, you can shop around for a better deal on the cost of services as well. Maybe it is cheaper to rent equipment instead of buying it. Look for alternatives to reduce the cost of these resource types and take into account special promotions and so on.

FINALIZING THE SCHEDULE

Once you have reviewed your schedule yourself but before you are ready to baseline it and move into execution, it is important that you perform several last steps in the project management process. Here are some things you should do before baselining your schedule:

- **Get feedback from other people**—After performing all of the schedule checks yourself, it is always a good idea to get someone else to review the schedule as well. You may be too intimately familiar with the project by the time you review it, so it is possible that you will not notice some mistakes you made. As a best practice, always have a "second pair of eyes" on all important documents that you produce.

- **Receive stakeholder approval**—Even if you have not made any drastic changes to the project schedule, it is always important to ensure that your project stakeholders approve the current plan. The best way to get approval is hold a review session with project stakeholders prior to the project kickoff. During this session you can discuss the changes and tradeoffs you made, bring up any outstanding issues with the contract, and discuss project risks.

- **Receive project team and organization buy-in**—Once you receive your stakeholders' approval to go ahead with the project, it is important that you meet with the parties involved in the project from your organization. This includes not only your project team, but also resource managers and other people who can have potential influence or impact on your project.

- **Secure the resources**—Ensure that the resources you scheduled to work on your project are available and there is no resource overallocation.

- **Prepare for the kickoff**—Once you have gotten approval from project stakeholders and sponsors and have received buy-in from the project team and your organization, you should prepare to hold a kickoff meeting, in which you bring together everyone who will be participating in the project execution. It is important that you discuss the scope of the project, highlight major deliverables and their deadlines, discuss major project milestones, and the consequences of those milestones not being met. In addition, you should set forth the expectations of each project participant, so that everyone is aware of his or her responsibilities.

BASELINING THE SCHEDULE

One of the last steps in preparing your project for execution is baselining it. A baseline represents a snapshot of all the planned data as it was outlined within the contract and approved by project stakeholders. Microsoft Project 2007 includes 11 baselines you can use to track authorized changes made to the project planned data. In addition, the baseline plays a very important role in the tracking and analysis of your project schedule. Microsoft Project uses the baseline values to derive variances in cost and schedule while comparing them to the actual data you record.

A baseline, according to the PMI's *PMBOK Guide*, is defined as "the original plan, plus or minus approved changes."

→ For more on PMI and the *PMBOK Guide,* **see** "Exploring Project Management Industry Standards," **p. 71**.

Baselining copies several key data types in your schedule and saves them for future reference and analysis. These data types include: all tasks, start and finish dates, durations, costs, assigned work, budget cost, budget work, fixed cost, accrued cost, deliverable start, and deliverable finish.

SAVING YOUR PROJECT BASELINE

You can save your project baseline by using one of two methods. First, you can use the Project Guide toolbar, which will guide you through the baselining process. To do so, follow these steps:

1. Display the Project Guide toolbar by selecting View, Toolbars, Project Guide. If Project Guide is not available as one of the options, open the Options dialog box by selecting Tools, Options. In the Options dialog box, select the Interface tab and select the Display Project Guide check box under Project Guide settings.

2. In the Project Guide toolbar, select Track and then select the Save a Baseline Plan to Compare with Later Versions option. The Save Baseline Project Guide is displayed on the left side of your screen, as shown in Figure 12.9.

3. In the Save Baseline Project Guide pane, click the Save Baseline button. The message "Baseline saved on <Day of the week>, <Date and Time>" is displayed under the Save Baseline button, indicating that your baseline was successfully saved on that day of the week and at that date and time.

Figure 12.9
The Save Baseline pane allows you to easily save your project baseline.

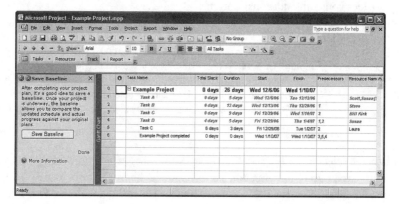

4. Click the Done button to complete the action.

You can also set the project baseline by performing the following steps:

1. Open the Set Baseline dialog box by selecting the menu sequence Tools, Tracking, Set Baseline.

2. In the Set Baseline dialog box, you can select to either save the entire project baseline or save the interim plan. Select the appropriate options and click the OK button, as shown in Figure 12.10.

Figure 12.10
Use the Set Baseline dialog box to select the baselining options for your project and to set the baseline.

Both of these options will accomplish the same thing. However, when using the Project Guide, you will only be able to save the default baseline, whereas the Set Baseline dialog box provides you with additional options.

NOTE

> Although Project records task splits, there is no explicit data field to show the split conditions. However, you can view these task splits in addition to the milestones and tasks that the baseline records using the Gantt Chart. In addition, task splits appear as time periods with zero hours of work in the time-phased data of the Usage views. The overall task duration shows the accumulated working periods disregarding the split sections.

When Project records a baseline, it saves the current schedule for all tasks, plus the start and finish date, duration, costs, and assigned work. There are also six new areas of information that Microsoft Project 2007 records: Budget Cost, Budget Work, Fixed Cost, Accrued Cost, Deliverable Start, and Deliverable Finish.

→ For additional information about the new baseline fields in Microsoft Project 2007, **see** Chapter 13, "Tracking Your Project Progress," **p. 443**.

You can save up to 11 different baselines. The first time you save a baseline, Project records it in the default baseline, named Baseline. If you create additional baselines after that, Microsoft Project names them Baseline 1, Baseline 2, and so on. Microsoft Project records the same fields for each baseline, so that they can be compared later. Additional baselines can be used to track additional authorized changes to the project once the execution has started. Often the changes reflected in the following baselines reflect change requests that are amendments to the original contract. This allows you to keep track of all changes, including the original plan that your project goes through. The process of revising your project schedule is known as *rebaselining*. If you do rebaseline, you should save the current baseline to one of the other available baselines and then set the new current baseline from your project schedule. To do so, select Tools, Tracking, Set Baseline, which opens the Set Baseline dialog box. The Set Baseline dialog box provides you with four different options:

12

- **Set Baseline**—This is the default selection when you open the Set Baseline dialog box. It saves the date from the current schedule into the baseline default setting. You can, however, select the down arrow to choose another baseline to save to.

- **Set Interim Plan**—This option is used for copying data from one version to another. For example, if you wanted to save the current default baseline to Baseline 1, you can select Baseline in the Copy text box and Baseline 1 in the Into text box.

- **For**—This option allows you to choose whether the baseline you are saving is for the entire project or for selected tasks only.

- **Roll Up Baselines**—This option is available only when you choose the For Selected Tasks option. When a baseline is saved, Project, by default, does not update that baseline for a summary task when a subtask is added, deleted, or modified. The two options under Roll Up Baselines allow you to choose to roll up the baseline changes for subtasks into their parent summary tasks. Select the To All Summary Tasks option, which includes the rebaselined subtask. If you want to update only the selected summary tasks, then choose those summary tasks along with the subtask(s) that you want to rebaseline (use Ctrl+click to add more than one subtask). Then choose From Subtasks into Selected Summary Task(s). You can click the Set as Default button to make your selection for either or both of these options the default on all new projects.

CAUTION

> The Multiple Undo feature of Microsoft Project 2007 allows you to undo the setting of a baseline. However, be cautious because some actions in Project, such as a Save operation, will clear the Undo list, after which you will no longer be able to undo the changes you have made.

The already used baselines have the "last saved" date next to the baseline version name. If you attempt to save your current baseline to the already used baseline version, Microsoft Project will display an overwrite warning message, as shown in Figure 12.11. If you are still in the process of making changes to the original project schedule plan, you can safely overwrite the baseline. However, if you are executing the project, it is recommended that you save your data to the next available baseline version.

It is a project management best practice to save the baseline after the project has been approved and before it has started execution. Also, the original approved baseline should always remain unchanged.

Figure 12.11
Be careful when overwriting an already existing baseline. If you are sure that you want to overwrite the previously saved baseline, then select Yes in the warning box shown here.

CONSULTANTS' TIPS

ARE YOU A PESSIMISTIC OR AN OPTIMISTIC ESTIMATOR?

Most people tend to either be pessimistic or optimistic in their work estimates, and this is an important factor to recognize and take into account when planning a project. It is imperative not only for the estimates you create yourself, but also for the estimates your team provides to you. Once you learn the nature of your team (or your own nature), future estimating will become a better predictor of reality, making your work and duration estimates more viable.

One way to determine the nature of your team is by figuring out the "reality ratio." Reality ratio shows you how much off someone's original estimate was from the actual execution and can be calculated from past projects. For example, you have a resource who estimates that it will take 30 hours to complete a certain type of task. Once the project is completed, the actual work for that task is 45 hours, which means that the original estimate the resource gave you was optimistic. The reality ratio in this case is 1.5 (that is, 45 / 30 = 1.5). Next time the same resource gives you an estimate for the same type of task or project, you can use the reality ratio to adjust that estimate, which will make the estimate more realistic and thus reduce the number of estimation errors in your schedule. If you do feel that you need to adjust a resource's original estimate, make sure to discuss the changes you would like to make with the resource and ensure that you are both in agreement with the change.

SCHEDULE PROBLEMS CHECKLIST

Table 12.1 provides some high-level questions that you need to answer as part of the schedule reality check process. This will ensure that your schedule does not contain any obvious mistakes and that you are ready to move into the Execution and Control phases.

TABLE 12.1 SCHEDULE PROBLEMS CHECK LIST

Question	Explanation/Example
Tasks	
Do the tasks in your project schedule accomplish all of the work you defined in your WBS and encompass the entire scope of your project?	Your organization should have a method to capture the business objectives with project scope and budget statements. A business plan is an example that can be used to determine if the schedule tasks perform all of the required scope.
Are all tasks in your project of appropriate size?	Are you required to follow project management best practices or other established standards for the length of tasks. For example, your tasks may be no less than a week in hours of duration and no larger than 2 weeks.
Do any tasks have fixed costs associated with them?	Some tasks may also have accrual at the beginning or end of the task activity.
Do tasks in your schedule have constraints? Are those constraint dates set in the future?	You may want to consider creating special milestones that precede a series of work activities. Use these milestones to set constraints such as Start no Earlier Than.

Question	Explanation/Example
Tasks	
Does your schedule contain any "dangling" tasks?	Dangling tasks are tasks that have no successors/predecessors and, therefore, are not connected with the rest of your project schedule.
Are the task naming conventions consistent and meet your project requirements (if there were any)?	Task names should reflect a deliverable item that can be clearly measured. A task name like "Research" is too ambiguous and cannot be clearly measured. Using a task name like "Write Research Report" enables you to clearly measure success regarding the completion of the task.
Resources	
Does your resource pool contain duplicate Resource Name entries?	For example, "Mary Smith" and "M Smith" may actually refer to the exact same person but Microsoft Project 2007 does not "know" this distinction.
Have you replaced all generic resources with actual resource names?	Project schedule templates often have generic resources on task assignments. Make sure you substitute the generic resources for named resources before you begin tracking schedule progress.
Do all of your resources have cost information associated with them?	Check your organization's policies before assigning cost data to resources. Some organization forbid the use of detailed resource costs.
Are any of your resources overallocated?	Always determine if resources are overloaded. If you ignore overload conditions, you dramatically increase your risk of project failure.
Which of your resources are scheduled for overtime, and was this intentional?	Analyze the workload conditions to ensure you have not accidentally overlooked overtime situations.
Schedule	
Are all of the tasks in your schedule baselined?	You need some basis of comparison when you execute the schedule details. Baselines are a very convenient way to compare performance to the original plan.
Does your project include correct and necessary milestones?	Use milestones as success markers within the lifecycle phases of the project.
Does your schedule reflect the latest scope information?	Check the business plan and change control logs to make sure the schedule reflects the full scope.
Calendar	
Does your project calendar include the accepted holiday information?	In addition to standard accepted holidays, also check for special "all company" events that should be included within the calendars.

12

continues

TABLE 12.1   CONTINUED

Question	Explanation/Example
Calendar	
Do your resource calendars correctly reflect the vacations and other non-working days for your project resources?	You need a general policy for maintaining resource calendars to reflect varying conditions throughout the the year.
Does your calendar include the correct working day length throughout?	You may also decide to use part-time, 24 hour, or other calendar variations as needed to reflect resources and/or project working conditions.

TIP

> You can perform the schedule reality check manually, but you should also consider the schedule auditing tools available as add-ins to Microsoft Project 2007, such as QuantumPM Schedule Auditor (QSA). These tools will simplify the tedious process of checking your schedule, so you can concentrate on estimation and technique used in your project schedule.

AVOIDING THE "WHILE YOU ARE HERE" SYNDROME

When creating your project schedule, avoid the "while you are here" syndrome—that is, do not add extra task activities that do not contribute to the measure of success of your project. The project manager must constantly monitor approved project scope and avoid unintentional scope creep by adding new tasks, even though those activities seem to be a logical progression of work. This syndrome is a common project manager trap that is responsible for many projects finishing over budget and behind schedule.

12

PART III

PROJECT EXECUTION THROUGH COMPLETION

CHAPTER **13**

TRACKING YOUR PROJECT PROGRESS

In this chapter

You have probably created a project schedule, assigned resources to tasks, captured baseline information, and then convinced yourself the schedule is ready to move into the execution lifecycle phase. Now you want to track progress and compare project performance to your original plans. This chapter helps you:

- Understand how to interpret progress compared to baseline data
- Use Microsoft Project 2007 functions to enter actual progress
- Understand how key Microsoft Project 2007 calculations work within the tool

OVERVIEW OF TRACKING

So you are finished creating your schedule. You have entered all the resources, assignments, and tasks, set the predecessors and successors, made sure that everything was correct, and set the initial baseline (see Chapter 12, "Performing a Schedule Reality Check," for details). You are ready to start using your project schedule, so now what? While this is a common stopping place for many project managers, it is not using Microsoft Project 2007 to its fullest potential. It would be like making a big print out of the schedule, hanging it up on the wall for everyone to admire, and just assuming that everything goes just as you planned. You made a perfect plan, so everything should work perfectly, right?

This chapter explores how to use Microsoft Project 2007 to track the progress of your schedule against the baseline and also spot scheduling issues if conditions deviate from your original plan. Your ability to identify and address problems early on will keep your project on track. There are several ways that Microsoft Project 2007 helps you to manage your project:

- You can open a view with your initial baseline to review the values that have been set. Remember, a baseline is a record of the project that can be used for comparison later on. The intent of a baseline is to establish a framework to measure schedule variance as you move through project lifecycles. You can use various features to clearly see how variations from your original plan may create high-risk conditions to the overall success of the project.

- You can use several data editing methods to enter and record information of what has actually happened during the execution phase of the project. This is called *tracking* in Microsoft Project 2007.

- As you enter tracking information, Microsoft Project 2007 will replace scheduled items, such as start and finish dates or costs, with the actual dates or costs. It will also recalculate entries such as task or assignment duration and/or adjust resource workload.

- Finally, Microsoft Project 2007 helps you snapshot incremental progress conditions to help you analyze overall performance during interim lifecycles or at the end of the project. This type of analysis can help you, and your organization, better understand how well you perform when compared to initial project scope and estimates.

→ For more information about end-to-end project analysis, **see** Chapter 14, "Analyzing Performance," **p. 473**.

USING PROJECT GUIDE FOR TRACKING

If you are new to Microsoft Project or tracking, you may find it helpful to use the Project Guide's Track pane, as shown in Figure 13.1. The Project Guide will help you with choosing how you want to track progress. The Project Guide will also help you with activities such as: setting up your custom view, creating your baseline, adding progress information, adjusting the project, and checking tasks.

→ More on Project Guide's Track pane can be found in the Sams book *Microsoft Office Project Server 2007 Unleashed*.

Figure 13.1
Use the Project Guide Track menu function to learn more about tracking options.

WORKING WITH PROJECT BASELINES

The key thing to remember when preparing to baseline your project is that neither the project nor the baseline is sacred. As much as you might like to think that your project is perfect, conditions will change—usually things outside your control. It is because of these changes that you need to baseline; using the baseline helps you to track these changes. While you should always make sure to keep a copy of your original baseline, as you make changes to the project, you can use one of the additional ten baselines to keep track of the changes.

According to PMI's *PMBOK Guide*, a baseline is defined as "the original plan, plus or minus approved changes." Setting a baseline allows you to use variance and earned value analysis to later understand how the work is performed and whether the project is proceeding according to plan.

→ For more information on the PMI and the PMBOK Guide, **see** "Exploring Project Management Industry Standards," **p. 71**.

→ For additional information on saving your baseline, **see** Chapter 12, "Performing a Schedule Reality Check," **p. 419**.

VIEWING BASELINES

Microsoft Project 2007 provides several methods to view baseline and tracking data. Each task and resources assignment contains many types of information like; task name, duration, work, cost, start and finish dates, and so forth. When you use the menu sequence Tools,

13

Tracking, Set Baseline feature, Microsoft Project 2007 copies key parts of the task and assignment data into special baseline fields.

Microsoft Project 2007 has several predefined combinations of view, table, groups, and filter settings to let you review task and assignment baseline data. You can also create and store your own combinations of views and tables that show you information in a familiar format. For instance, you can:

- Use the default views and tables to see baseline columns with additional columns you need.
- Use the Project Guide to show baseline and tracking data fields.
- Activate filters and groups to show important baseline and tracking data based on task completion status, assigned resources, and so forth.

Consider using the following helpful viewing combinations to review baseline and tracking information:

- View the default Tracking Gantt with the Baseline table to see baseline columns with Gantt bar overlay showing plan vs. baseline duration.
- View the Detailed Gantt with Delay table to see task slippage and free slack.
- View the Multiple Baseline Gantt if you are comparing several baselines side-by-side.
- View the default Tracking Gantt with the Variance table to show differences between the baseline and your current progress conditions.
- View the default Tracking Gantt with the Tracking table to see data field where you can enter progress information, such as: actual start, %Complete, actual work, and so forth.
- Use the menu Project, then Group by Complete and Incomplete Tasks.

TIP

> Remember to use menu viewing tricks such as: View, More Views; or Views, Table and More Tables; or Project, Group by; or Project, Filter functions. These tricks allow you to organize information and also see settings or options that may be hidden.

Figure 13.2 illustrates the combination of Tracking Gantt with the Baseline table. You can add your own data columns, such as: work, % Complete, physical % complete, and so forth to suit your needs. Notice how any task that does not have baseline data will show "NA" in the data field and also show missing bars within the Tracking Gantt view. Also notice how the baseline Gantt bars may be shifted to the past or future, compared to the current task start and finish dates.

Figure 13.2
Use View and Table combinations to see baseline data.

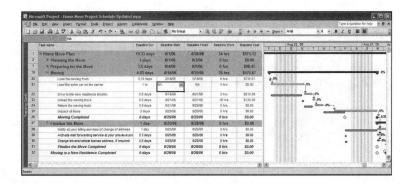

USING USAGE VIEWS TO SHOW TIME-PHASED DETAILS

Microsoft Project 2007 has very powerful viewing and editing functions that are enabled when you decide to use special display formats called Usage views. Usage views are located under the View menu. There are two major view types that show time-phased, sometimes also know as time-scaled, data details of resource assignments. You should become thoroughly familiar with the Usage views so that you can take advantage of several powerful features to view and edit data.

The Task Usage view displays tasks with each resource assigned within individual rows below the task. The Resource Usage view simply inverts the data, showing resources with a list of task assignments for each resource.

The left half of a Usage view can be arranged to show numerous data columns based on the Table that you select or you can insert any combination of task and assignment columns you need. The right half of the screen shows detailed breakdown of the assignment data, such as: Work, Cost, Baseline Work, and so on. Figure 13.3 shows a typical layout of a Task Usage view with the Baseline Table showing the columns on the left side and time-phased details on the right.

Figure 13.3
The Usage views show Time-phased Details.

13

You can see tasks with assigned resources listed below each task as you inspect the left side of the screen. Each task and resource assignment row on the left side of the screen can have one or more time-phased detailed rows on the right side of the display. You can right-click within the right-side data display to show more rows, and also include other hidden rows if you select the Detail Styles menu item.

> **TIP**
>
> You can right-click the calendar header of a Usage view to adjust the display characteristics, such as zoom factor and timescale column headers.

The time-phased data rows on the right side of the Usage view display show the internal details for each task and resource assignment. You can zoom into a level of detail that shows date and time information to 15 minute increments for each hour in each day. You can also zoom out to show data in a year-by-year rollup.

Many time-phased data fields on the right side of the Usage view can be directly edited, those field usually displayed with a white background. The numbers you enter are internally distributed between the task start and finish period for the selected cell according to factors like task and resource calendars. Therefore, you need to be cautious when directly editing data in the time-phased fields.

You should also be aware that most time-phased data fields immediately rollup to the associated tasks or summary task items or may also change the column data on the left side of the Usage view. When you type data into the time-phased data fields on the right, that data is captured and may roll up to rows up the list. However, some time-phased fields do not immediately roll up as you alter the time-phased data. Baseline data fields are an example of data that does not immediately roll up when you change the time-phased data.

Time-phased baseline data is copied from planning data fields when you use the menu function Tools, Tracking, Set Baseline. Essentially you can imagine that menu performs a general copy and paste operation from planning data into the time-phased baseline rows.

Some time-phased data field, such as Cost, may be derived or calculated from other conditions like individual resource settings. The derived fields can not be directly edited in the time-phased fields, even though the data cells may have a white background. Those data fields are calculated by factors like resource cost per hour, or cost per use settings.

You also need to be careful when editing Task Usage time-phased data within the task rows, generally shown with a yellow background. Some of those time-phased data fields, such as Work, can also be directly edited. Data you enter within a task row cell will be distributed, also called rolled down, to the resources assignments for that task. This type of edit can also transfer directly to the data columns on the left side of the display.

You are encouraged to create some simple schedule examples with resource assignments that you can use to experiment with Task and Resource Usage views. Watch how edits made in the left side of the display propagate to the right side time-phased data and visa versa. Then watch what happens to time-phased data when you perform functions like setting a baseline. You will learn a lot about how Microsoft Project 2007 stores and manipulates internal data when you learn how to use the Usage views.

TRACKING YOUR PROJECT'S PERFORMANCE AND COSTS

The key to tracking progress of your project is the feedback that you get back from your resources about their progress and then entering that information into your project. If you are using Microsoft Office Project Server, you can set up Microsoft Project Professional to automatically request progress updates from the team. Employees and other resources will receive a timesheet-style form to fill out and submit, then after review, you can update your project automatically.

> **NOTE**
>
> If you are not using Project Server, you will have to collect and enter the information manually.

UNDERSTANDING THE FIELDS USED IN UPDATING THE PROJECT SCHEDULE

As you begin building your schedule, you will enter information into the appropriate fields: Actual Start Date, Actual Finish Date, Actual Task Duration, %Complete, %Work Complete, and so forth. Plus, as you include resources, Microsoft Project 2007 will calculate amounts of work, overtime work, and cost for these resources. Microsoft Project 2007 recalculates your resource workload as you work with and change task conditions such as the starting date or duration during the planning phase. You can plan that you are going to start on a specific date, that it is going to take a specific amount of time, and that you will be finished on that date, but this is just guesswork until the tasks within the project are completed. Tracking is entering your results into the "Actual" assignment fields, such as Actual Start, Actual Finish, Actual Work, and Actual Cost. The various task and assignment data fields are interrelated so you need to understand those relationships before you enter tracking data.

The term "tracking" is what happens as you manually enter task and assignment actual data or if you use Project menu functions, such as Tools, Tracking, Update Project to update information. For example, when you enter the Actual Start date, Microsoft Project 2007 replaces the planned start with your new entry. This may now affect successor tasks, if you start early or late, and Microsoft Project 2007 will calculate the changes your actual start date makes to the schedule.

Two things happen in Microsoft Project 2007 when you enter an actual start date:

- The entry you made in the Actual Start field is copied into the (scheduled) Start field, and Microsoft Project 2007 recalculates the schedule for any successor tasks. Any other dates that are affected are highlighted with the change highlighting color control within the menu sequence Format, Text Styles, Changed Cells Background Color. This helps you to see if you need to make any changes down the road to the schedule, based on your early or late start.

- Microsoft Project 2007 sets the Start field as fixed, meaning that it cannot be recalculated. So once the Actual Start date has been entered, Microsoft Project 2007 will not change the value. However, you can manually edit that date if conditions require a change.

13

The same type of reaction occurs when you enter an Actual Finish date, except that Microsoft Project 2007 will also mark the %Complete schedule field as 100% complete for the affected tasks. You should be aware that Microsoft Project 2007 also updates other fields, such as Actual Duration, Actual Work, and so forth when you enter the Actual Finish date. Now your baseline is the only record of your originally scheduled project, so you can compare actual data to baseline data variances to see what went right and what did not.

There are several different ways of entering the actual values into your project. The following methods are listed in order from least exact to most precise, assuming that all data provided is valid. The method you choose depends on your need for precision and the expectations for reporting and lessons learned analysis.

- Update the %Complete task field to a fraction between zero and 100% without worrying about any of the actual schedule dates, work, cost, and so forth. While this is the fastest technique to update tasks, it is also the least accurate because this method assumes actual task activities occurred exactly as planned. This method gives you no information about how well you estimated or any information for future comparisons.

- Record when a task is started and finished, but do not include how much actual work or actual cost was involved. Microsoft Project 2007 assumes the work, cost, and other planned data occurred as originally planned when you enter actual date information. This will at least give you some idea for planning completion dates in the future.

- Record when a task starts, and then periodically enter estimates, such as Remaining Work and Remaining Duration, when you enter %Complete. This will help you spot tasks that are not making headway as planned and help you make adjustments to get things back on track.

- Collect timesheets from resources and enter how much actual work they did during each time period. This method allows the most information about progress and performance, but also takes up the most time because the data must be entered manually.

- Use Microsoft Office Project Server to request timesheet reports, and then have Microsoft Project Professional automatically update the fields from the data submitted. This takes much less time and is the one of the best ways to track your schedule progress.

> **TIP**
>
> Microsoft Project 2007 uses the term %Complete to mean the percentage complete along the start through finish timeline, that is duration. You should use the phrase "% Duration Complete" whenever you consider the meaning of the %Complete field.

> **TIP**
>
> You may also want to search the internet for timesheet entry tools that allow your team members to provide actual work information. Some tools allow the project manager to post actual work, cost, and so on into task data fields. Microsoft Office Project Server 2007 provides very robust schedule tracking and reporting functionality.

→ See *Microsoft Office Project Server 2007 Unleashed* to learn more about Project Server 2007.

Remember that when you enter data in Microsoft Project 2007, other fields may be modified by the scheduling engine, so it is important that you understand the potential impact of the method you choose for project status updates. Which method you choose depends on your need for precise information and how much time you can spend tracking your progress. No matter which way you choose to do it, you need to understand how the various fields interact so you should experiment with various methods and techniques before establishing a general schedule updating policy within your organization. You will learn more about these data fields in the following sections.

ENTERING TRACKING INFORMATION AT THE TASK LEVEL

This section covers how to use tracking fields at the task level to update task status. This is how you would manually enter progress, if you choose to use this method.

This section looks at the following task-tracking fields:

- Actual Start
- Actual Finish
- % Complete
- Actual Duration
- Remaining Duration
- Actual Work
- % Work Complete
- Remaining Work
- Time-Phased Work

You can view and edit most of these fields on the task by using the Gantt Chart view with the Tracking table columns showing (see Figure 13.4) . To display the table in a task view, right-click the Select All button and select Tracking. The % Work Complete and Remaining Work fields can be edited on the Work table, and time-phased work can be entered in the time-phased grid on the Task Usage view. See "Using Microsoft Project's Facilities for Updating Tasks" later in this chapter on how to open forms that make these fields available.

NOTE

> Keep in mind that Microsoft Project 2007 has different calculations for the "work" fields and the "%Complete" fields. By default, the %Work Complete for resource assignments and %Complete task fields are coupled such that an edit to either field updates the other field. You can decouple these two fields with the menu sequence Tools, Options, Calculation tab, and then clearing the Updating tasks status updates resource status check box. This means that it is possible to complete 100% of the work on a task and yet the % Complete for the duration field is not at 100%, but you then must manage each field individually for every task in the schedule.

13

Figure 13.4
The task Tracking table will give you access to many of the fields needed for tracking progress at the task level.

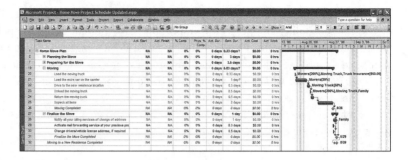

> All of the tracking fields can be affected by the Task Type conditions you select from the Task Information settings. Fixed Work, Fixed Duration, and Fixed Units tasks behave differently to data edit changes, so make sure you consider the task type settings as you update tracking data.

EDITING THE TASK ACTUAL START DATE

Project uses "NA" for the Actual Start date field value until you enter an Actual Start date or modify the %Complete field. Then, the date you enter or the planned start date replaces the NA. Additionally, any resource assignments to tasks with the same scheduled Start date as the task will be assigned the Actual Start date of that task. Microsoft Project 2007 then recalculates all assignments to that task and may also impact successor tasks and assignments.

TIP

> Make sure you enter the Actual Start date if the task does not begin on the scheduled Start date, before editing any of the other fields used for tracking progress. You may see unexpected results if you edit another field prior to entering the Actual Start date.

However, if the Actual Start date contains "NA" and you edit certain fields, such as %Complete, Actual Work, and so on, Microsoft Project 2007 will presume that the original planned Start date should be used as the Actual Start date.

EDITING THE TASK ACTUAL FINISH DATE

Just like the Actual Start date, the Actual Finish date contains "NA" in the entry until you edit information, indicating the task is complete. If you do not provide an explicit Finish Date, then Microsoft Project 2007 presumes the task is finished just as scheduled. If you enter an Actual Finish date, on the other hand, several data conditions may change on your schedule:

- Microsoft Project 2007 will replace the scheduled Finish date with the Actual Finish date.

- If you have not indicated the task has started, then all progress fields that still show NA will be replaced with the scheduled entry and the task will be marked as 100% complete.

Be careful if you enter an Actual Finish date that is later than the scheduled Finish date. In this case, Microsoft Project 2007 will increase the values in various data fields, such as task duration, costs, work, and other entries therein.

■ Based on the Actual Start and Actual Finish dates, Microsoft Project 2007 will calculate the Actual Duration and change the scheduled Duration to the same value, and then change the Remaining Duration to zero.

■ Both % Complete and % Work Complete will be changed to 100% for the task and all assignments.

■ The Actual Work and Actual Cost values for the task and assignments will be calculated, while Remaining Work and Remaining Cost will be set to zero.

■ If the tasks were on the critical path, they will be changed to non-critical and preceding linked tasks may also be set to non-critical.

In summary, if you enter an Actual Finish date, Microsoft Project 2007 assumes you are finished with the task and will calculate all of the unspecified actual values for tasks and assignments. You should experiment with examples so you can learn how Microsoft Project 2007 behaves in different situations.

Editing Task % Complete (Percentage Complete)

You can edit the task %Complete field to indicate a task has started or finished, so you need to become familiar with the behavior of Microsoft Project 2007 when you perform edits. Whenever you see the %Complete field, you should always mentally replace that name with the phrase "%Duration Complete," so that you recognize the meaning of this field. Therefore, task % Complete provides a method to track how much of the planned task duration, between the start and finish dates, has been finished.

Microsoft Project 2007 will assume that the task % Complete is zero until a task update has been entered, for example, Actual Work, Actual Duration, and so on. %Complete is then calculated with the following general formulas and rules:

$$\% \text{ Complete} = 100 \times (\text{Actual Duration} / \text{Duration})$$

$$\text{Duration} = \text{Actual Duration} + \text{Remaining Duration}$$

You can either enter the percentage complete yourself or let Microsoft Project 2007 handle the calculations by just entering the Actual Duration, the Remaining Duration, or any other field that calculates Actual Duration as greater than zero.

Several changes can occur when you edit the % Complete field:

■ When the Actual Start field is still NA, Microsoft Project 2007 will replace it with the scheduled Start date.

■ An entry of 100% will cause Microsoft Project 2007 to use the scheduled Finish date to set the Actual Finish date.

■ Actual Duration is set equal to % Complete × Duration, while Remaining Duration is set equal to Duration – Actual Duration.

13

- % Work Complete is set equal to $100 \times$ Actual Work / Work when the default menu Tools, Options, Calculation tab, Task status updates resource status check box is selected.

- Actual Cost and Actual Work are set the same as the scheduled time-phased work and cost for the time period set by Actual Duration.

- Remaining Work is set equal to the Work – Actual Work.

EDITING TASK ACTUAL DURATION

This field will allow you to display and enter the amount of task duration that has been used so far in the project. If you enter a value less than the total scheduled duration; then Project presumes everything is on schedule and will make the following calculations:

- The Actual Start field will be replaced with the scheduled Start date if Actual Start field is still NA.

- Remaining Duration is replaced by Duration – Actual Duration, while % Complete is calculated as $100 \times$ Actual Duration / Duration.

- Finally, Actual Cost and Actual Work are set the same as the scheduled time-phased work and cost scheduled for that duration.

If, on the other hand, you enter a value for Actual Duration that is longer than the scheduled Duration, Microsoft Project 2007 presumes the task is finished and took longer than scheduled and calculates the following:

- % Complete is set to 100%, while Remaining Duration is set to 0.

- Actual Finish is changed to match the longer duration.

- The scheduled Duration and scheduled Finish are set to match the Actual Duration and new Actual Finish.

- If the task type has been set to Fixed Units or Fixed Duration, any assignment scheduled to end when the task ends has their Actual Finish changed to match the task Actual Finish field. The Actual Work, Work, Actual Cost, and Cost fields for the aforementioned assignments are increased by the same proportion as the duration has been changed.

- If the task type is Fixed Work, then Actual Cost and Actual Work are set to equal the scheduled Cost and Work. Any assignments scheduled to finish when the task finishes get the same Actual Finish as the task. The Actual Cost and Actual Work fields are changed to the same as their scheduled Cost and Work fields.

- Any assignments that were scheduled to finish before the task is finished are presumed to have finished on time and their scheduled Cost and Work fields are copied into the Actual Cost and Actual Work fields.

13

EDITING TASK REMAINING DURATION

The Remaining Duration field is closely coupled with the task Duration and Finish date fields. If the Actual Start field contains NA, any editing done to the Remaining Duration field may have a direct effect on the other tracking fields. The task Finish date and Duration will change if you alter the Remaining Duration data before the Actual Start date has been declared. Furthermore, other calculated fields like Cost will be changed as the task duration is recomputed.

If the Actual Start field has an entry and you alter the Remaining Duration, then the following behavior occurs:

- A reduction in the Remaining Duration to a non-zero value results in a change to the task Duration and a recalculation of Finish date, Cost, Work, and so forth. If Remaining Duration is reduced to zero, then Microsoft Project 2007 will change the Actual Finish to the scheduled Start date, change the task to 100% complete, set the task Duration to zero, and recalculate other fields accordingly. This type of edit will also mark the task as a milestone.

- An increase in value in Remaining Duration, after the task has started, means that Microsoft Project 2007 presumes the scheduled Duration has increased and will calculate new values for scheduled Cost, Finish, Work, Remaining Cost, Remaining Work, % Complete, and so forth.

EDITING TASK ACTUAL WORK

The task Actual Work field shows the amount of work that has been completed by the resource or resources assigned to the task. The field is zero until tracking begins. If you enter any amount in the task Actual Work field, this entry is distributed between the resources according to their individual calendars. If the Actual Start date has not been declared, then the actual work data distribution begins on the planned start date for each resources.

For instance, Eric and Stacey are fulltime workers and scheduled to start task work on the same day, their work is distributed 30 hours and 10 hours, respectively. If you enter 20 hours in the task Actual Work field, then Microsoft Project 2007 will record 10 hours of Actual Work for Eric and 10 hours of Actual Work for Stacey. Eric will have 20 hours of remaining work while Stacey has zero remaining work. The task is not yet complete because Eric's work is not complete.

NOTE

> The calendar conditions for the project, tasks, and resources can also affect the end result of Actual Work edits. Task Actual Work data are distributed differently when you have a mix of fulltime and part-time resources. Make sure you experiment with variations so you can understand the tool behavior when you edit Actual Work.

13

Just like when entering Actual Duration, if you enter a value greater than the scheduled Work value, Microsoft Project 2007 assumes that the task is finished and recalculates data fields, such as Actual Start as scheduled (if it is NA), Actual Duration and Actual Finish commensurate with the added work, % Complete and % Work Complete are set to 100%, and Remaining Duration is set to zero.

Editing Task % Work Complete

When you edit the % Work Complete field when the Actual Start field is NA, Microsoft Project 2007 presumes that the task has started and sets Actual Work as a result. Microsoft Project 2007 then calculates Actual Work by multiplying % Work Complete by Work for the task. This assumes that the work scheduled was completed up through the amount of Actual Work, which determines Actual Duration. After that, % Complete is calculated by dividing Actual Duration by Duration. Actual Cost is then updated with the amount of cost scheduled for Actual Work.

Editing Task Remaining Work

You can use the Remaining Work field to indicate the amount of work to be completed in the future. If the Actual Start date is NA, then your edits to Remaining Work do not affect any of the other tracking fields but your edits can impact the task duration and finish date. Your edits also change conditions, such as scheduled Work, Cost, Duration, and so on.

For example, if you have a task that has started and accumulated an amount of Actual Work, Microsoft Project 2007 automatically calculates the Remaining Work for the remaining duration of the task. If you decrease that Remaining Work value, then you are indicating there is less work to do to finish that task. Microsoft Project 2007 may in turn recalculate conditions, such as % Work Complete, % Complete, Duration, Remaining Duration, Cost and so on.

If you increase Remaining Work, however, it means that the total work requirements for the task have increased, and Microsoft Project 2007 will recalculate scheduled Work, Duration, Finish, % Complete, % Work Complete, Cost, Remaining Duration, and so forth.

Editing Task Time-Phased Actual Work

If you open the Task Usage view, you can edit Actual Work and Actual Overtime Work for the periods in which they were performed. If you want to look at the time-phased Actual Work field, right-click in the grid on the right and select Actual Work. To record Actual Overtime work, right-click again and choose Detail Styles. Double-click Actual Overtime Work in the list on the left to place it in the list on the right, and then click OK.

Every cell in the grid is a time period, and any edits to a cell are distributed between the beginning and ending dates for that cell. So, if the bottom tier in the timescale displays weeks, and you enter 8 hours in a week that contains a 1-day holiday, Microsoft Project 2007 will distribute 2 hours of work in each of the remaining 4 days of the week. If you want to place all 8 hours in 1 day, then zoom in to display 1-day intervals in the timescale.

If the task Actual Start is NA, then the Actual Start will be established on the date of the cell period where you enter Actual Work.

If the entered Actual Work is less than the scheduled Work for that cell, remaining work is rescheduled into the future, after the planned end date for the task, therefore extending the task duration. If Actual Work is greater than scheduled Work for that cell, then the extra work is subtracted from the remaining cells in the task, and the duration shrinks.

If you skip any time-phased periods between your data edits for Actual Work, then those periods get zero time-phased task Actual Work, and the zeros will roll down to time-phased assignment Actual Work. Work scheduled for those zeroed days will be rescheduled at the end of the task, therefore extending the duration.

ENTERING TRACKING INFORMATION AT THE ASSIGNMENT LEVEL

The preceding sections of this chapter help you better understand how Microsoft Project 2007 behaves when you enter tracking data for tasks. Those sections also help you understand some of the tracking conditions regarding resource assignments on tasks. This section discusses how Microsoft Project 2007 calculates task progress when you enter tracking data for individual resources assigned to tasks. You need to understand a distinction between task-level data fields compared to similar data field for resource assignments on tasks, before you begin studying the details below.

You already know there are many task-level tracking fields with familiar names, such as Actual Work, Remaining Work, and so on. You will now learn that there are related tracking fields for each resource assigned to a task. The data details for these assignment-level fields are actually different even though they are spelled the same. You will also notice that task-level and assignment-level data cells are strongly associated so edits to a specific data cell may change the associated data.

This may seem confusing at first but there is an easy way to remember the distinction: any view showing a task row contains task-level tracking data cells, while resource rows contain data cells directly related to the specific resource. This is specifically true when you open a Usage view. Refer to Figure 13.3 for an illustration of a Usage view.

You will use the Task Usage or Resource Usage views to see and edit assignment-level data fields. Remember, these usage views have two major sections: the left and right sides of the screen. The left side contains Table columns that are associated with the time-phased period cells on the right side of the screen. You can use mouse right-click actions to add columns as desired on the left side and also add rows on the right side.

EDITING ASSIGNMENT ACTUAL START

Just as with task Actual Start, editing assignment Actual Start will cause Microsoft Project 2007 to change the assignment's scheduled Start to match the assignment's Actual Start. In addition, Microsoft Project 2007 will recalculate the assignment scheduled Finish date according to factors like the resource duration and calendar settings.

If the task has a single resource assignment and the task Actual Start is NA when you edit the assignment, then Microsoft Project 2007 will set the task Actual Start equal to the resource assignment Actual Start.

One of three actions will occur if there are multiple resources assigned to a task:

- If the assignment Actual Start is the same as the task scheduled Start, the task Actual Start will be set to the task scheduled Start.

- If the assignment Actual Start is later than the task scheduled Start, then the task Actual Start is set to the task scheduled Start. The task schedule finish may be delayed if the late assignment start is the critical resource on the task.

- If the assignment Actual Start is earlier than it was scheduled to start, and earlier than the task scheduled Start date, then the task Actual Start is changed to the assignment Actual Start. The task and assignment finish dates may also be changed per the overall duration settings.

EDITING ASSIGNMENT ACTUAL FINISH

Edit changes to the assignment actual finish have similar behavior to edits to the task Actual Finish. If the assignment Actual Start displays NA when you edit assignment Actual Finish, Microsoft Project 2007 presumes the assignment started on schedule and ended on the edited finish date. If the new Actual Finish date is different from the scheduled Finish date, Microsoft Project 2007 changes Cost and Work accordingly. If it is the only assignment for the task, the task- and assignment-tracking fields will be identical after the recalculations, except possibly Actual Cost, which may include some task fixed cost.

If the task has multiple assignments, editing Actual Finish for one assignment will cause Microsoft Project 2007 to recalculate the task Actual Work, Actual Cost, Actual Duration, % Complete, % Work Complete, Remaining Duration, Remaining Work, and Remaining Cost fields. The task type determines how work and duration are recalculated, as you can see in "Editing Task Actual Duration."

EDITING ASSIGNMENT ACTUAL WORK

If either the task or assignment Actual Start reads NA, any edits to the assignment Actual Work field cause Microsoft Project 2007 to set the assignment and task Actual Start dates to the assignment and task scheduled Actual Start dates. Microsoft Project 2007 will also recalculate both the assignment and task % Work Complete, Remaining Work, Actual Cost, Remaining Cost, and so on.

NOTE

The task Actual Duration is determined by taking the task Actual Work, which is the sum of all assignments' Actual Work, and calculating how long it would have taken to complete that amount of work if all of the assignments (not just the ones that show work complete) had completed work as scheduled. Then % Complete and Remaining Duration are both calculated by using the value for Actual Duration.

EDITING ASSIGNMENT % WORK COMPLETE

You may decide to track progress by updating the assignment-level %Work Complete for each resource on a task. Use the Task Usage view with the Work table to edit the assignment % Work Complete field.

If the assignment has not been started, any edits to this field will cause Microsoft Project 2007 to set the assignment Actual Start date equal to the scheduled Start date. Microsoft Project 2007 will also set the task Actual Start date to the task scheduled Start date, if that was NA. The assignment Actual Finish date is set to the scheduled Finish date if the edited value of % Work Complete is set at 100% and all resource assignments are also 100% complete.

Microsoft Project 2007 recalculates the assignment and task Actual Work, Remaining Work, % Work Complete, Actual Cost, and Remaining Cost fields. The task Actual Duration, % Complete, and Remaining Duration fields are updated as well.

EDITING ASSIGNMENT REMAINING WORK

Your resources may provide periodic estimates of remaining work to be performed for scheduled tasks. You can use the assignment Remaining Work field to capture those estimates. This field is also found on the Task Usage view with the Work table. Editing this field is similar to editing the Remaining Work field for tasks. If the assignment is not started, edits to Remaining Work change the scheduled Work for the assignment and thus change the scheduled Finish for the assignment. Make sure you review the task type when editing assignment-level Remaining Work field because the calculated results are different based on the task type settings.

Edits to an already started assignment that *reduce* Remaining Work leads to increases in assignment % Work Completed. This causes a ripple effect as described in the earlier section on edits to assignment Actual Work.

Edits to an already started assignment that *increase* Remaining Work will redefine the total scheduled Work for the assignment and lead to recalculated values for the tracking fields like: assignment scheduled Finish date, scheduled Cost, and % Work Complete. These new values mean recalculated values for the related task fields as well.

EDITING ASSIGNMENT TIME-PHASED WORK

If you provide resources with timecards that allow them to fill in the amount of actual work completed, and optimally the amount of overtime work as well, updating project with these timecards produces edits to the assignment time-phased fields Actual Work and Actual Overtime Work. Such edits mean recalculated values for assignment Actual Work, Remaining Work, % Work Complete, Actual Cost, and Remaining Cost. Those, in turn, mean recalculations for task-tracking fields, which you can read about in "Editing Assignment Actual Work," earlier in this chapter.

13

You might recall that each cell in the time-phased cells are for specific time periods, and any edits to the cell are distributed equally between the beginning and ending dates for the cell period. If the edited cell is the first actual work recorded (meaning the assignment Actual Start was NA), then Actual Start for the assignment is set to the begin date for the cell you edited. If no more remaining work exists after the edit, then assigned Actual Finish is set to the end date for the cell.

If the task type is Fixed Units or Fixed Work, and the entered Actual Work is less than scheduled Work for the cell you are editing, remaining work for the cell is rescheduled after the end date for the assignment. If the entered Actual Work is greater than the scheduled Work for that cell, any remaining work is moved to reduce the assignment finish date. If the task type is Fixed Duration, any differences between the scheduled and actual work for the period are divided equally among the remaining time periods in the assignment.

If you skip any periods when entering Actual Work, then the skipped periods will filled with zero time-phased Actual Work. Any work scheduled for these skipped periods is rescheduled at the end of the assignment, unless the task type is Fixed Duration, in which case the work for the assignments is reduced.

UNDERSTANDING THE CALCULATION OPTIONS THAT AFFECT TRACKING

Microsoft Project provides you several options that control default conditions used to calculate task and assignment results. You will learn more about those options within this section.

Looking back at "Entering Tracking Information at the Task Level" and "Entering Tracking Information at the Assignment Level," the descriptions of edits to task- and assignment-tracking fields assume default calculation options are enabled. Specifically, the edits to task status are also applied to assignments, and actual costs are calculated by Project. This section takes a look at the impact of those options on tracking calculations if these defaults are disabled, as well as other options that are disabled by default.

To disable or enable those options, go to Tools, Options and click the Calculation tab (see Figure 13.5). Project calls these "local" settings, meaning that the setting of the options, either enabled or disabled, is saved in the project file. You can change the default setting for each of the options by clicking the Set as Default Button on the Calculation tab.

Figure 13.5
Here you can see all the different Calculation options available to you that can affect tracking.

USING THE UPDATING TASK STATUS UPDATES RESOURCE STATUS OPTION

If you enable the option Updating task status updates resource status (which is the default setting), then edits to the task % Complete will cause Microsoft Project 2007 to calculate Actual Work and % Work Complete at both the task and assignment levels. The link behavior is reciprocal; any edits to assignment Actual Work causes Microsoft Project 2007 to recalculate task Actual Duration, % Complete, and Remaining Duration.

If you *disable* Updating task status updates resource status, then the following conditions will take effect:

- Edits to task % Complete affect only task Actual Duration and Remaining Duration. Actual Work, % Work Complete, and Remaining Work remain unaffected at both the task and assignment levels.

- Task Actual Work continues to be the rolled-up sum of assignment Actual Work. Edits at the task level to Actual Work, % Work Complete, and Remaining Work still roll down to assignments. Edits to those fields at the assignment level still roll up to the task.

- Edits to Actual Work, % Work Complete, or Remaining Work do not affect task % Complete, Actual Duration, or Remaining Duration.

13

CAUTION

> There is an exception to the last point on the preceding list. If you reset each assignment's Actual Work to zero, then Microsoft Project 2007 will reset task % Complete to 0%, which means you lose any manual edits to the % Complete field. This does not happen if you reset the task Actual Work to zero.
>
> Also, setting assignment or task % Complete to 100% has the opposite effect of setting % Work Complete to 100% when Updating task status updates resource status is turned off. This is the more common occurrence that users run into, and they do not understand why they have actual work on a task with the option is disabled.

If you are working with Updating task status updates resource status disabled and then change your mind and decide to return to working with the setting enabled, Microsoft Project 2007 does not recalculate previously edited work- and duration-tracking fields to align their values. Rather, it waits until you edit either a task duration–tracking field (Actual Duration, % Complete, or Remaining Duration) or a work-tracking field at either the assignment or task level (Actual Work, % Work Complete, or Remaining Work). If your first edit is to a duration-tracking field, Microsoft Project 2007 recalculates all the other duration-tracking fields, then recalculates all the work-tracking fields using the new Actual Duration. If your first edit is a work-tracking field, Microsoft Project 2007 recalculates all of the task assignment work-tracking fields and then recalculates the duration-tracking fields based on your edits to actual work.

TIP

> One of the tricks you can use by disabling Updating task status updates resource status is to compel Microsoft Project 2007 to calculate earned value fields using % Work Complete values instead of % Complete. To do this, save the file and perform the following steps with a copy of the file, so you can delete it when finished:
>
> 1. With the Updating task status updates resource status disabled, and both % Complete and % Work Complete displayed as columns in the task table, choose the column for % Work Complete and use Ctrl+C to copy the information.
>
> 2. Select the column for % Complete and use Ctrl+V to paste the information into that column.
>
> You can then conduct your analysis of earned value knowing that the earned value calculations are much closer, though not identical, to those you could get by using the traditional method of calculating earned value.

→ For additional information on earned value analysis, **see** "Analyzing Performance with Earned Value Analysis," **p. 491**.

13

USING THE ACTUAL COSTS ARE ALWAYS CALCULATED BY MICROSOFT PROJECT OPTION

When option Actual costs are always calculated by Microsoft Office Project is enabled (which is the default setting), Microsoft Project 2007 will calculate Actual Cost as you track progress on the task by adding accrued Fixed Cost to the sum of Actual Costs for all assignments.

Here is the formula for this behavior:

Assignment Actual Cost = (Actual Work × Cost Rate) + (Actual Overtime Work × Overtime Cost Rate) + Cost Per Use

The cost rate and overtime cost rate are taken from the cost rate table, defined for the resources assigned to the task.

When the Actual costs are always calculated by Microsoft Office Project option is enabled, you cannot edit Actual Cost at the assignment or task level until the task is 100% complete. However, when the task is complete, you can edit the task Actual Cost field, the assignment Actual Cost field, and the task or assignment time-phased Actual Cost field. The Remaining Cost field is always a calculated field and cannot be edited.

The effects of editing the actual cost fields after the task is completed, when Actual Cost has been calculated by Microsoft Project 2007, are listed here:

- Edits to assignment Actual Cost roll up to the task Actual Cost. As with other "Actual" fields, the value in Actual Cost is copied to the scheduled Cost field.
- Edits to the assignment time-phased Actual Cost also roll up to the task time-phased Actual Cost and then to task Actual Cost.
- The task Actual Cost field sums the rolled-up assignment Actual Cost field entries, so edits into the task Actual Cost field are *not* rolled down to the assignments. Instead, they are presumed to be actual fixed cost adjustments, and the difference between the edited value and the sum for the assignments is added to Fixed Cost, which is then added to the total in the Cost field. The end result is that the Cost field is equal to the Actual Cost field.

  Therefore, increasing task Actual Cost by $100 will cause the Fixed Cost field (and also the Cost field) to rise by $100. Decreasing the Actual Cost field by $100 causes the Fixed Cost field to fall by the same, and could result in a negative value.
- Any edits to the task time-phased Actual Cost field are distributed among assignments for that same time period in proportion to their share of existing Actual Cost for that time period. Microsoft Project 2007 also recalculates assignment Actual Cost for each assignment and rolls up the total to the task Actual Cost field. Therefore, edits to task time-phased Actual Cost do not lead to a change in Fixed Costs, like direct edits to task Actual Cost will.

13

You can view the Actual Fixed Cost in the time-phased Actual Fixed Cost field. The time-phased Actual Fixed Cost field is a calculated field only, so you cannot edit actual fixed cost in the time-phased cells.

If you disable the Actual costs are always calculated by Microsoft Office Project option, you are able to enter your own actual costs. In fact, you *have* to enter those values because Microsoft Project 2007 will no longer automatically calculate the field based on work completed.

The Cost field initially shows the estimated cost of completing a task or assignment. It is actually calculated as the estimated cost of work that remains to be finished, plus the actual cost already recorded. Before the task begins, the Cost field shows the same value as the Remaining Cost field, which you can see if you display the Cost table.

As you record work that is completed, the remaining cost normally falls and is replaced by the actual cost of the completed work. If Microsoft Project 2007 is not calculating Actual Cost, however, the effect on the Cost field when recording actual work is that Cost falls until you enter the Actual Cost field information yourself. Marking a task at 100% without entering Actual Cost causes the Cost field to fall to zero.

Editing the Actual Cost field, however, causes the Cost field to rise by the same amount as the Actual Cost field. Unlike when Microsoft Project 2007 is calculating actual cost, edits to the Actual Cost field never change the Fixed Cost field.

You are still unable to overwrite Microsoft Project's "scheduled" costs for an assignment, because they continue to be calculated based on resource work and cost rates plus cost per use.

If you edit the Actual Cost fields when Actual Cost is not calculated by Microsoft Project 2007, the following will happen:

- Edits to assignment Actual Cost or assignment time-phased Actual Cost roll up to the task Actual Cost and task time-phased Actual Cost and are also added to the assignment Cost.

- Edits to task Actual Cost roll down to the assignments and are distributed among the assignments in proportion to the Remaining Cost for the assignments, not counting Remaining Overtime Cost.

- Edits to task time-phased Actual Cost roll down to the assignments in the same time period, also in proportion to Remaining Cost, as shown in the time-phased Cost field.

Although disabling the option Actual costs are always calculated by Microsoft Office Project might give you more ability to match accounting costs in your project plan, it means a lot more work for you and hides the cost implications of the schedule.

When you enable Actual costs are always calculated by Microsoft Office Project option after it has been disabled, Microsoft Project 2007 will immediately overwrite any manually entered Actual Cost values with the calculated Actual Cost, based on Work and % Complete.

If Actual costs are always calculated by Microsoft Office Project is disabled, then the Edits to total actual cost will be spread to the status date sub-option will become available. The Edits to total actual cost will be spread to the status date option directs how Microsoft Project 2007 will distribute the time-phased values when you edit the assignment or task Actual Cost field yourself. Normally, Actual Cost edits are distributed from the start of the assignment or task, as planned in the scheduled cost distribution. If you enable Edits to total actual cost will be spread to the status date and then edit the task Actual Cost, the increase or decrease in task Actual Cost is distributed equally over the empty time-phased cells, starting after the last period in which time-phased Actual Cost was recorded up through the Status date (or Current Date if the Status date is undefined). Using the Edits to total actual cost will be spread to the status date option will smooth out the time-phased Actual Cost fields.

> **TIP**
>
> To define your status date, choose Project, Project Information and fill in the Status Date field.

USING THE EDITS TO TOTAL TASK PERCENTAGE COMPLETE WILL BE SPREAD TO THE STATUS DATE OPTION

The Edits to the Total task % complete will be spread to the status date option is disabled by default. The Edits to total task % Complete will be spread to the status date option only affects how time-phased % Complete is distributed when you edit the task % Complete field. Distribution of the time-phased % Complete field affects earned value calculations and how progress lines are displayed. It has no impact on how time-phased actual work is actually distributed among the time periods.

→ For more information on progress lines, **see** "Using Progress Lines," **p. 477**.

When Edits to Total task % complete will be spread to the status date is disabled, any edits you make to the task % Complete field will cause the amount of task Actual Work to be calculated and the time-phased Actual Work to be distributed from the start of the task, as scheduled for all assignments, until the Actual Work is accounted for. The time-phased % Complete field shows the percentage of total work completed in each time period, with the entries added up to the edited amount for % Complete.

When Edits to total task % complete will be spread to the status date is enabled, the time-phased Actual Work is distributed the same, but the time-phased % Complete field is equally distributed among the time periods from the last recorded time-phased % Complete value to the Status Date (or the Current Date if no Status Date is defined). This will smooth out the increments in earned value over time instead of causing discrete jumps. This option must also be enabled if you want progress lines to connect to tasks that have actual work completed ahead of schedule.

OPTIONS TO RESCHEDULE PARTS OF PARTIALLY COMPLETED TASKS

This section discusses the Calculations Options found in the menu sequence Tools, Options, Calculations tab that are shown in Figure 13.5. Since tasks are rarely completed exactly on

13

schedule, you often have tasks that should have been completed when you enter tracking information, but that still have incomplete work.

You can use the menu sequence Project, Project Information, then set the Status date to any date you desire, often different than the current date. The status date affects calculation and earned value results. As you can see in Figure 13.6, the status date is the end of Day 4. Task B was not scheduled to begin until Day 8. Microsoft Project 2007 shows that Task B has 2 days of actual progress already, so Microsoft Project 2007 assumes that the task had started as scheduled. Therefore, the task completed work falls into the future, after the Status date. The completed portion of the task should be moved back to the left of the status date to more accurately show what has happened to the tasks.

Task A was scheduled to be completed by the status date, but only 3 days of actual duration were reported for the status update. This remaining work needs to be completed, but is scheduled for days that are in the past. You need to move the incomplete part of Task A to start after the Status date.

Figure 13.6
You should reschedule unfinished work that is overdue to a more reasonable start date.

You can use the options below to automatically reschedule parts of a task like those in this example Note that each of these options functions only at the moment you enter a change to a task. These options will not impact tasks where you have entered tracking information before turning on the reschedule options.

NOTE

> The Split In-Progress Tasks check box, found on the Schedule tab of the Options dialog box, must be enabled (which is the default) for the following rescheduling options to work.

USING THE MOVE END OF COMPLETED PARTS AFTER STATUS DATE BACK TO STATUS DATE OPTION

As was discussed in the previous section, Task B in Figure 13.6 was scheduled for the future, but 2 days of work are already completed. If the Move end of completed parts after status date back to status date option is enabled (it is disabled by default) when you record the Actual Work, Microsoft Project 2007 moves the completed part of the task to the status date so that the task resumes on the status date. The rescheduled part of the task is shown by Task B in Figure 13.7. This option setting saves you the trouble of remembering to enter the actual start date for tasks that start early.

Figure 13.7
To correct your schedule, Project can automatically reschedule sections of partially completed tasks.

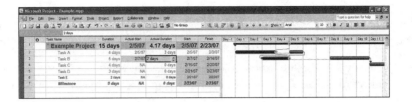

The option And move start of remaining parts back to status date sub-option is disabled by default, and becomes available only when the Move end of completed parts after status date back to status date option is enabled. This option will move task split conditions to the Status date.

USING THE MOVE START OF REMAINING PARTS BEFORE STATUS DATE FORWARD TO STATUS DATE OPTION

The option Move start of remaining parts before status date forward to status date (disabled by default) will automatically reschedule any unfinished work that was scheduled before the status date to start on the status date. That allows you to move the rescheduled part to a later date, if you set the Project Information Status date to a future period.

You can see that Task A, in Figure 13.7, started on schedule but still has unfinished work as of the status date. If this option had been enabled when the actual duration was entered, Microsoft Project 2007 would have entered the scheduled Start in the Actual Start field and automatically rescheduled the remaining duration to start on the status date, as shown in Task A. If work will not resume right away, you can drag the remaining duration further to the right to the date when you want to resume scheduled work.

When you enable Move start of remaining parts before status date forward to status date, the sub-option And move end of completed parts forward to status date becomes available.

When this option is enabled, Microsoft Project 2007 moves the completed section of the task to join the unfinished section at the status date.

13

USING MICROSOFT PROJECT'S FACILITIES FOR UPDATING TASKS

Microsoft Project 2007 allows you to select several views and forms to assist with recording your tracking. Here are some of the more common and frequently used options.

THE TRACKING TOOLBAR

There are several shortcuts that you can use while working with the Tracking Toolbar:

- **Quartile Percentage**—Use these buttons to set the % Complete for selected tasks.

- **Update as Scheduled**—This button is used to set the selected task's Actual Start to its scheduled Start, and to record Actual Duration complete through the Status Date (or Current Date if Status Date is undefined).

- **Reschedule Work**—This button is used to reschedule incomplete work to start on the Status Date (or Current Date if Status Date is undefined) for the selected task.

- **Add Progress Line**—Use this button when you want to add a line that highlights tasks that have unfinished work as of the date you select for placing the progress line. After you click this button, Project will wait for you to click a date on the timeline. You can then slide the mouse over the current date or the status date, and click to display the progress line. Peaks are drawn from the line to the left for any task that should be but is not finished, as of the progress date line. Use this to find tasks that might be missing their tracking information or that need to be rescheduled.

→ For more information on progress lines, **see** Chapter 14, "Analyzing Performance," **p. 473**.

- **Update Tasks**—This button will display the Update Tasks form for any tasks you select. See the section "The Update Tasks Form" for more details on how to use this form.

> **NOTE**
>
> Remember, these buttons will only affect the task or tasks you have selected. If a button does not work right the first time, make sure you have selected the right task.

THE UPDATE TASKS FORM

You can enter task-level tracking information for one or more selected tasks by using the Update Tasks form, which you can see in Figure 13.8. You can open this form by choosing Tools, Tracking, Update Tasks.

You may find it convenient to use the Update Tasks form instead of editing data in view that contains the Tracking table. You can edit task data in the Update Tasks form and then click OK to have Microsoft Project 2007 update the cells and recalculate the updates in a single action.

Figure 13.8
Use the Update Tasks form to view and edit any actual records for a selected task.

THE UPDATE PROJECT FORM

You can use the Update Project form to enter tracking information for all tasks scheduled throughout the project or a group of selected tasks. Use the menu sequence Tools, Tracking, Update Project to display the form shown in Figure 13.9.

Figure 13.9
You can update your project very quickly using the Update Project form.

You can perform two tracking functions with the Update Project form: You can update work as complete through the status date (or current date if status date is not set) or you can reschedule uncompleted work to start on the date you choose. Both of these options, by default, apply to all tasks in the project, or at least those tasks you have selected.

USING THE UPDATE WORK AS COMPLETE THROUGH OPTION

Use the Update work as complete through option to update all scheduled work as completed up through the specified date. By default, the status date you defined appears in the date box. The current date appears if you have not defined a status date. If you edit the Date box, any new date you enter will become the project's status date.

If you use this option, Microsoft Project 2007 will set the Actual Start date equal to the scheduled Start date, for all tasks that were scheduled to start before the status date. It also sets the Actual Finish date to the scheduled Finish date for tasks that were scheduled to finish before the status date.

If you choose to use the default sub-option Set 0% – 100% Complete, Microsoft Project 2007 will set the Actual Duration to complete through the selected date and calculate %

Complete. If you choose the Set 0% or 100% Complete Only sub-option, tasks that were scheduled to finish on or before the selected date are also marked 100% complete. Those not marked complete are left with 0% in the % Complete field.

The Entire Project button is selected by default, and all changes will be applied to all tasks in the project. Choose the Selected Tasks button when you want changes to only be applied to selected tasks. You will need to select the tasks you want before displaying the form, and then click the Selected Tasks option on the form.

USING THE RESCHEDULE UNCOMPLETED WORK TO START OPTION

You organization tracking standards may require you to use the Reschedule uncompleted work to start option to move incomplete work to resume after a selected date. Use the date drop down to set the date threshold to reschedule remaining work. The date box will show the current date (or status date, if defined) by default. Editing this date does not reset the project status date. When you click OK, Microsoft Project 2007 will reschedule any uncompleted work for tasks that have started to the date entered in the second date box.

> **NOTE**
>
> Remember you have to select your tasks first before you can use the Selected Task option on the Update Project form.

If a task has not started, but should, Microsoft Project 2007 will reschedule the entire task by giving it a Start No Earlier Than constraint for the date shown in the second date box. If this happens, a Planning Wizard dialog box will alert you to any constraints so you can look at the tasks individually for possible rescheduling (see Figure 13.10).

Figure 13.10
This Planning Wizard informs you when there is a task with a constraint on it that needs to be rescheduled.

You will need to deal with this Planning Wizard by rescheduling the constraint task manually. You can identify the tasks by applying the Should Start By task filter, as suggested by the dialog box. Choose Project, Filtered For, More Filters, select Should Start By, and click Apply to enact this filter. This is an interactive filter, and it will ask you to supply the start-by date (the date by which tasks should have started). Enter the current date or the status date if it is defined, since that is the date that was used in the Update Project command. The filter will then find all tasks not started, but that have scheduled start dates that are before the date you have entered.

If you select a constrained task and open its Task Information dialog box, you can reschedule its constraints. Change the Constraint Type setting on the Advanced tab to Start No Earlier Than, and enter the rescheduled date into the Constraint Date box. To remove all constraints and run the Update Project reschedule command again, you need to select all the constraint tasks, click the Task Information button to show the Multiple Task Information dialog box, then change the Constraint Type to As Soon as Possible and click OK.

CONSULTANTS' TIPS

ALWAYS KEEP THE ORIGINAL BASELINE

When working with baselines, it is important that you keep the original baseline for future comparisons. When you are finished setting your schedule, save the original baseline in the primary baseline (Baseline without a number) and also Baseline 1. The primary baseline can then be used as the "current" baseline information, and Baseline 1 ("original" baseline) is never changed.

REGULAR STATUSING OF TEAM ASSIGNMENTS

Proper statusing of team assignments in a project is critical to using Microsoft Project 2007 as a management tool. Although there are several ways to do this, from setting finish dates to setting % percent complete, you can get the most benefit from the tool if you establish a regular statusing cycle of weekly or bi-weekly updates. During these updates, get your project team together and get information on what started during the reporting period, what the progress is in terms of either percentage complete or effort spent, and what their estimate is of work or time to complete the remaining work on the task.

With this information, you can always have a clear picture of whether your project is performing to plan and whether your commitments will be met. For example, you can use the first half of the meeting to go through the current tasks in the project and update them in real time. Then, use the second half of the meeting to discuss the impact of this update to the critical deliverables of the project, to cover any issues that need to be addressed, and to set new objectives for the next cycle. Microsoft Office Project Server 2007 makes this process easier by providing a simple way to use statusing forms to enter progress information. These can then be sent electronically to the project manager. Now the entire status meeting can be used to analyze the results of the latest information and plan the remaining effort.

13

CHAPTER **14**

ANALYZING PERFORMANCE

In this chapter

ANALYSIS OVERVIEW

As a project manager, planning the project is only one phase of your overall objective. In fact, the process model supported by Project Management Institute (PMI) begins with initiation, followed by planning, executing, controlling, and closing the project. This is an excellent model to emulate to obtain the greatest success rate for managing your project. This chapter will focus on the controlling aspect of project management.

It is nearly impossible to plan a project with complete accuracy. That is why, for example, when durations are entered, they are referred to as "estimated durations." A project plan is the best estimate of how the project will proceed as approximated by the project manager(s) and other project stakeholders. Projects are bound to deviate from their original plans. Sometimes they take less time, less effort, or less cost than you originally called for; sometimes they take more. In either case, it is your responsibility as a project manager not only to keep track of a project's progress, but to react and adapt accordingly when things change.

The questions "How are things going?" and "How are we doing?" become crucial to managing the progress of a project. Ask early and ask often. Continuously monitor the progress from the project's start date. The more on top of the situation you are, the more prepared you will be to make necessary adjustments to the plan.

Often it is necessary to backtrack when following the PMI process model referenced previously. If, during the controlling phase, you need to make adjustments, your course of action may require you to go back to the planning phase, and continue to move forward from there. Do not get discouraged if this happens more than once; it may seem like you have made a mistake, but in reality you are a better project manager for making the adjustments than ignoring the need for them. Clients may be unhappy if the project has gone off schedule or off budget, but they will be much more appreciative to find out as it is happening (and that it is being accounted for) rather than at the end of the project.

This chapter will focus on different practices and procedures for analyzing the performance of your project.

REVIEWING THE CURRENT STATUS OF A PROJECT

Several features within Microsoft Project 2007 aid in reviewing and analyzing a project's current status. Views, reports, filters, as well as status fields and progress lines are all helpful analyzing tools. The next several sections will discuss these and other methods for analyzing a project's current status.

NOTE

> Capturing the baseline of your project is crucial to analyzing its progress. A baseline is more or less a snapshot of your project at any given time. That way, you have something to compare the project's current status to.

→ For more information about capturing baselines, **see** "Saving Your Project Baseline," **p. 435**.

REVIEWING THE STATUS VIA THE CURRENT SCHEDULE

The first step in analyzing a project's current status is to review the current schedule. Specifically, you are looking for tasks that are behind schedule. There are multiple ways of doing this. The Status and Status Indicator fields are immediate gauges of whether or not a task is behind schedule. Also, you can insert a progress line into the Gantt Chart view to display the information graphically. In addition, you can apply filters to find tasks that are behind schedule. All of these processes are described in the next three sections.

THE STATUS AND STATUS INDICATOR FIELDS

The Status and Status Indicator fields are excellent quick references as to a task's progress. These fields label the task as Complete, On Schedule, Late, or Future (for a task that has yet to begin). The Status Date in the Project Information dialog box is used as a reference point for the status indication. In other words, Microsoft Project 2007 compares the task's % Complete value (duration percentage complete) to the Status date, is able to calculate the progress based on that value, and labels the task based on that calculation.

For example, assume a task has a scheduled duration of 3 weeks and is scheduled to start on September 4th, 2007. Microsoft Project 2007 would calculate its finish date to be September 25th, 2007. Microsoft Project 2007 calculates the status of the task based on its % Complete versus its scheduled finish date. Therefore, if you entered a Status date of September 20th, 2007, and entered the % Complete as 60%, the Status and Status Indicator fields would show the task's status to be Late, because the task should be more than 60% complete by September 20th. If, however, the task was 60% complete and the Status date were September 12th, 2007, the Status and Status Indicators fields would show the task as On Schedule, because it is on pace to finish on or before the scheduled finish date (see Figure 14.1).

Insert the Status and Status Indicator fields into a table by right-clicking on a column, choosing Insert Column, and selecting Status or Status Indicator from the list. The column will be inserted where you selected, and all columns will move to the right to make room for it (except those already on its left, which will stay put).

The Status and Status Indicator columns primarily display the same information. The Status column displays the information in words (Complete, On Schedule, Late, or Future), whereas the Status Indicator field displays the graphical indicator (see Table 14.1). For this information to be accurate, you must enter an accurate % Complete value in the Task Information dialog box (right-click on a task and choose Task Information).

To enter a Status date, open the Project Information dialog box (select Project, Project Information) and enter a date in the Status Date field. Microsoft Project 2007 will use this date to base its calculations on. If no Status date is entered, the Current Date will be used to calculate the status of a task. You can also enter **NA** in the Status Date field to bypass the status date and use the current date.

14

Figure 14.1 shows the Gantt Chart view with the Status and Status Indicator fields displayed. Notice the different values in the two fields. The Status Date is set for September 6, 2007 and is represented on the timescale as a red vertical dashed line.

Figure 14.1

The Status and Status Indicator fields display status information for a task's progress.

NOTE

The status indicators are determined by the task status relative to the status or current date. It does not use the baseline values in the criteria to determine task status.

The values displayed in the Status and Status Indicator fields are useless if you have not accurately updated the progress of the task. If a task is 50% complete, but the % Complete field in the Task Information dialog box is not updated, you should update it with actual work or % complete as accurately as possible before notating the values in the Status and Status Indicator fields.

TABLE 14.1   STATUS LABELS, STATUS INDICATORS, AND THEIR MEANINGS

Status Label	Status Indicator	Meaning
Complete	✓	The task is 100% complete.
On Schedule	☑✓	The task is not yet complete, but all work that is scheduled for completion by the Status date is complete. The task is on pace to finish on or before the scheduled finish date.
Late	☑⊕	Not all work scheduled to be completed by the Status date is complete. The task is on pace to finish later than its scheduled finish date.
Future	(No indicator)	The task is not scheduled to start until after the Status date. This Status value has no indicator.

As an alternative to inserting the Status and Status Indicator fields, you can create custom fields that use a formula to determine the status of a task. You can also apply a graphical indicator to be displayed in the custom field that indicates a task's status. For example, the custom field could display the colors of a stoplight (red, yellow, and green) to indicate whether a task is late (red), on behind schedule (yellow), or on time or early (green), as shown in Figure 14.2.

Figure 14.2
The custom schedule and budget fields have been added to provide a quick at-a-glance status of your project.

→ For more information about creating custom fields with formulas and graphical indicators, **see** "Creating and Customizing Fields," **p. 801**.

USING PROGRESS LINES

The Status and Status Indicator fields are good references for a task's progress on the Task Entry table side of the Gantt Chart view. This section will discuss *progress lines*, which are graphical indicators of a task's progress on the timescale side. Progress lines are vertical lines on the timescale that spike out to the left and right to quickly call your attention to tasks that are ahead or behind schedule. They are customizable in their format and appearance.

You can choose to display a progress line at the current date, status date, or any other date of interest to you. The line will appear centered over the date you chose. You can also set up a progress line at specific intervals within the project schedule. For every incomplete taskbar that the progress line runs through (excluding completed tasks or tasks whose start date is later than the progress line date), it spikes out to the left or right, depending on the task's progress. If the task is ahead of schedule, the progress line spikes out to the right; if it is behind schedule, it spikes out to the left. This is of course very dependent on the % Complete field in the Task Information dialog box. The spike connects to the point on the taskbar that represents the task's percentage complete for its duration. In other words, if the task is 50% complete, the spike from the progress line will connect to the middle of the taskbar.

14

TIP

> To get the best usage of a progress line, be sure to update the progress for all tasks as accurately as possible by the tracking method used. Otherwise, the progress line(s) will not be accurate.

Figure 14.3 shows a progress line and several tasks. Notice how it spikes to the left for tasks that are behind schedule (late). For tasks that are on schedule, the line simply runs down the middle, as it does for completed tasks or tasks that begin after the progress line date and have not started yet (because progress lines call attention only to tasks that are ahead of or behind schedule). Also, notice how it spikes to the right for Task 8. Even though the start date for Task 8 is after the progress line date, the progress line connects to this taskbar because work has already started on this task. Tasks ahead of schedule (such Task 8) are only connected to the progress line if Edits To Total Task % Complete Will Be Spread to the Status Date option is selected (see the preceding Note).

Figure 14.3
A progress line is a visual indicator of tasks that are off schedule, either ahead or behind.

There are a few ways to display a progress line. One is to right-click over the timescale side of the Gantt Chart view and select Progress Lines. Another is to choose Tools from the main toolbar, then select Tracking, Progress Lines. Both methods will open the Progress Lines dialog box, as shown in Figure 14.4.

Figure 14.4
Define where and how often a progress line is displayed on the Dates and Intervals tab of the Progress Lines dialog box.

At the top of the Dates and Intervals tab of the Progress Lines dialog box, you can select Always Display Current Progress Line and choose whether you want the progress line on the status date or on the current date.

You can select another date other than the current or status date by selecting the Display Selected Progress Lines check box. Choose a date from the drop-down calendar in the Progress Line Dates field(s). You can enter multiple dates to display multiple progress lines, or delete a date by selecting it and pressing the Delete button. You can also temporarily hide the progress lines by clearing the Display Selected Progress Lines check box. This will hide the progress lines but keep the date list, so the next time you open the Progress Lines dialog box you simply have to select that check box to display them again.

As mentioned before, you can display progress lines at specific intervals. This may be helpful to analyze the pattern of deviation or progress over the course of your project. Select the Display Progress Lines at Recurring Intervals check box and define whether you want the progress line displayed daily, weekly, or monthly. Then, set the recurrence pattern. Your options are different depending on your interval selection (Daily, Weekly, or Monthly). By default, these recurring progress lines begin at the start of the project, but you can change them to begin on a specific date by selecting the date from the Begin At field at the bottom.

At the bottom-right corner of the Progress Lines dialog box is an option to display the progress lines in relation to the actual plan or the baseline plan. By default, Actual Plan is selected, meaning the progress lines are displayed in relation to the current schedule, including start and finish dates. If you choose Baseline Plan, the progress line is drawn to the date that represents the percent complete as applied to the baseline schedule. The progress line is drawn to the baseline bars if the Gantt Chart view displays baseline bars; if not, it is drawn on the calculated date anyway, even if the date does not fall on a scheduled taskbar.

TIP

> Once you have displayed a progress line, you can double-click the line itself to open up the Progress Lines dialog box and modify the display.

Figure 14.5 displays the Line Styles tab of the Progress Lines dialog box. On this tab, you have multiple options for setting how the progress lines will be displayed, including types, colors, shapes, and the date display.

Choose the Progress Line Type based on which of the four illustrations is most appealing to you. Then, in the Line Style fields, you can opt for different line types (solid, dashed, and so on), colors, point shapes (the point where the progress line meets the taskbar), and the point color for the current progress line and all other progress lines.

At the bottom of the dialog box, you can select the Show Date for Each Progress Line check box if you want to display the date at the top of each progress line. This may be helpful if your timescale is zoomed in a way that makes it difficult to see the date of the progress line. Next to that, you can choose which format to display the date, and change the font if you want.

14

Figure 14.5
Format the look of progress lines in the Line Styles tab of the Progress Lines dialog box.

When you are satisfied with your selections on both tabs of the Progress Lines dialog box, click OK to display the progress lines as you have defined them, or click Cancel to exit the dialog box without applying anything.

An alternative method of displaying progress lines without using the Progress Lines dialog box is to use the Add Progress Line button on the Tracking toolbar. Click the button, and your mouse pointer becomes a miniature progress line. As you move it across the timescale, a Progress Line information box appears displaying information relevant to your pointer's location on the timescale (see Figure 14.6). If you click where your pointer is, a progress line will be drawn according to the date in the Progress Line information box.

Figure 14.6
The Progress Line information box displays the date on which the progress line will be drawn if you click the mouse pointer.

FILTERING FOR SLIPPING TASKS

Filtering is another quick way to identify tasks that are not on schedule. Two built-in filters are good for this purpose: the Slipping Tasks filter for a task table, and the Slipping Assignments filter for a resource table.

In Microsoft Project 2007, a task is *slipping* when it is not complete, and its scheduled finish date is later than its baseline finish date. Therefore, if you have not yet captured the baseline for a task, the task will not be selected by the filter, even if it is behind schedule.

→ For more information about capturing baselines, **see** "Saving Your Project Baseline," **p. 435**.

To apply the Slipping Task filter to the Gantt Chart view (or any view with a task table), select it from the Filter drop-down list on the Formatting toolbar. Alternatively, you can choose Project, Filtered For, More Filters, and select Slipping Tasks from the list. Click Apply to apply the filter or Highlight to show all tasks but highlight those that meet the filter requirements (the slipping tasks).

Follow the same procedure for the Slipping Assignments filter, although it can only be applied to a resource table.

If you apply the Slipping Task filter to the Task Usage view, both the slipping assignments and their tasks are displayed. This allows you to determine the specific assignments that are causing tasks to slip. Similarly, if you apply the Slipping Assignments filter to the Resource Usage view, the slipping assignments are grouped by resource, and you are able to see if certain resources have a significant amount of slipping assignments.

REVIEWING THE STATUS VIA THE PROJECT PLAN

So far this chapter has described ways to pinpoint tasks that are off schedule (ahead or behind). But identifying these tasks is only part of the analyzing process; you must also know the implications of making changes to the schedule to account for the slipping tasks. The next several sections will examine the impact of schedule changes to the overall project.

DEFINING VARIANCE FIELDS AND PERCENTAGE COMPLETE FIELDS

Variance in Microsoft Project 2007 is defined as the difference between the actual value and the baseline. The related fields are Duration, Work, Cost, Start Date, and Finish Date. Thus, Microsoft Project 2007 automatically calculates field values for Duration Variance, Work Variance, Cost Variance, Start Variance, and Finish Variance. To get these values, Microsoft Project 2007 performs a simple subtraction calculation. For example:

Duration Variance = Current Duration − Baseline (Planned) Duration.

The same formula is applied to the other four variance fields.

NOTE

Like many topics covered so far in this chapter, this formula relies heavily on the assumption that you have captured the baseline.

14

If the result is zero, then there is no variance and your project is executing as planned. However, changes in the schedule will produce nonzero results, either positive or negative. If a positive number is produced, then the current value is greater than the baseline, which generally is unfavorable because the task is taking longer, starting or finishing later, taking more effort, or costing more than originally planned. On the reverse side, if a negative number is produced, the task is ahead of schedule, taking less effort, or costing less money than originally planned, which is a good thing!

You can display any of the five variance fields in any task table. Insert one by right-clicking on the column heading where you want it, choosing Insert Column, and choosing from the drop-down list in the Field Name field. Notice that you cannot change the value in a variance field; all calculations are done internally.

Until you enter actual values to track a task's progress, variances are calculated using the estimated values of the current schedule. Therefore, in order to display an accurate variance value, you must not only have captured your baseline, you must also enter actual values for a task. This can be done on most Tracking views, or on a task table such as the Task Entry table on the Gantt Chart. When these values are entered, the variance will reflect the difference between the planned value versus the actual value.

Similar to the variance fields are the percentage complete fields. The difference between these fields and variance fields is that variance fields compare scheduled and baseline values, whereas percentage complete fields compare scheduled and actual values.

The two percentage complete fields are % Complete and Work % Complete. % Complete measures the percentage of the duration complete, and Work % Complete measures the percentage of work complete. These values are not necessarily the same; you could have a % Complete of 20% but a larger Work % Complete value because multiple resources have worked on the task during that duration.

These fields can also be displayed and defined in a number of ways. You can insert a column in any task table (both fields are at the top on the drop-down list in the Field Name field in the Insert Column dialog box) or Tracking view. Also, you can enter the % Complete in the Task Information dialog box (right-click on a task and choose Task Information).

REVIEWING STATUS AT THE PROJECT LEVEL: DISPLAYING PROJECT STATISTICS AND THE PROJECT SUMMARY REPORT

Microsoft Project 2007 is equipped with several features that allow you to quickly view the overall progress of a project as compared to the original project plan. The Project Statistics dialog box and the Project Summary report both provide excellent references to the statistics of a project in one condensed image.

The Project Statistics dialog box can be accessed by clicking the Project Statistics button on the Tracking toolbar, or by opening the Project Information dialog box (Project, Project Information) and then clicking the Statistics button. Figure 14.7 displays an example of the Project Statistics dialog box.

Figure 14.7
The Project Statistics dialog box compares the current project plan to the baseline plan.

As you can see, the Project Statistics dialog box displays the current, baseline, actual, and variance values for the project's start and finish dates. Additionally, in the lower half, the current, baseline, actual, and remaining values are shown for Duration, Work, and Cost. The percent complete for % Complete and Work % Complete (labeled simply as "Work") are also displayed along the bottom.

The Project Statistics dialog box is the quickest way to view all this information together on one screen.

Another quick reference screen to the overall progress of a project is the Project Summary report.

To view the Project Summary report, follow these steps:

1. From the main menu, select Report, Reports.
2. In the Reports window, double-click Overview and then double-click Project Summary. Figure 14.8 demonstrates the resulting screen.

The Project Summary report displays the same information as the Project Statistics dialog box in a different format. In addition, it displays the variance values for Duration, Work, and Cost, as well as values for task and resource status.

The Project Summary report is displayed on a Print Preview screen, meaning that this report is ready to print if you desire. This may be beneficial to you if you want to share the summary information with other people involved with the project or for including in any other printed document, such as status report to the project sponsor or your manager.

Figure 14.8
The project Summary report displays similar information as the Project Statistics dialog box in a printer-friendly view.

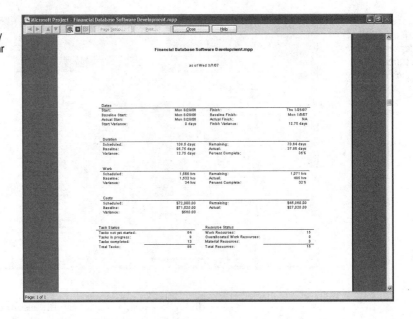

REVIEWING STATUS AT THE PROJECT LEVEL: USING THE PROJECT SUMMARY TASK

The project summary task provides yet another way to view most of the project information found in the Project Statistics dialog box and the Project Summary report. To display the project summary task, open the Options dialog box by selecting Tools, Options, selecting the View tab, and then selecting the Show Project Summary Task box on the right side near the bottom. The project summary task will appear at the top of any task table with an ID number 0 (zero).

TIP

As mentioned earlier in this book, it is a good practice to include the project summary task in your task list. That way, you have a summary task that encompasses the entire project, rather than several smaller summary tasks.

Unlike the Project Statistics dialog box and the Project Summary report, the project summary task does not display all of the project summary data on the same screen. In fact, you have to apply different tables to see the full range of summary data, or insert additional columns or fields to view all the information, such as some of the variance fields.

As an alternative, you can create your own project summary task by inserting a task with the project name at the top of the task list and indenting (demoting) all other tasks, but this method is not recommended because you would be duplicating information that already exists.

With your project summary task inserted, you can view various tables to view both specific (individual task) information as well as general (project summary task) information for different aspects of your project. For example, to view the Cost table, select View, Table and then choose Cost from the list. You can follow the same procedure to view the Work table or any other table of interest to you. Additionally, these tables are all customizable to fit your specific needs.

→ For more information about customizing tables, **see** "Creating and Customizing Tables," **p. 756**.

After reviewing specific aspects of your project, you can also collapse the tasks to review specific outline levels. If you have inserted a project summary task, it is the highest outline level by itself. The next level will be Outline Level 1 (since the project summary task is on its own level, think of it as Outline Level 0). Outline level 1 generally consists of the phases of the project, usually made up of summary tasks, but subtasks may be included as well.

To display specific outline levels, use the Show button on the Formatting toolbar. When you click it, a drop-down list will appear (see Figure 14.9). Select any of the outline levels from that list.

Figure 14.9
The Outline drop-down list is a quick and easy way to select a specific outline level.

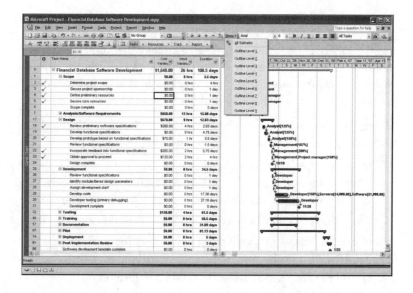

Alternatively, you can apply the Top Level Tasks filter to any task table to display the top outline level.

You can apply filters or use the Show button using different tables (Cost, Work, and so on) to more specifically analyze different aspects of your project.

REVIEWING STATUS AT THE TASK LEVEL

It is good practice to analyze variances as often as you record actual values. The reason you record actual values in the first place is to track progress on your project; therefore, it is not very productive to enter actual values if you do not pay attention to the significance of those values to your project's progress. Even if the actual values differ only slightly from the baseline, those differences can add up quickly, and if you do not monitor them regularly, they can make for quite an unpleasant surprise when you finally do get around to analyzing them.

You can examine variances by using a variety of views, filters, and reports. While you can apply these tools to the overall project or any phase in the project, this section will look at analyzing variances occurring at the individual task level.

The AutoFilter feature is a great tool to analyze variances. Remember that a positive number in the Variance field is unfavorable, meaning the actual value is greater than the baseline value. In other words, the actual value is later, longer, requires more work, or is more expensive than the planned baseline (depending on if you are looking at schedule, duration, work, or cost).

To use the AutoFilter, first apply the table you want to analyze (such as Cost, Work, Variance, and so on). Then, click the AutoFilter button on the Formatting toolbar, or choose Project, Filtered For, AutoFilter. When activated, the AutoFilter feature inserts drop-down menus in each of the column headings. In the Variance column, open the drop-down list and choose >0 (which means greater than zero). Project will filter for all variance values that are greater than zero (and thus, unfavorably off the baseline plan).

Depending on which table you have applied, you may have to create a custom filter to display variances greater than zero. To do this, follow these steps:

1. Insert the Variance column by clicking on any column in the view, right-clicking, and selecting Insert Column. In the Column Definition dialog box, select the Variance column you would like to insert from the Field Name drop-down.

2. Apply the AutoFilter by selecting Project, Filtered For, AutoFilter.

3. Above the Variance column name, select the filter drop-down and then select (Custom…). The Custom AutoFilter dialog box will appear, as shown in Figure 14.10.

4. Define the filter test by selecting Is Greater Than in the test field on the left side, and select $0.00 (zero) as the value field on the right side (refer to Figure 14.10). You do not have to define the optional second test; click OK to apply the filter.

NOTE

> The AutoFilter test for positive variance values assumes that the baseline was captured for all tasks; therefore, if the baseline was not captured, all the variances will be positive and the test is pointless.

Figure 14.10
Create a custom filter test for the AutoFilter feature in the Custom AutoFilter dialog box.

REVIEWING TASK START AND FINISH DATE VARIANCES

A date variance occurs whenever the current start or finish date estimates differ from the baseline dates. There are a number of reasons as to why this happens:

- The task began or finished at a different time than originally planned, so you entered the actual start or finish date as a different value than the baseline date.

- A predecessor task was delayed or finished earlier than planned, which in turn forced a successor task to be rescheduled accordingly.

- The task's duration and dates changed because you recorded more or less work than originally planned.

- You adjusted a task relationship, which altered the start or finish date.

Add the start variance and finish variance to review and analyze.

→ For more information about revising your schedule to get back on track, **see** Chapter 16, "Revising the Schedule," **p. 557**.

REVIEWING TASK COST VARIANCES

Cost variances become unfavorable when the current cost estimates are higher than the baseline estimates. Cost variances can happen for a number of reasons, and are not necessarily connected to the schedule. For example, a task can start and finish on time, but still have an unfavorable cost variance. If you assigned a resource when planning the project, but for some reason had to use a different resource with a higher cost rate, your cost variance may be affected unfavorably.

14

TIP

> Resource competency is not taken into account automatically in Microsoft Project 2007; assigning a more expensive resource will not shorten the duration of a task. When revising the duration, you should take into consideration the competency of the resource and make changes if necessary.

Apply the Cost Overbudget filter to the Cost table to filter for tasks with unfavorable cost variances. This filter tests for tasks that have captured baselines, and whose current estimated cost is higher than the baseline cost. You can apply the filter when viewing another table, but the Cost table will allow you to see the actual values.

TIP

> You may want to create a custom view that applies the Cost Overbudget filter to the Cost table. That way, you only have to apply that view, rather than apply both the table and the view; it saves you a step.

→ For more information about creating views, **see** "Creating and Customizing Views," **p. 764**.

REVIEWING TASK WORK VARIANCES

As with other fields discussed so far in this chapter, work variances are unfavorable if the Variance value is a positive number. This means that the resource will have to apply more work to complete the task than originally anticipated. The easiest way to view work variances is to apply the Work table (select View, Table, Work). The work variance values are displayed in the Variance column (see Figure 14.11).

Figure 14.11
View work variances by applying the Work table.

To quickly display all tasks that have an unfavorable work variance, apply the Work Overbudget filter. This filter behaves a lot like the Cost Overbudget filter, selecting tasks whose current work estimates are larger than the baseline values. Because this filter uses the Actual Work values when testing instead of the Work values, it does not account for tasks that have not started. These tasks still may have an unfavorable work variance, even though they have yet to begin. However, you can customize the filter to include these tasks by following these steps:

1. Select Project, Filtered For, More Filters, and choose Work Overbudget.
2. Click Copy.
3. Give the filter a unique name, such as **Work Overbudget (revised for Work)**. Since you are copying the Work Overbudget filter instead of editing it, the original Work Overbudget will remain intact.
4. In the first row under Field Name, change Actual Work to **Work**.
5. Click OK to finish the filter definition.
6. Click Apply to apply the filter, Highlight to show all tasks but highlight those selected by the filter, or Close to close the dialog box without applying the filter. The filter will now be in the More Filters list.

REVIEWING STATUS AT THE RESOURCE LEVEL

The previous sections described methods used to analyze variance for tasks. The methods are similar for analyzing variance and progress for resources.

As with tasks, Project saves the baseline date, work, and cost values for each assignment. The work and cost baseline values are the total baseline values for all of a particular resource's combined task assignments. Likewise, the resource's currently scheduled work and cost values, as well as actual work and actual cost values, are the total combined values for all task assignments for the resource (see the next section, "Reviewing Status at the Assignment Level," for information about analyzing variances for individual assignments). Therefore, the variance values are determined by comparing the total scheduled and total baseline values.

When analyzing resource variances, it is possible that certain resources are responsible for task variances. You may notice a pattern, caused by one of the following reasons:

- Tasks were assigned to resources whose skill level was not capable of completing the tasks within the planned duration.
- Resources arrived later than anticipated to work on the project, thus delaying all the start dates for their tasks.
- When planning the project, you underestimated (or overestimated) the amount of work for tasks assigned to a resource or resource group.
- A resource was overallocated and was not able to apply the percentage of time to the project you originally planned for.

14

- The original cost of a resource was underestimated or overestimated, or a different resource was later assigned to the task(s) that had a higher or lower cost than the original resource.
- A particular resource or resource group consistently had slipping tasks.
- A resource simply was not applying the appropriate effort needed to complete tasks on time and on budget.

Table 14.2 shows the tables and filters you can apply to show resource variances. Apply these tables and filters to the Resource Sheet view to identify the resource names selected by the filter, or apply them to the Resource Usage view to see specifically which assignments are contributing to the resource variances. Applying these tables and filters is a quicker way to analyze variances than the methods described for analyzing task variances.

TABLE 14.2 SUGGESTED TABLES AND FILTERS FOR RESOURCE VARIANCE ANALYSIS

Table	Filter	Displays
Cost	Cost Overbudget	Resources whose current estimated cost is greater than the originally estimated baseline cost.
Entry	Slipping Assignments	Resource assignments whose current estimated finish date is later than the planned baseline finish date.
Entry	Should Finish By (interactive filter)	Resource assignments that should have finished by the date you specified.
Entry	Should Start By (interactive filter)	Resource assignments that should have started by the date you specified.
Work	Work Overbudget	Resources whose current estimated work is greater than the originally estimated baseline work. The Work Overbudget filter uses work instead of actual work; you can edit the filter to use actual work if you prefer.

→ For more information about using interactive filters, **see** "Using Interactive Filters" **p. 793**.
→ For more information about editing filters, **see** "Creating and Customizing Filters," **p. 785**.

REVIEWING STATUS AT THE ASSIGNMENT LEVEL

As previously discussed, baseline assignment values for work and cost are combined and rolled up to the resource or task level. You can view individual assignment details by displaying either the Resource Usage or Task Usage views and applying the appropriate table (or inserting appropriate columns). The Task Usage view will display both the current estimates and the baseline estimates, they also display variance values for these fields. However, resource assignments do not have the start and finish variance fields available, only the work and cost variance values are displayed in the Resource Usage view.

To display assignment level details, select View and choose either Task Usage or Resource Usage. You can then display the Cost, Work, or Variance tables to see assignment variances. Choose View, Table and select the appropriate table to display. To see various time-phased baseline values for each assignment, right-click on the grid under the timescale and choose the appropriate value from the shortcut list. You may have to widen the row label's column to display the entire value name; drag the right boundary of the Details column header field.

ANALYZING PERFORMANCE WITH EARNED VALUE ANALYSIS

So far this chapter has discussed using variances as a means of analyzing progress on a project. However, variances are all measured in different units: dollar amounts (cost variances), hours (work variances), and time units (date variances). Variances also do not measure whether productivity is at the levels you planned for in the baseline; in other words, variances do not tell you the output per dollar cost, and whether or not there is enough money left in the project's budget to continue the project and finish as planned.

Earned value analysis evaluates work and cost performance. You can compare the value of the work completed with the cost of completing it. The primary purpose of earned value analysis is to try to measure the value you have earned based on the work that was planned and what was actually performed. These predictions are based on an estimated strategy, such as an educated estimate, a wild guess, scientific predictions, and so on. No matter how you end up with these estimates, you are going to capture them in a baseline at some point. So, earned value analysis compares how you are doing along the timeline of your estimates, and whether or not your project is likely to be on track with those estimates or if there are variances.

The reason you are looking for variances is to try to predict the future. You are trying to assess the likelihood of achieving your estimates by comparing your progress to them. Evaluation of the past performance is critical and used to determine the cost and schedule performance index which in turn is used to forecast the future performance. The future is where all the value is—all your effort and costs you have yet to expend.

Earned value analysis measures performance—or productivity—of a project as of a specific date (the status date, or current date if a status date is not identified). If a project is not producing the output per dollar cost that you had originally planned for, earned value analysis will detect the setback and call your attention to it.

Earned value analysis is based on earned money, because it is an accounting term. If you have $100, and you got your work done using only $80, you made a profit. Or, if you spent $150 to get the work done, you lost money. The other side of earned value analysis is work performance. If you have 100 hours worth of work (forget about cost for a minute), and you finish it in 80 hours, you have 20 hours profit of work remaining, or 20 hours of resource availability that you did not have when that work began. On the other hand, assume you have 100 hours allotted to complete the work but know now it will take 200. Of course, the

14

extra work chews up cost, but even worse, it uses resources and time. Earned value analysis predicts the future using a cost component and a schedule component to find your risk profile (low or high) for the remainder of the project.

NOTE

> The accuracy of earned value measurements dependent on the accuracy of your tracking methodology. You must record actual start and finish dates, actual cost, and actual work, and you must reschedule work that was not completed on time and completed work that was scheduled after the status date.

→ For more information about earned value and how it relates to Work Breakdown Structure (WBS), **see** Chapter 4, "Getting Started After the Business Initiative Is Approved," **p. 87**.

UNDERSTANDING EARNED VALUE MEASUREMENTS

In order to comprehend how earned value analysis works in Microsoft Project 2007, you must first understand its core measurements. Project tasks generate value as work is accomplished, and that value must be at least equal to the project's baseline cost of the work scheduled. If the two values are equal, then the task is progressing as expected. Thus, the baseline cost of project tasks acts as a measure of the project's productive output.

Earned value analysis in Microsoft Project 2007 lets you look at today or look to the past for synchronization points. Earned value analysis produces a quality measure if the following are true:

■ You have reasonable estimates of the work to be done, broken down into your task list.

TIP

> Using the Work Breakdown Structure (WBS) not only helps you logically split up your work, but also helps you better control scope and better estimate the work to be done. See Chapter 4, "Getting Started After the Business Initiative Is Approved," for additional information on using the WBS.

■ The baseline estimates for cost and effort for your tasks and resources were derived using a reasonable methodology.

■ You are collecting tracking data in a reasonable way and can depend on the data.

The word *reasonable* is mentioned throughout the preceding list because all of these factors contribute to quality of the EV measure.

Three core measurements are involved with earned value analysis, summarized in the following list:

■ **Planned value**—Planned value is the amount of baseline cost scheduled to be spent on work on the progress up to the status date. The field name for planned value in

Microsoft Project 2007 is BCWS, which stands for *Budgeted Cost of Work Scheduled*. When you see BCWS anywhere in Microsoft Project 2007, it is referring to the planned value. The BCWS value is calculated as soon as the baseline is saved. It is the cumulative sum of all baseline costs up to and including the status date.

- **Earned value**—Earned value is the value of completed work expressed in terms of the budget assigned to that work. The field name for earned value in Microsoft Project 2007 is BCWP, which stands for *Budgeted Cost of Work Performed*. When you see BCWP anywhere in Microsoft Project 2007, it is referring to the earned value.

  Earned value is calculated by the portion of a task or assignment that has been completed. For tasks, the calculation is done based on the percentage of duration complete (the % Complete field). For assignments, the calculation is done based on the percentage of work complete (the Work % Complete field). The percentage complete is based on the current schedule, and not on the baseline amount of duration or work.

- **Actual cost**—Actual cost is the actual cost of work completed as of the status date. The field name in Microsoft Project 2007 is ACWP, which stands for *Actual Cost of Work Performed*. Actual costs and planned costs may differ for several reasons. For example, resource cost rates may have increased since the baseline was captured, or more expensive resources may have been reassigned to the tasks.

Earned value and planned value are the same if work on a task has been completed as scheduled up to the status date. However, differences can arise due to several reasons. For example, assume a task was originally scheduled for 8 hours and to cost $500 (the planned value). If your resources have completed 5 of those hours, but the task's duration has changed to 10 hours, the duration is 50% complete (5 hours out of 10, not 5 hours out of 8) and the earned value is $250. Since the scheduled duration increased after the baseline was captured, the actual work generated a smaller value than planned (5/10 or 50%, instead of 5/8 or 63%).

Another example is if overtime was used but not scheduled, then more work was completed than scheduled, and earned value is greater than planned value (it cost more to complete the task than planned due to overtime work). Also, if a resource has been reassigned to a higher priority task or project, the earned value is less than the planned value, because, as of that status date, less work has been done to the task or project than planned.

Here is another way to think about earned value analysis: Resources create, or "earn," the value delivered by a project as they work on it. Therefore, "earned value" of any assignment, task, or project is the portion of planned value associated with completed work at any moment in the project's life cycle.

For example, you may have a project with a baseline cost of $200,000. This is the planned value for the project ($200,000), comprised of the baseline costs for all tasks and assignments. Now, on any specific date, you may find that 50% of all scheduled work for the project is complete; therefore, the earned value for the project as of that specific date is 50%, or $100,000. Perhaps the baseline schedule defined the project to be 40% complete on that date. The planned value for that date would be $80,000, and the project would be earning

14

value at a faster rate than planned. Suppose even further that the actual cost at that specific date is $90,000, meaning you have spent more on your project than you originally budgeted to spend. In other words, the actual cost ($90,000) is greater than the planned value ($80,000) on that specific date. So the question becomes, "Do I have enough money left in the budget to finish the project?" It is likely that you do, because the earned value of what has been produced thus far ($100,000) is greater than both the planned value ($80,000) and the actual cost ($90,000). Because the productivity is greater than you planned for, the project will likely finish on time (or early) and under budget. Then you can pat yourself on the back!

These core measurements (planned value, earned value, and actual cost) help you analyze progress better than simply analyzing variances. Earned value analysis creates earned value variances and productivity indexes that you can use to predict when the project will finish and the total cost upon completion.

In the previous example, and in the summary of the core measurements, a specific synchronization date, or status date, was mentioned. Earned value analysis uses this status date as a point of reference. By default, this date is the current date, taken from your computer's system date. This provides for the most accurate, up-to-date measurements. However, you must remember to track your progress so it is up to date. If you last updated tracking information a week ago, but use today's date for the earned value calculations, Project would not have any actual work and cost to compensate for the planned work and cost from the past week. Therefore, the status date for earned value measurements should be the date you last updated your actual values. Set the status date in the Project Information dialog box (Project, Project Information).

In Microsoft Project 2007, the three core calculations are performed at the assignment, task, and summary task levels. Calculations at the summary task level are rolled-up sums for their subtasks. At the task level, planned value (BCWS) and actual cost (ACWP) are rolled-up into combined sums for the assignments. Earned value (BCWP) calculations are performed using the % Complete (duration percentage complete) value for the task level and the % Work Complete value for the assignment level. This may result in a difference between the earned value of a task and the rolled-up earned value of its assignments.

Consider the following example and figures. Since this subject is advanced material, the details involved will be simple values to ensure that the concept is correctly conveyed and understood.

TIP

> Much of the following information is summed up in the upcoming section "A Summary of Using Earned Value Analysis in Microsoft Project 2007." It may be useful to review that section before re-reading this one.

Task 1 is scheduled to last 5 days (Wednesday 10-3-07 through Tuesday 10-9-07, excluding the weekend). The status date is set to Monday, 10-8-07, 4 days into the 5-day task, and you can assume it is also the current date. Ryan is the lone resource assigned 100% to the task

(5 days, or 40 hours). Ryan's standard rate is $10 an hour; therefore, the planned value for the task is $400. No work has been recorded yet on the task. Figure 14.12 illustrates this information.

Figure 14.12
Notice the Planned Value field (BCWS) has an entry of $320 (calculated through the status date, not the finish date), but the Earned Value (BCWP) and Actual Cost (ACWP) fields have an entry of zero because no work has been recorded.

In Figure 14.12, the top pane displays the Tracking Gantt Chart view with several Earned Value fields inserted into the table (right-click on a column header and insert the column to display these fields). The bottom pane displays the Task Usage view with the Earned Value table applied. The top row is the information for Task 1, and the bottom row is the information for Ryan (in italics). To save screen space, some of the column headers have been abbreviated (for example, Planned Value – BCWS has been abbreviated to just BCWS). On the right side of the bottom pane, several fields have been inserted. To re-create this, right-click on any of the fields under the Details column heading and choose Detail Styles. The Detail Styles dialog box will appear, as shown in Figure 14.13. Choose the desired field from the Available Fields column, and click the Show button to move the field to the Show These Fields column. The table will then display the field(s) you select in the order they are listed in the Show These Fields column.

In the top pane in Figure 14.12 are two taskbars: the bottom is the baseline taskbar and the top is the scheduled taskbar. The baseline taskbar, as well as the value for the BCWS field, are automatically displayed in the Tracking Gantt Chart view when you capture the baseline. 0% is next to the scheduled taskbar because no work has been recorded yet, which is also the reason the Earned Value (BCWP) and Actual Cost (ACWP) fields show zero as their entry. Also, the dashed vertical line going through the taskbars represents the status date.

14

Figure 14.13
Select detail fields to display in the Detail Styles dialog box by highlighting them in the Available Fields column and clicking the Show button.

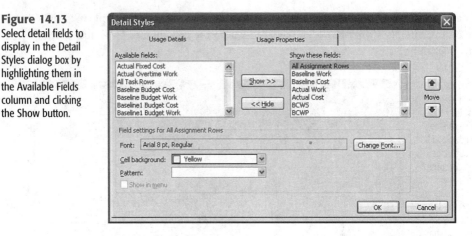

In the lower half of the screen, the Task Usage view displays time-phased details for the task. Notice how the planned value (BCWS) is calculated for each day up to and including the status date, and is cumulative. This calculation is performed instantly when the baseline is captured.

NOTE

> To display details for the task in the bottom pane, as shown in Figure 14.12, you must have the task selected in the top pane. If you have a field selected that is not in the task row in the top pane, the bottom pane will not display the details for the task.

Now, assume that at the end of the fourth day of the task (the status and current date), you discover Ryan has only worked 3 days on the task instead of 4, so you enter **60** in the % Complete field, because Ryan has worked 60% of the scheduled duration (3 days out of 5). Figure 14.14 illustrates the results.

Notice how on Day 4 (Monday, 10-8-07), no actual work or actual cost is displayed in the details side of the bottom pane. This is because Microsoft Project 2007 automatically calculates these values based on the entry of 60% in the % Complete field. 60% is equivalent to 3 days in this task; therefore, only 3 days of actual work are recorded.

The Earned Value (BCWP) field is marked as $240, because Ryan has earned $240 by doing 3 days of work at his rate of $10 an hour. Compare this to the planned value (BCWS) of $320, and you will see that Ryan has not earned as much as planned in the baseline, because he did not work according to the schedule.

Microsoft Project 2007 provides tables to help you analyze progress using earned value. You can apply the Earned Value Schedule Indicators table to deduce whether or not your project is earning value at the planned rate.

Figure 14.14
The Earned Value (BCWP) and Actual Cost (ACWP) fields have values now that actual work has been recorded. The Change Highlighting feature is enabled to point out the effects of entering 60% in the % Complete field.

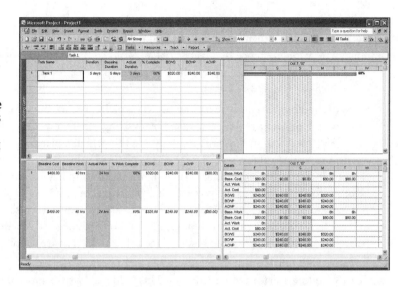

Figure 14.15 illustrates the Earned Value Schedule Indicators table as applied to both panes in the example of Ryan and Task 1. Again, some column headings have been abbreviated to save screen space, and the Detail Styles dialog box has been used to display specific detail fields on the timescale side of the Task Usage view (right side, bottom pane).

Figure 14.15
The Earned Value Schedule Indicators table helps you see the rate at which your project is earning value as compared to the planned rate.

Three important indicator fields are displayed on this table:

- **SV (Schedule Variance)**—This field displays the difference between planned value and earned value, calculated by subtracting planned value from earned value (BCWP – BCWS). In this example, ($80.00) is displayed. The parentheses indicate a negative number, because the earned value is less than the planned value. Therefore, the project has earned $80 less than what was planned for by this point, because less work has been done than planned (hence the name *schedule variance*). If the number was positive, then the earned value would be greater than originally planned for by this point in the project, which is good news for you.

■ **SV% (Schedule Variance percentage)**—This field displays the value of the schedule variance as a percentage. It is calculated by dividing schedule variance by the planned value (SV / BCWS). In this case, it is –$80 / $320, which equates to –25%. In other words, the earned value is 25% less than the planned value. Negative numbers such as this one indicate that something is keeping the work from being completed as scheduled, and because you are the project manager, this should signify to you that the matter is in need of investigation. Perhaps you need to assign additional resources. On the other side, a positive number may indicate that you are ahead of schedule, and you may be able to reassign some of the resources to other tasks that are slipping in order for them to catch up.

■ **SPI (Schedule Performance Index)**—This field displays the ratio of earned value to planned value (BCWP / BCWS). In this case, the value is 0.75 ($240 / $320). In other words, the task is earning $0.75 for every $1 of value that was planned to earn, or is .75 as productive as originally planned. Obviously this is unfavorable. Anything over 1.0 in this field would be favorable, and anything less than 1.0 provides the same indications to you as the project manager to fix the slipping task (in this case), assignment, or project.

You can also use the SPI to estimate the project or task's finish date. Divide the remaining duration by the SPI. You can insert the Remaining Duration column into the table as you wish. For example, in this case, you would divide 16 hours (remaining duration) by .75 (SPI), which equals 21.3 hours. Therefore, at this rate, it will take 21.3 more hours to complete the task, or 45.3 hours total. This is 5.3 hours (close to a full day) behind schedule if the progress rate continues to stay the same.

NOTE

> SV% and SPI are not calculated at the assignment level.

So far in this example, the earned value (BCWP) and the actual cost (ACWP) have been the same. They would change, however, if Ryan was moved off the task and another resource was reassigned to the task. Say, for instance, Chris is the new resource, but his rate is 50% more than Ryan's at $15 an hour. This will boost actual cost.

Figure 14.16 shows the calculations after Chris has replaced Ryan to work 100% on Task 1. The % Complete (60%) remains the same. Like the previous examples, column headings have been abbreviated to save screen space, and the Detail Styles dialog box has been used to display specific detail fields in the timescale side of the Task Usage view (right side, bottom pane).

Figure 14.16
When the Earned Value (BCWP) and Actual Cost (ACWP) fields differ, you can compare the two to see if you spent more than you earned.

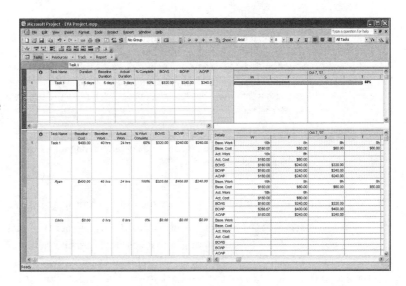

While the planned value (BCWS) and earned value (BCWP) are the same no matter which resource is used to work on the task, clearly the actual cost is different because Chris costs more than Ryan. Because Chris costs $120 a day and Ryan costs $80 a day, the actual cost increases by $40 a day, while the earned value remains the same. If this trend continues, you will be well over budget when the task or project concludes.

Again, there is a table to help indicate cost variance—the Earned Value Cost Indicators table. Figure 14.17 illustrates the Earned Value Cost Indicators table applied to the same example, with Chris working on the task instead of Ryan. As usual, the column headings have been abbreviated to save screen space and the Detail Styles dialog box has been used to display specific daily information on the timescale side of the Task Usage view.

Figure 14.17
The Earned Value Cost Indicators table helps to summarize the cost versus earned value thus far.

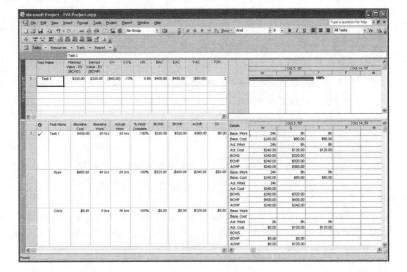

14

NOTE

> By default, the Earned Value Cost Indicators table does not include the Actual Cost (ACWP) field. It may be helpful to insert this field, as in Figure 14.17. Choose the column where you want to insert it and right-click on the column header. Choose Insert Column from the list, select ACWP from the drop-down list under Field Name, and click OK. You may also want to save this modification so all future uses of this table will include the ACWP column.

→ For more information about editing and saving tables, **see** "Creating and Customizing Tables," **p. 756**.

The cost indicators found in this table are defined in the following list:

■ **CV (Cost Variance)**—This field displays the difference between earned value and actual cost, calculated by subtracting actual cost from earned value (BCWP – ACWP). In this example, the cost variance is –$120, shown in parentheses as ($120.00), meaning the actual cost was $120 more than the earned value of the work (as of the status date). Again, this is an unfavorable result; the value of the work is lower than the cost of producing it. In other words, you are spending more than the work is worth. If the cost variance is a positive number, it is viewed as a favorable result.

■ **CV% (Cost Variance percentage)**—This field displays the value of the cost variance in terms of percent. It is calculated by dividing cost variance by the earned value (CV / BCWP). In this example, the value is –50%, meaning you spent 50% more than you planned so far. This is primarily because Chris is a much more expensive resource than Ryan. At this rate, you will not have enough money left in the budget to complete the remaining work.

■ **CPI (Cost Performance Index)**—This field displays the ratio of earned value to actual cost (BCWP / ACWP) for the actual work complete through the status date. CPI tells you how much cost value you earn for every dollar spent. In this case, the value is 0.67 ($240 / $360). In other words, the task is earning $0.67 of cost value for every $1 spent, about two-thirds as profitable as originally planned. Obviously this also is unfavorable, and the significant difference has much to do with Chris being a more expensive resource that Ryan, as well as being behind schedule. Anything over 1.0 in this field would be favorable, and anything less than 1.0 is not.

This field is used to calculate the EAC (Estimate at Completion) field, which is discussed later in this section.

NOTE

> CV% and CPI are not calculated at the assignment level.

The Earned Value Cost Indicators table includes additional fields to the right of the three fields just described. You may have to scroll to the right on the table to see them, but they are displayed in Figure 14.17.

- **BAC (Budget at Completion)**—This is the Baseline Cost field, displayed in this table as BAC. It represents the total planned value for the completed task.

- **EAC (Estimate at Completion)**—Earlier versions of Microsoft Project used to equate this field to the estimated total cost. Since Microsoft Project 2002, however, EAC is a calculated estimate of what the total cost will be when the task is completed if the CPI rate of performance remains constant through the end. In other words, the EAC calculation takes the actual cost as of the status date and adds an estimated remaining cost based on the CPI.

  The formula used to calculate this estimate is ACWP + (BAC − BCWP) / CPI. Microsoft Project 2007 begins by subtracting the earned value (BCWP) from the budget at completion (BAC) to get the remaining value yet to be produced. Next, that remaining value to be earned (BAC − BCWP) is divided by the CPI. CPI tells you the value you are currently earning for each dollar spent; therefore, dividing the remaining value to be earned by the value you are earning for each dollar gives you the number of actual dollars you will need to spend in order to produce the remaining value to be earned. Add that value (the amount you need to spend to produce the remaining value to be earned) with the money you have already spent (actual cost, or ACWP), and you have an estimated total cost at completion. In this case, it is approximately $600, which is $200 more than planned.

  Of course, the EAC will change over time as your CPI rate changes, but it is an estimate for the current status date.

- **VAC (Variance at Completion)**—VAC is the difference between the total baseline cost (BAC) and the estimated total cost (EAC), calculated by subtracting the total estimated cost at completion from the total planned value (BAC − EAC). If the VAC is a positive number, the cost estimate is lower than budgeted cost. If it is negative, like the example in Figure 14.15, the current cost rate is greater than the budgeted cost, and the project will complete over budget if the pattern continues. As a reminder, negative numbers are shown in parentheses.

- **TCPI (To Complete Performance Index)**—TCPI is the ratio of the value of remaining work to the budgeted funds remaining to be spent, as of the status date. The calculation uses this formula:

  (BAC − BCWP) / (BAC − ACWP)

  In other words, the value of remaining work is divided by the budgeted funds remaining to be spent.

  The TCPI formula calculates the value each dollar remaining in the budget must earn in order to stay within the budget. In other words, each remaining dollar spent must earn the TCPI value to stay within budget. In this example, each dollar spent must earn $4 to stay within the planned budget. Most of this discrepancy is due to using a resource that cost 50% more than planned, but it also has to do with being behind schedule.

  If you are currently over budget as of the status date, the TCPI will be greater than 1.0 in order to catch up. You will likely have to increase productivity or reduce the cost of work. If the TCPI is less than 1.0, then you are under budget and have the opportunity to increase the scope or quality of work, or save the money to use elsewhere in the project or in another project.

TIP

> Experience shows that clients are most appreciative when you deliver what is expected, not more and especially not less. In other words, even favorable variances are sometimes viewed as poor project management, simply because variances of any sort indicate a difference between estimated and actual values, and thus disprove your ability to accurately plan.
>
> It is wise to plan exactly as you see fit based on experience and research. Trying to impress your client with a low budget or quick schedule will only end up hurting you in the end when you cannot deliver the end result within the planned baseline. On the other side, do not cushion your estimates so your project finishes earlier or under the budget you planned. You may do this to look like an overachiever as a project manager, but finishing early will only leave your resources with nothing to do until their next project assignments begin, which have been scheduled to start according to your finish date estimates. Think of when an airplane arrives early—it has to simply sit on the runway and wait until its assigned gate is clear before the passengers can exit the plane. That particular flight may be early, but it still has to operate in synch with every other airport factor.

CONTROLLING THE CALCULATION OF EARNED VALUE

As mentioned previously, Microsoft Project 2007 calculates earned value at the task level using the duration percentage complete (the % Complete field). You have the option to use Physical % Complete instead. This may be more beneficial when calculating earned value for tasks that involve the production of physical units of output or the processing of physical units of input (tasks that produce or receive physical materials). This is because work on a task may not produce materials as consistently as duration uses time; duration is linear, but production levels vary. In other words, a task that takes 10 days to produce a certain number of material items may start slow, but after a few days, as the resources get more accustomed to the work, their productivity increases. Calculating earned value using Physical % Complete may, therefore, be more accurate because it measures the amount of materials produced at the status date, not the amount of time used.

To change the earned value calculation method, open the Task Information dialog box (double-click on a task), select the Advanced tab, and choose from the drop-down list in the Earned Value Method field at the bottom of the box. If you choose Physical % Complete, that field will be included on the Tracking table, and you can enter values there.

In Figure 14.18, the Earned Value table is displayed with the Earned Value Method and the Physical % Complete fields inserted. The two tasks are identical to convey the difference between the two earned value methods. Each version of the task is scheduled for 10 days, and the duration percentage complete is 50% (5 days into the task). However, only 25% of the work has been completed. You can see the difference in the earned value depending on which earned value method you select. Task 1a calculates the earned value using the duration percentage complete, and Task 1b uses the Physical % Complete value.

14

Figure 14.18
Notice the earned value difference if you use % Complete versus Physical % Complete.

You can also change the default calculation from % Complete to Physical % Complete if you feel that is more beneficial to your project. Select Tools, Options to open the Options dialog box, and on the Calculation tab, click the Earned Value button. The Earned Value dialog box will appear, as shown in Figure 14.19. In the top field, choose the Earned Value method. Underneath it is the Baseline for Earned Value Calculations field. Remember, Microsoft Project 2007 allows you to save a total of 11 baselines—the default baseline plus 10 additional baselines (Baseline 1 through Baseline 10). Select which baseline to use to calculate the earned value. For example, if a project schedule has been heavily revised since the original baseline was captured, you may want to use the revised baseline instead of the original.

NOTE

> Changing the baseline in the Earned Value dialog box affects earned value only; the duration, work, cost, start, and finish variances still use the standard baseline fields.
>
> Similarly, changing the Earned Value Method setting in the Earned Value dialog box affects tasks that are inserted after the default is changed. Click the Set As Default button to make your selection the default for all future projects.

Figure 14.19
You can change the earned value method and the baseline used for calculating the earned value in the Earned Value dialog box.

A SUMMARY OF USING EARNED VALUE ANALYSIS IN MICROSOFT PROJECT 2007

As previously stated, earned value analysis is an effective means of analyzing progress in your project. Its usage is best summarized as follows.

There are four basic steps you must follow to use earned value analysis in Microsoft Project 2007:

1. Use the Work Breakdown Structure (WBS) technique to plan your work. You must also ensure that the resources used have a cost rate.

2. Capture the baseline for the project. You can capture up to 11 different baselines; be sure you are using the most appropriate baseline in the Earned Value dialog box (described in the previous section).

3. Update the project with the latest tracking information. Be thorough in your tracking methodology, as it will improve the accuracy and significance of earned value measurements.

→ For more information about tracking your project, **see** Chapter 13, "Tracking Your Project Progress," **p. 443**.

4. Set the status date to the date you collect actuals and enter tracking information.

When using earned value analysis, the Gantt Chart view is the most common view to display, although other views can be applied that are helpful, such as the Tracking Gantt Chart view. Once the view is displayed, you can use three different tables to analyze the earned value calculations. To apply any of the following three tables, choose View, Table, and select More Tables. In the resulting More Tables dialog box, select one of the following tables:

> **NOTE**
>
> The fields in the following tables and their abbreviations are described in greater detail in the previous section, "Understanding Earned Value Measurements."

- **Earned Value**—This table, shown in Figure 14.20, displays the three core calculations: Planned Value (BCWS), Earned Value (BCWP), and Actual Cost (ACWP). The Earned Value table also displays the Earned Value Schedule Variance (SV), the Earned Value Cost Variances (CV), the Estimate at Completion (EAC), the Budget at Completion (BAC), and the Variance at Completion (VAC). Basically, this table displays all fields necessary for using earned value analysis. You may have to scroll to the right or move the vertical divider bar to view all columns together.

Figure 14.20
The Earned Value table displays the earned value calculations.

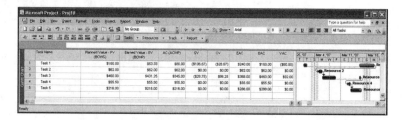

- **Earned Value Cost Indicators**—This table, shown in Figure 14.21, summarizes the effectiveness of cost thus far in the project in producing the planned value. The Earned Value Cost Indicators table displays Planned Value (BCWS) and Earned Value (BCWP), as well as Earned Value cost variance fields: Cost Variance (CV), Cost Variance percentage (CV%), and Cost Performance Index (CPI). It also displays the estimated final cost fields: Budget at Completion (BAC), Estimate at Completion (EAC), Variance at Completion (VAC), and To Complete Performance Index (TCPI). It may also be helpful to insert the Actual Cost (ACWP) column into the table.

Figure 14.21
The Earned Value Cost Indicators table summarizes the effectiveness of cost as of the status date.

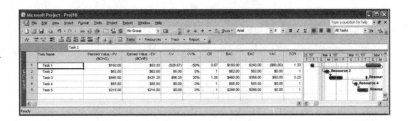

- **Earned Value Schedule Indicators**—This table, shown in Figure 14.22, displays the Planned Value (BCWS) and Earned Value (BCWP) columns, as well as the schedule variance and indicator calculations: Schedule Variance (SV), Schedule Variance percentage (SV%), and Schedule Performance Index (SPI).

Figure 14.22
The Earned Value Schedule Indicators focus on schedule variance as of the status date.

Alternatively, you can display the same fields as the Earned Value table in a custom form. To display the custom form, follow these steps:

1. Select a task (summary task or subtask).
2. Display the Custom Forms toolbar by right-clicking on the toolbar area and choosing Custom Forms to display that particular toolbar.
3. On the Custom Forms toolbar, click the Task Earned Value button (the fourth button from the left; hover the mouse pointer over the button for a ScreenTip as to which button it is). The Earned Value custom form for that particular task will appear, as shown in Figure 14.23.

Another way to open the custom form is to select the task, choose Tools, Customize, Forms, and then select Earned Value in the Customize Forms dialog box. Be sure that the Forms field at the top is set to Task, then click Apply.

14

Figure 14.23
View the same fields displayed in the Earned Value table for a specific task in the Earned Value custom form.

CREATING EARNED VALUE GRAPHS USING VISUAL REPORTS

NEW Visual reports are a new feature in Microsoft Project 2007 that provide many additional ways to display and analyze project data.

The Earned Value Over Time Report provides not only the table earned value data in a PivotTable format, but also includes the visual representation of what is known as the S-curve for at-a-glance earned value analysis. Figure 14.24 displays a modified Earned Value Over Time Report that provides the Earned Value graph, Earned Value PivotTable, and PivotTable field list on one page. You can use the PivotTable below the chart to expand or compress the level of detail you see, which is also reflected on the graph above. You can also use the PivotTable Field List to add additional fields to be displayed in the report.

The Earned Value Over Time visual report allows you to see Planned Value (BCWS), Actual Cost (ACWP), and Earned Value (BCWP). In Figure 14.24, you can see that through Week 39 of the project, all three values were around the same, meaning that the project was executing according to plan. After Week 39, however, the actual cost started to deviate from the plan, thus causing the earned value to be much lower than planned.

→ For additional information on the Earned Value Over Time visual report, **see** Chapter 15, "Using Reports for Tracking and Control," **p. 519**.

Figure 14.24
The Earned Value visual report allows you to graphically present the information and provide at-a-glance status to you and your project sponsors.

14

→ For additional information on customizing and working with Visual Reports, **see** Chapter 21, "Creating and Customizing Visual Reports," **p. 707**.

USING ANALYSIS VIEWS AND REPORTS

Microsoft Project 2007 comes equipped with dozens of views and reports that you can use for analyzing your project. All of these views and reports are customizable in varying degrees to mold them into exactly what you need.

→ For more information about customizing views, **see** "Creating and Customizing Views," **p. 764**.

→ For more information about customizing reports, **see** "Customizing Reports," **p. 672**.

As the project manager, your primary responsibility is to make sure the project runs as close to the project plan as possible. This responsibility involves a lot of constant analysis. Once the project begins to slip, you must fix it right away; the problem certainly will not fix itself, and will only get worse over time.

ANALYSIS VIEWS

The views that are found in Microsoft Project 2007 serve many purposes. Some views are designed for project data entry, and other views are designed for project data analysis. This section will discuss the various views found in Microsoft Project 2007 that can be used for project analysis. Each of these views is customizable and printable.

→ For more information about customizing views, **see** "Creating and Customizing Views," **p. 764**.

→ For more information about printing views, **see** "Printing Views," **p. 771**.

THE TRACKING GANTT VIEW

The tracking views and tables in Microsoft Project 2007 are typically very good for project analysis. The Tracking Gantt view is similar to the Gantt Chart view, but the timescale side also shows tracking information such as percentage complete. It also color-codes the taskbars. Tasks that are complete have a blue taskbar, and uncompleted tasks have a red task bar. The progress on a task is also illustrated within the taskbar, and the overall progress on a project is illustrated under the project summary taskbar (if the project summary task bar is not displayed, you can display it by selecting Tools, Options, and on the View tab, selecting the Show Project Summary Task check box). Below each taskbar is the taskbar for the baseline duration, so you can compare the baseline and actual duration side by side. Refer to Figure 14.25 to see how the Tracking Gantt view displays taskbars.

By default, the Entry table is applied to the Tracking Gantt view, but there are several other tables you can apply that will be useful for analyzing the project.

Figure 14.25
The Tracking Gantt view shows progress in the taskbars on the timescale side.

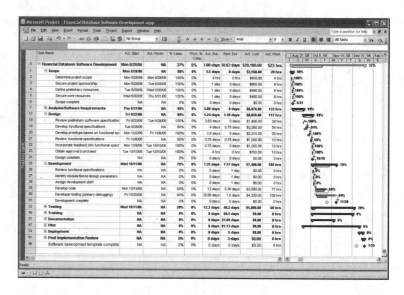

NOTE

While this section describes various tables applied to the Tracking Gantt view for analysis, these tables can be applied to most views in Project. The Tracking Gantt view is used in this discussion because its timescale side aids tremendously in analyzing progress for individual tasks as well as the entire project.

When you apply the Tracking table to the Tracking Gantt view, you combine the tracking timescale with the tracking information, all on one screen. That way, you are able to clearly view your tasks' progress on the timescale side, as well as the following columns of information: Actual Start, Actual Finish, % Complete, Physical % Complete, Actual Duration, Remaining Duration, Actual Cost, and Actual Work. To apply the Tracking table, first display the Tracking Gantt view (View, Tracking Gantt), then select View, Table, More Tables, and select Tracking. The Tracking table is applied to the illustration in Figure 14.25.

The columns of information found in the Tracking table are all practical for project analysis. These fields display a lot of actual information—that is, what is actually happening in each task, such as when it started or finished, how long it took, how much duration is remaining, how much it costs, and so on. Of course, to fully analyze this information, you must compare it to what was planned. That way, you have an idea of what has actually happened versus what was supposed to happen. If there is a lot of variance, you likely need to make some changes in the execution of your project.

The Baseline table provides several columns of information that display the baseline values for the project: Baseline Duration, Baseline Start, Baseline Finish, Baseline Work, and Baseline Cost. To display the Baseline table, choose View, Table, More Tables. Then, in the More Tables dialog box, select Baseline and click Apply.

Now, rather than actual information, you are viewing what was planned. Then, you can compare the baseline values with the actual values. There are two primary means of doing this using the two tables discussed thus far applied to the Tracking Gantt view. The first is to print two version of the Tracking Gantt view—one with the Baseline table applied and one with the Tracking table applied.

→ For more information about printing views, **see** "Printing Views," **p. 771**.

The second option is to insert baseline information into the Tracking table, or insert actual (Tracking) information into the Baseline table. To insert a column into a table, right-click on the column heading where you want the new column inserted and choose Insert Column. Choose the column name you want to insert from the Field Name drop-down list in the Insert Column dialog box and press OK. The new column will appear where you right-clicked, and all other columns will shift to the right. Repeat this process until you have inserted all the columns of information you wish to view.

Another helpful table to apply to the Tracking Gantt view to aid in project analysis is the Variance table. To display the Variance table, select View, Table, Variance. The Variance table is especially useful for analyzing a project's schedule because it summarizes the differences between the Baseline and Tracking (actual) tables for you. This table displays Start and Finish dates, Baseline Start and Baseline Finish dates, and Start Variance and Finish Variance dates. That way, you can examine each task's start and finish dates as compared to what was planned, and whether or not there is any variance. If desired, you can insert more columns of information, such as duration information, to further analyze the schedule.

The Work table is perhaps the most accommodating table to apply to the Tracking Gantt view for project scope analysis. Project scope is essentially the work that needs be done in order to accomplish the goal(s) of the project. Therefore, analyzing work on a project is vital to analyzing scope. To apply the Work table, select View, Table, Work. The Work table displays Work, Baseline (baseline work), Variance (work variance), Actual (actual work), Remaining (remaining work), and Work % Complete. You can evaluate each task or the project as a whole, and see how many work hours were planned, how many were actually performed, any variance between the plan and the actual values, and so on.

The Earned Value table is yet another useful table to apply to the Tracking Gantt view for project analysis. This particular table is best suited for analyzing project budget. The Earned Value table is discussed earlier in this chapter in the sections, "A Summary of Using Earned Value Analysis in Microsoft Project 2007" and "Understanding Earned Value Measurements."

NOTE

As mentioned previously, any and all of the tables described in this section are customizable. Furthermore, any of the columns of information found in these tables can be inserted into any other table. If you wish to combine information from two tables, you can insert the column using the right-click Insert Column command.

14

THE RESOURCE ALLOCATION VIEW

While the Tracking Gantt view and subsequent tables discussed in the previous section are all good for analyzing project tasks, schedule, budget, and scope, the Resource Allocation table is very helpful for analyzing your resource workload. To display the Resource Allocation view, select View, More Views, and in the More Views dialog box, select Resource Allocation.

The Resource Allocation view is a split window. The top pane is the Resource Usage view, which lists the resources and their assigned tasks, and the number of hours each resource is scheduled to work (total as well as per task). The bottom pane by default is the Leveling Gantt view, but you should change it to the Resource Graph view. Change the bottom pane to the Resource Graph view by clicking in the bottom pane to select it, and then in the main menu select View, Resource Graph. The screen will now display a split window: the Resource Usage view on top, and the Resource Graph on the bottom, as shown in Figure 14.26.

Figure 14.26
The Resource Allocation view with the Resource Graph in the bottom of the split window provides a clear view of which resources are over-loaded with work and which are not.

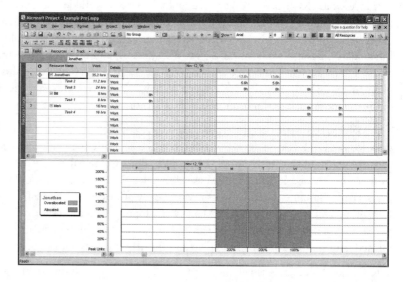

As indicated in Figure 14.26, the bottom pane (Resource Graph) provides a detailed illustration of the workload assigned to the selected resource in the top pane. In this case, Jonathan is overallocated; he is assigned more hours of work than are in a normal working day. On the bottom pane of the Resource Allocation view, the bar graph represents the hours per day he is scheduled to work. Notice that on Monday and Tuesday (November 13th and 14th, 2006), he is scheduled to work 9.67 hours. Since a normal working day is 8 hours, the remaining 1.67 hours are shown in red on the bar graph as overallocated.

→ For additional information on resource overallocations and techniques for resolving them, **see** Chapter 25, "Resolving Resource Allocation Problems," **p. 885**.

The Resource Allocation view is a great way to view all your resources simultaneously, and see whether or not their working hours and assignments are spread evenly across the board.

It is also a great view to examine to see if you can reassign certain assignments to other resources that may not have as large of a workload as some of your overallocated resources.

ANALYSIS REPORTS

Microsoft Project 2007 contains several basic and visual reports to aid in project analysis. These reports offer many options for analyzing project schedule, budget, and scope—the three main components of project analysis. As mentioned previously, all of these reports are customizable and intended for many different audiences. These reports are described in detail in other chapters of the book.

→ For more information about using the basic reports for project analysis, **see** "Using the Basic Reports for Project Analysis," **p. 521**.

→ For more information about using the visual reports for project analysis, **see** "Using Visual Reports," **p. 541**.

USING THE PROJECT GUIDE TOOLBAR

As mentioned throughout this book, the Project Guide is an excellent resource to walk you through various features and functions of Microsoft Project 2007. The same holds true for analyzing performance on your project.

To display the Project Guide toolbar, follow these steps:

1. Enable Project to display Project Guide by opening the Options dialog box by selecting Tools, Options.
2. On the Interface tab, be sure that the Display Project Guide check box is selected. If that box is empty, you will not be able to see or use the Project Guide, so select it and click OK to apply the change and exit the Options dialog box.
3. Right-click on the toolbar area at the top of your screen, and select Project Guide from the Toolbars list. The Project Guide toolbar will appear near the top of your screen.

Five primary buttons appear on the Project Guide toolbar (see Figure 14.27). The first is an icon that displays or hides the Project Guide when you click it. The Project Guide itself is a vertical pane that appears on the left side of the screen when displayed. Many users elect not to display the Project Guide because it takes up more screen space. The four buttons to the right of the Show/Hide Project Guide button are Tasks, Resources, Track, and Report. Clicking on any of these buttons will automatically open the Project Guide for that particular button and display a list of options. Figure 14.27 shows the result of clicking the Report button.

If you want to use the Project Guide toolbar without displaying the Project Guide itself, you can do that by clicking the drop-down arrows to the right of the Tasks, Resources, Track, and Report buttons. These arrows display the same list shown in the Project Guide if you were to click one of the buttons. Figure 14.28 shows this alternative way to choose a Project Guide function.

14

Figure 14.27
Clicking the Report button, or any of the other buttons on the Project Guide toolbar, opens the Project Guide on the left side of your screen and displays a list of options to choose from.

Figure 14.28
As an alternative to displaying the Project Guide options, click the arrow next to Report (or any of the other buttons on the Project Guide toolbar) to show the same list of options available for that particular button.

However, once you choose an option from the drop-down list, the Project Guide pane appears on the left. If you continue to use the Project Guide toolbar, you will need to keep the Project Guide pane displayed until you are finished.

Different panes will become available when using the Project Guide that were not origi-nally listed because they are cross-linked. Depending on which Project Guide pane is selected, additional options may appear indented in the drop-down lists next to the but-tons along the Project Guide taskbar. These additional options are not listed if you click the button itself; they are only listed if you have the appropriate pane already open.

For example, if you select Change the Look or Content of the Gantt Chart under the Report button and then click the arrow next to Report on the Project Guide toolbar, you will notice a new option in the drop-down list indented under the pane you have open called Add Columns of Custom Information. This is a link to another Project Guide pane (in this case, one found under the Tasks button).

ANALYZING PERFORMANCE USING THE PROJECT GUIDE

Most of the options for analyzing performance with the Project Guide are found under the Report button. However, one option under the Track button is significantly useful: Check the Progress of the Project. To display this option, click the Track button on the Project Guide toolbar (or click the arrow next to it) and select Check the Progress of the Project. The Project Guide pane will then walk you through this process (see Figure 14.29).

Figure 14.29
The Project Guide pane will walk you through the process of checking the progress of your pro-ject when you select that option from the Track button on the Project Guide toolbar.

When you select the Check the Progress of the Project option, the Project Guide Custom Tracking table is displayed to the right of the pane (see Figure 14.29). This table contains fields displaying the Status Indicator (as described earlier in this chapter, in the section "The Status and Status Indicator Fields"), % Work Complete, Work, Duration, Start date, Finish date, and Resource Names (due to limited screen space, not all these fields are dis-played in Figure 14.29). The Status Indicators are automatically inserted to help you view the status of each task (see Table 14.1).

14

In the Project Guide pane, the first inquiry you are presented with is to change the status date. You can also apply a filter or a group to display certain tasks or categorize them for more detailed analysis.

When you are finished, you can click Done at the bottom right to close the Project Guide, click the More Information hyperlink to read additional information about checking progress using the Project Guide, or choose another Project Guide option. You can always click the X in the upper-right corner of the pane to close the Project Guide.

TIP

> The various Project Guide pane screens contain helpful hyperlinks to further assist you with analyzing progress (or whatever particular function you are using). These hyperlinks are displayed in blue and have a question mark next to them on the left (see Figure 14.29). For example, there is often a More Information hyperlink at the bottom of each pane. These hyperlinks are quite helpful, and it is good practice to click on them and read their content, especially when you are confused about the process.
>
> Also, many terms found within these Project Guide screens are highlighted and in bold. Hover your mouse pointer over each one for a definition or detailed description of the term.

The rest of the helpful Project Guide functions for analyzing performance are found under the Report button. They are summarized as follows:

- **Select a View or Report**—When you select this option, you are prompted with the choice to display or analyze project information with a view or to create a project report. If you choose the first option, you are given a list of views to choose. Highlight a particular view for a brief summary of its contents. You can also click the See Additional Views hyperlink to open the More Views dialog box.

  If you choose the second option, Create a Project Report, you are given two hyperlinks: Display Visual Reports and Display Reports. Selecting Display Visual Reports opens the Visual Reports – Create Reports dialog box, which is discussed in greater detail in the previous section, "Creating Earned Value Graphs Using Visual Reports." Selecting Display Reports opens the Reports dialog box, in which you can access Microsoft Project's built-in reports, such as the Project Summary report discussed earlier this chapter (in the Reports dialog box, double-click Overview, then double-click Project Summary).

- **Change the Content or Order of Information in a View**—This option allows you to change the content or order of information displayed in a view by applying a filter or group to the view. A filter displays tasks or resources that meet a certain criteria, and a group categorizes tasks or resources depending by their characteristics. The More Filters and More Groups hyperlinks open the More Filters and More Groups dialog boxes, respectively, which contain additional filters or groups not in the primary drop-down lists. Filters and groups can be customized, or you can create new ones. You can then choose to sort the lists by their ID, Start date, Finish date, Priority, Cost, or other options found by clicking the More Sort Options hyperlink. You can also use this pane to change the view (by clicking the Choose a Different View hyperlink).

→ For more information about how to create or customize filters or groups, **see** Chapter 22, "Customizing Views, Tables, Filters, Groups, and Fields," **p. 755**.

- **Change the Look or Content of the Gantt Chart**—Perhaps you want to reformat the Gantt Chart to better analyze your project. Choosing this option displays the Gantt Chart to the right of the Project Guide pane (if it is not already displayed), and gives you four choices for reformatting it: Use the Gantt Chart Wizard, Change the Timescale, Change the Appearance of Gantt Bars, and Add Text to Gantt Bars. Depending on which option you choose, instructions and hyperlinks will be shown underneath the option list. The hyperlinks will open various dialog boxes to reformat the appearance of the Gantt Chart or its contents, or, in the case of the first option, open the Gantt Chart Wizard, which asks you a series of questions to format the Gantt Chart as you want it.

- **Add Columns of Custom Information**—This option becomes available on the Report drop-down list on the Project Guide toolbar when you have Change the Look or Content of the Gantt Chart displayed. It is a link to another Project Guide screen, which originally can be found in the Tasks drop-down list. If you select this option, the Project Guide will walk you through the process of adding default or custom fields to the Gantt Chart by inserting columns.

- **Print Current View as a Report**—This option will simply help you to print the current view you are displaying as a report. There are fours easy steps to this process. When you finish the first step, which is simply deciding on the number of pages in the report, click the Continue to Step 2 hyperlink at the bottom of the screen. Step 2 lets you modify your sizing options, Step 3 lets you insert a header, footer, and/or legend, and Step 4 gives you a final set of options for your report. At any time in this process, you can click the Print Preview button to see a preview of the printed report without actually printing it, or you can click Print to open the Print dialog box and print the report. Some of these options will link you to other printing dialog boxes, such as the Page Setup dialog box.

→ For more information about printing reports, including using the Page Setup dialog box, **see** "Printing Views," **p. 771**.

- **Compare Progress Against Baseline Work**—As mentioned throughout this chapter, capturing the baseline of your project is an imperative step in tracking and analyzing your progress. This option displays the Tracking Gantt Chart view, which will help you to compare the progress of each task to the baseline by inserting the baseline taskbar under the scheduled taskbar in the timescale side. It also displays the actual progress as a percentage (the % Complete value, which measures duration percent complete). Critical tasks are displayed in red, and variance values are shown in the Variance table to the left of the timescale. You can also apply a filter on this Project Guide screen.

- **Save a Baseline Plan to Compare with Later Versions**—This option becomes available in the Report drop-down list when you have the Compare Progress Against Baseline Work pane displayed. It is originally listed under the Track button in the

14

Project Guide toolbar. Selecting it will walk you through the process of capturing a baseline or multiple baselines, which is a very important part of analyzing the performance of your project.

- **See the Project's Critical Tasks**—Critical tasks dictate the finish date of a project. If they are delayed, then the project's finish date is delayed. Critical tasks' taskbars are by default displayed in red, but you can change that by reformatting the Gantt Chart (see the third option in this list, Change the Look or Content of the Gantt Chart). This option will give you the scheduled project finish date, as well as allow you to apply a filter. If you choose Critical from the filter drop-down list, the Gantt Chart will display only critical tasks. The next section, "Analyzing the Critical Path," discusses critical tasks in greater detail.

- **See How Resources' Time Is Allocated**—This option displays the Resource Usage view in the top pane to list all your resources and their assignments. It also lists unassigned tasks. The bottom pane displays the Gantt Chart view with the Earned Value Schedule Indicators table applied. Select a resource or assignment in the top pane to view its details in the bottom pane.

  This screen also displays resources that are overallocated, meaning that particular resource has more work assigned than it can handle in the given time frame. At the bottom of the screen is the hyperlink Resolve Overallocations by Leveling. Leveling delays or reassigns tasks to other resources to level out the workload. Leveling is based on a task's Priority value, set on the General tab in the Task Information dialog box, as well as its available slack time, its dependency relationships (predecessor/successor relationships), and its constraints. The Project Guide will walk you through the leveling process, or you can choose to have Microsoft Project 2007 automatically level your resources. To have Microsoft Project 2007 level your resources, choose Tools, Level Resources, and enter the appropriate commands in the Resource Leveling dialog box.

→ For more information about using the Resource Leveling dialog box, **see** "Using the Level Resources Tools," **p. 902**.

- **See Project Costs**—This option displays the Project Guide: Analyzing Cost table. The pane describes how the cost of a task is usually based on the cost rate(s) of the resource(s) assigned to work on the task. It also briefly discusses cost variance, and allows you to apply a filter to the table. The filters in the drop-down list are all helpful for analyzing cost. Additionally, the Slipping Tasks filter, found in the More Filters dialog box, allows you to view all tasks that are behind schedule. A previous section of this chapter, "Controlling the Calculation of Earned Value," discusses using the Earned Value Cost Indicators table to further analyze cost and its relationship to your project's progress.

ANALYZING THE CRITICAL PATH

Critical tasks drive the project; if they are delayed, then the project's finish date will be delayed. Therefore, when you are analyzing performance on a project, it is most efficient to first analyze the progress of the tasks within the critical path. If you can restore the slipping critical tasks, it is likely that you will reestablish the project back to its planned schedule or within its planned budget.

One way to quickly analyze the critical path is to apply a filter for critical tasks to a table that displays the analysis fields discussed throughout this chapter, such as any of the earned value tables or variance tables. Apply the critical tasks filter by selecting Project, Filtered For, More Filters, choosing Critical from the More Filters dialog box, and clicking Apply (or Highlight to show all tasks, highlighting only the critical tasks). Then examine which critical tasks are slipping and why. If they are over budget, maybe you need to cut back on resources working on the critical tasks to save money. If they are behind schedule, maybe you need to increase the number of resources, or increase the amount of work to get caught up.

When the overall project is slipping, it is good practice to concentrate first on fixing the critical path. This will certainly improve the project's progress, and likely bring it back up to speed.

→ For additional information on critical path analysis, **see** "Reviewing the Big Picture (Critical Path Analysis," **p. 427**.

CONSULTANTS' TIPS

PROJECT PERFORMANCE ANALYSIS PREREQUISITES

When analyzing the performance of your project, remember that you must have performed the following actions in order to properly perform the analysis:

- Spend a good amount of time planning out the work and breaking it down using the Work Breakdown Structure (WBS) technique to ensure that the full project scope has been captured.

- Ensure that the cost data in your project schedule is accurate and matches the financial data against which contract invoicing will be performed.

- Ensure that once you have completed planning, you save the baseline of the project to set a point to compare your project progress to.

- If you make any subsequent changes to the project schedule planned values, ensure that those are within the project scope or that the appropriate change request process has been implemented if the scope was changed. Resave another baseline to capture your project plan changing.

- Use the most accurate information and update your project progress regularly to ensure that the performance analysis you perform is based on the latest actual data.

PROJECT PERFORMANCE ANALYSIS AREAS

When analyzing your project performance, concentrate on the main aspects, which include the following:

14

- **Scope**—Ensure that the project still is within scope by reviewing the task list and scope statements, if you have captured them properly during the planning phase.

- **Budget**—Analyze views and reports described in this chapter to ensure that the budget variance in your schedule is under control and that you notice if the project budget begins to slip.

- **Schedule**—Analyze views and reports described in this chapter to ensure that the project is still scheduled to finish on time. Use any schedule variances you see as a red flag that the project schedule is deviating from the original plan. You can then use additional reports and views to drill in further to determine the source of the problem, so that it can be resolved. This will help you mitigate future risks as well as avoid the current problem getting out of control.

In addition, you want to analyze these areas:

- **Work**—Analyze the work fields, such as Planned Work, Actual Work, and Baseline Work, and Work Variance to ensure that the work being performed is in line with the original plan.

- **Resources**—Analyze the resource allocation and resource performance to ensure that the resources are performing the work as scheduled. This can help you determine whether your resource productivity is good enough. You can potentially replace them with other resources that would perform better. Resource views can also help you determine whether any resources are overallocated and resolve the problem by either redistributing work better, assigning additional resources, or delaying overlapping tasks.

PROJECT PERFORMANCE ANALYSIS OPTIONS

Microsoft Project 2007 provides several tools to help you analyze your project performance:

- Use the Project Information Statistics option to view high-level statistics about your project.

- Use the existing views, such as Tracking Gantt, Earned Value, and many others, as well as customized views achieved by adding more columns.

- Use reports to view additional data, such the Earned Value report and the Earned Value Over Time visual report.

- Employ the help of the Project Guide to view additional options for analyzing the performance of your project.

No matter what technique you use, just remember, that analyzing and tracking your project progress is as important as planning it. The more often you review the progress and performance, the more aware you will be of any problems that can potentially arise and the more prepared you will be to address them and still have your project finish within scope, budget, and schedule.

USING REPORTS FOR TRACKING AND CONTROL

In this chapter

15

This chapter provides background and real-world examples of reporting capabilities that are available in Microsoft Project 2007. Many of the reporting capabilities have been available in previous releases; new in 2007 are Visual Reports that use the power of Excel and Visio to enhance your analysis with graphics. This chapter focuses on reporting using standard reports and covers only the basic capabilities. It is a good starting point, but most projects will need some customization for their specific needs. Customization is not covered in this chapter.

USING BASIC REPORTS

The basic, out-of-the-box reports that come standard in Microsoft Office Project 2007 can be used in various ways by the project manager for tracking and controlling a project. A total of 29 basic reports come with Microsoft Project 2007, most of which fall into one of five categories: Overview, Current Activities, Costs, Assignments, or Workload. To access these reports, open the Reports dialog box by selecting Report, Reports from the main menu. The Reports dialog box will appear, as shown in Figure 15.1.

Figure 15.1
The Reports dialog box contains the basic report categories.

To open a specific report, select the category from the Reports dialog box (such as Overview, Current Activities, and so on) and click Select. The dialog box for that particular report category will appear, and you can select the report you wish to view.

Seven additional basic reports are not found in any of the five basic report categories. These remaining reports are listed in the Custom Reports dialog box. To open the Custom Reports dialog box, open the Reports dialog box (Report, Reports) and select Custom. The Custom Reports dialog box will appear, as shown in Figure 15.2.

Figure 15.2
The Custom Reports dialog box lists all 29 basic reports found in Microsoft Project 2007.

The list in the Custom Reports dialog box contains all 29 basic reports that are found in Microsoft Project 2007. Each of these reports is customizable; however, their degree of customization varies. A few reports are only able to be customized in their text format, whereas most other reports are able to be customized to include specific data that you wish to view on the report. Also, you have the option to design a new report from scratch if none of the existing reports satisfies your requirements. Customizing existing reports and creating new ones are excellent methods for constructing a report that contains exactly the columns of information you wish to display.

TIP

Take advantage of the customization options available for each report. You can reformat the heading text to make the report more visually appealing, add or take away various columns of information and other details found in the report, change the sort order for the items in the report, rename the report, modify the time period of information to display in the report, and so on. Before working extensively with reports, read through Chapter 20, "Creating and Customizing the Basic Reports," to familiarize yourself with all the customization options you have for each report.

→ For more information about customizing existing basic reports and creating new ones, as well as complete tables listing the basic reports found in each category, **see** Chapter 20, "Creating and Customizing the Basic Reports," **p. 657**.

The first part of this chapter will focus on using the existing basic reports for tracking and controlling your project, and later the chapter will focus on using visual reports for the same purpose.

The data contained in the basic reports can be advantageous for different purposes and different audiences. Some reports may be beneficial for project analysis, some may be useful for status reports for the project sponsor, and some may be useful for status meetings with your project team. The next several sections are organized by the basic reports' functionality with examples of who might find them useful and why.

NOTE

This chapter will provide insight regarding which standard reports are most useful for certain situations. It is advised that you read through Chapter 20, along with this chapter. Chapter 20 discusses how you can modify each report, change the page setup and print options you have available, and other options to make reports suitable for your audience.

→ For more information about common interaction within each report, **see** "Using the Common Customization Controls," **p. 678**.

USING THE BASIC REPORTS FOR PROJECT ANALYSIS

All of the preexisting reports in Microsoft Project 2007 are very helpful in analyzing the progress of a project's current resource utilization. As the project manager, your main focus is to keep the project moving forward as close to its estimates as possible. Basic reports provide a wide variety of ways to examine three key aspects of project analysis: schedule, budget, and resource usage. The upcoming sections discuss which reports are useful in examining these three core components of project analysis.

USING THE BASIC REPORTS FOR ANALYZING THE PROJECT SCHEDULE

Many of the reports for project analysis in Microsoft Project 2007 involve analyzing the schedule. When analyzing a project schedule, you are looking at how work is being completed on tasks compared to how it was planned and captured in the baseline. You do not want to see a lot of schedule variance, and you definitely do not want to see a lot of slipping tasks—especially slipping tasks in the critical path.

NOTE

> The accuracy of these analysis reports (and most reports in Microsoft Project 2007 for that matter) depends heavily on the accuracy of your tracking. For example, if a task has started but your tracking is not current, it will appear in the Unstarted Tasks report, even though in reality it has started.

→ For more information about accurately tracking your tasks' progress, **see** "Entering Tracking Information at the Task Level," **p. 451**.

The Current Activities report category contains six reports, all of which are great for analyzing your schedule. To access these reports, open the Current Activity Reports dialog box by opening the Reports dialog box (Report, Reports) and selecting Current Activities. The Current Activity Reports dialog box will appear, as shown in Figure 15.3.

Figure 15.3
The Current Activity Reports dialog box contains six reports, all of which can be used for schedule analysis.

THE UNSTARTED TASKS REPORT   The first report in the Current Activities category is the Unstarted Tasks report. This report lists all tasks that have yet to start, according to your tracking information, as well as any notes attached to the task and the resources assigned to it (see Figure 15.4).

Figure 15.4
The Unstarted Tasks report lists all unstarted tasks in the project.

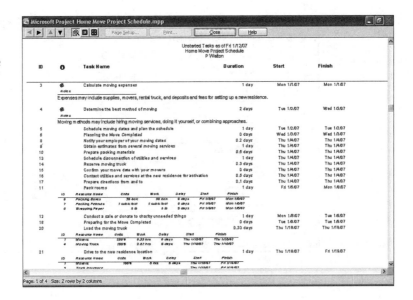

The Unstarted Tasks report provides a great look at which tasks are forthcoming. To view it, select Unstarted Tasks from the Current Activity Reports dialog box.

THE TASKS STARTING SOON REPORT   The second report in the Current Activities category is the Tasks Starting Soon report. This is an interactive report in which you define a date range, and Microsoft Project 2007 compiles a report listing all tasks that will start or finish within the date range you define. If, for example, you or other members of your project team will be away for a week, you may want to view the Tasks Starting Soon report for that particular week to see if any of the tasks need special attention before you go out of town. Or, if you know a particular upcoming date range will be extremely busy (or not busy for that matter), you may want to view this report to see if your hectic agenda will allow the project schedule to continue as planned. If not, you can make adjustments before it is too late.

To display the Tasks Starting Soon report, select Tasks Starting Soon from the Current Activity Reports dialog box, and Microsoft Project 2007 will prompt you with two interactive Date Range dialog boxes. The first will ask you to select a date to Show Tasks That Start Or Finish After (the selected date), and when you click OK, the second dialog box asks you to choose a date to close out the Date Range. For example, in Figure 15.5, the report's Date Range dialog boxes were used to define a 2-week date range from January 12th, 2007, through January 26th, 2007. The resulting report in Figure 15.5 lists all tasks that start or finish within that date range.

Figure 15.5
The Tasks Starting Soon report lists all tasks that start or finish within the date range you define.

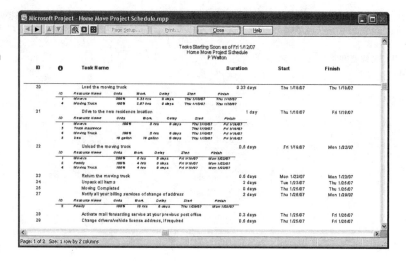

THE TASKS IN PROGRESS REPORT   The third report in the Current Activities category is the Tasks In Progress report. This report lists all tasks that have started but not yet reached completion. This report may be particularly useful to review what is currently being worked on. Since the report also lists the resources assigned to the tasks, the Tasks In Progress report can also serve as a guide to which resources are currently active, and which resources may be available for other assignments.

To display the Tasks In Progress report, select Tasks In Progress from the Current Activity Reports dialog box.

Figure 15.6 displays a Tasks In Progress report. In this particular example, two tasks are currently being worked on. Notice their finish dates; they were both scheduled to finish before this report was generated. The Tasks In Progress report can be very useful in quickly identifying tasks that are not on schedule.

Figure 15.6
The Tasks In Progress report lists all tasks that are currently being worked on, even if their scheduled finished date has passed.

THE COMPLETED TASKS REPORT The fourth report in the Current Activities category is the Completed Tasks report. This report lists all tasks that have been defined as complete. In the Gantt Chart view, these tasks would all have a check mark in the Indicators column, signifying their completion.

The Completed Task report also lists tasks' start and finish dates, duration, percent complete, cost, and actual work values. In Figure 15.7, the actual work values are not shown because they are on the next page of the report, but they are included in the report by default.

Figure 15.7
For a list of completed tasks, print the Completed Tasks report.

This report is a good reference if you want to quickly double-check whether a task has been completed. Or, if you know a task is complete, you may check this report to verify that you have updated its tracking information.

THE SHOULD HAVE STARTED TASKS REPORT The fifth report in the Current Activities category is particularly helpful: the Should Have Started Tasks report. This is another interactive report. To view the report, select Should Have Started Tasks from the Current Activity Reports dialog box. You will be prompted with a Should Start By dialog box, in which you enter a date. Microsoft Project 2007 then compiles a report that lists all tasks that should have started by the date you defined, but have no work recorded.

A good practice to follow with this report is to display the report as of the current Status Date (enter the status date in the Should Start By dialog box). Microsoft Project 2007 will then list all tasks that should have started by the status date, but have no progress recorded. This will indicate to you one of two things:

- The tasks on the report are slipping.
- You need to update your tracking information.

If the tasks on the report are slipping, and if they are critical tasks, then your project is slipping as well, because if critical tasks are late, then the project will finish late (remember, critical tasks are those that affect the project's finish date).

On the other hand, if there are tasks on the report that you are sure have started, then the report is a good indication that you need to update your tracking information, because Microsoft Project 2007 has no record of any work complete on the task(s).

By default, summary tasks are included in the report. Only those summary tasks that have subtasks that are late will be included in the report.

Figure 15.8 shows an example of a Should Have Started Tasks report.

Figure 15.8
The Should Have Started Tasks report shows you any tasks that were scheduled to start by a certain date but have not, indicating either that they are slipping (the case in this example) or that their tracking information is not accurately updated.

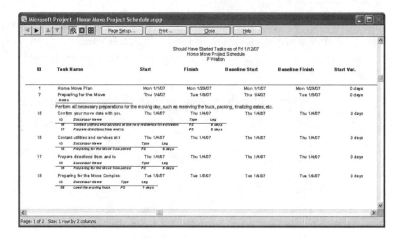

THE SLIPPING TASKS REPORT   The sixth and final report found in the Current Activities category is the Slipping Tasks report. A task is said to be slipping when it is running late, meaning that its actual finish date is later than the baseline finish. To display the Slipping Tasks report, select Slipping Tasks from the Current Activity Reports dialog box. The Slipping Tasks report will be displayed, as shown in Figure 15.9.

Figure 15.9
The Slipping Tasks report lists all tasks that are slipping.

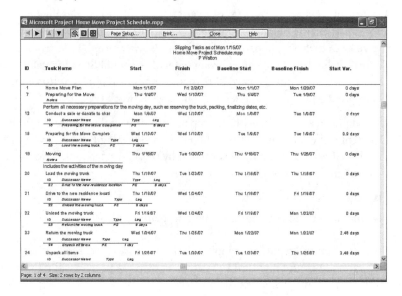

TIP

> Many of the basic reports depend on the use of the baseline fields for comparison. If you have not set a project baseline or have added tasks after the baseline was set, your reports may not have comparison data available.

If you do not have any tasks that are slipping in your project schedule, and you try to view the Slipping Tasks report, you will receive a warning box like the one shown in Figure 15.10. This box states that you do not have data for this particular report. In this case, you do not have slipping tasks. This warning box appears any time you try to view a report for which you have no data.

Figure 15.10
If no items are selected by a report's filter, the report cannot be generated, and you will receive this message.

THE OVERALLOCATED RESOURCES REPORT   Another report that may be useful for analyzing the project schedule is the Overallocated Resources report. This report lists all resources that have been assigned more work hours (effort) than their schedule can handle. It then lists their task assignments below the resource names.

In the example in Figure 15.11, the Movers resource has been assigned to work more hours over the course of 3 days than the baseline working schedule defines. Therefore, the Movers resource will have to work overtime, unless you reschedule the tasks or assign different resources.

To view the Overallocated Resources report, select the Assignments category from the Reports dialog box, and in the Assignment Reports dialog box, select the fourth report, Overallocated Resources. The Overallocated Resources report will be displayed, as shown in Figure 15.11.

Figure 15.11
The Overallocated Resources report lists all resources that have been assigned more work than their schedules allow for.

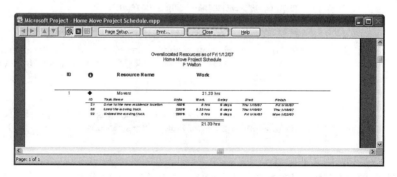

You should examine the Overallocated Resources report to see which resources are overallocated, and adjust the schedule or assign different resources to some of the tasks to resolve the overallocation. You also have the option of letting Microsoft Project 2007 level your resources. If you let the resource overallocations remain intact, they may not be able to complete the tasks as scheduled unless they work overtime to keep up with the schedule. By using the Overallocated Resources report, you can catch the problem before work on the tasks begins and make the adjustments so the tasks do not slip.

→ For more information about fixing resource overallocations, **see** "Strategies for Correcting Resource Allocation Problems," **p. 898**.

THE TASK AND RESOURCE USAGE REPORTS The fifth category, Workload, contains two reports that are helpful in analyzing your project schedule: the Task Usage report and the Resource Usage report. To access these reports, open the Workload Reports dialog box by selecting Workload in the Reports dialog box (Report, Reports, Workload). In the Workload Reports dialog box, select either the Task Usage report or the Resource Usage report.

The Task Usage report lists all the tasks in a project with all associated resources that have been assigned to work on each task. The columns are divided into weeks by default, and the amount of hours scheduled (for work resources) or units of measurement scheduled (for material resources) is listed for each week. The totals are calculated for both rows and columns as well. You can change the columns from Weeks to another time unit on the Definition tab of the Crosstab Report definition dialog box.

→ For more information about changing the time unit in the Task Usage report (or any Crosstab report), **see** "Using the Definition Tab to Customize a Crosstab Report," **p. 696**.

The Resource Usage report is similar to a Task Usage report in that it lists time-phased information (weekly by default) of the amount of hours (work resources) or other units of measurement (material resources) scheduled for each task. The row items are arranged by resources instead of tasks in the Resource Usage report. The report lists all resources and the respective task assignments below the each resource name. It also includes totals for each week, as well as totals for each task and for each resource.

TIP

> For complex projects, the use of filters and views may make analysis of task and resource data easier than using basic reports.

→ For more information about using filters and views for data analysis, **see** Chapter 11, "Using Standard Views, Tables, Filters, and Groups to Review Your Schedule," **p. 369**.

→ For more information about customizing filters and views, **see** Chapter 22, "Customizing Views, Tables, Filters, Groups, and Fields," **p. 755**.

USING THE BASIC REPORTS FOR ANALYZING THE PROJECT BUDGET

You can use several reports to aid in analyzing your project's budget. The majority of these reports can be found in the Costs reports category. To access them, open the Reports dialog box (Report, Reports) and select Costs. This will open the Cost Reports dialog box, as shown in Figure 15.12.

Figure 15.12
The Cost Reports dialog box contains five basic reports that are helpful in analyzing your project's budget.

THE CASH FLOW REPORT   The first report in the Costs category is the Cash Flow report. This Crosstab report lists the total amount of money needed each week for each task, as well as the weekly totals and the total cost for each task. Alternatively, you can arrange the columns to display information every day, month, or other time unit by customizing the report. This report is helpful for anticipating upcoming costs for tasks in your project.

→ For more information about customizing a Crosstab report's time unit, **see** "Customizing Crosstab Reports," **p. 695**.

Figure 15.13 shows an example of a Cash Flow report. Total cost by task is displayed in the far-right column, whereas total cost per week is displayed along the bottom row. To display this report in your project, select Cash Flow from the Cost Reports dialog box.

Figure 15.13
The Cash Flow report is a Crosstab report that lists each task in the row information and the weekly cost in each column.

THE BUDGET REPORT The second report in the Costs category is the Budget report. This report is very helpful in that it provides a quick overview as to where your project budget stands as compared to the baseline plan. The columns listed in the Budget report are Fixed Cost, Total Cost, Baseline Cost, Variance (between actual and baseline cost), Actual Cost, and Remaining Cost, all listed by task. With one report, you are able to view each task's actual cost as compared to the baseline. In other words, you are able to see how you are doing as compared to how you planned to do financially with each task and the overall project budget. The totals are calculated and displayed at the bottom of each column as well.

To view the Budget report, select Budget from the Cost Reports dialog box. Figure 15.14 shows an example of a Budget report.

Figure 15.14
The Budget report provides a quick look at the actual cost of your tasks as compared to the baseline.

THE OVERBUDGET TASKS REPORT The third report in the Costs category is the Overbudget Tasks report. This is a great report to view tasks that have gone or are on their way to going overbudget. The report lists the same columns of information as the Budget report: Fixed Cost, Total Cost, Baseline, Variance, Actual, and Remaining. It also totals all of these columns at the bottom.

Figure 15.15 shows an example of an Overbudget Tasks report. Again, the last two fields (Actual and Remaining cost) are cut off because the report does not fit onto one screen. To view this report, select Tasks Overbudget from the Cost Reports dialog box.

Figure 15.15
The Overbudget Tasks report lists all tasks that are going over budget and thus negatively affecting your project's overall budget.

The tasks in an Overbudget Tasks report are listed by default in order of their cost variance, from most variance to least. Therefore, the most problematic tasks in terms of their budget are listed at the top. The totals at the bottom of the report also give you an idea of how far off your project is from the baseline, especially the Variance total value. The report includes tasks that are complete as well as in progress.

If your project is going over budget, the Overbudget Tasks report is an excellent point of reference as to which tasks are causing it.

THE OVERBUDGET RESOURCES REPORT   The fourth report in the Costs category is the Overbudget Resources report. This report is similar to the Overbudget Tasks report, except it lists resources instead of tasks. The Overbudget Resources report includes the following column information: Cost, Baseline Cost, Variance, Actual Cost, and Remaining cost. Like the Overbudget Tasks report, the Overbudget Resources report is very helpful in determining which resources are going over budget in their assignments.

The resources are sorted by their cost variance values, from highest variance to lowest. The column information values are also totaled at the bottom of the report, giving you the sums of all resource overbudget information as well as individual data. This report will help you to establish which (if any) resources are considerably more over budget than the rest of your resources. This report can be very useful for material resources or other nonhuman resources where you are not able to see a direct correlation between amount of effort and cost.

Figure 15.16 shows an example of an Overbudget Resources report. To view this report, choose Overbudget Resources from the Cost Reports dialog box.

Figure 15.16
The Overbudget Resources report displays those resources that are going over budget in their assignments.

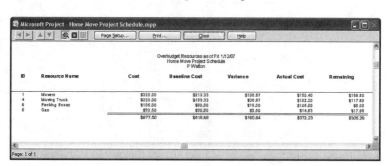

THE EARNED VALUE REPORT   The fifth and final report in the Costs category can be very effective for budget analysis: the Earned Value report. However, it is worth noting again that this report is useless unless you have captured your baseline and tracked all project data accurately. It is also very important that a correct WBS is in place and under change control; otherwise, the earned value statistics may be misleading.

→ For more information about capturing the baseline and accurately tracking your tasks' progress, **see** Chapter 13, "Tracking Your Project Progress," **p. 443**.

To view the Earned Value report, select Earned Value from the Cost Reports dialog box. Figures 15.17 and 15.18 show an example of an Earned Value report. They are separated into two illustrations because not all the fields fit onto one screen.

Figure 15.17
The Earned Value report measures what each task has earned compared to what it was expected to earn. This illustration shows the first screen in the report.

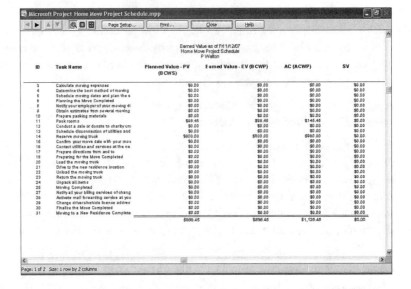

Figure 15.18
This illustration shows the second screen in an Earned Value report.

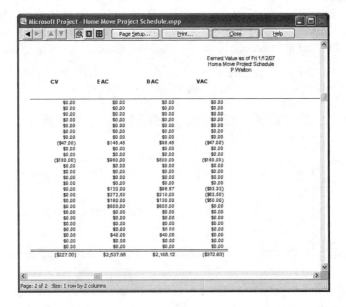

Earned value analysis can be a helpful tool for a project manager. As you may recall from Chapter 14, earned value analysis utilizes the concept of establishing a baseline value of the work being performed and comparing it to the planned value (schedule) as well as the actual value spent to date. All of these items use dollars as the common unit of measure. The Earned Value report shows the cumulative amount of Earned Value compared to Scheduled Value and Actual Cost of the project up to the Status Date. The report displays all of this information, providing you with an opportunity to quickly and easily compare earned, planned, and actual values for each individual task. The total summed values for all tasks are also included in this report. Although the report appears to roll up values at the Summary Tasks, Microsoft Project 2007 actually calculates earned value at all levels of the project.

Table 15.1 lists all the column headings in the Earned Value report. Since most of these fields are abbreviated, their full name is written out in the table, along with a brief definition.

TABLE 15.1   THE EARNED VALUE REPORT COLUMN INFORMATION

Abbreviation	Full Name	Brief Definition
PV (BCWS)	Planned Value (Budgeted Cost of Work Scheduled)	Amount of cost of scheduled work, captured in the baseline
EV (BCWP)	Earned Value (Budget Cost of Work Performed)	The percentage of Planned Value earned by the amount of actual work completed
AC (ACWP)	Actual Cost (Actual Cost of Work Performed)	The actual cost of work completed
SV	Schedule Variance	The difference between the Planned Value and the Earned Value (EV–PV)
CV	Cost Variance	The difference between Earned Value and Actual Cost (EV–AC)
EAC	Estimated At Completion	The estimated total cost for the task when it is completed
BAC	Budget At Completion	The total Planned Value for the task when it is completed
VAC	Variance At Completion	The difference between the total baseline (planned) cost and the estimated total cost (BAC–EAC)

→ For a more detailed explanation of earned value analysis, including more detailed definitions of the fields listed in Table 15.1, **see** "Analyzing Performance with Earned Value Analysis," **p. 491**.

If you have captured your baseline and tracked your progress accurately, the Earned Value report provides a very helpful reference to how each task in your project is earning value as compared to what was planned.

USING BASIC REPORTS FOR THE PROJECT SPONSOR

The project sponsor or other project stakeholders are primarily interested in how the project is doing overall: trends, whether or not it will finish on time, within budget, and if the project deliverables will be completed as defined in the project scope. Project sponsors should not be expected to review detail reports regarding the entire project. They hired or appointed you as the project manager so they would not have to worry about tracking and

15

controlling the project's details. Therefore, the basic reports that are typically presented to project sponsors show the three main areas they are concerned with: schedule, budget, and scope. They want to know how things are going as compared to the plan: what is working, what is not working, and what your plan is to bring unsuccessful areas of the project back to the level of success you planned for.

The best project sponsors use reports to understand the status of your project and monitor trends. They typically get more involved only when asked to support your decisions or to help when you need executive support to resolve problems.

The Overview reports category contains two reports that may be of significant interest to your project sponsor, described in the following sections.

THE PROJECT SUMMARY REPORT

The Project Summary report is a great snapshot of where the project is as of the current date. A project sponsor would benefit from periodically viewing the Project Summary report. On a single page, it displays Start and Finish Dates, Duration, Work, Costs, Task and Resource Status, and Notes for the project. In most of these areas, the Project Summary report lists baseline and actual data, as well as variance, allowing for the project sponsor to quickly read what was planned versus what is actually happening, and the difference between the two values. The Task Status area tells you how many tasks have finished, have not started, are in progress, and the total number of tasks, whereas the Resource Status area gives you the number of work and material resources, overallocated work resources, and total number of resources.

NOTE

> For the data to be entirely accurate in the Project Summary report, you must baseline your project and track your progress correctly.

→ For more information about baselining and tracking your project, **see** Chapter 13, "Tracking Your Project Progress," **p. 443**.

To display the Project Summary report, open the Reports dialog box (Report, Reports), select the Overview category, and then select Project Summary. The Project Summary report will be displayed, as shown in Figure 15.19.

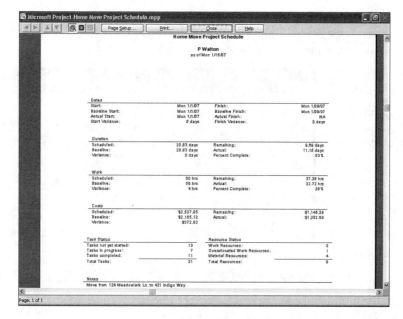

Figure 15.19
Project sponsors will appreciate the Project Summary report because it displays a snapshot of the project statistics as of the current date, and includes baseline, actual, and variance data.

→ For more information about the Project Summary report, including how to modify the header and text information, **see** "The Project Summary Report," **p. 662**, and "Customizing the Project Summary Report," **p. 683**.

THE MILESTONES REPORT

The project sponsor probably does not want to see the status of each task on a project, especially if the project involves a long task list. Instead, he or she can view the planned schedule for delivery of major components in the project.

The Milestones report is a good report to share with the project sponsor because it lists each milestone you define in the project schedule. A milestone should be created for the completion of deliverables and major phases within the project.

→ For more information about creating milestones, including a list of when to create a milestone, **see** "Defining Milestones," **p. 177**.

Milestones reports also include the summary tasks in the project. You can opt to not show summary tasks by editing the report using the Task Report definition dialog box.

→ For more information about editing the report using the Task Report definition dialog box, **see** "Customizing Task and Resource Reports," **p. 685**.

The milestone and summary task's ID number is displayed in the report, as well as notes attached to it. The Indicator column is also displayed, and indicates whether the milestone is finished (a check mark) or not, as well as whether or not the item is a summary task. In Figure 15.20, task numbers 2, 7, 19, and 26 are summary tasks. Notice the indicator for those items.

15

To view the Milestones report, open the Reports dialog box (Report, Reports) and select the Overview category. On the Overview Reports dialog box, select Milestones. The Milestones report will be displayed, as shown in Figure 15.20.

Figure 15.20
The Milestones report lists all project milestones and their start and finish dates, which may be of significant interest to the project sponsor. The check marks indicate that the milestones are complete.

USING BASIC REPORTS FOR THE PROJECT TEAM

Similar to reports for a project sponsor, there are a number of existing reports in Microsoft Project 2007 that will assist your project team. As the project manager, one of your main responsibilities is effective use of your resources by appropriate allocation of tasks across all members of your project team, and making sure they are completing their assignments on time and within budget. If situations arise that prevent them from completing their tasks, you must rearrange the schedule and solve the problem causing the delay.

To be a successful project manager, you must have an effective line of communication with your project team members. Every project manager has his or her own methods for maintaining communication with their team, but the one thing every project manager will agree on is you have to communicate regularly. Perhaps you hold status meetings every day, week, or month, or require your team members to submit written progress reports. No matter what your methodology is, the existing reports in Microsoft Project 2007 will help maintain the imperative line of communication, and thus help you effectively manage your project.

REPORTS FOR YOUR PROJECT TEAM IN THE OVERVIEW CATEGORY

The Overview reports category contains a few reports that your team would benefit from seeing and familiarizing themselves with. The Milestones report, discussed previously in this chapter, is a good report to print and post in your team's office, especially at the beginning of the project, because it displays all the major phases in the project and when the expected start and finish dates are. To view the Milestones report, open the Reports dialog box (Report, Reports), select the Overview category, and in the Overview Reports dialog box, select Milestones. When the Milestones report is open to the Print Preview screen, as in Figure 15.20, you can click the Print button to open the Print dialog box, define your print options, and print the report.

THE CRITICAL TASKS REPORT   The Critical Tasks report is another helpful report to print and post around the office. The Critical Tasks report displays all tasks that affect the project finish date. If tasks on the critical path slip, then the project finish date will likely be delayed. Making your team aware of the critical path tasks may help to avoid having any of the critical tasks slip, because your team will be more familiar with which tasks drive the project and their significance to an on-time project completion.

To display the Critical Tasks report, open the Reports dialog box (Report, Reports), select the Overview category, and choose Critical Tasks in the Overview Reports dialog box. The Critical Tasks report will be displayed in the Print Preview screen, as shown in Figure 15.21, and you can click Print to define your print options or Page Setup to modify the formatting of the report.

Figure 15.21
The Critical Tasks report lists all tasks in the critical path, which would be beneficial for your team to be familiar with.

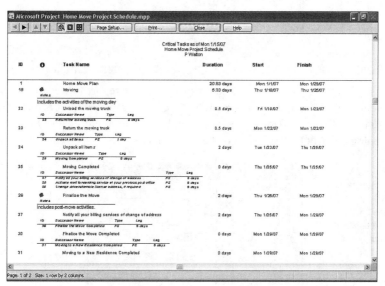

→ For more information about modifying the options in the Page Setup dialog box, **see** "Choosing the Page Setup Options for a Report," **p. 679**.

THE WORKING DAYS REPORT   The Working Days report is another helpful report to print and post around your office or workspace. The Working Days report displays the calendar of working time defined for each base calendar in the Microsoft Project 2007, including any exceptions (such as holidays). This will provide your project team members with a clear idea of when they are expected to be working on your project, and allow them to plan for any of their own personal exceptions to the working time.

To display the Working Days report, open the Reports dialog box (Report, Reports), select the Overview category, and choose Working Days. The Working Days report will be displayed, as shown in Figure 15.22, and you can print the report from the Print Preview screen by clicking the Print button to open the Print dialog box.

Figure 15.22
The Working Days report lets your team know exactly when the defined working hours for your project are.

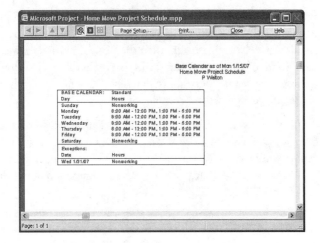

REPORTS FOR YOUR PROJECT TEAM IN THE ASSIGNMENTS CATEGORY

The Assignments category contains a total of four reports, three of which are very useful for your project team. To access them, open the Assignment Reports dialog box by opening the Reports dialog box (Report, Reports) and selecting Assignments. The Assignment Reports dialog box will be displayed, as shown in Figure 15.23.

Figure 15.23
The first three reports listed in the Assignment Reports dialog box are all useful for your project team to view.

THE WHO DOES WHAT REPORT   The first report listed in the Assignment Reports dialog box is the Who Does What report. This report lists the resources that have been assigned to tasks in the project, and underneath their names, it lists the tasks they are assigned to (see Figure 15.24). This is a good overview of resource assignments in the project.

The Who Does What report also indicates if a resource is overallocated (or more than one resource is needed) in the Indicator column, like the Movers resource in Figure 15.24. A quick look will show that the Units field is allocated at 200% for certain tasks. If only one resource is assigned, that resource is overallocated and you may need to reassign some of the overallocated resources' tasks to another resource who has availability.

Figure 15.24
Your project team should be familiar with the Who Does What report, which displays each resource and the tasks they are assigned to.

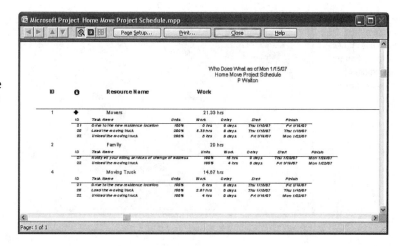

THE WHO DOES WHAT WHEN REPORT   The second report in the Assignment Reports dialog box is the Who Does What When report. This report is a Crosstab report, displaying resources and their assigned tasks as row information, and the amount of time scheduled for each task per time unit as column information. By default, the time unit is defined as Days. However, this can provide for a very lengthy report, so you may want to modify the time unit to Weeks, as in Figure 15.25.

Figure 15.25
The Who Does What When report lists the resources, their assigned tasks, and their scheduled time to work on each task.

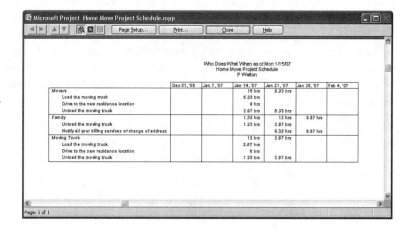

To modify the time unit to Weeks, follow these steps:

1. Open the Assignment Reports dialog box by selecting Assignments from the Reports dialog box.

2. Click on Who Does What When and then click Edit. The Crosstab Report definition dialog box will open, as shown in Figure 15.26.

Figure 15.26
You can define the time unit to use in the column information on the Definition tab of the Crosstab Report dialog box.

3. Under the Column heading, select Weeks from the drop-down list, as shown in Figure 15.26.

4. Click OK to apply the change and close the dialog box. You can then display the Who Does What When report by clicking it and then clicking Select in the Assignment Reports dialog box. The change will be applied.

→ For more information about modifying a Crosstab report, **see** "Customizing Crosstab Reports," **p. 695**.

The Who Does What When report is similar to the Who Does What report, only the Who Does What When report displays both the tasks assigned to the resources and the time they are scheduled to be working on them. This may be helpful for the project team members so they know which resources are working on certain tasks, and when they will be working on them. That way, if you or any of the project team needs to communicate with a particular resource, you can check this report to get an idea of where the needed resource is or what that person is working on.

THE TO-DO LIST REPORT   The third report in the Assignments category is the To-do List report. This is an interactive report, meaning that if you select it, the Using Resource dialog box will appear asking you to select which resource to create the report for. This dialog box is shown in Figure 15.27.

Figure 15.27
Select a resource and create the To-do List report for that resource in the Using Resource dialog box.

Select the resource from the drop-down list in the Using Resource dialog box, and a To-do List report will be created for that particular resource. In Figure 15.28, the resource called Family was chosen, and the resulting to-do list displays all tasks assigned to the Family resource, grouped by weeks.

Figure 15.28
The To-do List report shows all tasks assigned for a particular resource.

The To-do List report is useful for printing and passing out to the resources on your project team. That way, they know exactly what their assignments are, how long they are scheduled to complete each assignment, when it should start and finish, and what additional resources (if any) are assigned to the task.

> **TIP**
>
> If you hold regular status meetings with your project team, you probably review the overall upcoming schedule for each particular phase in the project. To emphasize each team members' roles even more, it may be beneficial for you to print out individual To-do List reports for the resources that lists all their assignments between the current meeting and the next. That way, at each meeting, you can give them a new To-do List report that lists all their assignments for the upcoming week, month, or whatever time frame you use.

→ For more information about changing the time frame in a To-do List report (or any Task or Resource report), **see** "Using the Definition Tab for Task and Resource List Reports," **p. 688**.

Some organizations use a technique called a *stand-up meeting* (named this because all team members remain standing during the meeting to keep it short) on a daily basis when they are in a critical phase of a project. During this short meeting, they will focus on the "Plan of the Day" and only discuss work that is to be done that day. The To-do List is an excellent report to use in this type of meeting.

USING VISUAL REPORTS

New to Microsoft Project 2007, visual reports are visual representations of project data. Visual reports are created using either Microsoft Office Excel or Microsoft Office Visio. The data is compiled into charts or graphs in each report, most of which offer three-dimensional functionality. All visual reports are customizable both in their appearance and in their content. You also have the ability to create a new template for a visual report if none of the existing templates meets your requirements.

15

TIP

> The greatest advantage visual reports have over basic reports is the fact that the graphical representation provides information in an intuitive, easy-to-read fashion. Microsoft Project's customization capabilities for visual reports provide a significant amount of room to modify the report exactly the way you want it to look. Therefore, take the time to customize these reports so their appearance is very appealing and their data is represented clearly and professionally. The figure illustrations throughout this section all contain reports that have been customized.

→ For more information about creating or customizing visual reports, **see** Chapter 21, "Creating and Customizing Visual Reports," **p. 707**.

Visual reports are excellent tools for tracking and controlling your project. Like the basic reports, visual reports provide detailed information about a particular aspect of your project. They are also very helpful to print and distribute to your project sponsor, team, or other project stakeholders. Whereas basic reports display data primarily in a text format, visual reports display the data in attractive charts, graphs, or other customizable formats, making them more exciting and more visually appealing than the basic reports.

To access the templates for visual reports, open the Visual Reports – Create Report dialog box by selecting Report, Visual Reports from the main menu. The Visual Reports – Create Report dialog box will appear, as shown in Figure 15.29.

Figure 15.29
The existing templates for the visual reports are divided into seven categories (tabs) in the Visual Reports – Create Report dialog box.

Seven tabs house the existing visual report templates found in the Visual Reports – Create Report dialog box: All, Task Usage, Resource Usage, Assignment Usage, Task Summary, Resource Summary, and Assignment Summary. You can choose to display visual reports created in either Excel or Visio by selecting the box next to either program at the top of the dialog box. If you check Excel, then only the Excel visual reports are listed. By default, both Excel and Visio are selected.

You can also define the time period that the data is displayed in by selecting Days, Weeks, Months, Quarters, or Years from the drop-down list in the Select Level of Usage Data to Include in the Report field, located near the bottom of the dialog box (refer to Figure 15.29).

Visual reports are OLAP (On-Line Analytical Processing) reports. OLAP databases are also known as *OLAP cubes* because they include several dimensions such as projects, tasks, resources, and time, with summarized data such as work, cost, and availability. Therefore, the visual reports in Project 2007 take various dimensions and create a three-dimensional cube, enabling you to slice into the data and analyze it based on more than one factor. Rather than an X,Y comparison, visual reports provide an X,Y,Z comparison.

→ For more information about Microsoft Project's visual reports, including a table listing all existing visual report templates and which type they are (Excel or Visio), **see** "Introduction to Visual Reports," **p. 708**.

The following sections discuss which of the existing visual reports are best suited for tracking and controlling your project. They are broken up by their audience: visual reports for project analysis, project sponsors, and the project team.

USING VISUAL REPORTS FOR PROJECT ANALYSIS

Like the basic reports, the visual reports in Microsoft Project 2007 can aid tremendously in analyzing your project. Visual report templates exist in Microsoft Project 2007 that will help you analyze the project schedule and budget. With the help of these reports, you will be able to clearly identify problem areas in your project and make the necessary adjustments to get things back on track.

As noted earlier, it is very important that you have captured your baseline correctly, and that you have accurately recorded your tracking information. If not, your analysis will be inaccurate, because your data is not current.

→ For more information about capturing the baseline correctly, **see** "Working with Project Baselines," **p. 445**.

→ For more information about accurately tracking your project's progress, **see** "Tracking Your Project's Performance and Costs," **p. 449**.

USING THE VISUAL REPORTS FOR ANALYZING THE PROJECT SCHEDULE

A handful of visual reports in Microsoft Project 2007 will come in handy when you analyze your project schedule. The main focus in analyzing your project schedule is to see how your resources are working as compared to what was planned. Are they finishing on time? Are they finishing early or late consistently? What you are hoping to see is very little deviation from the baseline schedule in either direction, because that means you planned very accurately in terms of your scheduling and duration or work estimates. As with most other reports, it is very important that your baseline was captured correctly and you have consistently updated your tracking information.

THE BASELINE WORK REPORT The Baseline Work report is found in the All tab as well as the Assignment Usage tab of the Visual Reports – Create Report dialog box. It displays Baseline Work, Work (planned work), and Actual Work for each task. Like many other visual reports, you can drill down into this report to display data at the project level, the phase level (summary tasks), or the task level. Generally, your Baseline Work and Work values will be the same or similar if you have captured the scope of work correctly.

Like the other reports, you can add other fields into the Baseline Work report to further aid in analyzing your schedule. Add fields in the PivotTable Field List, which appears on the right side of the graph when you click in it.

Figure 15.30 shows an example of a modified Baseline Work report. The data is displayed at the summary task level. To display individual task data, simply expand the summary tasks listed in the PivotTable underneath the graph.

Figure 15.30
The Baseline Work Report shows planned and baseline work compared to actual work values for each task.

→ For more information about modifying the appearance of Excel PivotTables and graphs in Microsoft Project's visual reports, **see** "Reporting Capabilities," **p. 719**.

THE RESOURCE WORK AVAILABILITY REPORT The Resource Work Availability report is found on the Resource Usage tab or the All tab of the Visual Reports – Create Report dialog box. It shows the amount of Work Availability (total amount of working time for all resources), Planned Work, and Remaining Availability for all resources combined over time. By default, the report data is displayed in quarters, but you can break it down into weeks if you like; Figure 15.31 shows the second quarter of 2007 (Q2) drilled down into weeks.

15

This report may be beneficial when analyzing your schedule to see if your resources have more availability in certain weeks than others, and if so, you can assign more work to make up for any possible slipping tasks that you have and use the available time to catch up.

Figure 15.31 shows an example of a customized Resource Work Availability report. Modifications made to this report are done by collapsing or expanding the time dimension fields in the pivot table below the graph.

Figure 15.31
The Resource Work Availability report shows total planned work and work avail-ability values for your resources over time. If there are times when you see more avail-ability, you may want to schedule any makeup work during those times.

→ For more information about modifying the appearance of Excel PivotTables and graphs in Microsoft Project's visual reports, **see** "Reporting Capabilities," **p. 719**.

THE RESOURCE WORK SUMMARY REPORT   The Resource Work Summary report is found on the Resource Usage tab as well as the All tab on the Visual Reports – Create Report dialog box. It is similar to the Resource Work Availability Report in that it lists Work Availability, Planned Work, and Remaining Availability. However, this report lists the data for each resource rather than total amounts over time. In addition, the Actual Work field is included, allowing you to see the actual work performed by each resource compared to the planned work. This can be very helpful for analyzing each resource's performance compared to what was expected as defined in the baseline schedule. You can also analyze each resource's work-load side by side.

Figure 15.32 displays an illustration of a customized Resource Work Summary report. As always, you can modify the fields listed in the report as well as the actual appearance of the data.

Figure 15.32
The Resource Work Summary report shows planned and actual work data, as well as remaining availability, for each resource in your project.

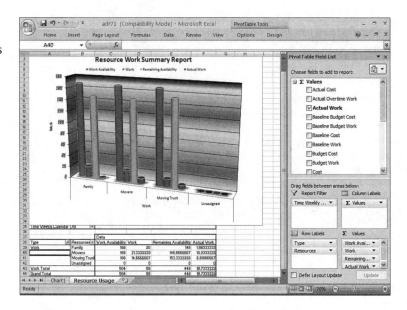

→ For more information about inserting alternate fields into the report or modifying the appearance of Excel PivotTables and graphs in Microsoft Project's visual reports, **see** "Reporting Capabilities," **p. 719**.

USING THE VISUAL REPORTS FOR ANALYZING THE PROJECT BUDGET

Analyzing your budget on a consistent basis is an important aspect of project management. You want to make sure the actual cost of the project is aligned with the baseline, that the project is earning value at the expected rate, and that your overall project is staying within its budget. Microsoft Project 2007 comes equipped with a number of visual reports to help you maintain an accurate budget analysis. Monitoring your budget closely and fixing any problems as soon as they arise will help you be more successful in properly managing your project's budget.

Three reports not mentioned in this chapter are helpful in analyzing project budget: the Baseline Cost report, the Cash Flow report, and the Earned Value Over Time report. These reports are discussed in the section, "Using Visual Reports for the Project Sponsor."

THE BUDGET COST REPORT The Budget Cost report should be used to analyze your budget. This report is found on the Assignment Usage tab as well as the All tab of the Visual Reports – Create Report dialog box. The Budget Cost Report shows Budget Cost, Baseline Cost, Cost (planned cost), and Actual Cost as a bar graph over time. As with the other visual reports, you can add more fields to the graph in the PivotTable Field List, or define different units of time on the PivotTable (years, quarters, weeks, and so on). With this report, you can quickly examine your actual cost as compared to your different planned and scheduled cost values side by side.

Figure 15.33 shows a customized version of a customized Budget Cost report.

Figure 15.33
The Budget Cost Report shows actual cost next to the planned and scheduled cost values.

→ For more information about inserting alternate fields into the report or modifying the appearance of Excel PivotTables and graphs in Microsoft Project's visual reports, **see** "Reporting Capabilities," **p. 719**.

THE RESOURCE COST SUMMARY REPORT   The Resource Cost Summary report is found on the Resource Usage tab as well as the All tab of the Visual Reports – Create Report dialog box. This is an Excel report that displays a pie chart showing the division of cost among the three resource types: work, material, and cost. If you only have one or two of the resource types in your project, then only data for those types is displayed. To further aid in analyzing a project's budget, you can add the Actual Cost field, or other helpful budget analysis fields, in the PivotTable Field List. Also, you can display data for all resources, or choose certain resources to analyze. The PivotTable Field List is used to define which resources to display data for.

Figure 15.34 shows a customized example of a customized Resource Cost Summary report. Notice how most of the cost is to work resources, and because no material resources have been assigned to tasks, there is no data on this report for material resources. Cost resources represent only a small fraction of the total resource cost.

Figure 15.34
The Resource Cost Summary report shows planned cost data for each of the three resource types, allowing you to quickly view which resource types are costing the most, and by how much.

→ For more information about using the PivotTable Field List to modify a visual report, **see** "Reporting Capabilities," **p. 719**.

USING VISUAL REPORTS FOR THE PROJECT SPONSOR

As mentioned earlier in this chapter, a project sponsor is generally not as concerned with project details as he or she is with the overall big picture. Therefore, the visual reports to share with project sponsors should include overall project information—how the project is doing as compared to the baseline.

THE BASELINE COST REPORT

The first report to discuss is the Baseline Cost report. This report is the first report listed in the All tab of the Visual Reports – Create Report dialog box. Also, it is found under the Assignment Usage tab. To access the Baseline Cost report, double-click it, or click it once and then click the View button.

The Baseline Cost report shows a project's baseline cost, planned cost, and actual cost, displayed in a bar graph. When you set your baseline, the Cost (planned cost) and Baseline Cost values start out the same. The Cost field may fluctuate as progress is reported but is typically expected to stay close to the baseline if problems have not occurred. As your project moves through its life cycle, you can analyze Actual Cost values against the Cost and Baseline Cost values. Projects that are in control are typically expected to have Actual Cost values within 10% (plus or minus) of the Cost or Baseline Cost values.

To view this data as text, click the Assignment Usage tab at the bottom of the screen. This will display the Excel spreadsheet that the graph represents visually. You can choose to expand or collapse some of the information, and the graph will reflect those changes. For example, the data is first displayed at the project level. There are three bars total (Cost, Actual Cost, and Baseline Cost) for the entire project. If you expand the data on the Assignment Usage tab to show project phases (summary tasks), then the bar graph will show the three cost values for each phase rather than the entire project. You can then expand each phase to the task level, and the graph will show the cost values for each task.

Alternatively, you can double-click on the legend underneath each bar on the Chart tab (the graph), and the bar will automatically expand. Or, you can right-click on a gridline in the graph and choose Format Axis, and define the level of data to display (project level, summary/phase level, task level) in the Format Axis dialog box.

CAUTION

> Expanding the data too much can cause the units underneath the graph to mix together and overlap, making it very difficult to read. To fix it, right-click on the unit text and select Format Axis, Alignment, Text Direction. From there you can rotate the text 270 degrees, so the text is displayed vertically instead of horizontally.

Also, you can include additional fields in the report by clicking on the spreadsheet. The PivotTable field list will appear on the right side of the screen, and you can select boxes next to fields you want included in the report, and clear boxes for fields you do not want included in the report. Then, click the Chart tab to return to the graph to view your changes.

Figure 15.35 shows an example of a customized Baseline Cost report. The report has been modified; the graph is copied and pasted above the PivotTable. Also, the PivotTable field list has been displayed on the right, where you can insert other fields to include in the report. On the PivotTable (underneath the graph), you can see that the task levels have been expanded in some areas, and the graph reflects those modifications. The appearance of the graph itself has been altered to look more three-dimensional.

→ For more information about modifying the appearance of Excel PivotTables and graphs in Microsoft Project's visual reports, **see** "Reporting Capabilities," **p. 719**.

Chart Area

PivotTable Field List

Figure 15.35
The Baseline Cost report shows a project's Baseline Cost, Cost (planned cost), and Actual Cost fields, which the project sponsor would be especially interested in.

PivotTable Area

Screen Tip

Figure 15.36 shows the same Baseline Cost report, only in this example, all the tasks have been rolled up in the PivotTable to display only project summary information.

Figure 15.36
This example of a Baseline Cost report displays only project summary information, rather than data at the task level, as defined in the PivotTable underneath the graph.

THE CASH FLOW REPORT

The Cash Flow report can be found on the All tab or on the Task Usage tab of the Visual Reports – Create Report dialog box. This report displays cost (planned cost) and cumulative cost data over time. The project sponsor may be inclined to view this report because it shows a bar representing planned cost as well as the total cumulative planned cost up to that point, so you get an idea of what was expected to be spent during each particular time period, as well as the total amount for the project up through that time period.

Figure 15.37 provides an example of a customized Cash Flow report. The report has been modified; the cumulative cost data is by default displayed as a line, but has been changed to be represented as a bar. Also, the bars are three-dimensional. Actual Cost data has been inserted as well.

→ For more information about modifying the appearance of Excel PivotTables and graphs in Microsoft Project's visual reports, **see** "Reporting Capabilities," **p. 719**.

As with the Baseline Cost report, you can drill down into the data in the PivotTable, and the graph will display data that reflects the PivotTable.

Figure 15.37
The Cash Flow report shows planned cost per time unit, as well as cumulative planned cost up through each particular time period.

TIP

You may want to add the Actual Cost field into the Cash Flow report, as in Figure 15.37. That way, you can compare what you spent with what you planned to spend in each time period. To insert the Actual Cost field into the report, select the Actual Cost check box in the PivotTable field list.

→ For more information about inserting additional fields into visual reports, **see** "Reporting Capabilities," **p. 719**.

THE EARNED VALUE OVER TIME REPORT

The Earned Value Over Time report is found on the All tab and the Assignment Usage tab of the Visual Reports – Create Report dialog box. This report compares planned value, earned value, and actual cost as a line graph. This may be important to a project sponsor for a visual representation of what value was planned, what value was earned, and what was spent to achieve the earned value. Since the graph is represented over time, it is easy to look back and see where the earned value measurements were at some point in the past, as well as examine the pattern over the course of your project.

→ For a more detailed explanation of earned value analysis, **see** "Analyzing Performance with Earned Value Analysis," **p. 491**.

Figures 15.38 and 15.39 show an example of a customized Earned Value Over Time report. Figure 15.38 displays the PivotTable, and Figure 15.39 shows the resulting graph that is based on the information defined in the PivotTable. As with the other illustrations in this section, this example has been customized to appear more visually attractive and represent the data more clearly.

→ For more information about modifying the appearance of Excel PivotTables and graphs in Microsoft Project's visual reports, **see** "Reporting Capabilities," **p. 719**.

Figure 15.38
Create the level of data displayed in the Earned Value Over Time graph by defining it in the PivotTable. The resulting graph is displayed in Figure 15.39.

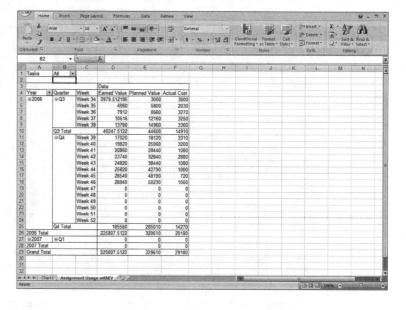

Figure 15.39
The Earned Value Over Time report shows earned value as compared to planned value and actual cost.

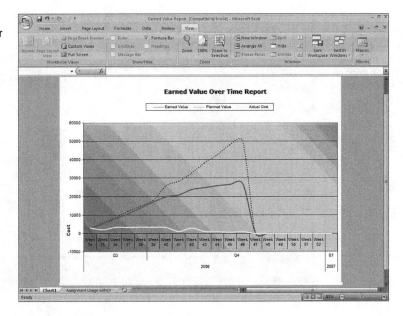

CRITICAL TASK STATUS REPORT

Critical tasks are those tasks whose finish dates affect the overall project finish date. If critical tasks are behind, it is likely that the project will finish late unless the problem is fixed. Therefore, a project sponsor may be very interested in seeing the Critical Task Status report. This report will give the project sponsor an idea of whether the project is running on time, early, or late.

The Critical Task Status report can be found on the All tab as well as the Task Status tab of the Visual Reports – Create Report dialog box. This is a Visio report that displays the critical tasks in a diagram. Each critical task's work, remaining work, and percentage complete values are shown. You will need to have Microsoft Office Visio 2007 installed for this report to function.

Figure 15.40 shows an example of a Critical Task Status report.

Figure 15.40
Project sponsors may want to see the Critical Task Status report, which can be modified to indicate the status of each critical task.

CUSTOM PROJECT SUMMARY REPORT FOR THE PROJECT SPONSOR

Microsoft Project 2007 does not come equipped with an existing visual report that summarizes the important information of a project. Recall the Project Summary report, a basic report discussed earlier in this chapter in the section, "The Project Summary Report." The Project Summary report displays Start and Finish Dates, Duration, Work, Costs, Task and Resource Status, and Notes for the project. In most of these areas, the report lists baseline and actual data, as well as variance, allowing for the project sponsor to quickly read what was planned versus what is actually happening, and the difference between those values. Most project sponsors would appreciate viewing this information as a visual report as well.

However, you will have to create the visual report because it does not exist as a template in Microsoft Project's visual reports. Your summary visual report should include the same information found in the Project Summary report: cost, work, and schedule information, all listed on the same report with baseline, actual, and variance values.

→ For more information about creating new visual reports, **see** "Reporting Capabilities," **p. 719**.

USING VISUAL REPORTS FOR THE PROJECT TEAM

While the project sponsor benefits more from overall project reports, your project team relies on specific, detailed reports about each phase of the project or their general assignments. Because team members are involved with the project on a daily basis, project overview reports that do not include specific detailed information do not encourage the team members to concentrate on their daily work. Instead, use the visual reports to break down work on a daily or weekly basis, giving the team members several small goals to achieve each day or week, rather than the overall big picture.

As a project manager, you must ensure your team members are staying current with their assignments and performing at the level they are expected to perform at. Use a visual report to illustrate the team's performance as compared to the project plan, which can serve as visual evidence of whether or not a team or team member is up to speed. Create a bar graph in a visual report that displays actual progress with baseline plans for work, schedule, and possibly for cost. A visual report may get your point across more effectively than just telling them what is going on. Talk to your team, and back up your points with a visual report.

TIP

> Remember, communication is very important to managing a successful project. Each team communicates differently; experiment and find the method of communication that works best for you and your team, and be consistent in maintaining it. Be sure you are available to answer any questions that will arise as work on a project progresses.

THE RESOURCE REMAINING WORK REPORT

The Resource Remaining Work report may be helpful for status meetings with your project team. This report displays each resource's actual work completed and remaining work, according to the amount of work planned for each resource. It provides a quick look at a resource's progress, as well as what still needs to be completed in terms of work. You can customize this report to also include Baseline Work or other fields that may be helpful in reviewing work for your project team. By default, the report lists data for all resources, but you can opt to include only certain resources, or even a single resource. These definitions are made in the PivotTable Field List (see Figure 15.41).

The Resource Remaining Work Report is found on the All tab as well as the Resource Summary tab of the Visual Reports – Create Report dialog box.

Figure 15.41
The Resource Remaining Work report lists actual work completed by each resource, as well as scheduled remaining work.

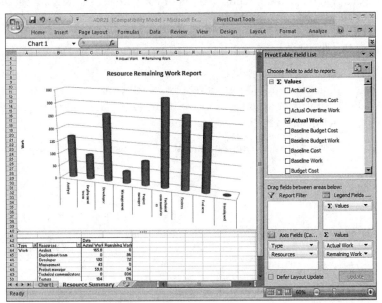

15

CUSTOM VISUAL REPORTS FOR THE PROJECT TEAM

You may also want to create visual reports similar to those discussed earlier in this chapter in the section "Using Basic Reports for the Project Team." Specifically, a to-do list for each resource, created in Visio as a timeline diagram, may be very beneficial for the resource to keep in his or her office or working area. That way, the resource not only has a list of task assignments that include all the necessary task information, he or she also has reports organized chronologically. You can create a to-do list for each resource that spans the entire project lifetime, as well as smaller to-do lists that span each day, week, or other time period throughout the project.

→ For more information about creating new visual reports, **see** "Reporting Capabilities," **p. 719**.

CONSULTANTS' TIPS

USING VISUAL REPORTS TO SHARE PROJECT STATUS

As you can see, Microsoft Project 2007 has added some excellent new capabilities for reporting and communicating your project status. The Visual Reports capabilities will help you focus both your team and your stakeholders on the correct information if you present the right information. Because the reports are now able to be created using Excel or Visio, they will be much easier to share via email or a project workspace. You will no longer need to spend so much time taking data and translating it into slide shows; much of this work has now been done for you.

Take advantage of this new capability and learn as much as you can about the basic reports and the interests of your stakeholders. Create a good standard set of reports when you are in the planning stages and gain agreement from your stakeholders so they know what to expect. A good pictorial representation of your project status is a great motivator, so use it to your advantage.

CUSTOMIZE THE OUT-OF-THE-BOX REPORTS FOR YOUR PROJECT NEEDS

You can create an almost endless set of variations of reports and analytical capabilities using the customization options for both the basic and visual reports. A small set of reports should be discussed with your project sponsor in the early stages of developing your project so that you can set them up for regular reporting.

Read Chapters 20 and 21 to learn about the vast array of reporting customization options.

CHAPTER 16

REVISING THE SCHEDULE

In this chapter

This chapter provides some insight into options that project managers should consider when there are signs of trouble. Depending on how the project plan and schedule were put together, alternatives can be considered to help the project manager get things back on track.

WHEN THINGS DON'T GO ACCORDING TO PLAN

A project schedule provides a roadmap, but it is not infallible; it is based on accumulated knowledge and best guesses, and it makes a set of assumptions that do not always work out. For example, if the schedule was put together without any weighted estimates for effort or budget, the chance for meeting the exact date and budget is approximately 50%. To increase those odds, more sophisticated estimation methods need to be used.

→ For additional information on estimation methods, **see** "Schedule Estimation Methods (PERT and Other Techniques)," **p. 421**.

There are hundreds, if not thousands of possible reasons that things do not go according to plan during project execution. The primary component is that projects rely on human resources to get work done, and human resources are not completely predictable. The best that a project manager can do is set up a robust and flexible plan and then be steadfast in monitoring all components of the project, and react as quickly as possible when the situation changes. Critical path analysis is an essential component of this analysis.

CRITICAL PATH CHANGES

Critical path analysis is one of the best tools available for analysis of a project schedule. When you monitor the critical path, you will notice changes to the tasks that show up on the critical path and possibly to the amount of lag time that is available on some important tasks. This is the normal process that takes place as work is accomplished on the project; some tasks will take longer than planned or start later than planned, whereas others may actually happen more quickly than expected. Most of these changes are subtle and not a cause for alarm as long as they do not continue to get further behind with each reporting cycle.

→ For additional information on how to set up critical path analysis, **see** "Reviewing the Big Picture (Critical Path Analysis)," **p. 427**.

When a schedule changes dramatically, the entire schedule needs to be reviewed carefully to understand the implications of the changes. In most cases, it is because work has been slipping and has impacted the project schedule finish date. The slip often comes as a surprise to a busy PM who does not have the time to monitor every task in the project. Once the work is late enough to change the critical path, other factors may be in play that will make the situation even worse. To avoid this surprise, the PM should also be monitoring tasks with a small amount of slack time because they have the potential to quickly become part of the critical path. To analyze the "near critical path" tasks, use the Total Slack field in a view or create a custom view or report that will help you monitor the amount of float time available. Tasks that have less than a specified amount of slack time should be analyzed to ensure that they will not be a problem. Additional views can be created to show tasks that are slipping or late. Figure 16.1 provides an example of a custom view that will help the project manager analyze the "near critical path" as well as the critical path. The near-critical tasks for this view have been defined to include tasks with slack of 1 days or less.

→ For additional information about customizing views, **see** Chapter 22, "Customizing Views, Tables, Filters, Groups, and Fields," **p. 755**.

Figure 16.1
Tasks with slack time of less than 1 day appear in this view.

WHAT CAN GO WRONG

The following is a set of items that might cause your project to run off course. There are no silver bullets to solve these problems, but there are some things that can be done to minimize their impact or at least help you determine how to recover.

- **Inaccurate estimates**—A common contributor to schedules that go awry is a set of activities with inaccurate estimates. Unless the organization has a solid history of good estimates, there is often little to go on for predicting the effort involved in a new project.

- **Resource issues**—There is always a fair amount of competition for experienced resources because inexperienced resources do not work as efficiently. Illness, job changes, and a myriad of other issues may cause problems with human resources. Most organizations have more requests for work than they have the ability to do, and the tendency is to take on more than is possible. Key resources are often asked to juggle multiple projects, so their attention is divided.

- **Budget issues**—Budget cuts, cost overruns, and higher costs for resources are just a few of the problems you may encounter.

- **Scope changes**—Scope creep (or fuzzy requirements) is one of the key causes of failure in project management. A large portion of schedule slippage and cost overruns is directly related to changes in the scope of the project after cost and time commitments have been made.

- **Risks, issues, and so on**—Natural disasters, labor strikes, regulatory requirements, and many other things that you are not able to predict can have an impact on the best of plans. You can have contingency plans for many of these issues, but even that is not always enough.

PREVENTION AND AVOIDANCE

Prevention and avoidance are obviously the preferred methods of dealing with adversity. You can find advice throughout this book to help you:

- Improved estimation (see Chapter 12, "Performing a Schedule Reality Check")

- Improved scope definition (see Chapter 4, "Getting Started After the Business Initiative Approved")

- Improved resource management (see Chapter 9, "Understanding Work Formula Basics," and Chapter 10, "Scheduling Single and Multiple Resource Assignments")

- Improved risk management and contingency planning (see Chapter 4 and Chapter 12)

In addition, Microsoft Project 2007 has some features to help you avoid problems and ways to determine what to do when a problem occurs. (It is recommended that you save a version of your project first so that you have a separate version for this activity. If you are using the Microsoft Project Professional 2007 version with Microsoft Project Server 2007, you can save several versions to the server as well.)

You can use the Multiple Undo feature and the Task Driver pane for what-if analysis. Make a set of changes to your project using these features and see what the ripple effect is. You can reduce effort or remove a resource, push out a set of tasks, and a variety of other things. With Microsoft Project 2007, you now have the ability to see how your changes make an impact on the project, and then you can undo these changes one by one.

TOO LATE FOR AVOIDANCE, NOW WHAT? RECOVERY

If your project is in trouble or you can see that it is heading that way, proactive management is your best bet to limit the extent of the problems and get back on track. When dealing with your Microsoft Project 2007 schedule, remember that you only have control of two of the three key components: scope, cost, and time. Go back and review the Measure of Success that you established to remind the team of which component is the most critical for your project. If quality and accuracy are most important, you may need to let the timeline slip to maintain the quality. If being "first to market" is key to success, you need to look at reducing scope or possibly increasing the budget to bring the project in on time (see Figure 16.2).

Figure 16.2
You can control only two of these three key components.

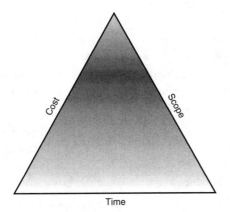

Whatever you decide, you will need to make tradeoffs, and you will need the support of your stakeholders and your team to accomplish this. The use of several "what-if" scenarios will help your team visualize the options.

REDUCING PROJECT SCOPE

Reducing scope to meet either budget or timeline requirements means that you must reduce functionality or potentially lower the quality for the finished product.

To remove functionality, review the project schedule to see if there are tasks (or preferably entire work packages) that can be removed from the scope without serious impact to other components of the schedule. If the schedule was put together using a WBS approach, it will be easier to find sets of functionality that can be isolated and removed. This is the preferred solution because it has the least impact on quality.

→ For additional information about the WBS, **see** "Work Breakdown Structure," **p. 92**.

If functionality cannot be completely removed, perhaps a substitute can be put in place that takes less time to build. In a manufacturing situation, substitution of a pre-built part for a custom-made component might solve the problem. This solution might increase project cost, but it would reduce the scope so that the project could come in on time.

The last choice would be to reduce the effort associated with tasks so that the final deliverable takes less time to produce. This is highly risky because of the potential impact on quality. For example, software projects that are running behind schedule often reduce the amount of time available for the final system test, thereby increasing the risk that the quality of the product will be lower than planned. A better solution would be removing a portion of the functionality for later delivery because the long-term effect of poor quality has a much larger impact.

REDUCING PROJECT COST

Reducing project costs may be necessary because the project is going over budget or because of outside factors such as an organizational budget cut. The reason for the reduction is extremely important in determining which options the project team should take. The team should first attempt to reduce the project cost without causing an impact to the timeline or the scope and quality of the project. There are several options to review:

- Substitute less-expensive resources or subcontract a portion of the project to an outside resource that is less expensive. The potential impacts of this option are to the timeline (less experienced or outside resources may require more time to perform the work) and to the quality (again, less experience may result in more errors).

- Review all fixed costs for supplies and for subcontracts to see if there are other products that can be substituted, costs that can be trimmed by using other vendors, or contracts that can be renegotiated.

- Review any contingency funding or reserve set-aside for possible use. This option adds risk to the project but may be a point for negotiation with stakeholders in the future.

- Negotiate changes in scope or timeline.

REDUCING SCHEDULED DURATION

As with the scope and budget components discussed previously, a reduction in the duration of the project comes with some tradeoffs. Because you are working inside a sophisticated scheduling engine, however, more options are available inside the tool to help you solve this problem.

As discussed in many of the earlier chapters of this book, there are several things that Microsoft Project 2007 uses to determine the total duration of your project. These include the relationships between tasks, calendars, resources, and the amount of work required to produce the deliverables.

- **Task relationships**—When schedules are initially built, the relationships between tasks are often set up as Finish-to-Start. In reality, tasks may not need to be related, or they can overlap so that one task does not have to be completely finished before the successor can begin. If different resources are required for the tasks (and the resources can be made available), a change in these relationships can speed things up significantly. To accomplish this, change the lag on the task from zero to a negative number. Note that this change reduces the total schedule duration only if the task is on the critical path, so you should focus on critical-path activities when using this approach (see Figure 16.3).

- **Resource changes**—Many options are available to reduce the duration of a schedule by adding and substituting resources. Review the schedule to determine which resources are the most critical on the project because they have the greatest impact on the overall schedule duration. Key resources are often used in multiple projects and can only devote a small percentage of their time to one. If other resources can perform some of their work or if the key resource can increase the percentage of commitment to your project, the timeline can be improved.

- **Calendars and resource allocation**—Scheduling overtime can be a short-term fix to a schedule problem. If the amount of time needed is extensive, however, overtime may not solve the problem. Look for other resources that are not overallocated to support some of the work to be done.

- **Work**—Reducing scope or the amount of effort required to complete certain tasks will have a positive impact on the schedule duration. It is easy to reduce the work in Microsoft Project 2007 by changing or eliminating tasks, so you must be careful to make sure that the new estimates are realistic. You do not want to repeat the same exercise in a week because the estimates were too optimistic.

Figure 16.3
Negative lag on critical-path tasks can reduce the project duration.

NOTE

If you need to reduce your schedule duration, also look at any recurring tasks that you have in your project. Often, recurring tasks or ongoing tasks (such as project management) will end up on your critical path and negatively impact the timeline.

REBASELINING STRATEGIES

In several earlier chapters, the concepts of baselines and change control were discussed. At some point in your project, you will need to decide if your project has changed enough that you need to reset the baseline and start fresh.

In general, it is recommended that the original baseline be kept and that new tasks (and some modified tasks) are baselined using the Save Baseline, For: Selected Tasks option. If your project scope has changed significantly, it may make sense to reset the baseline so that the baseline data is useful for comparison purposes.

If your project is under formal change control, there will be a process to follow to determine when a new baseline is required. A recommended best practice is to use one of the 10 available baselines to store your original baseline so that it is available for historical reference. Once it is stored in Baseline10, for example, you can then reset the baseline and move forward.

CONSULTANTS' TIPS

REGULARLY REVIEW YOUR PROJECT SCHEDULE

No matter what changes have impacted your project and what adjustments have been made, you need to regularly review your entire plan and schedule with both your team and your stakeholders. Surprises are not a good thing in the project management business and timely preparation of the stakeholders will help you when there is a significant change in plans. If you monitor the schedule carefully and are always accurate in what is going on, you will build credibility and you will have more support when problems arise.

PERFORM RISK MANAGEMENT AND CONTINGENCY PLANNING

Risk management and contingency planning are important activities in planning for success. When you determine that there are risks in your project, make sure that the mitigation plans make it into your project schedule. If the risk does not occur and you do not need to do mitigation, you will be a position to remove work from your schedule rather than add to it.

MAKE YOUR PROJECT ESTIMATES AS REALISTIC AS POSSIBLE

Try not to be too optimistic in your estimates. Things can and will go wrong, so use the "most likely" or "most pessimistic" estimates for the work packages that are difficult and critical to your project success. This will build some contingency time into your schedules that you will probably need. You will want your team to work with the shorter estimates as their goal, so make sure they have the incentive to go for the optimistic version while you plan for the worst.

Pay very close attention to both the critical and the near critical path of your project. This is one of the best early-warning systems you can have to minimize or mitigate the things that can go wrong.

CHAPTER **17**

CLOSING THE PROJECT

In this chapter

THE IMPORTANCE OF CLOSING YOUR PROJECT

One of the most important steps in project management is quite often overlooked: closing a project. Often times, project managers or teams do not take the time to officially close their projects for numerous reasons. Some people believe that once work on a project is completed, then the project is finished. Or, perhaps they have another project to start and feel their time would be better spent by just diving into the next project. All too often, work on a project finishes, but the project itself just trails away, because it was not properly closed.

At the end of any project, the team should be able to look back and judge its success against the criteria that were set at the beginning of the project. If set up correctly, the project will have clear measures of success. Microsoft Project 2007 has many built-in capabilities to help you with the evaluation. If the project schedule was structured correctly, baselined, and work/costs were tracked accurately, you can use Earned Value tracking and many other features to measure your project's success. These do need to be set up at the beginning of the project, but they are brought up here because you need to have the end game in mind when you begin.

Aside from formally completing all contract conditions and deliverables produced by the project, closing the project has several other benefits. You can perform a "lessons learned" analysis of the project, in which you and your team will analyze what did and did not go well during the various phases of working on the project, and retain that information to improve work on future projects. This also gives members of the team an opportunity to provide insight to their individual experience with the project, and share final data and other statistical or completion information. Keep in mind, however, that the lessons learned session should not focus on individuals, because that often leads to placing blame. Rather, team members should reflect on what they thought worked well and what did not, and more specifically what can be done differently next time to improve the project.

This chapter will examine the importance and methodology of closing a project.

THE PROJECT CLOSE PROCESS GROUP

The objective of the Project Close process group is to collect all deliverables and relevant artifacts produced by the project, and coordinate their acceptance by the client. If there are any contractual signoffs or stipulations, be sure those are resolved. Also, all tasks within the project schedule should be labeled as Complete. If for any reason a task has not been completed, you should attach a note explaining why, as well as what the expectations are for the unfinished task(s).

The Project Close process group has two major steps: closing the project itself, and closing the contract. Both of these steps break down into more specific actions, which are listed in this section and described in greater detail in this chapter.

The following is a checklist of what to do to properly close a project. It is based on information provided by the Project Management Institute's *A Guide to the Project Management Body of Knowledge, Third Edition* (ANSI/PMI) and the best practices identified by the QuantumPM team.

- **Obtain formal acceptance of the project**—This includes official signoff from the project sponsor and/or client to ensure that the contract conditions have been met. Some organizations have formal signoff documentation that needs to be completed by both parties, but it can be as simple as having a verbal acceptance.

- **Conduct a lessons learned session**—This includes a formal or informal meeting with the project team to discuss problems and successes as well as what can be done next time to prevent or mitigate the problems.

- **Organize and archive project files**—This includes the official close of the project schedule and archival of its files. During this part of the process, all project deliverables and other artifacts should be archived and moved to a designated location in accordance with the organization's operating procedure standards.

- **Celebrate success of the project**—It is important to acknowledge the completion of the project and celebrate its completion with the project team.

- **Transition to the operational phase of the product or system life cycle**—This includes the handling of project deliverables, as well as the support of a product or a system, if such was produced as a result of the project.

17

Closing the contractual agreement is the most important steps in the Project Close process group. The following list provides steps for properly closing any contractual agreement. It is also from the PMI's *A Guide to the Project Management Body of Knowledge, Third Edition* (ANSI/PMI).

- Provide formal written notice that the contract has been accepted.

- Conduct a procurement audit; implement warranty phase, if needed.

- Create a contract file to be included with final archived project files.

When closing a project, it is important that you ensure that all contractual agreements have been met, resolve any open items, and document the successful completion accordingly. Be sure to forward this documentation to all applicable parties.

Several things were recommended in the earlier chapters of this book to help you create a project with a successful end in mind. If you followed those recommendations, you now have three components to guide your evaluation of the project:

- Measure of Success (MOS)

- Work Breakdown Structure (WBS)

- Definition of Deliverables (DOD)

→ For more information about establishing these components, **see** "Organizing for Success," **p. 88**.

MEASURE OF SUCCESS

The Measure of Success that was created during the project initiation provides quantifiable criteria for measuring the project success. How do you know that your project met all required criteria? How do you know if you were successful?

You should revisit the MOS criteria at the project's close and determine whether your project was in fact successful. In some cases, the MOS cannot be evaluated completely until a longer period of time has passed because the product or service has not been available for enough time to allow an evaluation. If that is the case, the project manager should establish a date when the final measurements will be taken.

WORK BREAKDOWN STRUCTURE

Before you begin creating tasks in the schedule, you decomposed your project into a set of work packages that defined what would be accomplished during the project. During project closure, the WBS should be evaluated to determine if all work packages were completed as planned or if appropriate change control was in place so that changes to the original plan were documented and approved. The WBS is a key factor in scope control and the management of stakeholder expectations.

DEFINITION OF DELIVERABLES

One very important question to ask as the project manager is, "How do I know when my project is finished?" You must instill quantifiable measures and explicit criteria that declare, "I am finished with the project when X, Y, and Z happen." Teams that are comfortable with the use of WBS will identify these measurements in the WBS dictionary. If you did not use a WBS dictionary, you should at least have a set of deliverables defined for the components in your WBS.

As the project manager, you defined the criteria for the deliverables with your team after the WBS was decomposed into work packages. The deliverables can now be reviewed to see if they are in compliance with the plan. Here are some factors included when reviewing the deliverables to determine the completion of a project:

- **Fulfillment of the contract**—All contract deliverables and conditions have been met.

- **Completion of the entire project scope**—All work defined for the project has been completed.

- **Completion of all invoicing**—Final invoicing has been submitted and/or received and no outstanding balances remain on either party's side.

- **Review of all tasks**—All tasks, summary tasks, and milestones in the project should be marked as 100% complete with no remaining work. If this is not the case, an explanation should be made for any variances.

IMPLEMENTING PROJECT CLOSE CUSTOM FIELDS

As mentioned in many earlier chapters, the use of custom fields can help you maintain the status of tasks or project phases. Once you reach Project Close, it is time to perform a final review of the phases and tasks to ensure that all of them have been marked as complete.

→ For more information about creating custom fields, **see** "Creating and Customizing Fields," **p. 801**.

TIP

Defining the Phase custom field for every task may become tiresome. Rather, you can define this custom field at the summary task level.

In addition to the Phase custom field, you can create a Phase State custom field that provides an at-a-glance look at the state of the phase (open or closed). This will give you the ability to very quickly check the status of the project by maintaining the status of each phase. It could have three values: Not Started, In Progress, and Complete. Therefore, you can define which phase a task or summary task is in with the Phase custom field, and what the status is in the Phase Status custom field. You can, for example, have a summary task in the Close phase, with its status defined as In Progress.

To provide you even more insight into the state of your project, you can also create Budget and Schedule Status custom fields. These custom fields can be defined to display a graphical color indicators that help you determine whether your project is Under Budget, On Budget, or Over Budget. Similarly, you can create a field for Schedule Status to help you determine whether your project is Behind Schedule, On Schedule, or Ahead of Schedule. These status fields can help you throughout the life of the project and will provide an easy method to review the deliverables and see which contract terms have or have not been met.

→ For more information about creating custom fields, **see** "Creating and Customizing Fields," **p. 801**.

PERFORMING FINAL REPORTING

Creation of project closure reports is an important step to obtain formal acceptance of the project and to conduct lessons learned. Final reporting provides you with documentation as to how the project performed overall, as well as a documented explanation of any variances within the project. It may also be a requirement from your project sponsor to see the final statistics on the project, in which case running the correct reports can be an easy way to meet that requirement.

Microsoft Project 2007 supplies you with several different options for final reporting. You can compare your end results to the baseline plan, as well as perform final reporting on the critical path and the project's deliverables. You can also perform status reporting, where you can look at the project's status as of any given date (defined in the Status Date field in the Project Information dialog box).

The first screen to examine is the Tracking Gantt view (View, Tracking Gantt). You will want to modify the view to display baseline values versus actual values, as well as variance values. To modify the view in this manner, follow these steps:

1. Right-click on the column header in the table where you want to insert this information.

2. Choose Insert Column to open the Column Definition dialog box.

3. In the Field Name field, choose the column heading you wish to insert from the drop-down list and then click OK (or Best Fit).

Repeat this process until you have inserted all of the columns you want to include. Helpful columns to insert on this view are Actual Duration and Duration Variance. In addition, you may want to add Baseline Work, Actual Work, Baseline Start, Actual Start, Baseline Finish, Actual Finish, Baseline Cost, and Actual Cost. Your choice should not be limited to just the columns mentioned here, but driven by the requirements you have to meet in your reports.

→ For more information about modifying views, **see** "Creating and Customizing Views," **p. 764**.

→ For more information about variance and actual values versus baseline values, **see** "Reviewing the Status via the Project Plan," **p. 481**.

If you apply the Critical task filter to this view, it will show you variance for the critical path at the summary task and subtasks level (depending on whether or not your outline is collapsed). To apply the Critical tasks filter, select Project, Filtered For and then choose Critical. Only tasks in the critical path will be displayed. This view is recommended because it represents how the critical path was managed.

The Project Summary report is a very helpful report to examine as well. This report contains summary information for baseline, actual, and variance values for project start and finish dates, duration, work, and cost. It also provides task and resource status at the bottom. To view the Project Summary report, follow these steps:

1. Open the Reports dialog box by selecting Report, Reports.

2. In the Reports dialog box, double-click on Overview (or click it once and click Select). This will open the Overview Reports dialog box (see Figure 17.1).

3. Double-click on Project Summary (or click it once and click Select). The Project Summary report will be displayed.

Figure 17.1
The Overview Reports dialog box contains several helpful reports to use for final reporting.

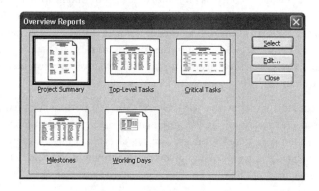

→ For more information about the Project Summary report, **see** "The Overview Reports Category," **p. 662**, as well as "Reviewing Status at the Project Level: Displaying Project Statistics and the Project Summary Report," **p. 482**.

When you have the Project Summary report displayed, you can zoom in or out for better viewing, as well as print it to distribute to your project team, project sponsor, and other project stakeholders.

The Overview Reports dialog box also contains additional reports you may find helpful for final reporting. Top-Level Tasks, Critical Tasks, and Milestone reports may all be useful. Double-click on any of these reports found in the Overview Reports dialog box to view them.

NOTE

> The Milestone report and the Critical Tasks report generate information based on the Task Entry table. Therefore, you should modify the Task Entry table to include baseline data before displaying these reports. You can modify the Task Entry table however you want, but be sure your modifications include displaying baseline data.

Another option for final reporting is to create a custom report. This can be done by selecting Custom in the Reports dialog box. Choose Report, Reports, and double-click on Custom. This will open the Custom Reports dialog box, as shown in Figure 17.2.

Figure 17.2
Use the Custom Reports dialog box to create new reports or modify existing ones.

In the Custom Reports dialog box, you can open any of the existing reports. Also, you can select a report and modify the formatting and layout, or its contents, by using the New, Edit, and Copy buttons.

→ For more information about customizing reports, **see** Chapter 20, "Creating and Customizing the Basic Reports," **p. 657**.

Resource Usage view is quite helpful for final reporting. Display the Resource Usage view and insert all baseline and actual data by right-clicking on the grid in the right pane and selecting the additional items you want to display, or by inserting the desired columns in the left pane. Then, you will be able to see if the schedule plan was achieved, which resources performed according to the plan, which resources were consistent, and whether the plan was accurate. If there is a significant amount of resources with schedule and work variances, it is likely that the schedule and work estimates were off.

Finally, the Earned Value report can be created to determine the project results. Earned Value is a very valuable method for calculating the variances in your planned and actual costs to determine whether the project brought value. The Earned Value report can be found in two different locations:

- **Using basic reports**—Select Report, Reports, and then select Costs and then select Earned Value.

- **Using visual reports**—Select Report, Visual Reports, Assignment Usage tab, and then select Earned Value Over Time Report.

Using visual reports provides you with more options, such as graphically displaying your project results in a chart. Visual reports are also highly customizable, so you can create the final project report containing any and all information you need.

→ For more information about customizing visual reports, **see** Chapter 21, "Creating and Customizing Visual Reports," **p. 707**.

→ For additional information about Earned Value and its importance in the project, **see** "Analyzing Performance with Earned Value Analysis," **p. 491**.

Performing final reporting is a necessary segue into the next step in the Project Close phase: performing a project retrospective.

PERFORMING A PROJECT RETROSPECTIVE (LESSONS LEARNED)

Like any major accomplishment in life, there are always lessons to be learned at the completion of a project. Performing a "lessons learned" (or a retrospective) is an important step in the Project Close phase because it enables you to take the necessary time to review the actions and events that impacted the project—especially those events that were not planned. This not only will help you and your project team uncover those details, but can also help you prevent them or mitigate them more efficiently in future projects.

Here are some questions to ask when performing a lessons learned, or retrospective:

- What went well, and why?
- What could be improved upon, and how?
- What were the major events that were not planned? Why did they happen?
- What were the causes of variances, either favorable or unfavorable?
- What action was taken when unplanned situations arose? Was it effective?
- What was the most challenging aspect of the project, for both you and for the project team?
- What was the most enjoyable aspect of the project, for both you and for the project team?

One idea to keep in mind while performing a project retrospective is to not put too much emphasis on the negative parts of the project. The negative points are important to discuss, but this is not supposed to turn into a blaming session and make you and your team feel bad. If the project finished late or over budget, try not to get discouraged. Rather, figure out what went wrong, talk about the issues with the people involved with the project, and keep in mind that similar projects in the future will go more smoothly because the project team will have more experience to work with.

It is important to determine when and why negative aspects occurred—not to assign blame, but to learn from them and figure out how to avoid similar problems in the future. Perhaps a particular resource naturally excelled in a certain area of the project; you would want to assign similar tasks to that resource in the future or at least provide cross-training if this was a skills problem. Also consider the opposite situation, if a particular resource struggled with an assignment. Was this a skills mismatch and would additional training help for the next project?

In any project, there will always be successes to celebrate as well as unsuccessful aspects you wish you could do over again; that is the nature of a project. Retrospective sessions should provide valuable lessons of what to do and what not to do, and those lessons should be used by not only you, but by other project managers, team members, and stakeholders for all future projects.

It is safe to say that the greatest amount of frustration project teams face is schedule related. Most schedule errors are errors in scope control and estimation, not in execution. Therefore, the retrospective can help determine where and why variances occurred, and prepare you to make much more accurate estimates for your future projects, especially those with a similar nature to the one you just wrapped up.

Microsoft Project 2007 provides quantitative data to support the lessons learned sessions, not only in the reporting described in the previous section, but also in the various views, tables, and filters you can apply. Determine what kind of data you want, and use the features within Microsoft Project 2007 to locate that data. The Tracking Gantt Chart view is very helpful to compare how the project was executed compared to how it was planned. Also, filter for tasks or phases in the project that have a lot of variance, and try to deduce why variance occurred so often in that particular aspect. It is helpful to use the reporting methods previously described and meet with your team, stakeholders, and/or clients to review. That way, everyone involved will learn from the retrospective session, not just you.

You can display the Task Usage view and insert the actual value and variance fields to show the estimated time and the actual time worked on each task. Tasks with large variances between actual work and planned work usually indicate that resources applied additional effort to complete the tasks on schedule, meaning that your planned duration values for those tasks were not accurate.

Finally, when performing a retrospective, be sure to examine the general process that was used between team members.

- Was the effort and quality delivered by the resources consistent throughout the project?
- Was the communication used within the team, as well as the communication with clients, effective and productive?
- Was everyone on the same page, or were resources or clients sometimes left in the dark about certain aspects of the project?

Remember that throughout this process, it is important to focus on events, and not peoples' mistakes. Collect and document the lessons learned, and implement any approved solutions in the future. It is also important to focus on positive aspects and make sure that they will also be able to be replicated on future projects.

ARCHIVING YOUR SCHEDULE

At the completion of a project, it is very important to archive your schedule for future reference. Perhaps you need to revisit a task or phase down the road to see how you handled a certain situation, or your client needs further clarification on an aspect of a completed project. It is also possible that you want to create a template from the project you just completed, to be used for future projects of the same type. If nothing else, you owe it to yourself and your team to properly save, store, and archive all of the hard work that was exerted into the project. It is also possible that your organization has standards for archiving your files that you must abide by.

As a project manager, you should think of each completed project as a learning tool. Performing a project retrospective, as discussed in the previous section, will provide you with lessons and insight to apply to all your future projects. Perhaps you learned that certain techniques or resources do or do not work well for you. Let your experience guide you. You have heard the phrase "Practice makes perfect." Well, nobody is perfect, but practice and experience will make you better, and you would be wise to take that into consideration.

Archiving your schedule can be especially important if the recently completed project is a type of project you work on often. If the project was especially successful, you should make it into a template—a guide or model to base future same-type projects on. That way, you will not have to re-create the project information over and over again. Save the template into a unique folder for quick and easy reference, and let your hard work and success carry through into your next project(s).

To convert your project schedule into a template, follow these steps:

1. Open the project file you want to save as a template.

2. Click File, Save As to open the Save As dialog box.

3. In the File Name field in the Save As dialog box, type in the name you want to save the template as (see Figure 17.3).

4. In the Save As Type field at the bottom of the Save As dialog box, choose Template from the drop-down list. This will change the filename from an .mpp file extension to an .mpt extension. You will not lose the original (.mpp) project file; it will remain where you had it saved originally, and the template will be saved in your Microsoft Templates folder (see Figure 17.3).

5. Click the Save button, which opens the Save As Template dialog box (see Figure 17.4).

6. The Save As Template provides you with options of item *not* to include in the template. Select any item you do not want included. Generally, you would not want to include actuals, baseline, and other tracking data. That data will be replaced with data from future projects; it is unique to the completed project, and now that it is a template, the project details are unnecessary. You may, however, want to include your planning estimates.

7. Click the Save button. The newly created template will be saved in your Microsoft Templates folder.

Figure 17.3
Name the template file and choose Template from the Save As Type field drop-down list.

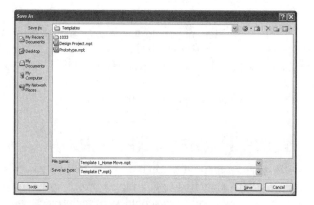

Figure 17.4
In the Save As Template dialog box, select the items you do not want included in the template.

→ For additional information about templates, **see** "Managing Project Files," **p. 581**.

After you have saved the file as a template, it may be helpful to review and edit it to ensure that there is no other schedule information that should not be included within the template. Remember, you are saving it as a guide for future projects, and specific project information that is saved within the template will not benefit you because you will want to define specific values for the new project, not use old values. Use the following list to guide you as you review the template:

- Tasks should not have a constraint attached to them other than As Soon As Possible or As Late As Possible. Use the icons in the Indicator column, or display the Constraints table to a task view to verify no other constraints are applied to the tasks.

- Display the Resource Sheet view. If there are any resources in the template, you may want to remove them or replace them with generic resources. This will help you or other project managers make the correct resource assignments, as well as ensure that resources are not automatically assigned to the same tasks.

- Review the project plan's logic (its WBS organization and its predecessor/successor dependency relationships). Does the WBS use a noun-based structure that is decomposed into work packages? Are the dependency relationships valid for the template?

- Review task durations compared to work. Do the planned and actual values match, or are they close? If they do match, or are close, you may want to leave the planned values in because they were accurate estimates. If they were not close, you will need to adjust the planned values based on the retrospective (described in the previous section).

When you are finished reviewing and modifying the template, click File, Save.

CELEBRATING YOUR PROJECT RESULTS

When a project is officially closed, do not skip out on celebrating your results. Hard work deserves to be recognized and celebrated, and closing a project is no exception. Plan to get together with your team, as well as other stakeholders in the project, and put the final stamp on the project with a party!

All too often, team members finish their work on a project and are assigned to work on other tasks for another project. Once the project they initially worked on closes, they often do not know about it because they are already immersed in something else. Take the time to invite these hard-working resources to a function of some sort, whether it is in your office or an outside location. Acknowledge the successes of the project, and make sure everyone knows that the project is finished, and they are officially free of responsibilities to it. Share the final reporting data with everyone, and be sure to also let them know about the lessons learned, so they can retain that information and become more efficient in the future.

Celebrating the project should be done even when a project was not totally successful. You should always make it a point to bring closure to the project for everyone involved with it, and focus on the positive areas of the project. Let the final interaction with the project be a constructive one for team members; they will feel much better about a project that may have been stressful for them, and leaving it on a good note will do well for you as a project manager when they are assigned to work on future projects with you.

A celebration is healthy for a team. It promotes team unity and brings a little light-heartedness at the end of what may have been a difficult stretch of work. People thrive off being rewarded for their efforts, and love to experience a sense of accomplishment. Taking an hour or two to celebrate a project's success will go a long way—especially if you serve food and drinks!

CONSULTANTS' TIPS

Everyone can cite reports about how few projects are considered to be successful (with success being defined as achieving the stated schedule, cost, and quality objectives), and the reasons for having a less-successful project are varied and also well documented. The project manager's role is to watch for challenges (issues and risks), detect them, address them, and then learn from them. That does not mean the issues will not happen again; it just means you will be better prepared to meet the challenges presented.

It is always good to approach the lessons learned sessions with enthusiasm. It is a chance to recognize the team's accomplishments with the stakeholders present, and it is a chance for everyone to learn. As long as everyone put their best effort into the work, there should be no hesitation about participating in a retrospective.

A lessons learned session that is supported by clear and objective data helps the stakeholders and the project team to focus on events, and not on people. Showing a Tracking Gantt chart that displays a lot of slipping tasks might not seem like a good decision, until you point out that the critical path was managed well. The data that Microsoft Project 2007 supplies, in the form of Gantt charts and reports, provides the visual focus to the story of the project told during the retrospective session.

The visual data needs to be backed up by facts, of course, including approved changes and major risk and issue events. It is often up to the project manager to apply his or her best skills in diplomacy to describe some events, but it cannot be stressed enough that lessons learned cannot focus on people in anything but a positive way. If a specific resource just did not perform his or her assignment, most of the project team members are probably already aware of that, and there is no need to focus on it. If a stakeholder micromanaged people and caused delays, you want to discuss the communication process issues, not the people issues.

And finally, you want to celebrate the project's completion. The retrospective brings closure to the project and, on some projects, marks the transition of people to other projects or to other organizations. Schedule an event to occur shortly after the lessons learned session and make sure everyone who was involved in the project is invited. Go and have fun, because your next project starts soon!

17

PART **IV**

TAILORING MICROSOFT OFFICE PROJECT 2007 TO YOUR NEEDS

CHAPTER 18

MANAGING PROJECT FILES

In this chapter

SAVING AND PROTECTING PROJECT FILES

When working with Microsoft Project 2007, you will want to know how to manipulate its important files and how file information is organized within the tool. This chapter explores how to manipulate project files, save and protect your work, create and use templates, and employ the Organizer feature to save and share common custom objects such as fields, calendars, or views in the Global for yourself or others within your organization.

You can save project files in many different formats when you are working with a group of people and sharing your files. Some of these options include Excel document and XML. When sharing your project file, it is important to protect the data within it and limit the control other people have over it. You may also create or need a custom object such as a calendar or view. The following sections discuss the options you have when saving, protecting, and sharing your project files.

DESIGNATING THE DEFAULT SAVE LOCATION AND FORMAT

When you are using Microsoft Project 2007 and save your project, it is saved to the default location—My Documents with the extension .mpp. However, you can modify the default location for storing your project files, as well as their type, by using the Options window. In addition, you can also designate the default save location for the user-defined templates that you create yourself.

NOTE
> Previous versions of Microsoft Project also supported a location for saving templates you share with others, referred to as *workgroup templates*. This feature has been removed from Microsoft Project 2007 and can no longer be accessed from the Tools, Options, Save tab.

To change the default save location for your files, follow these steps:

1. Open the Options dialog box by selecting Tools, Options from the main menu.

2. In the Options dialog box, select the Save tab (see Figure 18.1).

3. To modify the default save type for the projects you create, select the Save Microsoft Office Project files as drop-down list and choose between the three available options:
   - **Project(*.mpp)**—The default Project file type and the recommended option.
   - **Microsoft Project 2000–2003(*.mpp)**—Saves the Project file to be compatible with Microsoft Office Project 2000, 2002, or 2003.
   - **Template(*.mpt)**—The template file type; used to designate template files within Project.

4. To modify the default location for saving regular project files or templates, select the Projects row or User templates in the File types section respectively and click the Modify button. Browse to the new designated location and click OK to save your changes (refer to Figure 18.1).

TIP

> You should designate a new location for your project files under the My Documents folder on your computer. This will help you organize your files into one central location and keep them separate from other documents on your computer. Similarly, it is recommended to create a User Templates folder somewhere under My Documents as well. This will designate a single location for all of your Project templates and will make locating them much easier. If your organization has standards for organizing your personal files on your computer, this is a great place to integrate those standards and create additional folders to accommodate your project and template files. If your organization is sharing project templates, you could change the file location to the network drive where you all share your project templates. You will need to make sure that no one changes to location of the network drive without informing all project managers using the templates if you decide to do this.

5. You can also set the frequency that Project automatically saves your project file while you are working in Microsoft Project 2007. To do so, select the Save every check box under the Auto Save section and then enter the number of minutes in the minutes box. This option also allows you to select what kind of projects you want Auto Save to apply to, as well as whether you want to be prompted for each time there is an automatic save (see Figure 18.1).

6. Click OK to save your changes or click Cancel to exit without saving.

18

Regular project files default save location

Default Project save type

Figure 18.1
The Save tab of the Options dialog box allows you to set options for saving your project files, including the default file type, location, and Auto Save options.

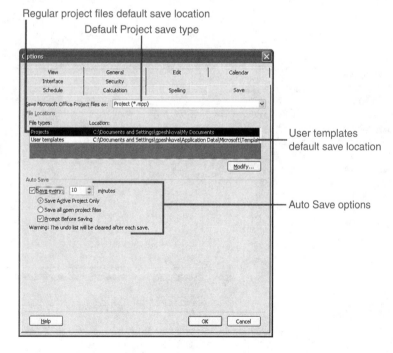

User templates default save location

Auto Save options

VERSION COMPATIBILITY

Like other software, Microsoft Project 2007 is backward compatible, meaning you can open files that have been created in previous versions of the tool in Microsoft Project 2007. However, some restrictions apply. For example, if a particular feature has been removed or modified from a previous version, modifications to the project file regarding that feature may not carry over into the new version.

Even though Microsoft Project 2007 is backward compatible, the same theory does not work when opening project files created in 2007 using the previous versions of the tool. Microsoft Office Project 2000, 2002, 2003, and 2007 do share the same file type for project files (.mpp). However, you have to specifically save the project file from Microsoft Project 2007 to the lower version of Microsoft Project in order for the files to be readable.

NOTE

> Microsoft Office Project 2000, 2002, and 2003 also had the capability to save project files to be compatible with Microsoft Project 98. However, this no longer applies in Project 2007.

To save a Microsoft Project 2007 file to be compatible with one of the previous versions of Microsoft Project (except Project 98), select File, Save As, and in the Save as type drop down box select the Microsoft Project 2000–2003 option, as shown in Figure 18.2.

Figure 18.2
Microsoft Project 2007 is compatible with Microsoft Project versions 2000–2003, and you can save the file down to those versions to ensure that they can be opened. The Save As dialog box allows you to select file name, location and file type for saving your project file.

The Save In drop-down box   Up One Level   Create
Back   New Folder

→ For additional information about version compatibility, **see** "Exchanging Project Files Across Microsoft Project Versions," **p. 914**.

SAVING A FILE

When saving a Microsoft Project 2007 file, you can select the File, Save As option from the main menu, which will open the Save As dialog box (see Figure 18.2).

TIP

> You can also save your project file by using the Ctrl+S keyboard combination. The second option works only if the project has not been previously saved. If the file has been previously saved, your latest changes will be saved to the previously designated location.

In the File Name box, enter a descriptive filename. This name will be used when printing reports, displaying your file, and any other viewing of your project, so ensure that the name conveys the purpose of the project.

CAUTION

> The project filename can be up to 200 characters in length, including spaces. Certain characters are not accepted for the filename. These include the following:
> / ? \ : * " < > |

The Save as type drop-down box provides several options for the file types, as described in Table 18.1.

TABLE 18.1 PROJECT 2007 SUPPORTED SAVE FILE TYPES

File Type	Extension	Description
Project	.mpp	The standard file type for individual project files for Microsoft Project 2007.
Microsoft Project 2000–2003	.mpp	The standard file type for individual project files compatible with Microsoft Office Project 2000, 2002, and 2003.
Template	.mpt	A special type of project file containing a group of tasks and/or resources to be used as a starting point for creating project schedules of similar type in Microsoft Project 2007. The templates will not be compatible with previous versions Microsoft Project versions.
Microsoft Excel Workbook	.xls	The file format used to export project data to Microsoft Office Excel 1997–2003. When you save a project file using this format, the Export Wizard is launched, allowing you to select the types of data (Task, Resource, and/or Assignment) and fields within those data types to be included in the Excel spreadsheet.

continues

TABLE 18.1   CONTINUED

File Type	Extension	Description
Microsoft Excel Pivot Table	.xls	The file format used to export data to Microsoft Office Excel in the form of a PivotTable. PivotTables are used to model data and allow a rich number of options for filtering and grouping in a table format. When this option is selected, the Export Wizard is launched, allowing you to select the data types (Task, Resource, and/or Assignment) and fields within each data type to be included in the PivotTable.
Text (tab delimited)	.txt	The file type used to export project data into a tab-delimited text file. This format can be useful if you are planning on importing it into another system, such as a database, that you can then use to model the data. When this file type is used, an Export Wizard is launched, allowing you to select the data types (Task, Resource, and/or Assignment) and the fields within those data types to be included.
CSV (comma delimited)	.csv	CSV stands for Comma Separated Values and represents a format commonly used by many databases, where each record is a single line and each field in the record is separated by a comma. This type of file format can be then imported into an external database system, as well as Excel. When this file type is applied, an Export Wizard is launched that allows you to select the data types (Task, Resource, and/or Assignment) and the fields within those data types to be included.

File Type	Extension	Description
XML Format	.xml	XML stands for Extensible Markup Language and is a widely used file format for manipulating data. XML is used for document creation and was developed to replace HTML, as it is more versatile and provides better document structure. When you save your project file in this format, the entire project information is exported, including all project details and statistics, calendars, tasks, resources, and assignments. Each part of the data is located on its own node, with the sub-values indented in the leaves below it. You can use this file type to export your project data to be used in any other external system for viewing and/or analysis.

NOTE

The allowed file types have been changed between Microsoft Project 2007 and previous versions. Microsoft Project 2007 no longer supports the Project Database (.mpd), Microsoft Access Database (.mdb), and ODBC Database file types. You can use the widely accepted standards of TXT, CSV, and XML, which can be read and imported into practically any database system.

→ For additional information about file formats and the export wizard, **see** "Exchanging Microsoft Office Project Data with Other Applications," **p. 916**.

PROVIDING SECURITY FOR SAVED FILES

When sharing project files among multiple people, it is important that you protect the highly sensitive data and the data you do not want other people to change.

You can use the password-protect feature by following these steps:

1. Launch the Save As dialog box by selecting File, Save As.

2. In the bottom-left corner of the Save As dialog box, select the Tools drop-down and choose General Options (see Figure 18.3).

3. The Save Options dialog box includes the following options:

    • **Always create backup**—You can create a backup of a previous version of a file every time you save the file. This option is very useful because it prevents you from overwriting the previous file version, allowing you to always roll back.

    • **Protection password**—You can password-protect the file by creating a password. If you apply this option, anyone attempting to open the file will be unable to, unless they know the password.

- **Write reservation password**—You can write-protect the file, which will allow any user to open a read-only copy of the file, but in order to save any changes to it, they must know the password. Although this does not prevent users from saving their changes under a different project name, it does allow you the control of who can change your project file.

- **Read-only recommended**—You can also save the project file with the warning that lets other users know that you prefer them opening the file in a read-only mode, forcing them to save any changes they make to a different filename and preventing potentially unwanted changes and/or loss of data.

4. Click OK to save your changes or click Cancel to exit without saving.

Save Options dialog box

Figure 18.3
Use the Save Options dialog box to protect your project file.

Tools drop-down

PASSWORD-PROTECTING A FILE

In order to password-protect a file, you can enter a password (up to 17 characters) in the Protection password field of the Save Options dialog box. The password you create is case sensitive and supports all text characters, including symbols, numbers, and spaces. When you click OK, a confirmation is displayed requesting you to reenter the password. Click OK to save your changes.

Every time you or anybody else opens your project file, the password must be entered in order to view the file. If the password does not match the password you entered in the Save Options dialog box, a warning is displayed, requesting that you or the other user try again. There is no limit to how many attempts for entering the password.

CAUTION

> It is recommended that you select a password you can easily remember or that you write it down in a safe location. If you happen to forget the password to your own project file, the data in that project file is completely unrecoverable until the correct password is entered, and there is no one who could help you open it without your password. So use this feature with caution, and always remember your password!

To remove a password from a password-protected file, follow these steps:

1. After opening the protected file using the password, from the main menu select File, Save As.

2. In the Save As dialog box, select Tools, General Options.

3. In the Save Options dialog box, simply erase all characters in the Protection Password box and click OK to save your changes.

SAVING A READ-ONLY FILE

Read-only files can be a great way to protect your project data from being edited by other people. It does not mean that others cannot make any changes to the file, however. They will just be unable to save it to the same project file name. The Write reservation password feature allows you to do just that. If you enter a write reservation password, when the project file is opened a warning is displayed, stating that the file is write-reserved (see Figure 18.4). If the user provides the correct password, he or she is able to view the project in regular mode and make changes to it under the same project name. In addition, if the user does not know the password, he or she has the ability to open the file in read-only mode. Read-only mode will prevent the user from making changes to the project file under the same name. However, the user can save the file under a different name to include the changes.

Saving the file with a write-reservation password ensures that only the users authorized to make changes to the project file can make any direct changes.

Figure 18.4
The write-reservation password warning is displayed when a user attempts to open the write-reservation protected project file.

To remove the write-reservation password after opening the protected file using the password, open the Save Options dialog box (select File, Save As, Tools, General Options), clear the text in the Write Reservation Password field, and then click OK.

SAVING A FILE AS READ-ONLY RECOMMENDED

The Read-Only Recommended feature does not prevent users from opening the project file in read-write mode. It only warns them of the preference you have added, and gives them a choice to accept it or bypass it. This option is not very effective when protecting your project file from being modified by other users.

USING THE ALWAYS CREATE BACKUP OPTION

The option for creating a backup file is activated by selecting the Always create backup check box in the Save Options dialog box (select File, Save As, Tools, General Options). When this option is selected, each time any user saves changes to the file, the original file is saved with the original name and the .bak extension. The active version of the file is then saved under the original project name with the .mpp extension. This option allows you to still access the previous version of your file, without overwriting the data.

SAVING THE WORKSPACE

A workspace in Microsoft Project 2007 is a pointer to all currently opened project files, although a separate copy of each file is not created in the workspace. This feature is very useful when working on multiple files. For example, if you have two projects open and leave the office to go home, you can save your entire workspace to reopen it where you left off in the morning. This feature can also be useful to capture the files that you work with regularly, bypassing you opening each project separately each time you work. Project does not let you select multiple files using the Open dialog box; therefore, creating a workspace is a great workaround for this issue.

To save a workspace, select File, Save Workspace. In the Save As dialog box, enter the name for the workspace and its location (by default, Resume.mpw displays). The workspace file will be saved with the .mpw extension. Microsoft Project 2007 prompts you to save changes to each file that was modified during that session.

NOTE

If you are saving a file that you just created and have not saved yet, you are prompted to include it in the workspace. New project files that are empty are not added to the workspace.

PROJECT 2007 SAFE MODE

Microsoft Project 2007, similar to the 2003 version, supports a safe mode features that is enabled when your system experiences instability, such as Registry corruption or an unexpected crash. This allows Microsoft Project 2007 to continue working on your project files in a safe mode, with some of the features disabled.

CAUTION

Continuing to work in an unstable environment can be risky. When instability occurs, save your work, close all open files, close all open applications, and restart Windows.

CREATING AND USING PROJECT TEMPLATES

In this section, you will learn how to create and reuse project templates.

A *template* is a project that has been specially designated to be used more than once by you or others. When you save a template file correctly, it has the file extension of .mpt rather than the .mpp extension which reflects a normal project file. A template has special characteristics, one being that it is saved into a special location reserved for templates.

Templates are especially useful for establishing consistent and repeated activities in a project so you do not have to start a project from scratch. For example, if you were in construction, you might be building condominiums and each condo project requires similar activities. You could set up the project once with all of the tasks already entered, and save it as a template to be used over and over for each condo project. As another example, suppose you are working on a major acquisition project; you can easily make a template that has custom fields that can be used by both the buyer and the seller. Project templates do not have to be very detailed or include all project information. Instead, project templates need to contain the common and repeatable project details that you can easily modify to fit to the new project you are creating.

A template can help you to set standards for projects within your organization, especially if the project structure and set up can be reused by several different project managers. A template allows you to reuse common tasks, project information, customized fields, calendars, and notes in a template project. It also lets you set up shared standard resources and equipment lists.

When you are building a template, you should strive for minimum threshold, not maximum. Build the template so that the basics are included, but let your project managers add their own tasks when they create their projects. If you have a template where project managers seem to be removing tasks over and over again, then those tasks do not belong in a template. Estimated durations can be included to establish standards. In the construction project example, it may be useful to include a task for wiring the condominiums and provide an estimated duration that represents the standard that you want to maintain.

Finally, you should try to include task relationships when designing a template. The closer the template reflects the actual activities and sequence of work performed on projects, the easier it is going to be for project managers to use the template, which will make them more productive. The purpose of building a template is to make it as useful as possible, so you can save time in the future.

CREATING A NEW PROJECT TEMPLATE

When you have a project you would like to use as a template, or have entered all of the project template details in a new project file, you can now save it as a template so that it will be available to be used in the future.

Follow these steps to save a project as a template:

1. From the main menu, select File, Save As.

2. In the File Name field, enter the name of your template. Try to provide as descriptive of a name as possible, so that will allow you to easily tell what the project template contains. You might even want to include Template at the end of name for easy identification.

3. In the Save as type drop-down box, select Template (which you can see is a .mpt file). Once you select the Template file type, Project will automatically change the location to the Templates folder. Do not change this location as you will not be able to use the process "Opening a Template File to Create a New Project" described later. This template location will sync up with the file location you left as default or changed as described in "Designating the Default Save Location and Format" earlier in the chapter.

4. Click the Save button.

5. In the Save As Template dialog box, select the values you want to be excluded from your template, as follows (refer to Figure 18.5). It is good practice to always select all the fields in the Save As Template dialog box, unless you have very good reason to include the values described in your template. If you leave the check boxes cleared and use this file as a template, every project based on the template will have the values left in the template.

    - **Values of All Baselines**—Select this box to remove any baselines that might have been set in the project (which you would have set using Tools, Tracking, Set Baseline).

    - **Actual Values**—Select this box to remove any actual values from the template. Selecting this item will remove data in the Actual Work, Actual Duration, Actual Cost, as well as other actual data fields.

    - **Resource Rates**—Select this box to remove any rates on resources that might be on the Resource Sheet or assigned tasks in the project. If you have added resources and their rates to this project, leaving this option cleared will save that resource information on the project schedules based on this template. You may want to leave this option cleared if you are using generic resources to initially calculate an estimated budget for the project using the template. Be cautious if you decide to leave resource rates in the template. In a couple of years, it is possible that resource rates will change and will need to be modified. If you fail to modify the rates, you risk having an inaccurate project budget.

    - **Fixed Costs**—Select this box to remove any Fixed Costs in the project template. In some templates, you might want to leave Fixed Costs in the template, although you should review the template occasionally to see if the fixed costs should be modified. For instance, there may be a fixed cost for inspections for the condo project template. You might want to leave the fixed cost in the template for others to use.

    - **Whether Tasks Have Been Published to Project Server**—Select this box to remove the designation that specifies whether the project has been saved to Project Server and, therefore, has dependencies with it. The Project Server is the enterprise-wide edition of Microsoft Project 2007, and if you are using the Standard edition of Microsoft Project 2007, you will most likely want to select this item.

Figure 18.5
The Save As Template dialog box allows you to choose what project data to exclude from the template.

6. Once you have made the desired selections, click the Save button to save your project as a template.

TIP

> It is important to note that you can save any project as a template, even the one you have created as a regular project—even if it has already been completed. The options described in step 5 are particularly useful if you are using an old project as a template. These options allow you to exclude the actual values, baselines, and other project-specific information that you do not necessary want in your template. However, you still want to be cautious of any other data you could save in a template. For instance, you may also have included hyperlinks in the file you are saving as the template, and those hyperlinks will be irrelevant for future projects using the template.

MODIFYING EXISTING TEMPLATE FILES

Microsoft Project 2007 provides no direct option to open an existing .mpt file. Therefore, in order to make changes to an existing project template file, you must open a copy of the template, make the desired changes, and resave it under the default name and .mpt extension. You must make sure to select the Project Template file type in the Save As dialog box; otherwise, a regular project file will be created by default. If you perform this action correctly, you will see a message saying the file name already exists. When the template file is resaved, it will overwrite the original copy, creating a more up-to-date one you modified.

OPENING A TEMPLATE FILE TO CREATE A NEW PROJECT

If you created a new template following the instructions in the previous section, and if you have used the Project default location, then that template will be available under the Templates dialog box in Project as shown in Figure 18.6. When you open a template file, you are opening a copy of the template file, not the original template file itself.

To create a new project based on a template, follow these steps:

1. Open Microsoft Office Project 2007.

2. In the main menu, select File, New.

3. In the New Project pane, select On Computer… (see Figure 18.6). This will open the Templates window and display all available project templates. Blank Project is the default template that automatically comes with Project. The Templates window contains two tabs—General and Project Templates. The General tab contains the Blank Project default template and any templates that you have created. The Project Templates tab contains Microsoft provided templates and includes different types of projects, so make sure to take a look and see if any of these templates might work for you.

Figure 18.6
You can use the New Project pane to access the predefined project templates in the General tab of the Templates dialog box.

NOTE

> If you are using Microsoft Project Professional 2007 connected to Microsoft Office Project Server 2007, the Templates window contains an additional tab—Enterprise Templates. Enterprise templates are enterprise-wide templates that are saved to the server and that can used by any project manager connected to that Project Server. Enterprise templates are a great way to create standards and project schedule consistency within an organization.

4. Select the template you would like to use and click OK. One of the first things you should do in the new project is select Project, Project Information and change the Start Date to the relevant start date of your project. Templates will retain all of the old dates that were saved in the original template.

WORKING WITH ORGANIZER AND THE GLOBAL FILE

When you modify an object in your project file, such as the Standard Task Calendar, or create a new custom view or report, they are only available and saved within the currently opened project file. Project 2007 provides the Organizer feature, which allows you to manage and reuse custom or modified objects. The Organizer is used to copy modified or custom objects from one project file to another or to GLOBAL.MPT.

To access the Organizer, select Tools, Organizer… (see Figure 18.7).

Figure 18.7
The Organizer feature allows you to access items that can be customized and shared in Project.

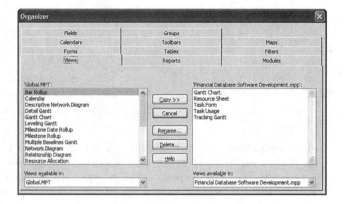

You can also access the Organizer by using one of the following options:

- Accessing the More Views dialog box by selecting View, More Views, Organizer
- Accessing the More Tables dialog box by selecting View, Table, More Tables, Organizer
- Accessing the More Filters dialog box by selecting Project, Filtered for, More Filters, Organizer
- Accessing the More Groups dialog box by selecting Project, Group by, More Groups, Organizer

Table 18.2 lists objects contained within the Organizer.

TABLE 18.2	ORGANIZER OBJECTS
Type	**Description**
Views	Views are tables and charts that are used to organize, categorize, and display project data. Views are used to view two main categories of data within project—tasks and resources. Project 2007 provides three different types of views: charts or graphs, sheets, and forms. You can customize views to create new views to fit your needs. For additional information about customizing views, see "Creating and Customizing Views" in Chapter 22, p. 764.
Reports	Reports are predefined, printable representations of project information. You can customize reports to create ones that best fit your needs. For additional information about customizing reports, see "Customizing Reports and Creating Reports" in Chapter 20, pp. 672 and 676.
Modules	Modules represent macros that you create within Microsoft Project 2007. Microsoft Project 2007 uses Visual Basic to create macros.
Forms	Forms are dialog boxes designed to allow you to enter specific data for a selected task or resource. You can customize forms to best fit your needs. For additional information about forms, see "Customizing Forms" in Chapter 23, p. 838.

18

continues

TABLE 18.2   CONTINUED

Type	Description
Tables	Tables are collections of fields, organized by rows and columns, reminiscent of a spreadsheet. Tables are used in many views, either by themselves or in conjunction with charts or graphs. You can customize tables to best fit your needs. For additional information about customizing tables, see "Creating and Customizing Tables" in Chapter 22, p. 756.
Filters	Filters are used to highlight or isolate specific information in the view based on the specified criteria. Microsoft Project 2007 supports two types of filters: task and resource. You can customize filters to best fit your needs. For additional information about customizing filters, see "Creating and Customizing Filters" in Chapter 22, p. 785.
Calendars	Calendars are used for specifying date exceptions and details to be used within the project schedule. Microsoft Project 2007 contains three types of calendars: project, task, and resource. You can customize calendars to best fit your needs. For additional information about calendars, see "Defining Calendars" in Chapter 5, p. 118.
Toolbars	Toolbars provide shortcut buttons to access Microsoft Project 2007 features and/or functionality. You can customize toolbars to best fit your needs. For additional information about customizing toolbars, see "Customizing Toolbars" in Chapter 23, p. 817.
Maps	Maps are used to track data exported to other programs. They are also used in the Export Wizard when saving project data to Excel or other export formats. For additional information about maps, see "Exchanging Microsoft Project Data with Other Applications" in Chapter 26, p. 916.
Fields	Fields are columns or boxes that contain a specific type of information about a task, resource, or assignment. You can create custom fields to best fit your needs. For additional information about customizing fields, see "Creating and Customizing Fields" in Chapter 22, p. 801.
Groups	Groups are tools to organize and summarize the display of project information. Microsoft Project 2007 supports two types of groups: task and resource. You can customize groups to best fit your needs. For additional information about customizing groups, see "Creating Custom Groups" in Chapter 22, p. 797.

THE GLOBAL.MPT FILE

GLOBAL.MPT is a special type of file in Microsoft Project that is a part of every new or existing project file. All projects inherit all of the features of the GLOBAL.MPT. The first time you launch Microsoft Project 2007, a copy of the GLOBAL.MPT file is created and becomes the active GLOBAL.MPT file. A backup of the GLOBAL.MPT is also created, called GLOBALbackup.MPT. The global contains all the default objects that Microsoft Project 2007 comes with, such as the Gantt Chart view or the standard calendar (see the list of objects in Table 18.2). It also contains the default selections in the Tools, Options dialog box. For instance, if you change the Default task type from Fixed Units to Fixed Duration in the Schedule tab of Tools, Options, and click the Set as Default on the screen, you have changed the GLOBAL.MPT. Whenever you make changes to the GLOBAL.MPT file, you affect all new project files created from that point forward. GLOBAL.MPT is stored in the default location on every computer under C:\Program Files\Microsoft Office\ OFFICE12\1033 directory.

When you open GLOBAL.MPT, you will see the Organizer but it will not act as a normal project file. There are two ways you could share the objects of the GLOBAL.MPT from your desktop with others: Send your GLOBAL.MPT to them to copy and use or send a project with the custom objects you have built. They can open the file on their desktop and move the custom objects into their own GLOBAL.MPT using the Organizer.

MANIPULATING OBJECTS USING THE ORGANIZER

You can use the Organizer to copy, rename, and delete objects in Microsoft Project 2007. Rather than opening the GLOBAL.MPT file directly, you can move custom fields or changes to default objects within any project file to the GLOBAL.MPT using the Organizer. The following sections explore the details of each one of these actions.

USING ORGANIZER TO COPY OBJECTS

To open an object by using the Organizer, open the file that contains the custom object and follow these steps:

1. To display the Organizer, from the main menu select Tools, Organizer. Note that if you are copying an object to a file other than GLOBAL.MPT, make sure that both the source and the target files are open.

2. Select the tab that contains the object you would like to copy. Figure 18.8 shows the Fields tab selected. The fields that have been used, modified, or newly created are listed on the right. The fields that would currently be included in the GLOBAL.MPT file are listed on the left.

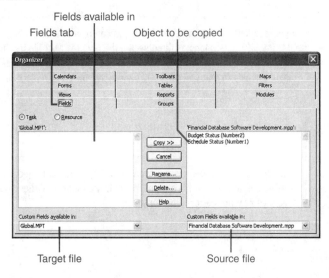

Figure 18.8
You can use the Organizer dialog box to copy an object from one project file to another.

3. Use the Custom Fields available in drop-down box on the left to specify the target file to have the selected object copied into.

4. Use the Custom Fields available in drop-down on the right to specify the source file to copy the selected object from.

5. Use the Task or Resource radio button to specify the type of field you would like to copy.

6. Select the field you would like to copy from your source file (on the right).

TIP

> You can copy multiple objects at once by selecting the first one and holding down the Shift key to select a range of objects. You can also select objects that are contained in the list out of order by holding down the Ctrl key and selecting each one.

7. Click the Copy button to copy the field. If a field with the same name already exists in the target file, Project will display a confirmation to replace the former field with a new one (see Figure 18.9).

Figure 18.9
Project displays a warning if you are attempting to copy an object with a name that already exists within the target file.

8. Click the Yes button to replace the field in the target file with the one from the source file. You can also click Cancel from the warning dialog box and then click the Rename button in the Organizer to provide another name that is currently not being used for the field being copied to the target file.

TIP

> If you accidentally overwrite an object, you can restore it by copying it from the GLOBAL.MPT file, as long as the object in the GLOBAL.MPT file has not previously been customized. You might want to make a backup copy of the GLOBAL.MPT before making major changes so that you can copy the original object to replace the edited one.

9. Click the Close button to close the Organizer dialog box and save your changes.

NOTE

> If the item you are copying is currently visible in Microsoft Project 2007 and you are copying the item from a file into the currently active project, then you will get a message saying you cannot perform the copy.

USING ORGANIZER TO RENAME OBJECTS

In addition to copying objects, you can also use the Organizer to rename existing ones.

To rename an object using the Organizer, follow these steps:

1. Open the Organizer by selecting Tools, Organizer in the main menu.
2. Select the tab for the object you would like to rename.
3. In the GLOBAL.MPT file that you want to reflect the change, select the object to rename.
4. Click the Rename button.
5. Provide the new name and click the OK button to save your changes.
6. Click Close to exit the Organizer window.

NOTE

> Objects in the GLOBAL.MPT file are not automatically updated. So, in order for your changes to be reflected in the new project files, the custom object must be copied in the GLOBAL.MPT. Any existing projects that contain the object must be manually updated as well.

USING ORGANIZER TO DELETE OBJECTS

You can use the Organizer to permanently delete objects. Note that you cannot delete objects currently in use. To do so, follow these steps:

1. Open the Organizer by selecting Tools, Organizer from the main menu.
2. Select the tab that contains the object you would like to delete.
3. In the GLOBAL.MPT file that contains the object, select the object to delete.
4. Click the Delete button. A confirmation box appears. Click Yes to confirm object deletion.
5. Click the Close button to exit the Organizer window.

CONSULTANTS' TIPS

GLOBAL.MPT

When working with Microsoft Project 2007, remember that there are underlying influences to how your project file looks and behaves. The GLOBAL.MPT file is the default template (not to be confused with project templates you create for building new projects) on which all new project files are based. GLOBAL.MPT contains all default and custom project information, such as fields, views, filters, reports, and so on.

In addition, make sure that you make a copy of the GLOBAL.MPT prior to making any changes to it, such as deleting objects, and so on. This is a good practice to ensure that you never lose data and can revert to the original if you have to.

USING THE ORGANIZER

Learn how to use the Organizer to copy favorite custom views for use in other projects. You or your organization may create a view that lets you see common project tracking information, such as % Complete and Actual Work. You can use the view for all of your projects by copying it into GLOBAL.MPT, and then you can use your file so others can copy the view into their GLOBAL.MPT. Using the Organizer is a powerful tool for creating common and standard processes within an organization.

PROTECTING YOUR PROJECT FILES WHEN SHARING

When sharing your project files among several people, it is important to protect your file from being edited without your knowledge. To protect your file, use either the Password Protect, Password Revise, or Read-Only Recommended option.

BASIC STEPS FOR STARTING A PROJECT

Whenever you start a project, either from a template or blank project, always begin with the same steps:

1. Set the project start date. If you are using the template, your project will use the start date the template has when it was saved, so it is unlikely you want that date to be your start date.

2. Set the project properties. This includes setting the project calendar. In addition, set the calendar in the Gantt section, unless you are using the "Standard" calendar in both.

3. Display the project summary task (Task 0).

USE TEMPLATES AND KEEP THEM SIMPLE

When creating templates, it is best to keep the project schedule as simple as possible. The more details you specify and create, the harder they may be to manage and edit in the future. Consider only putting generic/general information into your template and then customize it for each project accordingly.

CHAPTER **19**

FORMATTING VIEWS

In this chapter

USING THE COMMON FORMAT OPTIONS IN THE STANDARD VIEWS

Microsoft Office Project 2007 provides many "preformatted" views that you can use to look at project information. These views are organized into Gantt or graphical views, Usage or sheet views, and forms for task data entry. For instance, the Gantt views show schedule, tracking, and cost information in a combination view made up of a table of data items and the graphical schedule display with preset graphical formatting. Usage views are also combination views made up of a table of data items and a time-phased display of values, including work and costs. All three category formats can be modified and customized to meet individual requirements. This includes tables, Gantt styles, fonts, colors, and timescales. This chapter focuses on the various formatting features available for views.

You can use the Format commands to change the current view, and the new format will remain for all future displays of that view. If, for instance, you change the timescale on the Gantt Chart to show days instead of weeks, then that format change would be displayed until you modify it again. The Format Change is specific to the current view only. If you were to display another view that uses a timescale, however, that timescale would be based on changes you made the last time you displayed that view, not the changes you made to the previous view.

SORTING THE TASKS OR RESOURCES IN A VIEW

Sorting can be a fast-and-easy way to find specific information, especially for views that show tasks or resources using the table or list layout. You can also sort the order in which tasks and resources appear in form views as you scroll using the Next and Previous buttons. The only view you cannot sort displayed items in is the Relationship Diagram view.

You can use sorting to set up lists by several different predefined fields, as well as up to three columns or fields of your choice. Your predefined fields will change from view to view; for instance, when using a resource view, your predefined fields are By Cost, By Name, and By ID. In task views you can find By Start Date, By Finish Date, By Priority, By Cost, and By ID. If you want to sort through the entries in a view, select Project, Sort. A menu with the predefined sort fields will open, as shown in Figure 19.1. When you select one of these, your tasks or resources will be sorted by the field you selected into ascending order immediately. If you choose the Sort By option, the Sort dialog box- opens to offer you more choices, as shown in Figure 19.2.

SELECTING THE SORT KEYS

With the Sort dialog box, you can use the drop-down list in the Sort By area to choose which sort field you want to use, then you can sort it in ascending or descending order by selecting the appropriate button. You can then sort further by using up to two additional Then By sort field areas.

19

Figure 19.1
You can sort your tasks or resources using this cascading sort list.

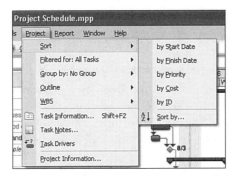

Figure 19.2
The Sort dialog box gives you many different options for sorting your tasks or resources.

Besides sorting by the predetermined fields, you can sort using custom fields, such as the Work Breakdown Structure codes you might have created. If you are using a custom field that has been renamed, both the generic field and the alias for it will show up in the sort key lists.

You can also use any of the columns in the table view as the sort by field. From any view that displays a table in it, click the column name to sort by that field. This will sort alphabetically in ascending order. Click the column name again to sort alphabetically in descending order. A small arrow indicator will appear in the column name to indicate the sort direction.

SELECTING THE SORT OPERATION

You should always save your project file before you sort. Although you can undo a sort, you should keep in mind that if the sorted tasks or resources are permanently renumbered (by selecting the Permanently Renumber Tasks or Permanently Renumber Resources check box, depending on your active view), they will be given new ID numbers. You should also choose to keep tasks under their summary tasks, and sort them within their summary tasks, by selecting the Keep Outline Structure check box. Clearing this check box will result in all tasks being sorted throughout the project.

While in resource views, you can sort your resources by their assigned projects (by selecting the Sort Resources by Project check box). This option is useful when using a pool of resources that are spread across several projects.

→ For additional information about resources, **see** Chapter 8, "Defining Project Resources," **p. 249**.

To sort a list after specifying its criteria, click the Sort button. If you want to return your sort to Microsoft Project's standard sort (by ID numbers), use the Reset button. However, the Reset button does not return the items to their original order if you have selected the Permanently Renumber Tasks/Resources check box. Also, if you have filters and macros set on tasks by their ID numbers, the Permanently Renumber Tasks/Resources check box will change everything. The only way to recover from this is to reopen a previously-saved project file.

FORMATTING TEXT STYLES FOR CATEGORIES OF TASKS AND RESOURCES

Many of the views in Microsoft Project 2007 allow you to set special formatting options to display text, such as changing font, type size, style, and color to help you display your data. You could, for instance, set all your critical tasks to display in red, or set apart your milestones by displaying them in italics. You can open the Text Styles dialog box by going to Format, Text Styles, as shown in Figure 19.3.

NOTE

A new feature of Microsoft Office Project 2007 now allows you to highlight task rows. You can do specific tasks or set highlighting formats for task types such as Critical or Milestone tasks.

NOTE

If you find that you cannot open the Text Styles dialog box from the Format menu, this is because you cannot change the text using the current view.

Figure 19.3
You can really spice up your text using the Text Styles dialog box by changing the font, size, style, and color.

CAUTION

Once you have made changes to the formatting of text, you cannot undo or reset those changes without going in and restoring the text back to its original formatting manually.

SELECTING AN ITEM TO CHANGE

When you click on the Item to Change drop-down list, you will find several different categories to choose from. If a task or resource belongs to two or more categories, then some of the items will take priority over others. The hierarchy of the Item to Change list, in descending order of priority, is as follows:

- Highlighted tasks
- Marked tasks
- Summary tasks
- Milestone tasks
- Critical tasks

For instance, if a milestone is also a critical task, then that task's display is controlled by the text format for milestones. If the same task is also selected by a highlight filter, then it will display the task using the Highlight task format, instead of the Milestone or Critical task formatting.

You can highlight a series of tasks when you need to make them stand out for any reason. The first step is to open the list of filters, under Project, Filtered For. This will give you a short list of filters; to see entire list, select More Filters... under the drop-down list. This brings up a list of all the filters you can choose from, as shown in Figure 19.4. Choose which filter you want to use, and then select the Highlight button instead of the Apply button. For instance, you could select Incomplete Tasks and click Highlight, and those tasks will now stand out in bold, blue font. To turn highlighting off, go back to the Project, Filtered For menu and select All Tasks.

The benefit to using highlighting instead of applying a filter is that highlighting will just change the text format of your tasks, instead of rearranging or hiding them. Microsoft Project 2007 has a default format already set in the Text Styles dialog. This format can be changed and saved as the default.

You can manually select tasks using the Marked field in the Microsoft Project 2007 database, because marked tasks have the logical value of Yes. You can use this to select tasks of interest without having to define a filter or custom field.

Milestone tasks have a logical value of Yes in the Milestone field. When you set a task to zero duration, it automatically becomes a Milestone (with a value of Yes in the Milestone field). You can also designate a task as a milestone by opening the Task Information dialog box, selecting the Advanced tab, and clicking the Mark Task as Milestone check box.

19

Figure 19.4
Using the Highlight option can make it easy for you to find tasks that meet specific qualifications quickly and easily.

Highlight button

You can change all of your tasks quickly and easily by selecting the All item in the Item to Change drop-down list in the Text Styles dialog box. Simply select All and make the formatting text changes you want. This will, however, override all other changes you have already made to specific tasks.

The items after All in the Item to Change list are specific to either tasks or resources, depending on the view you have open at the time. If the Gantt Chart view is your active view, then the first items are for tasks. Here are the text style items available for the Gantt Chart view:

- All
- Row & Column Titles
- Critical Tasks
- External Tasks
- Highlighted Tasks
- Marked Tasks
- Noncritical Tasks
- Milestone Tasks
- Summary Tasks
- Top, Middle, and Bottom Timescale Tier
- Bar Text – Left
- Bar Text – Right
- Bar Text – Top
- Bar Text – Bottom
- Bar Text – Inside
- Changed Cells

If you were using the Resource Usage view, on the other hand, your list would look like this:

- All
- Allocated Resources
- Overallocated Resources
- Highlighted Resources
- Row & Column Titles
- Assignment Row
- Middle, Bottom, and Top Timescale Tiers
- Changed Cells

CHANGING THE STYLE OF TEXT DISPLAYS

When you open the Text Styles dialog box (by selecting Format, Text Styles), you will notice that it is very similar to text formatting dialog boxes in other Microsoft applications, such as Word. The Text Styles dialog box allows you to change the assigned font, font formatting (that is, regular, bold, italic, and bold italic), font size, color, and, in Microsoft Project 2007, background color. You can also select the Underline check box for underlining text. To revert back to the default text style, click the Reset button.

You can use the Color drop-down list to change the color of your text. If you do not have a color printer, all text will print as black with grayscale shading. You can select the Clear Color option to make text transparent, although the item's row will still appear on the screen and paper. Even if you do not use a color printer, colored text can really make certain tasks or resources stand out when displayed onscreen.

FORMATTING FONT FOR SELECTED TEXT

Besides changing categories of styles, you can also change selected text items. Open the Font dialog box using the Format, Font command to change any text you have selected. The changes to text you make using the Font dialog box are the same as changes you make using the Text Styles dialog box, except that they will only affect preselected text. If you want to make just one specific task stand out, select that task, open the Font dialog box, and make the changes you need, such as making the text bold or changing the text color to red, to make it really stand out.

The Font dialog box is identical to the Text Styles dialog box, and you can make the same kind of changes with it that we covered in the last section.

 A fast way to copy formatting from one set of text to another is to use the Format Painter button on the Standard toolbar. Select the text, either a task or resource, that has the format you want to copy, and then click the Format Painter button. Your mouse will change to a cross with a paintbrush attached. Choose the text to which you want to apply the formatting, and then release the mouse button. If you want to change more than one set of text, you can click and drag your mouse to select multiple sets.

NOTE

The main difference between using the Text Styles dialog box and the Font dialog box is that with the Font dialog box, you are only making changes to specific selected text, whereas with the Text Styles dialog box, you are changing categories of tasks or resources. If you made a change to a task with the Font dialog box, for instance, it will only affect that task. However, if you change all of your incomplete tasks using the Text Styles dialog box, then any future tasks you enter that are incomplete will have the same formatting.

FORMATTING GRIDLINES

Gridlines are the guides on tables and timescales, and are usually added by default. They are the lines drawn between the rows and columns of a table, between column titles and between the units of a timescale. Gridlines can be added to views, such as adding a Project Status date line in the Gantt Chart view.

You can make changes to gridlines for your current view by selecting Format, Gridlines, which opens the Gridlines dialog box, as shown in Figure 19.5. You can also open the Gridlines dialog box by moving your mouse to any blank area of the Gantt Chart view and right-clicking, and then selecting the Gridlines option that appears on the shortcut menu.

Different options appear in this dialog box depending on which view you are using. Figure 19.5 shows the Gridlines dialog box for the Gantt Chart view. Figure 19.6 shows some of the common gridlines you could use; those not shown by default on the Gantt Chart view are marked with an asterisk.

Figure 19.5
Changing the look of the gridlines is easy using the Gridlines dialog box.

To change a gridline, select your choice from the Line to Change list. You can see which gridlines are in use if they have anything entered in the Normal, Type box. If there is nothing there, these are not default gridlines. Any changes you make will affect every line of the type chosen, unless the At Interval section has also been activated. The At Interval section creates gridlines to appear at regular intervals. Only a few of the line categories can use interval lines. In the Gantt Chart and Resource Usage views, for instance, the rows and columns can have interval colors and line types. In table views, the Sheet Row and Sheet Column gridlines can also have intervals.

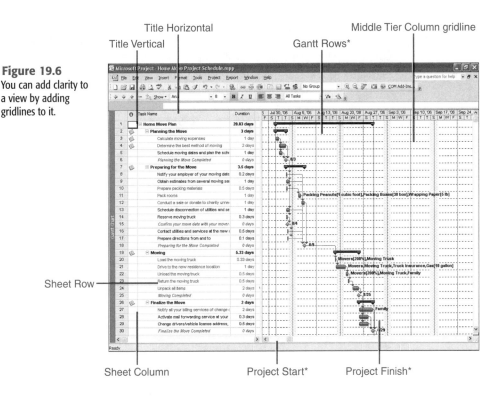

Figure 19.6
You can add clarity to a view by adding gridlines to it.

Five options appear in the Type drop-down list in the Normal section: no line, solid, dotted, small dashes, and large dashes. The Color drop-down list allows you to choose a color, with solid black the default. The At Interval line type, if available, allows you to choose the type and color you want. To activate the At Interval Type fields, simply choose an interval: 2 (for every other row or column), 3 (for every third row or column), 4 (for every fourth row or column), or Other (to set your interval number).

USING THE OUTLINE OPTIONS

Any view that shows tasks, such as the Task Sheet and Gantt Chart views for instance, can show information about the tasks' places in the outline structure. You can show or conceal those summary tasks, show subordinate tasks and their place in the outline through indenting, show outline numbers beside each task, and either exhibit, or not, the special symbol to show that tasks have subordinate tasks.

→ For additional information about outlines, **see** "Defining Summary Tasks and Subtasks," **p. 168**.

If you want to change the display of outlined tasks, go to Tools, Options, and then select the View tab on the Options dialog box. You can see all of the different options you have in Figure 19.7, whereas Figure 19.8 shows you the effects of the boxes you might select.

If you are not using a view that can display outlines, such as the Task Sheet or Gantt Chart view, you cannot access the Outline Options section in the View tab of the Options dialog box.

Figure 19.7
You can see the different display options you have for formatting your outline.

You can turn the Indent Name check box on and off; if you turn it off, all of the indentations are removed and tasks are aligned on the left margin.

The Show Outline Symbol check box displays either a plus (+) or a minus (–) sign preceding each summary task. A plus sign shows that this summary task has subtasks under it not currently shown, whereas the minus sign indicates that all tasks are being shown. If you are using the Formatting toolbar and the outline symbols are not available, the Show Summary Tasks option has been turned off. Turn that option on to use the outline symbols.

You can save space on printed reports by turning off the Indent Name option and turning on the Show Outline Number option. This way, all of the tasks are aligned to the left margin, but you can still easily tell their position in the outline by using the outline number option.

The project summary task is a specific type of task; it summarizes and rolls up the entire project. Selecting the Show Project Summary Task check box will show a project summary task at the beginning of your project's task list, with a task ID number of 0. This feature is very useful to sum up projects and consolidate projects. Some project managers prefer to set up their own summary task when they first create their projects, using task ID number 1.

Project Summary Task   Formatting toolbar outlining options

First-level summary task   Three-tiered timescale

Figure 19.8
Using Outline options and summary tasks can help you organize your project.

Outline number

Outline symbol   Second-level tasks indented

The Show Outline Number check box turns on and off the outline number that precedes an outline name, showing its location within the outline. The outline number for a task includes the related summary task number. This outline number is the same for the WBS codes in the Task Information dialog box, under the Advanced tab, unless you have created a custom WBS.

The Show Summary Tasks check box is always selected by default. If you clear the box using the Options dialog box's View tab, your summary tasks will not appear on the list. Also, if your subtasks are hidden when you turn off the summary task display, they will stay hidden. The outlining commands on the Formatting toolbar are not accessible when the summary tasks are not shown. Hiding summary tasks can be useful when you are applying a filter or sorting tasks.

FORMATTING TIMESCALES

A view that shows timescales, such as the Gantt Chart view, allows you the option of switching time units and date formats for each of the different levels of timescale display. Microsoft Project 2007 provides you with three tiers of the timescale: Top, Middle, and Bottom.

To make changes to the timescale, open the Timescale dialog box under Format, Timescale, as shown in Figure 19.9. In the sample display area, you can preview what the timescale will look like as you switch between different options.

19

TIP

Another way to access the Timescale dialog box is by double-clicking anywhere on the timescale itself or by right-clicking the timescale headings and choosing Timescale from the shortcut menu.

Under the shortcut menu you will also find the Zoom option. This lets you zoom in and out of your project at several different levels, such as 1 week, 1 month, or the entire project.

Figure 19.9
The Timescale dialog box gives you several options for displaying your timescale and lets you preview the look before deciding.

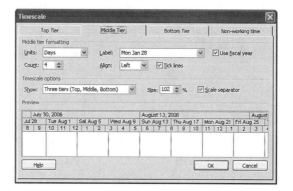

CHANGING TIMESCALE TIERS

The timescale has three tiers: the top, middle, and bottom. You can choose how many of them you wish to use, but you must select at least one tier. You will get a Timescale Error message if you try to close the Timescale dialog box with all three tiers hidden. If you select a single line on the timescale, it will be defined by the middle tier settings. Two tiers will be the middle tier and the bottom tier.

All of the tiers are defined on the same dialog box, but they are defined separately. The only real rule to remember is that any units assigned to a tier must be at least as large as the units for the tier beneath it. The time span of the lower tier (including the periods specified in the Count field) cannot be longer than the timescale of the higher tier. This means that you cannot set the middle tier at days if the bottom tier is set at weeks.

Use the Units drop-down list to select which time period you want your tier to display: Years, Half Years, Quarters, Months, Thirds of Months, Weeks, Days, Hours, or Minutes. Selecting a week will show 1 week, if you want more than 1 week, you can change the Count text box appropriately. A setting of 2 in the Count text box will show 2 weeks. You could get the same result by selecting days and setting the Count text box at 14.

TIP

If the tick lines that separate the units of the scales don't change in the sample area immediately after you change the Count setting, you might need to select the Tick Lines check box twice to refresh the tick line display.

The Label option allows you to decide how you want the timescale unit displayed, as shown in Figure 19.10. Your selection will depend somewhat on which units you decide to display. There are three types of labels for the time units:

- **The specific time period named**—This would show the year, quarter number, month name or number, or day number. There are many choices like this available, some with abbreviations, full or partial specifications, numbers, or words.

- **The number of time periods within the project**—This option allows you to either start from the beginning of the project (From Start) or count down from the end of the project (From End). For instance, if the unit is Week 1 (From Start), then the time periods are labeled Week 1, Week 2, and so on. You can set the same thing up using From End, only it will count backwards: Week 50, Week 49, and so on. This can be especially helpful when you are first setting up a long project, before your specific start and finish dates are set. This can also be helpful if you are setting the project up to be a template, and the start and finish dates will vary depending on who is using the project.

- **None**—You can also choose to have no label, which means Microsoft Project 2007 will display a timescale with tick marks only.

Figure 19.10
You can set the label options based on your chosen timescale units.

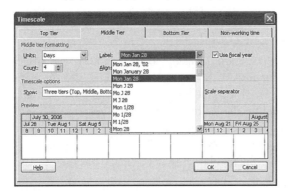

Using the Align drop-down list, you can align your time units labels—either left-align, right-align, or center. You can also choose whether you want separator tick lines between your larger time unit labels by selecting (or not) the Tick Lines check box.

Each tier can reflect calendar years (the default) or fiscal years. If you want to set displays and labels for periods according to fiscal years, you will need to change the Fiscal Year Starts In option, as shown in Figure 19.11. You can find it on the Calendar tab of the Options dialog box, under the Tools menu. Use the Fiscal Year Starts In option to set which month begins the fiscal year for your organization. The default is January, but you can use the drop-down list to change it to the month you need. If you use a month other than January, select the Use Fiscal Year check box on the Timescale dialog box to let Microsoft Project 2007 know you want to use the starting month for fiscal year numbering. You can similarly change the timescale to start on a day other than Sunday (the default) by using the Week Starts On option, which is also found on the Calendar tab of the Options dialog box.

19

Figure 19.11
You can set the Fiscal Year definition to display on the timescale on the Calendar tab in the Options dialog box.

COMPLETING THE TIMESCALE DEFINITION

Two more options on the Timescale dialog box to look at are the Size and the Scale Separator. These will modify the overall look of the timescale. You can modify the width of the timescale units displayed with the Size box by adjusting the percentage. For instance, if you cannot fit the values for the Resource Usage view into the cells of the lowest displayed timescale units, you can enlarge the unit space by using a value greater than 100, such as 120 or 150. On the other hand, if you want a smaller view so that you can fit more of your project on paper, then lower the number in the percentage box to less than 100.

Just like you can remove the ticks between the dates on your timescale, you can also remove the horizontal line between the labels. This is the Scale Separator, and you can turn it on and off using its check box.

Once you are finished with your changes to the timescale, click OK to make your changes active. Your timescale changes will only affect the display of the active view, just like with other formatting options. Every timescale view has its own options to format.

CAUTION

> If you have customized your timescale settings, specifically the labels, when you use the Zoom In or Zoom Out buttons in the Standard toolbar or apply a Zoom setting from the View menu, you lose your customized settings.

CHANGING THE DISPLAY OF NONWORKING TIME

Microsoft Project 2007 creates base calendars with working days, default and nondefault work times, and nonworking days. The Nonworking Time tab on the Timescale dialog box will let you make changes to the way your nonworking calendar time is displayed on the Gantt Chart, as shown in Figure 19.12.

CAUTION

The shortcut menu options displayed for nonworking time when you right-click the timescale bars are different from the options when you right-click the Gantt Chart. The shortcut menu from the timescale bars has the Change Working Time option. This option allows you access to the calendar and lets you redefine what should be considered non-working time. The shortcut menu for the Gantt Chart view simply changes the way non-working time is displayed. This is the same dialog box that opens when you double-click the timescale bars.

Figure 19.12
You can modify the look of the nonworking time display on the Gantt Chart view on the Nonworking Time tab in the Timescale dialog box.

You can also select which calendar you want to use when displaying nonworking time. Microsoft Project 2007 will default to the Standard calendar, since it is the driving calendar unless another has been selected using the Project, Project Information command. If you have other calendars defined, select one from the Calendar drop-down list.

→ For additional information about calendars, **see** "Defining Calendars," **p. 118**.

The three buttons in the Draw section of the Nonworking Time tab will modify the way the bars that span across the nonworking time are drawn. You can change the color and pattern in which nonworking time is displayed, but remember that you cannot see the non-working days unless at least one of your tiers in the timescale shows days or a smaller unit.

You also have options for the shading of nonworking time, which include Behind Taskbars (the default), In Front of Taskbars (which will leave a gap in the bars), and Do Not Draw. The Do Not Draw option will eliminate the shading on the nonworking time. In other words, the Do Not Draw option will not change the Gantt Chart view into a 5-day work week; the weekends are still shown, they just have nothing to differentiate them from the rest of the week.

The choice of displaying nonworking time in front of the task bars can indicate that tasks are not being worked on. This setting has no effect on the total duration of the task, just the display.

19

USING PAGE BREAKS

A page break will force the beginning of a new page when you print the view, but will have no effect on the screen display, except for the optional dashed line to show where that page break is located on the list. You can change the page break line format under the Format, Gridlines command.

If you want to force a page break in the permitted views, choose any cell in the row that falls below where you want your page break. This row now becomes the first row on the new page. Now go to Insert, Page Break to add the page break. If you want to remove it later on, choose the row below the page break and go to Insert, Remove Page Break. If you want to remove all of the page breaks, select all the tasks by clicking either the Task or Resource Name column heading. Alternatively, you can click the Select All square above the ID column and then go to Insert, Remove All Page Breaks.

Any of the page breaks you enter manually will only be honored by the Print command if you select the Manual Page Breaks check box in the Print dialog box. Clear it and Microsoft Project 2007 will ignore your page breaks.

→ For additional information about printing, **see** "Printing Views," **p. 771**.

FORMATTING THE GANTT CHART VIEWS

The Gantt Chart views are the most commonly used views for building projects and for presentations and reporting, so it makes sense that there are so many different choices available for formatting the Gantt Chart. You can format it manually or get help from the Gantt Chart Wizard.

FORMATTING THE GANTT CHART VIEW MANUALLY

Eight different options appear under the Format menu when you are using the Gantt Chart view: Bar, Bar Styles, Font, Gantt Chart Wizard, Gridlines, Layout, Text Styles, and Timescale. We have already looked at some of the ways you can manually change the Gantt Chart view, specifically the font, timescale, gridlines, and text styles. Now we are going to look at the remaining options.

USING THE BAR STYLES OPTIONS

One possible way to modify the bar chart section of the Gantt Chart view is use bar styles. Go to Format, Bar Styles on the menu bar. This will bring up the Bar Styles dialog box, as shown in Figure 19.13. You can also open the Bar Styles dialog box by double-clicking on the Gantt Chart view background or by right-clicking on a blank spot on the timescale portion of the Gantt Chart to open the shortcut menu and selecting Bar Styles.

Figure 19.13
The Bar Styles dialog box allows you to make changes to the different kind of task bars used in the Gantt Chart view.

The upper half of the Bar Styles dialog box shows the definition table, with rows for each of the bars and symbols that show up in the Gantt Chart view. The lower half has two tabs:

- The Text tab contains options for adding text to different locations around the Gantt Chart view bars.

- The Bars tab contains three different drop-down lists that set up the formatted look of the bars and symbols. You can make changes to the bar at the start, middle, and end. You can see examples of the defaults for each bar in the Gantt Chart view in the second column of the table located at the top of the dialog box.

To add a new type of bar into the table on the upper section of the Bar Styles dialog box, just choose the row you want to insert a new row above and click the Insert Row button. You can delete a bar by choosing the row it is in and using the Cut Row button. You can move your cut row to a new location by selecting the new location and clicking the Paste Row button.

TIP

You'll notice there are only three buttons: Insert Row, Cut Row, and Paste Row. There is no Copy Row. If you want to copy a row, you will have to cut and paste it. First select which row you want to copy, and click the Cut Row button, then immediately (without moving your selection) click the Paste Row button. That will return the original row right back to its starting place, and now you can move to where you want to insert the copy of the row and use Paste Row again. Once you cut the row, you can paste it as many times as you might need.

SUPPLYING THE BAR NAME   Enter the name of your new bar type in the first column of the definition table, located on the upper part of the Bar Styles dialog box. You can name your new bar anything you choose. This name will only be used in the legend, beside the bar symbol, when the Gantt Chart view is printed. If you add an asterisk (*) to the front of the name, it will not be printed.

DEFINING THE BAR APPEARANCE   You can see a preview of what the bar or symbol will look like when your Bars palette definition is applied in the Appearance column in the Bar Styles dialog box. To modify the look of the sample, you will be using the Start, Middle, and End sections of the Bars tab, on the lower half of the Bar Styles dialog box.

To change the color, shape, and type of shape at the beginning of the bar or at the end of the bar, use the Start or End column, respectively. You can choose which shape you want to use from the Shape drop-down list; the Type drop-down list lets you choose whether you want a dashed, framed, or solid shape. The Color drop-down list allows you to select which color you want for your shape.

The Middle section deals with the bars themselves. You can select which shape you want the bars on your Gantt Chart view to be by using the Shape drop-down list, what pattern you want them to use with the Pattern drop-down list, and what color with the Color drop-down list. Later in the chapter, we will look in more detail at the bars, in the section "Selecting the Row for the Bar."

> **TIP**
>
> Since projects are often just printed in black and white, you should consider using patterns for your bars, so that they will show up more easily, as opposed to just solid-color bars.

SELECTING THE TASKS THAT DISPLAY THE BAR   The third column of the upper section of the Bar Styles dialog box, Show For… Tasks, is used to define the type of tasks that will use the bar. You can click this column to display a drop-down list of bar categories. To use two or more categories, use a comma to separate the names.

Here are the task types you can select in the Show For… Tasks drop-down list:

- **Normal**—These are tasks that are neither Milestone nor Summary tasks. Most tasks fall into this category.
- **Milestone**—Milestone tasks are identified with Yes in the Milestone field; tasks set to zero duration are automatically defined as milestones. You can set a task as a milestone in several different ways; you can click Yes in the Milestone field, you can select the Mark Task as Milestone check box in the Advanced tab of the Task Information dialog box, or you can manually set your task to zero duration.
- **Summary**—Summary tasks have at least one or more subtasks indented under them and are identified with a Yes entry in the Summary task field.
- **Critical**—A Critical task is any task on the critical path. They are identified by a Yes in the Critical task field, and that entry is determined by the task's slack. If slack is zero or less, normally, then that task is set as critical. You can, however, change the cutoff point using the Calculation tab on the Options dialog box.
- **Noncritical**—A Noncritical task is any task not on the critical path.

- **Marked**—A Marked task is identified with a Yes entry in the Marked task field. You can set any task to Marked.

- **Finished**—A Finished task has an actual finish date (that is, Actual Finish does not contain NA).

- **In Progress**—An In Progress task has an actual start date, but no actual finish date.

- **Not Finished**—A Not Finished task has NA in its Actual Finish date field. Not Finished tasks include both In Progress and Not Started tasks.

- **Not Started**—A Not Started task has NA in its Actual Start date field.

- **Started Late**—A Started Late task has a scheduled start date later than its baseline start. These tasks may not have actually started.

- **Finished Late**—A Finished Late task has a scheduled finish date later than its baseline finish.

- **Started Early**—A Started Early task has a scheduled start date that is earlier than its baseline start.

- **Finished Early**—A Finished Early task has a scheduled finish date earlier than its baseline finish.

- **Started On Time**—A Started On Time task has a scheduled start date that is the same as its baseline start date.

- **Finished On Time**—A Finished On Time task has a scheduled finish date that is the same as its baseline finish date.

- **Rolled Up**—A Rolled Up task has its Rollup field set to Yes. Using the General tab of the Task Information dialog box you can set the Rollup field by choosing the Roll Up Gantt Bar to Summary check box. You will notice that summary tasks do not display subtask dates unless the Show Rolled Up Gantt Bars check box is filled for the summary task.

- **Project Summary**—A Project Summary task has a task ID number of 0, and is only displayed if you turn on the Show Project Summary Task option on the View tab of the Options dialog box.

- **Group by Summary**—A Group by Summary task is a temporary task, created by the Group By command, that has the rolled-up values for a specific set of tasks.

- **Split**—A Split task is any task that has been split into two or more sections.

- **External Tasks**—An External task is a phantom task. These represent tasks in other projects that have been linked as predecessors or successors to tasks in the current project.

- **Deliverable**—A deliverable is a tangible, measurable result, outcome, or item that must be produced to complete a project or part of a project. Bar styles for this task type, and the Dependency task type described next, can be defined as part of Project Professional and Project Server.

19

- **Dependency**—A dependency can be set to a deliverable that does not affect the project's schedule. Bar styles for this task type, and the Deliverable task type described previously, can be defined as part of Project Professional and Project Server.

- **Flag1...Flag20**—A Flag task has a custom Flag field set to Yes. You might add a Flag field to a task for data entry.

All tasks will fall into one of three categories: Normal, Milestone, or Summary. You should combine the other types of tasks on the list with one of these three, to give your tasks more definition. For instance, you could create Normal, Critical and Normal, Noncritical tasks instead of just the Normal tasks, which include both Critical and Noncritical.

When a task fits into more than one category, it will display the formatting of both. If one style of formatting, however, would overwrite another, the feature lowest on the definition table is applied last and will remain visible.

You can set it up to select all tasks except the one that is named by placing the word *Not* before the type name, as in Not Milestone or Not Summary.

SELECTING THE ROW FOR THE BAR   Every task can have up to four distinct, nonoverlapping bars drawn for it. Usually only row 1 is used, meaning there is only one row of bars for each task. If you decide to use multiple bar styles that apply to a task, then those styles will all show on the same row. Styles at the top of the table are drawn first, followed by the styles lower on the table, which can overwrite the styles higher up on the list. If the overwriting bar is as large or larger than the one it is overwriting, it will cover and hide that bar. If it is smaller, you will see them both, which is why the standard progress bar appears in the middle of the standard task bar.

You can show multiple styles side-by-side, if you set them up to occupy different rows. If you wanted to see a bar set for early start and finish dates for your task, another with late start and finish dates, and a third with scheduled dates, you would define three different rows, each one corresponding to early, late, and scheduled dates.

DEFINING THE LENGTH OF THE BAR   Microsoft Project 2007 uses the From and To columns in the definition table, in the upper part of the Bar Styles dialog box, to determine the length and placement of all bars and symbols. You can use several different options, either the date fields or one of several measures of time (such as Percent Complete, Total Slack, or Complete Through). You can choose these from the drop-down lists. The following is a list of your options and information on how they are calculated:

- **Start and Finish**—Times and dates when your task is scheduled to start or finish.

- **Baseline Start and Baseline Finish**—Planned start and finish dates based on your task's baseline. If you have not yet saved a baseline, these fields will show NA.

- **Actual Start and Actual Finish**—The recorded dates and times for the actual work start and finish on your task.

- **Start1–Start10 and Finish1–Finish10**—These are 10 custom fields you can use to store extra task start and finish date information. As you save interim schedules, they will be placed in these fields.

- **Baseline1–10 Start and Baseline1–10 Finish**—As you save your baselines, Microsoft Project 2007 will fill these fields with the start and finish dates, similar to the Start1–Start10 and Finish1–Finish10 mentioned earlier.

- **Deadline**—This is the date you set as a deadline for your task, instead of defining a date constraint for the task, to show when you want the task finished. Since it uses the deadline date as a single point in time, Microsoft Project 2007 uses the same field as the From and To entries.

- **Preleveled Start and Preleveled Finish**—These are the scheduled start and finish dates, before the last resource leveling was completed.

- **Early Start and Early Finish**—Early Start is defined as the earliest possible start date for a task, depending on the start of the project, the schedule of the task's predecessors, the calendar, and any other constraints that might have been imposed on the task. Early Finish is the earliest possible finish date, depending on the Early Start date, the task's duration, and any linking relationships it has.

- **Late Start and Late Finish**—Late Start is the latest start date possible for a task, without delaying the finish of a project. Late Finish is the latest finish date without delaying the finish of the project. If you set a Deadline date, it will be the Late Finish date.

- **Free Slack**—Free Slack is a duration value and is defined as the amount of time a task can be delayed without it affecting the schedule of another task. If you use the Leveling Gantt view, the Slack style is drawn from the Finish to Free Slack. This means that the bar begins at the task's finish date and is long enough to show the duration of Free Slack.

- **Negative Slack**—Negative Slack is the amount of time needed to be saved to avoid delaying any successor task. If there is not enough time scheduled for the task, then it is indicated with Negative Slack. It is usually the From column value and is paired with the Start date in the To column.

- **Physical % Complete**—The Physical % Complete field measures the work progress against a stated goal. It does not, however, affect duration or percentage-complete calculations. You will usually select this in the To value and pair it with the Actual Start in the From value.

- **Total Slack**—When you are using fixed start date projects, Total Slack is the time a task's finish can be delayed, without delaying the finish of the project or violating a successor task's constraint. You will usually use the To value and pair it with the scheduled Finish date in the From value.

SELECTING A PROGRESS BAR STYLE   A progress bar shows how much of a task has been finished, and should always be drawn from the Actual Start date.

Several of the To field options for progress bars are similar to other types of bars. Some of these fields should be looked at a bit closer:

- **% Complete**—Selecting this field will draw a progress bar that corresponds to the percentage your task duration is complete. So if your task % Complete is 65%, then this progress bar will be 65% the length between the task actual start and task finish. % Complete represents the time that has passed, not the actual work completed.

- **% Work Complete**—% Work Complete is normally calculated as Task Actual Work divided by Task Total Work, and represents the work finished, not just the time passed. This field will create a progress bar that is proportional in terms of % Work Complete to the task bar drawn from the task start to finish.

- **Complete Through**—This is a standard field for normal tasks. Microsoft Project 2007 adds the actual duration for a task to the actual start date, to determine the end of the bar. Microsoft Project 2007 normally only uses this Complete Through field internally, but you can select it in the From and To columns of the Bar Styles dialog box. You cannot display this field as text in any view.

- **Stop and Resume**—As you record actual work for a resource assignment, Microsoft Project 2007 places the time and date when the actual work is finished into the Stop field, and it places that same time and date in the task Resume field. Select Resume in the To column so that a progress bar will be created to show the earliest date when work needs to resume on an assignment. This Resume bar, however, gives very little information about overall progress of the task. You can also create a progress bar from the Resume date to the scheduled finish of the task, to show the span of time during which some of the work still needs to be finished.

- **Summary Progress**—This field applies to summary tasks. The Complete Through progress bar adds the actual duration to the actual start date, just like with normal tasks. The % Complete bar is drawn with exact proportion to the summary task duration that the % Complete field indicates. The % Work Complete bar compares the amount of completed and uncompleted work, whereas the Resume bar uses the earliest Resume date of any subtask.

> **TIP**
>
> Selecting values for From and To drop-down lists can be very difficult, and you need a thorough understanding of what each of the dates represents. You can read more complete descriptions of Microsoft Project 2007 database fields in the Reference section of the online help, under Help, Contents and Index.

PLACING TEXT IN A BAR CHART   Switch to the Text tab in the middle of the Bar Styles dialog box when you are ready to enter field data to be displayed on your bar, as shown in Figure 19.14. Text can be shown to the left, right, top, and bottom of the bar, plus inside. You cannot, however, enter text into these areas yourself; you will need to choose fields that contain data, such as dates, durations, percentages, and other numeric values. Any custom field you have defined and entered data into can also be displayed around the bars as well.

If you want to add text, but there isn't enough room on the row, simply add the text to a different row. A row does not require a bar, it can be used for text only. To add text to a different row, open the Bar Styles dialog box. Insert a row under the task type where you'd like to display text, such as under Normal, Noncritical. For Appearance, make the Start, Middle, and End shapes blank. In the Row column, select 2. Then, on the Text tab, set the text position as Inside and select the field to be displayed.

Figure 19.14
Text can be displayed by choosing one or more of the five different locations around the Gantt Chart bar in the Bar Styles Text tab.

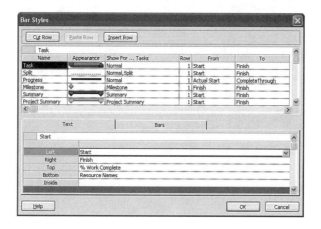

To enter text, choose the bar you want to use from the Bar Styles dialog box, then click the Text tab, choose where you want the text to be placed from one of the five rows, and then select the field name from the drop-down list. Click the OK button when you are finished, or click the Cancel button to close the window without saving changes.

A BAR STYLES DEFINITION EXAMPLE

It might be helpful, when using summary tasks, to define styles that clearly indicate the overall progress for the group of summarized subtasks. You could hide all of the subtasks, for instance, to help you see the bigger picture and focus on the major phases of your project. Since summary tasks look so similar, despite how many subtasks might be completed, this customization could provide more information than the standard display. With simply a glance, you can see which phases are complete, which are started but unfinished, and which have not begun yet.

For different summary task styles to effect different conditions, you first must set a different style row for each possible condition. Setting these custom styles for a single type of task means the conditions would have to always occur over the life cycle of the task, always in the same order. It is necessary that the final condition for a task is placed lowest in the rows of styles, so as to overwrite the earlier conditions. Three conditions are key in the summary task life cycle:

- **No subtasks have started**—Neither the Actual Start nor the Actual Finish fields for the summary task have dates in them.

19

- **At least one subtask must have started, but not all are finished**—An actual start date must be activated, but no actual finish date yet for the entire summary task.
- **All subtasks are finished**—Both actual dates are defined for the summary task.

You can see the style definitions required to draw summary bars representing changing conditions, in Table 19.1, with the results shown in Figure 19.15.

TABLE 19.1   SUMMARY TASK PROGRESS BAR STYLES

	Bar Appearance						
Task Name	Start	Middle	End	Show For	Row	From	To
Summary: Not Started	Framed, dark gray	Gray bar, solid	Framed, dark gray	Summary	1	Start	Finish
Summary: Started	Solid, black	Gray bar, solid	Framed, dark gray	Summary	1	Actual Start	Finish
Summary: Finished	Solid, black	Black bar, solid	Solid, black	Summary	1	Actual Start	Actual Finish
Summary: Progress	None	Black bar, solid	None	Summary	1	Actual Start	Complete Through

Figure 19.15
With the help of Microsoft Project 2007, you can create multiple styles for a single Gantt Chart bar, which can be applied to the formatting, based on changing conditions.

USING THE BAR OPTIONS FOR SELECTED TASKS

If you want to change the appearance of the bars for only selected tasks, instead of changing a bar style, you can open the Format Bar dialog box, as shown in Figure 19.16, by accessing the Format, Bar menu. You will see that the Format Bar dialog box is similar to the lower section of the Bar Styles dialog box. Microsoft Project 2007 omits the task definition portion because any changes made here would not be applied to all tasks types, but only the task(s) you select before you open this dialog box.

Any changes you make in the Format Bar dialog box are considered by Microsoft Project 2007 to be manual formatting, and will remain unless you reset the bar to the default. To change your task bar back to its original formatting, select it again, reopen the Format Bar dialog box, and click Reset.

Figure 19.16
The Format Bar dialog box allows you to make quick changes to selected task bar formats.

USING THE LAYOUT OPTIONS

To modify the way bars are displayed with the Gantt Chart view, select Format, Layout. This opens the Layout dialog box, as shown in Figure 19.17. You can also open the Layout dialog box by right-clicking an open area on the timescale side of the Gantt Chart and selecting Layout from the shortcut menu.

Figure 19.17
The Layout dialog box allows you to change the appearance of task bars in the Gantt Chart view.

19

If you find the task-linking lines to be distracting, you can easily turn them off. You also have the option of choosing between rectilinear line styles and straight line styles, which are the default.

You can make changes to the dates, displayed as text around the task bars, using the Date Format options. The drop-down list allows you to choose which style of date you want to use. The first option in your drop-down list is Default, which will use the format set on the View tab of the Options dialog box. Changes made here will not, however, change the default format for any date shown elsewhere in the project, such as the Start and Finish dates.

You can modify the height of your task bars using the Bar Height drop-down menu. You can set them between 6 and 24 points, with 12 points being the default.

You can easily set your project up so that all tasks will be rolled up and represented on summary tasks, by selecting the Always Roll Up Gantt Bars check box. If you select this check box, then all tasks will behave as if the Roll Up Gantt Bar to Summary option in the Task Information dialog box has been turned on. Your milestone indicators and bars connecting subtask start and finish dates will be shown in their respective summary tasks when you choose this option.

You can also use the Hide Rollup Bars When Summary Expanded check box if you want to hide the display of the summary bar when your summary tasks are collapsed. This will also hide the usual black bar with the down-pointing end shapes that shows up under the rolled-up bars and markers. Finally, when your summary tasks are expanded and the subtasks are visible, you will not see any roll-up indicators on the summary task bars.

Figure 19.18 shows the Always Roll Up Gantt Bars and Hide Rollup Bars When Summary Expanded options turned on.

Rollup bars hidden when summary task is expanded
Gantt bars rolled up to collapsed summary task

Figure 19.18
Here is an example of rolled-up markers for their subtasks set on Summary tasks.

If you have a task with a duration less than the time period in the lowest displayed timescale tier, you can modify how it is displayed with the Round Bars to Whole Days check box. If you had a task with a duration of 4 hours, for instance, being displayed in a Gantt Chart view, where the bottom tier has been set to Days and this box is not selected, then the bar will show the length for exactly 4 hours. If you do select the Round Bars to Whole Days check box, then the bar will be extended to a full day. This only affects the display, however; the calculated start and finish dates and actual duration are still the same.

You can also select the Show Bar Splits check box if you want Microsoft Project 2007 to actually show tasks being split in the Gantt Chart view. If the option is not selected, Microsoft Project 2007 will show the task bar extending the entire duration of the task, including the split, from start to finish. If you select the option, however, Microsoft Project 2007 will show a gap in the task bar for your split task, with the two parts connected by a dotted line.

If you want to be able to place graphics in the Gantt Chart, you will need to select the Show Drawings check box.

USING THE GANTT CHART WIZARD

You can use the Gantt Chart Wizard to help you with formatting bars, which makes it very easy. The wizard will help you through different formatting options, as it questions you about how you want your bars to be displayed. Your options are the same as was covered in the previous section "Formatting the Gantt Chart View Manually." However, the wizard will walk you through the process, step by step. You can open the Gantt Chart Wizard by selecting Format, Gantt Chart Wizard, by using the Gantt Chart Wizard button on the Formatting toolbar, or by selecting it from the Gantt Chart shortcut menu.

> **TIP**
>
> If you are unfamiliar with all of the multiple formatting options available, the Gantt Chart Wizard might be a good place for you to start. You can use it to set up your task bars and then exit the wizard and use the Bar Styles and Text Styles dialog boxes to make modifications to suit you.

After you open the wizard, the welcome screen appears. Click the Next button for your first screen of choices, as shown in Figure 19.19. As choices are made, you will move through the appropriate steps, depending on your choices. Simply select from your options, and then click Next to move on. You can use the Back, Cancel, and Finish buttons at any time. If you have any questions, you will need to get out of the Gantt Chart Wizard to use the Help button in the title bar, and then repeat your steps in the Gantt Chart Wizard to return to where you were.

Your first decision concerns the basic way tasks are displayed. You begin with the choices for setting up and formatting the bars on your Gantt Chart. Your five starting options are listed here:

- **Standard**—The default for Gantt Chart. If you have already run the wizard, you can run it again and choose Standard to undo your changes.

Figure 19.19
Setting up and formatting bars can be very easy with the Gantt Chart Wizard.

- **Critical Path**—This is the critical path option, which concerns tasks that must be completed on time to meet the project deadline. These are displayed in red and can be helpful when you are trying to reduce the duration of your project, also known as *crashing the schedule*.

- **Baseline**—With this option, you get two bars per task, showing the original and current schedules, such as the Tracking Gantt Chart view. This can be helpful for tracking a project already underway.

- **Other**—There are 13 predefined formats for you to select or modify as you choose.

- **Custom Gantt Chart**—This is your most extensive choice, and takes you through all the choices for formatting, step by step. You will get to choose colors, patterns, and shapes for the Critical, Normal, Summary, and Milestone tasks. You can also add bars for baseline information and place text next to the bars.

No matter what your starting format choice is, the wizard will prompt you for the type of text you wish to display in and around the task bars. Not all of the formats are available in the wizard's drop-down lists, but you can make custom choices to define distinct text formats for Normal, Summary, and Milestone tasks.

The last wizard question will ask you how you want linking lines drawn to display dependency relationships between your task bars. Once you have made all your choices, choose Finish, Format It, Exit.

CAUTION

Any changes that you make using the Gantt Chart Wizard will be applied to the Gantt Chart view currently being displayed. Running the wizard will cause default formatting to be lost. You should instead make a copy of the standard Gantt Chart, then use the wizard on your copy. Select View, More Views, Gantt Chart, Copy. Once you apply your copy, you will not have to worry about your changes; you can always go back to your original.

FORMATTING THE CALENDAR VIEW

The Gantt Chart view is not the only view to which you can easily make changes. The Calendar view can be modified in many different ways, depending on what you want to do with it. You can use the Zoom command in the View menu, or the Zoom In and Zoom Out buttons on the Standard toolbar to get in for a closer look or back off to see the big picture. This can also be very helpful if you have a lot of tasks occurring all at once.

With the Calendar view, you can change the height and width of the date boxes via your mouse, as shown in Figure 19.20. Move your mouse to point at any vertical line in the calendar, and the mouse pointer will change to a double-headed arrow. You can then drag this arrow left or right to widen or narrow your column. The same is true for horizontal lines, to make your date boxes taller or shorter.

TIP

If your Calendar view is set on Month, when you move lines vertically, you will affect the whole week, but when you move them horizontally, you will only affect that specific day of the week. For instance, if you widen Tuesday, then all of the Tuesdays in your month will become wider.

If you want to widen the entire calendar at once, instead of just week by week and day by day, select either the far-right vertical line, to widen the entire calendar proportionately, or the bottom horizontal line, to lengthen the calendar proportionately.

Figure 19.20
You can manipulate the size of the date boxes in the Calendar view, which allows you to see more tasks per day.

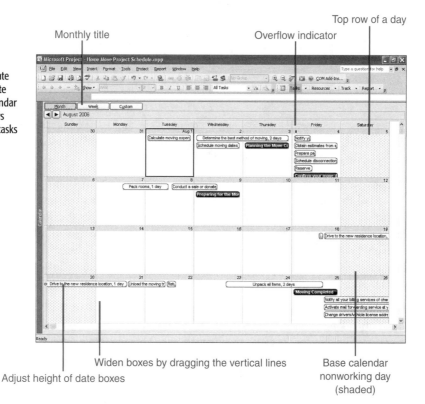

Monthly title

Overflow indicator

Top row of a day

Widen boxes by dragging the vertical lines

Adjust height of date boxes

Base calendar nonworking day (shaded)

19

Using the Format menu will open the following options for the Calendar view: Timescale, Gridlines, Text Styles, Bar Styles, Layout, and Layout Now. The Gridlines and Text Styles options are the same as mentioned in previous sections of this chapter, and are the same as the Gantt Chart view. Timescale, Bar Styles, and Layout/Layout Now for the Calendar view are unique, and will be covered in more detail in the following sections.

FORMATTING THE TIMESCALE FOR THE CALENDAR

You can open the Timescale dialog box by going to Format, Timescale, or by right-clicking any spot in the Calendar view, other than a specific bar or heading, to open the shortcut menu. You can see in Figure 19.21 that the Timescale dialog box for the Calendar view has three tabs: one for headings and titles, one for additional data elements that can appear in the date boxes, and one for shading on certain days.

Figure 19.21
The options in the Calendar view's Timescale dialog box are very different from the Gantt Chart view.

You can use the Week Headings tab to change your choices of labels for the month, days of the week, and the week itself. You can also set up either 5- or 7-day weeks, plus include smaller calendars for previous and subsequent months.

With the Date Boxes tab, you can set additional data information in the top or bottom row of each of the individual date boxes. You can also use colors and patterns for more emphasis. Microsoft Project's default setting for the Date Boxes tab omits the display of the bottom row, and on the top row it includes an overflow indicator and date. The overflow indicator lets you know when all tasks scheduled for that day cannot be displayed within the date box, because of lack of space. When printing your calendar, those overflow tasks will appear on a separate page.

With the Date Shading tab, you can make modifications to all of the categories for working and nonworking dates. With the Show Working Time For drop-down list, you can choose a base or resource calendar as your starting point. Then select an exception type, such as nonworking days or a resource's calendar, and set the pattern and color to create the visual distinction. You can see a sample of your work to the right as you set things up.

In Figure 19.22, a resource calendar for Eric Lutz has been used as the starting point. Eric's nonworking days are shown with horizontal stripes and the Using Resource… filter has been applied so only Eric's tasks are shown.

Figure 19.22
You can modify all categories for working and non-working dates for a selected base or resource calendar.

Resource's assigned tasks

Applied filter

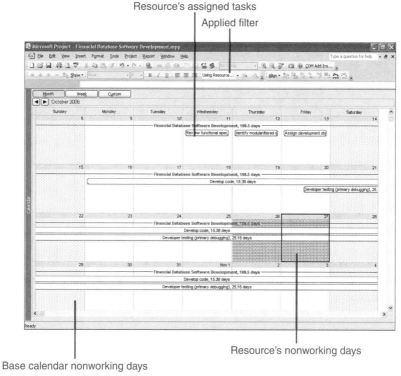

Resource's nonworking days

Base calendar nonworking days

SELECTING CALENDAR BAR STYLES OPTIONS

Just like with the Gantt Chart view, you can control how the bars in the calendar of your Calendar view appear, including text that can be added as part of the bars. To access the Bar Styles dialog box, shown in Figure 19.23, go to Format, Bar Styles, or you can right-click on the calendar to open the shortcut menu and choose the Bar Styles option.

Your first step is to choose which type of bar you want modified in the Task Type list box. Second, modify the bar type, color, pattern, and split pattern for the bar using the drop-down lists in the Bar Shape area. You can select either a bar or a line to represent the duration of a task. If you have chosen a bar, then you can also apply shadow for emphasis by selecting the Shadow check box. You also have a variety of patterns and colors to choose for your bars, and several different choices for different displays for split tasks.

If you select the Bar Rounding check box, then any task with a duration of less than a whole day will be rounded up to a whole day. So if you have a task that is a day and a half, it will be rounded up to show as 2 full days.

19

Figure 19.23
Use the Bar Styles dialog box to change the task bars display in the Calendar view.

The Text area allows you to choose the fields you want shown in the bar, by either typing in their names or choosing them from the drop-down list. If you want to enter more than one field on the bar and are typing them in, separate them with commas; if you are using the drop-down list, be sure to deselect the field name and enter a comma before choosing the next one from the list. If you do not, then the first field will be replaced by the second, instead of being added to it. You have the option of aligning your text either centered, left-aligned, or right-aligned. If your text is too long, you can select the Wrap Text in Bars check box. You can see results for choices made in the Sample box shown at the bottom of the dialog box, unless you have selected All in the Task Type categories list.

CAUTION

> You might get a warning message from Microsoft Project's Planning Wizard, depending on your choices in the Bar Styles dialog box, which will indicate you have calendar bars with different heights. The warning message will explain how to reposition those bars.

SETTING THE LAYOUT OPTIONS FOR THE CALENDAR VIEW

You can use the Layout dialog box (as shown in Figure 19.24) to display in which order your tasks will appear in the date boxes. You can open the Layout dialog box by either going to Format, Layout or right-clicking on the calendar to open the shortcut menu and choosing Layout. Microsoft Project's default method is Use Current Sort Order. You can also use Attempt to Fit as Many Tasks as Possible, which will do just what it says, without regard to the sorting. Select the Show Bar Splits check box to establish that a task that has been split displays differently from a regular task. A split task will show a dotted outline, by default, during the portion of the task when no work is underway. Selecting the Automatic Layout check box tells Microsoft Project 2007 to initiate the settings in the Layout dialog box automatically anytime tasks are edited, added, or deleted. If the Automatic Layout check box is not selected, you will need to go to Format, Layout Now or choose Layout Now from the calendar shortcut menu to apply any changes.

Figure 19.24
You can determine when and how tasks are sorted within each of the Calendar view's date boxes using the Layout dialog box.

FORMATTING THE NETWORK DIAGRAM VIEW

Getting a look at your project's logic and flow is easy with the Network Diagram view, which can be useful in the planning stages. There are several different customizations you can make to the Network Diagram view: You can change the borders, size, and shape of the nodes; you can create named data templates that specify the fields displayed in each node; and you can apply layout characteristics to task nodes.

Use of either the Zoom option on the View menu or the Zoom In and Zoom Out buttons on the Standard toolbar can help to change your perspective of the project, as will applying a filter.

The Format menu provides the following options: Box, Box Styles, and Layout. Making changes to the display of text in the Format menu for the Network Diagram view is just like the Gantt Chart view, and is covered earlier in this chapter. Although the Layout and Layout Now commands are similar and covered in other sections, summaries can be found in the following sections. Because of the differences between the Network Diagram view's use of the Box Styles dialog box and other views, it will be covered in more detail in the following sections.

➔ For additional information about the Network Diagram views, **see** "The Network Diagram View," **p. 384**.

USING THE BOX STYLES OPTIONS

Using the Box Styles dialog box allows you to customize the boxes that surround the nodes, changing between 10 different shapes, four different border widths, and a variety of border colors. You can also make modifications to the background colors and patterns. You can open the Box Styles dialog box by going to Format, Box Styles or by double-clicking anywhere in the open space of the Network Diagram view (see Figure 19.25).

Default box styles have been assigned according to their types of tasks. Any critical tasks, such as Summary or Milestone tasks, are outlined in red with a white background; noncritical tasks are outlined in blue with an aqua background. The shape defaults are rectangles for normal tasks, four-sided parallelograms for summary tasks, and six-sided boxes for milestones.

Figure 19.25
You have several different options you can apply to the node boxes of the Network Diagram view, using the Box Styles dialog box.

Select a task type to format   Preview the settings

Specify a task ID number to preview actual task data

Create or modify box templates

Set the border shape, color, and line width

Select the box background color and pattern

Microsoft Project 2007 sets the formatting of boxes displayed in an applied highlight filter, by default, to be the same shape as nonhighlighted nodes, but with a yellow background. Turn on the Set Highlight Filter Style option if you want to review or change the highlight settings for node types.

Seventeen different border colors can be applied to shapes, and they are great with a color printer to define different nodes. However, if you are not using a color printer, you should modify the border patterns to better distinguish between the types of tasks.

Turning on the Show Horizontal Gridlines and Show Vertical Gridlines options will help you view cell dividers in both the view onscreen and in print.

> **TIP**
>
> If you want to see how your styles will look with actual task information, instead of just the generic preview, you can enter a valid task ID number into the Show Data from Task ID entry box.

USING DATA TEMPLATES FOR NETWORK DIAGRAM NODES

Setting up a data template means that you will control the contents and the row and column layouts within each node. In a template, the node definitions include the following elements:

- Box cells laid out with up to 16 cells in a 4-row-by-4-column grid
- Cell width sizing for all cells in the box
- Vertical and horizontal alignment settings for the contents of each cell

- Up to a maximum of three lines of text to be displayed in cells
- Descriptive label inserted in front of data of each cell
- Font size, style, and color options for each cell
- Fields that appear in each of up to 16 cell positions
- Date formats for the Network Diagram view displays

The contents and layout of boxes are initially defined by the supplied templates. The standard template, which is used for normal critical and noncritical tasks, displays six fields of information on a 4-row-by-2-column grid: Task Name, Start, Finish, Resource Names, ID, and Duration. The Milestone template uses a 3-row-by-1-column format and lists the Task Name, Milestone Date, and Task ID. Summary tasks use a template with a 4-row-by-2-column grid with six fields of information: Task Name, Start, Finish, % Complete, ID, and Duration.

Use the following steps to create new Network Diagram data templates:

1. Go to Format, Box Styles to open the Network Diagram Box Styles dialog box.
2. Once the Box Styles dialog box is open, use the More Templates button. This will open the Data Templates dialog box, as shown in Figure 19.26.

Figure 19.26
With the Data Template dialog box, you can take a look at a generic sample of a data template or choose a valid task ID to see the actual task values.

3. Use the Import button to open a box style template definition within the current file or to open one that has already been created in another file. If a second file is needed, it must already be open to allow this import.
4. Click New for a new data template. If you want to use an existing template to start with, select either Copy or Edit.

NOTE

The Standard data template, provided by Microsoft Project 2007, cannot be edited. You can, however, make a copy of it and then edit the copy.

5. Use the Data Template Definition dialog box, shown in Figure 19.27, for setting your options on a new template.

Type a name for the template

Preview a generic box or data from a specific task

Figure 19.27
The Data Template Definition dialog box lets you set up the cell layout and settings for a new template.

Choose cell contents from the drop-down lists

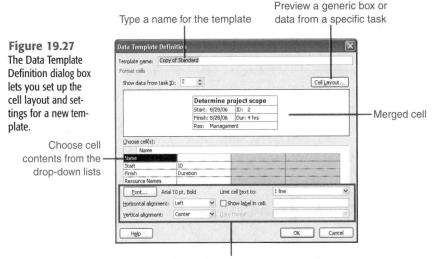

Merged cell

Formatting options are set for each cell

6. Name or rename the new template in the Template Name entry area.

7. Open the Cell Layout dialog box with the Cell Layout button, as shown in Figure 19.28.

Figure 19.28
Use the Cell Layout dialog box to change the box grid and cell width.

8. Choose the number of rows and columns for the new diagram box in the Cell Layout dialog box. You can also set the cell width.

9. You should also decide handling for cells that are left blank while in the Cell Layout dialog box. The Merge Blank Cells with Cell to the Left option has been used so that the Name field appears to occupy two cells, instead of one.

10. Once your layout is finished and you are ready to return to the Data Template Definition dialog box, click the OK button.

11. Choose your font, alignments, and number of text lines for each of the individual cells in the Data Template Definition dialog box. Select each cell in the Choose Cell(s) area and then add a prefix label to any or all cells. Finally, choose the date format for any date cells you might have.

> **N O T E**
>
> You can choose and change more than one cell at a time by clicking and dragging, or you can use Shift+click or Ctrl+click on the multiple cells you want to change.

12. Once you have finished with your template definition, first click OK and then click Close in the Data Templates dialog box to return to the Box Styles dialog box.

13. Back in the Box Styles dialog box you can apply your data template settings to nodes by selecting a task type in the Style Settings For list. Then choose a data template from the drop-down list.

14. Click the OK button when you have finished. The Network Diagram view will show your change immediately.

USING THE BOX OPTIONS

Using the Format Box dialog box is very similar to using Box Styles, but it only affects the box currently selected. A preview area is provided. You can select a data template and modify the border and background.

CONTROLLING THE NETWORK DIAGRAM LAYOUT

You can control the layout of the network diagram by setting options in the Layout dialog box. You can also use the Layout Now command if you want to force Microsoft Project 2007 to refresh the display. Once the general layout is defined and applied, you can then apply task filters and group definitions to the diagram, and collapse summary tasks in the outline to hide tasks.

SELECTING LAYOUT OPTIONS

You can use the Layout command, under the Network Diagram Format menu controls, to modify the overall look and feel of the Network Diagram, as opposed to just the appearance and contents of the individual network nodes. With the Layout command, you can select the options for box layout order and spacing, the style of the box connection lines, the color of the linking lines, the diagram background style and color, the drawing of task progress lines, and whether the diagram should be laid out automatically or manually.

19

Use these steps to set up the Network Diagram view's layout options:

1. Open the Layout dialog box, shown in Figure 19.29, by going to Format, Layout, or by right-clicking on a blank spot in the Network Diagram view and choosing Layout from the shortcut menu.

Figure 19.29
You can make changes to the Network Diagram view's overall appearance using the Layout dialog box.

2. Select Automatically Position All Boxes in the Layout Mode area, if you want Microsoft Project 2007 to maintain the onscreen layout. Alternatively, you can select Allow Manual Box Positions to allow click-and-drag movements of the boxes.

3. You can use the drop-down lists and spinners to set your row spacing, height, and alignment in the Box Layout area, as well as column spacing, width, and alignment. The settings are relative to those for other like elements; for instance, if you use a row alignment of Center to place all of the boxes in a single horizontal row, all of the box midlines will form a straight line. If you set the column alignment to Left, then all the boxes in a vertical column will align with the left box edges.

NOTE

> Your box sizes might vary, depending on the template settings applied to the box types. You can look back at the section "Using Data Templates for Network Diagram Nodes," earlier in this chapter, for more information.

4. You can use the Arrangement drop-down list in the Box Layout area to determine in what order Microsoft Project 2007 draws the diagram. The default arrangement is Top Down from Left. You can see in Figure 19.30 an example of Top Down from Left. This is a common arrangement for most network diagrams.

TIP

If you need to temporarily enlarge one of the Network Diagram boxes, you can move your mouse cursor over it and then pause, which will enlarge the box.

Figure 19.30
Top Down from Left, with dotted page breaks and rectilinear linking lines, is the standard diagram arrangement.

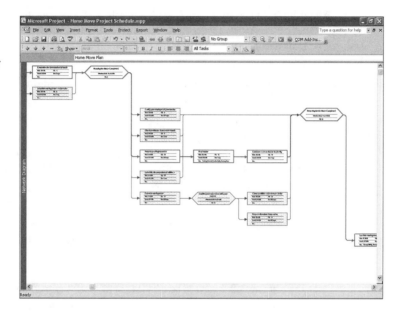

You can see in Figure 19.31, for comparison, how a Network Diagram view might look if the arrangement were set Top Down by Month. Each column of nodes represents a month; within columns, boxes are in ID order.

Figure 19.31
You can get a good picture of your project plan over time by using the Top Down by Month drawing of the Network Diagram view.

19

5. Use the Box Layout area in the Layout dialog box to make selections to keep tasks with their summaries when you are changing the layout arrangement, to show summary tasks, and to adjust for page breaks so that boxes cannot be split and printed partially on two different pages.

6. Decide which lines you want to use between diagram boxes—straight or rectilinear—and then select Show Arrows to indicate successor direction between nodes. Finally, select Show Link Labels if you want to include small dependency type labels (FS, SS, FF, SF) on each linking line.

7. Choose your pattern and color options for your linking lines and the diagram display background.

8. Two helpful options can be found at the bottom of the Layout dialog box. The first is the Show Page Breaks check box, which allows you to see onscreen how the printing will be laid out without having to go to the Print Preview. The second is the Mark In-Progress and Completed check box, which will draw a diagonal line (from the top left to the bottom right) across boxes for tasks with some progress, and an additional diagonal line through completed tasks.

9. If you are printing the overall structure of your plan and do not want to display any task details, you should use the Hide All Fields Except ID option, as shown in Figure 19.32.

TIP

There are two other ways to access the Hide All Fields Except ID option. You can also find it by right-clicking on the diagram background and selecting Hide Fields from the shortcut menu, or you can use the Hide Fields button on the Network Diagram toolbar.

10. Once you have made all of your selections and changes, click OK.

Figure 19.32
Hiding all fields except for ID allows you to print a nice condensed schematic of your plan.

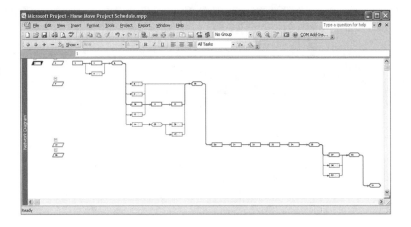

Predetermined logic exists behind each arrangement option in the Layout dialog box. If the Top Down from Left option has been chosen, Microsoft Project 2007 will redraw the Network Diagram view according to three standard rules of node placement:

- Successor tasks are always located to the right of, or below, their predecessor tasks.

- Summary tasks are always located above and to the left of their subordinate tasks.

- Linked task nodes are always connected with straight or diagonal lines, and an arrow is placed at the successor task's end of the line, to show the direction of the two tasks' relationship.

There are similar rules for other arrangement options.

Microsoft Project 2007 also includes a toolbar specific to Network Diagram view formatting. With the use of this toolbar, you can quickly apply many of the options in the Layout dialog box. Go to View, Toolbars, Network Diagram to turn the toolbar on. This toolbar is described in Table 19.2.

TABLE 19.2   THE NETWORK DIAGRAM TOOLBAR

Toolbar Icon	Tool Name	Action
Align ▾	Align	If manual positioning has been turned on, you can use this tool to line up task nodes by their edges, center, or midlines.
	Hide Summary Tasks	Toggles on and off to hide summary tasks.
	Show Progress Marks	Toggles to show (diagonal) progress marks on nodes.
	Show Page Breaks	Toggles to show page breaks onscreen.
	Show Link Labels	Toggles to show link labels (FS, SS, FF, SF) on lines connecting the nodes.
	Straight Links	Displays task-connecting links as Straight Links (toggles with rectilinear linking lines).
	Hide Fields	Hides all fields except task ID (toggles with full node displays).
	Layout Now	Instructs Microsoft Project 2007 to redraw the screen and apply the format or manual position changes.
	Layout Selection Now	Limits the application of changes to selected tasks only.

CONTROLLING BOX PLACEMENT IN THE NETWORK DIAGRAM VIEW

If you activate the Allow Manual Box Positioning radio button in the Layout dialog box, you can move the boxes of the diagram around, repositioning them for more clarity. To move a node manually, move the mouse cursor to the edge of the node, and then pause there until the cursor changes to a four-pointed arrow. You can then click and drag the border edge, moving the node to wherever you would like. You can also select the node and use the Ctrl+arrow keys to move it.

Any of your predefined or custom-built task filters can be applied to the Network Diagram view. With the diagram displayed, go to Project, Filtered For to apply one of the standard filters. You can also apply group definitions to the diagram. Go to Project, Group By. There are several predefined groups: No Group, Complete and Incomplete Tasks, Constraint Type, Critical, Duration, Duration then Priority, Milestones, Priority, and Priority Keeping Outline Structure. You can see in Figure 19.33 how task nodes have been grouped into critical and noncritical task sections, which occurs when you select the Critical option. You can also select More Groups and Customize Group By to define your desired grouping.

Noncritical tasks at the top   Critical group definition applied

Choose outline levels to display   Diagram reduced to ID-only format

Figure 19.33
Grouping capabilities can offer you several different ways to show tasks nodes.

Critical tasks at the bottom

You can also control the Network Diagram view display by setting up the outline detail level to be displayed. Use the Show button on the Formatting toolbar to select which level of subtasks you want to be displayed. You can also expand or collapse individual summary tasks on the screen. Just click the plus (+) or minus (–) symbol above each summary task.

USING THE ZOOM COMMAND

It can be very helpful to change the perspective of your view, especially using the Network Diagram view, by either zooming in to see the fine details or zooming out to see the bigger picture.

You can use the Zoom In and Zoom Out buttons to move through the various preset zoom levels. You can select Zoom from the View menu or right-click on the Network Diagram view, and select Zoom from the shortcut menu. The Zoom dialog box is displayed, as shown in Figure 19.34. There are several preset values for zooming, or you can enter a value between 25% and 400% in the Custom text box.

Figure 19.34
The Zoom dialog box allows you several different options on how to examine the Network Diagram view.

TIP

You can only zoom between 25% and 400% using the Zoom dialog box. If you have a large project, and use the Entire Project radio button, you will probably get an error box telling you your project cannot be displayed, because the view cannot be set below the minimum zoom of 25%.

FORMATTING THE TASK FORM AND RESOURCE FORM VIEWS

Since the Task Form and Resource Form cannot be printed, the formatting options for them are very limited. You can view all tasks or resources in the form when it is displayed full screen. To open these forms to full screen, go to View, More Views, and then choose either Task Form or Resource Form from the More Views dialog box. Use the Next and Previous buttons to move through the task or resource list.

If you want to split the screen, go to Window, Split. This will create another form in the lower pane of the split screen. The form in the lower pane of a split screen will display detailed information about the task or resource selected in the top pane.

→ For additional information about splitting Windows, **see** "Understanding Standard Views," **p. 378**.

SORTING THE FORM VIEWS

Task Form and Resource Form views can be sorted using the Sort option under the Project menu.

If a form view is displayed as either full screen or the top half of a split screen, the Sort option will change the order of the tasks and resources when the Next and Previous buttons are used. If the form is in the bottom half of the split screen, then applying a sort order will not have an effect; rather the sort order applied to the top half of a split screen controls the behavior of the Next and Previous buttons on the form.

FORMATTING DETAILS OF FORM VIEWS

The Details option under the Format menu offers different entry field combinations that you can place at the bottom of the form. The entry fields for the Resource Form and the Task Form have very similar options. Go to Format, Details when a form is active on the screen to pull up your choices. When you are using the Resource Form view, various tasks assigned to that resource are listed. If you change the details, it will alter which assigned task fields are displayed. A Task Form focuses on information about the task, including the resources assigned. So, if you change the details in the Task Form view, you are also changing what resource information or what detailed task information is shown for the selected task.

> **NOTE**
>
> You can right-click anywhere in a blank area of a form to open the shortcut menu and view a list of alternative formats for forms.

When the Task Form view is active, open Format, Details, Resource Schedule to see fields for when work is scheduled, plus the entry fields for imposing delay on either the task itself or on when the resource begins work on the task. You also have columns for Leveling Delay and Delay, as shown in Figure 19.35. The Leveling Delay field is a delay to the task itself, often caused when Microsoft Project 2007 applies resource leveling, and is the same field that appears on the Delay table on the Detail and Leveling Gantt Charts. The Delay field, however, is a delay to the resource only. This field shows delay if the resource does not start working at the beginning of the task.

The other form details show additional entry detail fields, as shown in Table 19.3.

TABLE 19.3 TASK AND RESOURCE FORM DETAILS

Task Form Detail	Resource Form Detail	Description
Resources & Predecessors	(Task form only)	Shows the default fields
Resources & Successors	(Task form only)	Focuses on upcoming tasks
Predecessors & Successors	(Task form only)	Shows the immediate links into and out of the task
Resource Schedule	Schedule	Shows the start, the finish, and any delays
Resource Work	Work	Shows the work fields for resources, including the Overtime field
Resource Cost	Cost	Includes Baseline, Actual, and Remaining resource costs

Task Form Detail	Resource Form Detail	Description
Notes	Notes	Shows any notes entered, usually through the Task or Resource Information dialog box
Objects	Objects	Shows any OLE objects that are attached to the task or resource

Figure 19.35
If you go to Format, Details, Resource Schedule, when a Task Form view is active, you can display assigned resource scheduling information.

FORMATTING THE RESOURCE GRAPH VIEW

The Resource Graph view is used when you want to look at values derived from the task assignments of one or more resources, as graphed along a timescale. You can open the Resource Graph by either going to View, Resource Graph or clicking on the Resource Graph icon on the View bar. In Figure 19.36, you can see a histogram or a bar chart in the lower pane of the allocated and overallocated task assignments for the resource Movers. The value displayed is peak units, or percentage of effort assigned during each time period.

You can graph several different measurements for a resource in a time period on each task:

- **Peak Units**—Highest assigned resource units in a time period
- **Work**—Amount of work assigned
- **Cumulative Work**—Running total of work assigned to date
- **Overallocation**—Work overallocation of the resource
- **Percentage Allocation**—Percentage of effort currently allocated
- **Remaining Availability**—Effort, in hours, still available for assignments

19

Figure 19.36
By using both the Resource Usage view and the Resource Graph view, you can see a visual representation of a resources peak unit.

- **Cost**—Cost of assignments
- **Cumulative Cost**—Running total of cost contribution to date
- **Work Availability**—Total work availability (does not reflect assignments)
- **Unit Availability**—Total percentage availability (does not reflect assignments)

You can use the graph to show these measurements for one resource, for a group of resources, or for the resource and the group together. Values can be shown for selected tasks or for all tasks in a given time period.

When a Resource Graph view is shown in the lower pane below a task view, the display values are for one resource only. You can show the values of a given resource's assignments either by selected task or by all tasks during any period that is measured using the timescale. You can see in Figure 19.37 the assignment bars for Movers for all tasks during each day, allowing a quick look at overassignment.

If a Resource Graph view is in the upper pane, or in the lower pane but with a resource view above it, then the values are shown for all tasks, and might be for one resource, for a group of resources, or for that one resource compared to a group of resources. If you are using group data for the display, then the group is defined by the current filter. For instance, if the All Resources filter, the default, is being used, then the data summarizes all resources for all tasks. You can see in Figure 19.38 the total costs associated with the Movers' task assignments, relative to the total costs for all resource assignments in the period.

Figure 19.37
You can use the Resource Graph view along with the Gantt Chart view to show bars for all tasks' work in that period for a single resource.

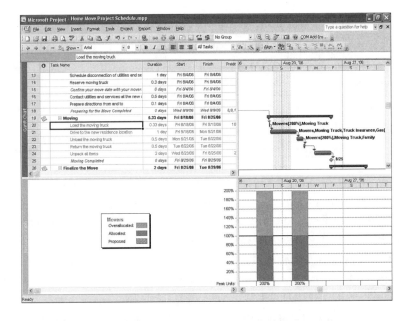

Figure 19.38
You can use the Resource Graph view to show costs associated with a single resource, as compared to the costs of all other resources.

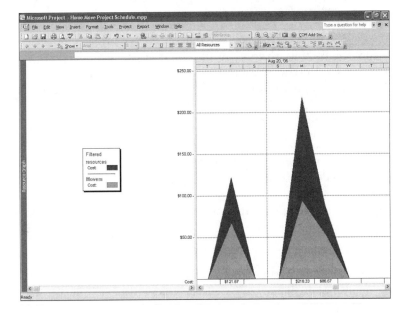

19

You can see a summarization of the values displayed for different placement locations for the Resource Graph view in Table 19.4.

TABLE 19.4   VALUES SHOWN IN THE RESOURCE GRAPH VIEW

Location of Graph	Graph Value	One Resource Value
Top pane or bottom pane below a resource view	Value is for all tasks for all filtered resources.	Value is for all tasks for the selected resource.
Bottom pane below a task view	Value is for one resource but for all tasks.	Value is for one resource but for only the tasks selected in the top pane.

REVIEWING THE FORMAT OPTIONS FOR THE RESOURCE GRAPH VIEW

The Zoom command for the Resource Graph view is available in the View menu, just like with other views, and is discussed previously in this chapter. The Zoom In and Zoom Out buttons on the Standard toolbar work the same also.

Also as in other views, the Format menu for the Resource Graph view contains dialog box options for formatting the timescale (provided the graph is not in the bottom pane), the gridlines, and the text styles.

Since the Bar Styles dialog box has unique features concerning the Resource Graph, it will be discussed in the following section.

You can also open a Details option from the Format menu. Your choices on this list of calculated values controls what information can be displayed in the timescale portion of the Resource Graph view. Since the Bar Styles dialog box options are based on these values, the Details options are discussed before the Bar Styles dialog box is covered.

SELECTING THE DETAILS TO DISPLAY

Go to Format, Details to open the choices you have on which values are calculated and graphed with the Resource Graph view. These choices are listed in the following sections with a brief description.

DISPLAYING PEAK UNITS DETAIL

The Peak Units option will measure the largest percentage of effort of a resource assigned during each time period on the graph, at any given moment.

Using the Peak Units measurement can be very useful with multiple-unit resources, when the number of maximum units available is more than one. The overallocation warning is more likely to be accurate in such a case.

DISPLAYING WORK DETAIL

The Work option is the number of units of each resource assigned to each task, measured in hours, and multiplied by the duration in hours of the task per time period display.

Microsoft Project 2007 determines the amount of work to be done by the resource by look-ing at the number of units of the resource, the resource calendar, and the resource availabil-ity contour during the time period. If total work for the time period surpasses the available amount of resource hours, Microsoft Project 2007 shows the surplus as overallocation.

NOTE

If Work is selected in the Details dialog box, the unit, be it hours, minutes, or days, is determined by the Work Is Entered In option on the Schedule tab of the Options dialog box. The show of costs is decided by the Currency Symbol, Currency Placement, and the Currency Decimal Digits choices on the View tab in the same dialog box.

DISPLAYING CUMULATIVE WORK DETAIL

Cumulative Work measures the total work since the beginning of the project for a resource. This also includes the work during the time period shown.

DISPLAYING OVERALLOCATION DETAIL

The Overallocation value shows how much work has been overallocated for the resource for the time period. This option only shows the amount of overallocation—not any work hours occurring during the normal work day. For an explanation on how work is measured, see the section "Displaying Work Detail," earlier in this chapter.

DISPLAYING PERCENT ALLOCATION DETAIL

The Percent Allocation value shows the allocated work versus available work. Percent Allocation shows the amount of work as a percentage of the amount available. See "Displaying Work Detail," earlier in this chapter, for a better idea on how work is mea-sured.

DISPLAYING REMAINING AVAILABILITY DETAIL

The Remaining Availability value shows unallocated work for the resource during the time period. This option displays the unused work time still available, and is a useful option if you want to see who still has available time to work on tasks, or to see who is available when new tasks need to be assigned.

DISPLAYING COST DETAIL

The Cost value option displays the scheduled cost of the resource work, during a given time period. If this cost is to be prorated, as defined in the Cost Accrual field in the Costs tab of the Resource Form view, then the cost will appear in the time period when the work is done. If a per-use cost is associated with the prorated resource, then that cost is shown at the start of the task. When the resource cost is to accrue at the beginning or end of a task, then the entire cost will appear in the graph at the beginning or end of the task.

19

DISPLAYING CUMULATIVE COST DETAIL

The Cumulative Cost option shows a running total of cost, based on adding each period's cost to the preceding period's cumulative cost. This measurement will show total cost over the life of the project, if you use only the group graph and include all resources in the group. See the "Using the Bar Styles Dialog Box" section, later in this chapter, for more information.

DISPLAYING WORK AVAILABILITY

The Work Availability option is a graphical representation of the total number of hours a resource is available in a given timeframe. Based on resource minimum units and the resource calendar, this display does not reflect any work assignments that might exist in the period.

DISPLAYING UNIT AVAILABILITY

The Unit Availability option shows the same information as the Work Availability option; however, the resource availability is shown as percentages.

USING THE BAR STYLES DIALOG BOX

The Bar Styles dialog box helps you to set up whichever type of graph you want to display, if any, and how it will look. Your choices for graphs are Bar, Area, Step, Line, Step Line, and Don't Show. You can also use the Bar Styles dialog box to set up whether you want to see selected resource information or groups of resource information. Open the Bar Styles dialog box for the Resource Graph by making sure the Resource Graph view is active and then going to Format, Bar Styles. Although a different Bar Styles dialog box appears for each of the value measurements just mentioned, they all have the same layout and are used the same way. You can see the Bar Styles dialog box for the Work value in Figure 19.39. Just like all of the Resource Graph view Bar Styles dialog boxes, this one has four main sections, plus three options at the bottom.

NOTE

> The different areas available in the Bar Styles dialog box depend on the Details options set in the Format, Details menu.

The upper two sections of the dialog box set up the display of overallocated amounts, if relevant, whereas the lower two sections set the display of the allocated value up to the maximum amount. The sections to the left side are for specifying the display of group data. The sections to the right side are for specifying the display of one selected resource. Some of the values on the Display menu can only display two of the sections.

Group Settings   Settings for selected resources

Formatting for overallocations

Figure 19.39
The Bar Styles dialog box will let you set options for displaying work on the Resource Graph view.

Once you are finished and the dialog box is closed, you might see sets of double bars, each possibly with an upper and lower segment. The upper segment represents the overallocation measurement, whereas the lower segment is the allocation up to the overallocation level. If you see pairs of bars, the left bar is the group measurement, whereas the right is the selected resource measurement. You will notice a similarity of the positioning of the bars to the position of options in the dialog box. Remember that the resource group is defined by the applied filter on the Resource Graph view (if the view is in the top pane or is displayed as a single pane). If no filter is applied, then the group will represent all resources.

You can see in Figure 19.40 that the bar on the right is for the resource (Movers) and the bar on the left is for the group (in this case, all resources). The striped upper portion of the resource's bars represents the overallocations, and at the bottom of the graph, work values are displayed in the same time periods where the resource is allocated.

Each of these different features was defined by the dialog box. You can go back and look at Figure 19.39 to see the settings of the dialog box that affects Figure 19.40. The Show Values check box has been selected, so Microsoft Project 2007 will display numeric data, along with the bars. The bars overlap by 20% to show that they are paired.

The graph shading patterns have been set by the selections in the four sections of the dialog box. For each section, you should select three features that establish how the value is displayed. You can use the Show As drop-down list to select the general format. You can choose from Bar, Area, Step, Line, Step Line, and Don't Show. Bar is the most common choice. If you select the Don't Show choice, Microsoft Project 2007 will suppress all representation of the value. You can then choose the color of the image, as well as fill either the bar or area with a pattern.

19

Total resource availability in this period

Overallocation amounts

Figure 19.40
You can review over-allocation of a single resource, compared to the entire resource pool, using the Resource Graph view.

Group Value — Individual resource values

Assigned Work

You can manage what is graphed by selecting what you want to be displayed, or not displayed, in each of the four sections of the Bar Styles dialog box. If you only want values from a selected resource, with nothing for the group values, select Don't Show from the Show As drop-down list for both left sections. If you only want the totals of all resources, select the Don't Show option for both right sections. If you select Overallocation on the Format, Details menu, then the Bar Styles dialog box will have both of the bottom sections grayed out, since these sections are not needed. When you are finished with your changes, click the OK button to execute them, or click Cancel to disregard the changes.

FORMATTING THE RESOURCE USAGE VIEW

If you would rather see number entries in a grid, instead of a graph, then use the Resource Usage view instead of the Resource Graph view. Figure 19.41 displays the Resource Usage view in addition to Resource Graph view, so you can see the similarity and the differences between the two views. In both cases, the value being displayed is scheduled Work.

You can use the options under the Format menu to define the following: Font, Timescale, Gridlines, Text Styles, Detail Styles, and Details for the Resource Usage view. You can also sort using the Project menu, just like with other views; plus you can insert page breaks with the Insert menu. Each of these subjects, except for Detail Styles and Details, work as covered earlier in this chapter. Detail Styles and Details are covered in the following sections.

Figure 19.41
By combining the Resource Usage view and the Resource Graph view, you can see both numeric values and their graphic representations.

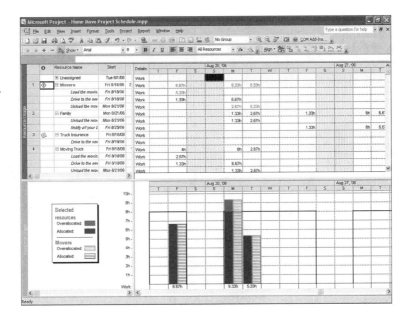

CHOOSING THE DETAILS FOR THE RESOURCE USAGE VIEW

You will find some of the same value choices in Format Details as are described in the "Formatting the Resource Graph View" section, earlier in this chapter. You can choose the value you want to show in the timescale grid by picking one of these options: Work, Actual Work, Cumulative Work, Overallocation, Cost, or Remaining Availability.

If you are using the Resource Usage view in the bottom pane, under a task view, then the only resources that will be displayed are resources assigned to the task that is selected in the top pane. Any work value displayed beside a resource name is the total scheduled Work for that resource, across all of the tasks in the project. You will also see a breakdown of other tasks assigned to that resource shown under the resource name. You can see in Figure 19.42 a Resource Usage view below a Gantt Chart view, and how the values in the usage table show the work assigned to Movers for all of the tasks during each time period.

FORMATTING THE DETAIL STYLES IN THE RESOURCE USAGE VIEW

To open the Detail Styles dialog box, shown in Figure 19.43, for your Resource Usage view, first make sure that the Resource Usage view is active. Then go to Format, Detail Styles. With this dialog box, you can select a wide variety of fields to display for each resource assignment on the Usage Details tab. Every field will show up on its own row in the timescale grid, and you can set them up to display in a different font, background color, and pattern. Go to the Available Fields list on the left, then choose a field to be displayed and click the Show>> button. If you do not want a field displayed, choose it from the Show These Fields list on the right, and then click the <<Hide button. If you want to change the order in which the fields will be displayed, use the Move up- and down-arrow buttons on the right side of the dialog box. The Usage Properties tab has options for aligning detail data and displaying headings for various columns and rows.

Resource's total work on the project

Figure 19.42
If you have a split window with the Gantt Chart view open over the Resource Usage view, you can see detailed work breakdowns, by time periods and task.

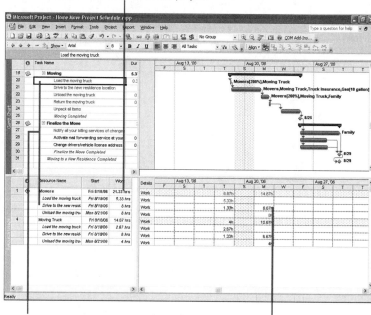

Work assigned for the task

Resource's work for all tasks in that period

Figure 19.43
You have several different options on how to display detail in the timescale grid with the Resource Usage view's Detail Styles dialog box.

FORMATTING THE TASK USAGE VIEW

Your options for formatting the Task Usage view are the same as those for the Resource Usage view. The primary difference between the two views is the focus; whereas the Resource Usage view looks at the information from a resource's perspective, the Task Usage looks at each task, providing totals for various details and then a breakdown of each resource assigned to work on the task. You can see in Figure 19.44 that the task has three resources assigned, and each one has its own hours and costs. Also shown are the work and cost totals for the task, the related summary task, and the project.

Figure 19.44
The Task Usage view can show you hours of work and costs for those work hours, which is useful information when you are making decisions about your project.

Summary task totals

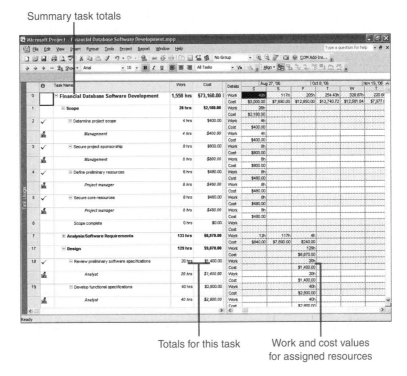

Totals for this task   Work and cost values for assigned resources

FORMATTING THE TASK SHEET AND RESOURCE SHEET VIEWS

If you want to show tables of field values for the lists of tasks and resources, the Task Sheet and Resource Sheet views are your best bet. Which columns are shown on the sheet views depend on the table applied to the sheet. You can use the Format menu for both of the sheet views, but the only options you have are changing font, gridlines, and the text styles. The Project menu includes options for sorting, filtering, and grouping. The Insert menu allows you a choice for inserting page breaks. All of these features are discussed earlier in this chapter.

CONSULTANTS' TIPS

Use the following tips to help you in formatting views within Microsoft Project 2007.

GET FAMILIAR WITH THE DEFAULT VIEWS FIRST, THEN CUSTOMIZE

Microsoft Office Project 2007 offers many ways to customize views and graphs to support just about any reporting requirement. The sheer quantity of options can be overwhelming to users until they have become more comfortable using the tool. A good approach is to start off using the default views, see where they do not meet your needs, and then make copies of views to customize. For example, before changing the Gantt Chart view, make a copy of it by selecting View, More Views. Select the view (Gantt Chart) and click the Copy button. Give it a name (such as My Gantt Chart) and click the OK button. This view is now displayed, ready for you to modify.

CUSTOMIZING THE GANTT CHART VIEW

It is easy to get carried away with customization of Gantt views. If your organization has a Gantt standard, it can be set up as a default view in a template and saved to each user's local templates using the Organizer. Most of the Gantt views follow industry-standard symbols for tasks, milestones, and summaries. Start off with simple modifications to these styles unless you have a formal standard that you follow.

SORTING VIEWS

When sorting your view, do not select the Permanently Renumber Tasks or Permanently Renumber Resources check box, depending on your active view. If this box is selected, the tasks or resources will be given new ID numbers. The Reset button does not return them to the original order, and filters and macros set on tasks by their ID numbers will not work. The only way to recover from this is to reopen a previously saved project file. Also, select the Keep Outline Structure check box. If this box is selected, tasks will stay under their summary tasks and be sorted within their summary tasks. Clearing this box will result in all tasks being sorted throughout the project.

A frequent modification made to Gantt charts is showing resources' initials, instead of the entire resource names, beside the tasks to which they have been assigned. This can make things less cluttered.

Adding rows for Actual Work and Actual Cost to the Task Usage or Resource Usage view provides an easy place to enter actual hours and costs while you are tracking project progress.

19

CHAPTER **20**

CREATING AND CUSTOMIZING THE BASIC REPORTS

In this chapter

This chapter will explore the basic reporting features of Microsoft Office Project 2007 and how to customize these reports to your individual reporting needs. You will also learn how to create and save new reports within your project or in your Global.MPT file for use with other projects.

UNDERSTANDING THE BASIC REPORTS

Microsoft Office Project 2007 contains several reports that are helpful during various stages of your project. Reports are an excellent way to view specific project information quickly, and are formatted in a printer-friendly fashion for easy distribution to other project stake-holders.

While much of the information contained in the various reports is displayed within the tables and views in Microsoft Project 2007, you will likely encounter circumstances when a view does not display the exact information you are after or is not formatted in the way you desire. Thus, the reports exist, providing you with detailed information across all aspects of your project, based on project data and presented in a textual format. Also, reports are customizable, giving you even more ability to display exactly the information you need in your report.

This chapter will examine how to use the basic reports in Microsoft Project 2007, as well as describe in detail how to customize or create new reports.

ACCESSING THE STANDARD REPORTS

Previous versions of Microsoft Project accessed the standard reports via the View menu. Microsoft Project 2007, however, has a new Report menu from which you can access the standard reports.

To open the Reports dialog box, select Report, Reports. The Reports dialog box will appear, as shown in Figure 20.1.

Figure 20.1
The Reports dialog box contains the six basic report categories.

Six report categories are found in the Reports dialog box: Overview, Current Activities, Costs, Assignments, Workload, and Custom. The first five categories contain various reports that are already created and automatically defined using the information you have entered into the project file. These reports are customizable and ready to print, and are discussed in greater detail in the upcoming sections.

The sixth category, Custom, allows you to access additional reports that are not available in the initial five report categories, as well as create your own custom reports. This process is described later in this chapter.

You can also use the Project Guide to open the Reports dialog box by following these steps:

1. On the Project Guide toolbar, choose Report.
2. In the Project Guide pane, click on the Select a View or Report hyperlink.
3. Choose the option Create a Project Report.
4. Under the section Select a Report, click on the Display Reports hyperlink, which will open the Reports dialog box.

NOTE

You can also open the Reports dialog box by using the drop-down menu. Click the arrow next to Report on the Project Guide toolbar. Then, choose the first option, Select a View or Report, from the drop-down list. Continue the process beginning with step 3, as described in the preceding list.

When the Reports dialog box is displayed, you can double-click on a category, or click it once and then click the Select button to open the particular category. No matter which of the six categories you choose, another dialog box will appear, containing the specific reports available for that category. In this new dialog box, select the report to display by double-clicking on it or clicking it once and clicking Select.

Figure 20.2 displays the Overview Reports dialog box, which can be opened by selecting Overview from the Reports dialog box.

Figure 20.2
Double-click on Overview (or click it once and then click Select) in the Reports dialog box to open the Overview Reports dialog box, which contains five different reports for the Overview category.

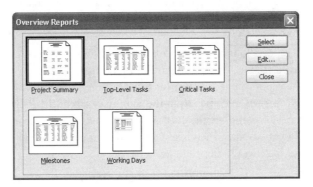

There are four basic report types in Microsoft Project 2007: Task, Resource, Crosstab, and Monthly Calendar. Most of the existing reports found in the five basic categories are variations of one of these four basic report types. However, there are two reports found in the Overview Reports category that are not: the Project Summary report and the Working Days report. These reports are described in greater detail in the upcoming section, "The Overview Reports Category."

The following list highlights the four basic report types:

■ **Task**—Task reports show all tasks, or those selected by a filter, and various details about those tasks (depending on which report you are displaying).

■ **Resource**—Resource reports show all resources, or those selected by a filter, and various details about those resources (depending on which report you are displaying).

■ **Crosstab**—Crosstab reports are shown in a table format measuring cost or work summaries by time period for tasks or resources. Tasks or resources are listed in the rows, time periods are listed in the columns, and cost or work values are summarized.

■ **Monthly Calendar**—Monthly Calendar reports are not found anywhere within the five report categories, but they can be used to create a new report (the Custom category). They are similar to the Calendar view, but formatted for printing.

The Task and Resource types are the most common report types found within the five basic categories. Crosstab reports are found in the Costs, Assignments, and Workload report categories.

As mentioned previously, choose a report category from the Reports dialog box. From that category, select a particular report to display by double-clicking it or highlighting it and clicking Select. The report will be displayed in Print Preview mode. You can place you mouse pointer over a certain area of the report to zoom in to read it, or use the magnifying glass button on the toolbar.

→ For more information about using the Print Preview mode, **see** "Using the Print Preview Button," **p. 782**.

COMMON REPORT ELEMENTS

Many of the basic reports found in Microsoft Project 2007 contain common elements or traits that are derived from the project data. For example, most reports have headers at the top that display the report name, the project title, and the project manager's name, among other items. This information comes from the Summary tab of the Properties dialog box (File, Properties). You can also set the current date in the Project Information dialog box (Project, Project Information), which is often included in the header of a report. The default value for the footer is generally the page number.

Therefore, if you want to display the project's title and/or manager's name in the header, make those changes on the Summary tab of the Properties dialog box, and make sure the current date is accurate in the Project Information dialog box. For each individual report, you can make changes to the header or footer in the Page Setup dialog box. Changes made are for that report only and do not encompass the entire project. See the upcoming section, "Choosing the Page Setup Options for a Report," for more information about using the Page Setup dialog box.

Other common elements appear in most reports, as defined in the following list:

- **Period**—The time period set for the information presented in the report, such as weekly, monthly, or quarterly.
- **Tables**—To gather the correct information for a report, assign the appropriate table to it. Task and Resource reports display columns of information based on the table assigned to the report. Custom tables can be used as well.

CAUTION

> If you have modified a table, those modifications are included in the report.

- **Filters**—For Task and Resource reports, all tasks or resources are displayed. Alternatively, you can apply a filter to the report to display only those tasks or resources that are filtered for.
- **Sort Order**—By default, reports display tasks or resources in their ID order. You can change the sort order as you see fit.

Notice these common elements as you explore the reports in Microsoft Project 2007. This chapter will explore how to change these elements in the upcoming section "Customizing Reports."

→ For more information about customizing tables, **see** "Creating and Customizing Tables," **p. 756**.

Sometimes you will receive a warning box that tells you there is no data to print. For example, if you try to display the Task In Progress report (Report, Reports, Current Activities, Tasks In Progress), but no tasks have actually started, you will see the warning box shown in Figure 20.3.

Figure 20.3
There must be data entered in order for Microsoft Project 2007 to compile a report; otherwise, you will see a warning.

20

TIP

> Familiarize yourself with all of Microsoft Project's standard reports. It may be helpful to open a project that has been completed or is well underway, and take the time to open and glance over all the reports. You will gain an understanding of which report contains what information, and how it may benefit you in the future. Refer to the next several sections as you review the reports.

THE OVERVIEW REPORTS CATEGORY

The first report category listed in the Reports dialog box is the Overview category. Select it, and you will see five reports: Project Summary, Top-Level Tasks, Critical Tasks, Milestones, and Working Days (refer back to Figure 20.2).

Table 20.1 describes these five overview reports. They all display summary information that spans across the entire project, and are useful as documentation of the scope of the project plan after the planning has been completed as well as status reports throughout the work on a project.

TABLE 20.1   OVERVIEW REPORTS

Report Name	Report Type	Usage
Project Summary	Not one of the standard report types	A snapshot of the project schedule (Dates, Duration, Work, Cost), as well as task and resource status information.
Top-Level Tasks	Task	Highlights the major phases (top-level summary tasks) of the project rather than each individual subtask.
Critical Tasks	Task	Highlights the critical tasks (those which control the project's finish date)
Milestones	Task	Highlights the tasks marked as milestones throughout the project in a similar fashion to the Critical Tasks report.
Working Days	Not one of the standard report types	Displays the base calendar working days and times. Identical to the Base Calendar report.

The Top-Level Tasks, Critical Tasks, and Milestones reports are all based on the standard Task report type. The tasks that apply to the report are listed, along with their data as defined by the report's accompanying table, as well as supporting task details (such as notes, resource assignments, and predecessor/successor relationships).

Figure 20.4 shows an example of the Critical Tasks report for a Home Move project schedule (the report is only partially shown due to screen size). The critical tasks are sorted by ID number. Notice the accompanying notes and successor relationships.

The other two reports in the Overview category—Project Summary and Working Days—are unique in that they are not based on any of the four standard report types. These are discussed further in the next two sections.

THE PROJECT SUMMARY REPORT

Like its name suggests, the Project Summary report summarizes the most important project information on one single page. It is more or less a re-creation of the information found in the Project Statistics dialog box, which you can open by clicking the Statistics button in the Project Information dialog box. However, the Project Summary report contains additional task and resource information and can be easily manipulated and printed.

Figure 20.4
The Critical Tasks report lists all tasks that determine the actual finish date of the project, and all their accompanying details.

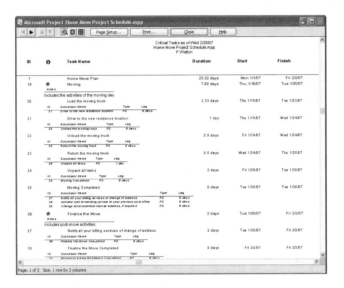

The Project Summary report is an excellent report to use for a status meeting, or as a means to update the project stakeholders as to the status of a project. It is also a good report to analyze at the beginning of a project, after the planning is completed but before actual work begins, because it lays out the entire project plan on a simple one-page document.

The Project Summary report is composed of six sections: Dates, Duration, Work, Costs, Task Status, and Resource Status. An additional seventh section, Notes, may be included. The Notes area of the Project Summary report is taken directly from the Comments field on the Summary tab of the Properties dialog box (File, Properties, Summary tab).

Each of the first four sections (Dates, Duration, Work, and Costs) includes baseline estimates, variance values, remaining values, and actual values. Therefore, you can quickly examine how the project is doing versus how it was planned.

The Task Status area gives you the number of tasks that have not started, the number of tasks in progress, the number of tasks completed, and the total number of tasks in the project. The Resource Status area provides the number of work resources, the number of overallocated work resources, the number of material resources, and the total number of resources.

The heading at the top of the report displays the project title, your company name, and the project manager, the values of which are defined in the Summary tab of the Properties dialog box. If you do not want these items displayed, remove them from the Properties dialog box before printing the report. You can add them back in if you want when the report is printed, but you will have to remove them again next time you print this report.

Below the heading information is the date. This date is taken directly from the Current Date as defined in the Project Information dialog box (Project, Project Information). This date does not act like a status date; only change the date if your Current Date is incorrect on your computer.

20

Figure 20.5 shows an example of a Project Summary report.

Figure 20.5
This particular Project Summary report contains a Notes area. If no comments are entered in the Properties dialog box, this area is removed from the report.

THE WORKING DAYS REPORT

The Working Days report lists all working and nonworking days and times for each base calendar used in the project, as well as the exceptions for each base calendar. The working days data is printed on a separate page for each base calendar. This report is a great way to verify that all the working times are set up correctly, and that all holidays and other exceptions to the base calendars are entered and accounted for.

The Working Days report is identical to the Base Calendar report, which is found in the Custom Reports dialog box (the Custom Reports dialog box is discussed in the upcoming section "Customizing Reports").

Figure 20.6 shows an example of a Working Days report.

Figure 20.6
The Working Days report provides a quick look at all base calendars and exceptions to working time in the project.

THE CURRENT ACTIVITY REPORTS CATEGORY

To view the Current Activity Reports category, open the Reports dialog box (Report, Reports) and select Current Activities. The six reports in the Current Activity Reports category will be displayed, as shown in Figure 20.7.

Figure 20.7
The Current Activity Reports category contains six reports.

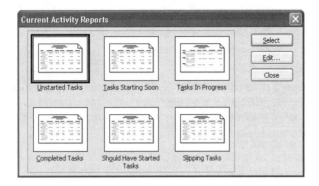

The Current Activity Reports category focuses on tasks. All six reports in this category are based off the Task report type. Some of the reports are interactive, requiring you to enter a date range from which Project calculates the report data. Refer to Table 20.2 for a list and description of the reports found in this category.

TABLE 20.2 CURRENT ACTIVITIES REPORTS

Report Name	Report Type	Usage
Unstarted Tasks	Task	Lists tasks that have yet to start. This report can be used to make sure resources and materials are in place before work begins.
Tasks Starting Soon	Task	An interactive report that lists tasks that occur within a date range you specify.
Tasks In Progress	Task	Lists tasks that are currently being worked on but are not completed. This report provides a good way to check the progress of the project.
Completed Tasks	Task	Lists tasks that are completed.
Should Have Started Tasks	Task	An interactive report that lists tasks that should have started by the date you enter. Provides a good reminder to update the status of tasks that have begun (if work has started but has not been entered). This report can also be a great tool in letting you know if your project is starting to slack and whether tasks that should be in progress are not.
Slipping Tasks	Task	Lists tasks that have started but are not scheduled to complete on time according to the planned duration. Use this report to determine which tasks run potential risks for delaying the project completion on schedule.

These six reports all provide quick updates about a project's progress. The Unstarted Tasks report tells you which tasks have yet to start; the Completed Tasks report tells you which tasks are finished; the Tasks In Progress report tells you which tasks have been worked on but are not yet completed. The other three reports in this category (Tasks Starting Soon, Should Have Started Tasks, and Slipping Tasks) are generally good indicators of whether the project schedule is on or off track, as they compare actual status to anticipated progress. They also allow you to pinpoint which tasks are at risk and address them before they cause potential project delay.

NOTE

Several of the reports in this category rely on accurate tracking to produce accurate data. For example, if a task is nearing completion, but you have not updated its percent complete, it will likely appear on the Slipping Tasks report, even though it is not slipping.

Figure 20.8 displays an example of the Unstarted Tasks report. All tasks that have not yet begun are listed.

Figure 20.8
The Unstarted Tasks report lists tasks that have yet to start. If you examine this report and notice a task listed that has begun, it is a good indication that your progress is not up to date.

CAUTION

If you have added tasks after saving the baseline, be sure to go back and update the baseline for recently added tasks and their effect on the other tasks. This is because several of the reports in this category rely on Baseline fields for comparison.

→ For more information about creating and adjusting baselines, **see** "Working with Project Baselines," **p. 445**.

THE COST REPORTS CATEGORY

The Cost Reports category contains five reports. To access them, open the Reports dialog box (Report, Reports) and select Costs (see Figure 20.9).

Figure 20.9
The Cost Reports category contains five reports.

The Cost Reports category includes five reports designed to provide an extensive assortment of cost data. Cost is one of the more significant factors in project management—that is, keeping cost under control and ensuring that the project finishes within budget. To successfully maintain and control the project's budget, you must accurately track the cost values. Table 20.3 displays all five Cost reports.

TABLE 20.3   COST REPORTS

Report Name	Report Type	Usage
Cash Flow	Crosstab (Task)	Shows the amount of money needed each week for each task, the totals for each week, and the totals for each task. This report can be useful for sharing with your project sponsor to ensure that the project budget is on track and executing per contract terms.
Budget	Task	Lists tasks, sorted by their total cost (highest to lowest), that are going over budget based on actual data.
Overbudget Tasks	Task	Lists tasks that have higher actual or scheduled costs than their baseline estimates, and sorts them by cost variance. This report can be a great way to identify the tasks that can cause your project to run over budget.
Overbudget Resources	Resource	Lists resources whose actual costs are higher than their baseline costs, generally because they are working more than expected on their assignments.
Earned Value	Task	Data is taken from the Earned Value table to compare each task's earned value (what the task has generated) to the planned value (what it was planned to generate) and actual cost.

The Cash Flow report gives you an idea of how much money you should anticipate spending on each task each week, and the Budget report shows you the current total budgeted amounts for each task. The Overbudget Task report shows you the tasks that are running over budget, and the Overbudget Resource report lists resources that are over budget, likely because they have spent more time on a task or tasks than originally planned, and thus cost more. Alternatively, the original resource could have been replaced with a more expensive one, thus deviating from the planned budget. The Earned Value report is an abbreviated, easy-to-read version of the Earned Value table, displaying actual cost of tasks and the dollar value earned for the cost spent performing the work compared to what was planned. The Cash Flow report and the Earned Value report are discussed in greater detail in this section.

The default Cost reports require a baseline to be set, because cost variance is the difference between scheduled cost and baseline cost. Therefore, be sure to set the baseline. Furthermore, be sure to enter appropriate resource cost rates for these reports to be accurate. It is recommended that you synchronize the resource cost data with your financial system to ensure that the rates are correct and that the cost used for project invoicing matches that in your project schedule.

→ For more information about setting the baseline, **see** "Working with Project Baselines," **p. 445**.

→ For more information about entering appropriate resource rates, **see** "Defining Resource Costs," **p. 265**.

The Cost table determines the data within most of the Cost reports. If you find that some of the data is irrelevant for your report, you can hide the particular field in the Cost table, and it will not be included in your report. To hide the field, resize it in the Gantt Chart view by dragging the column's border so that it is no longer visible. For example, you may want to hide the Fixed Cost Accrual field because it is not as crucial as some of the other fields.

CAUTION

> You can delete a column, or choose Edit, Hide Column, and the field will not appear on the report. However, you should remember to reinsert it after you print the report. If you hide the field by dragging the column boundary as mentioned previously, you do not have to reinsert it.

THE CASH FLOW REPORT

The Cash Flow report is the first report thus far that is a Crosstab report type (it is also a Task report type because it lists tasks). The report is arranged in a spreadsheet or grid format, and the data is taken from the Task Cost table. The cost information is the sum of resource usage costs and fixed costs associated with each task.

The first column lists rows of tasks, with each task displayed below its summary task. The remaining columns are arranged in weekly intervals, and in each row the cost information is listed per task per week. The final column lists the total costs for each task, while the bottom row lists the total costs for each week. Therefore, the cell in the bottom-right corner displays the total cost of the project, as shown in Figure 20.10.

Figure 20.10
The Cash Flow report lists weekly costs for each task in a Crosstab format.

THE EARNED VALUE REPORT

Earned value analysis is a process first developed by the U.S. Department of Defense to determine what value has been earned to date within the project life cycle as compared to what was expected to be earned to date. The Earned Value report takes its data from the Earned Value table within Microsoft Project 2007. It compares the cost of what is being produced or generated with each task to what was planned up to the Current Date (set in the Project Information dialog box).

In order for the Earned Value report to be valuable, you have to ensure that the project baseline has been captured and all tracking information updated. The reason being, Earned Value data will only be calculated if a baseline has been saved on the project. If a baseline has not been saved, then the Earned Value (BCWP) will be blank.

All subtasks are displayed in the Earned Value report, sorted by their IDs, whereas summary tasks are not displayed. The report contains several columns and is too wide to fit onto a single screen; therefore, the illustration in Figure 20.11 does not show all the columns in the report.

→ For more information about using earned value analysis, **see** "Analyzing Performance with Earned Value Analysis," **p. 491**.

THE ASSIGNMENT REPORTS CATEGORY

The Assignment Reports category contains four reports, as shown in Figure 20.12. To access them, open the Reports dialog box (Report, Reports) and select Assignments.

Figure 20.11
The Earned Value report conveys whether each task is earning value at the planned rate or not.

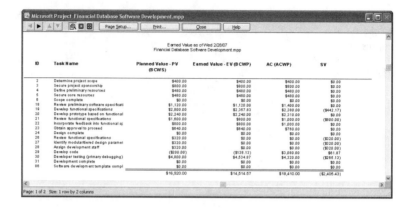

Figure 20.12
The Assignment Reports category contains four reports and provides assignment-related information from your project schedule.

The reports in the Assignment category display various information regarding resources' assignments to tasks. Refer to Table 20.4 for the list of Assignment reports.

TABLE 20.4 ASSIGNMENT REPORTS

Report Name	Report Type	Usage
Who Does What	Resource	Lists the resources working on the project, and shows the tasks each resource is assigned to.
Who Does What When	Crosstab (Resource)	Lists each resource and their work assignments for each day of the project. This may be a useful report to print and display somewhere the rest of the project team can see to ensure everyone is aware of his or her assignments and what tasks other project team members are responsible for.
To-do List	Task	An interactive report—you select the resource, and the report displays that particular resource's task assignments, listed chronologically by weeks. This report is a great way to print out a to-do list for each individual resource, to ensure that they are all aware of their responsibilities in your project.

Report Name	Report Type	Usage
Overallocated Resources	Resource	Lists all resources that are overallocated—that is, those resources that are assigned to more hours of work than the Max Units field specifies. The report can help you identify resources that are overallocated, and therefore may not finish their assignments on time. In turn, you can take an action of adding more resources to the overallocated resource's tasks to lighten the load, or to reschedule the tasks so that the work does not overlap.

The Who Does What and the Who Does What When reports are great references to all the resources assigned to tasks on the project, and when they are scheduled to work on them. The To-do List report is an excellent way to quickly view a single resource's assignments in chronological order. A filter is automatically applied to the Overallocated Resources report that excludes resources that are fully allocated or underallocated.

→ For more information about resource overallocation and techniques used to resolve it, **see** Chapter 25, "Resolving Resource Allocation Problems," **p. 885**.

All reports in the Assignment category focus on resources and their various assignments. They provide data as to the work that the resources are assigned to do, and in what time periods they are scheduled to work.

TIP

> The Who Does What When report can be very lengthy because it is arranged by day. Preview the report before printing it, and consider restricting the printout to a short time period, rather than printing the length of the entire project. After you decide on the appropriate time period, enter the dates in the From and To boxes in the Timescale area of the Print dialog box.

THE WORKLOAD REPORTS CATEGORY

The Workload Reports category contains only two reports, both of which are Crosstab reports. The two reports focus on how resources are being used. Refer to Figure 20.13 and Table 20.5.

20

Figure 20.13
The Workload Reports category contains two Crosstab reports.

TABLE 20.5   WORKLOAD REPORTS

Report Name	Report Type	Usage
Task Usage	Crosstab (Tasks)	Shows the hours of work or units of material to which each task is assigned, broken down into weekly intervals and sorted by summary tasks, with subtasks underneath.
Resource Usage	Crosstab (Resources)	Shows the hours of work or units of material to which each resource is assigned, broken down into weekly intervals and sorted by resources, with their assignments listed below their names.

Both reports list the number of hours or units of material for each task or resource in weekly intervals, and give the weekly totals along the last row of the reports. Project totals are listed in the last column for each task or resource. Workload reports are very useful in determining which resources are not assigned to their full capacity. Display the Resource Usage report, and look through each week along the bottom. If certain resources are only assigned to a few hours of work during a given week, they may be available to work on other tasks to help overallocated resources or to speed up the completion of a task. They may also be assigned to other projects.

In addition to these two reports, four other reports are available that allow you to focus on either work or material resources (these two Workload reports include both work and material resources). These four additional reports are available in the Custom Report category. In the Reports dialog box select Custom, which will open the Custom Reports dialog box (discussed and illustrated in the next section). In the Custom Reports dialog box, select one of the following four additional work or material resource reports:

- **Resource (material)**—A list of all material resources, such as machines.
- **Resource (work)**—A list of all work resources, such as people.
- **Resource Usage (material)**—A list of all material resources and their tasks, displaying their unit of measurement allocations arranged in weekly intervals.
- **Resource Usage (work)**—A list of all work resources and their tasks, displaying their time allocations (hours assigned) arranged in weekly intervals.

CUSTOMIZING REPORTS

Reports in Microsoft Project 2007 are customizable to varying degrees. Some reports can only be customized in their format, while others are able to be customized in their content. Similar to views and tables, reports are customized in three different ways:

- Modifying the existing report
- Creating a copy of an existing report and modifying the copy
- Creating a new report from scratch

All of these customization methods begin in the Custom Reports dialog box. To access it, open the Reports dialog box (Report, Reports) and choose the Custom option. The Custom Reports dialog box will appear, as shown in Figure 20.14.

Figure 20.14
The Custom Reports dialog box allows you to create custom reports from scratch or based on the list of already existing reports.

The next several sections will discuss the three different methods for customizing reports, as well as how to customize the information within a report and the format it is presented in.

CUSTOMIZING AN EXISTING REPORT

Many reports can be edited from the Custom Reports dialog box, as discussed in the previous section. As an alternative method, you can also use the Edit button from the specific report category you have open.

TIP

Even though this option is available in Microsoft Project 2007, it is not recommended, simply because you would lose the original version of the report when you edit it if you do not change the report name before saving it. It is always a good practice to maintain the original files, and modify the copy instead.

The preferred method for customizing an existing report is to copy the original report and then edit the copy. This allows you to retain the original and the modified copy together. This method is discussed in the upcoming section, "Creating a New Report Based on an Existing Report."

To modify an existing report without first making a copy, you must select the specific report from the appropriate report category dialog box and then click the Edit button. For example, Figure 20.15 shows the six different reports for the Current Activities category. You can click once on any of them, and rather than clicking Select, you can click Edit, which will open a definition dialog box that allows you to modify that particular report. This dialog box is shown in Figure 20.16.

20

Figure 20.15
In any report category, such as Current Activities, select a particular report and click the Edit button to modify it.

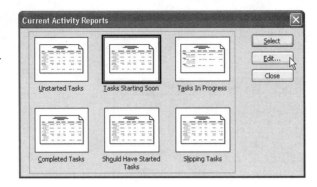

Since the Tasks Starting Soon report selected to edit in Figure 20.15 is based on the Task report format, the resulting dialog box in Figure 20.16 is a Task-specific dialog box, from which you can modify the Task report.

Figure 20.16
Clicking the Edit button opens up a dialog box in which you can customize an existing report.

The modification options vary from report to report. The options in Figure 20.16 are identical to the options you are presented with if you edit the report through the Custom Reports dialog box. These options will be discussed in greater detail in the upcoming section "Customizing Specific Report Types."

USING THE CUSTOM CATEGORY OF REPORTS

As mentioned previously, the Custom Reports dialog box is where you can create, copy, and edit reports. All reports are listed in the Custom Reports dialog box, including some that are not listed in the five report categories. To access the Custom Reports dialog box, select Report, Reports. Then in the Reports dialog box, choose Custom and click Select. The Custom Reports dialog box will open. Refer back to Figure 20.14 for an illustration.

20

The eight buttons in the Custom Reports dialog box are described in the following list:

- **Preview**—This button opens the Print Preview screen, which displays a preview of what the selected report would look like as a printed document. In the Print Preview screen, you have the opportunity to click the Page Setup button, which allows you to change the format of the report. See the upcoming section "Using the Common Customization Controls."

- **Setup**—This button opens up the Page Setup dialog box for the selected report (same as clicking the Page Setup button on the Print Preview screen). The Page Setup dialog box allows you to change the format for the report, such as modify the headers, footers, margins, and so on. See the upcoming section "Using the Common Customization Controls."

- **Print**—This button will open the Print dialog box to print the report in its current state (it will print as it appears in the Print Preview screen). See the upcoming section "Using the Common Customization Controls."

- **Cancel**—This button closes the Custom Reports dialog box.

- **New**—Click this button if you are creating a new report. It opens the Define New Report dialog box, which begins the process by asking you to choose from the four basic report types: Task, Resource, Monthly Calendar, or Crosstab. See the upcoming section "Designing a New Report."

- **Edit**—This button opens the dialog box in which you edit the report, as described in the previous section. Changes you make using this function change the original report. It is recommended that you use the Copy button, which copies the original report, and modify the copy, in order to keep the original report intact. See the previous section "Customizing an Existing Report."

- **Copy**—This button opens the same dialog box as the Edit button, only you are modifying a copied version of the original report, rather than modifying the original report itself. This enables you to have both the original and modified version of the report. See the upcoming section "Creating a New Report Based on an Existing Report."

- Organizer—This button opens up the Organizer dialog box to the Reports tab, allowing you to import or export reports (including custom reports) from or to your Global file for use on other projects. You can also delete unused reports from the Custom Reports dialog box to keep your list uncluttered. See the upcoming section "Saving and Sharing Custom Reports."

20

NOTE

> You cannot use the Copy button for the Base Calendar and Project Summary reports. These reports can only be edited for simple formatting changes to the text.

The New and Copy buttons create new reports that are added to the list in the Custom Reports dialog box. Use the New button to create a report from scratch, or the Copy button to modify an existing report without losing the original.

The following sections will describe in greater detail the functions of the buttons listed.

CREATING REPORTS

Reports are created by copying existing ones and modifying them, or by building them from scratch. The new report appears on the list in the Custom Reports dialog box, and you can further customize it as you would any other report.

TIP

> Reports are composed of information generated mainly through tables and filters. It is good practice to first create, format, and test your tables and filters before creating the reports that will incorporate their data.

The next two sections will describe the process of creating new reports. Following that, there are several sections that describe the actual customization process.

CREATING A NEW REPORT BASED ON AN EXISTING REPORT

You will likely find yourself in a situation where there is a report that comes close to meeting your needs, but not completely. One option is to edit that report to your specifications, but the major disadvantage to this approach is that you lose the original version when you save the changes.

As an alternative to that, Microsoft Project 2007 allows you to make a copy of the existing report, enabling you to save the existing report and create a new one based on its characteristics. By making a copy of the existing report, you take advantage of its features and create an opportunity to change the aspects that do not meet your requirements.

TIP

> It is in your best interest to copy an existing report if one exists that comes close to your specifications, because most of the work in creating the report is already done. If none of the existing reports meets your needs, you will have to create a new one from scratch (described in the next section).

Follow these steps to create a new report based on an existing report:

1. Open the Reports dialog box by selecting Report, Reports.

2. Click on Custom and then click Select (or simply double-click Custom), which opens the Custom Reports dialog box.

3. Select the existing report that you wish to copy and then click Copy. The definition dialog box for the new report appears (see Figure 20.17). Its features are identical to the report that you copied, except in the Name field it reads "Copy of [existing report]." For example, if you selected Budget Report, the Name field in the newly created report's definition dialog box would read "Copy of Budget Report."

Figure 20.17
Define the character-
istics for the new
report in the report's
definition dialog box.
In this case, a copy of
the Budget report has
been created.

4. Modify the Name field to give the report a more descriptive name—one that is specific to your needs and reflects the contents of the report.

5. Complete the report definitions within the dialog box, and click OK when you are finished (instructions for making changes to various types of reports are provided later this chapter). The new report will appear in the report list in the Custom Reports dialog box, and you can make further modifications in the future if necessary.

The preceding procedure describes only how to create the new report from an existing one; further instructions for modifying it are found later in this chapter.

DESIGNING A NEW REPORT

If none of the existing reports come close to providing the information you desire, then you will likely have to create one from scratch. If you want to create a Monthly Calendar report, you must use this method, because there are no existing reports of this type that are available for copying or editing.

Follow these steps to create a new report:

1. Open the Reports dialog box by selecting Report, Reports.

2. Click on Custom and then click Select (or simply double-click Custom), which opens the Custom Reports dialog box.

3. Click the New button. The Define New Report dialog box will appear, as shown in Figure 20.18. The new report must be modeled after one of the four report types listed in the Define New Report dialog box.

4. Select a report type and click OK. The report definition dialog box for that particular type will be displayed with the default settings. A default report name (such as Report 1) appears in the Name field, as shown in Figure 20.19.

20

Figure 20.18
When designing a new report, you must base it off one of these four report types.

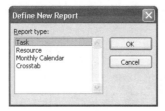

Figure 20.19
In this example, the Resource Report definition dialog box is shown, because Resource was selected as the report type.

5. Enter a descriptive name in the Name field, replacing the default.

6. Complete the report definitions within the dialog box, and click OK when you are finished (instructions for making changes to various types of reports are provided later this chapter). The new report will appear in the report list in the Custom Reports dialog box, and you can make further modifications in the future if necessary.

USING THE COMMON CUSTOMIZATION CONTROLS

One aspect of the customization process for reports is to alter the format. Specifically, this entails modifying the text format, the page setup options, and/or the order in which the report information is sorted. These are the common custom options, because they apply to all reports, regardless of how they were created (edited, copied, or new). The next few sections describe these common custom options.

CONTROLLING PAGE BREAKS IN A REPORT

You are not able to insert page breaks directly into a report. However, reports by default maintain the manual page breaks you have inserted into a task or resource list. To insert a page break in a task or resource list, display the list, select where you want the page break, and choose Insert, Page Break. Then, when you print the report, the page break will be honored where it is inserted in the task or resource list. In other words, insert page breaks into the list before printing the report, and double-check with the Print Preview screen (click the Preview button) before printing to ensure that the report will be printed correctly.

If you do not wish to include specific page breaks in your report, you do not have to go through the task or resource list and extract them. Rather, simply clear the box next to Manual Page Breaks in the Print dialog box (see Figure 20.20). If you have inserted page breaks but they are not shown in the Print Preview screen (or did not print correctly), double-check to make sure this box is selected. If it is cleared, manual page breaks will not be taken into consideration.

Figure 20.20
Be sure to select or clear the Manual Page Breaks box in the Print dialog box, depending on whether or not you want the inserted page breaks included in your report.

CHOOSING THE PAGE SETUP OPTIONS FOR A REPORT

The Page Setup dialog box is where you can change the margins of the report or change the appearance of the header or footer, among other things. To access the Page Setup dialog box from the Custom Reports dialog box, select the report you wish to modify and click the Setup button. If the Print Preview screen is displayed, you can click the Page Setup button at the top to open the Page Setup dialog box.

The Legend and View tabs on the Page Setup dialog box are generally not accessible for any reports.

→ For more information about using the Page Setup dialog box, **see** "Using the Page Setup Dialog Box," **p. 773**.

FORMATTING TEXT IN A REPORT

While some reports are able to be modified more than others, you can modify the appearance of the text in any report in Microsoft Project 2007. To do so, open the definition dialog box for the report, as described previously, and click the Text button. If the definition dialog box has multiple tabs, the Text button is found on each tab. Once you click the Text button, the Text Styles dialog box appears, as shown in Figure 20.21.

NOTE

> The Text Styles dialog box is opened automatically when you choose to edit the Project Summary report, because the only option for customizing that particular report is to modify the text. In this case, it is called the Report Text dialog box, but functions the same as the Text Styles dialog box. As previously stated, the header information for the Project Summary report is taken directly from the Summary tab of the Properties dialog box (File, Properties).

Figure 20.21
In this example, a copy of the Unstarted Tasks report has been created, and in the definition dialog box, the Text button was clicked to open the Text Styles dialog box.

In the Text Styles dialog box, you can select special formatting for any or all of the text found in the report. The box itself resembles the dialog box that appears when you choose Format, Text Styles on the main menu.

You can change the font, font style, size, and color to emphasize certain types of information found in the report or to better distinguish specific sections of text data. The specific choices found in the Text Styles dialog box vary depending on which report you are modifying. Generally, the default setting is 8-point type without any distinguishing characteristics (such as bold, underlined, or italics).

At the top of the Text Styles dialog box, choose which areas of text you are modifying from the drop-down list in the Items to Change field. By default, All is selected, meaning the changes you make will affect all the text in the report. You can alter different areas in different ways. For example, in a task report, you can italicize the summary tasks to help them stand out, or change their color, and so on.

It is important to note that there is no connection between the text format in a view and the text format in a report. If, in a view, summary tasks are displayed in bolded blue, they will not be displayed as such in the report unless you actually define them that way in the Text Styles dialog box.

CHANGING THE SORT ORDER FOR A REPORT

The sort order can be modified for all Task, Resource, and Crosstab reports. To do so, open the report's definition dialog box by selecting it from the Custom Reports dialog box and clicking Copy (or Edit, to modify the existing report). Then select the Sort tab. Figure 20.22 illustrates the Sort tab for a Crosstab report. The Sort tabs for a Task or Resource report look almost identical.

Figure 20.22
Use the controls on the Sort tab of the report's definition dialog box to change the sort order of the items in the report.

The controls in the Sort tab of the report definition dialog box allow you to sort the items in the report by as many as three fields, and each field can be sorted in ascending or descending order. In the Sort By field, select the value from the drop-down list you want the report to be sorted by first. Then, you have the option to sort the items two more times, as defined in the remaining Then By fields.

For example, if you defined a Copy of Unstarted Tasks report to be sorted by Duration, then by ID number, with both values sorted in ascending order, the report would sort the items from lowest duration to highest. If some of the tasks had the same duration, such as 2 days, then those tasks with the same duration would be listed in the order of their ID number, from lowest to highest, before the next item(s) with durations of more than 2 days. This is shown in Figure 20.23.

Also, the field used for sorting, which you define in the Sort By and Then By fields, does not have to be included in the report itself. Therefore, you can sort a task list by Start date, even if the Start date is not displayed in the report.

There is no connection between the sort order displayed in a view or table and the sort order displayed in a corresponding report. In other words, if the tasks are sorted by ID number on the Earned Value table, they can be sorted by a different value, such as Actual Cost, in the Earned Value report. Changing the sort order of the report will not affect the sort order for the view.

20

Figure 20.23
This report has been sorted in ascending order, first by Duration, then by ID number. Notice the tasks with the same duration. They are sorted in order of their ID numbers.

COLLAPSING TASK DETAIL IN A REPORT

Task outline levels and filters are the two settings that affect whether or not tasks are displayed in a Task, Crosstab, or Monthly Calendar report. If you print a report while the outline is collapsed in the current view, then only those tasks that are displayed at the time the report is printed will be included in the report. You must expand your outline before you print the report if you want it to display the entire task list. Therefore, be sure your current view displays the correct outline level for the task list before you print your report, and always click the Preview button to open the Print Preview screen to verify that the report looks correct before you print it.

However, reports ignore any filter that has been applied to the current view. If, for example, you have applied a Date Range filter to your current view to only list tasks that start or finish within a certain time period, your Task Usage report will still include all the tasks whose summary tasks are expanded, regardless of whether or not they meet the filter criteria applied to the view. But, you can apply filters to reports in the report definition dialog box by selecting the filter on the Definition tab. This process is further discussed in upcoming sections.

NOTE

> Collapsing an outline in the current view overrides the filter applied to the report. Even if a task hidden on the current view is selected by the report's filter, it will not be included on the report because it is hidden in the current view. Again, be sure your outline is expanded to your satisfaction in the current view before printing the report.

→ For more information about collapsing and expanding outlines, **see** "Indenting and Outdenting Tasks," **p. 170**.

→ For more information about applying a filter to your task list, **see** "Understanding Filtering and Grouping," **p. 399**.

CUSTOMIZING SPECIFIC REPORT TYPES

As previously described, there are four types of reports in Microsoft Project 2007 (Task, Resource, Crosstab, and Monthly Calendar), plus two reports that do not fall under these four types (the Project Summary report and the Working Days report). Of these four report types, Task and Resource reports have the most versatility for customization; they have the most amount of customization options. In each of these reports, you can modify the columns of information to display, the filter to apply, the table to use, and the amount of supporting detail about the tasks or resources listed in the report.

With Crosstab reports, you can select which task or resource detail you wish to display over a unit of time (weeks, days, quarters, and so on) defined by you, as well as edit the column and row information. Most of the Task, Resource, and Crosstab reports also allow the addition of gridlines and gray bands.

The remaining reports (aside from Task, Resource, and Crosstab reports) are more case-specific.

All of the existing reports in Microsoft Project 2007 allow you to modify the text formatting (as described in the previous section "Formatting Text in a Report"). This chapter has already described the common customization controls for all reports, such as modifying the page breaks, page setup, sort order, and collapsing or expanding the outline to show or hide tasks. The following sections will describe in greater detail the customization options for each specific report type.

CUSTOMIZING THE PROJECT SUMMARY REPORT

The Overview Reports category holds the most unique preexisting report in Microsoft Project 2007: the Project Summary report. This report cannot be copied. In fact, the only editing you can do to this report is to modify the text.

The Report Text dialog box (the same as the Text Styles dialog box) opens automatically when you select the Project Summary report and click Edit. The Report Styles dialog box is displayed in Figure 20.24.

Figure 20.24
Change the text formatting for the Project Summary report in the Report Text dialog box.

In the Report Text dialog box, select which item(s) you would like to modify from the drop-down list in the Item to Change field. You can choose to modify All items, Project Name, Company Name, Manager Name, or Details (all the other text in the report). When you have selected the item to change, make your modifications to the item's Font, Font Style, and Size fields. When you have made selections in these three fields, a sample is displayed of what the text will look like in the Sample box. You can also opt to underline the text and change its color. When you are finished, click OK to apply the changes or click Cancel to exit without changing anything.

TIP

It may be helpful, or at least more visually appealing, to make the heading items (such as Project Name, Company Name, and Manager Name) stand out more by making them bold, or in a larger font size. This is a matter of personal preference.

NOTE

The heading information for the Project Summary report is taken directly from the Summary tab of the Properties dialog box. Open the Properties dialog box (File, Properties) to the Summary tab, and insert or delete this information to your satisfaction. If you do not want the Project Manager's name listed in the heading of the Project Summary report, remove it from the Summary tab before printing the report. Remember to go back and reenter it after the report is finished (if you choose to keep the manager's name documented in the project file).

In Figure 20.25, the Project Summary report's text has been edited. The project name is 14-point bolded Arial Black, the company name is 12-point italicized Arial Narrow, and the project manager's name and remaining text details are 9-point regular Arial.

Figure 20.25
Formatting the text for the Project Summary report can be more visually appealing, but the text formatting is the only customizing you can do to this report.

CUSTOMIZING THE CALENDAR REPORTS

There are two Calendar reports listed in Microsoft Project 2007—the Working Days report in the Overview category and the Base Calendar report in the Custom category. They are in fact the same report. So in actuality, there is only one existing Calendar report, but it is found in two different places.

Every report that is found in the five basic report categories is also listed in the Custom Reports dialog box, *except* for the Working Days report. It is replaced by the Base Calendar report in the Custom Reports list. These reports display the working days, working times, nonworking days, and exceptions for each base calendar defined in the project file. Furthermore, each base calendar is listed on a separate page in these reports.

Like the Project Summary report, the Base Calendar report cannot be copied, and the only modifications you can make are to the text. In the Custom Reports dialog box, select Base Calendar and click Edit. The Report Text dialog box appears, like when editing the Project Summary report (refer to Figure 20.24). In the Report Text dialog box, you can change the Calendar Name text, the Detail text, or all the text simultaneously. When you have made your modifications, click OK to apply them, or click Cancel to exit without changing anything.

As mentioned in the previous section, choosing a different format for the calendar name to distinguish it from the rest of the text may help your report to be more visually appealing.

CUSTOMIZING TASK AND RESOURCE REPORTS

Task and Resource reports account for the majority of preexisting reports in Microsoft Project 2007. These are also referred to as *List-type* reports because the reports are composed of lists of tasks or resources.

The data found in Task and Resource reports comes directly from a table in the project database. Filters are also applied to narrow the focus of the report in some cases. Those reports that list all tasks or resources still have a filter applied (the All Tasks or All Resources filter), even though all items meet the filter criteria. You also have the option to group the task or resource list by the time period in which they are active.

Some Task or Resource reports come with supporting details, such as totals, notes, assignment schedules, successors, and so on. While not all of the preexisting reports are equipped with supporting details, you have the option to include them when you customize the report. For example, in a Task list report, it may be beneficial to display the predecessor and successor relationships for each task. You can enable this feature in the report definition dialog box. You may also want to include resource assignment schedules and work summaries for each task in a Task list report, or details about each resource's cost rate and resource notes in a Resource list report.

The process of customizing Task and Resource reports is very similar. The small differences between the two will be noted throughout the upcoming sections, but generally the description applies to both.

20

Table 20.6 displays each Task list report that exists in Microsoft Project 2007, the table and filter used to generate the data, and any supporting details included in the report by default.

TABLE 20.6   PREEXISTING TASK REPORT SETTINGS

Task Report Name	Table Used	Filter Applied	Default Details (If Any)
Budget Report	Cost	All Tasks	Show totals
Completed Tasks	Summary	Completed Tasks	None
Critical Tasks	Entry	Critical	None
Earned Value	Earned Value	All Tasks	Show totals
Milestones	Entry	Milestones	Task notes
Overbudget Tasks	Cost	Cost Overbudget	Show totals
Should Have Started Tasks	Variance	Should Start By... (interactive filter)	Task notes; successors
Slipping Tasks	Variance	Slipping Tasks	Notes; successors
Task	Entry	All Tasks	None
Tasks In Progress	Entry	In Progress Tasks	Assignment schedule
Tasks Starting Soon	Entry	Date Range... (interactive filter)	Assignment schedule
To-do List	Entry	Using Resource... (interactive filter)	None
Top-Level Tasks	Summary	Top Level Tasks	Task notes
Unstarted Tasks	Entry	Unstarted Tasks	Task notes; assignment schedule

NOTE

Table 20.6 (Task report settings), Table 20.7 (Resource report settings), and Table 20.8 (Crosstab report settings) list 27 of the 29 preexisting reports found in Microsoft Project 2007 (listed in the Custom Reports dialog box). The remaining two reports are the Project Summary report and the Base Calendar report, which can only be customized in their text formatting. Refer to the preceding sections "Customizing the Project Summary Report" and "Customizing the Calendar Reports."

Similarly, Table 20.7 displays each Resource report that exists in Microsoft Project 2007, and summarizes the table and filter used to generate the data, as well as the supporting details included by default.

TABLE 20.7   PREEXISTING RESOURCE REPORT SETTINGS

Resource Report Name	Table Used	Filter Applied	Default Details (If Any)
Resource	Entry	All Resources	None
Resource (material)	Entry-Material Resources	Resources – Material	None
Resource (work)	Entry-Work Resources	Resources – Work	None
Overallocated Resources	Usage	Overallocated Resources	Show totals; assignment schedule
Overbudget Resources	Cost	Cost Overbudget	Show totals
Who Does What	Usage	Resources – Work	Assignment schedule

Essentially, the main differences between Task and Resource list reports are found in the choices of supporting details available for each type. Task reports can include both task and resource details for a particular task, whereas Resource reports focus on resource and assignment details for the particular resource.

As discussed earlier in this chapter, there are three ways to customize Task and Resource (and most other) reports: edit the existing report, copy the existing report and edit the copied report, and create a new report altogether. All three methods are described earlier in this chapter, and the descriptions all lead to the report definition dialog box. What you do to the report dialog box is discussed in the next few sections.

The report definition dialog box for Task and Resource reports has three tabs (refer to Figure 20.26):

- **Definition tab**—This tab is used to set the overall definition of the report, such as the report name, table, filter, and time period grouping.

- **Details tab**—This tab is used to define the drill-down details for the report. There is a wide assortment of options that differ between Task and Resource reports.

- **Sort tab**—This tab is used to rearrange the way items in the report are sorted (listed). See the section "Changing the Sort Order for a Report," earlier in this chapter.

Figure 20.26 shows an example of a Task report definition dialog box. While Resource report definition dialog boxes have the same tabs, some of the options vary.

The next two sections describe in greater detail how the Definition and Detail tabs function.

Figure 20.26
The Task and Resource report definition dialog boxes have three tabs: Definition, Details, and Sort.

USING THE DEFINITION TAB FOR TASK AND RESOURCE LIST REPORTS

As previously stated, the Definition tab on the definition dialog box for Task and Resource reports allows you to make modifications to the report's name, time period, count, table, and filter. The following list describes the functionality of the options on the Definition tab:

- **Name**—Enter a new, descriptive name for the report. This is especially helpful for copied or new reports. By default a generic name is given, such as "Copy of (Report)" or "Report 1." It is especially helpful to specifically rename the report if it is to be used often over long periods of time, or saved to your GLOBAL.MPT (via the Organizer) file for use on other projects.

→ For additional information about GLOBAL.MPT and the Organizer, **see** "Managing Project Files," **p. 581**.

- **Period**—This field defines the time period for the report. By default, Entire Project is selected, meaning the data spans the entire project with no grouped intervals. From the drop-down list, you can select Years, Half Years, Quarters, Months, Thirds of Months, Weeks, or Days. If you select one of these options other than Entire Project, the report items will be grouped by your choice. For example, if you select Weeks, the report will separate the items into weekly intervals.

- **Count**—This field defines the interval of the time period you select in the Period field. For instance, if Weeks was selected in the Period field, and you select 2 for the Count field, the items will be grouped in 2-week intervals. This may be helpful if you want to group resource assignments by pay periods, such as every 2 weeks (see Figure 20.27).

- **Table**—The columns of data that appear to the right of the line items in a report are defined by the Table field. For example, if Entry was selected, the columns would display the same information found in the columns of the Entry table. You can choose any table from the Table drop-down menu for your report. The Table drop-down menu lists all the tables from the More Tables dialog box, including any tables you have created or customized in the project file.

→ For more information about creating and customizing tables, **see** "Creating and Customizing Tables," **p. 756**.

- **Filter**—To apply a filter to the report, select the filter from the Filter drop-down menu. The Filter drop-down menu lists all the filters from the More Filters dialog box, including ones you have created or customized. If you choose an interactive filter, the interactive prompt appears each time you print or preview the report. The default interactive filters have an ellipsis (...) at the end of their name. If you want to create a new interactive filter, you have to put the ellipsis on the end of the name manually. Also, select the Highlight box if you want the report to display all tasks or resources, but visually highlight those that meet the filter criteria.

  Remember, applying a filter to the view does not automatically apply the filter to a report. You must define the filter for the report in the definition dialog box's Definition tab.

→ For more information about creating and customizing filters, **see** "Creating and Customizing Filters," **p. 785**.

NOTE

> If you want to apply a custom filter or table to a report, you must create or customize that filter or table before defining it in the report. That way, it will be included in the drop-down menus on the Definition tab of the report definition dialog box.

To display summary tasks in addition to subtasks on a Task report, select the Show Summary Tasks check box. Displaying summary tasks may be useful for organizational purposes; having descriptive summary tasks may explain the subtasks more completely than just displaying the subtasks. This option is not available for Resource reports.

If you have defined time periods in your report (the Period field described in the previous list), and you want to visually separate those time periods with gray bands, select the Gray Bands check box. Gray horizontal lines will appear on your report, separating the time periods.

Figure 20.27 shows the Definition tab of a copy of the Unstarted Tasks report's definition dialog box. The name has been changed to "Unstarted Tasks (Bi-weekly)" to differentiate it form the original Unstarted Tasks report and to describe that this copied report is grouped into bi-weekly intervals. Figure 20.28 shows the resulting report as defined in Figure 20.27. Take a moment to analyze the two figures and get a feel for the options in the Definition tab of the report definition dialog box.

20

USING THE DETAILS TAB FOR TASK AND RESOURCE LIST REPORTS

The Details tab on the report definition dialog box looks very similar for Task and Resource reports, but the information displayed on the report varies between the two significantly. Microsoft Project 2007 tracks distinctly different task and resource fields; therefore, the supporting information defined on the Details tab of Task and Resource reports reflects those differences.

Figure 20.27
The Definition tab has been customized to group the list items bi-weekly, separated by a gray band. The Highlight box is cleared; if it were selected, all unstarted tasks would be shown as highlighted in gray on the report.

Figure 20.28
This report was defined in Figure 20.27. Notice the gray bands separating the item list in 2-week intervals.

The Details tab is where you decide what and how much specific information is included on your Task or Resource reports. This information is defined by selecting or clearing the check boxes on the tab.

The Details tab for a Task report is displayed in Figure 20.29.

The following list describes the functionality of the Details tab of a Task report definition dialog box:

- **The Task Heading**—Select from the following four boxes:

  Notes—If you have entered any text in the Notes field for any of the tasks (via the Notes tab on the Task Information dialog box) and you want to include those notes on the report, select the Notes box. Notes can be a great way to include more details about a task, as well as capture task scope.

  Objects—If you have inserted any objects you have created using another Windows application (such as Microsoft Word or Excel) and want to indicate those objects in the report, select the Objects box. An icon will appear indicating the report, signifying the existence of the object attached to the task.

→ For more information about inserting objects into a project, **see** "Placing Objects into Microsoft Project 2007," **p. 974**.

Figure 20.29
Define specific detail information by selecting or clearing the boxes on the Details tab of the report definition dialog box.

Predecessors—If you want to include a list of predecessor task information under each task, select the Predecessors box.

Successors—If you want to include a list of successor task information under each task, select the Successors box.

- **The Assignment Heading**—Choose to display specific resource assignment information by selecting from the four boxes shown in Figure 20.29 and listed next. The details are displayed in subcharts below the tasks in the report. The following list shows what fields are displayed for each subchart:

Notes—Displays the Assignment Notes field (assignment notes are separate task or resource notes and are entered in the Task Usage or Resource Usage views).

Schedule—Displays Resource ID, Resource Name, Units (of Resource Assigned), Work (Scheduled Work), Delay, Start (Scheduled), and Finish (Scheduled) fields.

Cost—Displays Resource ID, Resource Name, Units (of Resource Assigned), Cost (Scheduled Cost), Baseline Cost, Actual Cost, and Remaining (Scheduled Cost) fields.

Work—Displays Resource ID, Resource Name, Units (of Resource Assigned), Work (Scheduled Work), Overtime Work, Baseline Work, Actual Work, and Remaining Work (Scheduled Work) fields.

The Work (Scheduled Work) field is not repeated if both the Schedule and Work boxes are selected. Also, if you choose two or three detail options for the subchart, Microsoft Project 2007 combines the fields into one subchart if the report's orientation is set to Landscape (defined on the Page Setup dialog box).

- **Border Around Details**—To enclose the subchart in border lines, which may make it easier to read and distinguish, select the Border Around Details check box.

20

- **Gridlines Between Details**—To show gridlines between each task, which may also make the report easier to read, select the Gridlines Between Details check box.

- **Show Totals**—To display totals at the bottom of the report for all columns that contain numeric values, select the Show Totals check box.

Figure 20.30 displays the Details tab of the Task report definition dialog box for a copied version of the Task report, and Figure 20.31 displays the resulting report. Notice the information selected in Figure 20.30 and how it is displayed in Figure 20.31.

Figure 20.30
The Detail tab has been customized to display each task's notes, predecessor task information, and successor task information, as well as Schedule and Cost resource assignment details, which are enclosed with borders. Notice also the gridlines separating each task.

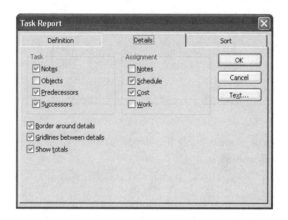

Figure 20.31
This illustration is taken from the third page of the report to display all information defined in Figure 20.30.

Customizing the Detail tab for a Resource report is much like customizing a Task report. The Details tab looks very similar, and the process is the same: select the check boxes next to the information you wish to display on the Resource report. Figure 20.32 shows the Details tab of a Resource report definition dialog box.

Figure 20.32
The Details tab of a Resource report definition dialog box looks similar to that of a Task report.

NOTE

The following fields are grayed out unless you have chosen Entire Project in the Period field on the Definition tab: Resource Notes and Objects; Assignment Notes, Cost, and Work; and Show Totals. In Figure 20.32, these fields are not grayed out because Entire Project is defined as the time period.

The following list describes the functionality of the Resource heading on the Details tab of a Resource report definition dialog box:

- **Notes**—If you have entered any text in the Notes area for any of the resources, and you want to include those notes on the report, select the Notes check box.

- **Objects**—If you have inserted any objects you have created using another Windows application (such as Microsoft Word or Excel) and want to include those objects in the report, select the Objects check box. Perhaps you have created an Excel spreadsheet of work hours for a group of resources assigned to a group of tasks. By selecting the Objects check box, an icon will appear in the report indicating the existence of objects attached to the resource.

- **Calendar**—If you want to include the resource calendars in the report, select the Calendar check box.

- **Cost Rates**—If you want to include the cost rate tables for each resource, select the Cost Rates check box.

The Assignment heading of the Details tab in the Resource report definition dialog box functions the same as that of a Task report, and is described earlier in this section. Select the Notes, Schedule, Cost, and Work check boxes to include subcharts of this information on the report. The fields found in the subcharts are the same as those described for a Task report.

Also similar to Task reports are the three boxes at the bottom of the report. You can add borders to the resource details and use gridlines to separate the resources in the report for easier viewing. You can also opt to show totals at the bottom of numeric columns in the report.

20

CHANGING THE TEXT FORMATTING AND SORT ORDER FOR TASK AND RESOURCE REPORTS

As mentioned previously, the Text button appears on all three tabs of the Task and Resource report definition dialog boxes. Click the Text button to open the Text Styles dialog box. Use this dialog box to make changes to the text, as described earlier this chapter in the section "Formatting Text in a Report." Customizing the text can make certain items stand out more and create an overall more visually appealing report.

Here is a list of the categories in the Items to Change drop-down list available for special formatting in Text reports:

- All (the default category)
- Noncritical Tasks
- Critical Tasks
- Milestone Tasks
- Summary Tasks (the default style is bold)
- Marked Tasks
- Highlighted Tasks (shaded)
- Column Titles (the default is bold 9-point type)
- External Tasks
- Task Details (the default is italic 7-point type)
- Totals

Here are the categories in the Items to Change drop-down list available for special formatting in Resource reports:

- All (the default category)
- Allocated Resources
- Overallocated Resources
- Highlighted Resources (shaded)
- Column Titles (the default is bold 9-point type)
- Resource Details (the default is italic 7-point type)
- Totals

The default text format for each category is 8-point type with no distinguishing characteristics, unless otherwise noted in parentheses.

When using the Sort tab on a task or report, you are defining the criteria in which Microsoft Project 2007 sorts the Task or Resource list in the report. The functionality of the Sort tab is discussed earlier in this chapter in the section "Changing the Sort Order for a Report."

After you have modified all three tabs to your satisfaction, click the OK button on any of the tabs, which will apply the changes and close the report definition dialog box. Then, you can select the newly customized report in the Custom Reports dialog box and click the Preview button to see your changes.

> **TIP**
>
> If after previewing your customized report you decide to customize it further, select the customized report and click Edit (instead of Copy). That way, you are editing the report you have already been customizing. If you click Copy, you will create a copy of the customized report, leaving you with the original, the customized copy, and a second copy you just created (three versions total). If you copy a report, customize it, and decide it will not work, simply edit the copied report further rather than creating a new one. This will save you the hassle of having to look through several versions of the same report later.
>
> Of course, if you want to keep the customized report, as well as make a copy of it to customize again, then click Copy.

CUSTOMIZING CROSSTAB REPORTS

Crosstab reports are set up in a grid format. They display tasks or resources down the rows and cost amount or work hours along the columns. Table 20.8 lists the preexisting Crosstab reports that are available for customizing and the data that they include.

TABLE 20.8   PREEXISTING CROSSTAB REPORT SETTINGS

Crosstab Report Name	Row Setting	Data Values
Crosstab	(Tasks or Resources)	None
Who Does What When	Resources	Resources – Work
Cash Flow	Tasks	Cost
Resource Usage	Resources	Work
Resource Usage (material)	Resources – Material	Work
Resource Usage (work)	Resources – Work	Work
Task Usage	Tasks	Work

As with Task and Resource reports, you can customize a Crosstab report by selecting it from the specific category it belongs to (such as the Workload Reports dialog box) and clicking Edit. Alternatively, you can select the report from the Custom Reports dialog box and choose Copy. The latter method is the recommended method, as it is preferred to first make a copy and edit the copy rather than editing—and thus losing—the original version of the report.

Whichever method you choose, the Crosstab Report definition dialog box appears, as shown in Figure 20.33.

Figure 20.33
Customize a Crosstab report in the Crosstab Report definition dialog box, which has the same three tabs as the Task and Resource report definition dialog boxes.

USING THE DEFINITION TAB TO CUSTOMIZE A CROSSTAB REPORT

As shown in Figure 20.33, the Crosstab Report definition dialog box contains the same three tabs as Task and Resource report definition dialog boxes. However, they function quite differently.

Use the Definition tab to set the type of information to be displayed in a Crosstab report. First, rename the custom report (if you are customizing a copy of an existing report or creating a new report) to something unique and descriptive. Then, under the Crosstab heading, select whether you want tasks or resources down the rows of the report by choosing Tasks or Resources from the drop-down list in the Row field (refer to Figure 20.33).

In the Column field, you can set the time period for the report, which functions much like the Period and Count fields on the Definition tab of Task or Resource report definition dialog box. Select from Years, Half Years, Quarters, Months, Thirds of Months, Weeks, and Days, and define the interval in the number field to the left. In Figure 20.33, the time period is set for Weeks, and the interval is 1, meaning that the columns will be grouped to display information on a weekly basis.

Below the time period fields is another drop-down list. Choose a selection from this list, which will define what information is presented in the columns. The choices in this list vary depending on whether you have defined the rows as tasks or resources.

For tasks, you have the options listed in Table 20.9 available for inclusion in the column data.

TABLE 20.9 COLUMN SETTINGS FOR TASK CROSSTAB REPORTS

Option	Definition
Actual Cost	Actual dollar cost incurred
Actual Overtime Work	Actual overtime work hours incurred

Option	Definition
Actual Work	Actual work hours incurred
ACWP	Actual Cost of Work Performed (actual value in dollars)
Baseline Cost	Baseline dollar value
Baseline Work	Baseline work hours
BCWP	Budgeted Cost of Work Performed (Earned Value)
BCWS	Budgeted Cost of Work Scheduled (Planned Value)
Cost	Planned dollar cost
Cumulative Cost	Scheduled cost, time-phased
Cumulative Work	Scheduled work, time-phased
CV	Cost Variance that represents the difference between the planned and actual cost values
Fixed Cost	Planned fixed cost
Overtime Work	Planned overtime work hours
Regular Work	Planned regular work hours
SV	Schedule Variance that represents the difference between the planned and actual values
Work	Planned work hours

For resources, you have the options listed in Table 20.10 available for inclusion in the column data.

TABLE 20.10   COLUMN SETTINGS FOR RESOURCE CROSSTAB REPORTS

Option	Definition
Actual Cost	Actual dollar expenditures incurred
Actual Overtime Work	Actual overtime hours incurred
Actual Work	Actual hours incurred for each task
ACWP	Actual Cost of Work Performed (actual value in dollars)
Baseline Cost	Baseline dollar value for each task
Baseline Work	Baseline hours for each task
BCWP	Budgeted Cost of Work Performed (Earned Value)
BCWS	Budgeted Cost of Work Scheduled (Planned Value)
Cost	Planned dollar value
Cumulative Cost	Scheduled dollar value, time-phased

20

continues

TABLE 20.10 CONTINUED

Option	Definition
Cumulative Work	Scheduled hours, time-phased
CV	Cost Variance that represents the difference between the planned and actual cost values
Overallocation	Percentage of resource availability
Overtime Work	Planned overtime hours
Peak Units	Highest allocation amount in the schedule
Percent Allocation	Percentage of resource total available time that is being used on a task assignment
Regular Work	Planned regular hours excluding any planned overtime hours
Remaining Availability	Remaining resource availability based on the difference between resource availability defined in the resource calendar and the work scheduled for the resource within the project
SV	Schedule Variance that represents the difference between the planned and actual values
Unit Availability	Resource units that resource is available to work
Work	Planned hours a resource has been assigned to work
Work Availability	Available hours a resource has to perform project work

If you would like to include assignment details in the report, select the And (Task or Resource) Assignments check box. If the Row field is set to Resources, the option will be And Task Assignments, and if you select it, each resource's task assignment(s) will be listed under its name in each row, along with the corresponding information in each column. If the Row field is set to Tasks, the option will be And Resource Assignments, and selecting it will include all the resources assigned to each task listed on the report.

As with Task and Resource reports, you can apply a filter to a Crosstab report. In the Filter field, choose the filter from the drop-down list. If you have chosen Tasks in the Row field, then a list of task filters is presented to you. If you chose Resources in the Row field, then a list of resource filters is presented to you. These lists are taken from the More Filters dialog box, and include any custom filters you have already defined. Check the Highlight box if you want to list all items and highlight those that meet the filter criteria.

Figure 20.34 shows the Definition tab of a customized version of the Crosstab report, and Figure 20.35 shows the resulting report. Notice the time period is set to bi-weekly, the rows display resources with their task assignments, and the columns display values for Baseline Work.

Figure 20.34
Define the type of information to display in a Crosstab report on the Definition tab of the Crosstab Report definition dialog box.

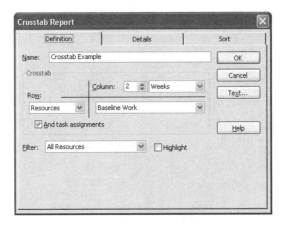

Figure 20.35
This is the customized Crosstab report defined in Figure 20.34.

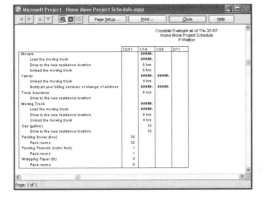

USING THE DETAILS TAB TO CUSTOMIZE A CROSSTAB REPORT

Like Task and Resource reports, you can add details to a Crosstab report in the Details tab of the Crosstab Report definition dialog box. Whereas the detail information for a Task or Resource report is descriptive, the detail information for a Crosstab report is primarily numeric.

Figure 20.36 shows the Details tab in the Crosstab Report definition dialog box.

The following list describes the functionality of a Crosstab report's Details tab:

- **The Show Heading**—Under the Show heading, you can choose to show row totals at the end of each row by checking the box next to Row Totals. Similarly, you can display column totals at the bottom of each column by checking Column Totals. If both boxes are selected, an overall total amount is included on the bottom-right corner of the grid, where the row totals and column totals intersect.

  If you selected Tasks for row information on the Definition tab, you have the option of displaying summary tasks in the report by selecting the Summary Tasks check box. If you have chosen Resources as row information, this option is unavailable and dimmed (as in Figure 20.36).

20

Figure 20.36
Add details to a
Crosstab report on
the Details tab of the
report's definition dia-
log box.

- **The Gridlines Heading**—Under the Gridlines heading, you can opt to display horizontal gridlines on the report, which may make for easier viewing of the data. The gridlines will be placed between tasks or resources, depending on whether you are
  displaying tasks or resources in the rows. If both tasks and resources are listed, you can
  select both boxes. Vertical gridlines separating each column are automatically displayed.

- **Show Zero Values**—If a value is zero (0) anywhere on the report, you can choose to
  either display the number 0 and the unit of measurement, or just have that field left
  blank. To show the zero value, select the Show Zero Values check box. To show a blank
  field, clear the check box.

- **Repeat First Column on Every Page**—If your Crosstab report extends horizontally to
  more than one page, it may be beneficial to always show the first column. That way, as
  you are reviewing the report, you do not have to go back to the first page and verify
  which row item the column data is about. To show the first column on every page, select
  the Repeat First Column on Every Page check box.

- **Date Format**—In this field, you can choose the date format that appears along the top
  of the grid. Several options are available in the drop-down list, ranging from the written
  month and date, abbreviations, numeric abbreviations, days of the week, and so on.

Figure 20.37 shows the Details tab of a Crosstab Report definition dialog box, and Figure
20.38 shows the resulting report. Tasks are listed as row information, and Baseline Work is
the column information (defined on the Definition tab). Notice the horizontal gridlines are
drawn between tasks, but not between the resources assigned to them. Also, the zero values
are shown. If your report contains a lot of zero values, as does this one, it may appear
cleaner to not show them.

Figure 20.37
The details of this Crosstab report example have been customized, and the resulting report is shown in Figure 20.38.

Figure 20.38
This illustration is the result of the modifications made in Figure 20.37.

CHANGING THE TEXT FORMATTING AND SORT ORDER FOR A CROSSTAB REPORT

You can click the Text button on any of the tabs in a Crosstab report to access the Text Styles dialog box. You can change the text format for certain types of information found in the report by selecting the specific type from the Items to Change drop-down list and then altering the font, font style, size, and any distinguishing characteristics. The default format of each text category is 8-point type with no distinguishing characteristics. Refer back to the section "Formatting Text in a Report," earlier in this chapter, for more information. Remember that even if the text formatting has been modified in the current view, you have to define the modifications again in the Text Styles dialog box for a report.

20

The Sort tab for a Crosstab report is identical to the Sort tab on any of the custom report definition dialog boxes. See the section "Changing the Sort Order for a Report," earlier in this chapter, for more information.

Once you have made all the modifications on all three tabs and in the Text Styles dialog box, click OK to apply the changes. Then, select the newly customized report in the Custom Reports dialog box and click the Preview button to view the results.

CUSTOMIZING THE MONTHLY CALENDAR REPORT

If you would like to report task information in a calendar format, you have the option of creating a Monthly Calendar report. No preexisting Monthly Calendar reports exist in Microsoft Project 2007, so you will have to create one from scratch.

While a Monthly Calendar report offers fewer formatting options than the Calendar view, you do have the ability to print an individual resource's calendar, which you cannot do in a Calendar view.

Access the Monthly Calendar report by clicking the New button on the Custom Reports dialog box. This will open the Define New Report dialog box. Select Monthly Calendar from the Report Type list and then click OK (see Figure 20.39).

Figure 20.39
To begin creating a Monthly Calendar report, select Monthly Calendar in the Define New Report dialog box.

The monthly Calendar Report Definition dialog box will appear, as shown in Figure 20.40.

Figure 20.40
Define the name, filter, base calendar, and other formatting options in the Monthly Calendar Report Definition dialog box.

The first thing you want to do is give your Monthly Calendar report a specific, descriptive name in the Name field. Then, you can choose a filter to apply from the drop-down list in the Filter field. For example, you may apply a Using Resource filter to print a calendar to give to a certain resource, displaying the scheduled working and nonworking times and task assignments for that particular resource. You can check the Highlight box to list all tasks but highlight those that meet the filter criteria. If you choose an interactive filter, the interactive prompt appears each time you display or print the report.

The main advantage to printing a Monthly Calendar report over a Calendar view is the ability to print an individual resource's calendar to view his or her working and nonworking times. In the Calendar field, you can choose to display any of the base calendars or resource calendars that are found in the project file. Select the base or resource calendar you wish to display from the drop-down list in the Calendar field.

The remaining options in the Monthly Calendar Report Definition dialog box allow you to modify the report as follows:

- You can distinguish working days from nonworking days by opting to display nonworking days in gray. Check the box next to Gray Nonworking Days to do so.

- If you display taskbars across the scheduled duration for the tasks, you can choose to display breaks in the bars from one week or month to the next with dotted or solid lines at the bar ends. To display solid bar breaks, select the Solid Bar Breaks check box. Leave it empty to display dotted lines.

- If more tasks are assigned on a day than can fit on the calendar, an asterisk is displayed beside the day number, and the unprinted tasks appear in a list at the end of the report. If you wish to separate the dates in that task list with gray bands, select the Print Gray Bands check box.

- Under the Show Tasks As heading, you have the option to show tasks across the calendar as bars (taskbars), lines, or by their start and finish dates. Select the option you would like to display. It may be helpful to preview all three and choose which one you like best.

- Under the Label Tasks With heading, you have the option of including the task ID number, name, and duration when the task is labeled on the calendar. You can select all three, or any combination.

- To format the text in the report, click the Text button, which will open the Text Styles dialog box. You can choose to format different task types uniquely to visually differentiate between tasks. To do so, select the task type from the Items to Change drop-down list, and make your changes. For more information, see the section "Formatting Text in a Report," earlier this chapter.

After you have finished designing the Monthly Calendar report, click OK to apply the definition and return to the Custom Reports dialog box. From there, you can select the newly created Monthly Calendar report and click Preview to view the results of your definition.

20

The report will be saved to the list as soon as you click OK and exit the Monthly Calendar Report Definition dialog box.

Figure 20.41 shows a Monthly Calendar Report Definition dialog box, and Figure 20.42 shows the resulting report. In this example, a calendar has been created, showing the working and nonworking time for the resource called "Family." Examine the definitions in Figure 20.41 and their applications in Figure 20.42.

Figure 20.41
Create a Monthly Calendar report in the Monthly Calendar Report Definition dialog box. The results of this example are shown in Figure 20.42.

Figure 20.42
This Monthly Calendar report displays the working and nonworking time for the resource called "Family," as defined in Figure 20.41.

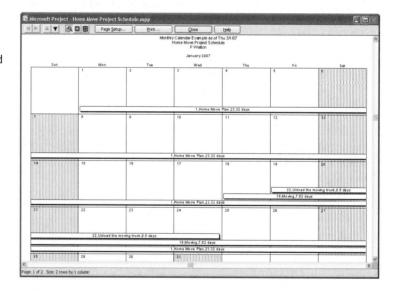

SAVING AND SHARING CUSTOM REPORTS

Whenever you create or customize a report and click the OK button, the report is automatically saved into the Custom Reports dialog box list. However, you must also save your project file before ending your current session; otherwise, you will lose the customized report (and any other work you did in that session). Always save the file before exiting.

There is no option to save the results of the reports. However, you can print the reports to share them with other project stakeholders or your project team.

It is also possible (and recommended) to make custom report definitions available to use in all your project files or share with other people working with the same project. To do so, use the Organizer to copy the reports from your project file into the Global.MPT file. You can access the Organizer from the Custom Reports dialog box by clicking the Organizer button. The Organizer appears, as shown in Figure 20.43.

Figure 20.43
Use the Organizer to copy custom reports from your project file to the Global.MPT file, or import reports from the Global.MPT file to a new project file.

To copy reports from your project file, select them from the list on the right and then click the Copy button, as indicated in Figure 20.43. The same process works for importing reports from the Global.MPT file: Select the report from the list on the left and click the Copy button to copy it into your project file. You can also delete or rename reports in the Organizer by selecting a report and clicking the Delete button or Rename button. The various tabs on the Organizer open other areas of the project (such as Tables, Views, and so on).

→ For additional information on GLOBAL.MPT and the Organizer, **see** Chapter 18, "Managing Project Files," **p. 581**.

CONSULTANTS' TIPS

Most of the people interested in your project are not used to looking at or interpreting Gantt Project schedules. They usually want to see the information in a table or summary format that shows dates, hours, and cost for different parts of the schedule.

Reports are an excellent way to share information with your project stakeholders. The Project Summary Report and Cost Report categories provide most (if not all) of the information commonly asked for by clients and project sponsors. This is especially true for your financial audience who will be more interested in the numbers rather than the schedule.

It is common to also tailor the assignment reports to include baseline information so that your project team can have a clear picture of the budget and planned effort you expect from their assignments. Distributing these reports on a regular basis can be a useful communication tool with the resources on your project.

20

CHAPTER **21**

CREATING AND CUSTOMIZING VISUAL REPORTS

In this chapter

INTRODUCTION TO VISUAL REPORTS

Visual reports are perhaps the most significant new feature in Microsoft Office Project 2007. Like the basic reports, visual reports provide project data for all aspects of your project. They are fully customizable in both their content and their appearance. Also, you have the ability to create a visual report from scratch. Whereas the basic reports provide information in a text format, visual reports display information in graphs, charts, tables, diagrams, and other visual mediums. They are much more versatile than the basic reports in their functionality and customization options.

This chapter discusses how to fully utilize Microsoft Project's visual report templates, how to customize them to work best for you, and how to create new visual reports from scratch.

An important subject to initially address is why you would want to use a visual report. Oftentimes, you generate reports for your own analysis as the project manager, or to share project data with your team or project sponsors. In comparison to basic reports, visual reports have the ability to include more project data, such as fields that are unavailable within basic reports. In addition, visual reports provide a lot more flexibility in data manipulation, such as filters, grouping, as well as graphical representation of the data. Whereas a basic report may serve the purpose of summarizing certain aspects of your project, a visual report can take that data and present it in a much more appealing, professional manner. Many people react better to visual depictions of data rather than numeric charts and lists. A visual report allows you to present your project data in an eye-catching way, while at the same time keeping the level of dignity and professionalism your team or clients expect.

TIP

> For the maximum result of clarity and professionalism in your reporting, present the source data table in your visual reports. That way, you can present your data and back it up visually with a visual report, doubling the impact of your reporting presentation.

→ For more information about customizing and creating basic reports, as well as complete tables listing the basic reports found in each category, **see** Chapter 20, "Creating and Customizing the Basic Reports," **p. 657**.

→ For more information about using basic and visual reports for tracking and reporting to specific audiences, **see** Chapter 15, "Using Reports for Tracking and Control," **p. 519**.

The existing visual report templates in Microsoft Project 2007 can be accessed by opening the Visual Reports – Create Report dialog box. To open the Visual Reports – Create Report dialog box, choose Report from the main menu, and select Visual Reports. The Visual Reports – Create Report dialog box will appear, as shown in Figure 21.1.

The Visual Reports – Create Report dialog box houses 22 visual report templates, contained in seven tabs: Task Usage, Resource Usage, Assignment Usage, Task Summary, Resource Summary, Assignment Summary, and All. The 22 visual reports are divided among the first six tabs, while the All tab holds all 22 visual reports. Therefore, each report can be accessed from two locations: once from one of the first six tabs, and again from the All tab.

Figure 21.1
The Visual Reports –
Create Report dialog
box contains existing
visual report tem-
plates.

Visual reports can be generated in one of two formats: Microsoft Office Excel 2007 or Microsoft Office Visio 2007. Notice in Figure 21.1 that some reports have the Excel icon next to them, and others have the Visio icon, representing which tool the report is created in. Each of the formats will be discussed in more detail later in this chapter.

Table 21.1 lists all 22 existing visual reports, which tab they are found under, their type (Excel or Visio), and a brief description of the report data. To view a visual report, double-click on it, or select it and click View.

TABLE 21.1   THE EXISTING VISUAL REPORT TEMPLATES IN MICROSOFT PROJECT 2007

Visual Report Name	Tab Location (Besides the All Tab)	Report Type (Excel or Visio)	Brief Description
Baseline Cost Report	Assignment Usage	Excel	A bar graph that displays baseline cost, planned cost, and actual cost for tasks (can be drilled down to project, phase, or subtask level).

continues

21

TABLE 21.1 CONTINUED

Visual Report Name	Tab Location (Besides the All Tab)	Report Type (Excel or Visio)	Brief Description
Baseline Report (Metric)	Assignment Usage	Visio	A diagram that compares planned work and cost to baseline work and cost, broken down by quarter, then by task. Indicators show when planned data surpasses baseline data. Units use the metric system of measurement.
Baseline Report (US)	Assignment Usage	Visio	A diagram that compares planned work and cost to baseline work and cost, broken down by quarter, then by task. Indicators show when planned data surpasses baseline data. Units use the U.S. system of measurement.
Baseline Work Report	Assignment Usage	Excel	A bar graph that displays baseline work, planned work, and actual work for tasks (can be drilled down to project, phase, or subtask level).
Budget Cost Report	Assignment Usage	Excel	A bar graph that displays budget cost, baseline cost, planned cost, and actual cost over time.
Budget Work Report	Assignment Usage	Excel	A bar graph that displays budget work, baseline work, planned work, and actual cost over time.
Cash Flow Report	Task Usage	Excel	A bar graph with cost and cumulative cost displayed over time.
Cash Flow Report (Metric)	Resource Usage	Visio	A diagram that shows planned and actual costs over time, broken down by resource type (work, material, or cost), with indicators if planned costs exceed baseline costs. Units use the metric system of measurement.
Cash Flow Report (US)	Resource Usage	Visio	A diagram that shows planned and actual costs over time, broken down by resource type (work, material, or cost), with indicators if planned costs exceed baseline costs. Units use the U.S. system of measurement.

Visual Report Name	Tab Location (Besides the All Tab)	Report Type (Excel or Visio)	Brief Description
Critical Tasks Status Report (Metric)	Task Summary	Visio	A diagram that shows work and remaining work for both critical and noncritical tasks. A data bar shows the work percentage complete. Critical tasks are separated from the noncritical tasks. Units use the metric system of measurement.
Critical Tasks Status Report (US)	Task Summary	Visio	A diagram that shows work and remaining work for both critical and noncritical tasks. A data bar shows the work percentage complete. Critical tasks are separated from the noncritical tasks. Units use the U.S. system of measurement.
Earned Value Over Time Report	Task Usage	Excel	Displays actual cost, planned value, and earned value over time.
Resource Availability Report (Metric)	Resource Usage	Visio	A diagram that shows Work and Remaining Availability for each resource. Resources are separated by type (cost, work, and material). Units use the metric system of measurement.
Resource Availability Report (US)	Resource Usage	Visio	A diagram that shows Work and Remaining Availability for each resource. Resources are separated by type (cost, work, and material). Units use the U.S. system of measurement.
Resource Cost Summary Report	Resource Usage	Excel	A pie chart that displays the division of resource cost between the three resource types (work, material, and cost).
Resource Remaining Work Report	Resource Summary	Excel	A bar graph that displays remaining work and actual work for each work resource.

continues

21

TABLE 21.1   CONTINUED

Visual Report Name	Tab Location (Besides the All Tab)	Report Type (Excel or Visio)	Brief Description
Resource Status Report (Metric)	Assignment Summary	Visio	A diagram showing the work and cost values for each resource. The percentage of work complete is indicated by the shading in each box on the diagram, getting darker as the resource approaches completion of his or her assignments. Units use the metric system of measurement.
Resource Status Report (US)	Assignment Summary	Visio	A diagram showing the work and cost values for each resource. The percentage of work complete is indicated by the shading in each box on the diagram, getting darker as the resource approaches completion of his or her assignments. Units use the U.S. system of measurement.
Resource Work Availability Report	Resource Usage	Excel	A bar graph that displays total work availability, work, and remaining availability over time for work resources.
Resource Work Summary Report	Resource Usage	Excel	A bar graph that displays total work availability, work, remaining availability, and actual work for work resources.
Task Status Report (Metric)	Task Summary	Visio	A diagram showing tasks' work and percentage of work complete. Indicators show when work surpasses baseline work, when work equals baseline work, and when baseline work surpasses work. Units use the metric system of measurement.
Task Status Report (US)	Task Summary	Visio	A diagram showing tasks' work and percentage of work complete. Indicators show when work surpasses baseline work, when work equals baseline work, and when baseline work surpasses work. Units use the U.S. system of measurement.

21

UNDERSTANDING OLAP CUBES FOR VISUAL REPORTS

OLAP cubes are specially constructed databases. Normal databases are organized to reduce the space the data they contain takes up. Normal databases (or normalized databases) trade off performance for storage. OLAP databases are not so much concerned with reducing storage as they are concerned with organizing data for fast finding and fast retrieval (in support of dynamic and immediate data analysis needs). The information is organized in a single table and cross-indexed across all attributes so that a query's data results can be immediately presented rather than spending precious time searching through, organizing, and aggregating linked information. OLAP databases are referred to as *OLAP cubes* to reflect the mental picture of an analyst looking at the data first in one way, on one side of a cube, and then another—tipping the cube in various ways to examine different attributes and angles on the data. The term *cubes* also reminds you that many more dimensions are possible than the two dimensions usually considered in flat reports and spreadsheets.

Visual reports are built on a local OLAP cube (a file ending in .cub and containing the OLAP database). It is called a *local* cube because it is physically located on your local machine, rather than being served out to you from a remote database server machine. You can save this cube in your project file or export it to use elsewhere (see the section "Sharing and Saving Visual Reports," later this chapter). The data found in a visual report comes from the Microsoft Project 2007 file database. From that project data, a local OLAP cube is built, which is then attached to a PivotTable and PivotChart in Excel, or a PivotDiagram in Visio (refer to the next section, "Introduction to Microsoft Office 2007").

The 22 existing visual report templates have already been constructed. Later sections in this chapter will describe how to customize these templates to better suit your needs. You can choose not to use a template, meaning that you wish to create a new visual report data query and presentation view from scratch. To create a visual report from scratch, you must first define the OLAP cube dimensions. This process is also discussed later in this chapter, in the "Reporting Capabilities" section.

INTRODUCTION TO MICROSOFT OFFICE 2007

Because visual reports are created using either Microsoft Office Excel or Microsoft Office Visio, it is important to have an understanding of each of these tools, and how they are used to create and customize visual reports in Microsoft Project 2007.

Many project managers have little to no experience with Visio, and their experience in Excel is often not much more than data entry on a spreadsheet. This chapter is written with the assumption that your experience with these two tools is limited. Regardless of your skill level with Excel or Visio, this chapter provides enough detailed information that you can comfortably use them while working with visual reports. However, it is important to note that by no means does the information in this chapter give you thorough instructions on how to fully use Excel or Visio. In other words, this chapter touches on some of the concepts that will aid you in creating successful visual reports, but does not go into great detail about either Excel

21

or Visio beyond the purposes relevant to this chapter. For a much more detailed guide to these two Microsoft Office tools, consult outside sources or other manuals written about them directly.

USING EXCEL 2007 WHILE WORKING WITH VISUAL REPORTS

Ten of the preexisting visual report templates are Excel reports. Each Excel report includes two sheets: the PivotTable and the PivotChart. The PivotTable is essentially the data, which comes from the project file database, displayed in an Excel spreadsheet. A PivotTable has more functionality than just a sequence of rows because the data rows are listed and aggregated, allowing you to expand or collapse groups of data in the PivotTable. The PivotChart is the visual graph or chart that illustrates the same data. A PivotChart is always associated with a PivotTable (although the PivotTable may be hidden) and when you expand/collapse entries in one or the other, the action is automatically reflected in the linked partner.

For example, the Baseline Cost Report is the first report listed in the All tab of the Visual Reports – Create Report dialog box. It is an Excel report. To open it, double-click on its name in the Visual Reports – Create Report dialog box, or click it once and then click View. The Baseline Cost Report will be displayed, as shown in Figure 21.2.

PivotChart Tools ribbon

Figure 21.2
The Baseline Cost Report is an Excel report that displays Baseline Cost, Cost, and Actual Cost data.

PivotTable and PivotChart tabs   Adjust the scale of the graph

When you open the Baseline Cost Report, the screen displays the PivotChart, or the graph, as shown in Figure 21.2. There are several items to point out in this illustration. First, at the bottom-right corner is a scale you can use to enlarge or decrease the size of the PivotChart on your screen. In Figure 21.2, the scale has been reduced to 90% to make room for the entire graph and options above.

At the top of the screen, above the graph, is the main menu toolbar ribbon. You can choose to display or hide this ribbon. To display it, click on PivotChart Tools at the top of the screen. To hide it, right-click somewhere along the tabs and choose Minimize the Ribbon.

This area provides several customization options for the PivotChart, which will be discussed in greater detail later in this chapter. For now, it is important to grasp the functionality of the PivotChart Tools ribbon. Along the toolbar, several tabs are displayed: Home, Insert, Page Layout, Formulas, Data, Review, View, Design, Layout, Format, and Analyze. If you click on any of these tabs, all your customization options for that particular tab will be displayed below the toolbar. In Figure 21.2, the Design tab is selected, and all the design options are displayed underneath it.

NOTE

If you hide the PivotChart ribbon by right-clicking and selecting Minimize the Ribbon, the tabs will still be displayed along the top of the screen. You can click on any of the tabs to display their customization options.

At the bottom-left corner of the screen are three folder tabs: Chart1, Assignment Usage, and a tab to open a new sheet (refer to Figure 21.2). In Figure 21.2, the Chart1 tab is selected, meaning the screen is displaying the PivotChart. If you click on the Assignment Usage folder tab, the screen will display the PivotTable for the particular report. In this case, since the Baseline Cost Report is in the Assignment Usage category, the PivotTable is called Assignment Usage.

Figure 21.3 illustrates the PivotTable of the Baseline Cost Report, which is displayed by clicking the Assignment Usage sheet tab at the bottom-left corner of the screen.

The PivotTable screen may be more familiar to project managers with some experience in Excel. It is set up as an Excel spreadsheet, with rows and columns of information. Notice the scale at the bottom-right corner, as well as the sheet tabs in the bottom-left corner.

Like the PivotChart, there are several tabs along the top of the screen that hold various customization options. You can choose to display the tab details by clicking PivotTable Tools at the top, or hide them by right-clicking along the tabs and selecting Minimize the Ribbon. In Figure 21.3, the option for minimizing the ribbon is displayed by right-clicking where the mouse is located.

Expand/Collapse data

Figure 21.3
The Assignment
Usage sheet displays
the PivotTable for the
Baseline Cost Report.

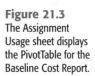

Figure 21.3
The Assignment
Usage sheet displays
the PivotTable for the
Baseline Cost Report.

PivotTable and PivotChart tabs   Adjust the scale of the graph

PivotTables provide dynamic views that allow you to analyze project data by sorting, grouping, filtering, and pivoting. You can add or remove data fields to include in a report, and drill down into the report data. Notice in Figure 21.3 there are plus signs (+) next to the tasks in column B. In this illustration, only the phases (summary-level tasks) are listed down this column. However, you can choose to expand some or all of the summary tasks to show data at the subtask level by clicking on the plus sign and expanding the list. Because the PivotTable and PivotChart display the same data, the graph in the PivotChart will also expand to show report data at the task level.

Similarly, you can collapse the data from the phase level to project level by clicking the minus sign (–) next to the project summary task in column A. The PivotTable will collapse to show data at the project level, as will the graph in the PivotChart.

In Figure 21.4, the PivotTable has been collapsed to show data at the project level. The graph has been copied and pasted underneath the PivotTable to view both at the same time. You can see that the graph displays only one bar for each item in the PivotTable (Baseline Cost, Cost, and Actual Cost). Whereas in Figures 21.2 and 21.3, the data in the graph and PivotTable was drilled down to the phase level, in Figure 21.4 it is displayed at the project level.

Figure 21.4
Collapse or expand the data in a PivotTable, and the graph will adjust to match your definition.

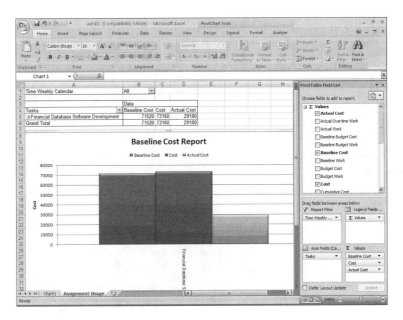

TIP

It may be helpful for you to copy and paste the graph into the PivotTable screen. That way, you can view both simultaneously without having to switch back and forth on the folder tabs. To do so, select the graph in the PivotChart, copy it (Ctrl+C), switch to the PivotTable tab, and paste it (Ctrl+V) under or on top of the PivotTable.

TIP

Use ScreenTips to your advantage when working with PivotCharts and PivotTables. Hover your mouse pointer over a button, tab, or cell, and a ScreenTip will appear, describing the feature, function, or cell contents. ScreenTips are also displayed for the chart view of the visual reports.

To add or remove data fields from a report, use the PivotTable Field List. To display the PivotTable Field List, right-click on the PivotTable, and choose Show Field List. Alternatively, you can select the Options tab along the top of the screen and select Field List in the Show/Hide heading. If you are on the PivotChart screen, select the Analyze tab and click on Field List in the Show/Hide heading.

Figures 21.2, 21.3, and 21.4 all have the PivotTable Field List displayed on the right side of the screen. Figure 21.5 shows how to display the PivotTable Field List using the Options tab of the PivotTable Tools menu.

The first heading in the PivotTable Field List is Choose Fields to Add to Report. To add a field, select the box next to the field name, or clear the check from any fields you want to remove from the report. The rest of the PivotTable Field List pane areas will be discussed

21

later in this chapter; the upcoming section "Customizing Excel 2007 Visual Reports" goes into greater detail about the specific features you can use in PivotTables and PivotCharts to customize your visual reports or create new ones.

Figure 21.5
Add or remove data fields in a visual report by using the PivotTable Field List, which you can choose to show or hide on the Options tab.

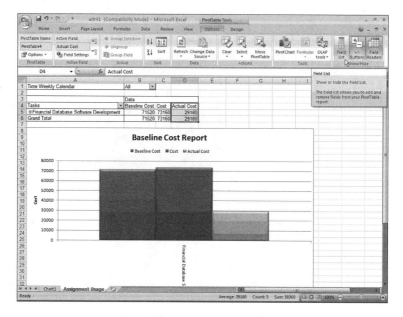

USING VISIO 2007 WHILE WORKING WITH VISUAL REPORTS

Six of the visual report templates are Visio reports, and each one has a U.S. measurement and a metric measurement system version, making for a total of 12 Visio reports.

Visio reports are composed in PivotDiagrams. A PivotDiagram is an assortment of shapes assembled in a tree structure, creating a visual format to help you summarize and analyze data. These shapes are also called *nodes*. A PivotDiagram begins with one node, called the *top node*, which is broken down into lower, subnode levels that specify aspects of the top node. For instance, a top node could be a project summary task, the next level could be the subtasks, and each subtask node can hold another level of summary tasks.

Figure 21.6 shows the Task Status Report (US), where the top node represents the entire project. The next level lists the phases, or summary tasks, of the project. The section "Customizing Visio 2007 Visual Reports," later this chapter, discusses how to drill into the data even further to display the subtask level.

Like Excel, Visio provides the capability to add or remove data fields from the report. You can also add shapes to certain nodes to represent information about the particular node's data, such as how a task is operating compared to the baseline.

A more detailed discussion on customizing Visio visual reports can be found later in this chapter; see the section "Customizing Visio 2007 Visual Reports."

21

Figure 21.6
The Task Status Report (US) is a Visio report, with data displayed in a PivotDiagram.

REPORTING CAPABILITIES

Like the basic reports, there are many customization options for visual reports you can use to sculpt an existing template into something much more suited for your reporting purposes. In Excel, you can modify the data fields to include in a report, drill down to specific levels in the data, and completely rework the appearance of the graph in the PivotChart. In Visio, you can modify the data in the report, as well as change the look and feel of the PivotDiagram. Customizing the content and appearance of visual reports can help make them more comprehendible and visually appealing to both you and the audience you are reporting to.

Furthermore, if none of the existing visual report templates comes close to meeting your criteria for a visual report, you can create a new one from scratch.

→ For more information about customizing existing basic reports and creating new reports, **see** Chapter 20, "Creating and Customizing the Basic Reports," **p. 657**.

The following sections describe in detail the processes used to customize existing Excel and Visio visual reports, as well as create new visual reports.

NOTE

The upcoming sections describe the theory and processes associated with customizing and creating visual reports in general. Data content in the forthcoming examples is irrelevant.

→ For more information about which existing visual report templates are appropriate to use for various tracking and control purposes, or which ones to use for specific audiences (project sponsors, project team, and so on), **see** "Using Visual Reports," **p. 541**.

21

CUSTOMIZING EXCEL 2007 VISUAL REPORTS

Excel visual reports are extremely versatile in their customization options. This section first discusses how to edit or customize that data within a report, and then how to customize the appearance of the report.

CUSTOMIZING DATA IN AN EXCEL VISUAL REPORT

Three major steps are involved in editing the data found in an Excel visual report. The first two are done before you actually open the report, and the third is done within the PivotTable screen. You may find that you need to use all three methods to fully achieve what you are after.

The first step is to use the Visual Reports – Field Picker dialog box to insert or remove fields to include in your report. To open it, first open the Visual Reports – Create Report dialog box (Report, Visual Reports). Refer to Figure 21.1. Then, click the report you wish to customize and click the Edit Template button. The Visual Reports – Field Picker dialog box will appear, as shown in Figure 21.7.

Figure 21.7
Edit the contents of a visual report in the Visual Reports – Field Picker dialog box.

TIP

In the Visual Reports – Create Report dialog box, you can choose to display only Excel reports or only Visio reports by selecting the boxes underneath the Show Reports Created In heading at the top of the dialog box. This may make it easier to decide which report you want to edit.

As illustrated in Figure 21.7, the Visual Reports – Field Picker dialog box has two areas: Select Fields and Select Custom Fields. In the Select Fields section, at the top, are two headings. The first heading is Available Fields, which lists all the available Microsoft Project

2007 predefined fields you can insert for use in your report. To select a field for your report, click on it in the Available Fields list and then click the Add button. The field disappears from the Available Fields list and appears in the Selected Fields list on the right.

The Selected Fields column lists all fields that have been selected to be included on the PivotTable Field List. Fields found in the Selected Fields list are not automatically included in the report; you must select them again from the PivotTable Field List to actually include their data in your report. This mechanism is intended to allow you to preselect a set of fields that could be valid for inclusion in the report (simplifying the Field set later presented when you are actually working with Data content in the report—a great help!). You can opt to remove a field from the PivotTable Field List if you know that you will not use it. To do so, select it from the Selected Fields list and click the Remove button. The removed field will now appear highlighted on the Available fields list. Because it is highlighted, it is still selected, so if you removed it from the Selected Fields list by mistake, just click Add and the field will be returned to the Selected Fields list.

You can also remove all of the fields from the Selected Fields list by clicking the Remove All button. This will clear the Selected Fields list, so you can start over with exactly the fields you want to be able to include in your report. However, if you click the Remove All button by mistake, all the removed fields will remain highlighted in the Available Fields list, and you can undo the action by clicking the Add button immediately after, returning them to the Selected Fields list.

You will notice that some of the fields listed in the Visual Reports – Field Picker dialog box have the word *dimension* next to them in parentheses (see Figure 21.7). This indicates that the particular field represents a major category in the OLAP cube; it is a significant field in report data and analysis.

CAUTION

It is important to select no more than six dimension fields for your report. Selecting more than six dimensions will significantly increase the amount of data and complexity of the PivotTable and therefore decrease the performance and usability of your report.

The bottom half of the Visual Reports – Field Picker dialog box functions the same as the top half, but is dedicated to custom fields only.

NOTE

The Selected Custom Fields list has a maximum limit of 130 custom fields.

→ For more information about creating and modifying custom fields, **see** "Creating and Customizing Fields," **p. 801**.

21

NOTE

> Not all fields are available in both Excel and Visio reports. Some fields are only available in one or the other. Furthermore, if you are unable to locate a field you want to include in your report, it may be stored in a different data category.
>
> For example, some fields you may think of as Task Summary fields are actually Assignment Summary fields. If you cannot find a particular field from a report under the Task Summary tab of the Visual Reports – Create Report dialog box, try to look at reports under the Assignment Summary tab.

When you are finished selecting or removing fields from the Visual Reports – Field Picker dialog box, click Edit Template to close the box and apply your changes. To close the box without changing anything, click Cancel.

NOTE

> Defining the time period of the report is the second of the three major steps of editing the visual report.

Once you have selected the fields to include in your report's PivotTable Field List, it is time to define the time period of the report. This is the second of the three major steps of editing the data in a visual report.

In the Visual Reports – Create Report dialog box, underneath the list of existing report templates, you will see the heading Select Level of Usage Data to Include in the Report, followed by a drop-down list. The drop-down list contains the following options: Years, Quarters, Months, Weeks, and Days. Select from one of these five options to define the level of information to drill down into your report. By default, Microsoft Project 2007 selects the level most appropriate for that particular report. If Weeks is selected, then you can drill into the report to view weekly data.

For instance, the Earned Value Over Time Report shows Earned Value, Planned Value, and Actual Cost data over time. If you select Weeks from the level of usage data drop-down, you can drill into the data to weekly information. However, if you select Days, you can drill even further, into daily information. This does not mean that you *have* to display daily information; you can still show Earned Value data for the quarter or year. But, if you select Days, then you have the capability of drilling down to daily information. Therefore, it is recommended that you select a smaller time unit, such as Weeks or Days, if you plan on drilling into that data. If not, it is recommended that you select a larger time unit, such as Quarters or Years.

21

NOTE

> The level you choose will impact the performance and complexity of the report. Lower levels increase the amount of data presented by the report (reducing performance). Lower levels may also present too much detail, confusing your audience or focusing their attention on a level of detail that detracts from the main point of the report.

To define the time unit for your report, first click on the report in the Visual Reports – Create Report dialog box and then make your selection from the drop-down list.

NOTE

Organizing the filtering, layout, and presentation of the report is the last of the three major steps of editing the visual report.

The third step in editing the data in your report is performed in the PivotTable. To access it, open the report by double-clicking on it or clicking it once and then clicking View in the Visual Reports – Create Report dialog box. The report will then be displayed.

For this discussion, the Baseline Cost Report is used. Figure 21.8 shows the PivotTable for the Baseline Cost Report, with the graph copied and pasted underneath.

Figure 21.8
Make data modifications to an Excel visual report in the PivotTable. In this case, the Baseline Cost Report is being edited.

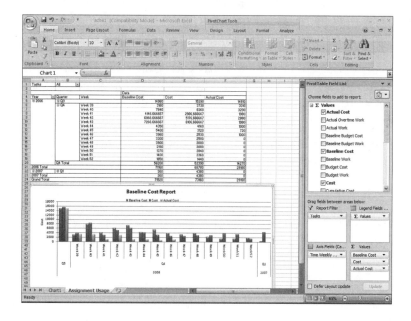

A previous section in this chapter, "Using Excel 2007 While Working with Visual Report," briefly described how you can drill into data by collapsing or expanding the information on the PivotTable. Click the plus sign (+) to expand the data, and the minus sign (–) to collapse it. The graph will adjust itself to match your choices. For example, notice in Figure 21.8 that the fourth quarter for 2006 (Q4) has been expanded to show weekly data. The PivotTable shows the weekly data for Q4, as does the graph.

The PivotTable Field List was also mentioned previously. Items that are selected in the PivotTable Field List will appear as field data in the PivotTable and on the graph. In Figure 21.8, Actual Cost, Baseline Cost, and Cost are selected, and thus appear as field data in the

21

report. Budget Cost is by default selected for this particular report, but has been cleared and thus removed from the report.

All the data field options listed in the PivotTable Field List are taken directly from the Selected Fields and Selected Custom Fields lists in the Visual Reports – Field Picker dialog box, discussed earlier in this section.

NOTE

> You must define the Selected Fields list and the time unit level (as discussed earlier in this section) before opening the visual report to edit. Otherwise, those definitions will not be included in the visual report.

In the bottom half of the PivotTable, underneath the Choose Fields to Add to Report area, are four other areas: Report Filter, Column Labels/Legend Fields (Series), Row Labels/Axis Fields (Categories), and Values. Drag fields into the Report Filter section to filter for any attributes before inserting the data into the PivotTable. You can add fields as column information by dragging and dropping them into the Column Labels box (sometimes called the Legend Fields box on the PivotChart screen), or as row information in the Row Labels box (or the Axis Fields box on the PivotChart screen). The Values box can hold any of the value fields from the PivotTable Field List; drag and drop them into this box or place check marks in their corresponding boxes.

You can make changes to the PivotTable by dragging and dropping fields from the Field List into or between these areas or to location-sensitive areas in the PivotTable itself.

NOTE

> You can get comfortable with the location-sensitive areas in the PivotTable by dragging fields from the Field List directly to a location-sensitive area in the PivotTable and seeing where the field shows up in the four quadrants at the bottom of the Pivot Table Field List pane.

Underneath these four areas is the option Defer Layout Update. Select this box if you want to make changes to the PivotTable but do not want the changes to happen immediately. To defer the update of the PivotTable, select this box, make your changes, and when you are ready to update the PivotTable, click Update.

At the top of the PivotTable Field List is a button with a drop-down list that allows you to choose the layout of the PivotTable Field List. Click the button, and your layout options will appear, as shown in Figure 21.9.

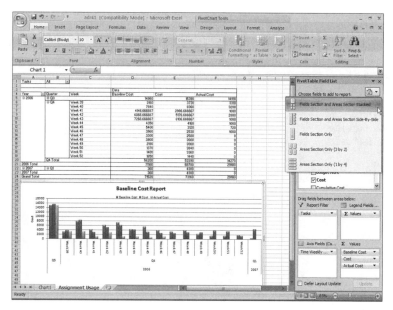

In the PivotTable itself, you can also make adjustments using the drop-down arrows that
appear in some of the cells. For example, in Figure 21.8, at the top of the PivotTable is a
drop-down arrow next to the word *All*. In that particular illustration, the word *All* coincides
with the cell to the left of it (Tasks). In other words, in this example, the data is filtered to
include all tasks. If you click that drop-down arrow, you can expand the filter option from
All, to the project level, then phase level, and finally the subtask level. Use this to display
only specific project data, rather than data for the entire project.

For example, in Figure 21.10, the PivotTable has been selected to filter for only tasks in the
Scope phase of the project. You can select the box next to Select Multiple Items to filter for
more than one phase or task. When you have made your selection, click OK, and the
PivotTable will only display data for what you selected.

The same concept applies to the drop-down list in the Year cell. Select it and choose which
year to display data for, or drill into each year and choose the quarter or week.

If you are viewing the PivotChart screen, you can display the PivotTable Field List, and drag
and drop data fields directly from the PivotTable Field List into the PivotChart. They will
then be included in the chart, and thus the report.

CUSTOMIZING THE APPEARANCE OF AN EXCEL 2007 VISUAL REPORT

Like modifying the data of a visual report, the appearance of an Excel visual report can be
altered significantly. There are many reasons why you may want to spend time modifying
your visual report. The graphs in the PivotChart screen at first appear quite simple when
compared to a graph with a few basic modifications. Therefore, improving the appearance of
your visual report will make it more professional looking and impressive.

21

Figure 21.10
Choose specific task levels to filter for by clicking the drop-down arrow at the top of the PivotTable. In this case, only Baseline Cost data for the Scope phase level has been displayed.

TIP

Incorporate organizational presentation standards when generating your reports. Many clients, team members, or other project stakeholders will react more positively to a report that appears in a standard corporate format or that just appears more polished than what they are accustomed to. On the other hand, spending too much time on the appearance of a report can overshadow the data it holds. Find a comfortable compromise between style and necessity. With a few simple touches, you can make your report stand out much better than originally designed.

Another reason to modify the appearance of an Excel visual report is to clarify or better emphasize the data. Perhaps you feel a column will make the report easier to understand than a line graph or pie chart. Excel reports allow you the capability to choose different visual representations of the data in the report. Experiment to find what works best for you and be consistent in your reporting techniques for best results.

CUSTOMIZING THE APPEARANCE OF CHART TYPES   The Cash Flow Report is an Excel visual report that displays Cost as columns and Cumulative Cost as a line over time. You can change not only the appearance of this data (from a line to a column, and so on), you can also change the appearance of the chart types (columns or lines) themselves.

For instance, perhaps you do not like having columns and lines on the same graph. You could opt to display Cumulative Cost as a column rather than a line. To do so, right-click on Cumulative Cost in the legend, or on the line itself, and choose Change Chart Type from the list options. This will open the Change Chart Type dialog box, as shown in Figure 21.11.

Figure 21.11
Select the type of line, bar, column, or other chart type for your data in the Change Chart Type dialog box.

In the Change Chart Type dialog box, you can choose from Column, Line, Pie, Bar, Area, X Y (Scatter), Stock, Surface, Doughnut, Bubble, or Radar chart types, as well as from a template, for your chart data. In this case, because the Cost data is displayed as a column, you may also want to choose one of the Column options for the Cumulative Cost data as well.

Figure 21.12 shows what the Cash Flow Report looks like if you changed the original line chart type for Cumulative Cost to the first Column option in the Change Chart Type dialog box.

You can change the chart type in any of the Excel PivotChart visual reports by following the same process:

1. Right-click on the chart type you wish to change and choose Change Chart Type. This will open the Change Chart Type dialog box.

2. In the Change Chart Type dialog box, choose from the many different options for each chart type.

3. When you have made your selection, click OK to apply the change and close the dialog box.

21

Figure 21.12
Changing the Cumulative Cost data from a line to a column may improve the clarity of the data in your report.

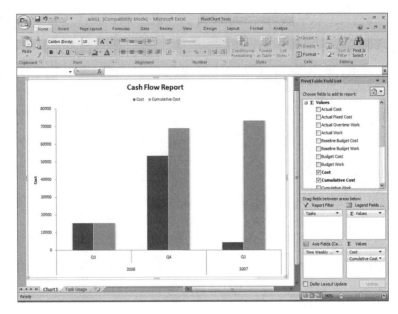

Once you have chosen the chart types to visually represent your data, you can make further modifications to the chart types themselves. In Figure 21.11, you probably noticed that there are many options for each chart type. For example, there are 19 different Column options. Some of them are square at the top, some are rounded, and some come to a point.

Also, many of the Column chart types are three-dimensional. If you choose a three-dimensional chart type but your data has only two dimensions, a warning box will appear, as shown in Figure 21.13.

Figure 21.13
If you mistakenly choose a chart type that requires more data dimensions than the chart type you are changing from, Visual Reports will prompt you to add the needed information (usually by requesting the missing data series in a two- or three-dimensional chart).

In Figure 21.13, because the data series had only two dimensions and a three-dimensional chart type was chosen, the warning box appeared. Figure 21.14 shows the results of selecting Yes in the warning box in Figure 21.13.

Figure 21.14
Choosing Yes in the warning box in Figure 21.13 creates a three-dimensional data series in your chart.

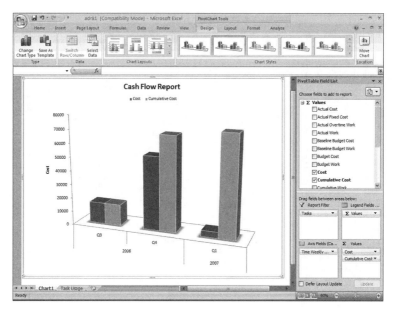

The Design tab of the PivotChart Tools option tabs also provides options to change the chart type in your graph. Click on the Design tab to list the options available to you in the ribbon underneath the tabs, as shown in Figure 21.14. The Design tab lists alternative ways to customize the look of your data chart types.

You can open the Change Chart Type dialog box by clicking on the Change Chart Type option all the way on the left side of the Design ribbon.

CUSTOMIZING THE WALLS, BORDERS, AXES, AND TEXT OF AN EXCEL CHART Although the data chart types generally are placed in the foreground of a PivotChart, you also have the ability to customize the background and sides of the graph. Adding a few minor changes to the background and side walls of a visual report can give it a bit of an artistic flare while helping the data in the foreground stand out.

To modify the background and side walls of a graph, you must open the Format Walls dialog box. To do so, right-click on one of the walls in the graph, and select Format Walls from the list. Alternatively, you can click on the Format tab, and on the Current Selection heading on the left side of the Format ribbon, choose Walls from the drop-down list, and click Format Selection. Both methods will open the Format Walls dialog box, as shown in Figure 21.15.

The Format Walls dialog box has several formatting options, listed on the left. The Fill option will allow you to customize the appearance of the walls themselves. Choose from No Fill for empty white space, Solid Fill for a solid color, Gradient Fill for a gradient color scheme, Picture or Texture Fill to insert a picture or preset texture, or Automatic to use the default Excel choice.

21

Figure 21.15
Change the background and walls for your graph in the Format Walls dialog box.

The Border Color and Border Styles options allow you to format the border lines of the graph. The Shadow option provides customization capabilities for the graph's shadow, and the 3-D Format and 3-D Rotation selections allow you to customize the three-dimensional options for the graph.

The floor of the graph can also be formatted. To do so, select the Format tab, and on the Current Selection heading on the left side of the Format ribbon, choose Floor from the drop-down list and then click Format Selection. The Format Floor dialog box appears, which operates in the same fashion as the Format Walls dialog box.

Figure 21.16 shows an example of a graph after making modifications in the Format Walls and Format Floor dialog boxes. A gradient fill has been selected with some slight shadowing effects. It is best to take a little time to experiment with all of these options and determine what works best in your reports.

NOTE

The illustrations in this book appear in black and white. However, many of the customization options for Excel PivotCharts include color. If you are printing a report on a color printer, be sure to take advantage of the colorful customization options.

For more information about printing a visual report, see the section "Sharing and Saving Visual Reports," later in this chapter.

21

Figure 21.16
The walls and floor have been given a gradient fill and a light shadowing effect, which helps to make the data stand out more and improve the overall appearance of the graph.

Besides the walls and floor, you can customize every aspect of the graph by selecting a particular option from the drop-down list on the Current Selection heading of the Format tab. Once you choose which aspect you wish to modify, click the Format Selection button, and a dialog box will appear in which you can make the changes. You can also open an item-specific dialog box by right-clicking directly on the item you want to modify, such as the legend or axis lines, and choosing the Format (item) option at the bottom of the list. This opens the appropriate dialog box for that particular item.

Here are the items you can customize on your PivotChart:

- Back Wall
- Chart Area
- Chart Title
- Floor
- Horizontal (Category) Axis
- Legend
- Plot Area
- Side Wall
- Vertical (Value) Axis
- Vertical (Value) Axis Major Gridlines
- Vertical (Value) Axis Title
- Walls
- Series (there may be several of these, depending on the chart data in your graph)

NOTE

> You do not need to modify all walls in the same fashion. That is why you have the options to customize the back wall and the side wall. Choosing the Walls option will customize both together.

CUSTOMIZING LABELS ON AN EXCEL PIVOTCHART   The Layout tab provides several customization options for specific areas of your PivotChart. The Axes and Background headings allow you to customize these items similarly to the methods described in the previous section.

The Labels heading on the Layout tab can be very useful to customize the Chart Title, Axes Titles, and Legend information. Also, you can change the display of the Data Labels, and choose to display the Data Table, which is similar to the PivotTable, only it is not interactive.

Figure 21.17 displays the Layout tab opened and the various options found under the Labels heading. In this illustration, Show Data Table with Legend Keys has been selected, and you can see the Data Table displayed underneath the graph with the legend keys included.

Figure 21.17
Customize the layout and appearance of the various labels found in your graph with the Labels heading on the Layout tab.

RESOLVING TEXT OVERLAPPING IN AN EXCEL PIVOTCHART   Sometimes, when you drill into your data, the text along the horizontal axis will overlap, simply because there is not enough room to display it (see Figure 21.18). All the text data along the horizontal axis is overlapping.

Figure 21.18
Drilling into the data can cause the text data to overlap, making it nearly impossible to read.

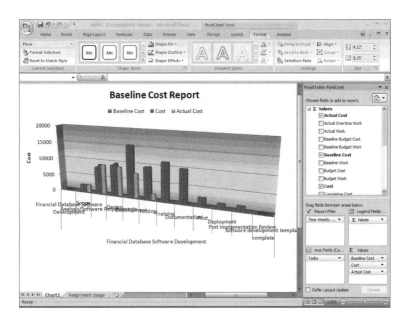

You can fix this problem by right-clicking on the text and choosing Format Axis. This will open the Format Axis dialog box. In the Format Axis dialog box, choose Alignment, and then rotate the text either 90 or 270 degrees, as shown in Figure 21.19. The text will then be displayed vertically, so it does not overlap, as shown in Figure 21.20.

Figure 21.19
Rotate the text data in the Format Axis dialog box to fix the overlapping problem.

Figure 21.20
The text data has been rotated 90 degrees, making it much easier to read.

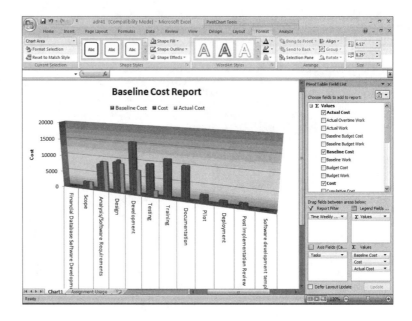

CUSTOMIZING VISIO 2007 VISUAL REPORTS

As mentioned previously, Visio reports are built using a PivotDiagram. Therefore, to customize a Visio visual report, you must understand the essentials of customizing a PivotDiagram.

NOTE

> Microsoft Office Visio 2007 does not come standard with Microsoft Office 2007. In order to use the Visio visual reports in Microsoft Office Project 2007, you will need to install Visio as well.

FORMATTING A PIVOTDIAGRAM

When you open an existing Visio report, several toolbars are displayed at the top of the screen, many of which are similar to the toolbars in Microsoft Office Word or other Office tools. To display or hide any particular toolbar, right-click on the toolbar area, and select it from the list to display it (or to hide it if it is already selected).

As with other Office tools, you can hover your mouse pointer over any button or feature in Visio, and a ScreenTip will appear that describes that particular item.

On the right side of the Standard toolbar, you will see a Zoom field. Generally, when you open a Visio visual report, it chooses a zoom factor that will show the entire diagram. Usually it is too small to read, so you will need to zoom in to work with it. To do so, click the drop-down list in the Zoom field and choose how much you want to zoom in, or just type in the percentage. The PivotDiagram will then zoom in accordingly.

The PivotDiagram toolbar is unique to Visio visual reports. It contains nine command buttons and a drop-down list. Figure 21.21 shows the PivotDiagram toolbar. If it is not displayed when you open the Visio report, right-click on the toolbar area and choose PivotDiagram.

Figure 21.21
The PivotDiagram toolbar provides several formatting options for the Visio PivotDiagram.

Zoom Field   PivotDiagram Toolbar

Table 21.2 shows the icon, name, and a brief description of the nine command buttons found on the PivotDiagram toolbar.

TABLE 21.2 THE PIVOTDIAGRAM TOOLBAR BUTTONS AND FUNCTIONS

Toolbar Icon	Name	Brief Description
Apply Shape...	Apply Shape	Inserts a shape into the PivotDiagram. Select the node(s), click Apply Shape, and in the Apply Shape dialog box, choose the shape you wish to apply and click OK.
Refresh Data	Refresh Data	Refreshes the data in a PivotDiagram.
	Merge	Merges two or more nodes.
	Unmerge	Unmerges merged nodes.

continues

21

TABLE 21.2 CONTINUED

Toolbar Icon	Name	Brief Description
	Re-layout All	When you manually move nodes by dragging them to other areas on the PivotDiagram, this button resets them to their last predefined location. This action applies only to the manually moved nodes.
	Move Left/Up	Moves selected item(s) left or up.
	Move Right/Down	Moves selected item(s) right or down.
	Layout Direction	Changes the node layout direction: Top-to-Bottom, Bottom-to-Top, Right-to-Left, or Left-to-Right.
	Layout Alignment	Changes the node layout alignment: Left, Center, Right, Top, Middle, or Bottom.

Besides the nine command buttons, the PivotDiagram toolbar has a drop-down list, in which you can Sort, Promote, Collapse, or Edit Data Graphic for particular nodes. Not all nodes can be customized with all these options; you cannot collapse a node that does not have "children" (other nodes attached to it at lower levels).

Also in the drop-down list is the Options choice. Select this, and the PivotDiagram Options dialog box will open, as shown in Figure 21.22. In the PivotDiagram Options dialog box, you can choose from many different formatting options for both the diagram and the data, including showing the title, legend, connections, and breakdown shapes.

Figure 21.22
The PivotDiagram Options dialog box provides several basic formatting options for the PivotDiagram.

21

Many formatting options are also available when you right-click any node or shape in the PivotDiagram. You can list tasks or resources associated with a particular node, apply a shape, or apply other Format, Data, and Shape formatting options listed when you right-click. For the Format option, you can edit the node's text, connecting line, or fill (the fill is the appearance of the node box). For the Data option, you can edit or remove a data graphic, which is used as an indicator to the status of the data. The Shape option lets you format any shapes in the PivotDiagram.

NOTE Data graphics can be used to indicate the status of the data represented by a Visio shape.

CHANGING THE LOOK AND FEEL OF A PIVOTDIAGRAM   As with the Excel PivotCharts, you can change the background appearance of a PivotDiagram. When you first open a Visio visual report, a pane appears on the left side of the screen (see Figure 21.21). If you collapse the PivotDiagram heading, it will reveal five additional tabs: Background, Borders and Titles, Department, Workflow Objects, and PivotDiagram Shapes. Each of these tabs holds several items you can insert into the PivotDiagram by dragging them from the pane and dropping them into the PivotDiagram.

Therefore, to change the background of a PivotDiagram, collapse the PivotDiagram heading on the pane and click on the Background tab. The background options will appear under the tab heading. Select from any of the 19 background options: Click on the desired background and drag it into the PivotDiagram. The background will automatically be inserted into the diagram.

Use this same methodology for the other four tabs: Borders and Titles, Department, Workflow Objects, and PivotDiagram Shapes.

Figure 21.23 shows a PivotDiagram with the Background World inserted. Notice the Background tab on the left pane.

To remove a background, you can use the Multiple Undo feature on the Standard toolbar. Or, you can open the Page Setup dialog box. To do so, select File, Page Setup. On the Page Properties tab of the Page Setup dialog box, choose None from the Background field drop-down list, click Apply, and then click OK. The background will be removed.

NOTE By default, the report's title is displayed in the upper-left corner of the PivotDiagram. You can select it and move it, as well as format the title's text like you would in Microsoft Word.

21

Another way to change the look and feel of a PivotDiagram is to apply a theme to it. To do so, click the Theme button, located on the Formatting toolbar. The Theme pane will open on the right side of the screen, as illustrated in Figure 21.24.

Figure 21.23
Drag and drop any of the 19 backgrounds into the PivotDiagram from the options listed under the Background tab on the left task bar.

Figure 21.24
Apply a theme to the PivotDiagram to change the colors of the nodes, using a predefined color scheme.

The Theme pane has two options: Theme Color and Theme Effects. The Theme Color option provides a number of different color schemes for the nodes themselves. The Theme Effects option provides different selections for the shapes and styles of the nodes. Click on any of the options listed in the Theme pane, and it will be applied to your PivotDiagram. Click the Theme button again on the Formatting toolbar to close the Theme pane.

CUSTOMIZING THE DATA IN A PIVOTDIAGRAM

Like the Excel reports, you can insert data fields to be included in your PivotDiagram using the Visual Reports – Field Picker dialog box. To access it, open the Visual Reports – Create Report dialog box (Report, Visual Reports), select the Visio report you wish to customize, and click the Edit Template button. This will open the Visual Reports – Field Picker dialog box, in which you can add fields to or remove fields from the list in the same way as discussed in the previous section "Customizing Data in an Excel Visual Report." Click OK when you are finished, and open the Visio report.

There are two main areas to add data to a Visio PivotDiagram: Add Category and Add Total. Both are located on the pane on the left side of the screen, as illustrated in Figure 21.25.

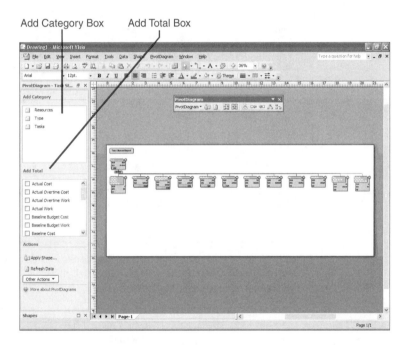

Figure 21.25
You can use the Add Category and Add Total panes to add additional fields and categories of fields to your Visio report.

In the Add Category area, you can choose the level of tasks or resources to display in the diagram. For example, if you are working with the Task Status Report, the diagram lists the Work and Cost values for each summary task, along with indicators of how the data compares to the baseline data. You may want to drill further into the subtask level, or display resource information for each summary task. Furthermore, you can select specific nodes to add categories to, or add them to the entire diagram.

Figure 21.26 shows the Task Status Report (US), with the resources displayed for the Scope summary task and the subtasks displayed for the Design summary task. To display resources for a node, select it, and in the Add Category box, choose Resources. A tree extension is inserted underneath the node(s) you selected, labeled "Resources," and the resources associated with that particular node will be displayed (refer to Figure 21.26). Similarly, to display another level of tasks, choose the node(s) you wish to expand, and select Tasks from the Add Category box. A drop-down list will display the levels of tasks you are able to drill into (Tasks 01, Tasks 02, Tasks 03, and so on). Select the level you wish to display, and those subtasks will be displayed underneath the node(s) you selected.

Figure 21.26
Use the Add Category box to display additional category information, such as resources and other task levels.

> **NOTE**
>
> By default, lower levels of tasks or resources are displayed underneath the node you selected. However, you can change the layout and alignment of the tree structure in a PivotDiagram using the PivotDiagram toolbar.

To remove the newly inserted category, select the node(s) that the tree is attached to, and in the PivotDiagram toolbar, select Collapse from the drop-down list.

The Add Total box functions similarly to the PivotTable Field List of an Excel PivotChart. Select the boxes next to the data fields you wish to include in the PivotDiagram, or clear the selections you wish to remove. For example, in the Task Status Report, you may wish to include Actual Cost and Actual Work into the diagram to compare with the Cost and Work values. Select the Actual Cost and Actual Work check boxes, and they will appear in each node, as illustrated in Figure 21.27.

21

Figure 21.27
Use the Add Total box to display additional data fields or remove fields from the PivotDiagram.

Underneath the Add Category and Add Total boxes is the Apply Shape command. This is also a command button on the PivotDiagram toolbar. To add a shape to a node, select it and click the Apply Shape button (either on the PivotDiagram toolbar or on the pane under the Add Total box). The Apply Shape dialog box will appear, as shown in Figure 21.28. Choose the shape you wish to apply and click OK. The shape will then be attached to the node.

Figure 21.28
In the Apply Shape dialog box, choose the shape you wish to apply to the node you selected.

21

TIP

> Shapes can be very helpful graphical indicators of the data or category of a particular node or group of nodes.

The Refresh Data button underneath the Apply Shape button is also found on the PivotDiagram toolbar. It will refresh the data in the PivotDiagram to apply any changes made to the project file.

The Other Actions drop-down list under the Refresh Data button is the same list as the drop-down list in the PivotDiagram toolbar.

THE SHAPE DATA DIALOG BOX   If you want to examine all the information related to a node, you can do so in the Shape Data dialog box. To display it, right-click on a node and choose Data, Shape Data. The Shape Data dialog box will appear, as shown in Figure 21.29.

Figure 21.29
The Shape Data dialog box allows you to view specific data information for any particular node.

Shape Data	
Tasks:	Financial Database Software Development
Tasks 01:	Scope
Member:	Scope
Actual Duration:	3.5
Actual Finish:	0
Actual Start:	8/28/2006 8:00:00 AM
Baseline Duration:	3.5
Baseline Finish:	8/31/2006 12:00:00 PM
Baseline Fixed Cost:	0
Baseline Start:	8/28/2006 8:00:00 AM
Constraint Date:	0
Created:	8/12/2006 9:37:00 AM
Deadline:	0
Duration:	3.5
Duration Variance:	0
Early Finish:	8/31/2006 12:00:00 PM
Early Start:	8/28/2006 8:00:00 AM
Finish:	8/31/2006 12:00:00 PM
Finish Slack:	105
Finish Variance:	0

(Note: Additional properties not shown)

Prompt

[?]   Define...   OK   Cancel

The Shape Data dialog box is an excellent way to view all the information associated with a node, as it is sometimes difficult to see everything in the node itself.

Although the Shape Data dialog box is primarily intended for viewing specific information, you can change some of the data by typing directly into a particular field. Also, if you click the Define button, located at the bottom of the Shape Data dialog box, the Define Shape Data dialog box will appear, as shown in Figure 21.30. Use the Define Shape Data dialog box to define further information about the node you selected.

Figure 21.30
In the Define Shape Data dialog box, you can define additional information regarding the node you selected.

HELPFUL TIPS FOR CUSTOMIZING VISIO 2007 VISUAL REPORTS   Visio provides the capability to create a report within a report. That is, you can create another type of report that includes data fields from your original report, outside of the Visio PivotDiagram format. To do so, select Data, Reports from the main menu. This will open the Report Definition Wizard, which will walk you through the process of creating an alternate report via Visio. These reports can be generated using Excel, HTML, Visio Shape, or XML format.

CREATING VISUAL REPORTS USING EXCEL 2007

If none of the existing visual reports completely meets your needs, you can create a new report from scratch. To create a new Excel visual report, you must first open the Visual Reports – Create Report dialog box by selecting Report, Visual Reports from the main menu.

In the Visual Reports – Create Report dialog box, click the New Template button. This will open the Visual Reports – New Template dialog box, as shown in Figure 21.31.

To create a new Excel visual report, follow these steps:

1. In the Visual Reports – New Template dialog box, select Excel from the Select Application area.

2. In the Select Data Type area, choose from Task Usage, Resource Usage, Assignment Usage, Task Status, Resource Status, and Assignment Status. To help make the right decision, ask yourself if the report will primarily focus on task, resource, or assignment data, and make your selection based on that decision.

21

Figure 21.31
Create a new Excel visual report by selecting Excel in the Visual Reports – New Template dialog box.

TIP

> If you would like to include time-phased data in your report, then choose Task Usage, Resource Usage, or Assignment Usage as your data type. These three data types will allow you to display time-phased data.

3. Once you choose your data type, select the fields to include in your report by clicking the Field Picker button, which will display the Visual Reports – Field Picker dialog box (refer back to Figure 21.7).

4. In the Visual Reports – Field Picker dialog box, choose which fields you want to include from the Available Fields or Available Custom Fields boxes, and click Add to insert them into the Selected Fields or Selected Custom Fields boxes. These fields will then be available for you to include in your report data by selecting them from the PivotTable Field List. You can also remove fields that you do not want to use in your report. When you have finished choosing your data fields, click OK to close the Visual Reports – Field Picker dialog box and return to the Visual Reports – New Template dialog box. Refer back to the previous section "Customizing Data in an Excel Visual Report" for more information about the Visual Reports – Field Picker dialog box.

5. To complete the creation of your new visual report template, click OK in the Visual Reports – New Template dialog box. This will open a blank Excel PivotTable, as shown in Figure 21.32.

To insert data fields into the blank PivotTable, you can drag and drop them onto the table itself, select them in the PivotTable Field List, or drag and drop them into the Values box at the bottom of the PivotTable Field List. Scroll down past the data fields in the PivotTable Field List to find Tasks, Resources, or Time options, depending on the data type you chose when creating the report. You can drag these category fields into the Report Filter, Column Labels, or Row Labels boxes at the bottom of the PivotTable Field List, or select them in the list. If the Defer Layout Update option is cleared, the PivotTable will change based on the modifications you make as you make them.

Figure 21.32
When you create a new Excel visual report, a blank PivotTable appears, in which you can place your data fields to construct the report.

Perhaps you want to create an Excel report that shows your Actual Work and Actual Cost over time thus far in your project. You would select the boxes next to these fields in your PivotTable Field List. Also, you can insert Tasks and Time by selecting those boxes and dragging them into the areas where you want them to be displayed.

TIP

> It is best to have a general idea of how you want to organize your report and what data and categories you wish to include. Then, as you are building your report in the PivotTable Field List, experiment with the formatting of the data by dragging and dropping the data fields and categories into different rows or columns until you are happy with the results.

You will also notice a blinking Office Button in the top-left corner of your screen. Place your mouse pointer over it, and a ScreenTip informs you to click the button to open, save, print, or see everything else you can do with your document. If you click the Office Button, the box in Figure 21.33 appears.

Saving and printing your report will be discussed in greater detail in the section "Sharing and Saving Visual Reports," later in this chapter.

As you are constructing your PivotTable, you can also create the PivotChart for your report. To do so, select the Insert tab from the main menu and choose what kind of PivotChart you want to create from the Charts section of the Insert ribbon. You can choose from Column, Line, Pie, Bar, Area, Scatter, and Other Charts (see Figure 21.34). Each chart type will have several two- and three-dimensional options.

21

Figure 21.33
Clicking the blinking Office Button will open this box, in which you can save, open, print, or perform other Office commands.

In Figure 21.34, a PivotTable has been created to display Actual Work and Actual Cost for all tasks in the project over time. The Tasks category is collapsed to show total project data (but can be expanded to show lower task levels). Also, the Time category has been expanded to show the third quarter data for 2006. A PivotChart has also been defined to show the data in a three-dimensional column format.

Figure 21.34
Insert a PivotChart to your PivotTable using the Chart area on the Insert tab.

If you want to place your PivotChart on a separate sheet than your PivotTable, select the PivotChart, and on the main menu, select the Design tab. At the right side of the Design ribbon is the Move Chart option. Click on this option, and a Move Chart dialog box will appear, in which you can opt to move the chart to a different sheet.

You can continue to modify your PivotTable and PivotChart using the methods discussed previously in the section "Customizing Excel 2007 Visual Reports."

CREATING VISUAL REPORTS USING VISIO 2007

Creating a new Visio visual report is similar to creating a new Excel report. To create a new Visio visual report, follow these steps:

1. Open the Visual Reports – Create Report dialog box by selecting Report, Visual Reports from the main menu.

2. Click the New Template button to open the Visual Reports – New Template dialog box.

3. In the Visual Reports – New Template dialog box, select either Visio (Metric) or Visio (US Units), depending on which measurement system you want to use in your report.

4. Select your data type from the six options in the Data Type drop-down list, and use the Field Picker to add data field options to or remove them from your report.

5. When you have finished selecting the fields to be included in the report, click the OK button to create the report. A new PivotDiagram will open.

Figure 21.35 shows a new PivotDiagram that has been created to display Actual Work and Actual Cost for each quarter in the project. Theme colors and effects have been applied using the Theme button on the Formatting toolbar.

Figure 21.35
Use the Add Category and Add Total boxes to insert data into your new Visio report.

You can define which categories to include as nodes (tasks, resources, and so on) using the Add Category box, and define the data each node holds in the Add Total box. You can also format the nodes themselves by right-clicking on them and choosing from the available formatting options, or by using the PivotDiagram toolbar or Theme options.

If you want to change the title, right-click on it to format the text. You can also move it by dragging it.

Continue to modify your PivotDiagram using the methods discussed previously in the section "Customizing Visio 2007 Visual Reports."

SHARING AND SAVING VISUAL REPORTS

The 22 existing visual report templates are designed to contain specific project data, and are excellent starting points for customizing your own visual reports using the methods discussed throughout this chapter. When you make changes to a report template, or when you create your own, you have the ability to share not only the data but the format of the report you have modified. That way, if you or other project managers want to use the same report format for future project files, it is saved and stored properly and does not have to be recreated.

You can save the modified or new report as a template using both Excel and Visio. Also, you can save it as a cube (to open in Excel) or a database (to open in Excel or Visio). Whereas a template saves the report's format definition with no actual data, a cube includes the specific project reporting data. That way, you can access the report, including the project information, from Excel or Visio without having to open Microsoft Project 2007. A database also includes specific project data, but is smaller and more specific than a cube.

SAVING A VISUAL REPORT TEMPLATE USING EXCEL 2007

If you have customized or created a new Excel visual report, and you find that the report format works very well, you may want to save the format for use in future projects. To do so, follow these steps:

1. In the Excel or Visio, from the File menu select Save, which will open the Save As dialog box. Type in a specific name for your new report template that describes the functionality of the report and is unique from the other existing Excel report templates. When you have entered the template's name, click Save.

2. A box will appear asking you if you want to clear the data before saving the template. Click Yes, and the template will be saved as specified in the Save As dialog box.

By default, when you click Save and close the Save As dialog box, the report template will be saved along with the other existing visual report templates. It will appear on the list in the Visual Reports – Create Report dialog box, not only for your current project file, but for all project files you open or create.

21

NOTE

> The new report template does not appear in the Visual Reports – Create Report dialog box until you close the box and reopen it after the template has been saved. Once you reopen the dialog box, the report will appear in the list.

However, you may choose to save it in another location on your computer or network. If that is the case, the new template may not appear in the Visual Reports – Create Report dialog box automatically; you may have to browse for it. To do so, select the Include Report Templates From check box in the Visual Reports – Create Report dialog box and click the Modify button to browse for the template.

NOTE

> Sometimes, selecting the Include Report Templates From box is enough to display the new report template; you may not have to browse for it when you check this box.

SAVING A VISUAL REPORT TEMPLATE USING VISIO 2007

To save a customized or new Visio report as a template, repeat the process described in the previous section. Click the Save button, which will open the Save As dialog box. Name your report, and click Save. By default, it will be saved in the same folder as the other existing visual reports, and will appear every time you open the Visual Reports – Create Report dialog box (if the box is currently open, you will have to close it and reopen it to see the new template).

If you choose to save it elsewhere, you will have to select the Include Report Templates From check box in the Visual Reports – Create Report dialog box and browse for it using the Modify button if it did not automatically appear when you checked the box.

SAVING A REPORTING CUBE

There will be times when you want to save the reporting data in your project file outside of your project. You can save the data as a cube, which is larger than a regular database, to be opened later in Excel. To do so, follow these steps:

1. Click the Save Data button on the Visual Reports – Create Report dialog box. This will open the Visual Report – Save Reporting Data dialog box, as shown in Figure 21.36.

   In the Visual Reports – Save Reporting Data dialog box, you can choose to save reporting data as either a cube or as a database. As previously mentioned, a cube is larger than a regular database.

2. To save your reporting data as a cube, use the drop-down menu to choose from Task Usage, Resource Usage, Assignment Usage, Task Summary, Resource Summary, and Assignment Summary.

21

Figure 21.36
Save reporting data
as a cube or as a
database using the
Visual Reports – Save
Reporting Data dialog
box.

3. Click the Field Picker button to open the Visual Reports – Field Picker dialog box and select your fields as described previously in this chapter.

4. When you have chosen the cube and its accompanying fields, click Save Cube. The Save As dialog box will appear, and you can designate the location you wish to save your cube.

To access the saved reporting data, follow these steps:

1. Open Excel. On the Insert tab, select either PivotTable or PivotChart from the Tables heading. This will open the Create PivotTable or Create PivotChart dialog box, depending on what you selected on the Insert ribbon (see Figure 21.37).

2. Select Use an External Data Source, and click Choose Connection. This will open the Existing Connections dialog box.

3. Click the Browse For More button, and browse for the location where you saved the cube. When you find it, select it and click Open, then click OK on the Create PivotTable (or Create PivotChart) dialog box.

4. A blank PivotTable or PivotChart will appear, and when you select data fields from the PivotTable Field List, the reporting data from the project file will be displayed as the data values in the chart.

Figure 21.37 shows the Create PivotTable dialog box.

SAVING A REPORTING DATABASE

To save the reporting data as a database, open the Visual Reports – Save Reporting Data dialog box as instructed in the previous section and click Save Database. This will open the Save As dialog box, which you can use to define the name and location where you wish to save the reporting database.

Figure 21.37
To import data from a saved cube, select Use an External Data Source. Then browse for your saved cube by clicking the Choose Connection button on the Create PivotTable (or Create PivotChart) dialog box.

After you have saved the database, you can open it in either Excel or Visio.

To open it in Excel, follow these steps:

1. Open Excel, and on the Insert tab, choose PivotTable or PivotChart on the Tables heading. This opens the Create PivotTable or Create PivotChart dialog box (see Figure 21.37).

2. In the Create PivotTable (or PivotChart) dialog box, select Use an External Data Source and then click Choose Connection.

3. In the Existing Connections dialog box, select Browse For More, find your saved database, and click Open. This will open the Select Table dialog box.

4. In the Select Table dialog box, choose the database table to insert into the PivotTable or PivotChart and then click OK. Click OK on the Create PivotTable or Create PivotChart dialog box, and the blank PivotTable or PivotChart will be inserted.

5. Select the data fields from the PivotTable Field List, and the reporting data from your original project will appear as data values in those fields.

To open the reporting database in Visio, follow these steps:

1. Open Visio, and choose Data, Insert PivotDiagram. This will open the Data Selector dialog box.

2. On the Data Selector dialog box, choose Microsoft Office Access Database and click Next.

3. Browse for your existing database by clicking Browse on the next screen. Select it and click Open.

4. Click Next to advance to the next screen, and choose your rows and columns to include. By default, All Columns and All Data are selected. Click Next and then click Finish.

5. Select the data fields from the Add Total and Add Category boxes to include on the PivotDiagram. The reporting data from your project will be displayed as data values.

21

PRINTING A VISUAL REPORT

When you have finished customizing or creating your report, and you have saved it appropriately, you may also want to print a copy of your report to share with your project team or other project stakeholders. Printing a report is slightly different for Excel and Visio.

In Excel, click the Office Button in the top-left corner of your screen. A list of options will appear, as illustrated previously in Figure 21.33. Scroll down to the Print option, which will give you three print choices: Print, Quick Print, and Print Preview. The Print option opens the Print dialog box, in which you can define which printer to use, how many copies to print, the page range, and so on. The Quick Print option prints the report as is, without allowing you to choose the printer or make any changes (it prints on your default printer). The Print Preview option opens the Print Preview screen to give you a preview of what your printed report will look like before you actually print it.

Using the Print Preview screen is highly recommended because it enables you to verify that the report is indeed ready to be printed and needs no further modifications. From the Print Preview screen, you can also open the Page Setup dialog box by clicking Page Setup at the top of the screen. The Page Setup dialog box allows you to make additional formatting modifications to your printed report.

Once you have verified that you are ready to print your report, open the Print dialog box either by clicking the Print option from the Office Button or by clicking Print from the Print Preview screen. Be sure that the definitions in the Print dialog box are those you are intending to implement before you click the Print button. The report will print out as you specified, exactly as it appeared on the Print Preview screen, on the printer defined in the Print dialog box.

CAUTION

> Not all printers are capable of printing color documents. If you must have a printed report in color, be sure to verify on the Print Preview screen that it will in fact be printing in color. If it shows up black and white on the Print Preview screen, you will need to change the printer to use in the Print dialog box to a printer that can print in color.

To print a Visio report, select File and choose either Page Setup, Print Preview, or Print. The Page Setup option displays the Page Setup dialog box, in which you can make additional formatting modifications to your printed report. The Print option opens the Print dialog box, and the Print Preview option displays the Print Preview screen. Again, it is highly recommended that you view the Print Preview screen before actually printing your report to verify that everything is exactly as you want it to appear. Otherwise, you will have to reprint your report, which is a waste of time, ink, and paper.

When you have verified that the report is ready to be printed, open the Print dialog box and click Print. The Visio report will print on the printer defined in the Print dialog box.

CONSULTANTS' TIPS

80/20: CHOOSE THE RIGHT DATA RESOLUTION FOR YOUR REPORTING GOALS

Successful reports communicate information within the correct context. The wrong context can cause confusion, which in turn can sometimes only be cleared through an amazing amount of effort that could have been avoided if the context had been provided. Data resolution is often a critical part of providing the right context. For example, tracking project status daily is a waste of effort if the team is only updating the status weekly. Worse, reporting that daily status and drawing conclusions from it is an even bigger waste of time. When you present information, presenting more than is needed causes miscommunication. People naturally look for patterns from which to draw conclusions. Presenting too much information provides the opportunity to look for patterns that are irrelevant. But the assumption by your audience is always going to be that if you provide the information, it must be relevant.

SAVE CUSTOMIZED REPORTS AS TEMPLATES FOR LATER USE

Microsoft Project 2007 visual reports provide a variety of customization options; therefore, when you identify report definitions that work best for you, it is important that you save them as templates for future use. Using visual reports' templates can be a great way to save time in your future projects. In addition, templates can be used to standardize the format and data across your organization as your project managers can share the templates they create. Having consistent, informative reports can help you effectively communicate your project information to your project team and project sponsors, as well as help you better understand problems occurring in your project.

21

CUSTOMIZING VIEWS, TABLES, FILTERS, GROUPS, AND FIELDS

In this chapter

22

THE RELATIONSHIPS BETWEEN VIEWS, TABLES, FILTERS, GROUPS, AND FIELDS

This chapter focuses on creating and customizing elements within Microsoft Project 2007 that will help make your own project unique to your needs. Views, tables, filters, groups, and fields are all helpful ways of organizing specific aspects of your project. They are useful for displaying or reporting various characteristics or phases within your project. Furthermore, they are all related. Views are composed of different kinds of tables. Tables can be filtered or grouped to display common traits within the table entries. Tables can also include custom fields, which contain specific project information, such as customized schedule "stop light" indicators driven by formulas. Each of these elements can help you to more effectively manage your project based on the specific information each provides and how they are formatted or configured. All of these concepts will be discussed in greater detail throughout this chapter.

Another thing to keep in mind while reading this chapter is the difference between tasks (work that needs to be done) and resources (the people, tools, and equipment necessary to get the work done) and how they apply to views, tables, filters, groups, and fields. For instance, different tables are available to view tasks rather than resources, and vice versa. This is important to remember because while the methods for customizing and creating views, tables, filters, groups, and fields for tasks and resources are the same, the end result often is not, simply because tasks and resources are two different entities within Microsoft Project 2007. For example, Resource Names is a field in the default Task Entry table, but several resource tables have fields in which you define the resource name.

→ For additional details on what you can view in Microsoft Project 2007, **see** "What Can I View Using Microsoft Project 2007?" **p. 370** and "Viewing Strategies," **p. 371**.

In short, all the methods and concepts discussed within this chapter are related; some processes may require an understanding of other processes, such as creating a custom table to insert into a custom view. Also, bear in mind that different views, tables, filters, groups, and fields will appear or function differently for a task than a resource.

TIP

> Most of the dialog boxes discussed in this chapter have a Help button. The Help button can be a great resource for answering questions or guiding you through a process you may be confused about.

CREATING AND CUSTOMIZING TABLES

As previously mentioned, Microsoft Project 2007 contains tables that hold and define a wide variety of information within a project. Tables are composed of rows and columns that are customizable in many aspects, and are the foundation for sheet views within Microsoft Project 2007. In any table row, column, or field, you can define not only the information it houses, but also its appearance within the table. You can adjust the width, height, and text alignment of a table's columns. Furthermore, you can add, delete, and move columns to better suit your needs.

To create and customize a table, select View, Table, and then More Tables. This opens up the More Tables dialog box, with the currently displayed table highlighted, as shown in Figure 22.1.

Figure 22.1
The More Tables dialog box is the starting point for creating and customizing a table.

The More Tables dialog box looks quite similar to the More Views dialog box discussed later in this chapter. The major difference is the choice of displaying Task and Resource tables, which is found at the top of the dialog box. Selecting Task will display all the task tables, and selecting Resource will display all the resource tables. One or the other is selected automatically, depending on the view you were displaying when you opened the More Tables dialog box. If it was a Task view, then the Task tables are listed, and vice versa if it was a Resource view.

To change a table on your current view, highlight the table you want to display and click Apply. Microsoft Project 2007 will only let you display applicable tables for the current view; you cannot display a Task table on a Resource view, and vice versa.

The rest of the More Tables dialog box works like the More Views dialog box. If you want to edit a table, saving the changes and replacing the original table, highlight the table and choose Edit. If you want to edit a table but do not want to replace the original, choose Copy. To copy a table to or from the Global.MPT file, choose Organizer (this feature is discussed at the end of this chapter in the section, "Organizing Views and Other Custom Elements in Project Files").

To create a new table, follow these steps:

1. Open the More Tables dialog box by selecting View, Tables, More Tables.
2. In the More Tables dialog box, select New. This opens the Table Definition dialog box, as does choosing Edit or Copy. Notice how all the fields are blank; you create the new table by entering values in these fields. If you chose Edit or Copy, these fields would already be defined based on the original table you were editing, and you would edit the original table by changing the entries in these fields (see Figure 22.2).

22

Figure 22.2
Create a new table or
edit an existing one in
the Table Definition
dialog box.

The following sections will discuss the various fields in the Table Definition dialog box and the process for creating and customizing tables.

ENTERING A TABLE NAME

As with any name in Microsoft Project 2007, your table name should be unique and specific to what is defined in the table. This applies to new tables and edited ones. Even if you are making minor adjustments, you want the name to reflect those modifications. If you are copying an existing table, you need to make sure you give it a new name; otherwise, you will end up with two different tables that have identical names.

As with views, you can include an ampersand symbol (&) directly before any letter you want to designate as the hotkey. This way, if you save the table to the main Table menu (View, Table), you can type the hotkey letter as a shortcut to the table. For more information about hotkeys, see "Entering the Name of the View" later in this chapter. To save the table to the main Table menu, select the Show in Menu check box before you click OK.

ADDING AND CHANGING THE COLUMNS IN THE TABLE

To add a new column in your table, there are several fields in the Table Definition dialog box to define information about the column. The following list describes each of these fields:

- **Field Name**—Choose the field name by clicking in the Field Name field and selecting from the drop-down list (see Figure 22.3). You cannot create your own; you must use one from the drop-down list. You can, however, rename it so the name is displayed the way you want it to read. (See the "Title" section of this list.) Once you choose a field name and click in another area of the Table Definition dialog box, three other fields are automatically filled in with default values: Align Data, Width, and Align Title.

22

- **Align Data**—In this field, you have three choices available in the drop-down list: Left, Center, and Right. The one you choose is how the data in each cell will be displayed. If you choose Right, it will be as far to the right in the cell as possible. Choosing Center will center the data in the cell, and Left will line it up all the way to the left. The default choice is Right.

- **Width**—In the Width field, you simply define the width of the column. The default is 10 characters and you can increase or decrease that value by using the up and down arrows on the right side of the field or by typing in the number of characters you want the width to be.

- **Title**—The Title field is where you would define the text you want displayed as the header of the column. For example, in the Task Entry Table Definition dialog box, the third entry under Field Name is Name, but its Title entry is Task Name. You can see that Task Name appears at the top of the column in that particular table. Thus, the Title field is where you would change the display name that you selected as your field name. You can leave the Title fields blank, and the column header will be displayed as its field name.

- **Align Title**—This field is similar to the Align Data field. Again, you have a drop-down list with three options: Left, Center, and Right. Your choice determines how the text in the column header (the top of the column in the table) will be displayed. This alignment does not have to match the alignment you chose for the data. You could have the title aligned to the right and the data in its subordinate cells aligned in the center. It may be helpful to visually align the title and the cell data differently to emphasize the column header.

- **Header Wrapping**—In this field, you have two choices in the drop-down list: Yes and No. This only applies if you have a long column header title that does not fit in the cell. If you select Yes, Microsoft Project 2007 will automatically wrap the title to fit in the cell.

Figure 22.3
Click in the Field Name field to choose from the drop-down list. Other fields in the Table Definition dialog box also have drop-down lists to select from.

22

TIP

If you have never created a new table before, it may be a good idea to open a familiar table's Table Definition dialog box to see how it is defined. For example, you are probably familiar with the Task Entry table (the left side of the Gantt Chart view).

To view its Table Definition dialog box, switch to the Gantt Chart view and choose View, Table, More Tables. Then select Task at the top of the More Tables dialog box, select Entry, and click Copy. The Table Definition dialog box will appear, with all the Task Entry table's characteristics defined. You can play around with it and see the effects of your modifications without losing the original Task Entry table.

Any time you make an entry in the Field Name field, you create a new column. Furthermore, the columns are displayed in order. Reading them from top to bottom is the same order they will be in from left to right on the table. Therefore, you want to keep the order in mind as you are creating or customizing your table. If you want to insert a column somewhere in the middle of the table, select any field where you want to put it, and click the Insert Row button. A blank row will be created for you to enter the column information, and all other rows, including the one you had selected, will move down to make room for it.

To delete a column from the table, select a field in its row and click the Delete Row button. Or, if you want to replace the deleted column, you do not have to delete it. Simply click in the Field Name field for the column you want to delete, and select the field name you want to replace it with. Then fill in all the information for the new column.

You can also cut and paste the rows to rearrange columns in the table. Select any field in the row for the column you want to move, and click the Cut Row button. Then, select any field in the row you want to move it to, and click the Paste Row button. The new column information will be pasted in the row you selected, and all other rows beneath it, including the one you selected, will move down to make room for the pasted row.

COMPLETING THE DEFINITION OF THE TABLE

You can select the date format to use in the table if you want to change it from the default. The default date format is defined on the View tab of the Options dialog box (Tools, Options). Changing the date format applies only to the table and not to other tables or views within the project.

Next to the Date Format field is the Row Height field. By default, it is set at 1, which means one row of text is displayed for each task or resource row in the table. You can change this by entering a number or using the up and down arrows, which will make all rows on the table that height. Alternatively, you can change the height of individual rows without changing all the rows on the table. This is done outside of the Table Definition dialog box by clicking and dragging on the individual row dividers.

→ For more information about changing individual row height in a table, **see** "Adjusting the Height of Task Rows," **p. 162**.

Selecting the Lock First Column check box is useful when working with a table that has columns displayed to the right that you have to scroll to see. If selected, this feature will always display the first column as a means for you to keep track of the row information. For instance, if your first column (the top column entry row in the Table Definition dialog box) is Task Name, and you have the Lock First Column box checked, you can scroll all the way to the right and your task names will always be displayed.

By default this box is checked. The disadvantage, however, is that this column cannot be edited in the table itself, because it is locked. Also, the column header (the Title) is not displayed in the table when this box is checked.

By default, the check box is selected for Auto-adjust Header Row Heights. This feature is applied when you change the width of a row. If you decide to make a row narrower, the column header (the Title) may not be able to fit with the smaller width. If this box is selected, Microsoft Project 2007 will wrap the header to fit by using more rows. If it is not selected, the header will only be partially displayed (as much as will fit with the new, narrower width).

Figure 22.4 shows a Table Definition dialog box. A table has been customized from the standard Task Entry table. To re-create this, follow these steps:

1. Set the Task Sheet as your view by selecting View, More Views, and then Task Sheet.
2. Select View, Table, More Tables. Entry will be highlighted in the More Tables dialog box.
3. Choose Copy to customize the Task Entry table without losing the original.
4. The Table Definition dialog box will appear and you can define the table based on the information in the previous sections. In the example in Figure 22.4, the % Complete and % Work Complete fields have been added to view the task's progress.

NOTE

> The example in Figure 22.4 is meant to convey the theory behind customizing a table; it is not necessarily the best way to view task progress. While the newly customized table in this example is called "Task Progress," there are other tables already built into Microsoft Project 2007 that may be more beneficial for tracking a task's progress.

Figure 22.4
The Task Entry table has been customized into a new table, called Task Progress, by inserting the % Complete and % Work Complete fields.

22

Figure 22.5 shows the newly customized Task Progress table itself as applied to the Task Sheet view.

Figure 22.5
The Task Progress table is displayed in the Task Sheet view. This is the table defined in Figure 22.4.

CHANGING TABLE FEATURES FROM THE VIEW SCREEN

Many of the table customization or creation modifications can be made without using the Table Definition dialog box. The Column Definition dialog box can be accessed to make changes to particular columns in the table.

To open the Column Definition dialog box, double-click the column header. The Column Definition dialog box will appear, as shown in Figure 22.6. Notice that the entry fields in the Column Definition dialog box are quite similar to those found in the Table Definition dialog box.

Figure 22.6
Modify column information in the Column Definition dialog box.

You can change column information in the following fields: Field Name, Title, Align Title, Align Data, and Width. While in a slightly different order, these are the same fields in the Table Definition dialog box. Header Text Wrapping is also an option, only here it is a check box instead of a Yes/No field.

The major difference between defining this information in the Column Definition dialog box versus the Table Definition dialog box is the Best Fit button in the Column Definition dialog box. When you have entered all the information you want, you can click OK to apply the changes and close the box. Alternatively, you can click the Best Fit button, which applies all the information and closes the box, but the column width is automatically calculated by Microsoft Project 2007. The width will be defined to fit the longest entry in the column.

CAUTION

> Choosing the Best Fit button fits the longest entry onto one long line of text. This can make for very wide columns if you have long entries such as the task name.

You can also insert a new column in the table without using the Table Definition dialog box. To do so, highlight the column where you want to insert the new one by clicking its header. Then, insert it in one of several ways:

- Select Insert, Column from the menu bar.
- Right-click the column title and choose Insert Column.
- Press the Insert (Ins) key.

The Column Definition dialog box will appear. Define the new column's information and click OK. The new column will be inserted in place of the one you highlighted, and all columns to the right will shift over to make room for the new one.

To hide or delete a column without accessing the Table Definition dialog box, do one of the following:

- Highlight the column by clicking its header and then press the Delete (Del) key, or choose Edit, Hide Column. This removes the column from the table entirely.
- Right-click the column header and choose Hide Column. This also removes it from the table entirely.
- Drag the right divider line for the column from right to left until the column is hidden. This does not remove the column from the table, but sets its width to zero.

If a column was hidden or deleted, you must reinsert it to get it back using any of the methods described in this section or using the Table Definition dialog box. If you used the mouse to drag the width to zero, you can use the mouse to reopen it. This may be tricky because the column is not displayed; slowly drag the mouse over the area where it was hidden in until the pointer becomes a vertical line with horizontal arrows, then drag it open.

CAUTION

> You must remember if you hid a column using your mouse because Microsoft Project 2007 gives no indication of a hidden column.

Row heights can be changed as well by dragging the border of a row with the mouse.

> **NOTE**
> There are advantages to changing table features from the View screen as opposed to the Table Definition dialog box. The Table Definition dialog box is beneficial to making changes to multiple rows at once, while other methods such as accessing the Column Definition dialog box aid in modifying columns one at a time.

CREATING AND CUSTOMIZING VIEWS

Microsoft Project 2007 is equipped with dozens of views, all of which are beneficial depending on specifically what you want to display on the screen. Moreover, these views are divided into single-pane views, in which the view is displayed on the entire screen, and combination views, which are composed of two different views combined onto one screen separated by a divider bar.

In addition to these views, you have the ability to copy and/or edit the existing views to create new ones, or create new views entirely from scratch. Editing existing views and creating new ones is done in the More Views dialog box, shown in Figure 22.7. To open it, select View, More Views.

> **NOTE**
> A view is composed of a table, a filter, a group, and a screen. It is not necessary to create a new filter and table for a new view; you can use existing ones, but they must be defined in the New View dialog box.

Figure 22.7
Edit and create views using the buttons along the right side of the More Views dialog box.

Four buttons appear along the right side of the More Views dialog box:

- **New**—Use the New button to create a new view from scratch.
- **Edit**—Use the Edit button to edit an existing view, replacing the original view with the newly edited version.

■ **Copy**—Use the Copy button to edit an existing view without replacing the original, so you are left with both the original and your edited version.

TIP

It is wise to use the Copy button to create a copy of a view for further edits instead of customizing one of the out-of-the-box views. That way you do not replace the original view after you edit it. Unless you are positive you will never need the original view, use the Copy button. Once you select the Copy button, the first thing you should do is change the view name so it does not get confused with the original.

■ **Organizer**—Use the Organizer button to open the View tab Organizer dialog box, where you can rename or delete views, and copy them to or from the Global.MPT file or any other Microsoft Project 2007 file that may be opened in your current session. This is helpful if you create or customize a view and want to use it in other projects, or to use a view you have created or customized in a previous project that was copied to the Global.MPT file. This is discussed more at the end of this chapter in the section, "Organizing Views and Other Custom Elements in Project Files."

→ For additional information about Global.MPT and the Organizer, **see** Chapter 18, "Managing Project Files," **p. 581**.

Regardless of which option you choose to customize or create your view (New, Edit, or Copy), the process is very similar. If a view is almost, but not completely, what you are looking for, choose the Edit or Copy button to customize that view to your specific needs.

If none of the views in Microsoft Project 2007 meets your needs, then create a new view by clicking the New button. The Define New View dialog box appears, as shown in Figure 22.8.

Figure 22.8
In the Define New View dialog box, you can create a new Single view or Combination view.

Depending on which option you choose (Single view or Combination view), another dialog box appears. If you are creating a Combination view, you must define the new view's name and choose the two views to be displayed in the top pane and the bottom pane, as shown in Figure 22.9.

Figure 22.9
To create a new combination view, enter the name and choose which existing views to display in the top and bottom panes.

This is a brief summary of creating a Combination view; the process is discussed further in the upcoming section "Creating a Combination View," later in this chapter.

NOTE

> If one or more panes in your new Combination view are to include another customized or created view, you must customize or create that view first, then select it from the drop-down list when selecting the top and bottom panes in the View Definition dialog box.

If you are creating a new Single view, a different version of the View Definition dialog box appears (see Figure 22.10). This is the same dialog box you will use if you select Edit or Copy. You would, of course, define the name in the Name field, then choose the screen, table, group, and filter from their respective drop-down lists. These will all be discussed in greater detail in the following sections.

Figure 22.10
Create a new Single view in this version of the View Definition dialog box.

ENTERING THE NAME OF THE VIEW

Similar to naming tasks or resources, it is important to choose a name for a view that is unique and clearly identifies the features the view incorporates. Otherwise, a few months down the road you may find yourself wasting time searching through ambiguous view names for the one you want.

If you want to include your view in the main drop-down list that appears when you select View, select the Show in Menu check box. If not, leave it unchecked. The view will still appear in the More Views list (View, More Views).

Also, just like with tables, you can designate a hotkey letter to use when selecting the view as a shortcut if you select Show in Menu. Simply put an ampersand symbol (&) before the letter you want to designate as the hotkey. Then, in the main View drop-down list, the hotkey will be underlined, and you can type that letter to select the view. The hotkey can be any letter in the view's name, not just the first letter. Be sure that this letter is unique; otherwise, you will still have to select from all the views that have identical hotkeys. This hotkey shortcut only applies in the main View list; in the More Views list, you can press the first letter of the view name you are looking for, and select from all views that begin with that letter.

SELECTING THE STARTING FORMAT

When customizing or creating views, you must start with an existing screen and make your changes from there. All views must use one of the basic screens as its foundation, and all basic screens are already defined in Microsoft Project 2007. Choose this "starting point" screen from the drop-down list in the Screen field of the View Definition dialog box (see Figure 22.10).

You are only able to define the starting view in the Screen field if you are creating a new view. If you are editing or copying an existing view, the Screen field is automatically filled in because you cannot change the view you are editing or copying.

Fourteen basic screens are found in the drop-down list, as shown in Figure 22.11. Notice that some of them are resource screens, and some are task screens. Be sure to have a clear idea of whether the view you are creating is a resource or a task view.

Figure 22.11
Choose from the Fourteen different default views, which are the foundation of any new view you create in Microsoft Project 2007.

Some views can be modified more than others; you just have to experiment to see which one is most suitable for your needs. You can also change the formatting on most of the screens. Over time, you will become more familiar with the basic screens and will know which one to select to meet your specific view requirements.

→ For more information about formatting screens and views, **see** Chapter 19, "Formatting Views," **p. 601**.

SELECTING THE TABLE FOR THE VIEW

Depending on the view you have selected, you may have to select a table. Not all views display tables, but many do. If the view you have selected does not display a table, the Table field in the View Definition dialog box is grayed out so you cannot make a selection. The following screens require a Table field entry:

- Gantt Chart
- Resource Sheet
- Resource Usage
- Task Sheet
- Task Usage

If you are using one of these screens, select the table you want from the drop-down list in the Table field in the View Definition dialog box (refer to Figure 22.10). The list will display all the tables that can be used with the screen type you have selected. For instance, if you chose a resource screen type, such as Resource Usage, the Table drop-down list will display all the possible tables to use for that particular screen, and will not include task tables.

Also, if you have any customized tables that would apply to the screen type, they will be in the drop-down list. If you want to select a customized table, you must create it before you create your view. This process is described in the section "Creating and Customizing Tables," later in this chapter. The same applies to custom groups and filters.

SELECTING THE GROUP FOR THE VIEW

After defining a table for your view, the next option is the Group field. Your selection in the Group field determines how Project will arrange the table entries in your view. You can opt to choose No Group, and the tasks or resources will be sorted according to their ID number. If you choose a custom group, it must exist prior to selection, as discussed in the section "Creating Custom Groups," later in this chapter.

SELECTING THE FILTER FOR THE VIEW

The last step in creating or customizing your view is defining the filter to apply to it. The options in the Filter drop-down list are all of the possible filters you can use based on your other entries in the View Definition dialog box. Depending on your screen type, the top choice in the Filter drop-down list is All Tasks or All Resources. Select this option if you do not want Microsoft Project 2007 to filter the task or resource list for anything more specific.

Once you have chosen your filter, you can also select the check box next to Highlight Filter. If this option is selected, Microsoft Project 2007 will display all the tasks or resources, and the ones that the filter applies to will be highlighted. For instance, if you chose the Completed Tasks filter and select the Highlight Filter check box, all of the completed tasks will be highlighted in the list. The method of highlighting (bold, underline, italic, and so on) can be defined in the Text Styles dialog box. Choose Format, Text Styles to open the Text Styles dialog box.

As with tables and groups, you can create a custom filter and apply it to your custom view, but you must create the custom filter before you create the custom view. This process is described in the section "Creating Custom Filters," later in this chapter.

NOTE

You must define all fields in the View Definition dialog box except for when a field is grayed out. However, once you create your view, the entries in these fields are really just starting points when you first launch the view. You can apply different tables, groups, or filters, just like any other view in Microsoft Project 2007, after you have created and applied the custom view.

DISPLAYING THE VIEW NAME IN THE MENU

Once you have created a view, it will appear in the More Views dialog box (View, More Views). If you want it to appear in the main View menu, select the Show In Menu check box (refer to Figure 22.10).

You probably want to include the new view in the main View menu if you will be consistently using it. If not, you may not want to clear the Show in Menu check box, just to keep it out of the way until you need it.

SAVING THE VIEW DEFINITION

After you have entered all applicable information in the View Definition dialog box, click OK (or Cancel to exit without making any changes). The More Views dialog box is still displayed, and the view you just created or edited is highlighted in the list. To display the view immediately, click Apply. To exit the More Views dialog box without displaying the new view, click Close. The new view is saved and ready to be applied.

You can also continue working with any of the views by clicking the New, Edit, or Copy button.

Alternatively, click the Organizer button to open the Organizer dialog box to save the new view to the Global.MPT file for use in other projects. As previously mentioned, this is discussed further at the end of this chapter in the section "Organizing Views and Other Custom Elements in Project Files."

CREATING A COMBINATION VIEW

The previous sections described copying views, editing views, and creating new Single views. This section will focus on creating new Combination views.

As mentioned previously, a Combination view displays two Single views on the screen simultaneously. Creating Combination views is similar to creating Single views. To create a Combination view, follow these steps:

1. Open the More Views dialog box by selecting View, More Views.
2. Open the Define New View dialog box by clicking the New button (refer to Figure 22.8).

3. In the Define New View dialog box, select Combination view and click OK. A version of the View Definition dialog box will appear, and this time it is designed to create a Combination view rather than a Single view as discussed in the previous sections (refer to Figure 22.9).

4. Name the new Combination view as you would a Single view. Choose a name that is descriptive and unique, and place an ampersand symbol (&) directly in front of the letter you choose to be the hotkey. If the view appears in the main View menu, you only have to type that hotkey to select the view from the list.

5. The next step is to select the top and bottom panes for the Combination view. Use the drop-down lists in the Top and Bottom fields to do this. All Single views are displayed in these two lists, including any recently created or customized views. You cannot display the same view in both panes; you must select different views for the Top and Bottom settings.

6. When you have made your selections, decide if you want to display the new Combination view in the main View menu by selecting Show in Menu. Leaving it blank still saves the new Combination view in the More Views dialog box.

7. Click OK to save the view and exit back to the More Views dialog box, where you can immediately apply the new Combination view, or any of the other options described in the previous section "Saving the View Definition."

This process can become slightly more complicated if you want to create a new Combination view but the Single views you want to use are not yet defined. Essentially, you have to start at the bottom and work your way up.

You must first create the Single views you want to use. But before you can do that, you must create any custom tables, groups, and filters (remember, a Single view requires you to define all of these fields unless they do not apply to the screen type). Creating custom tables, groups, and filters are covered in the following sections. If the tables, groups, and filters you plan to use for the Single views already exist, you do not have to create new ones.

Once you have an idea of the tables, groups, and filters you plan to apply to your Single views, you can create your Single views. Select View, More Views, and click the New button. Choose Single View, click OK, and follow the process described in the previous sections.

If you want to format either of the Single views, do that as well before creating the Combination view.

→ For more information about formatting views, **see** Chapter 19, "Formatting Views," **p. 601**.

When all that is finished to your satisfaction, create the Combination view using the process described earlier in this section. The newly created Single views will appear in the Top and Bottom drop-down lists in the combination View Definition dialog box.

TIP

> If you have edited a standard view and saved it, thus replacing the original standard view with the edited view, and you want to get the original view back, you can do that in the Organizer dialog box. Click the Organizer button on the More Views dialog box, select the original view from the Global.MPT file, and click Copy. This will bring the original view back into your project and overwrite your new view unless you have changed its name. It is assumed that the original view in the Global.MPT file has not been over-written.

PRINTING VIEWS

Sometimes you may want to print a hard copy of the data within a view. Hard copies can be helpful for preparing reports or presentations, showing other people who do not have immediate computer access, and analyzing while traveling—or you may just be the type of person who prefers paper to computer screens. Whatever the case may be, the following sections will discuss how to print views in Microsoft Project 2007.

PREPARING YOUR SCREEN AND CHOOSING FUNDAMENTALS FOR YOUR PRINTED VIEW

When you print a view, the printed paper will display the exact data that is on your screen when you print it. Therefore, before printing your view, be sure that all tables, fields, filters, and groups are applied or displayed exactly as you want them to be. You will learn how to customize and display all these items throughout this chapter.

The first step is to choose the appropriate view to print. If you are printing a view with a timescale, such as the Gantt Chart, the timescale that is displayed is what will be printed. You can zoom in or out using the Zoom In and Zoom Out buttons on the Standard toolbar, which look like magnifying glasses with a plus sign (+) or minus sign (–) inside the glass. Zooming will change the time units; zooming in will display smaller units, such as hours and minutes, and zooming out will display larger units, such as days, weeks, thirds of months, months, quarters, half-years, and years. Alternatively, you can change the time units by choosing Format, Timescale, and selecting the time unit you want from the drop-down list in the Unit field. When you click OK, Microsoft Project 2007 will adjust the timescale accordingly, based on your selection. When viewing the entire project timescale, select Zoom, Entire Project.

If your screen is split into two panes, you must choose which pane to print. If you choose the top pane, all data is printed (unless it is filtered, in which case only the filtered data is printed). Since the bottom pane shows data based on the selection in the top pane, only data related to that selection is printed if you choose the bottom pane.

TIP

> As mentioned before, a column must be completely visible on the screen to be printed. If a column is hidden and you want the data to print when you print the view, move it so it is displayed on the screen by inserting it somewhere else or dragging a divider bar that may be hiding it. Alternatively, on the View tab in the Page Setup dialog box (which will be discussed in the upcoming sections), you can choose to print all columns, whether or not they are displayed. Select File, Page Setup, and on the View tab select the Print All Sheet Columns check box.

FILTERING, SORTING, GROUPING, AND ENHANCING THE DISPLAY

You may want the printed view to focus on a more specific aspect of the project and not all of the tasks or resources. In this case, apply a filter to the display before you print it. Applying and customizing filters are covered later in this chapter.

Similarly, you may want your printed view to display task or resource data in a different order than what is on your screen. You can apply a custom group, which will be discussed later in this chapter, or use the Sort or Group By command.

→ For more information about using the Sort and Group By commands, **see** Chapter 11, "Using Standard Views, Tables, Filters, and Groups to Review Your Schedule," **p. 369**.

Formatting the text data can enhance your printed view and make it easier to examine. You can highlight selected tasks or resources, display items in bold, italics, or underlined, or change the font and size. Also, you can customize gridlines, as well as column and row separator lines. All of these formatting options, as well as additional ones, must be performed before you print your view.

→ For more information about formatting views, **see** Chapter 19, "Formatting Views," **p. 601**.

USING PAGE BREAKS

Like other Microsoft tools, page breaks are inserted automatically for multiple-page printed views. You can, however, insert them yourself in specific areas. For instance, if you are printing a task or resource list, you may want a certain task or resource to be at the top of a page. When you insert a page break at a specific task or resource, that page break is tied to that item, and not the location in the list. In other words, if you move the task or resource, or filter, group, or sort the list, the page break stays with the task or resource, wherever it moves to within the list.

Furthermore, you can insert page breaks, but still opt to ignore some or all of them in the final dialog box before you print. This feature is handy in case you want to print a special version of the view without having to insert the page breaks again later.

To insert a page break, select the row directly underneath the intended page break and then choose Insert, Page Break. The manually inserted page break will appear as a dashed line.

To remove a page break, select the row just below the existing page break and then select Insert, Remove Page Break. The dashed line will disappear. You can also remove all page breaks by selecting all rows (click the upper-left column heading) and choosing Insert, Remove All Page Breaks.

TIP

By properly inserting page breaks, you can print different aspects of the same project to give to different people. For instance, you could print different parts of the overall task list for different resources that are responsible for those specific tasks, without having to print the entire list for them and without having to create separate project files.

USING THE PAGE SETUP DIALOG BOX

The Page Setup dialog box is where you can change the appearance of printed view pages. You can modify margins, orientation (landscape vs. portrait), headers and footers, and so on. Changing a view's page setup applies to that view only, not to any other views within the project.

To open the Page Setup dialog box, choose File, Page Setup. Not all views can be printed; if the view you are using cannot be printed, this option will not be available. Alternatively, you can click the Page Setup button in Print Preview. Figure 22.12 displays the Page Setup dialog box.

Figure 22.12
Change the appearance of printed pages in the Page Setup dialog box. This dialog box has the Page tab active.

There are multiple tabs in the Page Setup dialog box. Choose one to display and edit the specific settings for that particular tab. The usage of these tabs is covered in the following sections. While the functionality of the tabs will go in order (beginning with Page and moving left to right), the section headings refer to the action and not necessarily the Tab title.

TIP

At any time when working in the Page Setup dialog box, you can preview what the printed pages will look like by clicking the Print Preview button, located at the bottom of every tab.

NOTE

You can use the custom page setup settings in other projects. To do so, save the customized view to the Global.MPT file, which is done in the Organizer. This process is discussed later in the section "Organizing Views and Other Custom Elements in Project Files."

SELECTING THE ORIENTATION

Under the Page tab, the first choice you can make is the Orientation field. The orientation refers to the layout of the printed page. You have two choices: Portrait (taller and narrower) and Landscape (shorter and wider). If you are printing a long list, or if you are adding the printed view to another document, you may want to choose Portrait because that is the normal orientation for most other text documents and because you can fit more rows in your list onto one page. On the other hand, if you have a large timescale, you would probably want to use the Landscape orientation because it can accommodate more of the timescale.

SCALING THE PRINTOUT

Also under the Page tab is the Scaling field. Scaling is used to enlarge or reduce the size of your printouts. You can use a percentage in the Adjust To box, or specify a number of pages in the Fit To boxes.

For instance, if you click the Print Preview button, and see that your list runs just over one page, you may want to reduce the size so that it fits onto one page rather than print the extra page just for a few items.

Also, you can print multiple pages onto one sheet of paper. To do so, click the Options button and change the Pages Per Sheet field to however many pages you want on each printed sheet of paper. For example, if you entered 2 pages wide by 1 page tall, and change Pages Per Sheet to 2, your printed sheet would have two pages—one on the left half of the page and one on the right (see Figure 22.13). If you entered "1 page wide by 2 pages tall," it would still print two pages onto one printed page (if your Pages Per Sheet was set to 2), only this time they would be on the top and bottom rather than the left and right.

TIP

Use the Print Preview button relentlessly until you have scaled the printout exactly how you want it. This saves time and paper! If you are enlarging or reducing the scale to fit on one or more pages, try the Adjust To % field. If you are trying to fit multiple pages onto one sheet, try the Fit To fields with the Pages Per Sheet field defined correctly. Once you are comfortable using these features, you can experiment more to find the method you prefer.

Figure 22.13
If you defined the Scaling field of the Page tab in the Page Setup dialog box as 2 pages wide by 1 page tall, and the Pages Per Sheet field was set to 2 (found by clicking the Options button), each printed page would have two pages on it—one on the left and one on the right.

22

DESIGNATING PAPER SIZE AND PAGE NUMBERING

At the bottom of the Page tab in the Page Setup dialog box, you can set the paper size as well as the first page number. To set the paper size, choose from the drop-down list in the Paper Size field. You can also use the printer Properties dialog box to set the paper size (choose File, Print, Properties).

Set the page numbering by entering the first page to print in the First Page Number field. By default, Auto is selected. Do not change this field unless you want Microsoft Project 2007 to begin printing on another page besides the first one. For example, if you have a multipage view to print but do not need the first two pages, enter **3** in the First Page Number field, and the first page to print will be the third page.

SPECIFYING MARGINS AND BORDERS

The second tab in the Page Setup dialog box is the Margins tab. Like its name suggests, you set the margins using this tab. The default margin for all four borders is one-half of an inch (0.5"), meaning that there will be at least one-half of an inch of space between the edge of the printed page and the data it contains (see Figure 22.14).

Borders surround the page with a box. You can opt to display borders, which will place a box around the data at the specified margin measurement (in this case, one-half inch from the edges of the paper), or not to display borders, leaving the area outside of the margin blank. You can also opt to display borders around the outer pages only, which makes it easier to find the beginning and end of a multipage list or other view. This is done on the bottom of the Margins tab under the Borders Around field. By default, borders are selected to be displayed.

Figure 22.14
Set margins for the printed view under the Margins tab of the Page Setup dialog box.

N O T E

Project always places a margin of one-quarter of an inch (0.25") on all printed views, even if you set the margins to zero.

USING THE HEADER AND FOOTER TABS

The Header and Footer tabs look almost identical, except for the fact that the Header tab is for headers (that is, summary displays at the top of the page), and the Footer tab is for footers (that is, summary displays at the bottom of the page). Both tabs have a Preview box at the top that will display in real time the header or footer you are creating. You cannot make entries in this box, but you can make entries in the box below it (see Figure 22.15).

Figure 22.15
Define header and footer information for your printed view in the Header and Footer tabs. This example shows the Header tab.

22

You can enter a maximum of five lines of header text and three lines of footer text on each page of a printed document.

The Alignment field gives you three options: the left side of the page, the center, or the right side. You can enter different data in all three alignment areas, and the header or footer will display it all.

Below the Alignment field is the header or footer entry box. Use this box to enter any text you wish to define as the header or footer for the Alignment area you selected above the box.

Directly below the entry box is a row of seven buttons that you use to format, insert system codes, or insert pictures into the header or footer (see Figure 22.15). Hover over any of these buttons for a ScreenTip to help you identify the button's purpose. The seven buttons are described in the following list, moving from left to right:

- **Format Text Font**—When you click this button, the Font dialog box appears, allowing you to format the font, font style, size, color, and script for the text in the header or footer. If you want to format only part of the header or footer, highlight it using the mouse, and click the Format Text Font button. Your definitions in the Font dialog box will apply only to the highlighted items. You can format different text in different ways on each of the Alignment tabs.

- **Insert Page Number**—When you click the Insert Page Numbers button, Project inserts the following code: **&[Page]**. While this is displayed, only the page number is actually printed. Therefore, if you want the word *Page* to be displayed, you must type it before the page number code. For example, for the printed view to display "Page 5" on the fifth page of the document, you would enter **Page** (including a space after the word *Page*) and then click the Insert Page Number button, so it would look like this in the Preview box: **Page &[Page]**. The result would be "Page 5" on either the header or the footer (depending on which tab you were working in).

- **Insert Total Page Count**—This button is similar to the Insert Page Number button in that it displays a code when you click it: **&[Pages]**. This code represents the total number of pages *only*, and not the current page number. Therefore, if you wanted the header or footer to display "Page 3 of 5" on the third page of a five-page document, you would enter **Page** (including a space after the word *Page*), click the Insert Page Number button, then enter **of** (with a space before and after the word *of*) and click the Insert Total Page Count button, so the Preview field would look like this: **Page &[Page] of &[Pages]**.

- **Insert Current Date**—This button also displays a code: **&[Date]**. When printed, the current date, according to your computer, will be displayed in your header or footer. The date displayed is the date that the document is printed.

- **Insert Current Time**—This button displays the code **&[Time]**. Again, this is only a code; the time (based on your computer) will be printed in its place. The time displayed is the time the document is printed.

TIP

> Printing the date and time as a header or footer can be very useful, especially when you produce several revisions of the document.

- **Insert File Name**—This button inserts the code **&[File]**. As with the other codes, this will not actually be printed, but the project file name will be, as displayed in the Preview box. Unless you have Windows set to display file extensions (such as .mpp), the extension is not displayed with the filename.

- **Insert Picture**—When you click this button, the Insert Picture dialog box opens, from which you can browse your files for the picture or image you are looking to insert. This can be any type of picture file, such as WMF, PCS, CGM, TIF, BMP, or GIF. This button is especially useful when inserting a company logo into a header or footer.

TIP

> A good way to please your client is to insert their company logo as a header or footer on your printed documents for the project they have hired you to manage.

USING THE DROP-DOWN LISTS IN THE HEADER AND FOOTER TABS

Below the seven buttons in the Header and Footer columns are drop-down lists for the General and Project Fields boxes. These can be used in addition to the seven buttons for entering project data into a header or footer.

The first drop-down list, General, contains the same data provided by the seven insert buttons (such as Total Page Count), as well as information from the project Properties dialog box (such as Project Title), which can be defined by selecting File, Properties.

→ For more information about the project Properties dialog box, **see** "Set Project Attributes," **p. 44**.

The Project Fields drop-down list can be used to insert many fields found within the project. This list includes any fields regarding cost, duration, work, and dates, as well as custom text and custom number fields.

To insert project data into a header or footer using these two drop-down lists, make the selection and click the Add button next to the appropriate box.

USING LEGENDS

Besides headers and footers, you can insert legends into your printed views or reports to further describe the contents of the document. A legend can be especially helpful in explaining graphic elements in your document, such as the timescale on the Gantt Chart view.

Figure 22.16 shows the Page Setup dialog box open to the Legend tab. This is the area where you define the settings for the legend. Notice the similarities to the Header and Footer tabs.

Figure 22.16
Define legend information for your printed document in the Legend tab.

The Legend tab has an Alignment field in which you can enter up to three lines of text in each area (Left, Center, and Right). These three lines of text can be different for each of the three Alignment options. By default, the project name and date are entered on the left side of every page, as defined in Figure 22.16.

Below the Alignment field is the text box in which you can type in text, or use the same seven buttons as the Header and Footer tabs. The buttons are used exactly as described in the bulleted list in the section "Using the Header and Footer Tabs" to format, insert system codes, or insert pictures into the legend. Also, the two drop-down lists, General and Project fields, below the seven insert buttons function the same as described in the previous section to insert specific project information into the legend.

Under the Legend on field, you can choose where to display the legend. Choosing Every page displays the legend at the bottom of every page in the document. Choosing Legend page prints the legend once on a separate page at the end of the document. Choosing None displays no legend anywhere.

As much as half of the legend area can be occupied by text. The width of the legend text area is defined in the Width box by choosing a number between 0 and 5 inches. This number represents the amount of space devoted in the legend area to text. Therefore, if you enter **0**, the entire legend area is devoted to graphics and no text. If you type **5**, the entire legend area is devoted to text. By default, the entry is 2 inches.

SELECTING SPECIAL OPTIONS FOR VIEWS

The View tab is the final tab on the Page Setup dialog box (see Figure 22.17). In the View tab, you set specific options for printing different views. Not all of these options are available for all views; some options may be dimmed out if they are unavailable.

Figure 22.17
Set special view
options in the View
tab.

NOTE

When you're printing the Calendar view, the View tab in the Page Setup dialog box
appears different from the one shown in Figure 22.17. The Calendar view version of the
View tab is covered later in this section.

The following list describes the options in the View tab. Place a check in the box next to
each option to activate it.

- **Print All Sheet Columns**—Select this check box when printing a sheet view (such as
  Gantt Chart, Task Sheet, Resource Sheet) to print all columns in the view, regardless of
  whether or not they are displayed on the screen when you are ready to print.

- **Print First X Columns on All Pages**—This option allows you to print the first three
  (or any number you specify) columns on all pages. This overrides the default of printing
  the first three columns (ID number, Indicators, and Task Name columns) on the first
  page only. This is a great feature to enable if you have a table in your printed view that
  extends multiple pages, and you are not going to fasten it together. When you get to
  page 5, for example, you will not have to go back and look at page 1 to see which task is
  in a certain row because the first few columns will be printed on all the pages.

- **Print Notes**—This option prints the notes you have attached to tasks or resources. The
  notes are printed on a separate page.

NOTE

It is always good practice to attach notes to tasks or resources, especially to communicate scope, constraints, assumptions, and limitations.

- **Print Blank Pages**—By default, all pages are set to print. You can clear this box if you do not want any blank pages that may exist within your document to print.

- **Fit Timescale to End of Page**—Select this box to ensure that a timescale unit does not break across two pages. For example, on the timescale, if a week begins on one page and ended on another, you could select this box to make sure that the entire week is printed on the same page rather than being broken up over two pages.

- **Print Row Totals for Values Within Print Date Range**—This feature adds a column at the end of the printout that houses data totals for each row within the date range you specify in the Print dialog box (which is discussed in a few sections). The row totals column always prints on a separate page, after the timescale and before the notes.

- **Print Column Totals**—This feature adds a new row at the bottom of the printout, which houses the totals for each column.

As mentioned before, when you're printing a Calendar view, the View tab in the Page Setup dialog box contains different options, as displayed in Figure 22.18.

Figure 22.18
The View tab in the Page Setup dialog box for the Calendar view contains different options.

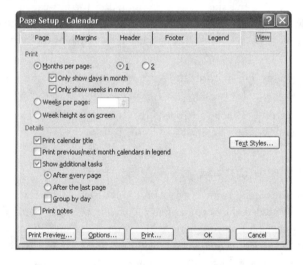

The following list describes the options for the View tab when printing the Calendar view.

- **Months Per Page**—Choose to print either 1 or 2 months on each page. Selecting Only show days in month means that if the month starts in the middle of a week, the days before it in the same week (the last days of the previous month) will be displayed as blank boxes. Selecting Only show weeks in month means that weeks from other months will not be printed.

- **Weeks Per Page**—If you have many tasks, and want to print only one or a few weeks on each page, choose this option and specify the number of weeks per page to print. However, if you select 8 weeks or more, it becomes unreadable (the same reason you can only select up to 2 months per page in the previous option).

- **Week Height as on Screen**—This option matches the printed calendar with the week height on the screen display.

> **NOTE**
> You can only select one of these three options: Months Per Page, Weeks Per Page, or Week Height as on Screen.

- **Print Calendar Title**—This feature prints the calendar title at the top of each page.
- **Print Previous/Next Month Calendars in Legend**—This feature prints a miniature version of the previous and next months' calendars to appear in the legend. Only the dates are displayed and not any project information. Be sure the legend is set to something other than "None" in the Legend On field on the Legend tab.
- **Show Additional Tasks**—Sometimes you may have more tasks than can fit on the calendar. Select this box, and Microsoft Project 2007 will print an overflow page containing these extra tasks. Choose to print an overflow page after every page (After every page check box), or at the end of the printout (After the last page check box). Also, you can select Group by day, which lists the extra tasks for each day on the overflow page. If a task is worked on over several days, it is listed every day if the Group by day box is selected.
- **Print Notes**—This option prints the notes for tasks on a separate page after the calendar or overflow page (if it exists). The Task ID and name appear with the note.
- **Text Styles button**—This button opens the Text Styles dialog box, which allows you to format the font type for any text within the printout.

USING THE PRINT PREVIEW BUTTON

As previously mentioned, the Print Preview button is a very useful feature. The Print Preview button is located at the bottom of all the tabs in the Page Setup dialog box. You can play around with various formatting options and print styles, and always click this button for a preview of what the actual printed version will look like without having to print it. Alternatively, you can choose File, Print Preview (see Figure 22.19).

Use the arrows at the top left of the screen to scroll through various pages in the print preview. Next to the arrow buttons is the Zoom button, which you can use to zoom in or out to examine the data from a closer or farther perspective. Alternatively, you can click on the screen to zoom in or out of that particular area.

The buttons next to the Zoom button are for displaying one or multiple pages on the same screen. Next to those are buttons to open the Page Setup dialog box, print the document, close the print preview, and provide help. Hover over any button for a ScreenTip to identify the function the button performs.

Figure 22.19
Click the Print
Preview button to
preview what the
actual printout will
look like.

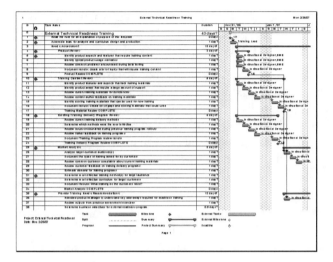

USING THE PRINT COMMAND

After you have selected all of your print options, it is finally time to print your document. To
do so, open the Print dialog box by selecting File, Print. You can also open this dialog box
by clicking the Print button on the Print Preview screen or along the bottom of any tab in
the Page Setup dialog box (see Figure 22.20).

CAUTION

There is a Print command button on the Standard toolbar, but if you click this button, the
document will print without first opening the Print dialog box.

Figure 22.20
Choose what to print
and the number of
copies in the Print
dialog box.

22

As with other dialog boxes discussed throughout this chapter, some of the options in the Print dialog box will not apply to all views. Those options that do not apply to your particular view will be grayed out and inaccessible.

At the top of the Print dialog box, you can choose the printer to send your document to. Be sure you are using the correct printer. If the printer you want is not an option from the printer Name drop-down list, you may have to add it by using Start, Printers and Faxes, and selecting Add a Printer in the Printer Tasks panel. If you are unsure of a network printer setup, it may be beneficial to contact the person in your organization who is responsible for such issues, or consult the printer manual.

SELECTING THE PAGES AND NUMBER OF COPIES TO PRINT

In the Print Range area, select the pages you want to print. Generally, you want to print them all, so All is selected as the default. But you may only want to print some pages within the document. Select the starting page number in the Page(s) From field and the ending page number in the To field. If you only want to print one page, enter the page number in both fields.

To the right of the Print Range area is the Copies area. In the Number of Copies field, choose how many copies of the document you want to print.

PRINTING VIEWS THAT CONTAIN TIMESCALES

Under the Print Range area is the Timescale area. This is similar to the Print Range area in that you define a range to print; only in this case, you define the date range for the timescale instead of the page numbers. By default, All is selected, meaning Microsoft Project 2007 will print the entire timescale from the project's start date to its finish date. However, you can define a more specific date range in the Dates From and To fields.

As discussed in the previous section, "Preparing Your Screen and Choosing Fundamentals for Your Printed View," be sure that the correct time units are displayed on your timescale screen before you print.

Choose the Print Left Column of Pages Only option to print only the pages in the left column of a multiple-page layout in the Print Preview screen.

If you have inserted manual page breaks, as described in the previous section "Using Page Breaks," be sure that there is a check in the box next to Manual Page Breaks. Otherwise, they will not be applied.

SENDING THE VIEW TO THE PRINTER

Once you have set all your print options, it is time to print. Since you have come this far, it is wise to click the Preview button one more time, just to double-check that everything looks good before you commit it to paper.

NOTE

> If you have specified a limited number of pages to print in the Print Range area of the Print dialog box, the Print Preview will still display all pages in the document. Do not panic. As long as the Print Range area is accurate, your printed view will be accurate as well.

22

To begin printing, click the OK button in the Print dialog box. Alternatively, click the Print button on the standard toolbar, which sends the document to the printer immediately without opening the Print dialog box.

CREATING AND CUSTOMIZING FILTERS

Just as tables define which columns and rows are displayed for tasks or resources, filters define which tasks and resources are shown in a table or view. A filter is always applied to any view. By default, the initial filter is All Tasks or All Resources (depending if you are displaying a task or resource view), which shows all of the tasks or resources in a project (as their titles suggest). If you apply a highlighted filter, all tasks or resources are displayed, and those selected by the filter are highlighted.

NOTE

> In a Combination View, no filter can be applied to the bottom pane because the bottom pane is already filtered and controlled by what is selected in the top pane.

As with views and tables, there is a More Filters dialog box you use to edit, copy, or create a new filter (see Figure 22.21). To open the More Filters dialog box, select Project, Filtered For, and then choose More Filters.

Figure 22.21
You can edit, copy, or create a new filter in the More Filters dialog box.

As with the More Tables dialog box, you can choose to display either the Task or Resource filters at the top of the box. The same buttons appear on the right: New, Edit, Copy,

22

Organizer, and Help. Choosing New will create a new filter, Edit will modify an existing filter and replace the original, Copy will modify an existing filter, saving both the original and the modified version, and Organizer will aid in saving filters to the Global.MPT file (as well as other features described at the end of this chapter).

The Help button is a good resource if you are confused about any part of creating or customizing filters.

Before you begin to customize or create a filter, you want to have a good idea of exactly what you want the filter to do. It may be helpful to view the functionality of the existing filters to give you a better idea of what you already have available. If you find a filter that comes close to meeting your needs, you should use the Copy command to modify the filter appropriately without losing the original. If none of the filters are close to what you are looking for, then create a new one with the New button on the More Filters dialog box.

To view the functionality of an existing filter, choose it from the list, and click the Copy button (or the Edit button if you want to replace the original). This will open up the Filter Definition dialog box, and the definitions for the filter will be displayed. If you click the New button, the Filter Definition dialog box will appear with no information defined. Figure 22.22 displays the Filter Definition dialog box opened as if you were going to modify a copy of the Date Range filter.

NOTE

If you select All Tasks or All Resources, you cannot choose Edit or Copy. These filters are permanent, because they really do not filter for anything. Instead, they display all of the tasks or resources in your project.

Figure 22.22
You can make changes to the Date Range filter or most of the other filters, or create a new filter, in the Filter Definition dialog box.

The upcoming sections will refer back to Figure 22.22 while discussing the different fields used to create or customize a filter.

Naming a Filter

As with naming views and tables, choose a name for your filter that is definitive and unique. Select the Show in Menu box if you want the filter to be in the main filter list (Project, Filtered For) as well as the filter drop-down list on the Formatting toolbar. Place an ampersand symbol (&) directly in front of any letter in the name you want as the hotkey (see the Name field in Figure 22.22; the ampersand symbol is in front of the letter *R*). That way, in the main filter list, you can press the hotkey as a shortcut to select that particular filter and then press Enter to apply it.

Defining Filter Criteria

For each test Microsoft Project 2007 is to conduct within the filter, you must create a row in the Filter Definition dialog box. For example, the Date Range filter performs two tests, and each test is defined on its own row in Figure 22.22. Microsoft Project 2007 internally tests all tasks to the criteria, and if they meet the criteria, they are displayed when the filter is applied.

Four columns are used to define the criteria for a filter:

- **And/Or**—This column is used if multiple tests are performed in the filter. The top row is blank because it is the first test. Beginning in the second row, you would define this column by choosing And or Or from the drop-down list. If you choose And, the test criterion must be met for the task or resource to be included in the filtered list. If you choose Or, this indicates that only some of the tests must be met. In Figure 22.22, And is chosen, meaning that the task must meet criterion for both tests to be included in the filtered list. If Or was chosen, the task would only have to meet the criteria for one of the tests.

- **Field Name**—In this column, select the name of the field you are testing. The field relates to the task or resource table you will apply the filter to. For example, in Figure 22.22, in the first row, Finish is selected because the first test will be performed on the Finish field for all tasks. You can type in the field name or choose from the drop-down list.

- **Test**—This column defines the actual test that is to take place. Make your Test selection from the drop-down list. In Figure 22.22, the filter is defined to test whether the Finish field is greater than or equal to the entry in the Value column, and whether the Start field is less than or equal to the entry in the Value column in the second row. If a task's Start and Finish fields contain an entry that is within these defined boundaries, then that task is displayed when the filter is applied.

  The table at the end of this list (Table 22.1) describes all of the Test options and their meanings. The various Within and Contains tests are described in the upcoming section "Using More Filter Criterion Tests."

- **Value(s)**—This is the final column used in defining the criteria for the test. In this column, you enter a value for what the test is actually testing for. To make an entry in the Value(s) field, you can type it in, choose from the drop-down list, or create a prompt for interactive filters. Interactive filters open a dialog box asking for input when the filter is executed. This is discussed in greater detail in the upcoming section "Using Interactive Filters."

In Figure 22.22, in the first row, the test is whether the Finish field of a task is greater than or equal to a value. In this case, you would enter a date in the Value(s) field, thus completing the criteria for that particular test. Therefore, the complete test would be whether the Finish field is greater than or equal to the date you entered in the Value(s) column. In other words, if the task's finish date is the same date or later than the date you specify in the Value field, it has met the criteria for that particular test. If it meets the criteria for all other tests as defined in the Filter Definition dialog box, it will be displayed when the filter is applied.

You will have to enter two values in this column if you are defining the Test column as Is Within or Is Not Within. In this case, separate the two value entries with a comma, and include them on the same row.

TABLE 22.1 FILTER TEST OPTION NAMES AND THEIR MEANINGS

Test Name	Meaning
Equals	The entry in the Field Name column must match the entry in the Value(s) column exactly.
Does Not Equal	The entry in the Field Name column must differ from the entry in the Value(s) column.
Is Greater Than	The entry in the Field Name column must be more than the entry in the Value(s) column. If the entries are dates, the date in the Field Name column must be later than the date in the Value(s) column.
Is Greater Than or Equal To	The entry in the Field Name column must be equal to or more than the entry in the Value(s) column. If the entries are dates, the date in the Field Name column must be the same date or later than the date in the Value(s) column.
Is Less Than	The entry in the Field Name column must be less than the entry in the Value(s) column. If the entries are dates, the date in the Field Name column must be earlier than the date in the Value(s) column.
Is Less Than or Equal To	The entry in the Field Name column must be equal to or less than the entry in the Value(s) column. If the entries are dates, the date in the Field Name column must be the same date or earlier than the date in the Value(s) column.
Is Within	The entry in the Field Name column must be on or between the range of the two entries in the Value(s) column.
Is Not Within	The entry in the Field Name column must be outside the range of the two entries in the Value(s) column.

22

Test Name	Meaning
Contains	The entry in the Field Name column must contain the string of characters in the Value(s) column.
Does Not Contain	The entry in the Field Name column must not contain the string of characters in the Value(s) column.
Contains Exactly	The entry in the Field Name column must contain the exact string of characters in the Value(s) column. There may be more than one string of characters in the Value(s) column; if this is the case, the entry in the Field Name column must contain exactly one of the strings of characters in the Value(s) column. The strings of characters in the Value(s) column are separated by commas.

To insert a test row before one that already exists, select the existing row and click Insert Row. A new blank test row will appear above the existing one.

When you apply the filter, you can also opt to display the summary data for the filtered tasks by checking the box next to Show Related Summary Rows. This can apply to a resource filter as well; if you are filtering for tasks assigned to a resource, selecting this box will display the summary data for the resources' assigned tasks.

Once you are satisfied with your entries in the Filter Definition dialog box, click the OK button to return to the More Filters dialog box. The newly customized or created filter will be highlighted. Click Apply to apply the filter immediately, or click Close to save the filter for later use. You can also click Highlight to apply the filter immediately, displaying all the tasks or resources and highlighting the filtered ones.

TIP

You may want to practice creating a new filter that displays all the subtasks of a project. This will help you get familiar with the process of creating and customizing filters, and leave you with a useful custom filter. To do so, remove all summary tasks and milestones (see Figure 22.23).

Figure 22.23
In this newly created filter called Subtasks, the Summary and Milestone tasks are defined as "No," meaning they are not displayed when the filter is applied.

USING MORE FILTER CRITERION TESTS

As you are creating or customizing a filter, you will have limitations in your definitions, depending on the tests you are creating. For example, many entries in the Value(s) column will be a choice between Yes and No only. If you have entered invalid information into any of the columns when defining tests in the Filter Definition dialog box, Microsoft Project 2007 will warn you and instruct to go back and fix the problem (see Figure 22.24).

Figure 22.24
This warning box appears when you have created an invalid test in the Filter Definition dialog box.

Table 22.1 displays all of the Test options available when defining filters. The first few are easy to understand, but the last five (Is Within, Is Not Within, Contains, Does Not Contain, and Contains Exactly) are slightly more complex.

IS WITHIN AND IS NOT WITHIN TESTS

When using the Is Within or the Is Not Within tests, you are defining the filter to test according to a range of values. You define this range in the Value(s) column, entering the endpoints for the value range together in the same row, separated by a comma. The endpoints you enter are included as part of the value range. Thus, if you use the Is Within test, you are filtering for a value within the value range you define, including the endpoints. If you are using the Is Not Within test, you are filtering for a value that is outside the endpoints for the value range you define.

Refer back to the Date Range filter example from Figure 22.22. Perhaps you want to filter for tasks that have a finish date within a range of dates. You would enter those dates in the Value(s) column, separated by a comma. Microsoft Project 2007 would then filter for all tasks whose finish dates are within the defined date range—including the first and last date entered in the Value(s) column—and display those tasks when the filter is applied, as shown in Figure 22.25.

The same methodology applies to the is not within test; if you want to filter for tasks with finish dates outside of a certain range, use the is not within test and define the date range in the Value(s) column.

CONTAINS, DOES NOT CONTAIN, AND CONTAINS EXACTLY TESTS

The Contains test filters for a specific string of characters you enter in the Value(s) column. This test is especially helpful when you want to filter for words in a task or resource name, or in any text field.

Figure 22.25
To filter for tasks with a finish date within a specific date range, use the is within test and define the date range in the Value(s) column.

Type the word or string of characters in the Value(s) column when using a Contains test. When you apply this filter, Microsoft Project 2007 will display all tasks or resources whose name contains the word or string of characters you entered. For example, if you wanted to display all tasks that have the word *expense* in their name, you would type **expense** in the Value(s) column, as shown in Figure 22.26. You could define this test in a new filter or as an additional test to an existing one.

Figure 22.26
To filter all task names for the word *expense*, type it in the test's Value(s) column.

NOTE

Microsoft Project 2007 filters for plural versions of words when using the Contains test, as long as the plural version contains the string of characters you define in the Value(s) column. In the preceding example, if you had tasks that contain the word *expenses* in their names, Microsoft Project 2007 would select those when the filter is applied as well as tasks with the word *expense*, because both actually contain the string of characters that spell out "expense." The contains exactly test, however, would not select both; it would only select the exact string of characters in the tasks' names.

If you were to perform the preceding test using Does Not Contain, Microsoft Project 2007 would list all tasks whose names do not have the word *expense* anywhere in them.

The Contains Exactly test performs much like its title suggests. If you enter a string of characters in the Value(s) column for a Contains Exactly test of the task names and then apply the filter, Microsoft Project 2007 displays all tasks whose names contain *exactly* the string of characters you defined. Therefore, if you enter **expense**, Microsoft Project 2007 will not display tasks whose names have the word *expenses*, because the string of characters is not exact.

Similarly, if you have two or more words in the task name, and only enter one word in the Value(s) column, the words in the task name will have to be separated by a comma (see Table 22.2).

TABLE 22.2   EXAMPLES OF TASK NAMES THAT WOULD BE SELECTED WITH THE DIFFERENT CONTAINS FILTERS USING "EXPENSE" IN THE VALUE(S) COLUMN

Task Name	Contains	Does Not Contain	Contains Exactly
Calculate May 2007 Expenses	X		
Calculate May 2007 Expense	X		
Expenses, May 2007	X		
Expense, May 2007	X		X
Calculate May 2007 Expenditures		X	

In Table 22.2, the five listed task names are all filtered for the word *expense* using the three different Contains tests. If the test displays the task when the filter is applied, it has an X in that column.

In short, the Contains Exactly test is useful for fields that have comma-separated entries and for finding fields that have the string of characters exactly. The Contains test is useful for searching for fields that contain the string of characters somewhere, regardless of what else is in the field.

NOTE

The string of characters is not case sensitive. In Table 22.2, you could filter for "Expense" or "expense," and the results would be the same.

USING WILDCARDS IN THE VALUE(S) COLUMN

You may encounter a situation where you want to filter for a string of characters, but the string of characters may have slight variations within your project. To solve this problem, you can use wildcards in your definition. However, to use wildcards, you must use the Equals or Not Equals tests only.

22

A wildcard in Microsoft Project 2007 is similar to a wildcard in a game of Poker; it can represent any character in the string. During an intense game of Poker, the dealer may call "deuces wild," meaning that all the "two" cards in the deck are wild and you can play them as any card you want (such as an Ace, King, and so on). In Microsoft Project 2007, the same theory applies. You can use the wildcard characters to represent any other character.

The wildcard characters you use are the asterisk (*) and the question mark (?). The asterisk represents any number of missing characters, including no characters, and the question mark represents a single missing character.

When you define a string of characters, the characters that are not wildcards must be in the places you defined them in order to be selected in the filtering process. The wildcards can be any character, or number of characters, as long as the non-wildcard characters are in place.

For example, if you enter **t?p** in the Value(s) column using an Equals or Not Equals test, Microsoft Project 2007 would filter for fields that have such entries as top, tip, t4p, t0p, and so on. Similarly, if you enter **t*p**, Microsoft Project 2007 will filter for t55p, tp, temp, t739stp, and so on.

Furthermore, you can search using a wildcard character. To do so, place a caret symbol (^) directly before the wildcard character. You must begin and end the string with an asterisk. For example, to search for fields that have a question mark (?), you would type ***^?***.

USING INTERACTIVE FILTERS

As previously mentioned, you can create a prompt for an interactive filter in the Value(s) column of the Filter Definition dialog box. An interactive filter is a flexible filter that does not always search for the same value when the filter is applied. Instead, you are prompted for input, and your response provides the value(s) to test for. You can distinguish interactive filters from regular filters because they have an ellipsis (…) after their name.

To create an interactive filter, type a message in the Value(s) column when creating a filter test in the Filter Definition dialog box. Surround your prompt with double quotes ("") and end it with a question mark (?). Then, when the filter is applied, the prompt is displayed in a dialog box, and Microsoft Project 2007 waits for you to answer the prompt. You will receive a separate dialog box prompt for each test you create in the Filter Definition dialog box.

In addition, you can enter more than one prompt on the same row if you are using an Is Within test or another test that requires two values. Enter each prompt surrounded in double quotes and ending with a question mark, and place a comma in between prompts, so it looks like this: **"Prompt 1"?, "Prompt 2"?**. Both prompts will be included in the same dialog box when the filter is applied.

Microsoft Project 2007 already contains several interactive filters. You can view any of them. For example, open the More Filters dialog box (Project, Filtered For, More Filters) and choose any of the filters that have an ellipsis at the end of the name, such as Created After…. Click the Copy button to display the Filter Definition dialog box, as shown in Figure 22.27.

Figure 22.27
Define value prompts
for interactive filters
in the Filter Definition
dialog box.

Notice the Value(s) column in this example. This is how a value prompt for an interactive filter should be displayed.

If you were to apply this filter, a small dialog box would appear, prompting you to choose a date as the value. Microsoft Project 2007 would then filter for all tasks created after the date you specified (see Figure 22.28).

Figure 22.28
When you apply an
interactive filter,
Microsoft Project
2007 prompts you
with dialog boxes like
this one to define
value information for
the filter.

Perhaps you want to change a filter to an interactive filter. To do so, simply change the Value(s) column entry or entries to the appropriate interactive filter format. For example, open the Filter Definition dialog box for In Progress Tasks and follow these steps:

1. If you are copying the filter, give it a unique name.

2. In the Value(s) column for the first test row, replace NA with the interactive prompt. Whatever you put inside the double quotes will be prompted in the dialog box. Type something like this: **"Define the start date:"?**.

3. Define the interactive prompt for the second test row in the Value(s) column. Type something like this: **"And the finish date:"?**.

4. Select the Show in Menu box if you want the interactive filter to be displayed in the main Filtered For menu. It will automatically be displayed in the More Filters list. Click OK, and then click Apply. The first dialog box will appear, prompting you to define the start date for the filter. Then, the second dialog box will appear, prompting you to define the finish date.

CREATING CALCULATED FILTERS

A calculated filter compares the values of two different fields of a task or resource. Cost Overbudget and Work Overbudget are both examples of a calculated filter. Figure 22.29 shows the Filter Definition dialog box for Work Overbudget. Notice that the Value(s) column in the first test row is Baseline Work surrounded in brackets ([]). The brackets indicate that this is a calculated filter, because the test value is also a field name, as indicated on the second test row.

Figure 22.29
The Baseline Work is a test value as well as a test field in this calculated filter.

When creating a calculated field, you enter a task or resource field in the Value(s) column surrounded by brackets ([and]), and then you must define the value for that field. In other words, the example in Figure 22.29 defines Actual Work as being greater than Baseline Work in order for the task to be selected when the filter is applied. However, you must also give Baseline Work a value, which takes place on the second line. You cannot compare two fields unless they both have a value.

CREATING MULTIPLE CRITERIA FILTERS

As previously mentioned, if you have more than one test in a filter, each test is defined on its own row in the Filter Definition dialog box. The And/Or column is used to define the relationship of the tests. The order of the tests is important; if you have two or more tests, the And/Or column of the second row determines its relationship to the test above it, and so on. If you enter **And**, then both tests must be met. If you enter **Or**, then either test must be met to be selected when the filter is applied.

Furthermore, you can group multiple criteria together when defining a filter. Look at the Incomplete Tasks Filter Definition dialog box in Figure 22.30.

Figure 22.30
Define multiple criteria for filter tests by inserting a blank row with only the And/Or column defined.

The first test states that for a task to be incomplete, its % Complete must not equal 100%. But, there is another way to define a task as incomplete, as the second test criterion indicates. Following the first test criteria, there is a row that only reads "Or," and is shaded in gray. This row indicates that multiple criteria are used to define this filter, and because it reads "Or," only one of them must be met. The second set of criteria, on the third and fourth rows, has two tests that must be met, indicated by the And in the fourth row. They state that % Work Complete must not equal 100%, and that the task is assigned to at least one resource. If a task meets both of these criteria, it will be selected when the filter is applied, just as it will be selected if it meets the criteria defined on the first line.

To insert a row similar to row 3 in Figure 22.30, simply select a blank row, and either choose And or Or. Define nothing else in the row. When you click out of that row, it will be shaded in gray, and the And or Or entry will be in bold and placed all the way to the left of the row, indicating that there are multiple criteria tests for that particular filter.

TIP

> Remember, the order in which you define the tests is the order in which the tests will be performed in Microsoft Project 2007. The And/Or column relates directly to the row above it.

CREATING CUSTOM FILTERS WITH AUTOFILTER

Another option for creating custom filters is the AutoFilter. To use this feature, click the AutoFilter icon on the Formatting toolbar, or select Project, Filtered For, AutoFilter. No dialog box will appear just yet, but you can tell you have turned the AutoFilter feature on if the column headings on the table you are displaying now all have drop-down arrows in them (see Figure 22.31). If you click on one of those drop-down lists and select Custom, the Custom AutoFilter dialog box appears (see Figure 22.31).

Figure 22.31
The Custom AutoFilter dialog box is another option for defining test criteria for a filter. Notice behind the dialog box the drop-down arrows in all the table column headings.

The first field in the dialog box is already defined as a filter test, depending on which column's drop-down list you opened. If the field you chose was a task name, then Contains is the test used, because you are filtering the task names for a string of characters. If you chose a field such as Duration or Start, then Equals is entered as the test in the first field.

Next to that field is the Value(s) field, although it is not labeled as such. In Figure 22.31, the Custom AutoFilter dialog box was selected from the Task Name column, so you would define the string of characters in the second box. Then, you have the option to define another test in the filter. Choose And or Or, and repeat the process on the second row in the dialog box.

When you have defined your tests in the Custom AutoFilter dialog box, click OK to apply the filter. The next time you access the dialog box from the Task Name AutoFilter drop-down list, the criteria you defined will be in place, and you can edit it if you want.

If the custom AutoFilter is one you find particularly useful, you may want to save it for later use. Click the Save button, which will open the Filter Definition dialog box with the tests already defined. Enter the remaining information in the Filter Definition dialog box, and select the Show in menu checkbox if you would like the filter to show in the Filtered for menu found by going to Project, Filtered for.

CREATING CUSTOM GROUPS

Grouping is a great way to organize your task or resource list to better assess your project. When you organize the task or resource list into groups, the individual data for each item is rolled up to display the information for the group instead, temporarily hiding some of the clutter on your screen and generating useful summary information.

Creating a custom group is similar to creating a custom filter. The following sections describe the process of creating custom groups.

ACCESSING CUSTOM GROUPS

Like other topics in this chapter, you start creating a custom group by opening the Group Definition dialog box. To do so, open the More Groups dialog box by selecting Project, Group By, More Groups. In the More Groups dialog box, you are presented with familiar options. Select from a Task or Resource list, and click one of the buttons to the right. As usual, New opens the Group Definition dialog box to create a new group, Edit lets you edit an existing group (replacing the original), and Copy lets you edit an existing group without replacing the original. Click one of those buttons, and the Group Definition dialog box appears (see Figure 22.32).

Figure 22.32
Create and customize groups in the Group Definition dialog box. In this example, the New button was clicked to create a new group.

As with views, tables, and filters, choose a unique and descriptive name for the group you are customizing, and enter it in the Name field. Select the Show in Menu box to display the group in the cascading main Group By menu. It will automatically appear in the More Groups dialog box list, whether you check the box or not.

SELECTING GROUPING FIELDS

Select the grouping fields from the drop-down lists in the Field Name column of the Group Definition dialog box (see Figure 22.32). You can select up to 10 grouping levels, with each selection defining a more detailed grouping criteria. Therefore, the top selection is the broadest group, and the more fields you select, the more refined the group definition becomes.

After you have selected the field name in the Group By row, there are two more columns to define. The Field Type is filled in automatically based on the Field Name, and usually cannot be modified. By default, Ascending is entered in the Order column. You can change it to Descending from the drop-down list, depending on the order you want the group to be displayed when it is applied to the screen. Continue these selections on the following Then By rows up to 10 times. There is no preview; you must click the OK button to view the result.

NOTE

It is important to point out that the Group field for a resource is different from the concept of grouping. When you create a resource list, you have the option to define a group the resource falls into using the Group field. This is not the same as the grouping feature that is being described in this chapter.

Underneath the Group By and Then By rows is the check box Group Assignments, Not Tasks/Resources (depending on whether you are working with a task or resource list). This box is cleared by default, so each assignment for each task or resource is displayed in the group. Decide which is best for you, and then format the grouping with the Font, Cell Background, and Pattern fields.

DEFINING GROUP INTERVALS

In the Group Definition dialog box, you have the option to define the group intervals. To do so, select a field name from the Group By or Then By rows, and click the Define Group Intervals button. The Define Group Interval dialog box will appear, as show in Figure 22.33.

Figure 22.33
Define group intervals in the Define Group Interval dialog box.

Field Name is automatically entered using the field name selected when you open the Define Group Interval dialog box. In the Group On field, Each Value is selected by default. You can change this entry using the drop-down list, which will give you different options based on the Field Name setting. Depending on your Group On selection, you can define the Start At and Group Interval fields. For instance, date values can be grouped by intervals of minutes, hours, all the way up to years. Numeric values can be grouped in any interval, and the grouping can start on a number other than 1 (sometimes including negative numbers). Text values can be grouped by the first few characters, and so on.

You can use Group Interval to define intervals for the groups and the starting value for the selected field. For example, if you are grouping on the amount of work instead of a different grouping for each different work value (1 hour, 2 hours, 3 hours, and so on), you can specify groupings in 4-hour intervals. The first grouping, defined in the Group By field, would be 0-4 hours, the second grouping (defined in the first Then By field) would be 5-8 hours, the third grouping (defined in the second Then By field) would be 9-12 hours, and so on.

When you have completed your entries in the Define Group Interval dialog box, click OK. Once you are finished with the Group Definition dialog box, click OK, and you are back to the More Groups dialog box. Click Apply to apply the group immediately, or click Close to save it for later use. It will always be displayed in the More Groups dialog box and possibly in the main Group By list if you checked the box next to Show in menu.

FORMATTING GROUP DISPLAYS

As previously mentioned, you can format the group display in the Group Definition dialog box. Each group level has its own setting for font size, background color, and pattern.

Groups look and behave like outlines. As with an outline, you can show or hide levels of the group using the Show button on the Formatting toolbar. Also, you can use the Show and Hide buttons on the screen, which look like plus (+) and minus (–) symbols as shown in Figure 22.34.

Figure 22.34
Show (+) and Hide (-) buttons using Group by on % Complete.

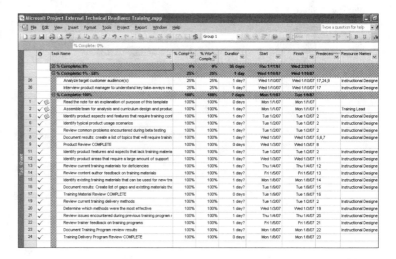

NOTE

It is important to use cell background colors sparingly to ensure your Group by screen does not become unreadable and overwhelmed with color. This is especially important when you are grouping on multiple fields.

SAVING CUSTOM GROUPS

The group is always saved to the More Groups list, and it's saved to the main Group By list if you selected Show in menu. You can also save it so it is available in other project files using the Organizer. This is discussed in greater detail in the section, "Organizing Views and Other Custom Elements in Project Files," at the end of this chapter.

CREATING AND CUSTOMIZING FIELDS

As you must be aware by now, Microsoft Project 2007 is equipped with dozens of different task and resource fields in which you store all of your various project data. In addition to those existing fields, you can create and customize fields to better suit your project and make your life as a project manager less hectic. The process for customizing custom fields has been improved for Microsoft Project 2007.

For example, you may want to have a field to define the status of a task besides % Complete, such as whether or not the resource has approved the assignment. Or, perhaps your organization has a unique system of classifying resources, and you want to implement that system into your tables. A variety of custom fields and field types within Microsoft Project 2007 are available for you to customize.

There are separate sets of custom fields for task and resource information. The default names are identical, and you can give them different aliases as you are customizing them. The numbers in the following list represent the number of available custom fields for that particular type:

- **Text1–Text30**—Alphanumeric text up to 255 characters
- **Number1–Number 20**—Any positive or negative number
- **Cost1–Cost10**—Number values (formatted)
- **Date1–Date10**—Any valid date value
- **Duration1–Duration10**—Any duration value, such as 4w (4 weeks)
- **Start1–Start10**—Any valid start date value
- **Finish1–Finish10**—Any valid finish date value
- **Flag1–Flag20**—Yes/No values
- **Outline Code1–Outline Code10**—User-defined alphanumeric outline structures

→ For details about custom fields, **see** "Defining Custom Fields," **p. 127**.

The following sections discuss defining custom fields.

ACCESSING THE CUSTOM FIELDS

Technically, custom fields already exist. They are present in every drop-down list that contains predefined fields, such as in the Field Name column of the Group Definition dialog box, even if you have not given them a specific value.

Therefore, you cannot actually create custom fields; rather, you modify—or *customize*—the ones that already exist. Each type has at least 10 different fields, so there should be an ample amount of fields to customize within your project.

Define values for custom fields in the Custom Fields dialog box. To access it, choose Tools, Customize, Fields (see Figure 22.35).

Figure 22.35
Define values for custom fields in the Custom Fields dialog box.

When you open the Custom Fields dialog box, select the custom field general type by choosing Task or Resource and selecting one of the category types from the drop-down list in the Type field. The drop-down list contains all nine field types from the list in the previous section. Once you have selected the type, the names of all the available custom fields are displayed in the Field box. Select the one you want to customize.

NAMING CUSTOM FIELDS

The custom field names, such as Cost1, Cost2, and so on, are permanent. However, you can give them an alias; that way each custom field has a much more descriptive name associated with it. To do so, click the Rename button, and enter the name you want as the alias. After you click OK, the new name will be displayed with the old one in parentheses next to it.

The new name/old name pair will now appear in all drop-down lists. However, only the new name will be displayed anywhere the custom field is used—even if the field was used before it was renamed.

CREATING CALCULATED CUSTOM FIELDS

A custom field's data can be derived from values in other fields in your project. Also, you can apply calculations or custom formulas to a custom field to determine its value. This is done on the bottom half of the Custom Fields dialog box.

Specify value behaviors in custom fields in the Custom Attributes section of the Custom Fields dialog box. By default, None is selected. You can opt to create and assign a lookup table or formula to obtain the value of the custom field.

To apply a lookup table to the custom field, click the Lookup button. A lookup table is a value list that the user can select from to enter a value in the custom field. The options as you define appear in a drop-down list in the field. Figure 22.36 displays the resulting Edit Lookup Table dialog box.

Figure 22.36
Create and edit a lookup table for a custom field in the Edit Lookup Table dialog box.

In the Edit Lookup Table dialog box, you can define default values, define and restrict available entries for the custom field, or import a lookup table. Enter acceptable values on as many rows as necessary. You can also add optional descriptions of the values to the right in the Description column.

Select the check box next to Use a Value From the Table as the Default Entry for the Field if you always want the selected value to appear in the field as the default entry. Then, select the Display Order for Lookup Table: By Row Number (the order in which you entered the rows), Sort Ascending, or Sort Descending. Click the plus sign (+) button if these options are not already displayed. When you choose, click Sort. Below that, set the data entry options. If you want to allow users to enter values that are not on the value list, check the box next to Allow Additional Items to be Entered into the Fields. The value they enter will then be added to the list.

You can also import a lookup table by clicking the Import Lookup Table button and following the instructions in the Import Lookup Table dialog box.

When you are finished, click Close.

Alternatively, you can apply a formula to the custom field to compute and enter their values. A formula is especially useful to calculate values that you might use to determine variance from the plan. For example, you may want to have graphical indicators calculated based on the task progress compared to the baseline. You could create a custom field to track the task baseline finish and actual finish dates, and display the status of the task accordingly. That

22

way, you can easily view which tasks have no baseline, are on schedule, or are late by more than 5 days.

To apply a formula, click the Formula button, which is next to the Lookup button in the Custom Fields dialog box. The Formula dialog box will appear, as shown in Figure 22.37.

Figure 22.37
Define formulas for custom fields in the Formula dialog box.

Type in the formula you want to use, or import it from another source on your computer as you would import a custom field or lookup table. If you are building a formula, type it directly into the Edit Formula area. You can use the Insert Field drop-down menu, which lists all allowable Microsoft Project 2007 fields, or the Insert Function drop-down menu, which lists all possible predefined functions that can be used in custom field calculations, to assist you. You can also use the operator buttons.

> **NOTE**
>
> You do not have to type in the equal sign (=) in the Edit Formula area; Microsoft Project 2007 automatically adds it.

When you are finished, click OK. A warning box appears. You will always get this warning when you complete a formula: "Existing data in the custom field will be deleted, because all values will now be calculated by the formula." If that is okay with you, click OK; if not, click Cancel.

CONTROLLING CUSTOM FIELD BEHAVIORS

The Calculation for Task and Group Summary Rows section in the Custom Fields dialog box enables you to control custom field calculations for summary rows and for use in custom groups. By default, no value is entered on summary or group rows for custom fields.

You can set the summary and group-level fields to use the formula set for the custom field if you have defined one. Or, at the roll-up level, you can set them to perform single mathematical operations. The choices for math operations are Average, Average First Sublevel,

Maximum, Minimum, and Sum. The Average First Sublevel option, which is applicable to grouping, prevents a field value from being carried up in the calculations from very detailed groups into less detailed groups.

NOTE

> You can only select Use Formula if the custom field uses a formula, defined in the Custom Attributes section of the Custom Fields dialog box.

The Calculation for Assignment Rows section of the Custom Fields dialog box has only two options. Select the None radio button if the assignment row has no rolled-up values or formulas associated with it. The other option is Roll Down Unless Manually Entered.

CREATING CUSTOM INDICATOR FIELDS

Rather than display the actual values, Microsoft Project 2007 enables you to display graphical indicators instead, which you customize to represent a range of values. This is useful to save space on your screen by avoiding clutter, as well as to preserve confidentiality; you may not want people to view the exact values, but just an overview represented by an indicator. For example, if you have created a formula to calculate the schedule status of a task compared to baseline, you can then create indicators to display the status in a graphical format.

In the Values to Display section of the Custom Fields dialog box, select the Data radio button to display actual data in the field contents in all views in which the field appears. Alternatively, select the radio button next to the Graphical Indicators button and click the Graphical Indicators button to specify the criteria and associated indicator images to be displayed in the field in place of data. The Graphical Indicators dialog box will appear, as shown in Figure 22.38.

Figure 22.38
Graphical indicators, defined in the Graphical Indicators dialog box, are useful when you do not want to display actual values in custom fields.

In the Graphical Indicators dialog box, you can define the indicators to use for certain values of the custom field. Use the drop-down lists to guide you through the process.

You can also import the graphical indicator criteria by clicking the Import Indicator Criteria button and choosing the criteria to import from another project or the Global.MPT.

Click OK when you are finished to apply the graphical indicator, or click Cancel to exit the dialog box without making the changes.

TIP

> A common practice in Microsoft Project 2007 is to use graphical indicators for schedule status or budget status. Use the colors of a traffic light: a green indicator means your schedule or budget status is on schedule, yellow means it is late, and red means it is significantly late.

CREATING OUTLINE CODE CUSTOM FIELDS

It is a reoccurring theme for many companies to want to capture specific job codes or cost accounting codes associated with their organization. To accomplish this, an Outline Code should be used, especially if you need to control input so that the codes conform to a predefined hierarchical structure.

Similar to many of the custom field types listed in the beginning of this section, a specified lookup table can be created for the Outline Code. In fact, all the other options on the Customize Field dialog box, when creating the other types of custom fields, are not available such as the Calculation for task and group summary rows, Calculation for assignment rows, and Values to display options, as shown grayed out in Figure 22.39.

Unlike the other field types, each Outline Code must have a predefined Code mask as shown in Figure 22.40. The code mask is used to define the format, sequence, length, and separator of each level and value in the lookup table. When entering the structure and values in the lookup table, each value is matched up against the defined code mask to ensure there is not a mismatch. Another option exclusive to Outline Codes is the ability to "Allow only codes that have no subordinate values." If this option is chosen, you will only be able to enter additional values into the Outline Code custom field if it is at the lowest level. If you do not want any additional values entered into the Outline Code lookup table, then both of the options underneath Data entry options must be cleared.

TIP

> Ideally, you will want to define the code mask for the lookup table first and then begin to enter the values into the lookup table as needed. If any of the values you have entered do not match the code mask, the item will be displayed in red in the lookup table. In addition, if you try to save the lookup table and at least one of the values does not match the code mask, you will receive the following message, "One or more code values in the lookup table is invalid. A value is invalid when it does not match the mask defined for the code, includes the separator character, is a duplicate of another value, or exceeds 255 characters in length."

Figure 22.39
Outline Code field type with the Lookup table option available.

Figure 22.40
Ability to define code mask for Outline Code field type

There are five action buttons that are specific to the Outline Code custom field. They make up the last five buttons under the Lookup table section in Figure 22.40. Each of these buttons can be used to manipulate the lookup table during the active working session:

- **Outdent**—Decreases value or parent code of the selected item by moving it to the left
- **Indent**—Increases value or parent code of the selected item by moving it to the right

22

- **Show Subcodes**—Displays all the subcodes underneath a selected parent code
- **Hide Subcodes**—Hides all the subcodes underneath a selected parent code
- **Show All Subcodes**—Displays all the subcodes in the lookup table regardless of the item selected

An example of a Cost Center look up table can be found in Figure 22.41. You can see that the code mask consists of two levels, different characters (letters and numbers), and a period (.) as the value separator.

Figure 22.41
Cost Center lookup table is an example of an Outline Code defined in Microsoft Project 2007.

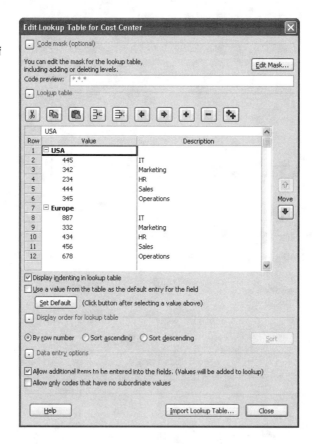

To put the code to use, it needs to be inserted into an existing view by one of the methods described in this chapter. For simplicity, just right-click a column in your existing view and select Insert Column. Choose the new field you want to include in the view (in this case, it is Cost Center Outline Code1). Once the field is included in your active view, then a selection can be made from the Cost Center field. Figure 22.42 shows this process. You can see that all the values in the drop-down appear as they did in the lookup table with one exception; the description is attached to the code value. Once a value is selected, the parent level value is concatenated with the separator and selected value. This concatenation holds true regardless of the number of levels you have designated.

Figure 22.42
The Cost Center code column is added to the Gantt Chart view and allows you to select a value for each task in the view.

TIP

> Be sure to give outline code values appropriate descriptions. This will ensure that whenever you or someone makes a selection from the outline code field, there will not be any confusion as to what the value means. This is especially important when the defined values contain only numbers.

MANAGING CUSTOM FIELDS

Once you are done with the Custom Fields dialog box, click OK. Your custom field will be stored in the project, and you can insert it anywhere you can insert fields. You can also save it to your Global.MPT file for use in other projects. The next section will describe that process.

ORGANIZING VIEWS AND OTHER CUSTOM ELEMENTS IN PROJECT FILES

Throughout this chapter, you have read about saving your views, tables, filters, groups, and custom fields not only to the project you are working on, but to your Global.MPT file, for use in other project files. Finally, the moment has arrived when you will better understand what that means.

Every time you open Microsoft Project 2007, the Global.MPT file loads with the project file. After you have worked on your project file, everything you saved and/or created is saved to the project file, but not the Global.MPT file. However, you can save items to the Global.MPT file, thus allowing them to be used in other project files. To do so, follow these steps:

1. Click the Organizer button, which is found on the More Views, More Tables, More Filters, and More Groups dialog boxes. This will in turn open up the Organizer dialog box, as shown in Figure 22.43. You can also click Tools, Organizer to open the Organizer dialog box.

Figure 22.43
The Organizer aids in saving customized items such as views, tables, filters, groups, and fields.

2. The Organizer dialog box has several tabs for custom items. Click on the appropriate tab (if you want to save a custom filter, click the Filters tab). If you opened the Organizer dialog box from the More Filters dialog box, you will already be on the Filters tab. You must select the Fields tab to save custom fields since there is no corresponding More Fields dialog box. The left side of the box shows all items applicable to that particular tab that are saved in the Global.MPT file. The right side shows all custom items for that tab that you have created in the current project file, plus all the standard items you have used during the current session (in other words, if you were in the Filters tab, it would show all the custom filters you have created as well as all the filters you have used in the current session).

3. Select all the items from your project (on the right side) that you want to save in the Global.MPT file, and click the Copy button. The items are then copied to the Global.MPT file. You can copy multiple items at once by holding down the Ctrl key as you select the items.

4. The Cancel button will change to Close once the items are copied. You can copy additional items, choose a different tab, or click Close to complete the copy process.

TIP

As mentioned before, all customized items are displayed in the Organizer dialog box, as well as items that have been used during your current session. It may be helpful to keep track of the items you have customized; that way, they will not be confused with the standard items that appear with them. This is in case you want to copy custom items only.

CAUTION

Be sure to copy custom items that relate to each other. For example, if you copy a custom view, be sure to also copy any tables, filters, groups, and so on, that were customized for that particular view.

Now, any time you create a new project file, these items will be available.

In addition, you can use the Organizer dialog box to rename or delete items from the Global.MPT file or other current project files. To delete an item, simply select it from the appropriate list, and click the Delete button. Microsoft Project 2007 will ask you to confirm the deletion; select Yes to delete the item and No to cancel the deletion. If you want the item deleted from both lists, you must delete it from both lists (Microsoft Project 2007 will not do it automatically).

To rename an item, simply select it and click the Rename button. Type the new name in the Rename dialog box that appears, and click OK.

NOTE

You cannot rename a custom field in the Organizer dialog box. To rename a custom field, open the Custom Fields dialog box (Tools, Customize, Fields).

You can also use the Organizer dialog box to copy items from one project file to another without using the Global.MPT file. Be sure both files are open, and at the bottom of the Organizer dialog box, select them from the drop-down lists on the left and on the right. Then, follow the same procedure described previously.

TIP

If you are working with several project files, it may be beneficial to designate a project file as a holding vessel for storing and retrieving your customized items. This is especially practical if you run a shared copy of Microsoft Project 2007 on a network and you cannot save items to the Global.MPT file that is used by everyone else on the network.

The Organizer is updated if you upgrade to Microsoft Project 2007 from an earlier version. Your old Organizer still exists, combined with the new one.

→ For additional information about the Organizer, **see** "Manipulating Objects Using the Organizer," **p. 597**.

CONSULTANTS' TIPS

Use the tips provided in this section of the chapter to help you with customizing views, tables, filters, groups, and fields.

CREATE VIEWS THE RIGHT WAY

Microsoft Project 2007 comes with a number of very helpful views, but of course, no one can anticipate everyone's needs. Creating new views may seem to be a complex task at first, but if you map out what you want to see and how you want to see it, it is not that difficult.

Just remember that a view is composed of a table, filter, group, and screen. A good approach is to find a "like" view whenever possible, and then copy and modify the view to meet your needs. This will ensure that the default view is never overwritten. If you cannot find a "like" view, then create a new one. Similarly, if you cannot find a "like" table to build your view off of, then create a new table. Next, go back to the view definition to add the filter and group information.

Test it to make sure it works correctly and, assuming it does, use the Organizer to put the view into the Global.MPT file, so it will always be available in future projects.

NAME ORGANIZER OBJECTS APPROPRIATELY

It is critical to ensure all views, tables, fields, filters, and groups are named appropriately with easily recognizable and descriptive names. This will ensure that whenever you or someone else accesses these items, there will not be any confusion as to what the object's true intention is.

RESOLVE UNEXPECTED VIEW RESULTS

While analyzing a project view, you may not see the expected results or it may appear that information that should be present has disappeared. When this occurs, first check to make sure that there is not an active filter applied to the view. Most likely, changing the Filtered for option to All Tasks will resolve the issue.

KNOW YOUR AUDIENCE WHEN USING GRAPHICAL INDICATORS

When selecting graphical indicators associated with a custom field, be cognizant of the fact that there may be users who are color blind and will not benefit from certain ones such as "stop light" schedule indicators with red, yellow, and green circles. If this is the case, consider using another set of indicators such as schedule indicators with faces (smiley face for on schedule, straight face for late, and a sad face for substantially late).

In addition, when setting up your custom fields for cost and/or schedule status, be sure to include a No Baseline value to identify those projects and/or tasks that do not have a baseline. Otherwise, the values that do not have a baseline will show an error. In addition, this will enable you to identify those tasks that do not have a baseline and take the appropriate actions to baseline them.

KEEP AN EXCEL CONFIGURATION WORKBOOK

You should keep a personal list of all the customized objects you have created so that you know what is available to you and other users. You might consider creating an Excel configuration workbook with a worksheet for each type of object (tables, views, groups, filters, and fields). This will save you time in the long run in that you will not have to jump directly into a particular project schedule and navigate around until you find the object you are looking for. With a central configuration table, you can open the Excel spreadsheet and immediately locate the customized item you are looking for. In addition, you will want to make sure you keep the configuration table constantly updated.

CHAPTER **23**

CUSTOMIZING TOOLBARS, MENUS, AND FORMS

In this chapter

Project managers are busy people who must plan, adjust, and communicate change quickly and efficiently. This chapter will show you how customization of toolbars, menus, and forms can save time and improve your ability to find the schedule information you need, when you need it.

ADJUSTING THE BEHAVIOR OF PERSONALIZED MENUS AND TOOLBARS

Microsoft Project can provide you with a lot of information, so much so that at times it is difficult to see all of it. When you have more needed information than can fit on the screen at once, you have a problem with your screen "real estate." One of the ways to get more real estate is to modify your toolbars, menus, and forms, moving things around or making new versions that allow you to access what you need, while hiding what you do not want. There are many toolbars and it would be impractical to have all of them showing at one time, as shown in Figure 23.1, so you need to decide which ones make the most sense for you.

Figure 23.1
There are many toolbars available; if you understand their uses, you can pick the ones that are most important for you.

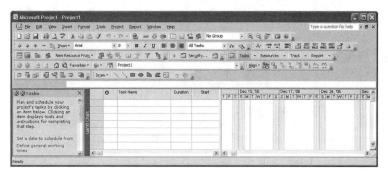

This chapter will help you learn how to better manage your toolbars, menus, and forms. Since you use some commands regularly, some on occasion, and the rest not at all, personalizing your toolbars and menus will help you increase your efficiency. Also keep in mind that Microsoft Project will automatically determine which items you use most, and will show or hide these based on a complex formula. You can let Microsoft Project make those decisions for you, or you can decide for yourself what works best for you, and personalize things the way you want them to work.

ADJUSTING THE BEHAVIOR OF MENUS

If you need to access an item in a menu that Microsoft Project has decided you do not use enough to show, simply double-click the menu name to bring up all the options in the menu. You can also turn this option off by right-clicking on a menu or toolbar, then choosing the Customize option from the shortcut menu. Within the resulting dialog box, choose the Options tab (see Figure 23.2) and then click on the Always Show Full Menus option.

Figure 23.2
You can turn the personalized menus on and off using the Customize dialog box.

Remember that this change will affect all of your other Microsoft Office applications also. Later in the chapter, you will learn more about the other options found under the Customize dialog box.

ADJUSTING THE BEHAVIOR OF TOOLBARS

Project will display three toolbars at the top of the window automatically when starting up: the Standard toolbar, the Formatting toolbar, and the Project Guide, as seen in Figure 23.3. If you hover your mouse over the area known as the *move handle*, the mouse will become a four-headed arrow, and you can then move the toolbar around as needed. You can use this feature to adjust the order and placement of your toolbars for optimum usability.

Activate Toolbar Options/
Toolbar Options drop-down list

Standard Toolbar

Figure 23.3
The three standard toolbars in Microsoft Project are the Standard, the Formatting, and the Project Guide toolbars.

Move Handle   Formatting Toolbar   Places Standard and Formatting
Project Guide Toolbar   toolbars on one row

To save screen real estate, you can make both the Standard and the Formatting toolbars appear on one row. Just left-click in the area known as the Toolbar Options drop-down list area and you will see the option Show Buttons on One Row, as shown in Figure 23.3. You can also change this option under the menu Tools, Customize, Toolbars, Options tab. Just click the Show Standard and Formatting Toolbars on Two Rows check box to turn the option on or off.

Keep in mind that when these two toolbars appear on only one row, some of the options are hidden. Buttons used most often will be displayed. Hover your cursor over the Toolbar

Options area, then left-click to see the rest of your buttons along with the Toolbar Options drop-down list. This is an application-specific option, and it will not affect your other Microsoft applications.

NOTE

> In Project 2007, the Project Guide toolbar is available via the drop-down list as well as via a new option, Turn On (Off) Project Guide, in the View menu. In addition, you can control display of the Project Guide and customize the content of the Project Guide through the Tools, Options, Interface tab.

QUICKLY CUSTOMIZING PERSONALIZED TOOLBARS

When you use the Toolbar Options drop-down list, it shows the hidden buttons and the option to have the Standard and Formatting toolbars on one row or two; it also gives you the Add or Remove Buttons option. If you hover your cursor over the Add or Remove Buttons option, a list of the toolbars on that row will appear—in this case, the Standard and the Formatting toolbars. You can then move your cursor over to highlight those toolbars, and another list will appear showing all of the buttons typically located under that toolbar. If there are any arrows at the top or bottom of the list, more buttons are available than are currently visible. You can then select which of these buttons you want on the toolbar. You can also choose the Reset Toolbar option at the bottom of the list to show the original set of default buttons. You can see an example of the list in Figure 23.4.

Any buttons with check marks are the default buttons, while buttons that are grayed out are ones that have been added to the toolbar. Adding buttons to your toolbars is discussed later in this chapter in the section "Adding and Removing Command Buttons."

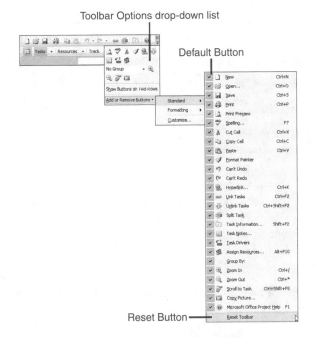

Toolbar Options drop-down list

Figure 23.4
The Standard toolbar has many buttons to choose from.

Default Button

Reset Button

CUSTOMIZING TOOLBARS

Toolbars are collections of buttons, each toolbar grouping together buttons to do specific kinds of tasks. The Standard toolbar covers buttons such as Open, Save, Print, Copy, and Paste, whereas the Formatting toolbar deals with text options such as Bold, Indent, Text Type, and Text Size. Microsoft has set up these toolbars in all of its applications, thus allowing users to be comfortable with their look and feel regardless of the application being used.

As you grow familiar with Project, you will find that there are some buttons you use often, and others you use rarely or never. You might also find that there are some things you use in Project for which there are no buttons. Customizing the toolbars, or building a toolbar that meets all of your requirements, is an easy way to collect all the buttons you find yourself needing.

If you use macros or create macros for Project, you can also assign or even design buttons to add to your toolbars. That way, you only need to click your button to execute a particular Project feature.

Chapter 22, "Customizing Views, Tables, Filters, Groups, and Fields," discusses the topic of creating special views, tables, forms, filters, and groups, and you learned that if you want to use these in another project, you have to copy them into the new project file or into the Global.MPT file. However, when you customize menus and toolbars, they are automatically stored to Global.MPT, and will be available in all of your projects. If you want to send your customized menus or toolbars to someone else, you will need to include them in the file you forward.

REVIEWING THE BUILT-IN TOOLBARS

There are built-in toolbars already set up for Project 2007, in addition to the menu bar that is available in all Office applications. Three of these toolbars (the Standard, Formatting, and Project Guide toolbars) are loaded automatically when you start up Project 2007 (see Figure 23.5).

- **The Standard toolbar**—You can use this toolbar to access many of the primary Project features. On the left side of this toolbar are the buttons standard to most other Microsoft programs, whereas the buttons on the right are Project specific.

- **The Formatting toolbar**—With this toolbar you can get to Project's features, filters, and the text-formatting options. Similar to the Standard toolbar, many of the buttons found here are standard to other Microsoft applications; those buttons are found on the right side of the toolbar, whereas the Project buttons are on the left.

- **The Project Guide toolbar**—The toolbar will lead you through many functions and features within Project. It contains two parts: the toolbar that appears at the top and the task pane that appears on the lefthand side of the screen. The toolbar and task pane will help you set up your project, work with tasks and resources, track progress, and report your information.

23

Project Guide toolbar

Standard toolbar | Formatting toolbar | Menu bar

Figure 23.5
The three default tool-bars, task pane, and menu bar are available when you first open Project.

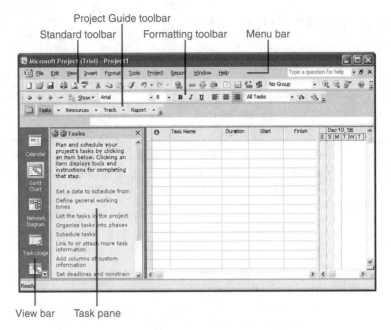

View bar   Task pane

NOTE

> **The Task Pane**—The task pane appears to the left of your main screen and sets up shortcuts to many common operations (see Figure 23.5). It is a component of the Project Guide toolbar and can be hidden by clicking the button in the righthand corner of the pane. If hidden, it can be displayed by clicking on one of the four command options in the Project Guide toolbar.

There are seven additional toolbars available with the default installation of Project Standard. You can find these toolbars by selecting View, Toolbars:

- **The Custom Forms toolbar**—Use this toolbar to customize your tasks or resource information entry screens.

- **The Drawing toolbar**—Use this toolbar to access your graphic drawing tools for drawing figures and text boxes in the Gantt Chart view.

- **The Resource Management toolbar**—This toolbar is used to assist with resource allocation issues.

- **The Tracking toolbar**—This toolbar supports the functions of managing project progress and rescheduling work.

- **The Visual Basic toolbar**—Use this toolbar to show buttons for running, recording, and editing your macros.

- **The Web toolbar**—Use this toolbar to open your web browser, move through the Internet, and track your favorite sites.

- **The Network Diagram toolbar**—Use this toolbar to show analysis, viewing, and your layout tools for use with your Network Diagram view.

There are four additional toolbars that are available with the default installation of Project Professional:

- **The Collaborate toolbar**—You can set up workgroup communication and enterprise project management information views with this toolbar to support your use of Microsoft Office Project Server 2007.
- **The Analysis toolbar**—Use this toolbar to gain access to installed add-in programs.
- **The Compare Project Versions toolbar**—Use this toolbar to create your reports when comparing two Project files; then you can drill down to more specific information.
- **The PERT Analysis toolbar**—Use this toolbar to get access to the PERT estimating tools.

> **NOTE**
> The PERT Analysis and Compare Project Versions toolbars are also available in Project Standard 2007. However, they are not part of the default installation. See the Manually Activating Toolbar Add-ins section under Consultants' Tips at the end of the chapter for steps on displaying the PERT Analysis and Compare Project Versions toolbar add-ins.

Finally, there are two additional toolbars that are available but are not installed by default in Professional 2007:

- **The Database Upgrade Utility toolbar**—This toolbar facilitates the upgrade of project schedules from a 2003 version of Microsoft Project.
- **The Euro Currency Converter toolbar**—This toolbar allows the use of alternative currencies for cost fields.

> **NOTE**
> **View Bar**—Although not a toolbar, this is another handy tool available in Project that is controlled from the menu bar. Select View, View Bar to show or hide the graphic representation of shortcuts for many common views that are available in Project (see Figure 23.5).

DISPLAYING TOOLBARS

Like so many other things in Microsoft applications, there is more than one way to show and hide your toolbars in Project. The easiest way is to use a shortcut by right-clicking on the toolbar area. Another way is to open the toolbar using the View, Toolbars command.

If you hover your mouse over one of the toolbars, then click the right mouse button, you can open your selected toolbar, as shown in Figure 23.6. The Standard, Formatting, and Project Guide toolbars all have check marks next to them, as you can see in Figure 23.6, meaning that they are turned on, or activated. The toolbars without check marks are not in use.

Figure 23.6
Use the Toolbar short-
cut to activate and
deactivate your tool-
bars.

Toolbars currently active

Toolbars currently inactive

Opens the Customize dialog box

Inactive toolbars can be activated by simply clicking on the toolbar name; clicking it a second time will hide the toolbar.

You can also show and hide toolbars by using the Views, Toolbar command. Once you have selected your toolbar shortcut menu by using this command, showing or hiding the toolbar is identical to the previous instructions.

NOTE

You can now turn the Project Guide on or off from the Views menu. The option appears directly below the Views, Toolbars menu choice.

POSITIONING TOOLBARS ON THE SCREEN

When activated, most toolbars are placed in a preestablished docking location at the top of the screen. Once the toolbar is displayed, you can move it around the screen to any location that's best for you. You can move the toolbar around its designated area (or dock) at the top of the screen, or you can pull it off the dock to float in the middle of the screen. You can also change your dock area to the side of the screen. If a toolbar is in its dock, but does not extend all the way across your screen, you can move another toolbar up beside it, saving yourself some screen real estate.

However, some of your toolbars are combination boxes, which means they have buttons with a text box and an entry-list arrow, such as the Font drop-down box on the Formatting toolbar. If you use the side screen dock area, these combination boxes will not be displayed.

You can see both a docked and floating toolbar in Figure 23.7. The floating toolbar has a title bar and Close button. You can return your floating toolbar to its assigned place in the dock with a double-click of the mouse. If you click the Close button, the toolbar will be hidden. You can also resize a floating toolbar just like you would resize a regular window. If you hover the mouse on the border of the toolbar window, it will change to a double-headed arrow, and you can use that to resize the floating toolbar as needed.

23

Resource Management toolbar docked along the edge
Move handle   Floating Drawing toolbar

Figure 23.7
Microsoft Project allows you to move toolbars around your screen to suit your taste.

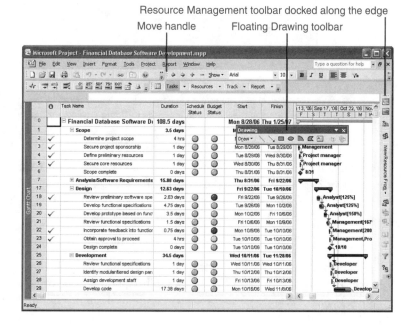

USING THE CUSTOMIZE DIALOG BOX

The Customize dialog box is used to create or customize toolbars. With the Customize dialog box, you are able to create new toolbars, add or remove buttons from any active toolbar, rearrange the order of the buttons, resize your combo boxes, and set up new toolbar options, such as setting your Standard and Formatting toolbars in one row. Remember, if you want to customize a window, it must be the active window. Figure 23.8 shows you the toolbars you can activate with the Customize dialog box.

Figure 23.8
You can create new toolbars or customize your existing toolbars by using the Customize dialog box.

TIP

If you want to customize a toolbar, but it is being covered by the Customize dialog box, you can drag the title bar to move the Customize dialog box around.

As previously mentioned, there is more than one way to display the Customize dialog box. You can right-click any toolbar and choose Customize from the Toolbar shortcut menu. You can choose View, Toolbars, Customize, or Choose Tools, Customize, and then choose Toolbars from the cascading menu.

The Customize dialog box contains the following three tabs:

- **Toolbars**—You can show or hide toolbars with this tab by checking or unchecking the toolbar name. You can also create new toolbars, plus rename or delete your custom toolbars. Finally, any toolbars you have customized can be reset to their original buttons using this tab.

- **Commands**—This tab allows you to add a command to any toolbar.

- **Options**—Use this tab to change the size of your toolbar buttons, show what is in the toolbar button ToolTips, and set up how you want your menus animated.

ORGANIZING TOOLBAR BUTTONS

Besides using the Customize dialog box to add, remove, and rearrange the buttons on your toolbars, you can also change each button's underlying function, change the image, and move buttons around until you have them set into groups that make sense to you.

To modify a toolbar, you must first activate it. Then you can open the Customize dialog box and choose the Commands tab so you can see which commands are available (see Figure 23.9).

Figure 23.9
Open the Commands tab in the Customize dialog box to see all the commands you can use to modify your toolbars.

On the left side of the Commands tab is the list of categories of commands you can work with. In Figure 23.9, the Edit category has been selected. When you choose a category, the commands available will appear in the list on the right.

When you are ready to change the action of a specific command button on the active toolbar, click the Modify Selection button. It is only active when you select a command on the toolbar, not on the Commands list box. You can also right-click the button to change it if the Customize dialog box is open. Any command you add to the toolbar may or may not have a corresponding icon button. If there is no icon for a button, it will appear as a text button.

ADDING AND REMOVING COMMAND BUTTONS

Adding a command button to a toolbar or menu is as simple as dragging the button from the Commands list to the desired location, as shown in Figure 23.10. If you place the button between two other buttons, it will drop into place and the existing buttons will move to allow it to fit. If too many buttons are on a toolbar, the buttons at the far right will wrap to a new line for the toolbar, but only while the Customize dialog box is open. When you close the Customize dialog box, Project will automatically hide the least-used buttons on the right side of the toolbar to make room for the new ones. The hidden buttons appear on the Toolbar Options drop-down list for that toolbar. You can read more about this in an earlier section of this chapter, "Adjusting the Behavior of Toolbars."

NOTE

There is a category under the Commands tab of the Customize dialog box that will show all of the macros in your project, including the ones you have created. This makes it easy to find and drag a macro name onto the toolbar you want to use to run it. You can also create a new button for the toolbar, instead of using the text name. Creating new buttons is covered later in this chapter.

Figure 23.10
You can add commands to any toolbar using the Customize dialog box and selecting the Commands tab. Some of these will include an icon whereas others will appear as text only.

Formatting toolbar

Text Styles button added to the Formatting toolbar

Text Styles command

You can remove command buttons you never use from your toolbars to make room for new or other buttons. Just open the Customize dialog box, drag the button off its toolbar, and then release it in the center of the screen away from other toolbars.

REARRANGING COMMAND BUTTONS

You can also use the Rearrange Commands dialog box to add, remove, and rearrange commands quickly on your toolbars and menu bars. Click the Rearrange Commands button on the Commands tab of the Customize dialog box to pull up the Rearrange Commands dialog box. Choose the toolbar or menu bar you want to change, make your changes, and then close it. You can see in Figure 23.11 the Rearrange Commands dialog box open with the Format menu's controls shown.

It is also possible to move the buttons on a toolbar by dragging them to a different location. As mentioned earlier, if you want to move buttons around, the Customize dialog box must be open. Select the button to move on the toolbar, and a heavy border will show that the button has been selected. As you move it, the cursor will change to a heavy uppercase *I*.

You can also move buttons from toolbar to toolbar by using the steps mentioned earlier. In addition, you can drag the buttons from one toolbar to the other. If you move a button from one toolbar to another, both of them must be on display and the Customize dialog box must also be open.

Figure 23.11
The Rearrange Commands dialog box allows you to quickly make changes to your toolbars and menu bars.

The Customize dialog box must be open

The menu being changed

List of controls

Reset button

23

NOTE

While some of the buttons on the toolbar are recognizable or easy to identify, it is not true with all of them. However, you can easily identify a button's function by hovering your mouse over the top of it for just a moment, and the name of the button will pop in as a Screen Tip.

GROUPING COMMAND BUTTONS

The Command buttons on your toolbars are organized by group. Vertical separator lines appear between each group. To add a new separator bar, you should be in the Rearrange Commands window, under the Customize window, with the Commands tab active, as shown in Figure 23.11.

Select the command button you want your separator to appear in front of, then click the Modify Selection button, which will open a drop-down menu. Then you want to choose Begin a Group. This will create a new separator bar above the command button you have made active, and it will appear on the toolbar you have altered. If you want to delete that separator bar later, you can do it two ways: either activate the command button as before, then go to Modify Selection and clear the Begin a Group option, or simply click on the bar and then use the Delete button in the Rearrange Commands window.

RESIZING A COMBO BOX

Combo boxes combine a text box with a drop-down list arrow that you can use to choose options, such as Group By in the Standard toolbar, or Font in the Formatting toolbar. You can change the width of a text box portion when the Customize dialog box is open.

Just follow these steps to increase or decrease the size of your combo boxes:

1. With the Customize toolbar dialog showing, activate the toolbar that contains the combo box you want to change, then open the Customize dialog box. You can have any tab open on the Customize dialog box when you resize.

2. Select the combo box in the toolbar. A dark black border will appear around the combo box to show that it has been activated.

3. Hover your mouse over the left or right side of the combo box; it will change to a dark two-headed arrow.

4. Drag the edge of the combo box to the desired size.

5. Close the Customize dialog box.

CREATING NEW TOOLBARS

When you find yourself needing to have several different toolbars open, but only using a few buttons from each of them, you are wasting your screen real estate. Rather than having several toolbars open, you can build one or two toolbars that hold most, if not all, of the buttons you might need to use to save on your real estate. With Project you can make new toolbars containing the command buttons you need without having to change any of the existing toolbars.

One of the easiest ways to make a new toolbar is by simply selecting the toolbar that has the majority of the buttons you use over and over, then make a copy of that toolbar and give it a new name. You can then add or delete buttons as you want without ever changing the original. You can also, of course, start with a blank toolbar and build it as you prefer.

MAKING A NEW TOOLBAR FROM THE COPY OF AN EXISTING TOOLBAR

To create a copy of a toolbar, you must open the Organizer. You can read more about the Organizer (see Figure 23.12) later in this chapter, but once you have a copy of a toolbar, you must open the Customize dialog box and use the steps previously mentioned to modify your copy.

Figure 23.12
The Organizer with the Toolbars tab open allows you to copy files from Global.MPT to your personalized project.

BUILDING A NEW TOOLBAR

To create a new toolbar that is empty and floating on your screen, follow these steps:

1. Open the Customize dialog box by right-clicking any toolbar and choosing Customize from the shortcut menu, or you can select View, Toolbars, Customize.

2. Once the Customize dialog box is open, select the Toolbars tab, and then choose New to open the New Toolbar dialog box. Project will assign your new toolbar with a sequential number and generic name, such as Custom 1.

3. Type in the new toolbar name. The name must be unique and can only be up to 51 characters (including spaces).

4. To include commands in your new toolbar, in the Customize dialog box select the Commands tab, browse for the commands you would like to add, and drag and drop them onto your newly created toolbar.

Your new toolbar name will now appear on the list in the Toolbars tab, and a new empty toolbar will appear in the Project window, as you can see in Figure 23.13. You can now use the Commands tab to drag new buttons to your new toolbar, which will enlarge as the buttons are added. You can either leave the toolbar floating on your window, or add it to your dock.

Figure 23.13
Your new toolbar will always start out floating in the Project window.

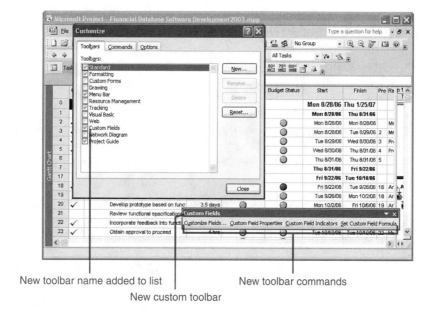

New toolbar name added to list | New toolbar commands
New custom toolbar

DELETING YOUR CUSTOM TOOLBARS

Toolbars included with Project cannot be deleted; they can be customized or reset. Any user-defined toolbars can be deleted. Open the Customize dialog box, click on the Toolbars tab, select the toolbar to be removed, and then click Delete.

RESTORING THE BUILT-IN TOOLBARS

As you modify the built-in toolbars, you might later decide that they do not fit every project you create, or you might find yourself needing to make changes for another reason.

If you want to restore a toolbar to its original settings, open the Customize dialog box, select the Toolbars tab, choose the toolbar to be reset, and click Reset. Project will then warn you that all customizations are about to be lost. It is important to remember that using the Reset button will reset all changes to the original settings; you will lose *any* customizations you have made to the toolbar, no matter when the changes were made. If you intended this, click OK; if not, try making a copy of the toolbar and renaming it to something like "Custom Toolbar 2." Then reset the original. That way you can track anything you might have lost.

CUSTOMIZING COMMAND BUTTONS

Some commands in the Customize dialog box have no button image. If you add any of these commands to your toolbars, only the name of the command will be displayed in text form (see Figure 23.13). Also, there might be a command or a macro you have named that has no button associated with it. If you create a macro, that name will be shown on the Commands tab in the Customize dialog box, but there is no button associated with it. If you put that macro onto one of your toolbars, only the text name will be shown.

There are two ways to create images for a command button that has no image: either use a copy of an existing command button, or create your own using the button display options.

USING THE BUTTON DISPLAY OPTIONS

If you want to modify an existing button, follow these steps:

1. Activate the toolbar that contains the command button you want to change.
2. Bring up the Customize dialog box by clicking the Tools Options arrow on any toolbar. Select the Add or Remove Buttons and then select Customize. You can also open the Customize dialog box by selecting View, Toolbars, Customize.
3. Select the Commands tab.
4. Select the button you want to change directly on the toolbar and then in the Customize dialog box click Modify Selection. The Modify Selection button will list all available options. Select the desired one to modify the button.

CUSTOMIZING A BUTTON FACE

You can use the Customize dialog box to either copy an existing button or open the Editor dialog box where you can build your own custom button. If there is another command button similar in design to what you are looking for, you can copy the design of the button to the clipboard, then paste it back onto a blank button.

To modify your new button or build a new one from scratch, follow these instructions:

1. Bring up the toolbar that contains the button you want to change.

2. Open the Customize dialog box from either the Toolbar shortcut menu or from View, Toolbars, Customize.

3. Right-click on the toolbar button that you want to change. A black border will appear around the button to show it has been selected, and the list of button display options will appear:

- Use the Copy Button Image option to place a copy of the selected button on your Clipboard.

- Use the Reset Button Image option to remove any immediate previous editing, returning it to the original display button.

- Use the Edit Button Image option to open the Button Editor and make changes to your selected button.

- Use the Change Button Image option to choose a design from the Project image library and then use it as your selected button.

4. Close the Customize dialog box when you are finished making your changes.

The Paste Button Image option only becomes active after you have copied an image. Select another button and paste the new image into it. It does not have to be a blank button; you can paste over an existing button.

Project has an existing library you can choose from for a new button face instead of having to create your own, as shown in Figure 23.14.

Figure 23.14
You can choose a new button face from the library of existing images that Project maintains.

Finally, you can design your own images to turn into buttons. You can either start with an image of an existing button you want to edit, a picture from the Project library to edit, or a blank button you want to build yourself. To make these changes or make your own button, you must use the Button Editor dialog box. Your image will be enlarged, allowing you to see each individual pixel. This will make it easier to either change an existing image, or create a new one.

Figure 23.15 shows a copy of the Save button from the Standard toolbar. Here, a macro has been created that will save the project to a separate drive. Instead of having to select Save To... every time, you can save the button that will run the macro.

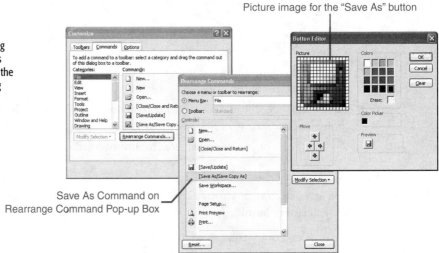

Picture image for the "Save As" button

Figure 23.15
Creating or changing an existing button is easy when you use the Button Editor dialog box.

Save As Command on
Rearrange Command Pop-up Box

Thev "move" arrows let you move your cursor around one pixel at a time, whereas the Colors box gives you a palette for choosing colored pixels for your new image. The Preview area allows you to see what your button will look like at button size.

Here are some tips for changing your image:

- If you want to change the color of your pixels, choose a color in the Colors box and click on the pixel, or drag the color across a section of the image.

- If you want to erase part of the image, choose the Erase box and then click all of the pixels you want cleared by dragging your mouse across them or by clicking one pixel at a time.

- If you want to move the picture on the button, clear an area along the edge you want to move towards and then click the desired move arrow button.

- If you want to clear the whole image and start over, click Clear. If you want to cancel your changes and start over, you can either click Cancel or press Escape.

Once you are done, click OK and the new image will appear on the new button. Figure 23.16 shows the new Save button image.

Figure 23.16
The new image now looks similar, but not exactly like the Save button. This helps the user to recognize that it is to be used to save, but to save to a different area.

CHANGING THE ACTIONS OF A BUTTON

Once you have added a command button or modified a button's image, you might want to change the command that is associated with that button. Highlight the command in the activated toolbar and right-click or choose Modify Selection to see the Assign Macro option. The Customize Tool dialog box will appear, as shown in Figure 23.17.

Figure 23.17
You can change a button's behavior using the Customize Tool dialog box.

The Command drop-down list will show you all of the forms and macros that can be assigned to a button, so if you wanted to assign a macro to a button, scroll down the Command options until you find the macro that most suits your needs. If you want to activate a custom form, choose which form best fits your needs from the list. Forms are set off with double quotes, such as Macro "Rollup_Formatting," as shown in Figure 23.18.

There is an additional method to access the Customize Tool dialog box from the Project window without using the Modify Selection button. Press the Ctrl key and then right-click on the button you want to change. The Customize Tool dialog box will appear to allow you to make your changes.

Figure 23.18
You have a number of predesigned macros to choose from using the Customize Tool window.

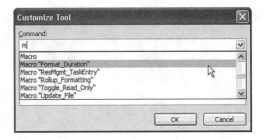

CUSTOMIZING MENU BARS

A menu is a collection of commands that focus on a set of actions or topics. For instance, the View menu shows a variety of options you can use to change your views, modify toolbar views, or zoom in on your view. There are also submenus, such as the Toolbars submenu under the View menu (see Figure 23.19).

Figure 23.19
The View menu has two built-in submenus: Table and Toolbars.

All menus contain commands, such as Print, to direct actions within the program. Microsoft tries to use the same or similar menus throughout its suite of programs to allow users to feel comfortable with each new program they open and use. For instance, Word 2007 and Project 2007 both contain the following menus: View and Insert. Although the commands within these windows will vary from Word to Project, you can see how many of the items across the menu bar are consistent across Office applications. Previous versions of Word had a lot more menus like Project, but since the addition of the ribbon style menus to the Office 2007 suite, they now differ in the organization and style.

The menu bar is managed in the same manner as a toolbar, with a few additional options. You can add new menus, change the existing menus, and customize a menu the same way you can change a toolbar. If you want to add a command to a menu, use the steps from the previous section on adding commands to toolbars. The rest of this section is spent on options that are specific to customizing menus.

There are two main reasons for customizing menu bars: to make the hidden ones more available and to create new ones. Customizing menus allows for a lot of flexibility because you can attach commands, frequently used views, filters, and macros to an existing menu.

NOTE

> Unlike views, tables, and filters, menus are part of the application file rather than the project file. Therefore, modifying the menus makes a global change, visible within all project files on your computer. Menus are stored in the GLOBAL.MPT file.

23

ADDING NEW MENUS TO A MENU BAR

You can either create a new menu or add a submenu to an existing menu. To do so, follow these steps:

1. Open the Customize dialog box by selecting View, Toolbars, Customize.
2. Choose the Commands tab on the Customize dialog box.
3. Scroll down the list of categories until you find the New Menu option. When you click on it, the only thing that will appear in the Commands column is New Menu.
4. Drag your new menu command to a place on the main menu bar, or into one of the existing menus to create a submenu, as shown in Figure 23.20.
   - If you are inserting a new menu directly onto the menu bar, a thick uppercase *I* will appear on the menu bar. This *I* will show you where the menu will be placed when you release your mouse button.
   - If you want to insert a new menu into an existing menu, basically creating a sub-menu, then drag the New Menu command up to the menu bar and hover your mouse over the menu into which you want to place your new menu. The menu will open and activate; then you can drag your new menu down to where you want it to exist.

Figure 23.20
You can add new menus or create submenus with only a few easy steps.

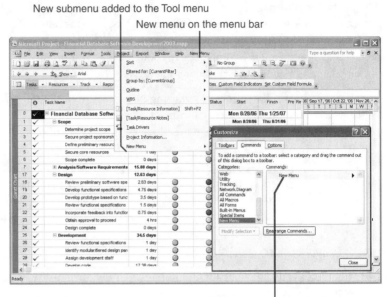

New submenu added to the Tool menu

New menu on the menu bar

Dragging "New Menu" from the Commands list will create a new menu or submenu

RENAMING MENUS AND COMMANDS

Once you have placed your new menu in the location you like, you should rename it. To do this, you must have the Customize dialog box open. Right-click on the new menu text to open the display menu, and then scroll down to the Name option to enter the new name. It works the same for submenus; you just need to open the main menu first.

You can also assign a keyboard hotkey to your menu or command, so you can open or use it with just a quick click on the keyboard. For instance, Alt+V is the hotkey for View, allowing you to open the View menu quickly and easily. You can set up a hotkey in the Name text box by using an ampersand symbol (&) in front of the letter you want to use as a hotkey. For View, it would be **&View**.

Make sure, however, that you are not using an existing hotkey. If you are adding a new menu, these keys are already in use: F (File), E (Edit), V (View), I (Insert), O (Format), T (Tools), P (Project), R (Report), W (Window), and H (Help). You can easily avoid duplication by looking at the underlined letters in the menu name, which represent which letters are being used as the hotkeys.

CAUTION

> If you do accidentally duplicate a hotkey, the first command will be highlighted, but you must now click Enter to active it. If you enter the hotkey again, it will bring up the second option, which must also be activated by the Enter key.

ADDING ITEMS TO A MENU

Once you have created your new menu, you can add items to it by using the same process you used to add buttons to toolbars. Open the Customize dialog box, select the category and item to add, and then drag it to the menu bar. As you drag your selected item, a small box will appear next to it as a status box. It will let you know that you can drop your item somewhere by a plus sign appearing in the box (or that you are unable to drop your item in a specific spot by showing an X in the status box). Also, a large, heavy "I" shape will show you where your dropped item will be placed. You can see an example of an item added into a new menu in Figure 23.21.

Figure 23.21
You can customize your new menus by clicking and dragging items to it from the Customize dialog box.

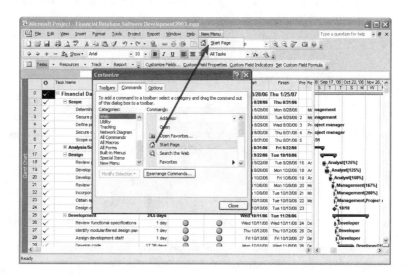

There are three different items you can add to a menu:

- **Commands**—You can add any commands from the Customize dialog box to your menu. The All Commands category shows every command in Project listed in alphabetical order.

- **Built-in menus**—Like the All Commands category, you can select the Build-In Menus category to show all the built-in menus available in Project.

- **Special items**—Some menus have special items other than commands or menus. For instance, the File menu has a list of previously opened projects.

REMOVING AND RESTORING MENUS AND COMMANDS

If you ever decide you are finished using one of your custom menus or want to remove it, you have two options: you can either drag it off the menu bar, allowing it to disappear, or you can use the following steps. Remember, the Customized dialog box must be open when using either option.

CAUTION

> Because menus, like toolbars, are saved to the Global.MPT file, when you reset your menus, you are resetting them for all of your projects.

To return the menu bar back to its original configuration, use the following steps:

1. With the Customize dialog box open, select the Toolbars tab.
2. Choose Menu Bar from the list of toolbars.
3. Click the Reset button. You will see a warning message appear to let you know you are resetting the menu bar.
4. Click OK and close the Customize dialog box.

MOVING MENUS AND COMMANDS

Just like with toolbars, you can easily rearrange the commands under a menu using the Rearrange Commands dialog box. Simply select the menu you want to change from the category list and then click the Rearrange Commands button. For more information about the Rearrange Commands dialog box, see "Rearranging Command Buttons," earlier in this chapter.

CHANGING THE ATTRIBUTES OF A MENU OR COMMAND

You can change several attributes within a menu. The first is the name, which was discussed earlier in this chapter in the section "Renaming Menus and Commands."

You can also change how the commands within the menu are divided into groups, such as how the File menu has separated the New and Open commands, the various Save commands, the Print commands, and others. You can add a divider bar by using Rearrange Commands, Modify Selection and clicking on Begin a Group. A separator bar will then appear above whichever command you have chosen. If the location of the separator bar is not where you want it, just highlight the bar and use the Move Up or Move Down button to change its place in the menu. You can also delete the separator bar by using the Delete button.

MANAGING MENUS AND TOOLBARS WITH THE ORGANIZER

Toolbars and menus are global objects for Microsoft applications, which means that any toolbar or menu you create or modify for one project will be saved to the Global.MPT file and will be used for every project that you open with that version of the program.

If, however, you want to access a toolbar or menu you have created from another version of Project (for example, when working at home or sending a copy over to a co-worker), you will have to copy it from the Global.MPT file to a project file.

→ For additional information about the Global.MPT file and the Organizer, **see** Chapter 18, "Managing Project Files," **p. 581**.

You can create a copy by using the following steps:

1. From the menu bar, choose Tools, Organizer.

2. Choose the Toolbars tab. On the left side of the window is the Global.MPT file, and to the right is the active Project file. Usually there are no listings in the Project1 file. If you have multiple copies of Project open, and Project1 is not the file you want to use, you can find the file you want using the Toolbars Available In drop-down menu.

3. Select the name of the toolbar you want to copy and click the Copy button. This will create a copy of the toolbar or menu you have customized. For example, if you have made changes to the Project Guide toolbar, you will need to save a copy of the Project Guide toolbar. The copy will now appear in the left Project1 column, as you can see in Figure 23.22.

Copy button to copy the toolbar to a local file

Local copy of the toolbar

Figure 23.22
Using the Organizer will let you transfer files from the Global.MPT file to your personal copies.

Toolbars tab in GLOBAL.MPT

4. Since you are copying a toolbar or menu from the Global.MPT file over to a copy of Project, the file will already exist, so you need to change the name. For instance, if you are saving a copy of Custom Fields, you should click the Rename button and use a variation such as "Custom Fields Copy" for the name of the new toolbar. After you have entered in the new name, click OK. You can see an example of this in Figure 23.23.

In Figure 23.24, the new Custom Fields Copy toolbar copied into the Financial Database Software Development2003.mpp file. When you open this new Project file in another version of Microsoft Project, you must open up the Organizer and copy the new file into that version's Global.MPT file. If the file is not in the Global.MPT file, you cannot access it.

Figure 23.23
Rename your custom toolbars and menus to prevent them from being mixed up with the originals.

Figure 23.24
The Organizer will let you move files back and forth between copies of Microsoft Project.

CUSTOMIZING FORMS

A form is a pop-up data entry window, similar to a dialog box. Forms allow you easy access to information that might not be displayed using the standard views. You can build a custom form so that you can look at a field with information you might need without ever having to change views.

Microsoft Project has several built-in forms for you to use on your most common tasks. To display the built-in forms toolbar, select Views, Toolbars, Custom Forms. With Project you can modify the built-in forms by moving information, but you cannot add or delete any existing fields in the built-in forms. You can, however, build your own forms using the Custom Form Editor.

You can attach your new custom forms to Project in three ways: using a toolbar button, a menu, or a hotkey. The tasks or resources selected when you activate a form will be affected by your entries into the form. Custom forms cannot be placed in a pane to use for scrolling through either the task or resource list. Clicking the OK or Cancel button will remove the form from display.

NOTE

Forms display information for one specific task or resource at a time and must be opened, updated, and then closed before you can move on to another task or resource. For this reason, it is not a very efficient way to update fields. The best way to have continuous access for update purposes is to create a view that incorporates a custom table. For guidelines on creating custom views, see Chapter 22, "Customizing Views, Tables, Filters, Groups, and Fields."

REVIEWING THE FORMS SUPPLIED WITH MICROSOFT PROJECT

Microsoft Project provides you with several different forms for both task data and resource data. You can display the custom forms toolbar to quickly see the available forms.

There are eight standard forms for task data:

- **Cost Tracking**—This form will track the cost information for your tasks and will provide some progress information.
- **Earned Value**—This form will look at your project performance using the planned, scheduled, and actual cost of work data.
- **Entry**—This form shows basic task information.
- **PERT Entry**—This form submits your three duration estimates: Optimistic, Expected, and Pessimistic.
- **Schedule Tracking**—This form shows duration, percentage complete, and scheduled task dates and variances.
- **Task Relationships**—This form shows the predecessors and successors for a selected task.
- **Tracking**—This form tracks task duration.
- **Work Tracking**—This form shows duration and tracks actual work progress.

There are four forms available for resource data:

- **Cost Tracking**—This form shows cost information.
- **Entry**—This form is used to enter basic resource information.
- **Summary**—This form shows the overall cost and work-tracking variances.
- **Work Tracking**—This form shows the work-tracking information.

Because forms, like all other aspects of Project, are either task or resource based, the forms display will depend on what kind of view you have open. For instance, if you are working in a Gantt Chart view, the available forms will be the eight listed above for task data. If you highlight a task and then select one of the forms, it will appear in a pop-up window and allow entries for the selected form as shown in Figure 23.25.

Figure 23.25
The Organizer will let you move files back and forth between copies of Microsoft Project.

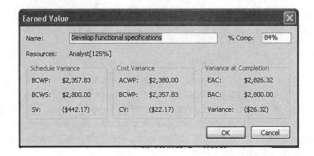

USING CUSTOM FORMS

If the set of forms from the previous section is not sufficient for your needs, you can create a custom form using the Tools, Customize, Forms menu. If you want to show the information for a specific task or resource, choose the task you want displayed before opening the form. You can display multiple tasks or resources the same way by choosing all of the tasks and resources beforehand. Keep in mind that if you make changes to a form while having multiple tasks or resources selected, the changes will affect all of your choices.

To display a custom form, follows these steps:

1. Choose the task or resources you want to edit. If you want to make changes to multiple tasks or resources, choose all of them beforehand.

2. Open the Customize Forms dialog box by selecting Tools, Customize, Forms, as shown in Figure 23.26. Choose Task or Resource to display the current set of forms.

Figure 23.26
Task and Resource forms are available using the Customize Forms dialog box.

3. Choose the form you want and then click the Apply button to open it.

4. You can now view or edit any of the field values you want. Click OK when finished.

ASSIGNING A HOTKEY TO SHOW A FORM

If you find that you use a specific form on a regular basis, you can create a hotkey that will shorten the steps needed to bring up that form. Follow these steps to create a hotkey:

1. Open the Customize Forms dialog box through Tools, Customize, Forms.

2. Choose the form you want to add a hotkey to, then click Rename.

3. The Define Custom Form dialog box is now open (see Figure 23.27). Change the name of the form or add a hotkey in the fields provided.

4. Enter a single letter in the Key box for the hotkey shortcut. It must be a letter; any other key will not work. When you are finished, click OK to apply your changes.

Figure 23.27
The Define Custom Form dialog box will let you rename a form or set up a hotkey for that form.

Change the form's name

Enter a single letter for the hotkey

→ Once the key is setup, the user presses the Ctrl key with the designated letter and the form will be displayed. To learn more about using hotkeys, **see** "Renaming Menus and Commands," **p. 834**.

ASSIGNING A TOOLBAR BUTTON TO DISPLAY A FORM

You can set up forms to be linked with toolbar buttons, making it much easier to open the forms. Simply click on the right button instead of digging through the Tools menu. To do this, you have to open the Customized Tool dialog box, which was discussed earlier in this chapter. You can also reference the "Adding and Removing Command Buttons" section if you need to create or add a button to the toolbar. Once you have created the button, follow these steps to link it to a form:

1. Open the Customize Tool dialog box (see Figure 23.28) by holding down the Ctrl button and clicking on the button you wish to link to a form.

2. Using the Command drop-down list, scroll to the Form commands to find which form you want to link to your chosen button.

3. Using the Description text box, enter the text you want displayed when the cursor is hovered over your chosen button. Click OK when you are finished.

Figure 23.28
The Customize Tool dialog box will let you link together toolbar buttons and forms for easier access to your forms.

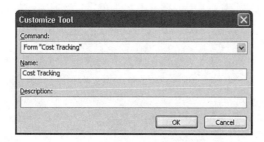

CREATING A NEW CUSTOM FORM

Just like with toolbars and menus, it is possible to set up your own custom form if the forms provided by Project do not include the fields of information that you feel you might need. The easiest way to do this is to copy an already existing form and then customize it to fit your needs, just like you can with a toolbar or a menu. However, you always have the option of creating your own form from scratch.

USING THE CUSTOM FORM EDITOR TO OPEN A FORM

To customize an existing form or create your own, you will need to use the Custom Form Editor. Use the following steps to open a form with the Custom Form Editor:

1. Open the Customize Forms dialog box by selecting Tools, Customize, Forms (refer to Figure 23.26).

2. If you want to make a new, custom form, click the New button (see Figure 23.29 for an example of a new form).

Figure 23.29
A new custom form only includes the OK and Cancel buttons when first opened.

3. If you want to modify an existing form, click the Copy button. A pop-up window, Design Custom Form, will appear. Click OK on this window and a "Copy of" pop-up window will appear as shown in Figure 23.30.

Figure 23.30
A copy of a form can be customized into an entirely new form using the Custom Form Editor.

23

SIZING AND POSITIONING A CUSTOMIZED FORM

Resizing your form works just like resizing a window or other dialog box. Drag the borders or corners to the new size you want to use. To move your form, simply click on the title bar and drag it around the screen.

Like most things in Project, there is another way to resize and move your form. You can open the Form Information box (see Figure 23.31) by either double-clicking on your form or using Edit, Info. The Form Information box allows you to reposition your form using the X and Y text boxes, or resize it using the Width and Height boxes.

Auto boxes will center your form for you

Figure 23.31
The Form Information dialog box allows you to move and resize your custom form.

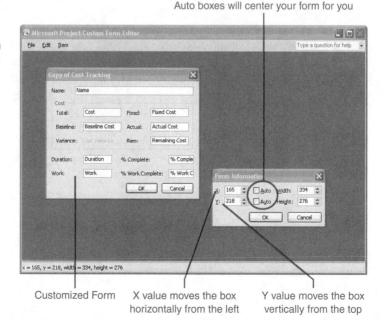

Customized Form   X value moves the box   Y value moves the box
                       horizontally from the left   vertically from the top

Moving your box around the screen is simple using the X and Y text boxes. Remember that X starts horizontally from the left, which means a value of 1 will put it on the left edge of the window, whereas Y is the vertical value starting from the top. A value of 1 in the Y text box places the box at the top of the screen. Your limits are the same as your screen resolution, so if your screen is set at 600 by 800, this is the visible limit you can use. You can go over these values, but your window will essentially appear off the screen, unseen.

PLACING ITEMS ON A FORM

You can add several types of items to a form: buttons, check boxes, fields with values from the database, groups, and text. New forms will also automatically include OK and Cancel buttons.

One of the things to keep in mind when using the Customized Form Editor is that there are no alignment options. You have to know the X, Y locations of the items on your form to keep them aligned and prevent overlap. You can click and drag them, but you can also double-click them to open the Item Information dialog box and enter the X, Y locations.

CAUTION

> When you are adding items to your form, be aware of their locations. It is possible to place one item on top of another, especially when you are first adding them, and only the top item will be visible. This makes it possible to lose items that are still on your form.

PLACING TEXT ON A FORM

Text items are labels that are typically used to identify information contained in the fields. For instance, if you set up a field for % Work Complete, you would use the text label to identify the field.

Selecting Item, Text will place a text box on your form. You can move it by either dragging it around or using the Item Information dialog box, as explained earlier. To replace the default *Text* word, click on the text box and type in your desired text. The text placeholder can be resized if your label is too long using the Item Information dialog box. Once you have positioned the text correctly, click on a neutral area of the form to deselect the text item.

Figure 23.32 shows an example of a text box added to a new form.

Figure 23.32
A text box must be added to the form before you can enter your own customized text.

Item menu listing the four types of objects you can place on a form

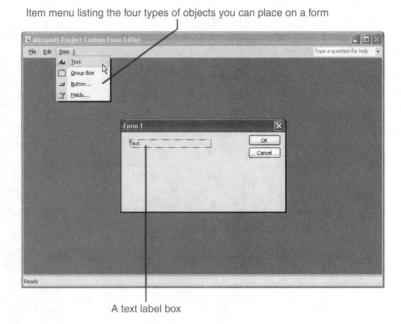

A text label box

PLACING FIELD VALUES ON A FORM

You can add field values to your custom form, which will show reports about specific tasks or resources within your project. You can allow the user to edit the fields and also design static fields that cannot be edited by selecting the Shows as Static Text check box when you set them up.

Follow these steps to set up a field value item:

1. Open a field via Items, Fields. The Item Information dialog box will open (see Figure 23.33).

2. Choose a field from the Field drop-down list. This will cause the information about your chosen field to be pulled from your project and reported in that field.

3. Either leave the field editable, or make it uneditable by choosing the Show as Static Text check box.

4. Click OK when you are finished. You can go back by double-clicking on the field to pull the Item Information dialog box back up, which can also be used to move your Field value box around your form.

New field added

Figure 23.33
Setting up Field Value boxes is easy using the Item Information dialog box.

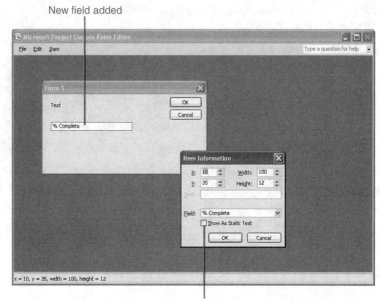

Check box to make the field read-only

PLACING A GROUP BOX ON A FORM

A group box is simply a formatting tool that allows you to create a boundary to separate information on your form. Once you create a group box, you can place text or fields within the box. To add a new box, use Item, Group Box (see Figure 23.34).

Once you have created a group box, manipulating it is similar to how you placed text on a form. Simply clicking on the box will allow you to change the text, whereas double-clicking on it will open the Item Information dialog box to change the size and reposition it. Always make sure your box is big enough to fit the items you want to put inside. Also, be careful with placement because it is possible to lay a group box over another item and hide it.

Figure 23.34
A group box can be used to display a logical grouping of form items.

PLACING A BUTTON ON A FORM

You can only add two buttons to a form—the OK and Cancel buttons. Project places those buttons on the form automatically when it is set up. You have the option of deleting the buttons or moving them to different locations in the form. If you delete a button and later decide you needed it, simply add it back by using Item, Buttons. You will be given the choice of OK or Cancel; just select which one you want to add.

SAVING A FORM

When you are finished and want to save your form, click File, Save. If you try and exit before saving, you will be prompted with the Save dialog box.

RENAMING, EDITING, DELETING, AND COPYING CUSTOM FORMS

Unlike toolbars and menus, any form you create is specific to the project for which it is created. If you want to use your customized form on another project, you should save it to the Global.MPT file through the Organizer. You can open the Organizer through the Customize Forms dialog box, then simply follow the same steps mentioned in "Managing Menus and Toolbars with the Organizer," earlier in this chapter. You can also use the Customize Forms dialog box to edit an existing form, make a copy of a custom form, or rename a form.

RENAMING CUSTOM FORMS

A custom form can be renamed in either the Customize Forms dialog box or with the Organizer. If you are using the Customize Forms dialog box, open it through Tools, Customize, Forms, then choose the form you wish to rename and click the Rename button.

EDITING OR COPYING CUSTOM FORMS

You can make changes to your custom-built forms just like you would Project's supplied forms. To copy a form, simply open the Customize Forms dialog box through Tools, Customize, Forms, and after selecting the form you want to copy, click the Copy box. This will open the Define Custom Form dialog box, where you can rename your copy. If you want to change your custom form, it is probably best if you make a copy of it first, so that if there are problems, you still have the original. Once you make a copy, the Custom Field Editor will open, and you can make changes as described in "Placing Items on a Form," earlier in this chapter.

DELETING A FORM

If you make a mistake or want to delete a custom form that is no longer needed, choose Tools, Organizer, Forms. Locate the form that should be deleted and click the Delete button. A warning pop-up will appear; click Yes and the form will be removed from the list.

MANAGING FORMS WITH THE ORGANIZER

As mentioned earlier, forms, unlike toolbars and menus, are project specific. If you want to access them in your other projects, you must save a copy of them to the Global.MPT file using the Organizer. You can open the Organizer through the Custom Forms dialog box.

→ For additional information about the Organizer, **see** Chapter 18, "Managing Project Files," on **p. 581**.

CONSULTANTS' TIPS

MANUALLY ACTIVATING TOOLBAR ADD-INS

If you are using Project Standard and PERT Analysis and Compare Project Versions toolbars are not available under View, Toolbars, then it is possible it is disabled in the registry.

NOTE

> The procedure described here contains information about modifying the registry. Before you modify the registry, make sure to back it up and make sure that you understand how to restore the registry if a problem occurs.

In order to have additional toolbars appear under Project toolbars, follow these steps:

1. Select Start, Run, and type in *regedit*.
2. In the Registry Editor, expand the tree on the left. Expand HKEY_CURRENT_USER, Software, Microsoft, Office, MS Project, Addins. The Addins folder contains all of the add-ins available for Project.
3. To activate the PERT Analysis toolbar add-in, select the PERTAnalysis.dsrPERT Analysis12 folder. On the righthand side, right click on the LoadBehavior and, if the value is not currently 3, select Modify Binary Data. In the Edit Binary Value window, replace the 09 bit with 03.
4. To activate the Compare Project Versions toolbar add-in, repeat step 3.
5. Close the Registry Editor and reopen Project.

MASTER THE BASICS, THEN CUSTOMIZE FOR EFFICIENCY

Project managers are very busy people and they need to save time whenever possible. They also need to communicate quickly and efficiently to their teams and their stakeholders.. Not every project manager uses customized toolbars and menus, but many do, and they do it to save time. The less time that is spent searching for or updating information, the more time is available to lead the project. Once you have mastered the basics, take a look at the items in the toolbars you use and think about removing items you hardly ever use and replacing them with other items that you use frequently. This saves screen space and allows you to quickly find the tools you need. Do not forget to leave room in your toolbars for the QuantumPM Schedule Auditor! It is a great time-saver when you want to review the quality of your schedule.

USING PROJECT GUIDE FOR GUIDANCE

If you are a new project manager, spend some time reviewing the Project Guide. It is very useful for new project managers who may need guidance in managing the features of Project and can be easily hidden when no longer needed by using the techniques identified in this chapter. It can also be customized to include your organization's workflow. You can save some space by hiding the left-side task pane using the first button on the left and leaving the Project Guide toolbar at the top. Then, when you need some quick help, click on the menu item and the Task Pane will appear.

USING THE VIEW BAR FOR QUICK ACCESS TO VIEWS

Also remember to use the View Bar as a quick method to find and move from one view to another. The View Bar is controlled from the menu item: View, View Bar.

23

MICROSOFT OFFICE PROJECT 2007 KNOWLEDGE IN DEPTH

CHAPTER **24**

WORKING WITH MULTIPLE PROJECTS

USING WINDOWS COMMANDS

There may be various instances when you need to work with more than one project at a time. Here are some examples:

- You might have two tasks in different projects that are dependent on each other—for instance, if the start date for a task in one project is dependant on the finish date of a task in another project.

- You might have several projects placed under your supervision. For example, if you are a program manager and need to see the status of projects within the program, you can create a program-level master project. Even if the projects within the program are managed by different project managers, the master project allows you to get an overall status and insight into how the entire program is executing.

- You might have a project that is too large and has become difficult to manage. You can break this project down into smaller, more controllable projects and then link them back together into one master project to see the high-level status. This has a similar benefit to outlining a project, but on a larger scale.

- You find yourself with several projects using the same set of resources, which need to be coordinated to prevent overallocations.

- Although this is a rare scenario, you might have a project that is too large to fit your organization's computer memory capacity. You can break it down into smaller projects to bypass these confines.

Microsoft Project 2007 can have up to 1,000 files open at the same time in 50 separate windows. When inserting projects to make a master project, you may have up to 1,000 files open, in total, if your computer processor and memory can support it. Practically however, you will want to use the least amount of files required to manage your master project. If multiple projects are open simultaneously, you can use the Window menu to move between your open files. The Ctrl+F6 key also allows you to move between active project windows. The list of open project files appears at the bottom of the Window menu, as shown in Figure 24.1. The active window is designated by a check mark, and if you have more than nine files open at a time, there will be an option of More Windows at the bottom of the Window menu; selecting More Windows will show all of the open project files. You can then select the project file you want to activate, and all other files will be moved to the background.

Figure 24.1
You can switch between all open project files by using the list at the bottom of the Window menu.

NOTE

You also have a list of files found at the bottom of the File menu. This list shows the most recently accessed files, but does not mean that these files are currently open. You can control the number of files in this list by selecting Tools, Options. Under the General tab, you can turn this option on and off with the Recently used file list check box and can set the number of entries in the same location.

24

Besides switching between screens, you can also use the Window, Split command to divide the screen for combination views of a single project. These can be very useful when dealing with different areas of a large project file. For instance, you can open the Resource Usage view in the upper section of the screen, and the Gantt Chart in the lower. You can then view and change specific resource assignments in the upper view while reviewing the effects in the Gantt Chart view in the lower part of the screen.

→ For additional information on working with views, **see** Chapter 11, "Using Standard Views, Tables, Filters, and Groups to Review Your Schedule," **p. 369**.

VIEWING ALL THE FILE WINDOWS AT THE SAME TIME

If you would like to view multiple files at the same time, you can open them all onscreen, in their own distinct window, by using the Window, Arrange All command. The Arrange All command will create windows for every project you have open, so remember to only open the projects you want to view in this arrangement. When you use the Window, Arrange All command, the last project opened will appear in the top-left corner of your screen. The number of windows opened depends on your processor, memory, and screen size, but managing more than five or six projects in one multi-tiled screen would be impractical.

Each window is sized and moved so they can be seen onscreen at the same time. This process tiles your windows, depending on how many projects are open at the same time. Each filename is shown in its title bar and the active window is identified by the active pane indicator and active window color scheme, as shown in Figure 24.2.

Figure 24.2
The Window, Arrange All command makes it easy to open several windows with different projects at the same time.

TIP

The Window, Arrange All command can be very useful when you want to compare a saved version of a project with a current project, side by side. For example, if you wanted to compare last month's status with the current status of the project, you can open both files with the Window, Arrange All command, and compare specific tasks using the AutoFilter function. This provides a side-by-side comparison of the changes made over time. While you can save up to 11 full baselines at a time, some project managers prefer saving versions of the same file, perhaps at the end of the month, to allow for review, comparison, contrast, and analysis of project data.

You can also use the Compare Project analysis tool. If the Compare Project Versions toolbar is not open, go to Views, Toolbars, Project Versions to open it, and then click the Compare Project button. This allows you to open two files and then build a comparison file by merging your two selected files, displaying their differences, discussed later in this chapter.

TIP

When viewing multiple project windows in one screen using the Window, Arrange All command, you can use the shortcut menu for quick options for a particular project file. To access the shortcut menu, right-click on the file's title bar. The commands available in the shortcut include Save, Save As…, Print…, Page Setup…, Spelling…, New Window, Arrange All, Zoom…, Split…, Project Information…, and View Code.

If you maximize one of the open windows, all other windows will become maximized as well. You cannot, however, see the other files, because the active window covers the whole screen. To switch between project files when the window is maximized, use the Window menu.

HIDING AND UNHIDING OPEN WINDOWS

You might come across a situation where you have open project files, but do not want to include them in the Arrange All display. Rather than closing them, you can use the Hide command to hide them. To hide a file, it must first be the selected, active file. Then, select Window, Hide. That file will be hidden and the next file will become the active project in the window. To unhide a file, choose the Window, Unhide command, and the Unhide dialog box will open, showing you the list of any and all files you have hidden. Select the file you want to unhide and click OK; it will become the active file. If you have any hidden files when you exit Microsoft Project 2007, you will be prompted to save them, if necessary.

USING THE SAVE WORKSPACE COMMAND

When you are working on several files at once, and want to be able to go back to what you are working on later, you can save the workspace. The workspace includes all of the files you have open and saves your current setup in addition to saving the individual files. The workspace does not save a second copy of the files, but rather creates a pointer to the originals. Follow these steps to save a workspace:

1. From the top menu, select File, Save Workspace.
2. If you have any unsaved changes to the individual files, the File Save dialog box will open, prompting you to save those individual files. Click Yes to close the File Save dialog box.
3. In the Save Workspace As dialog box, browse to the directory you want to save your files to on the right, if you do not want to use the default directory. Microsoft Project 2007 automatically provides a default Resume.mpw name. You can change it by entering a new name in the File Name box.
4. Click the Save button when you are finished.
5. Reopening these files is as easy as going to File, Open and selecting the workspace file.

> **NOTE**
>
> Microsoft Project 2007 automatically saves all workspace files with the .mpw extension.

→ For additional information about workspaces, **see** Chapter 18, "Managing Project Files," **p. 581**.

COMPARING PROJECT VERSIONS

Microsoft Project 2007 makes it easy to compare the first draft of your project with a revised version, letting you analyze the differences between cost, duration, resources, work, and other data. This will help you to look at and report the net effect of your changes. Once you have made your revisions, you can use File, Save As to save your new version.

CAUTION

> If you are using Microsoft Office Project Professional 2007 in conjunction with Microsoft Project Server, you can run into a special situation with the resource pool. Keep in mind that if you are using a resource pool, when you create two versions of a project, they are both drawing from that common pool, which causes duplication of your assignment information, and invalidates your available information. Once you are done comparing your versions, make sure you select the version you do not plan to use and break the link it has to your resource pool.

To compare the new project schedule to your original, follow these steps:

1. Open the newest version (Version 2) first, then open the original (Version 1), and then reactivate Version 2. This will position Version 2 as the later version when you use the Compare Project Versions dialog box.

2. Display the Compare Project Versions toolbar by selecting View, Toolbars, Compare Project Versions or by right clicking the toolbar area and selecting Compare Project Versions.

3. Click the Compare Project Versions button to open the Compare Project Versions dialog box (Figure 24.3).

Figure 24.3
Use the Compare Project Versions dialog box to select options for comparing two versions of a project.

4. Choose the correct task and resource tables in the section, and then click OK. A third project schedule is created that contains the data from both version 1 and version 2 files. This is not a full-fledged project schedule and is used as a placeholder for the comparison information.

5. In the Compare Project Versions – Done dialog box, select Yes to view the legend for comparing project (see Figure 24.4) or select No to skip the legend and just view the project version comparison report (see Figure 24.5).

Figure 24.4
The Project Versions legend helps you to compare and contrast your two different projects.

Figure 24.5
The Comparison Report table uses Gantt bars and a custom table to compare the two versions of a project.

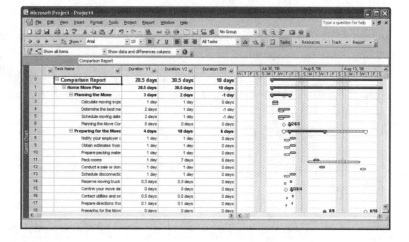

When you are using the Comparison Report project, a custom table is applied to the task sheet. For every table selected from Version 2, it displays three custom fields. For instance, if you had selected the Entry table in Version 2, the Comparison Report will show three Entry tables: Version 1, Version 2, and the difference version.

Table 24.1 provides the breakdown of how this would work.

TABLE 24.1   THE COMPARISON REPORT: TASK ALL COLUMNS TABLE UTILIZES SEVERAL USER-DEFINED FIELDS

Field Label	(Actual Field Name)	Version: Data Type
Duration: V1	(Duration 1)	Version 1: Duration
Duration: V2	(Duration 2)	Version 2: Duration
Duration: Diff	(Duration 3)	Comparison version: Duration
Start: V1	(Start1)	Version 1: Date
Start: V2	(Start2)	Version 2: Date
Start: Diff	(Duration 4)	Comparison version: Duration
Finish: V1	(Finish1)	Version 1: Date
Finish: V2	(Finish2)	Version 2: Date
Finish: Diff	(Duration 5)	Comparison version: Duration
Predecessors: V1	(Text1)	Version 1: Text
Predecessors: V2	(Text2)	Version 2: Text
Predecessors: Diff	(Text3)	Comparison version: Text
Resource Name: V1	(Text4)	Version 1: Text
Resource Name: V2	(Text5)	Version 2: Text
Resource Name: Diff	(Text6)	Comparison version: Text

You can use the More Information button on the Compare Project Versions toolbar when you want to view the legend.

If you try to have too many user-defined fields when you use Compare Project, you may receive the warning, because Compare Project has a limited number of custom fields available to show all of the data.

Since Comparison Report project uses its own set of custom fields, it will not change any of the custom fields in your project files. Custom fields will be listed the same as all of the other fields when run through Comparison Report, showing Version 1, Version 2, and the difference version.

DISPLAYING TASKS FROM DIFFERENT PROJECTS IN THE SAME WINDOW

Microsoft Project 2007 supports two viewing techniques for displaying tasks from different projects in the same window. You can use the Insert, Project command to combine multiple project files. This allows you to edit, view, print, and even link multiple projects' tasks in one view. You can change the view to add a column to identify the project file each task came from, such as a column with Project field selected, which will allow you to see the origin project of each task. You can sort and filter the task list the same way you would a regular project file. You can apply any table or view to the combined file, including the Network Diagram view, and insert and delete tasks. In addition, you can print views or reports from the merged project.

There are two different ways you can combine projects into one window. First, you can use the Window, New Window command. This assumes that all of the files being combined are already open. The second process uses the Insert, Project command to access files not currently open. These are not true merged files; you cannot select or link tasks across the displayed windows, even from within the same project schedule.

You can read more about the second approach in the "Combining Projects into One File Using the Insert Project Menu" section, later in the chapter.

USING THE NEW WINDOW COMMAND

The New Window menu has two major functions. First, you can use it to open a new window for the same file. This new window will be designated with a colon and number; for instance, if you had a file titled New Project, and opened a copy with the New Window menu, you will now have a window for the file named NewProject:2.

The other major function of the New Window menu is for creating master and sub relationships between two or more files. A master file is one or more files combined together from several sub files.

> **TIP**
>
> The New Window menu can also be helpful for editing the same file in two different windows. For instance, you can show a summary task in one window and make edits to tasks in another.

Follow these steps to combine tasks from multiple sub projects into one master file:

1. Open the New Window dialog box by selecting Window, New Window in the top menu, as shown in Figure 24.6.

Figure 24.6
Use the New Window dialog box to combine multiple projects into a one-window view.

2. Select all of the files you want included from the Projects list, holding down the Shift key to highlight them. You can use the Ctrl key if you need to add nonadjacent filenames to your selection.

3. You can select which view you want your new window to open by using the View list box at the bottom of the dialog box. The Gantt Chart is the default, but you can always go back and change the view later, after the new window has opened.

4. Select OK when you are finished and ready to display your new window.

Your new window will be named Project(*number*), where (*number*) is the consecutively assigned number given each time you create a new project. You can save your new file by using the File, Save command. A separate entry for Project(*number*) is also added under the Window menu, in addition to the project files you already have open.

When any of the task sheet views are active, including any of the Gantt Chart views, the Indicators column will display an icon for an inserted project, as shown in Figure 24.7. If you hover your mouse cursor over the icon, the name of the source file and its location is displayed. The icon simply tells you that the inserted project is pointing to the source file that contains the tasks. If you use the Gantt Chart view for each inserted file, then the corresponding project summary task name will be shown and the task ID for this project summary task will indicate the order in which the selected files were merged. Use the outline symbol in front of the project summary task name if you want to hide the details of the task, just as though you were working with the tasks in an outline. You will also see a gray task bar in the timescale side of the Gantt Chart view, which represents the Project Summary task and looks just like the regular summary task bar.

Figure 24.7
Holding your cursor over the icon in the indicator column will show information about the inserted projects.

NOTE

You can use the Show command on the Formatting toolbar to choose the level of outline detail you want displayed.

TIP

> If you would like to see a different view of a project quickly, without losing all of your layout information in the current view, you can create a new window with the new view. This way, you could have the Gantt Chart view open with a split screen showing the Task Usage view in the lower half, and then open a new window with the Resource Sheet view, allowing you to use filters on the Resource Sheet view without changing the layout information you have set up for your Gantt Chart view.
>
> To do so, select Window, New Window and only highlight your current project. That will open another window with your current project as the active one. It is, essentially, creating more than a standard combination view—you can now see two separate combination views, two full-screen views, or one combination view and one full-screen view, all from the same project. When you do this, you will be opening another copy of the same file with the same name, with an addition of :2, such as Home Move Project and Home Move Project:2. You can then use either the Window menu or Ctrl+F6 to move between them. Any changes you make and save are saved to both versions of the file. You have, in essence, only one file open; it is just displayed in two separate windows.

24

FILTERING AND SORTING CONSOLIDATED PROJECTS

When you first create a consolidated project, the tasks are grouped by the file they originally came from. You can sort the list using the Sort command, or filter tasks with the Filter drop-down list or AutoFilter method. If you want to sort the list, go to Project, Sort, Sort By. This opens the Sort dialog box. At the bottom of the Sort dialog box is the Keep Outline Structure check box. If you want to want to change the order of tasks from their original grouping of which project they came from, you will need to clear this box. You can now, for instance, sort your list by start date, and the tasks from all of the consolidated project files will move out of their original start date. Remember that your predefined sort options on the Sort menu are set to sustain the outline structure, and if you turn off the outline structure, the subtask level expanding and collapsing will not work.

Figure 24.8 shows that the task list for the two inserted projects has been sorted by start date. The Project field column has been added to the table, so you can see the name of the source project for each task. The outline indenting option has been turned off and the summary tasks and project summary tasks have been hidden. You can make the same changes using the View tab of the Options dialog box.

Many of the task names in Figure 24.8 are duplications of one another. Many managers find that common tasks occur in almost all similar-type projects. Following good project management practices and creating project files from existing files or templates will cause some repetition of task names when you combine projects into a master file. Adding the Project column is an easy way to identify the source of each task.

Figure 24.8
You can sort a file with inserted projects to make it easier to find when tasks from different projects are scheduled.

...then by project name

Besides using filtering and sorting, there are other formatting options you can use with your consolidated file, such as Bar Style formatting and layout commands.

Microsoft Project 2007 will treat individually inserted files as summary tasks with subtasks in new consolidated files. Each will have its own critical path.

If you want to set up a critical path across all of the projects and tasks within a combined file, follow these steps:

1. Open the Options dialog box by selecting Tools, Options from the top menu.
2. Select the Calculation tab.
3. In order for inserted projects to be calculated like summary tasks, turn on this feature by selecting the Inserted Projects Are Calculated Like Summary Tasks check box, shown in Figure 24.9. Your files do not have to be linked to use this feature.

TIP

> The cross-project task dependencies are very important, if you really want to manage the critical path. If you do not establish the task dependencies, then your critical path simply becomes the point where the two projects happen to converge. To use the critical path properly, you must establish your task dependencies.

→ For additional information about task dependencies, **see** "Linking Tasks," **p. 201**.

Figure 24.9
If you treat your inserted files as summary tasks, you can show the critical path across your combined files.

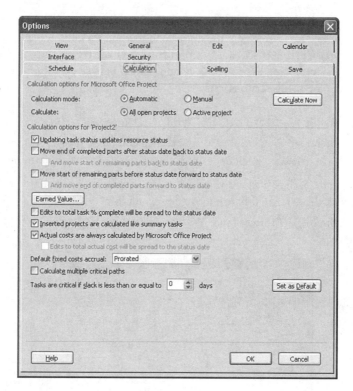

CREATING MASTER PROJECTS

You will find several advantages to managing large and complex projects in smaller, separate files. You can more easily share files among coworkers, and you can print and transmit several small files faster than one large file.

CAUTION

One issue with using master and sub files is the potential of having broken connection links. For example, if you have the sub files stored in a shared location on the network and the project manager moves a linked project to a different location, then the link within your master will be incorrect and Microsoft Project 2007 will not be able to open that project.

When you need to analyze, review, and report on your project, you can take each of the individual files and create a master/sub project structure, combining the files into one. You can save this consolidated file and use it later, so you will not have to re-create it each time. An advantage of this approach is that these master/sub projects can be multilevel: you can show consolidated projects at different levels, such as the departmental, functional, regional, and perhaps even the national or international level.

You can use two methods to combine files into a master/sub project structure. The first method, using the New Window command, was discussed earlier in the chapter. For more information, see the "Displaying Tasks from Different Projects in the Same Window" section. The following sections discuss the second method for combining files: inserting files into a new master project schedule. Important master file issues, such as maintaining the combined file, removing the sub project, and linking between combined files are also discussed in the following sections.

COMBINING PROJECTS INTO ONE FILE USING THE INSERT PROJECT MENU

To insert one project into another, or to create a combined project from two original projects, use the Insert, Project menu. Follow these steps to insert an entire project into another:

1. Choose the task row where you want to insert the new project. When the new tasks are inserted, the existing task will move down one row.

2. Open the Insert Project dialog box by selecting Insert, Project, as shown in Figure 24.10.

Figure 24.10
The Insert Project dialog box will assist you in opening and inserting one project file into another.

3. Choose which of the files you want to insert.

4. If you want to insert a read-only copy of the project into the file, use the Insert drop-down list at the lower-right corner of the Insert, Project dialog box to select that option. This allows you to make changes to the source project in the master project, but you will not be able to save those changes back to the source copy. This option could be helpful, for instance, if you want to allow someone to see the effect of the changes he or she would like to implement. That person cannot actually make the changes; rather he or she will need to discuss them with the individual project managers in charge of the source project. This prevents project managers from inadvertently making changes to another project manager's project. If you do not use the read-only option, it will always default to the regular Insert with Full Read and Write Permissions.

5. You will create a link to the inserted project unless you clear the Link to Project option. If you clear the Link to Project option, you will, in effect, be copying tasks from the source project. Any changes that are made to the master files will also be made to the inserted file, on a bidirectional basis. If the file was inserted as read-only, then any updates from the source to the master project files work, but updates from the master

file back to the source files will not work. If the files are inserted in a full read-write capability, you will still have the option of not saving changes to individual files.

6. Click OK when finished. This newly created file is now a master file and is separate from your original sub file.

NOTE

> The ODBC button on the Insert Project dialog box is for inserting data stored in a database. You can read more about this topic in the section in Chapter 26 called, "Creating Import Maps for Access and ODBC Sources."

TIP

> When inserting multiple files into the same location of a master project file, click them in the order you want them displayed. Select the first one and then press and hold the Ctrl key while you pick your other projects in the order you wish for them to appear. If you simply want to select an adjacent block of files, and do not care about their order, choose your first file, hold down the Shift key when selecting your last file, and all files between the two will be automatically chosen to be placed in the master project file.

24

WORKING WITH INSERTED PROJECTS

 For information about your inserted project, you can use the Advanced tab on the Task Information dialog box. You can open the dialog box either by using the Task Information button on the Standard toolbar or by double-clicking the Project Summary task of the inserted project. Once you have accessed the Task Information dialog box for a task from your inserted project, the title of the dialog box will change to Inserted Project Information, and the Advanced tab will display the details of the source project file. The title bar indicates that you have selected the task from an inserted project, as shown in Figure 24.11.

Figure 24.11
You can see the link to the source file and gain access to project information using the Task Information dialog box for an inserted project.

You have the option to maintain a link with the individual files or not. You can choose whether or not changes made to the master file will link back to your original file by using the Link to Project check box. When the Link to Project check box is selected, any content-related changes you make to the new master file will also be made to the original inserted files. The link between your original source file and the new file is created by default. However, any changes made to the formatting in the new window will not be reflected in the source files. This allows you to make formatting changes in the new window, to assist in telling the two combined projects apart or printing reports for different audiences, without your changes being saved back to the original working file.

As mentioned previously, the read-write option is the default, but you can change that to read-only, if you prefer. To do so, select the Read Only check box to protect your original source files from changes. If you use the Read Only check box, then your inserted files will show an icon in the Indicators column of the Gantt Chart view. This icon is an exclamation point and indicates that the file is read-only. Hovering your mouse cursor over the icon brings up information about this condition.

If you need to change the link to another file, or fix a link for a file that has been moved or renamed, the Browse button will allow you to select a new, moved, or renamed file. Later sections in the chapter cover moving, deleting, and renaming of the inserted projects.

You can also click the Project Info button to open the Project Information dialog box for your source file. You can find the Project Info button in the lower section of the Inserted Project Information dialog box.

NOTE

> The original source file location reference is stored in the Subproject field for inserted project tasks. If the Read Only check box has been selected, then a Yes is stored in the Subproject Read Only field. These fields can only be seen if you add them to a table. If you clear the Link to Project check box, then the inserted source project becomes a normal summary task and file location references are not shown.

Not only can you create inserted projects at any level of an outline, you can then insert that consolidated project into another project. Microsoft Project 2007 will make sure that there are no circular references existing within the levels.

BREAKING A LARGE PROJECT APART USING INSERTED PROJECTS

Now that you know how to insert projects, you can also create inserted projects by moving tasks from a large project into new project files, and then designating these new files as inserted projects. When you move one or more tasks that are linked to tasks that remain behind, you will lose those links and have to reestablish them later. It is easier, therefore, to copy the tasks that are going to become new project files and paste the copied tasks to a new file. Then you will insert the project file, change the links, and finally delete the original copied tasks.

Follow these steps to move tasks to a new project file:

1. Highlight the entire row of task IDs for the tasks you are planning to move. This guarantees that all fields are selected and that all of the relevant data will be copied. If your selected tasks include a summary and all the subtasks indented underneath, you can just select the summary task instead.

2. Go to Edit, Copy Tasks, or use Ctrl+C, to copy the task data to the Clipboard.

3. Select File, New to create your new project file. If the Prompt for project info for new projects check box is selected on the General tab of the Options dialog box, then the Project Information dialog box will open.

4. Select the Name field of the first task in the new file, then go to Edit, Paste, or use Ctrl+V, to paste the new task data into the new project.

5. Save your new file by selecting File, Save. Fill in the name in the resulting dialog box and click Save.

6. Open the Window menu and select the filename in the list at the bottom to return to your original file. You can also press Ctrl+F6 until the project reappears.

7. Choose where you want your inserted tasks to appear, and insert those tasks as described earlier in the chapter in the "Working with Inserted Projects" section.

MASTER PROJECTS USING HAMMOCK TASKS

A *hammock task* is a task dependent on external dates for the start date, finish date, and duration. These tasks are called hammock tasks because of the hammock shape created, as shown in Figure 24.12, which determines the distance between the points to which the task needs to be attached.

Figure 24.12
Hammock tasks are named so because of the way one task is slung between two other tasks.

As scheduled dates in other tasks change, the duration and start and/or finish dates of the hammock task will change as well. If you have three tasks (Tasks A, B, and C), as shown in Figure 24.12, then Task C must start on the finish date of Task A, and must finish by the finish date of the Task B.

The span of time between the dates of Tasks A and B will dictate the available time to accomplish Task C. For example, if the date for Task A changes, then the start date for Task C will change as well. If the date for Task B moves, then Task C must finish appropriately. The difference between the dates on Tasks A and B determines the duration for Task C.

If you have Tasks A, B, and C linked together in a predecessor relationship, and you create a new task, Task D, with the start date coming from Task A's start and the finish date coming from Task B's finish, then Task D acquires the start date of Task A and the finish date of Task B. If Task C is delayed (the duration changes), then the duration of Task D will also change.

TIP

> Hammock tasks can be useful at the top of a project schedule to reflect key milestones within your schedule. Use the hammock method to duplicate task names and start and finish dates. Then, when the parent milestone changes, the hammock task will show the updates.

Use the following steps to establish a hammock task:

1. Right-click the cell that contains the date that will determine when the hammock task starts and select Copy Cell.
2. Right-click the hammock task start date cell and select Paste Special.
3. In the Paste Special dialog box, select Paste Link and then click the OK button.
4. Right-click on the cell containing the date that will determine when the hammock task finishes and then select Copy Cell.
5. Right-click the hammock task finish date cell and select Paste Special.
6. In the Paste Special dialog box, select Paste Link and then click the OK button.

To use hammock tasks in a master project, use the following steps:

1. Using the procedures previously described, create a master project containing one or more sub-projects so that each sub-project is a Summary task.
2. Add a new Summary task called *Dynamic links* (the name is not important, but it makes it easier to find) in the workspace and create several blank rows beneath the summary.
3. Create the hammock tasks as described above.
4. After all of the hammock tasks are created, continue to expand the master project and copy (from the Dynamic Links section) the linked tasks and paste them into the master. This creates "double-hammock tasks" or "duplicated existing links."

Once all of the desired links have been created in the master project, save the "dynamic master schedule" file. Click "Yes to all" to save the master, with the newly added links. Once dynamic links file and linked hammock tasks are created, opening the master project will cause the dynamic links file to be opened in the background. Subsequently, all of the linked enterprise projects that feed the updates to the master project are opened. The master project will now include duration-based schedule data from the sub-projects, rather than using links between tasks or milestones.

TIP

> To test your hammock task, change the duration of the task that provides the start or finish date of the hammock task, to see if the hammock task reflects the changes.
>
> You can also double-click on the small triangle in the lower-right corner of hammock task. This will open the parent cell.

You should not specify a predecessor for a hammock task. Only Paste Linked dates will determine start and finish. You may, of course, specify predecessors for the tasks from which dates are paste-linked into the hammock task.

CAUTION

> The hammock tasks will necessarily contain a date constraint. You cannot clear this type of constraint.
>
> Also, if you later go back and directly edit any one of the hammock task's Pasted Link fields, then the hammock relationship is removed for that field.

24

MAINTAINING INSERTED PROJECTS

To replace an inserted project, you can change the name in the source project by selecting the Advanced tab of the Task Information dialog box. Use the Browse button to find the file instead of typing it in. If you just delete the filename, you will sever the link between the two projects, and your inserted project task will become a single task with a 1-day duration by default. If you change the filename to an already existing file, then that file will be used as the source project file, instead of the previous file. If you enter a filename Microsoft Project 2007 cannot find, Microsoft Project 2007 will automatically open the Browse dialog box, shown in Figure 24.13.

Figure 24.13
The Browse dialog box will open if you need to re-identify an inserted project when the original is moved, deleted, renamed, or cannot be found.

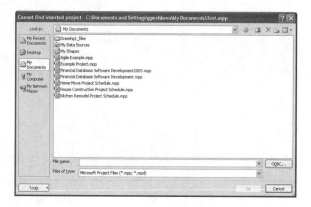

Be careful when moving or renaming projects used as inserted projects. If you want to try to open a project that contains an inserted project and Microsoft Project 2007 cannot find the file, the Browse dialog box from Figure 24.13 will open. Locate the file before proceeding to maintain your links.

CAUTION

> Microsoft Project 2007 will not alert you of a lost link on inserted project files until the outline for the file is expanded in the combined file. A combined file always opens collapsed down to a single summary line for every inserted project, regardless of whether the outline was expanded when the combined file was saved and closed.

TIP

> If you plan to maintain several sub projects rolled up into a master file, it would be useful to investigate how best to organize and catalog the repository of files. Just as with a filing cabinet or a computer hard drive, you can save a lot of time by setting up an appropriate filing system to organize your files, as well as maintaining the linkages built into the master project.

IDENTIFYING TASKS THAT ARE INSERTED PROJECTS

Besides the inserted projects indicator in the Indicators column, you can also use the Subproject File field, which stores the name of the inserted project. You can set up a table displaying that field to help you identify the tasks.

Every Subproject File field entry has to contain a filename and extension, which are separated by a period. Figure 24.14 demonstrates a filter definition for displaying inserted projects, which filters the Subproject File field for any entry containing a period. Enter a period into the *contains* test to find the value you are looking for.

→ For additional information about filter definitions, **see** "Creating and Customizing Filters," **p. 785**.

Figure 24.14
You can create a filter to find inserted projects by searching for the period in the Subproject field.

REMOVING INSERTED PROJECTS

Removing an inserted project is identical to the way you remove a summary task. Select the inserted project and either press the Delete key on the keyboard or right-click the task ID and select Delete Task from the shortcut menu. A warning message is displayed to let you know you are deleting more than one task, as shown in Figure 24.15.

Figure 24.15
This warning dialog box will appear when you attempt to delete inserted projects.

CREATING LINKS BETWEEN TASKS IN SEPARATE PROJECTS

Links can be easily created between projects. One method is to link tasks of one project together as the predecessor or successor to a group of tasks in another project. For example, a detailed landscape project cannot begin until the home construction project is completed and the lot is cleaned of construction debris. If you need to monitor the construction project's progress in order to efficiently schedule your workforce, you might want to link a group of tasks. Another way to accomplish this is to link a single task from one project to a single task in another.

The method for creating these links is the same no matter which method you use. If you have already inserted one project inside another, you can simply expand the inserted project task list, and then choose the tasks to be linked. To do so, select Edit, Link Tasks command or use the Link Tasks tool on the Standard toolbar. Use Window, New Window if you want to display both projects at the same time, and then select the tasks you want linked. You can also enter the full path of the project file and task ID into the Predecessors or Successors task fields, as follows:

Drive:\directory\subdirectory\filename.ext\taskIDnumber

If, for instance, your predecessor is Task 13 in the project file newproduct.mpp, stored in the directory C:\Projects\Development, you would enter the following into the Predecessors field:

C:\Projects\Development\newproduct.mpp\13

While this functionality can be used, in practice it is rare to see it used due to the possibility of making entry errors.

> **NOTE**
>
> With networked computers, it is not necessary to use a drive name; you can use a network share instead. The format for this could be the following:
>
> *\\sharename\directory\subdirectory\filename.ext\taskIDnumber*
>
> You can even keep files on an FTP site, and then insert them into a project using the Insert Project dialog box, by pulling up the predefined FTP site in your drop-down list box for the Look In field.

A cross-link between files can use any of the standard relationships (Finish-to-Finish, Finish-to-Start, Start-to-Finish, or Start-to-Start), plus lag and lead times are supported.

→ For additional information about creating links between tasks, **see** "Linking Tasks," **p. 201**.

Once the link is established, the name of the task being linked to, along with the duration, start, and finish, appear in gray text. If the linked task has a duration, a task bar will also appear in gray. If the linked task is a milestone, the milestone marker will be gray. Double-clicking on the linked task opens the original project plan that contains that task. If the source project for the linked task is open, the linked task from the destination project plan will also appear in gray, and you can double-click it to return to the original project file. When you open the Task Information dialog box for either of the two grayed-out tasks, information about those tasks will be displayed, but you can only change the Note entries.

> **CAUTION**
>
> Any notes or other data column changes entered for a grayed-out task will not be saved back to the original task.

24

NOTE

> If you create a link to a task in another project file, the External Task field is set to Yes. This allows you to create a filter for all tasks with external links. A filter like this, plus a table including the Predecessors and Successors column, will provide a view of all the external links and their sources.

For instance, suppose you are using separate files for two new projects in development. The design work for the second product prototype begins once the prototype for the first product is finished. If the two tasks from separate files have been linked together, Microsoft Project 2007 will include placeholder tasks for both files. An external successor task in the First New Product file would look as shown in Figure 24.16.

Figure 24.16
You can set up predecessor or successor tasks that are linked back to another project. These tasks will be shown in gray.

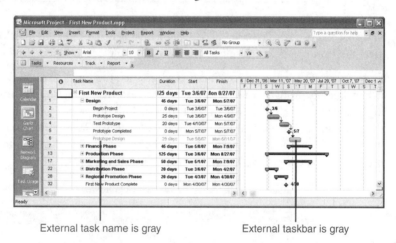

External task name is gray   External taskbar is gray

Notice the gray text of the task named Prototype Design. The second Prototype Design task is part of the New Product file only to the extent that it is a successor to the Prototype Completed task. You can double-click these tasks, and the New Product 2 file will open, as shown in Figure 24.17. In New Product 2, you will see the gray text from the first Prototype Completed task. Once again, this task is part of the New Product 2 plan only to the extent that it is a predecessor to beginning the Prototype Design task. Double-clicking the gray Prototype Design task will return you to the New Product file.

CAUTION

> Make sure you do not delete the gray task, because this will break the bidirectional links between the files the next time they are opened.

Figure 24.17
You can easily jump back and forth between projects by double-clicking on the grayed-out cross-linked tasks.

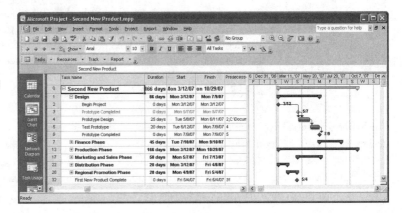

Now that the two projects are linked together, any changes to the New Product file that affect the Prototype Complete task will also affect the Second New Product file.

If you open a file that has cross-linked predecessors, the Links Between Projects dialog box will open if any changes have taken place to the external tasks. You can also open this dialog box by going to Tools, Links Between Projects. This dialog box not only refreshes any changes made to the external files, but also reestablishes file locations or deletes links. You can see which changes have occurred in the Differences column, and in Figure 24.18, you can see that the full path is shown for the selected tab in the title bar.

Figure 24.18
You can see if there have been any changes made in cross-linked tasks with the Links Between Projects dialog box.

Task in current file   Linked filename

External predecessor task information

If you accidentally create any links that might cause a circular relationship between tasks, such as one task acting as the predecessor and successor for another, then a warning dialog box will appear, as shown in Figure 24.19. You will need to remove the conflicting link to prevent this from reappearing.

Figure 24.19
If you accidentally create a circular relationship, a warning will appear and you will need to remove the conflicting link.

SHARING RESOURCES AMONG PROJECTS

Project managers who have several projects executing at the same time often use the same set of resources. It can, however, be very difficult to manage the same resources in several different projects. You cannot always see which resources have been assigned and what they are doing for all projects. You can have Microsoft Project 2007 store that resource information into one file, and only the assignment information into the project files. You can enter all of the resources into one project file and instruct other project files to use resources defined in this file, your shared resource pool file. The project file that contains your shared resource pool does not require or should contain any tasks.

If several projects share the same resource pool, you can open all of your projects at the same time to display the allocation of resources across your projects. Microsoft Project 2007 will warn you when a resource is being overallocated because of conflicting assignments in different projects. You can then use the leveling feature to resolve resource overallocation by delaying tasks in different projects.

→ For additional information on resolving resource overallocations, **see** Chapter 25, "Resolving Resource Allocation Problems," **p. 885**.

The steps shown in this section for sharing resources will only work with Project Standard 2007 or Project Professional 2007 if it has not been linked with Microsoft Office Project Server 2007.

CREATING THE SHARED RESOURCE PROJECT

The easiest way to create a resource pool is to create a project file with no tasks, simply containing a list of all your resources. To create the resource pool, follow these steps:

1. Open a blank project schedule by selecting File, New, Blank Project.
2. Switch to the Resource Sheet view by selecting View, Resource Sheet.
3. Enter your resource data, including resource names, types, rates, and so on.
4. Save this file with a recognizable name that indicates the file is the resource pool, such as Shared Resource Pool.

USING THE RESOURCE POOL

Use the menu command Tools, Resource Sharing, Share Resources to associate the resource pool file to your project schedule file. When both files have resources defined in them at the time the link is established, the resource pool will be enlarged to include all of the resources in both files. If both projects use the same resources (although this is not recommended) but have different definitions, you must select which file will take precedence. You can set this up using the Share Resource dialog box, which provides a check box to set precedence.

Once your resource pool sharing link is established, look at the Resource Sheet view of either file to see the complete list of resources. You can change the resource definitions in either file if needed. Once you close the files, make sure each one includes a copy of the entire resource pool. This allows you to open the project file that uses the resource pool independently of the file that actually contains the resources, if needed, to change and manage that project file.

Follow these steps to allow a project file to use resources from another file:

1. Open both of the projects files: the file containing the resource pool and the file that will be sharing the pool. Confirm that the active project is the file sharing the pool, not the pool itself.

2. Open the Share Resources dialog box by selecting Tools, Resource Sharing, Share Resources (see Figure 24.20). Select the Use Resources option button, and then select your resource pool from your currently open files using the From: drop-down box.

Figure 24.20
The Share Resources dialog box will help you to link your resource pool to other project files.

3. Choose the Pool Takes Precedence option button to avoid conflicting definitions between your two pools (the resource pool and the file sharing the pool). If you want your sharing pool to control resources, select the Sharer Takes Precedence button.

4. Click the OK button to finish.

If your resource pool file is not open when a connected file opens, the Open Resource Pool Information dialog box is displayed, as shown in Figure 24.21. Here, you can choose to have Microsoft Project 2007 open the resource pool, plus all other project files that use those resources.

TIP

You can select the shared resource pool and display the Resource Usage view to see all of the resources shared with other schedule files. Insert the Project column to see associated schedules. Split the screen with Resource Usage on the top and Resource Graph on the bottom to see assignment workload profiles for selected resources.

Figure 24.21
You can open your resources with the Open Resource Pool Information dialog box.

You have a few different options with the Open Resource Pool Information dialog box, as shown in Figure 24.21. The Open Resource Pool Information dialog box appears once you open the Microsoft Project 2007 file containing your shared resource pool. Using the first option, you can open the resource pool and see assignments across all shared files. Any changes made to the shared file will be immediately reproduced in the resource pool file. Microsoft Project 2007 may claim that the pool file will be opened as read-only, but this is a bit misleading. The truth is the resource pool will accept changes to resource assignment information, so it is not entirely read-only. The pool is temporarily locked, however, to prevent other sharer files from making changes to the pool. The shared resource pool is changed to read-write, saved, and then returned to read-only status when you save your project file and click OK to the Save Pool challenge dialog box.

The other option in the Open Resource Pool Information dialog box lets you open and work on a project file without having to also open the resource pool. With only one file open at a time, this should increase your computing performance.

CAUTION

When you open a file that shares resources with the resource pool, but do not open the resource pool, any changes you make will be saved to the file, but the resource pool will not be immediately updated. Any changes made are not included until the resource pool and all sharing files have been opened at the same time, or you have saved all of the projects. Your options for opening the resource pool are shown in Figure 24.22.

Figure 24.22
How you open your resource pool file will determine the access to and behavior of that file.

If you open the resource pool file without opening another linked file first, the option you select on the Open Resource Pool dialog box will establish your accessibility and how the pool will be updated. If you use the read-only option, you can make changes and see the results instantly in a copy of the last-saved version of the pool file, but any changes made in real time by another user will not be reflected until the pool has been closed and reopened. You can refresh the pool with current information, however, when you have multiple users working on it. Go to Tools, Resource Sharing and select the Update Resource Pool option. This will save changes to the stored resource pool, and then you can go to Tools, Resource Sharing, Refresh Resource Pool to load a fresh copy of the pool into your open resource pool window. When these two options are grayed out and unavailable, this means that the file-sharing environment is updated, and refreshing is unnecessary.

The second option when you open your resource pool file is to open the file with read-write capabilities. The read-write option itself has two choices—you can have complete editing control over the pool file, but will lock out other users while you have the file open. Alternatively, you can open the resource pool as read-write, along with all of the shared files. These force Microsoft Project 2007 to retrieve the last saved versions of all of the attached files, and rebuild the pool.

> **TIP**
>
> It is a good idea to occasionally open your resource pool file and all of the sharer files along with it, to force the most up-to-date information into all of the files. This can also alert you if any files have lost or corrupted links.
>
> Open only the shared resource pool and then use the Resource Sharing menu. A dialog box is present to allow you to select any or all associated project schedules. You can also use the Break Links option to remove resource sharing. A copy of the shared resources is saved within the selected schedule(s) if you break the sharing link.

Once a project has been set up to share another project's resource file, if the resource pool is open in read-write mode, then any changes made to the resource pool while both files are open will be saved back into the shared pool, and both files are updated immediately.

However, when you are working with a dependant project file alone, and changes are made in the resource sheet of that project, then the changes will not be saved back to the resource pool until you try to either close or save the file. If you only add new resources with different names, these resources are added to the resource pool when it is next opened in read-write mode.

If you make changes to the definition of the resource, such as the pay rate, maximum units, or working days on the resource calendar, it is possible those changes might be lost if both files are loaded in memory together the next time. If you have selected the Pool Takes Precedence option button in the Share Resources dialog box, then changes will be lost if you make them in the sub file. If, however, you selected the Sharer Takes Precedence option button in the Share Resources dialog box, your changes will be updated within the resource pool. The Pool Takes Precedence option is the default button, so changes to the definitions of your resources should always be made to the resource pool, if possible.

TIP

> For best practices, the resource pool is the only file where the underlying resource details are changed. In most cases, organizations only have one or two people to serve as resource managers, custodians of the resource pool, and they should be the ones entering and making changes to resource details, such as maximum units, pay rates, calendars, and so forth. Sharing files should be connected to the pool, and the Pool Takes Precedence option should be selected in the Share Resources dialog box.

DISCONTINUING RESOURCE SHARING

You can quit sharing resources whenever you choose. To do so, open the file using another file's resources, and then go to the Share Resources dialog box by selecting Tools, Resource Sharing, Share Resources. In the Share Resources dialog box, select the Use Own Resources option button. The resource pool will be no longer available to this file. However, if any resources that were assigned to tasks in the file have been copied into the file's resource list, they are now saved with that file. Also, any resource in the file being shared from the resource pool of another project will be copied into the local resource sheet and will remain there after sharing has been disconnected.

Follow these steps to discontinue a project file's dependence on another file's resource pool:

1. Open the file you want to make independent and use its own resources.
2. Set up this file as the active file window.
3. Open the Share Resources dialog box by selecting Tools, Resource Sharing, Share Resources.
4. Select the Use Own Resources option button.
5. Click the OK button to finish. A confirmation of resource connection removal between your sharing file and the resource pool file is displayed, as shown in Figure 24.23.

Figure 24.23
This dialog box will confirm your decision to remove the connection between your project file and your resource pool.

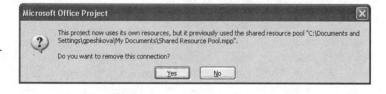

NOTE

> It is also possible to break a sharing link in the other direction by opening the resource pool file, bringing up the Share Resources dialog box, and clicking on the Break Link button.

IDENTIFYING RESOURCE POOL LINKS

Resource sharing connections are recorded both in the resource pool file and the file that uses the resource pool. You can open the Share Resources dialog box (Tools, Resource Sharing, Share Resources) to show the linking information in both file types. The layout of the dialog box will also show you which of the two files types is active.

Microsoft Project 2007 knows which files is the resource pool file, and will change the Share Resources dialog box when you need link-management options.

TIP

> As you experiment with inserted projects, cross-project links, and shared resource pools, it might be helpful to include columns for External, Linked Fields, Predecessors, Successors, Subproject File, Subproject File Read-Only, and Notes. This way, as you are trying different options, you can see what is happening and where Project is storing the information.

VIEWING RESOURCE LOADS WITHOUT SHARING A POOL

With a larger organization, having multiple project managers attaching their files to a single resource pool might cause problems. Too many attached projects might cause performance to be negatively affected, and other managers might have problems making and saving changes to their files, especially if someone has opened all of the sharer files by mistake. If your primary reason for pooling is to summarize and report on the resource assignments for several different files, Microsoft Project 2007 gives you another option that does not require links to the resource pool.

If two or more projects have been linked together, as mentioned earlier in the chapter, Microsoft Project 2007 will create a combined list of resources that are assigned to each of those files. If you break those links, Project will re-create a list of resources from all of the linked files. Resource names from each of the files will be matched up, and the assignments will be totaled. You can then use the Resource Usage view to show the sharing of work by resource between all of the linked projects in a particular file.

If you want to build this combined resource list, select Tools, Options, View option to show the project summary line. Open the Task Information dialog box, go to the Advanced tab, and in the Source Project area clear the Link to Project option, as shown in Figure 24.24. Your Gantt Chart view will now show tasks renumbered consecutively and duplicate task IDs will no longer exist. You can now create a separate consolidated file, with file links included, to edit projects from this level.

Figure 24.24
You can use the Task Information dialog box to create a combined resource list across projects by unlinking your consolidated files.

TIP

> If you decide to use the aforementioned method to create a consolidated resource list, make sure that you have a separate file acting as your resource information pool. You should have someone in your organization keep the resource detail information (pay rate, nonworking time, and so on) in a separate and up-to-date file. When updates are then made to that file, all project managers should open their Project files, link them to this resource file to upload the most recent resource information, and then break the resource sharing link and save their files.

SAVING MULTIPLE FILES IN A WORKSPACE

Microsoft Project 2007 supports a concept of workspaces. A workspace represents all of the files you have currently open in Microsoft Project 2007 and allows you to capture a work setup that you can easily access by opening a previously saved workspace. Workspaces do not create copies of the project files, but rather provide pointers to the file locations that are opened once you open the workspace.

If you are using a shared resource pool, you can save the pool and resource-sharing files into a workspace file simultaneously. To do so, select File, Save Workspace from the top navigation menu. This will save all open pool and sharer files together; this workspace file is assigned the name resumen.mpw by default.

You can open files attached to the resource pool quite easily by opening the resource pool first, and then using the Share Resource dialog box by going to Tools, Resource Sharing, Share Resources. This will display a list of all of the sharing files attached to your resource pool in the Share Resources dialog box, and you can open all of them at the same time, using the Open All button, as shown in Figure 24.25. To open individual sharing files, simply choose the filename in the Sharing links area and then select Open.

Figure 24.25
The Share Resources dialog box lets you open one or all of your resource pools' sharing files.

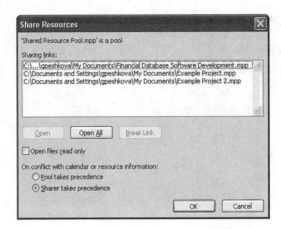

CONSULTANTS' TIPS

USING MASTER FILES

Using master project files can be a useful technique when you need to view the high-level status of multiple projects. Master files are often used for program-level information. Although this feature can be very helpful, it should be used with caution. To avoid broken links, ensure that the location of the source (sub) files inserted into the master is well maintained. In addition, if you have multiple people working on the project files, including the master, establish file-sharing policies so that the changes made to files are not overwritten.

HOW DO I TELL WHICH TASK IS FROM WHICH PROJECT WHEN THEY HAVE THE SAME NAMES?

Make sure that you only have the files that you need open; it will simplify the look of your workspace. You can also insert the Project field into your view that will help you distinguish the source of each task.

SHARING RESOURCES BETWEEN PROJECTS

If you are not using Microsoft Office Project Professional 2007 in conjunction with Microsoft Office Project Server 2007 and you work in an environment with multiple project managers, it is highly recommended that you set up a shared resource pool. Resource over-allocation problems can be some of the hardest ones to diagnose and can be really hard to detect in an isolated environment. The sharing resource pool allows you and other project managers in your organization to view where and which resources have already been allocated, contributing to a more accurate and realistic planning, tracking, and reporting.

Even if you are not sharing your resource pool with other project managers, it can be beneficial to set one up. It can save you time from re-entering the resources you use often and also predict resource availability more accurately.

CHAPTER 25

RESOLVING RESOURCE ALLOCATION PROBLEMS

In this chapter

One of the most difficult conditions facing project managers is how to identify and correct resource workload conditions. Project schedules contain tasks and resources assigned to those tasks. This chapter helps you with the following:

- Understanding how resources allocation problems can occur
- Determining how to visualize resource workload problems
- Selecting strategies to correct overallocation conditions

UNDERSTANDING HOW RESOURCE ALLOCATION PROBLEMS OCCUR

You should have a firm understanding regarding how resource allocation problems can occur. Some of the problems are driven by business goals for the project; other problems will be attributable to a lack of knowledge about a Microsoft Project 2007 feature. This chapter introduces you to a wide range of techniques and cross-references to other chapters in this book.

→ For additional information on simplified project management and tracking, **see** Chapter 2, "Microsoft Project 2007 Quick Start," **p. 29**.

→ For a discussion about detailed progress tracking, **see** Chapter 13, "Tracking Your Project Progress," **p. 443**.

25

WHY SHOULD I CARE ABOUT RESOURCE WORKLOAD CONDITIONS?

The combination of task types and resource assignments can cause overload conditions within your project schedule. As you change one conditions on a task, the various factors may combine to cause a resource overloading condition. Overloaded resources threaten the outcome of the task deliverables because a resource just cannot be in multiple places at one time. This can make your scheduled project finish date invalid.

Most schedules depend on people performing identified activities expressed as tasks within a project schedule. The performance of each resource on those tasks determines the overall success or failure of the project, so it is to your best advantage to understand how resource workload levels affect the project outcome. You may dramatically increase the risks to your project if you choose to ignore these resource allocation issues.

Your schedule probably has named resources you plan to use throughout the project life cycle. Some resources may report directly to you during the normal course of business, so you have direct responsibility to apply those resources in ways that satisfy overall project and staff management goals.

Some resources may report to other staff managers, so those resources are shared by multiple projects throughout the organization. Chances are you must negotiate to use shared resources. Therefore, you must build a compelling business case showing how those resources can advance your project goals.

Organizations often need to provide project life cycle budget forecasts. Typical financial forecasting models are done using a tool such as Microsoft Excel to show expected spending levels in the future. You can also use Microsoft Project with a resource cost structure to make these forecasts. This may be a paradigm shift for you as you consider how to use Microsoft Project 2007 instead of Excel to predict workload effort and costs for the project.

You can use the robust features of Microsoft Project 2007 to forecast resource workloads and costs for overall task delivery. These resource forecasts help you build a strong business case while also strengthening your argument to use certain shared resources that perform project task activities.

WHAT IS THE PROBLEM?

The key challenge for the project manager is to identify the resource workload conditions and then decide how to correct those conditions.

Exaggerated actual work and cost are also common problems that can occur with overloaded resources. % Complete updates to your schedule can show false or unexpected actual work and cost for any resource that is overloaded. These false data can also show unexpected errors in overall budget forecasts.

Figure 25.1 shows a simple example of an overload resource condition. Notice how the resource graph shows that the Russ resource is clearly overloaded for a period of time. If the project manager changes the % Complete on the summary task, then Actual Work and Actual Cost data are exaggerated.

Figure 25.1
A combination view of Gantt Chart and Resource Usage is a simple way to see how resources are allocated for each task within your schedule.

Another common, but less obvious, condition is the effect on your project when other project managers overload the same resources you expect to use in your project. This can cause your project unexpected high-risk conditions when the resources become unavailable because they are overbooked on other projects. You would be wise to examine the resource loading conditions of all other projects that may compete for the resources you need.

WHAT CAUSES RESOURCE OVERALLOCATION?

There are many common problems that can cause resource overallocation issues. A major cause for this condition is an arbitrary deliverable date being established or modified that must be met. Some of the other reasons are due to other normal business interests, such as competing projects, unexpected discoveries, emergency conditions, and so forth. Project managers instinctively understand these conditions, so the trick is expressing those conditions within a tool such as Microsoft Project 2007.

Many of the common problems are attributed to lack of knowledge regarding the use of Microsoft Project 2007 features, such as the following:

- Using Task Type settings that affect the way resource workload is calculated
- Not understanding the relationship between a task's Duration, Work, and Resource Units
- Creating a task assignment on more than one task during a specific overlapping time period (for example, tasks running in parallel)
- Assuming resources are 100% dedicated to each task
- Not using Microsoft Project 2007 views, groups, and filters to isolate overloaded resources
- Ignoring task links and overlapping tasks

SHOULD I IGNORE RESOURCE ALLOCATION PROBLEMS?

You can generally ignore resource allocation issues if you have the following project conditions:

- If you have dedicated teams under your complete control and they just do what you tell them
- If you are using the project to simply collect actual work by resources, i.e. time collection buckets on application support tasks
- If you have unlimited budget and no specific delivery timelines
- If your resources are generally sitting around with nothing to do

All other project conditions probably demand your attention to resource workloading conditions.

The bottom line is simple and straightforward: Ignore resource workloading conditions, and you increase the risk of facing very embarrassing project and budget failures in the future.

VISUALIZING RESOURCE ALLOCATION CONDITIONS

Microsoft Project 2007 provides several mechanisms to view and manipulate resource allocation data. This section shows you features commonly used to examine resource workload conditions, including the following:

- Resource Max Units and calendars
- Resource graphs
- Resource sheet
- Split views
- Resource usage time-phased data
- Grouping, filtering, and sorting tasks and resources
- Review task relationships

The simple example shown in Figure 25.1 will be used for the remainder of this chapter to demonstrate these concepts. You may want to create your own version of this example to follow along in the upcoming sections.

RESOURCE MAX UNITS, CALENDARS, AND OTHER SETTINGS

Each resource in your project schedule has certain settings that allow you to specify the general properties for those resources. Each one of the properties is an attribute about the resource—for example, calendar, availability dates, cost, email address, and so forth.

→ For additional information about calendars, **see** "Defining Calendars," **p. 118**.

One of those properties is called Max Units, which allows you to set a maximum capacity for resource availability. The default setting for the Max Units field is 100%. The Max Units setting does not prevent you from overloading a resource, but rather gives you a visual queue when overload conditions are present.

Figure 25.2 shows a Resource Sheet view with a list of individual named resources with a variety of settings. Max Units for Russ is set to 100%, indicating this resource is generally available as a full-time worker. Becky is set to 50%, indicating a half-time worker, and G_Implementer is a generic resource set to 500%, indicating five full-time workers are available from a general pool of system implementers.

Figure 25.2
The resource row color and font will change when the resource workloads exceed the Max Units threshold value.

Resource calendars in combination with the Max Units also affect the amount of work a resource can be scheduled to perform during a given point in time. The individual resource calendars allow you to specify the expected working schedule for the resource. The calendar settings also allow you to specify exceptions to working periods.

TIP

> Use shared resource pools to establish Max Units, working calendars, exceptions, and so forth. Then you do not have to alter every resource calendar in every schedule when resource vacations are planned. Just remember to open and resave each effected schedule to update the effected tasks. Another way to handle this shared resource condition is to use the Microsoft Project Server 2007 Enterprise Global Resource Pool features.

TIP

> Another shared resource tip: Open one project schedule and use the Resource Usage view to see all the projects related to the selected resources. Then you will see which project schedules should be updated when a resource calendar changes.

The resource calendar has a direct impact on work when you assign a resource to a task. By default, the resource calendar drives the task duration, work, or resource units. If, however, you change the task attributes to Ignore Resource Calendars, then you can create a resource overload condition. Figure 25.3 illustrates before and after conditions when you use this setting.

Each of the tasks is Fixed Work, and each resource uses a standard calendar. You can create an overload condition if you force a 12-hour-per-day calendar on each task and also set the flag for the task to ignore the resource calendars. Now each resource is forced to work longer hours per day to get the job done, thus overloading the resource allocation.

CAUTION

> Notice how the resources on the task in Figure 25.3 are now overloaded. You need to be careful about using this task feature that ignores resource calendars.

Figure 25.3
Before and after—the
task ignores resource
calendars.

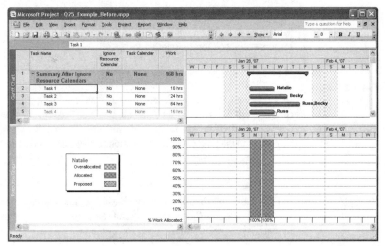

RESOURCE GRAPHS

Resource Graph views are very helpful to get a quick overview of resource workload conditions. This type of view is especially helpful when you split the window, showing the Gantt Chart view at the top and the Resource Graph in the bottom half. Figure 25.4 shows an example of a split window with the Resource Graph. The resource list in the Resource Graph changes as you select a single task or multiple tasks from the Gantt Chart view. You can easily see the overall workload conditions for each resource across a given timescale.

Figure 25.4
Split window with Resource Graph where you can use the horizontal scroll bar on the left side of the Resource Graph to switch between resources.

TIP

Remember to pan right and left in the Resource Graph's Names section to see each resource condition for the selected tasks.

CAUTION

Be aware the Resource Graph color may indicate overloading conditions, based on the current zoom factor for the time display. Microsoft Project 2007 stores data at a minute-by-minute resolution, so you may see overallocation conditions when work overlaps anywhere within the time period, such as month, week, day, and so forth.

TIP

Did you know that you can change the Resource Graph format and details if you right-click in the Resource Graph area? You can select from a variety of graph styles and color formats. Try using the Percent Allocation display.

RESOURCE SHEET

The Resource Sheet view provides a quick way to find overallocated resources, which display in red. You can inspect various resource settings such as Max Units, Standard and Overtime Rates, and Base Calendars.

You can quickly see overallocation conditions by looking for the following:

- Red-colored rows indicate that the cumulative resource workload exceeds the Max Units value in a time period.
- The information Indicators column shows a graphic icon under which you will see a warning message about leveling.
- If you display the Overallocated column and see the Yes condition, the resource is over-allocated.

Figure 25.5 shows an example of useful display features for overallocated resources.

Figure 25.5
You can drill into additional details when you double-click a resource to inspect conditions such as Availability From Units for specific date ranges, Work Time, Effective Dates for Costs, and so forth.

→ For additional information about resources, **see** Chapter 8, "Defining Project Resources," **p. 249**.

TIP

> Use the menu command Format, Text Styles to alter the display colors for overallocated resources. Try using background cell colors and font settings to highlight important resource conditions.

SPLIT VIEWS AND WINDOWS

The preceding sections show simple examples of using split views to see a combination of task and resource information. This section explores this powerful feature in greater detail.

→ For additional information about resource views, **see** "Working with Resources," **p. 271**.

You should already be familiar with the various ways to split the screen into two sections. But did you know there are several combinations of split views that are helpful for determining resource workloading conditions?

Figure 25.6 shows an example of a Resource Sheet view in the top half of the screen and with projects and task listed in the bottom half of the screen. You can see a lot of helpful information in the lower half of the screen as you navigate to each resource in the Resource Sheet. You can also see cross-references to other projects and tasks if you are using a shared resource pool.

Figure 25.6
The Resource Sheet view with Task Details is a great way to navigate each resource in the Resource Sheet.

Figure 25.7 illustrates a good use of both the Resource Sheet and Resource Graph. You can select one or more resources in the top half of the screen and then see the graph in the lower half.

Figure 25.7
You can also combine Resource Sheet and Resource Graph views in a split window, which allows you to select and view overallocation conditions for more than one resource.

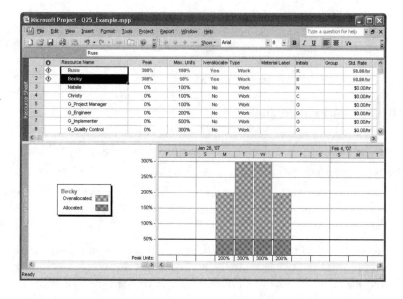

You can also use another helpful viewing method whereby you divide the Microsoft Project 2007 session screen into multiple individual windows. Figure 25.8 shows an example where the single Microsoft Project 2007 session has two windows reference the same schedule. You will notice each window's title bar has the name of the project with a suffix window number.

This window arrangement is easily created by using the menu command Window, New Window to indicate another view for this project. You can then use that same menu's Arrange Windows command so you can see each active window within the same Microsoft Project 2007 session.

A key point to understand is that when you make a change within any project window, those edit changes are applied to the project in all windows.

This multiwindow option gives you a lot of flexibility in viewing resource allocation issues.

Figure 25.8
You can use the multiple-windows feature in Microsoft Project 2007 to view resource allocation within your project schedule.

25

CAUTION

Be aware that the timescales are controlled independently in each window and are not synchronized.

RESOURCE USAGE TIME-PHASED DATA

You may be familiar with the basic Microsoft Project 2007 usage data, whereby you can drill into greater detail for resource assignments on tasks. Usage data is central to the core data about all assignments. This core data is typically called *time-phased* or *time-scaled* data and is stored within Microsoft Project 2007 at the minute-by-minute level of detail.

➔ For additional information about assigning resources to tasks, **see** "Modifying Resource Assignments," **p. 332**.

The Resource Usage view is very helpful if you need to see the details about resource allocation. You can use this view to isolate overallocation issues.

Figure 25.9 illustrates a typical Resource Usage view showing several helpful data fields. You can add data columns on the left side of the screen or add data rows to the right side. You can also split the screen to show a combination of Resource Usage and Resource Graph information. The combination of these data fields and viewing layouts gives you a lot of resource allocation information.

Figure 25.9
Adding more field columns to the Resource Usage view is a great way to combine information and analyze the resource allocation conditions.

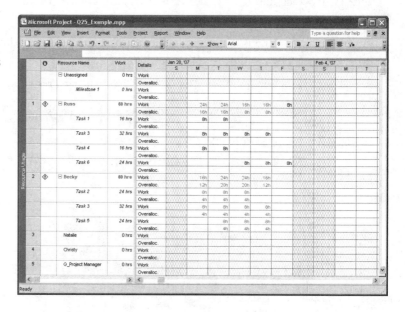

TIP

Right-click in the Resource Usage detailed data to add more data fields, change the color display, and so forth. Use the menu command Format, Text Style to show overallocated resources using special colors and font characteristics.

TIP

You can copy/paste data in the detailed data display within a usage view. Try copying data rows and then paste that data into Microsoft Excel for additional analysis. You can also use Visual Report to export data to Excel.

GROUPS, FILTERS, AND SORTING TASKS WITH RESOURCES

Microsoft Project 2007 provides several helpful features to rearrange the resource data. You can use combinations of these features to view resource overallocation conditions:

- Grouping
- Filtering
- Setting colors
- Sorting
- Resource allocation fields

Figure 25.10 shows an example of a Resource Sheet with a customized group applied. The group has some simple criteria used to rearrange resource information display with key structures at the top of the list. This group uses the data fields Overallocation, Peak (units), and sort criteria to arrange the resources in a simple view. The menu command Format, Text Style was also used to create a color schema showing overallocated resources in bold text.

Figure 25.10
You can group the list of current resources based on the overallocation and/or peak units.

→ For additional information about using groups in views, **see** Chapter 11 "Using Standard Views, Tables, Filters, and Groups to Review Your Schedule," **p. 369**.

You should consider using creative combinations of features to group, filter, and color resource information to make flexible views for analyzing resource allocation conditions.

REVIEW TASK RELATIONSHIPS

The structure you select for your activity breakdown list also has a direct impact on resource allocation. You can overload resources if you assign those resources to multiple parallel activities. You may also create resource overallocation conditions if you are using features to create task-level overlap conditions. Therefore, you should examine the task's relationships to resource assignment information.

Consider combining a task Gantt Chart view with a Resource Usage view if you want to examine overallocation issues. Figure 25.11 provides an example of viewing task relationships and resource allocation. This view uses another simple tactic—selecting multiple tasks within the top view and then scrolling through the resources in the bottom view.

Figure 25.11
Analyzing the task relationships in the top part of the split Gantt Chart view and the resource allocations in the bottom can help you determine the source of resource allocation problems.

STRATEGIES FOR CORRECTING RESOURCE ALLOCATION PROBLEMS

Microsoft Project 2007 provides several techniques you can consider for correcting certain resource overallocation conditions. You may decide to use one or more of these techniques to address the issues you observe within your project schedule. You should also know that a single feature may not provide the total solution you seek, so you may need to explore multiple strategies such as the following:

- Review the business goals
- Replace resources
- Split tasks
- Link tasks
- Adjust resource units
- Use automated resource leveling
- Use manual strategies such as assignment contouring

PROCESS CHECK: REVIEW PROJECT SCOPE AND OTHER BUSINESS ISSUES

A review of the business goals is always the first thing you should consider when you have project scheduling or resource allocation issues. Consider business conditions, such as overall project scope, budget, timeline, and so forth.

You may decide that resource overallocation is caused by intermediate or final milestone timelines, but the budget cannot withstand additional overtime costs for workers to meet those dates. This condition may cause you to simply extend the project timeline. You should use a formal change-management process to record this information as important artifacts of the project history.

The overall business issues may require that you take steps within tools such as Microsoft Project 2007 to correct these conditions. The remainder of this chapter provides guidance on strategies to address resource overallocation conditions.

REPLACING OR ADDING RESOURCES

One obvious strategy to relieve overbooked resources is to add resources or use resource-substitution techniques. You may decide to replace overloaded resources with those that have greater availability to work on specific tasks.

The first action you will take is to understand which resources could be used for substitution. You can use various viewing techniques shown in the beginning of this chapter to find the resources that are overallocated. You can then use the Microsoft Project 2007 Assign Resources feature to replace overloaded resources.

Figure 25.12 shows a simple example using the Assign Resources feature to replace one resource with another. The technique is straightforward:

1. Select the task containing the overloaded resources.
2. Use the menu command Tools, Assign Resources (or use the menu icon) to open the assignment dialog box.
3. Select the target resources for replacement and click the Replace button.
4. Select the substitution resource, optionally set the resource units, and then click OK.

Figure 25.12
You can use the Assign Resources feature to replace resources if a resource overallocation scenario occurs.

TIP

> Click the Graph button in the Resource Assignment dialog box to see Assignment Work graphs with Availability information.

You should also consider the impact to resource workloading when you replace a resource on tasks. You may accidentally overload the newly assigned resource on other tasks within your project or other projects using that same resource.

TIP

> Use the menu command Project, Filter and Using Resource to rearrange the task list to show those tasks with the overallocated resources. You can select some or all of these tasks and use the Assign Resources function to do a mass-substitution.

→ For additional information about manipulating resource assignments, **see** Chapter 10, "Scheduling Single and Multiple Resource Assignments," **p. 313**.

SPLITTING TASKS

You may find opportunities to use task slack when you examine the overall schedule critical path. One of the ways you can use task slack is to split task work into multiple segments. This technique should only be used on those tasks that do not require continuity of work and can be stopped and started easily. Figure 25.13 shows a simple example where task work activity has been split into multiple segments to correct overallocation for a specific resource. This simple example also illustrates how the critical path and related milestone can still be achieved by using this split task technique. This example shows how Becky could have started working on a task, paused on that task to do the original critical path work, then resumed work on the original task.

Figure 25.13
You can split tasks into smaller segments to lighten the work load and correct resource overallocation issues.

TIP

> You will notice that a split task condition retains the original Duration value but the finish date will move.

LINKING TASKS

A simple way to clear some resource overallocation issues is to manually change the task linkage sequence. Figure 25.14 shows a simple overallocation condition where tasks are scheduled in a parallel sequence; this parallel activity condition overloads resources.

Figure 25.14
Parallel scheduled tasks can often cause resource over-allocation.

You should review the critical path of tasks to see if you have activity slack that can be used to shift dates by linking tasks. Figure 25.15 shows the effect of linking tasks. This relieves some overallocation conditions but may have a direct impact on final milestone delivery dates.

Figure 25.15
You can also use a technique of linking tasks to solve resource overallocation issues.

25

ADJUSTING RESOURCE UNITS

You may decide to assign a single resource to multiple task-parallel activities. You must be careful to examine the resource Units factor for each of these work assignments so that you can understand resource overallocation issues.

You can use a few manual techniques to adjust the resource Units factors for resource assignments. Examples of these techniques include the following:

- Change the resource Units within the Resource Names column in a Gantt Chart, as shown in Figure 25.16.
- Split the screen and adjust the resource Units for selected tasks.
- Use the Assign Resource window to change Units.
- Use a Task Usage view to alter the resource assignment Units.
- Use a Resource Usage view to alter the resource assignment Units.

Figure 25.16
Resource Units can be adjusted to reduce overallocation conditions for specified resources.

USING THE LEVEL RESOURCES TOOLS

Microsoft Project 2007 has a specific feature called *leveling* that allows you to automatically alter resource assignment timelines, thus adjusting overall resource overallocation conditions.

The leveling feature adjusts the tasks/assignments within your schedule with two basic actions:

- Setting a delay on the task/assignment
- Splitting a task

This feature is found in the Tools, Level Resources menu. You need to understand the basic features of the Level Resources tool before you use those features to alter your schedule.

You should become familiar with every feature of the Level Resources dialog box to gain confidence before applying this tool to your project schedules. You will then recognize typical scenarios where this tool can be very helpful in solving resource overallocation conditions. Consider using the leveling features for conditions such as these:

- The schedule may have several parallel tasks, with slack, assigned to a given resource.
- You may choose to level the schedule and then later clear the leveling on selected tasks for subsequent manual intervention.
- You may choose to level task assignments within a specific date range.

You should now ask the question, What does the leveling tool do with my schedule? The resource leveling tool uses a simple strategy to reduce workload conditions for resource assignments by altering the start and finish dates. The following general actions are taken to resolve resource assignments considered overallocated compared to the Max Units setting for the resources:

- Apply a tasks or resource assignment leveling delay factor, thus adjusting the start and finish dates for a given resource on a task.
- Split a task's work activities into multiple segments, effectively moving some assigned work to the future. This action will alter the finish date for the task.

You also need to understand that the Level Resources tool has certain limitations (that is, actions it will not perform). These are summarized as follows:

- Resource assignment Work is not altered.
- Resource assignment Units are not adjusted.
- Will not make assignment changes to fully utilize resources.
- Resource calendars and Max Units settings are not modified.
- One resource is not substituted for another.
- Task Duration data fields are not directly modified.
- Task Type settings are not changed.
- Generic, budget, cost, and material resources are not leveled.
- Some combinations of resource assignments, actual work, date constraints, and so forth can create conditions that cannot be resolved by the leveling algorithm. These conditions can cause error or warning messages that you must acknowledge.
- Will not move a task/assignment to start earlier to resolve an overallocation.

TIP

Use the embedded Help button to understand details about each feature within the Level Resources dialog box. Look for the key phrase "about resource leveling."

CAUTION

> The Level Resources tool does *not* optimize resource workload conditions, so the tool will not alter a combination of factors you may desire. You may need to use manual editing techniques to tune resource assignment details beyond the automated leveling results.

The Level Resources tool has internal limitations that cannot solve certain overallocation conditions. Figure 25.17 illustrates an example of unresolved resource allocation conditions. You will need to examine these conditions and take manual action.

Figure 25.17
Unresolved resource allocation conditions.

The next section allows you to practice with some simple leveling examples so that you can learn more about this tool. You should build yourself some simple schedule examples to practice with the tool and learn about the features.

TIP

> Make a copy of your schedule and experiment with different resource leveling settings to see the effects on your schedule timeline. Try variations of the leveling settings to understand what this tool will do to the task and resource conditions. Save intermediate copies and then use the Compare Schedules Wizard to see the differences among the schedules.

SCENARIO 1: SIMPLE LEVEL EXAMPLE

Let's say you want to use the leveling tool to redistribute the workload for the Russ resource. Use the menu command Tools, Level Resources to review the defaults before clicking on the Level Now button. You may see scheduling warnings, in which case you should see a result similar to the one shown in Figure 25.18. The unresolved scheduling issues will be discussed later.

Notice how the Gantt Chart has been changed to show conditions, such as the task date shift due to leveling delays, the change to the overall critical path, possible task-split conditions, and so forth. Also notice how the lower half of the screen shows a resource assignment delay factor that adjusted the finish date for a specific resource on a specific task. These are examples of how the leveling tool might alter the resource assignments to reduce overallocation conditions.

Use the menu command Tools, Level Resources, Clear Leveling to undo the leveling delays.

> **TIP**
>
> Show the Leveling Delay column to see any delay factors applied to tasks.

Figure 25.18
Simple leveling example with default settings.

SCENARIO 2: LEVEL EXAMPLE WITHIN SLACK

This example illustrates how the leveling tool produces different results, with possible warning messages, when you restrain the solution to within the available critical path slack. Use the menu command Tools, Level Resource and then check the box titled Level Only Within Available Slack in the resulting dialog box. The purpose of this setting is to attempt to level the resources without pushing out project or intermediate milestone dates. Click Level Now to see the results.

You may have to acknowledge warning messages indicating a unique solution can not be found. Click the Skip button to watch a series of messages appear. Figure 25.19 shows an end-result example of this solution. Take some time to carefully examine task and resource assignment leveling delays. Use combination view layouts to visualize the results.

Figure 25.19
Leveling example constrained within available slack.

SCENARIO 3: CLEAR LEVELING ON SELECTED TASKS

Let's say you like some of the leveling results but you want to override certain task results. Run the leveling tool again, but this time click Clear Leveling and then select Selected Tasks. The tool will remove the leveling delay conditions from the selected tasks, so you can perform other manual operations for those resource assignments, as shown in Figure 25.20. You might then fine-tune some of the tasks by using other techniques.

Figure 25.20
Clear Leveling for selected tasks to manually change the leveling conditions.

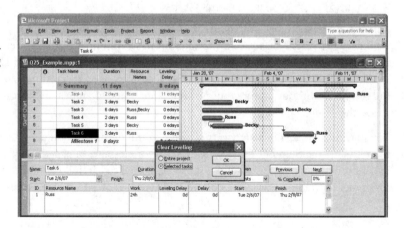

SCENARIO 4: LEVELING AFTER RESCHEDULING UNCOMPLETED WORK

Let's say your schedule is in progress and some tasks have started but are behind schedule. Furthermore, you have a business process that requires rescheduling uncompleted work into the future weeks. You may want to use the Level Resources tool after that action.

This example shows the following:

- Some actual work has been posted on certain tasks.
- Incomplete work has been rescheduled using the menu command Tools, Tracking, Update Project, "Reschedule uncompleted work after date:" (status date).
- You may have set task-level priorities and then used the leveling feature Priority, Standard.

You may want to reexamine the resource-loading issues that could have occurred as a result of these actions. You might want to use the Level Resources functions to mitigate overallocation conditions, as shown in Figure 25.21. This example focuses on the tasks assigned to Russ, so the Task Priority has been adjusted so that those tasks are considered before other tasks.

WARNING

> The leveling tool will produce different results for tasks with posted actual work. Sometimes the Clear Leveling function may not remove all leveling conditions previously established. This may cause the leveling tool to create conditions that you may not expect. You should practice leveling schedules that contain actual work.

Figure 25.21
Releveling after posting actual work.

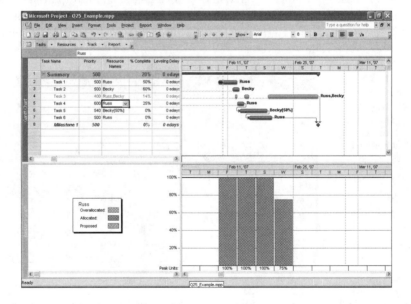

You should now have a better overall understanding of how the Level Resources tool works. Use the tips in this section and refer to the "Consultants' Tips" section at the end of this chapter for more discussion of this topic.

MANUAL STRATEGIES TO CORRECT RESOURCE ALLOCATION PROBLEMS

There are three additional manual edit strategies you can explore within Microsoft Project 2007. Each of these strategies requires a lot of detailed investigation and editing, so you should consider them as a last resort to reduce resource overallocation conditions. These strategies involve the following general features:

- Using resource assignment contour patterns to structure work
- Editing resource work details in the Usage views
- Inserting manual delays or dates for resource assignments

The following sections summarize each of these strategies.

STRATEGY 1: USE RESOURCE ASSIGNMENT CONTOURS

Microsoft Project 2007 provides a specialized set of detailed work contour patterns for each resource assignment. You can only see the contour options if you are using a Resource or Task Usage view. Figure 25.22 shows the list of predefined Work Contour settings. The standard default is Flat, but you can alter the work distribution profile by selecting one of the alternative structures.

You can use this feature if you want to set one task assignment to Front Loaded and another assignment to Back Loaded. This would allow you to redistribute the work on tasks. The Usage Work data is redistributed for the effected task, so you should carefully inspect the impact on task duration dates.

Figure 25.22
You can use the resource assignment contour profiles to help you manually level the distribution of work.

Figure 25.23 shows an example of how a single resource is initially overloaded for two tasks, shown at the top of the screen. The overallocation condition is reduced after Front Loaded and Back Loaded contours are applied. Also notice the dates for the tasks have been shifted as a result of recontouring the assigned work.

CAUTION

> The predefine work contours will redistribute all of the task work for the selected
> resource. This may result in a task duration change. You may also see unexpected results
> if you alter individual resource assignment contours on tasks that have actual work.

Figure 25.23
Resource assignments
using front and back
loading.

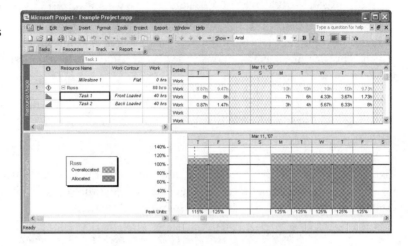

STRATEGY 2: MANUALLY EDIT RESOURCE ASSIGNMENT WORK IN USAGE VIEWS

You can also manually edit the specific work details within a Usage view to distribute the
workload on task assignments. The Indicators messages for assignments will show that data
has been edited, and the Work Contour profile will show Contoured when you perform a
manual edit on the Usage data.

Figure 25.24 shows an example of manual edits to an overloaded resource condition. This
method allows you to explicitly modify the work profile details to create any overall workloading condition you want to schedule.

Figure 25.24
Manually edited
resource assignment
work contours.

CAUTION

> Manually contoured assignment work details will be erased if you use one of the predefined contour types.

STRATEGY 3: USE MANUALLY EDITED ASSIGNMENT DELAYS AND DATES

Microsoft Project 2007 provides another method for you to set individual assignment delays or dates. You can split the screen, showing the Resource Schedule in the lower half of the screen. This view arrangement allows you to set conditions individually, such as the following:

- Resource work and units

- Assignment start and finish dates

- Assignment delay factors

Figure 25.25 illustrates this kind of view and controls, but it may take you a long time to fine-tune a result that is optimum for your situation. You will see task-split conditions if you establish delay factors or fix individual resource start dates.

Figure 25.25
Split-screen assignment edits.

CAUTION

> Certain detail edits may result in warning messages about scheduling conflicts. Edits may also create constraint date conditions that show as messages within the Indicators column.

CONSULTANTS' TIPS

This section provides some suggestions you should consider.

ESTABLISH GUIDELINES FOR RESOLVING RESOURCE ALLOCATION ISSUES

Consider establishing some general-process guidelines for project managers to resolve resource allocation conditions. The following items are recommended:

- Examine task sequence links starting from or leading to intermediate or terminating milestones. Use these milestones to establish deadlines or constraints.

- Use a standard set of multiple views and windows to review resource allocation issues. Consider using a common Global.mpt file shared among Microsoft Project 2007 users in your organization.

- Determine which edit and update strategies are most likely to produce the desired results for tracking project progress and managing resource allocation.

- Use temporary copies of schedules to practice solving resource allocation problems. Use the Compare Schedules Wizard to see the before and after details in an overlaid view.

EXAMPLES OF RESOURCE-LEVELING SCENARIOS

You may discover or wish to test many different resource-leveling scenarios. The following list should give you some ideas:

- **Scenario 1**—Use basic leveling on schedules that do not use task links of constraints.
- **Scenario 2**—Level with resources that have calendar exceptions for working periods.
- **Scenario 3**—Level tasks containing Actual Work or nonzero % Complete.
- **Scenario 4**—Level tasks with fixed-start-date or start-no-later-than-date constraints.
- **Scenario 5**—Level tasks with various Task Priority settings from 1 to 999. A variant scenario includes tasks with Priority set to 1000, meaning the leveling tool ignores these tasks.
- **Scenario 6**—Level tasks with several resource assignments that include full-time and part-time units.
- **Scenario 7**—Level tasks that ignore resource calendars.
- **Scenario 8**—Level schedules with a mix of task types, such as fixed duration, fixed work, and fixed units.

25

RECEIVING AN OVERALLOCATION CANNOT BE RESOLVED WARNING

If you are receiving an overallocation cannot be resolved warning, perform the following:

- Check for resources that are assigned over their set Max Units
- Check for constraints that prevent a task/assignment being delayed
- Remove the option Level only within available slack on the leveling dialog box

RESOURCE(S) INDICATE OVERALLOCATION CONDITION AFTER LEVELING

If your resources indicate overallocation condition after leveling, change the leveling calculation option to a smaller time interval (hour by hour).

25

CHAPTER 26

EXPORTING AND IMPORTING PROJECT DATA

In this chapter

You may occasionally have the need to exchange project data with other applications or file formats. For instance, you may have a resource list in an Excel spreadsheet you want to import into the Resource Sheet of Microsoft Project 2007 to build your project team. Or, you might need to send a simple project task list to others, but you cannot use an .mpp file because the people who need the file do not have Microsoft Project 2007. In another case, you may need to export particular project data such as actual resource hours or costs, so that other systems can use the data for reporting purposes.

This chapter covers the various forms of importing and exporting data to other applications or file formats to help you with similar situations. In some cases, you may want to consider a simple cut and paste for data exchange. Weigh the time and cost benefits of performing an elaborate import/export process, something that may be occasional or difficult. This chapter focuses on a built-in feature of Microsoft Project 2007 which uses maps to translate data from one file or application format to another. In many cases, creating a map to export data is simple for some applications, whereas creating a map to import data may be a bit more difficult. In addition, maps can be saved and reused, so the data maps may be well worth your time if you have a consistent data import or export requirement. Microsoft Project 2007 has a handy wizard to help guide you through your data mapping decisions for the various file formats or applications you may use.

In previous versions of Microsoft Project, exporting data was also useful for creating reports, but with the new visual reports feature in Microsoft Project 20007, you should consider exploring its capabilities for some of your reporting needs.

→ For additional information about visual reports, **see** "Introduction to Visual Reports," **p. 708**.

EXCHANGING PROJECT FILES ACROSS MICROSOFT PROJECT VERSIONS

First, you might wonder about sharing project files (.mpp file format) with other versions of Microsoft Office Project. Microsoft Office Project 2007 is backward compatible with many of the older versions of Microsoft Project (2000, 2002, 2003, and even 98), allowing you to open and use older versions of Microsoft Project files. When you open an older version of a project file in Microsoft Project 2007, there may be some changes to the layout, and the Gantt Chart will now appear as the new 2007 version, but all of the schedule's data from the previous version will be included.

If you have created a file in Microsoft Project 2007, you will have two options to open it later with an older version of Microsoft Project. First, you can simply save your project as a 2007 version, and then open it with an older version of Microsoft Project. If you do open the 2007 project with an older version, Microsoft Project will warn you that you are opening a newer version file, and you will need to download a converter, as shown in Figure 26.1. The warning box will open Internet Explorer and take you to the Microsoft site for the download.

Figure 26.1
In order to open a Microsoft Project 2007 file with an older version of Microsoft Project, you must download the converter from the Microsoft Office website.

This file was created by a newer version of Microsoft Project and a converter is needed to open it. Do you want to download the converter from the Microsoft Office Web site?

Yes   No

<blockquote>
CAUTION

At the time of writing this book, the converter to open Microsoft Project 2007 files in Microsoft Project 2003 was unavailable. Converters for opening Microsoft Project 2007 files are expected to be available during the last quarter of 2007.
</blockquote>

Your other option when you need to open a Microsoft Project 2007 file in an older version of Microsoft Project is to save your project file into the 2000–2003 format while you are in Microsoft Project 2007. When you select this option, Microsoft Project will warn you that this format may leave data out due to incompatible features, as shown in Figure 26.2. You will have the choice of continuing with saving your file or canceling the save operation.

Figure 26.2
Microsoft Project 2007 warns you about the changes that will be made to your 2007 version file when you try to save it to the 2000–2003 format.

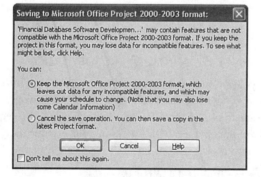

Saving to Microsoft Office Project 2000-2003 format:

'Financial Database Software Developmen...' may contain features that are not compatible with the Microsoft Office Project 2000-2003 format. If you keep the project in this format, you may lose data for incompatible features. To see what might be lost, click Help.

You can:

○ Keep the Microsoft Office Project 2000-2003 format, which leaves out data for any incompatible features, and which may cause your schedule to change. (Note that you may also lose some Calendar Information)

○ Cancel the save operation. You can then save a copy in the latest Project format.

OK   Cancel   Help

☐ Don't tell me about this again.

26

<blockquote>
CAUTION

When you save a 2007 version file to the 2000–2003 format, you will lose any data in Microsoft Project 2007 fields that are not available in the older versions. This includes anything entered as a Cost or Budget Resource. These resources will be changed to either work or material resources, depending on how you set them up in your 2007 version. In addition, fields in the 2007 version, but not in the 2003 version, will be included as "unavailable" with the values listed as "NA" when viewing them in Microsoft Project 2003.
</blockquote>

→ For additional information about compatibility of other versions of Microsoft Project, **see** "Version Compatibility," **p. 584**.

EXCHANGING MICROSOFT PROJECT DATA WITH OTHER APPLICATIONS

Sharing information with other Microsoft Office applications, such as Excel, Word, Access, and Visio, is easy in Microsoft Project 2007. There are several alternatives for sharing project data between the different applications.

First, you can use the Copy and Paste commands to transfer project data into any of the Microsoft Office programs and many other applications as well. You should use this method for simple and occasional data transfer. However, remember that when you paste an entire task row of data from Microsoft Project, you retain the data in the fields, but lose some of the calculation capabilities that exist in Microsoft Project (such as Duration * Resource Units = Work). And if you copy and paste task data from another application (such as Excel), Project will start applying its pertinent calculations to key fields.

→ For additional information about using Copy and Paste in Microsoft Project, **see** Chapter 27, "Manipulating Data Using Other Applications," **p. 959**.

You may be using a particular file format or a particular application to exchange data. In most cases (importing tasks from Outlook uses its own method), when you start the import or export process, Microsoft Project 2007 provides an import/export wizard that can help you map fields between Microsoft Project 2007 and other applications such as Excel or other file formats such as text- or comma-delimited. Later sections in this chapter discuss the wizard and other methods for exchanging data with applications such as Excel, Outlook, and other file formats such as Text and XML.

IMPORTING MICROSOFT PROJECT DATA INTO MICROSOFT VISIO

In Microsoft Visio 2007, you can import Microsoft Project 2007 data into either a Timeline view or a Gantt Chart view. These options can be very useful when you want to create reports and you do not want to use all of your options in Microsoft Project 2007, or when you want to be able to share information with others in your organization who do not have Microsoft Project installed on their desktops but do have Visio available.

Follow these steps to open the Import Timeline Wizard:

1. Open Microsoft Visio 2007 and from the top menu select Data, Insert Data Solutions, Timeline. This will open the first screen of the Import Timeline Wizard. Use the Browse button to find the Project data you would like to import. Click the Next button when you have found your project.

2. The next screen gives you the option of what kind of task types you want to include: All, top level tasks only, Milestone only, Summary tasks only, or Top level tasks and milestones, as shown in Figure 26.3. Each can be useful in its own way to create reports. In this example, the option Top level tasks and milestones has been selected. Click the Next button to move to the next screen.

Figure 26.3
You can select the task types you want to include in your Visio report using the Import Timeline Wizard.

3. The next screen gives you some options to configure the look of your timeline. You can change how the timeline looks, the appearance of milestones, and how the intervals are represented. You have four or five options for each shape, so you may want to experiment with them at first until you decide which option meets the requirements of your report. In this example, the default shapes are used. Click the Next button to continue to the next wizard screen.

4. In this last screen, you can see which options you have selected—your timeline type, your timescale type, your filter type, and the name of your source file, as shown in Figure 26.4. This is your last chance to review your choices and go back and make changes before Visio creates your timeline. Click the Finish button when you are ready to create your Timeline report.

Figure 26.4
The last screen of the Import Timeline Wizard displays all of the options you selected.

26

TIP

> The Microsoft Project 2007 application may become the active window when it pulls the data needed to create your timeline or Gantt Chart in Visio. If you end up looking at a Microsoft Project file, expecting to see a Visio report, you might need to minimize Microsoft Project to find Visio behind it.

After the data is imported into Visio using an import wizard, you may need to make some adjustments to get the exact look you need, as shown in Figure 26.5. You can easily move around the tasks and milestones, or remove them to simplify as necessary. However, you will want to make sure your information remains true to the project data when making changes to the Visio drawing.

Figure 26.5
Because of the small size of the Visio drawing, you will probably have a lot of data stacked on top of other data, and you will need to move some information around to make it more readable.

In addition to creating a timeline, you can also create a Gantt Chart with Visio. Follow these steps to bring up a Gantt Chart view in Visio:

1. Open Visio 2007 and in the top menu select Data, Insert Data Solutions, Gantt Chart. This opens the Import Project Data Wizard. On the first screen, you have two choices. You can either open a preexisting project file or create a Gantt Chart by entering information. Creating your own Gantt Chart involves entering task information into an Excel spreadsheet and will not be covered here. Select the option of using a preexisting project file and click the Next button to continue.

2. The next screen of the Import Project Data Wizard allows you to pick your data format—Microsoft Office Project File, Microsoft Office Excel File, Text File, or MPX File. In this example, the Microsoft Office Project file has been selected. Click the Next button to continue to the next screen.

3. On this screen, use the Browse button to find which Project file you wish to use; select it and click Open. Click the Next button.

4. The fourth screen allows you to choose the timescale that Visio will use to display your Gantt Chart. Choose the Major units (Days, Weeks, Months, Quarters, or Years), the Minor units (Hours, Days, or Weeks), and the Duration option (Weeks, Days, Hours, Days Hours, Weeks Days, or Weeks Hours). In this example, the defaults have been left selected, as shown in Figure 26.6. The Advanced button allows you to make formatting changes to your task bars, milestones, and summary bars. Click the Next button to continue.

Figure 26.6
You can select the Major and Minor units in the timescale, and the format for the Duration options using the Import Project Data Wizard.

5. The next screen allows you to choose which task types you want to include, and is identical to the screen used to import Timescale data into Visio, as shown previously in Figure 26.3. Similarly, this example uses the Top Level Tasks and Milestones option. Click the Next button to continue to the next screen.

6. The last screen in the Import Project Data Wizard is identical to the last screen of the Import Timeline Wizard, shown previously in Figure 26.4. This screen displays all of the choices you have selected to set up your Gantt Chart, and allows you to go back and make any changes. Click the Finish button to create your new Gantt Chart.

The Visio Gantt Chart looks similar to the Microsoft Project Gantt Chart, showing the ID, task name, start date, finish date, and duration, plus the Gantt Chart itself, as shown in Figure 26.7. Visio will try to fit the Gantt Chart into the best layout possible. To make changes to the Gantt Chart, use the Gantt Chart floating toolbar. It allows you to link and unlink tasks, create new tasks, and indent or outdent tasks. You can also move the chart around the drawing and resize it as necessary.

26

Figure 26.7
The Gantt Chart created in Visio using Microsoft Office Project 2007 data looks similar to the Gantt Chart in Microsoft Project 2007.

FILE FORMATS SUPPORTED BY MICROSOFT OFFICE PROJECT 2007

Although you will almost always save your files as Microsoft Project 2007 files (.mpp files) for your usual project operations, occasionally you may want to use a different file format for opening and saving project data using the File, Open and File, Save As commands. When you select one of these other file formats presented when using one of the commands, you can open, read, write, and save project data into formats other than the .mpp Microsoft Project 2007 format.

All Microsoft Project 2007 nonnative file formats can only support a portion of the Microsoft Project data, and you will use the Import/Export Wizard and the mapping process to guide you through setting up the fields for data exchange as described in the section "Working with Import/Export Maps to Select Your Project Data." You might also use the same process for just selecting particular fields in Microsoft Project 2007 to export. Some file formats, such as Excel Workbook, allow you to transfer an Excel template of basic project data or all project data (by selecting the Add All button during the mapping process). The process of selecting how you want to exchange project data is described in the section "Working with Import/Export Maps to Select Your Project Data." If you plan to use a nonnative file format for exporting project data, you should experiment with it to understand its capabilities and limitations.

→ For additional information about the different file formats supported in Microsoft Office Project 2007, **see** Chapter 18, "Managing Project Files," **p. 581**.

As of version 2007, Microsoft Project no longer supports using import/export maps with Microsoft Access. Data transfer between Microsoft Project and Access will now occur though simple cut-and-paste operations or through the use of visual reports. Also, Microsoft Office Project 2007 does not support exporting to HTML.

→ For additional information about visual reports, **see** "Introduction to Visual Reports," **p. 708**.

WORKING WITH IMPORT/EXPORT MAPS TO SELECT YOUR PROJECT DATA

Import/export maps specify which tables and fields from a foreign data format correspond to the correct tables and fields in Microsoft Project's native format. You can use the predefined maps, but you can also set up your own map, defining tables to match Microsoft Project 2007. In some file formats, you can only export selected fields from the project file, such as with text formats. Although in other cases, such as with the Excel file format, you can save almost the entire project. It may be impractical to do this, so you may choose instead to save selected information. For instance, if a fellow project manager asked for only a few fields such as a simple list of task names, scheduled work, and actual work from your project, you could save just the requested data from your project into an Excel format using the Export Wizard and an export map.

NOTE

When exporting all project data to a Microsoft Excel format by selecting the Add All button, you may receive a warning that the project contains too many fields. The maximum number of fields to be imported is 255.

When selecting fields of project data using one of the export formats, you will use an export map to define which of the fields you want to export from Microsoft Project 2007. An example of this process is shown in Figure 27.11. You will also need to name the table or tables where the fields will be stored.

If you make changes to the values in another format when exporting it, and then import the data back into Microsoft Project 2007, you will need to make sure you use the same map, or set up a new one with the same changes you made when exporting. This import map will help Microsoft Project 2007 know where the data being imported needs to be inserted within the Microsoft Project 2007 data structure.

NOTE

Time-phased data cannot be imported from or exported to Microsoft Project 2007 using the import/export maps.

26

TIP

In Microsoft Project 2007, only four file formats use maps when you are exporting data:

- Microsoft Excel Workbook (*.xls)
- Microsoft Excel PivotTable (*.xls)
- Text (Tab Delimited) (*.txt)
- CSV (Comma Delimited) (*.csv)

In the previous versions of Microsoft Project, additional formats were supported and used the export maps. Those options are no longer available.

However, when importing data back into Microsoft Project 2007, you have three additional data type options that use maps:

- Project Databases (*.mpd)
- Microsoft Access Databases (*.mdb)
- XML Format (*.xml)

UNDERSTANDING IMPORT/EXPORT MAPS

You can define three tables when building your own import/export map:

- An assignment table for values matching Microsoft Project 2007 assignment fields
- A resource table for values matching Microsoft Project 2007 resource fields
- A task table for values matching Microsoft Project 2007 task fields

For each table in a map, you must specify the field name in Microsoft Project 2007 and the equivalent data location in the foreign format. You can add all of the Microsoft Project 2007 fields to a table or add the same set of fields from an already defined table in Microsoft Project using the Option button.

When exporting maps, you can select a subset of tasks or resources in the project using the predefined filters.

→ For additional information about predefined filters, **see** "Understanding Filtering and Grouping," **p. 399**.

When building import maps, you must decide how the imported data will fit into an open Microsoft Project 2007 file. You have three options, as follows:

- You can insert your imported records into a new Microsoft Project 2007 document. A new .mpp file will be created with the field values you have chosen. This is a standard .mpp file with no links to the source of the imported data. When you save it, the source data is not updated.
- Your imported records can be appended to the tasks, resources, and assignments that already exist in the open project file. These new tasks, resources, and assignments will be added below the existing corresponding fields.

26

- You can have your imported values merged into the existing project to update the existing tasks, resources, or assignments. If you use this option, Microsoft Project 2007 will attempt to match the records being imported with those in the current file. You will have to define one field as the key field when matching the records. For instance, you could be importing resource names and standard rates to update the pay rates for resources on the project team. In such a situation, you would most likely use the resource name as the key field.

CAUTION

The default installation of Microsoft Project 2007 will not allow you to save a project file in xls format. Unless you change the Legacy Formats option to Allow loading files with legacy or non default file formats under Tools, Options, Security tab, you will get an error message stating "You are trying to save a file in an older file format. Your settings do not allow you to save the file in older file formats. To change your setting, navigate to the "Security" tab in the Options dialog box."

Import/export maps may be used for different file formats. If you create a map for importing data from Excel, you can use the same map to import data from a text file. Keep in mind that different file formats can often convert non-text fields into different field types and values.

NOTE

If you decide to save Microsoft Project 2007 data into a non–Microsoft Project format, Microsoft Project 2007 will change the options shown on the import/export map to match the format you have selected. If, for instance, you choose Save As for a text format and then use an import/export map designed for working with an Excel workbook, then the workbook options will be replaced with text options.

26

Caution is advised when importing data into Microsoft Project 2007 using a map. Maps are designed for one database or worksheet, with specific tables or fields that might not work in another data source. Be sure to check the structure of the map before using it to import data.

When import/export maps are created, they are saved in the GLOBAL.MPT file instead of the active project file. To change the name of a map, you do not need to use the Organizer; you can change the map name when you are editing it. You will, however, have to use the Organizer if you want to delete a map.

TIP

If you want to share a map with other users, use the Organizer to copy your map into an open project file and then save the project. Other users who can open your project file can copy the map to their GLOBAL.MPT files using the Organizer.

→ For additional information about the Organizer and the GLOBAL.MPT file, **see** Chapter 18, "Managing Project Files," **p. 581**.

REVIEWING THE PREDEFINED IMPORT/EXPORT MAPS

Microsoft Office Project 2007 contains 10 predefined import/export maps. They are listed and described in Table 26.1.

TABLE 26.1   PREDEFINED IMPORT/EXPORT MAPS

Map	Description
"Who Does What" report	Exports a table that lists resources and their task assignments
Compare to Baseline	Exports a table that lists all tasks with scheduled and baseline values
Cost Data by Task	Exports a table that lists task costs
Default Task Information	Exports or imports the basic task fields included in the Task Entry table
Earned Value Information	Exports the task's earned value fields
Resource "Export Table" map	Exports all the fields in the predefined resource's Export table
Task "Export Table" map	Exports all the fields in the predefined task's Export table
Task and Resource PivotTable report	Creates Excel PivotTables for tasks and resources
Task List with Embedded Assignment Rows	Exports a table of tasks and their assigned resources
Top Level Tasks list	Exports tables with data for tasks at the top outline level

The next sections of this chapter discuss each map in more detail, covering how they were created and how to get the most efficient use out of them. Each of these maps was designed to export data from Microsoft Project 2007 into another format. While some were designed for specific file formats, any map can be used to export any format. Of course, they work best when used with the format for which they were created. Some of the maps were also designed for importing, but can be used to export. Take caution when using any map to import data because you may receive an unexpected result.

NOTE

> Microsoft Project 2007 exports values for duration and work fields as text and not as numeric data. Microsoft Project 2007 will attach a time unit as part of the text value, such as "5d" representing 5 days.

Any time you exchange data using an import/export map with a file of another format, the external file supplying or receiving the data will be added to the list of recently used files, shown at the bottom of the File menu in Microsoft Project 2007. For instance, if you exported data to an Excel worksheet named EarnedValue.xls using the Earned Value Information map, you will find an entry titled EarnedValue.xls. You can then click on this file listing and Microsoft Project 2007 will import the Excel file EarnedValue.xls, copying its data into a Microsoft Project 2007 document, using the Earned Value Information map when deciding which fields will receive the imported data.

All of the Microsoft Project 2007 predefined import/export maps place imported data into a new Microsoft Project 2007 document by default. Clicking the aforementioned link causes Microsoft Project 2007 to create a new document with Excel data in it. You should not save this project file when you are finished, because it is built on a map designed for exporting (and not importing), and it is not a complete project file.

Imported data placed in a new Microsoft Project 2007 document does little harm because it is a new document and you can simply close it. On the other hand, imported maps can also be set up to append imported data into an active file, or merge the imported information to an existing task or resource record. This will update the existing field values with data from external documents. When the map in the file listing is set to append or merge, activating the file listing will alter the data in your open document when you click the listing. If there is any unsaved data in your active document, you might lose some or all of your changes when opening the listing on the File menu.

CAUTION

> Use caution when opening a foreign-format map file from the File menu. Imported data can alter active, open projects in unexpected ways. Always save any active document before opening a foreign-format map file, to be on the safe side.

USING THE "WHO DOES WHAT" REPORT MAP

A good use of the "Who Does What" report is to export Microsoft Project 2007 data to an Excel format using the map. It is similar to the printable "Who Does What" report you will find by selecting Report, Reports, Assignments, Who Does What. The Excel spreadsheet, similar to the Resource Usage view in Microsoft Project 2007, shows the list of resource names and task assignment names, in the same column, but does not indent the assignment names under their resource names. Included under each assignment are columns for Start, Finish, and Scheduled_Work field values. The exported data for the Scheduled_Work field is text data, instead of numerical, and the unit "hrs" is added as part of the text value.

Although this map works well when saving to an Excel spreadsheet format, you can also save to a text or comma-separated values (CSV) file. If you save it to one of these formats, your resource rows will be identical to the assignment rows and the data is separated by a tab (default selection) or another separator that you specified, such as a space or a comma. These two formats are useful when you plan on importing the data into another system or a database.

26

TIP

> When saving your data to an Excel, text, or CSV format, you should change the Who Does What report map, adding the field named Assignment to the table, to help distinguish resource names from task assignment names. The resource rows in the list have No in the Assignment field, whereas the assignment rows have Yes. By applying Excel's conditional formatting, you can bold the resource rows, because of the No value found in the Assignment column. For more information, see the section "Exporting Microsoft Project 2007 Data to an Excel Worksheet" later in this chapter.

USING THE COMPARE TO BASELINE MAP

The Compare to Baseline map exports a table titled Baseline Comparison, which lists all tasks, including their start and finish dates, plus their scheduled, baseline, and variance values for duration, work, and cost. This map works the same for spreadsheet and text formats.

USING THE COST DATA BY TASK MAP

The Cost Data by Task map exports a table titled Task Costs, which lists all of the tasks (fixed cost, cost, baseline cost, cost variance, actual cost, and remaining costs), plus their cost values.

USING THE DEFAULT TASK INFORMATION MAP

The Default Task Information map exports or imports basic task fields that are included in the Task Entry table: ID, Name, Duration, Start Date, Finish Date, Predecessors, and Resource Names. This map will work the same for all file formats.

USING THE EARNED VALUE INFORMATION MAP

The Earned Value Information map exports the earned value fields for tasks into any file format. This includes Task ID, Task Name, BCWS, BCWP, ACWP, SV, CV, Cost (EAC), Baseline Cost (BAC), and VAC.

USING THE RESOURCE EXPORT TABLE MAP

The Resource Export Table map exports the fields included in the predefined resource's Export table. This Export table is an inclusive list of 24 resource fields, covering the definition of the resources, as well as scheduled, baseline, and tracking sums for work and cost for each resource.

USING THE TASK EXPORT TABLE MAP

The Task Export Table map exports almost all of the fields included in the predefined task's Export table. This Export table contains over 70 fields, including the task definition fields: values for scheduled, baseline, actual work, cost, duration, start, and finish, as well as several user-defined fields, such as cost, duration, number, and flag.

Using the Task and Resource PivotTable Map

The Task and Resource PivotTable map will create an Excel document with two PivotTables summarizing the total costs of the resource assignments. Each PivotTable is organized by resource groups, and in each group by resource name. Four sheets will be included in each Excel file:

- The Tasks sheet provides all of the data for the Task PivotTable and includes the following columns: Resource Group, Resource Name, Task Name(s), Duration, Start, Finish, and Cost. If you have outlined your project, a Task Name column for each outline level will be included, plus all summary task names for a subtask will appear on the row for the subtask. Outline level 1 summary tasks will be placed in a column named Task Name1, outline level 2 summary tasks will be placed in a column named Task Name2, and so on.

- The Task PivotTable sheet displays, for each resource group, the tasks that each resource in the group is assigned, plus the task duration, start, and finish. Cost for each assignment is the PivotTable's Data field, and includes summary costs for each task and summary task, for each resource, and for each resource group.

- The Resources sheet lists data for the Resource PivotTable and includes the Resource Group, Resource Name, Work, and Cost fields.

- The Resource PivotTable displays the work and cost totals for each resource group and each resource within the group. Totals are not broken down by task.

NOTE

> When a project has more than two outline levels, Microsoft Project 2007 will create data sheets and PivotTables, but cannot lay out the fields for the Task PivotTable, which causes that sheet to appear empty. To fix this, you will have to manually lay them out in Excel. To do this, select all the information in the Tasks data sheet you want to include as part of the PivotTable and click Insert. Next, click the PivotTable button. From here, you can select where you want the PivotTable to be created. You will most likely want to create a new worksheet and click OK. A new blank PivotTable will appear where you can drag and drop the fields you want included into the PivotTable.

26

You can read more about working with PivotTables later in this chapter, in the section, "Exporting Microsoft Project 2007 Data to an Excel PivotTable."

Using the Task List with Embedded Assignment Rows Map

The Task List with Embedded Assignment Rows map exports a table of tasks and their assigned resources. The best use of this map is for exporting a table that includes all of the resource assignments for each task, along with the Work, Duration, Start, Finish, and % Work Complete fields for each assignment. In addition to using this map to export to Excel, you can also use it for the text and CSV formats.

USING THE TOP LEVEL TASKS LIST MAP

The Top Level Tasks map exports a table showing only the outline level 1 tasks. This includes the following fields: Task ID, Name, Duration, Start, Finish, % Complete, Cost, and Work. This map works with all file formats.

CREATING AND USING AN EXPORT MAP

An export map is easier to create than an import map, because Microsoft Project 2007 field names are the source of the data, and it is easy to create field names in the target format similar to Microsoft Project 2007 field names. It can be much harder to relate imported field names in the source format with the field names in Microsoft Project 2007.

The following steps take you through creating an export map by using an example of exporting Microsoft Project 2007 cost data to an Excel worksheet:

1. Open the Microsoft Project 2007 file containing the data you want exported.
2. In the top menu, select File, Save As.
3. Choose the directory location from the Save In list box.
4. In the Save as Type list box, select Microsoft Excel Workbook (*.xls).

TIP

> If you plan to add data to overwrite an existing document, you should create a copy of your document for testing as you create your new map. If there are problems, you will not lose your previously saved document, and if your map works as planned, you can keep the newly created document and delete the previously saved version.

5. Click the Save button to open the Export Wizard dialog box.
6. Click the Next button to open the Data dialog box.
7. Choose the Selected Data option and click the Next button. This will open the Map dialog box.
8. Choose the New Map option and click the Next button. This will open the Map Options dialog box.
9. Choose one or more data types to be exported: tasks, resources, or assignments. Since this is being exported to an Excel file, you also have the options of exporting the headers and including assignment rows. In Figure 26.8, all three have been selected, and the Export Includes Headers option has been selected as well.
10. Click the Next button to open the Task Mapping dialog box.
11. Enter a name for your table into the Destination Worksheet Name field. The more descriptive the name for your table, the easier it will be to remember what you built it for later on.

Figure 26.8
You can select which type of data table you want to create with the Map Options dialog box in the Export Wizard.

12. You can limit any of the tasks being exported by selecting one of the filters in the Export Filter field. You can choose any of the Microsoft Project's predefined filters, or any you might have defined ahead of time, but you cannot design a new filter at this point. If you find you need a filter that is not included in the list, you will have to cancel out of the Export Wizard, create your new filter, and then start again at the beginning of the Export Wizard in step 1.

→ For additional information about creating filters, **see** "Creating and Customizing Filters," **p. 785**.

13. You will now need to define which task fields you want to export in the mapping table. List each of the fields you want to be exported in the From: Microsoft Office Project Field column.

    You can use the drop-down menus listing Microsoft Project's predefined fields by clicking on the cell that displays the Click Here to Map a Field prompt, as shown in Figure 26.9. Once you have selected a data field, you can click on the corresponding cell under To: Excel Field, and Microsoft Project will automatically create a name for your worksheet field, as shown in Figure 26.10.

14. Once you have chosen the fields you will be exporting from the list of Microsoft Project fields, you can either press the Enter key after selecting each field, press the Tab key on your keyboard, or click on the corresponding To: Excel Field cell. Any of these will insert a default field name into the cell. You can see a sample of the fields you have added and their data in the Preview box below the mapping table.

    You can change your export field name if you want, instead of using the name supplied by the Microsoft Project 2007. If you do, however, make sure that you do not violate any of the field-naming rules for the format you are creating, such as using periods, exclamation points, or square brackets.

26

Figure 26.9
Name your destination document and choose an Export filter in the Task Mapping page of the Export Wizard.

Enter a name for this table

Choose a predefined filter here

Figure 26.10
Choose which fields you will be exporting with the Task Mapping page of the Export Wizard.

Drop-down list of Microsoft Project's field names

Names for exported fields

Move selected field up or down in the list

Tools to help manage the field list

Sample data for selected fields

15. Several buttons can help you manage the field mapping table, as shown in Figure 26.10:

   - If you need to move a field row in the list, highlight the row you want to move and use the Move arrows to the right of the mapping table. They will move the row up or down the list.

   - Use the Add All button to insert all of the Microsoft Project 2007 task fields. Microsoft Project 2007 has a limitation of 255 fields for exporting. If you are selecting several tables, you will want to use this selection with caution. If your selection exceeds 255 fields, the Export Wizard will display an error message and you will be required to decrease the number of fields in the map.

- Use the Clear All button to clear the mapping table.

- Use the Insert Row button if you need to place a blank row into the middle of the list. Select a row, click the Insert Row button, and all of the rows will move down to create an empty row above the one you selected.

- Use the Delete Row button to remove a field row.

- You can add a predefined map to your mapping table by using the Base on Table button. Clicking this button will pull up a list of the Microsoft Project 2007 defined task tables in the Select Base for Field Mapping dialog box, as shown in Figure 26.11. Choose which table you want to use and click OK. Any entries previously made in the mapping table will be cleared and the fields defined in the table you choose will be placed in the mapping table instead.

Predefined list of task tables

Figure 26.11
The Select Base Table for Field Mapping dialog box will let you fill in your mapping table with one of the Microsoft Project 2007 predefined tables.

16. Once you have finished with the task mapping table, click the Next button to move on to the next table to include in the export. Since all three data types were chosen for this example (refer to Figure 26.8), your next window is the Resource Mapping page, shown in Figure 26.12. You will need to fill out this mapping table by repeating steps 11 through 15. Click the Next button to continue through the wizard.

17. Your next page will be the Assignment Mapping page, because this example used all three types of data. When building your own export map, you may or may not use this many steps. Filling out the assignment mapping field is like using the first two mapping fields. Assignment records are created from combined task and resource cost summaries. Since there is no table in Microsoft Project 2007 for assignments (they appear in the Task Usage and Resource Usage views, and some other forms), you will not be able to select a table as a template for the fields to be included. There are also no filters defined for assignments. You will notice that both of these options are grayed out.

26

Resource table name

Figure 26.12
You can define the
resource mapping
table the same way
you defined the task
mapping table.

Sample data for chosen fields

18. Once you have finished with the Assignment Mapping page, click the Next button. You will now see the End of Map Definition page.

19. Click the Save Map button to open the Save Map dialog box, as shown in Figure 26.13.

Names of existing maps

Figure 26.13
It is always a good
idea to save your
map, even if you do
not plan to use it
again. This will save
you from having to
create it again.

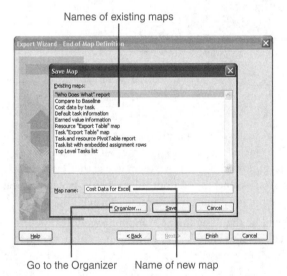

Go to the Organizer   Name of new map

20. Enter a name for your map in the Map Name field and click the Save button. This will return you to the End of Map Definition dialog box. You should use a descriptive name to help you remember why you created this map.

21. Click the Finish button to export your chosen data to a new Excel document.

TIP

> When you are building a map for one file format, such as Excel in the last example, and then use the same map to exchange data with another application in a different format, such as text, you will get varying results. For example, the formatting in the Excel format will be lost and depending on the separator chosen, each data field will be separated by the designated delimiter (tab, space, or comma). For specialized maps such as the one you just created, it is a good idea to include the application type in the map name, as shown in Figure 26.13.

TIP

> If you are planning on using your export map later to import data into Microsoft Project 2007, as described in the next section, you should include the Unique ID field in your export. Since the Unique ID number will not change after a task has been created, this makes it a very reliable key field when importing data at a later time.

CREATING AND USING AN IMPORT MAP

If you want to import data into Microsoft Office Project 2007 from another source application, you will need to either find a workable import map or create your own. If the data was exported from Microsoft Project 2007 originally, you can import your data with the same map you used to export it. You can also edit your export map if you want to make some changes and then save it as a new import map.

Your options for an import map are a little different from those used when building an export map:

- Your source tables are already defined, unlike in the export map, where you had to define your target tables. There may be, for instance, several tables in the source document with task information included in them. You will have to select which table contains the task data you need. You will also have to identify the source tables appropriate for supplying your resource or assignment fields.

  If your source was created with an export map, it will be easier to import it back into Microsoft Project 2007 because the field names will be recognizable. If your source table was created by some application other than Microsoft Project 2007, you will have to match your field names with Microsoft Project 2007 internal fields.

- Microsoft Project 2007 will filter data during an import. If you only want to include some of the records from your source, you will have to filter the source first to create a new data source document and then import it into Microsoft Project 2007. Otherwise, you will have to import all of the data into Microsoft Project 2007 and then delete the necessary data.

- When you are using an import map, you can select whether you want the imported data to be stored in a new project file or inserted into an existing one. You can add the imported records to information that already exists in Microsoft Project 2007, or you can merge the imported data, using it to update selected fields for already existing tasks or resources.

26

As an example for importing from another file format, you will see how to import the cost Excel spreadsheet created earlier in the section "Creating and Using an Export Map."

If you want to add your imported data to an existing project, you will need to open that project before beginning the import process. If you do not want to add your imported data to an existing project, it will not matter which project documents are open, because Microsoft Project 2007 will create a new document. Follow these steps to import data using an import map:

1. In Microsoft Project 2007, select File, Open.

2. Choose the location of your data source in the Look In list box. If importing from an ODBC data source, click the ODBC button instead, and choose the data source in that dialog box, as shown in Figure 26.14.

Figure 26.14
The Select Data Sources dialog box allows you to select external data sources to import data into Microsoft Project 2007.

3. In the Files of Type list box, choose the format of your data source.

4. Select the data source file from the file list and click the Open box. This will open the Import Wizard dialog box.

5. Click the Next button to move to the Map dialog box.

6. Choose the Use Existing Map option, as shown in Figure 26.15. To create a new import map, choose the New Map option, then follow the techniques shown for creating an export map in the previous section "Creating and Using an Export Map." Click the Next button to move to the Map Selection dialog box.

7. Choose the map you wish to use to import your data. Be careful choosing a map; it will define the way you import your data. In this example, the export map created in the previous section, "Creating and Using an Export Map," is used to import the data. Click Next to move to the Import Mode dialog box.

Figure 26.15
You can either create a new map from scratch and select the tables and fields to include in the import or use an existing map in Microsoft Project 2007.

8. You have three options in the Import Mode dialog box: Import your file As a new project, Append the data to the active project, and Merge the data into the active project. Once you have decided which of these options works best for you, click the Next button to move to the Map Options dialog box.

9. Select the types of data you want to import: Tasks, Resources, or Assignments. If you are using an export map you have already set up to import your data, Microsoft Project 2007 will enter this data for you, although you can amend it if you choose. Once you are finished, click the Next button.

> **TIP**
>
> If you are importing an existing text delimited document, you will only be able to choose a single type of data to import (Task, Resources, or Assignments). You will be prompted with radio buttons instead of check boxes when importing other formats. You can read more about importing text delimited documents later in this chapter, in the section, "Working with Text File Formats."

26

10. Microsoft Project 2007 will now open the Mapping dialog box for the first type of data you chose in step 9. So, if you selected to import task data, Microsoft Project 2007 will open the Task Mapping dialog box.

11. Look through the Mapping dialog box for each type of data that is being imported to make sure your settings are exact. You can check the list of names in the Source worksheet name field to confirm that the right table has been chosen for the type of data in each Mapping dialog box.

As you can see in Figure 26.16, the Task Mapping dialog box for the importing map is the same as the export map created in the previous section. The Source Worksheet Name list has been highlighted to show the tables available.

Figure 26.16
The mapping fields box that you set up as an export map has a few different options when it is used as an import map.

Source data table names

12. Click the Next button to move to the Resource Mapping or Assignment Mapping dialog boxes. Confirm your settings in each of these.

13. If you decided to merge your imported data, the Set Merge Key button will appear on each of the Task, Resource, and Assignment Mapping dialog boxes. You must use this merge key button in each of the Mapping dialog boxes you have active. Merge Key is a field with identical values in both the existing Microsoft Project 2007 file and the imported tables. The task ID field, for instance, matches tasks as long as the task list has not been changed since the data was exported. This is why you should use the Unique ID field, as mentioned in the tip at the end of the section "Creating and Using an Export Map."

Once you have chosen your key field, click the Set Merge Key button. The field name will change to MERGE KEY:*field name*. The ID field has been chosen as the merge key in the Task Mapping dialog box, as shown in Figure 26.17. If you later find that you need to change the Merge Key field, choose a new key field and click the Set Merge Key button again.

NOTE

> You must use the Unique ID field if you want to merge assignment data.

14. Click the Next button to move to the End of Map Definition dialog box. If changes have been made to the map, and you wish to save it by a new name, click the Save Map button.

15. Click the Finish button to import your data into your project.

Some errors may appear in the mapping tables if you select the wrong map, as shown in Figure 26.18. If your map source field names do not exist in the file you have opened, the field name entries will appear in red and have an "OUT OF CONTEXT:" prefix in the From: Excel Field column.

Figure 26.17
You will need to choose a field to serve as the merge key field, to help identify matching records when you are importing data to be merged with the existing data.

Selected key field   Set Merge Key button

Wrong map selected

Figure 26.18
If the wrong map has been chosen to import data, you will see several OUT OF CONTEXT errors in your mapping fields.

Field names in map are not found in the source data

Creating Import Maps for Access and ODBC Sources

It is fairly easy to create an import map once you understand the process, because Microsoft Project 2007 does most of the work for you. When importing data from an existing Access file, an import map is used, similar to the one used for Excel. The difference is that you will need to select the Microsoft Project 2007 database table name to map each data type to. When using an ODBC data source to import data, you will need to select an existing data source connection or create a new one and define the mapping.

EXCHANGING DATA WITH MICROSOFT EXCEL

You have two options when exporting field data into Microsoft Excel—you can either export it as worksheet data or as PivotTable data. You can also import table data from Excel worksheets, but not from PivotTables. When you export to Excel, Microsoft Project 2007 will create an Excel file in the Excel 2007 (.xlsx) format. You can import Excel 4.0 format documents or later, including Excel 97–2003.

You can also exchange data between Microsoft Project 2007 and Excel using visual reports.

→ For additional information about visual reports in Microsoft Project 2007, **see** "Using Excel 2007 While Working with Visual Reports," **p. 714**.

If you create an import/export map for the Excel format, there are a few differences you should keep in mind:

- You can export using either an export map or an Excel template. The Excel template will export a predefined set of Task, Resource, and Assignment fields, and will create a separate worksheet for each of the data types.

- You have the option of exporting field names as the first row of each worksheet. If you choose not to export field names, the field data will be entered in row 2 of the worksheet, and if you want column titles, you will have to add them in separately later on.

- You can include assignment rows, like those shown in the tables of the Task Usage and Resource Usage views. These worksheet rows will not be outlined and indented automatically in the Excel workbook as they are in Microsoft Project 2007.

Excel's Group and Outline commands can be used to group assignments under the task or resource, making it possible to display or hide the assignment rows, as in Microsoft Project 2007. However, you will have to group each set of assignments by hand, and they will not be indented when the assignment rows are shown.

TIP

> You should change Excel's grouping direction before using Excel's Group and Outline command. In Excel 2007, open the Data tab and then click on the small box in the lower-right corner of the Outline box. This will open the Settings dialog box, and you will need to clear the Summary Rows Below Detail check box. This will place the outline symbols for grouping, the plus and minus indicators, to the left of the task or resource name, as in an Assignment view, instead of at the bottom of the list of assignments in each group.

CAUTION

> Sort in Excel with caution. If you sort the rows in a worksheet, you might not be able to tell which assignments go with which tasks or resources.

EXPORTING MICROSOFT PROJECT 2007 DATA TO AN EXCEL WORKSHEET

Import/export maps that have been created for another format, including any of the predefined maps, can be used to export the Microsoft Project 2007 data into Excel. If you use an existing map, you may then want to save it with a different name, so you know it was used for exporting data to Excel.

Follow these steps to export Microsoft Project 2007 data to an Excel workbook:

1. Open the Microsoft Project 2007 file containing the data you want exported.

2. Open the Save As dialog box by selecting File, Save As in the top menu. Choose the location of your new file in the Save In list box, then change the Save as Type to Microsoft Excel Workbook 2007 (*.xlsx), enter a name in the File Name text box, and click the Save button.

3. Microsoft Project 2007 will open the Export Wizard dialog box. Click the Next button to open the Data dialog box.

4. Choose the Selected Data button, and then click the Next button to go to the Map dialog box. The Project Excel Template button will be discussed later in this chapter.

5. Choose the Use Existing Map button. To create a new import map, choose the New Map option and then use the same steps for creating an export map as outlined in the section "Creating and Using an Export Map," earlier in the chapter. Click the Next button to open the Map Selection dialog box.

6. Select an export map, and click the Next button to open the Map Options dialog box.

7. Three types of data can be exported to Excel—tasks, resources, and assignments. Not all options will be active, depending on the type of export map you selected. The options for the Default Task Information export map in the Map Options dialog box are shown in Figure 26.19.

26

Include column headings

Figure 26.19
For help identifying which records are tasks or resources and which are assignments, use the Include Assignment Rows in Output check box.

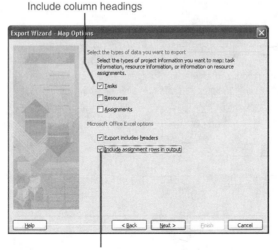

Include assignments with tasks and resources

8. Select the Export Includes Headers check box. With this option selected, the first row of data on each sheet in the workbook will now display field names as column headers. If it is not active, there will be no label at the top of each column.

9. Select the Include Assignment Rows in Output check box if you want your tasks and resources to show details by assignment, as in the Task Usage and Resource Usage views. Remember to include the field named Assignment in the Task Mapping dialog box, so you can distinguish assignments from tasks or resources. Click the Next button to move to the Task Mapping dialog box.

CAUTION

> When you are exporting the rows for the assignment details in a task mapping, the assignment rows will appear to be extra tasks in the workbook that is created. If you later import the data back into Microsoft Project 2007, your resource assignments will now be listed as tasks, even if you include the Task Assignment field in the exported data. Also, any exported assignment details in a resource mapping will result in the assignments being treated as additional resources, and you will not be able to import them back into Microsoft Project 2007.

10. Select your task fields that are being exported to Excel to confirm that the settings are correct. You will see a destination worksheet name for the worksheet that receives the task data, as shown in Figure 26.20.

The Task_Data worksheet title in the Destination worksheet name

Figure 26.20
The Task Mapping dialog box lets you confirm that your exported data is going into the correct worksheet and that you are exporting all of the fields you want to use, plus you can add any extras to a predetermined export map.

The Assignment field adds assignments from tasks and resources

11. If you selected to include resource and assignment data in the Map Options dialog box, in step 7, you will need to continue through the Resource Mapping and Assignment Mapping dialog boxes. Once you are finished with your data mapping dialog boxes, you will reach the End of Map Definition dialog box.

12. Click the Save Map button and give your export map a unique name when the Save Map dialog box appears, so if you ever want to import the data back into Microsoft Project, you will already have the exact Import/Export map set up. Click the Finish button when you are done to export your data to an Excel workbook.

When you export data into Excel, the application will create a worksheet for each of the tables defined in the export map in Microsoft Project 2007, as shown in Figure 26.21. Since the option Export Includes Header was selected, the field names will appear in the first row of the worksheet, and the assignments for each resource will be listed under the row for that resource.

Figure 26.21
Microsoft Project 2007 exports data into an Excel workbook, listing the assignments for each task below the task name.

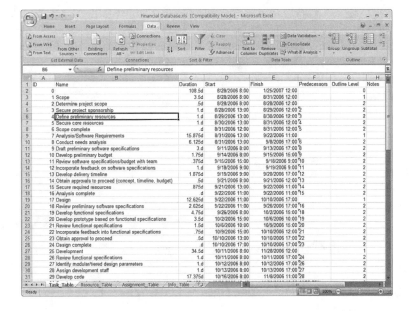

When you open the Import/Export Wizard, the option for Project Excel Template will appear in the Data dialog box and is used for exporting data into Excel. The option will export data to Excel easily, using a standard list of fields for task, resource, and assignment information. These fields are listed here:

- **Task fields**—ID, Name, Duration, Start, Finish, Predecessors, Outline Level, and Notes.

- **Resource fields**—ID, Name, Initials, Type, Material Label, Group, Email Address, Windows User Account, Max Unites, Standard Rate, Cost Per Use, and Notes.

- **Assignment fields**—Task Name, Resource Name, % Work Complete, Work, and Units.

The Project Excel Template option exports data to four Excel worksheets—Task_Table, Resource_Table, Assignment_Table, and Info_Table. The first three show data described by the worksheet name, whereas the Info_Table worksheet contains general information about using the Project Excel template. You can see in Figure 26.22 an Excel workbook created with the Project Excel Template option, then formatted by the user.

Figure 26.22
Using the Microsoft Project Excel Template option is a quick and easy way to export data from Microsoft Project into Excel.

A worksheet for information about the template

Worksheets for task, resource, and assignment data

EXPORTING MICROSOFT PROJECT 2007 DATA TO AN EXCEL PIVOTTABLE

An Excel PivotTable will summarize data in cross-table calculations, offering flexibility to change the layout of the PivotTable quickly. If you export to a PivotTable format, the export map allows you to choose which fields will be included for one or more of the three data categories: tasks, resources, and assignments. Microsoft Project 2007 will create a separate PivotTable for each category, which will be stored in the same Excel workbook. Using the Save operation will not only copy the data into Excel data sheets, but will create the PivotTables on separate worksheets based on the data sheets.

Microsoft Project 2007 can also exchange data with Excel PivotTables using visual reports. Building a PivotTable involves exporting the data and then fine-tuning the PivotTable in

Excel in order to create the results you desire. Exporting in Microsoft Project 2007 creates only the simplest of PivotTables, but you can edit it to get the desired formatting results.

→ For additional information about using visual reports in Microsoft Project 2007, **see** "Using Excel 2007 While Working with Visual Reports," **p. 714**.

Follow these steps to export Microsoft Project 2007 data to an Excel PivotTable:

1. Open the Microsoft Project file containing the data you want exported.

2. Open the Save As dialog box by selecting File, Save As in the top menu. Choose the location of your new file in the Save In list box. Then, change the Save as Type to Microsoft Excel PivotTable 2007 (*.xlsx), enter a name in the File Name text box, and click the Save button.

3. Microsoft Project opens the Export Wizard dialog box. Click the Next button to continue to the Map dialog box.

4. Select New Map, and then click the Next button to go to the Map Options dialog box.

5. Use the Map Options dialog box to choose one or more of the types of data (tasks, resources, or assignments) you want exported to your PivotTable, as shown in Figure 26.23.

CAUTION

> You can only select one category for each PivotTable. If you try to export fields from all three categories, you will end up with three separate, unrelated PivotTables in your Excel Workbook.

Figure 26.23
Using the Microsoft Project Excel Template option is a quick and easy way to export data from Microsoft Project into Excel.

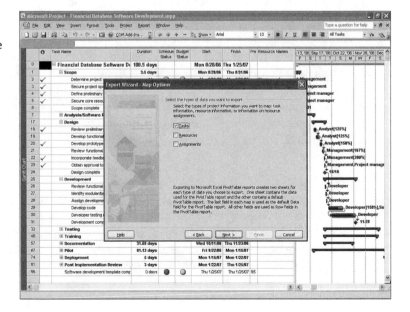

6. Click the Next button to proceed on to the Task Mapping dialog box.

7. Enter a name for your worksheet into the Destination Worksheet Name text box, as shown in Figure 26.24.

Worksheet name for Excel

Figure 26.24
Microsoft Project 2007 turns the last field in the mapping table red, with the Pivot Data Field prefix, to let you know that this is the field used as the calculating body of the PivotTable.

The last fields in the mapping table is the data area in the PivotTable

8. Select the names of the Microsoft Project 2007 fields to be exported in the From: Microsoft Office Project Field column. Microsoft Project 2007 automatically supplies a field name for the To: Worksheet Field column when you enter a Microsoft Project field name. These can be changed if desired.

Microsoft Project 2007 designates the last field entered in the mapping table as the field Excel will use for the table data, the calculated summary numbers in the body of the PivotTable. Microsoft Project 2007 designates this field by showing it in red and adding the "Pivot Data Field:" prefix before the export field name. As you continue adding fields into the mapping table, Microsoft Project 2007 will automatically designate the last one as the Pivot Data field. If you need to go back and add a field, but do not want it to be the last field, use the Insert Row button.

TIP

If you want to group the data in the PivotTable by Major categories, with Minor category details underneath, place your Major category fields above the minor category fields in the field mapping.

Make sure that the field you want to use for calculations is the last field in the field mapping list. Cost is the last field listed in this example, because the calculations of this example will be based on its values in the PivotTable.

9. Once your field map is finished, click the Next button to move to the End of Map Definition dialog box.

10. Click the Save Map button to open the Save Map dialog box. Give your new map a unique name, such as Cost Export to PT, so that in the future if you need to re-create your PivotTable, you will know which map to use. Once you have named your map, click the Save button to return to the End of Map Definition text box.

11. Click the Finish button to export your data into an Excel PivotTable.

Open the newly created Excel document to see the data generated from the exported data in a PivotTable, as shown in Figure 26.25. You will have two sheets in Excel; the first sheet shows the raw data you exported, whereas the second contains the default PivotTable created by Microsoft Project 2007, as shown in Figure 26.25.

NOTE

> If you added the Task Name field in the Task Mapping list of fields, Microsoft Project 2007 will set up multiple Task Name columns in the worksheet, one for each outline level. For each subtask, the outline level 1 summary tasks will show up in the Task Name 1 column, the outline level 2 summary tasks will show up in the Task Name 2 column, and so on, as shown in Figure 26.25.

Figure 26.25
All of the data you export will be placed into a plain worksheet, the source for the PivotTable.

Top-level task names

Third-level names (subtasks)

Resource names

NOTE

When you add the Resource Names field into the Task Mapping list of fields, Microsoft Project 2007 will create separate records for each resource name assigned to the task, as shown in Figure 26.29.

The data in the first sheet could be used to create a PivotTable on your own, but Microsoft Project 2007 and Excel have already done the work for you, and stored it in the second sheet, as shown in Figure 26.26. You will need to format the column width, number display, layout of the PivotTable. The default PivotTable does not have any column categories, but you will probably want the resource names to appear in column headings. In addition, there is only one calculation in the data area, and you will want to show the percentage distribution plus the sum of the costs.

Second-level task names (summary tasks and subtasks)

Top-level task names | Third-level task names (subtasks) | Resource names

Figure 26.26
Microsoft Project 2007 creates a PivotTable that may not show the project information in the way you want to see it, so you will need to modify your PivotTable to build the finished product you are looking for.

Raw data tab | Default PivotTable tab | Separate records for each assigned resource

IMPORTING MICROSOFT PROJECT 2007 DATA FROM THE EXCEL FORMAT

Use caution when importing data from Excel into Microsoft Project 2007. Your data must be mapped correctly to the Microsoft Project 2007 fields, and the data types must be correct for each field; otherwise, you will run into problems.

CAUTION

> As mentioned previously in this chapter, if the Excel workbook was created by exporting tasks or resources from Microsoft Project 2007, and if the option to include rows for resource assignments was used, some of the rows in the workbook will be tasks or resources, whereas others will be assignment details. Do not import data from a workbook with assignment details included. Find and delete the assignment details before you import the data back into Microsoft Project 2007.

The following example will show you how to add a list of new employees to the resource sheet in a Microsoft Project 2007 file. The list has been created and stored in Sheet 1 of an Excel workbook. The names will be imported to the Resource data in the New Product Microsoft Project 2007 file. The column headings are not perfect matches for the Microsoft Project 2007 field names, and the Overtime Rate field uses text entries, whereas Microsoft Project 2007 expects numbers. You can see an example of the worksheet in Figure 26.27.

Figure 26.27
Information such as new resources and their pay rates can be imported into Microsoft Project 2007 from Excel, using an import map.

Follow these steps to import data from Excel into an Microsoft Project 2007 file:

1. Open the Microsoft Project 2007 file you want to import your data into. If you do not have a file open, Microsoft Project 2007 will create a new document for your imported data.

2. It is a good idea, but not required, that you change your project to a view that will show the data you are importing. Having the view open can be useful if you are unsure of which Microsoft Project 2007 field names are needed for your imported data. In the

example set up earlier, opening the Resource Sheet view will show you that the employee's name should go into the Resource Name column, but the name of that field is simply Name. You can find the real field name for a column by double-clicking on the column heading to open the Column Definition dialog box, shown in Figure 26.28.

Official name of the field

Figure 26.28
You can learn information about Microsoft Project's columns, such as their field names versus their titles, in the Column Definition dialog box.

Title displayed in this table

3. Select File, Open to show the Open dialog box, then change to file type in the Files of Type selection box. In this case, you would change it to Microsoft Excel Workbook.

4. Select the location where your Excel workbook has been saved in the Look In list box and then find your file and click the Open button. This will open the Import Wizard dialog box.

5. Click the Next button to move on to the Map dialog box. Select the New Map option and click the Next button to open the Import Mode dialog box.

   The Import Mode dialog box is where you have the option of how you want to import your data into Microsoft Project 2007: As a new project, Append the data to the active project, or Merge the data into an active project.

6. Select how you want to place your import data into Microsoft Project 2007. For this example, click the Append the data to an existing project option. Click the Next button to move on to the Map Options dialog box.

   The Map Options dialog box contains options for what kind of data you want to import: Tasks, Resources, or Assignments.

7. Click the Resources box as the type of data to import. Although this example shows how to import data containing new employees and their pay rates, you could just as easily create task data listing the tasks in your project.

   Confirm that the Import Includes Headers box is selected. If this box is cleared, the map's field list will not show the Excel column headers; it will simply number the columns. This creates difficulties, so you need to find out which Excel column maps to which Microsoft Project 2007 field, as shown in Figure 26.29.

8. Click the Next button to move to the Resource Mapping dialog box.

9. Choose the source worksheet name in the Source Worksheet Name list. This is the worksheet you have saved your information to, most often Sheet 1, which is what will be used for this example also.

Type of data to be imported

Figure 26.29
Importing the headers from your Excel worksheet will help you match your imported data with the correct Microsoft Project 2007 fields.

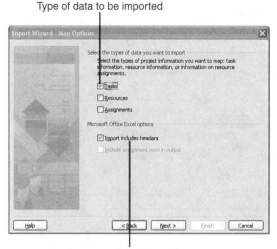

Import will include headers

Once the worksheet has been chosen, Microsoft Project 2007 will fill in the From: Excel Field columns on the left side of the mapping field with the column headings you set up in your worksheet. Microsoft Project 2007 will also try to find matching field names from the project to enter into the To: Microsoft Project Field column on the right side of the mapping field. Not all of the Excel field names used were matched in the Microsoft Project Resource Field column, as shown in Figure 26.30.

Column titles in Excel worksheet

Figure 26.30
Microsoft Project 2007 matches the column headings from your Excel document when possible, but it may not always find the right match, and you will have to enter them yourself.

Matching Project field names not found

10. Enter the correct field names in the To: Microsoft Project Field column of the mapping table for each of the fields in the From: Excel Field column, as shown in Figure 26.31.

Figure 26.31
Use the Microsoft Project 2007 drop-down list of field names to find the correct field for your imported data.

11. Once you have finished filling in the field names, click the Next button to move to the End of Map Definition dialog box. Click the Save Map button if you want to save your import map. Do not forget to give it a unique name. If you do not want to save it, click the Finish button to import your data. In this example, it will be added to the end of the Resource sheet list, as shown in Figure 26.32.

Figure 26.32
Microsoft Project 2007 adds new resources to the project resource list, with the use of an Excel import map.

New resources added to the resource list

When Microsoft Project 2007 has a problem importing data, you may receive a warning message, as shown in Figure 26.33. Microsoft Project 2007 is very rigid when importing task data, as you can see from this warning, where Microsoft Project 2007 found a mismatched Duration value in the imported data. If you happen to see one of these error messages while importing data, you have three different options:

- Click Yes to keep importing data, and to continue receiving error messages if more exist. This is your best option, unless you know specifically what the problem is and how to correct it in Excel. This option will continue importing the data, and you can find and fix the problem in Microsoft Project 2007 once the import is complete.

- Click No if you want to continue importing data, but do not want to receive any more error messages. This option can create problems, because you will not know if there are any more errors in your imported data.

- Click Cancel to quit importing your data.

Figure 26.33
If Microsoft Project 2007 encounters a problem with mismatched data during an import, it will warn you of the problem and give you three options for continuing.

If your imported data does contain mismatches, it will not be imported into Microsoft Project 2007 even if you select Yes from the warning dialog box (see Figure 26.33). Microsoft Project 2007 will instead show a default value, and you will need to find the holes left by this mismatched data and enter the correct information.

If you do encounter the warning dialog box, you should save the source references listed. These references can assist you when you go back to find and fill in the holes left by the missing data.

26

WORKING WITH WEB-ENABLED PROJECT DATA

With Microsoft Project 2007, you can export project data in the XML format, but you can no longer export into HTML. Exporting into XML allows you to publish Microsoft Project 2007 data onto web pages, which can be used for reviewing most all of the project information on either the Internet or a corporate intranet. Unlike with HTML, you can import XML data into Microsoft Project 2007 as well. XML is a versatile format because of its structured form and can be easily imported into many other applications and formats.

Follow these steps to save a project to an XML file:

1. Open the Microsoft Project file containing the data you want to export.

2. Go to File, Save As to open the Save As dialog box. Then select the directory for your new XML file in the Save In list box, and name your file.

3. Choose the XML Format (.xml) file format, then click the Save button. Your project has now been saved as an XML file.

NOTE

When you are saving a project into the XML format, you cannot export selected data only; you must export the entire file. The Project data within the file is structured by nodes. You can expand each node to view the groupings of data, such as Task, Resource, and Assignment.

WORKING WITH TEXT FILE FORMATS

Microsoft Project 2007 supports two ASCII text formats: the tab-delimited format and the comma-separated values (CSV) format. Import/export maps for these formats are nearly identical to the import/export maps of Excel, with one important difference. In Excel, you can import or export all three data table types at the same time: tasks, resources, and assignments. When you import/export text formats, you can only select one of these three data tables at a time.

EXPORTING PROJECT DATA IN THE TEXT FORMATS

Follow these steps to export a list of summary tasks with their start and finish dates to a text file:

1. Open the project from which you wish to export your summary tasks.

2. Go to File, Save As, and browse to the directory for your new text file in the Save In list box.

3. Choose the file format you want to use in the Save as Type list box. If you want a tab-delimited file, select Text (Tab Delimited) (*.txt). This format will place tab characters between each of the data fields in the record, with paragraph marks to separate the records (a carriage return and line feed).

   If you want a comma-delimited file, select CSV (Comma Delimited) (*.csv). This format will place commas between each of the data fields in the record (with quote marks surrounding field values that contain commas themselves) and separate the records with paragraph marks.

4. Click the Save button. This opens the Export Wizard dialog box. Click the Next button to go to the Map dialog box.

5. In the Map dialog box, choose whether you want to use an existing export map or create a new one. This example creates a new map. Click Next to move to the Map Options dialog box.

6. Choose which type of data you want to import from the Map Options dialog box: tasks, resources, or assignments. You will only be able to choose one of the three, unlike in an Excel export map. See Figure 26.34 for more details.

Figure 26.34
You can only choose one data table at a time in the Map Options box when you are saving your data to a text file.

Only one type of data can be selected   Export field labels

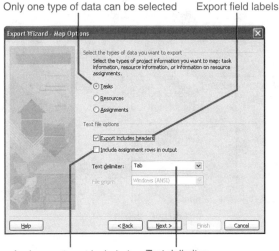

Assignments not included   Text delimiter

7. If you want your exported data labeled, leave the Export Includes Headers box selected.

8. If you want your assignments included, select the Include Assignment Rows in Output box. Keep in mind that your assignments will be indistinguishable from your tasks or resources, unless you include the Assignment field in the field mapping box to identify them.

9. Choose your text delimiter from the drop-down list if you want to use either a comma or a space as the delimiter, instead of the tab character, which is the default.

10. Click the Next button to open the Mapping dialog box. You may now select the data type you want to include in your text file. This example includes the Name field, the Start_Date field, and the Finish_Date field, while using the Summary Task export filter, as shown in Figure 26.35. You will also notice that the Destination Table Name text box is unavailable when importing or exporting text-formatted data.

11. Click the Next button to proceed on to the End of Map Definition dialog box.

12. If you made a new export map and want to save it, click the Save button, and then give the map a unique name, such as Export Summary Tasks to Text, so you can identify it more easily next time you choose to use it.

13. Click the Finish button to create the file.

26

Figure 26.35
The Summary Task filter will limit the tasks exported, thus making data management easier.

Destination Table Name
text box not available   Summary Tasks filter

Microsoft Project field names

Exported field labels

You can open the text file in Notepad or any other text editor. It can also be imported into any application that can import tab-delimited text files. You can see how the example, with some minor formatting, creates a nice list of your summary tasks and their start and finish dates, as shown in Figure 26.36.

Figure 26.36
With a little bit of formatting to create better spacing between the summary task names and the start and finish dates, you can create an easy-to-read text file in Notepad.

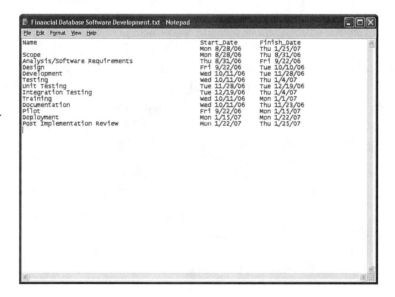

IMPORTING PROJECT DATA FROM TEXT FORMATS

You can import a text file in a similar manner as importing an Excel file. However, as when you are exporting, you can only import one type of data at a time. This means you will have to import your tasks, resources, and assignments separately. Also, as with Excel formats, you will probably encounter problems matching field names if your import source file was not exported originally from Microsoft Project 2007. (See the earlier section "Importing Microsoft Project 2007 Data from the Excel Format" for more information.)

When you are importing a text file, there is one additional option you will have that was grayed out for exporting (see Figure 26.35). The File Origin text box will let you specify whether a different character set has been used as the source data. The default is Windows (ANSI), but you can also choose DOS, OS/2 (PC-8), or Unicode. This will assist you in importing your data more correctly, if the text files originated in an OS/2 environment or an international environment using Unicode.

IMPORTING A TASK LIST FROM OUTLOOK

Because many organizations use Outlook to track their calendars and to-do lists, Microsoft Project 2007 is set up so you can import your tasks straight from Outlook. You can see in Figure 26.37 a list of tasks that have been entered into Outlook.

Task list

Figure 26.37
With the help of Microsoft Project 2007, you can enter a task list in Outlook and then import it into a project file.

26

Figures 26.38 and 26.39 show additional information you can enter into an Outlook task, such as notes and the duration for tasks. Double-click on the task when you want to add more information.

Figure 26.38
You can add notes in Outlook through the Task tab.

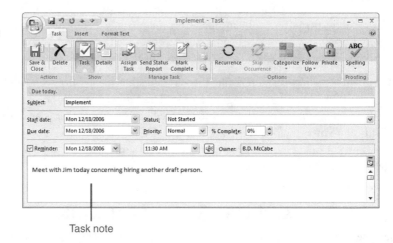

Task note

Figure 26.39
You can specify details about the task(s) by clicking the show Details button in Outlook.

Total work (duration) for the task

Follow these steps to import a task into Microsoft Project 2007 from Outlook:

1. Enter your task information in the Tasks section of Outlook. You can add the start date, duration, due date, and even notes if necessary.

2. Open the project you wish to import the Outlook tasks into, or a blank project file to start a new project.

3. Go to Tools, Import Outlook Tasks to open the Import Outlook Tasks dialog box, as shown in Figure 26.40.

Select the tasks to be imported   Notes

Figure 26.40
Use the Import
Outlook Tasks dialog
box to select and
import tasks to be
imported into
Microsoft Project
2007.

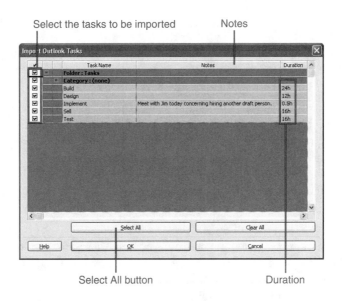

Select All button   Duration

4. Choose which tasks you want to import by filling the check box in the first column for each task. Use the Select All button to choose every task on the list.

5. Click the OK button to import the Outlook tasks.

Microsoft Project 2007 will import your Outlook tasks in alphabetical order, as shown in Figure 26.41. Once you have imported the tasks into Microsoft Project 2007, you can drag them into the preferred order, plus set their dependencies and constraints, and so on. You will also see that the start date for each imported task has been set to the start date of the project. The dates associated with the tasks, when created in Outlook, will not be imported.

26

Imported tasks, in
alphabetical order

Figure 26.41
You can see how
Microsoft Project
2007 imports tasks
from Outlook in
alphabetical order,
including the duration
and any notes that
were added in
Outlook.

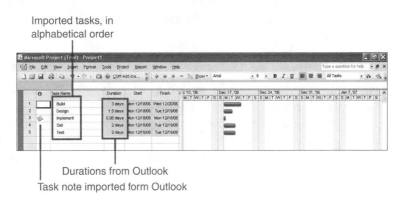

Durations from Outlook

Task note imported form Outlook

Consultants' Tips

The following tips might help you when working with importing/exporting project data.

Design the Data Layout Prior to Import/Export

Even if on paper only, you should design the data layout for the information you want to import or export before trying to import/export it. The mapping process can be frustrating without some preliminary thinking. You might use the data exchange process to create some reports for yourself in other applications, such as in Excel, to help you analyze issues with your projects offline. For instance, you could use the Compare to Baseline map to print an Excel report, then review it later for analysis.

Using Export/Import vs. Copy/Paste

Although this is a rare situation, if you have ever seen Microsoft Project data crash in a previous version for a given file, then consider cutting and pasting the data you need rather importing the data. The original data set up may be corrupt, and by importing the data, you may be taking some of the issues with you.

Copying and Pasting Using Excel

If you decide to copy and paste using Excel as the transfer agent, then think ahead to get the intended summary/task/assignment structure set up. Map the exact columns to use for the copy-and-paste operation.

Be Aware of Additional Data When Importing/Exporting

A project file has hundreds of fields, and sometimes you will be unaware of certain data in the project file by viewing only a few columns. For instance, you will often miss transferring data in the actual work and cost or baseline fields to other file formats if you do not know it is there. Prior to data transfer, consider displaying extra columns to determine whether "hidden" data exists.

Using the XML Export Will Not Keep Some of the Usage Data

If you are using XML output, you may *not* get all the detailed data in the Usage views. For example, when viewing the Resource Usage view, you can see time-phased data for each resource assignment, but when the project is exported into XML format, it will not contain this time-phased data. Specifically, a resource may have worked 8 hours a day for the past three weeks, but you will not be able to see this when the project data is exported to XML format.

CHAPTER **27**

MANIPULATING DATA USING OTHER APPLICATIONS

In this chapter

COPYING DATA BETWEEN APPLICATIONS

In this chapter you will learn how to exchange individual field values and objects between files, and use the Copy and Paste and Insert Object commands. You will discover that data you paste into Microsoft Project 2007, plus any objects you might insert, can be linked back to their original source. This allows you to update the Project document to show the most current values in a source file. Although in some cases you might need the rigor and preciseness of using an Import/Export map to exchange data between fields, as described in Chapter 26, "Exporting and Importing Project Data," the cutting and pasting or linking of objects often suffices for most of your project needs. For instance, you might need to just link a Word document that contains the specifications associated with a task in your project that indicates the "Create Specifications Document" task is complete. Or you might need to copy and paste the same set of tasks for a phase that a colleague created in an Excel spreadsheet, and it simply is not worth the time and trouble to perform the data mapping.

NOTE

> Time-phased data is not handled by Import/Export maps, and time-phased reports can only be viewed or printed using Microsoft Office Project 2007. Copy and Paste may be your best option to copy Microsoft Project's time-phased data into other applications if you are not comfortable using VBA (Visual Basic for Applications) to write macros for the time-phased reports.

Use the Clipboard to copy and paste data from one application's document (the source) into another application's document (the destination) if you do not need to transfer all of the information in a file (for instance, you only need one or a few values from your source document). In such a case, Microsoft Project 2007 can be either the source or the destination document when exchanging data. Simply paste a copy of your values. Alternatively, you can paste a permanent link that shows the current value from the source document that can also be updated as needed to show changes in the source document.

If you are using the Clipboard to paste data into a table (a series of cells, such as the list of resources in the Gantt Chart view) in Microsoft Project 2007, it is important to choose the correct field receiving the data. When importing files with the Import/Export map, you can define which field the data will be placed in, but when you are using Copy and Paste, the location depends on which field you select.

When pasting a single value, it is easy to pick the right recipient field, but if you are copying a block of two or more columns of values, you will need to be in a table view in Microsoft Project 2007 that has the appropriate columns along side one another in the same order as your copied block of values. This often requires you to define a custom table in Microsoft Project 2007 to show the data field columns in the same order as the data being copied. When pasting data into Microsoft Project 2007, you might also have to have a custom table with like columns of data from the source open in the current view.

→ For additional information about custom tables, **see** "Creating and Customizing Tables," **p. 756**.

In Figure 27.1, the Excel worksheet layout contains fields for resource names as well as the cost rates for each resource. If you opened the Entry table in the Resource Sheet view, you will see that it does not match this layout. There are five other columns between the Resource Name and the Standard Rate columns. Therefore, if you want to cut and paste your information from your Excel worksheet into a Resource Sheet view, you will need to create a custom Entry table in Microsoft Project 2007 that looks like your Excel sheet and hides the five columns, so your information can be pasted correctly, as shown in Figure 27.2.

Figure 27.1
If you want to correctly paste your spreadsheet data into Project, you must create a custom table with the columns laid out identical to your spreadsheet.

Correctly formatted text entries

N/A is an unrecognized rate

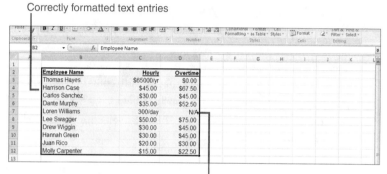

Resource Sheet view set up with a custom Entry table
Text data successfully changed to numeric data

Figure 27.2
You can create a custom resource table to accept the data pasted from the spreadsheet shown in Figure 27.1.

N/A changed to zero

Be sure to select the cell that should receive the upper-left cell of your block of pasted cells before you execute the Paste command. The cell containing Thomas Hayes was chosen before pasting, as shown in Figure 27.2.

COPYING DATA FROM OTHER APPLICATIONS INTO MICROSOFT PROJECT 2007

Follow these steps when copying data into Microsoft Project 2007 from another application:

1. Choose your source data. You can choose a single value, or several values, as shown in Figure 27.1. When choosing several values, be sure the layout of your values matches the order of the values in the Microsoft Project 2007 table serving as the destination.

2. Move the data to the Clipboard using Edit, Copy, Ctrl+C, or the Copy button on the Standard toolbar.

3. Open Microsoft Project 2007 and choose which view contains the table with the columns in the same order as the data you are copying, as shown in Figure 27.2.

4. Choose the resource or task row and field in the table that will be receiving the data. If you choose blank rows, Microsoft Project 2007 will create new resources or tasks with the copied data. If you select rows that already contain data, Microsoft Project 2007 will replace the existing data with the newly copied data.

5. Paste your data to Microsoft Project 2007 by selecting Edit, Paste, Ctrl+V, or the Paste button on the Standard toolbar.

CAUTION

> If, while copying and pasting, you overwrite an existing resource, you are simply changing field values for that resource. Any tasks that have been assigned to that resource will still be assigned to it, even if the resource name may have changed.

Using the Paste command places a static copy of the current value from the source document into your selected field. Microsoft Project 2007 will not automatically update this value if the source document is changed.

If you paste into a field that does not support the data type you are importing, you will see a pasting error such as the one shown in Figure 27.3. For instance, the data from Figure 27.1 contained the text value N/A in cell D7, and in Figure 27.3, Microsoft Project 2007 tells you that it is unclear what to do with that value in the Overtime Rate field. The error message shows you that the error was detected in ID 2 in the Overtime Rate column. Error dialog boxes give you three option buttons:

Figure 27.3
Microsoft Project 2007 opens an error message dialog box to tell you where the error occurred and what kind of data is expected.

- **Yes**—Choose Yes to continue pasting and receiving error messages. Your mismatched value will be pasted into the cell, and Microsoft Project 2007 will try and make sense of it.

- **No**—Choose No to continue pasting, but without receiving any more error messages. Microsoft Project 2007 will paste the mismatched value into the cell and ignore any more mismatched values it encounters.

- **Cancel**—Choose Cancel to terminate your pasting operation. If you are pasting a block of values and some have already been pasted, using the Cancel button will cause the already pasted values to remain in the Microsoft Project 2007 document, but no more of your values will be added.

NOTE

> When you are pasting data from another application into Microsoft Project 2007, Microsoft Project 2007 will give you an error if you use a slash (/), such as in Figure 27.1. The only exception to this would be if you used it as an abbreviation for a time period at which an amount is earned. For instance, $10 per hour would be represented as 10/h.

CAUTION

> When you are pasting dates into the Start or Finish fields for a task, you will create soft constraints for those tasks (Start No Earlier Than constraints in projects scheduled using a start date, and Finish No Later Than constraints in projects scheduled using a finish date). To change those constraints, go to the Task Information dialog box and select the Advanced tab. If you select As Soon As Possible, you can reset the constraint type to the least constrained.

→ For additional information about types of constraints and their removal, **see** "Defining Constraints," **p. 223**.

COPYING MICROSOFT PROJECT 2007 DATA INTO OTHER APPLICATIONS

Follow these steps when you want to copy data from Microsoft Project 2007 into another application:

1. Choose a view and apply a table displaying the data you want to copy to another application.

2. Choose your source data; you can select a single value, several adjacent values, whole rows or columns, or all of the cells in the table:
   - If you want to select an entire row, click the ID number for the row or rows.
   - If you want to select entire columns, click the column headers.
   - If you want to select all the cells in the table, click the Select All button above the ID numbers and to the left of the other column headers.

3. Copy the data to the Clipboard by either selecting Edit, Copy Cell (if you have selected a whole task instead of a cell, Microsoft Project 2007 will show you Edit, Copy Task), pressing Ctrl+C, or clicking the Copy button on the Standard toolbar.

4. Open the other application and choose the location to which you want to paste your data.

5. Select Edit, Paste (or press Ctrl+V) to paste the data into your selected application.

In Figure 27.4, a block of data is copied from the Resource Usage view into an Excel worksheet. Before the data to copy was selected, the Cost table in Project was changed to include the Assignment field. Once the data was pasted into Excel, the user added the heading at the top of each column in the worksheet (Resources and Assignments, Cost, and Assignment?). Final formatting on this worksheet might include using the Assignment? column to separate the rows containing resource data from those containing assignment data.

Manually entered titles

Figure 27.4
Data copied from Microsoft Project's Resource Usage view has been pasted into Excel, and is now ready for final formatting.

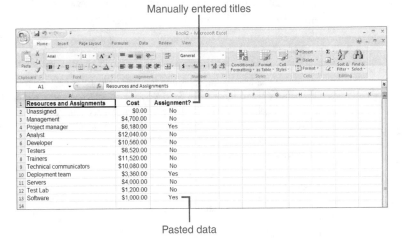

Pasted data

TIP

There are three steps you must follow if you want to copy and paste information contained in the time-phased grid of either the Resource Usage view or Task Usage view:

1. Choose the desired information in the table, then copy and paste it to the destination application.

2. Choose the desired date in the time-phased grid, making sure to match the data in the grid with the correct rows from the table before copying this information and pasting it to the destination application.

3. Enter the column headings for both the table information and the time-phased data into the destination application.

LINKING DATA BETWEEN APPLICATIONS

This section discusses how to make static copies from one application to another; copies that will not change if the source data changes. You are now going to learn how to paste a value from one application to another that will change and update based on the changes of the source document. These are known as *linked references*. A linked reference can be updated to show the changes in the value stored in the source document.

LINKING MICROSOFT PROJECT DATA FIELDS FROM EXTERNAL SOURCES

When pasting a link from an external data source into a Microsoft Project 2007 table, you can use another application, such as Excel or Word where you can maintain reference data efficiently, or you can link from another Microsoft Project 2007 document. For instance, you could use an Excel workbook to keep track of resource names and cost rates, linking that document to your Microsoft Project 2007 document.

Follow these steps to link Microsoft Project 2007 field values to values stored in other sources:

1. Choose your source data, such as a cell or range of cells in an Excel worksheet. You can choose a single value or several values; if choosing several values, confirm that the order of the values you are copying matches the order of the values in the table into which you are pasting your data.
2. Copy the data to the Clipboard.
3. Activate Microsoft Project 2007 and choose which view has the table with the columns arranged to match the order of the data you will be copying into Microsoft Project 2007.
4. Choose the row in the table that will receive the data.
5. Select Edit, Paste Special, opening the Paste Special dialog box, as shown in Figure 27.5.

Figure 27.5
You can specify the format for the data that will be pasted into a receiving file using the Paste Special dialog box.

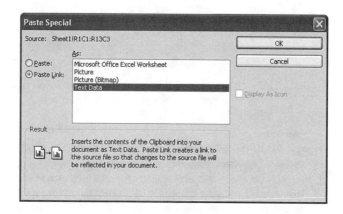

27

6. Select the Paste Link option.

7. Select Text Data in the As box as the type of link, if you want the data to become text in the table. Microsoft Project 2007 will attempt to convert text data into numeric data in the number field, or into a date in the date field.

8. Click OK to set up the link. Microsoft Project 2007 will display, by default, a small triangle in the lower-right corner of each cell linked to a source for its data. You can see the link indicator for the Name, the Standard Rate, and the Overtime Rate values in Figure 27.6. The resource names and cost rate information has been dynamically linked to an Excel worksheet, where the resource information is maintained.

Link indicator

Figure 27.6
Microsoft Project 2007 indicates which cells in a table are linked cells by a small triangle in the lower-right corner of the cell.

TIP

If you expect to see a link indicator, but do not, go to Tools, Options and click the View tab in the Options dialog box. You can make sure that the OLE Links Indictors check box is in use.

If you try to paste a link that contains mismatched data, you will receive an object linking and embedding (OLE) error message to let you know the operation cannot be completed. Unlike with the regular Paste command, if data is mismatched while you are pasting a block of values, Microsoft Project 2007 will stop the operation and remove all of the values that might have been pasted during the operation. These values are grouped together since the block of cells is considered one link. If even one cell has a mismatch, the entire block of data will be ignored.

→ For additional information about attaching hyperlinks, **see** "Attaching Hyperlinks to Tasks," **p. 183**.

REFRESHING LINKED DATA IN MICROSOFT PROJECT 2007

When you save a project file that contains linked values, Microsoft Project 2007 saves the current value of your linked files, as well as a reference to the source for the value. This means that when you open a file with linked values, Microsoft Project 2007 will show the most recent values.

If you open a Microsoft Project 2007 file that contains links to other files, Microsoft Project 2007 will ask you if you want to reestablish those links upon opening the file. Microsoft Project 2007 will refresh the values in the linked cells with the current values in the source files, as shown in Figure 27.7. If you choose Yes, Microsoft Project 2007 will retrieve the current or saved values of each link's source. If you choose No, Microsoft Project 2007 will open the Microsoft Project 2007 document and show the last saved values for the linked cells. If you decide later to go back and update these links, you can.

Figure 27.7
If you open a Microsoft Project 2007 file with links to other files, Microsoft Project 2007 will refresh the links or use the last values saved in the Microsoft Project 2007 file.

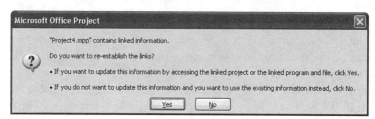

To update the linked values of a Microsoft Project 2007 document at any time, go to the Edit, Links command to open the Links dialog box. Your source application does not need to be open when your linked values are refreshed. When you open the Links dialog box, it will list all the external links in the current document, as shown in Figure 27.8.

The Links list displays the path of the source, the document type of the source file, and the update status of each link. All three items are displayed in greater detail at the bottom of the dialog box for the selected link. If you do not see these items on display, you may need to use the Update Now button. When the filename and link reference are too long, the path to the source will be condensed. Links in Microsoft Project 2007 to external data sources utilize Dynamic Data Exchange (DDE) to manage the source and target locations of the data. The source is usually referred to as the DDE Server.

Figure 27.8
The Links dialog box will show you all of the external sources of linked data in a project.

Selected link   List of all the links in the Project file

Details for the selected link

The chosen item in the Links list shows the path to the file condensed, since it is too long for the display, as shown in Figure 27.8. The details also show the filename and the location of linked data in the file, as well as the cell range. The type has been identified as a Microsoft Word Document, and the update status is Automatic, which means you do not have to click the Update Now button if you want to refresh the values in Microsoft Project 2007. If it was set to Manual, you would have to use the Update Now button to refresh the values.

If your update status is set to Automatic, and the file is open in memory and supports an automatic update, then changes in the source will appear immediately in the document while it too is open in memory. However, some source applications do not support the automatic update choice, and the Update column at the top of the dialog box shows Unavail, short for Unavailable. The update status will also be set to Unavail when the Microsoft Project 2007 document has not been updated during the current editing session.

TIP

When an object's Update field at the bottom of the dialog box has the Automatic button set, and you want to change to the Manual button, do not make the change if the update status for the link in the list is unavailable. You need to update the link with the Update Now button before any changes are made to the updating method.

There is only one link reference in the Links dialog box for a whole range of Excel cells pasted in the link operation, as shown in Figure 27.8. If you want to maintain each of the cells as separate links, you need to copy and paste each cell independently.

Follow these steps if you want to update links to external sources:

1. Open the Links dialog box by selecting Edit, Links, as shown in Figure 27.8.

TIP

When the Links command is grayed out, the document has no linked values.

2. Choose all of the links you want refreshed.

3. Click the Update Now button. This will refresh all of the data links you have chosen. The source for each selected link is searched for among the current values.

4. To open the application document named in the chosen link reference, click the Open Source button. You must choose only one link when using the Open Source button; multiple links are invalid. You can, however, open multiple linked source documents simultaneously by opening each of them independently. Here are some other options in the Links dialog box:

   - To remove a selected link, click the Break Link button. The current value will remain in the link location, but the external source reference will disappear.

   - To change the source of a selected link, click the Change Source button. This will open the Change Source dialog box, as shown in Figure 27.9. Use the Browse button to select another file to link to.

Figure 27.9
Use the Change Source dialog box to redefine a link's source.

TIP

While you can browse the files directly to find the filename of a new source to link to, you might also need to establish the location within the new source file to finish the change. Because of this fact, it is usually better to paste new links over the old ones, instead of using the Change Source dialog box.

DELETING LINKS TO EXTERNAL SOURCES

As mentioned in the previous section, when you break a link to an external source, Microsoft Project 2007 saves the current value that was linked, but disassociates the value from the external source. Likewise, if you try to type over a field value already linked to an external source, you are warned that the link will be lost, and then given the choice to proceed or cancel the entry. Select No if you want to cancel your editing changes and keep the link. If you select Yes, the dynamic data exchange (DDE) link reference will be lost. You can, however, undo the change using the Edit, Undo command.

If you want to delete the data and its link to an external source, select the file whose link you want removed and go to Edit, Clear, Contents, or use Ctrl+Del. You will be asked to confirm your deletion.

TIP

> If you delete the link in a cell that is part of a block of linked values, the link for all of the cells in that block will be removed, not just for one cell. Use the Edit, Undo command to restore these links if they are deleted accidentally.

IDENTIFYING TASKS OR RESOURCES WITH LINKS ATTACHED

You can find out which of your tasks or resources use linked data from other sources by filtering them. Choose the Linked Fields filter from the Filters drop-down list in either a task view or resource view. You can also find the linked values by looking for the links indicator triangle in the lower-right corner of the cells.

PASTING LINKS TO MICROSOFT PROJECT 2007 DATA IN OTHER APPLICATIONS

Both Microsoft Excel and Microsoft Word will accept pasted links to individual data cells in Microsoft Project 2007 tables. To copy a single linked value into one of these applications, display a table with a cell for the value you want to use, select the cell, and use the Copy Cell command. Once this has been completed, activate either Word or Excel, go to the Edit, Paste Special command, and select the Paste Link option to paste the data as text. To copy a block of values, make sure you modify a table in Microsoft Project 2007 so the values you choose to copy are adjacent to one another, just as you copied from another application into Microsoft Project 2007. Choose the entire block and, as before, go to Edit, Paste Special and use the Paste Link command to enter the block of values into Word or Excel. A pasted block of data is treated as a single entity in both applications, and when you update the links in Microsoft Project 2007, all the values of the block are updated.

NOTE

> There can be formatting issues related to displaying the Microsoft Project 2007 data in other applications. For instance, the duration fields can display the duration in minutes, multiplied by 10 (so an hour appears as 600), and the work fields display the work as minutes, multiplied by 1,000 (so an hour appears as 60,000). These durations can also be considered text by other applications, since the unit can be copied with the value. The data should be processed after it is copied to provide a meaningful display for the users.

WORKING WITH OBJECTS

Microsoft uses the term *object* to represent data, usually a group of data or a special format for data, that has been formatted by another application. Objects are most frequently used to show graphical data, such as placing Excel charts, PowerPoint slides, sound files, video clips, or other graphics into Microsoft Project 2007. You can also use the Gantt Chart view or the Network Diagram view from Microsoft Project 2007 and place them into other applications.

When working with objects, it is common to refer to the application that generates an object as the *server* application, and the application into which the object has been pasted as the *client* application. The client document can also be known as the *container* document. These terms are important in the following discussions, where they should help clarify which application is being discussed.

PASTING OBJECTS

As with text data, you can copy data as an object from an external application and paste it as an object in Microsoft Project 2007 by using the Edit, Paste or Edit, Paste Special command. You could, for instance, paste an Excel chart into the Gantt Chart view. If you use the Paste Special command, the chart can be linked back to its server Excel document. As with linked text data, a linked object can be updated, either automatically or manually, depending on the settings used in the Links dialog box.

When the object is not linked, but placed permanently into a client document and cannot be updated, it is called an *embedded* object. An embedded object is stored in the client document, and because the format is foreign to the client application, any editing of the embedded object requires activating the server application. Once editing is finished and the server application is closed, the revised object remains in the client application.

Once an object has been pasted, you can move and resize it using Microsoft Project 2007, as if it were a piece of clip art. It is also possible to edit some object formats directly from within Microsoft Project 2007 by double-clicking on the object. For instance, if an Excel chart has been pasted in as a linked object, as shown in Figure 27.10, you can double-click on the object to open Excel for editing. When you close Excel and save any changes, the revised object will be visible in Microsoft Project 2007. If the chart in Figure 27.10 were embedded, instead of linked, double-clicking would open the object for editing, and Excel's menu bar and toolbars would be visible instead of Microsoft Project's menu bar and toolbars, as shown in Figure 27.11. You would still, however, be working within Microsoft Project 2007. Once you make your changes, click outside the object onto the Microsoft Project 2007 workspace to exit from editing mode, and return to Microsoft Project's menu bar and toolbars.

27

Source data for chart

Figure 27.10
You can use Microsoft Project 2007 data for each phase, paste-linked into an Excel worksheet, and that data can be used to create an Excel chart, which can be paste-linked back into Microsoft Project 2007 as an object on the Gantt Chart view.

Excel chart object

Figure 27.11
If you double-click on an embedded chart, it will be opened for editing within Project, but using the source application, such as Excel in this example.

Open Excel application for editing chart in Project

NOTE

> While in editing mode, you can switch from Microsoft Project 2007 to another applica-
> tion, and when you return your editing mode is still active so you can continue with your
> changes.

When you paste in a media object to Microsoft Project 2007, such as a video clip or sound
file into the Gantt Chart, it will show up as an icon, and you must double-click it to active
and run the media.

When Microsoft Project 2007 is a source or server, and you paste copies of data cells from
the Gantt Chart view table into another application document as text, every row of task
information will become a row of ordinary text in the document. If, however, you copy the
selection as an object, it will be displayed as a graphic figure in the client document.

Figure 27.12 shows how the same Microsoft Project 2007 task rows have been pasted as
both text and as a picture object into a Microsoft Word document. The task field text
appears as a simple tab-separated data in Word. The graphic of the tasks include the Gantt
Chart view table cells, plus the taskbars and the timescale above the taskbars. You can read
more about this in "Placing Objects into Other Applications," later in this chapter.

Figure 27.12
With Microsoft Word,
you can show the
same information as
both pasted text and
as a Microsoft Project
2007 image on the
same page of a docu-
ment.

Task data pasted as text

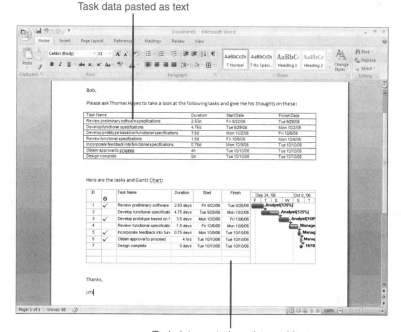

Task data pasted as picture object

INSERTING OBJECTS

To place objects into a client document, use the Insert, Objects command. This command inserts existing files that have been created by a server application into the client document. You have the choice of the object being linked or embedded.

With the Insert, Object command you can also open a server application from within the client document. This lets you create new embedded objects that exist only within the client document. You could, for instance, insert a new, blank Excel spreadsheet into a Microsoft Project 2007 document; whatever data you want to enter into the spreadsheet, you could do so using the Excel application's menu and toolbars. When you are finished, you can click on the Microsoft Project 2007 workspace in the background and the object will remain embedded in Microsoft Project 2007. The data only exists saved in the Microsoft Project 2007 document. You could also insert a Microsoft Project 2007 object into Word or Excel, such as a Gantt chart you want to update and use for multiple meetings. When you are finished updating, click outside the object, and it will remain embedded in the container document.

PLACING OBJECTS INTO MICROSOFT PROJECT 2007

You can paste or insert objects to Microsoft Project 2007 in four locations:

- The graphics area of the Gantt Chart view
- The Notes box of the Task, Resource, or Assignment Information Form view
- The special task Objects box of the Task Form view, or the resource Objects box of the Resource Form view
- The Header, Footer, or Legend area of a view's Page Format dialog box

PASTING OBJECTS IN THE GANTT CHART VIEW

The Gantt Chart view is the primary view when looking at a graphically depicted Microsoft Project 2007 file. You can enhance this view by pasting objects from other applications into the timescale area. Follow these steps to paste an object into the Gantt Chart view:

1. Activate the server application, then select the source data, copying it to the Clipboard using the Edit, Copy command.
2. Activate Microsoft Project 2007 (the client application) and open a Gantt Chart view.
3. Select Edit, Paste Special to open the Paste Special dialog box, as shown in Figure 27.13.
4. Select Paste if you want to embed the object, or Paste Link if you want to link it.

Figure 27.13
Use the Paste Special dialog box to embed or link objects into Microsoft Project 2007.

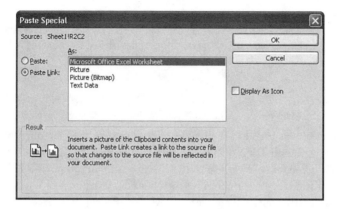

5. With the As list, you have the option to include the server application's name. You might also have the option called Picture. These choices will produce picture images that look similar. The server application's name option allows you to open the object in the server application, to edit or modify the object. With the Picture option, Microsoft Project 2007 will place a picture of the object into the document that cannot be edited with the client application. In short, select the server application's name if you want to be able to go back and edit the object in Microsoft Project 2007, or select Picture if you do not want it to be editable.

6. Click OK to paste the image into the document.

Once the object is in the Gantt Chart view, you can move and resize it as you like. To move it, simply click the object to select it, dragging it to a new position. To resize the object, select it and drag its resizing handles to change the size. If you want to remove the object, select it and press the Delete key.

TIP

When you resize a picture object, regardless of whether it is linked, you might cause the picture to appear distorted. This is because resizing can cause the horizontal and vertical dimensions to change proportionally relative to one another. To keep the dimensions in proportion, hold down the Shift key as you drag the object's corner handles.

CAUTION

Keep in mind that you cannot undo resizing or deleting of an object. Make sure to save your Microsoft Project 2007 document before you begin experimenting with either of these actions.

27

TIP

When you have more than one object placed on the Gantt Chart view, you can scroll through your objects quickly by using the Tab key. You can use the Tab key to select any other objects in that pane, one at a time.

INSERTING OBJECTS IN THE GANTT CHART VIEW

You saw the examples used in the previous section, where the data of an object was created as part of a server application document, then copied and pasted to the client application. Another option you can use is the Insert, Object command, to place a linked or embedded copy of an entire source document into the client document as an object. Keep in mind that embedding an entire source document into Microsoft Project 2007 will increase the Microsoft Project document's file size and your embedded document will be cut off from updates to the original source document.

Another option when using the Insert, Object command is that you can create an object without using an existing file. You could create a new object by using the formatting capabilities for server applications that support Microsoft OLE 2.0 or higher. You can open the server application's interface from within Project to create the new data. Once the server is closed, the object remains embedded in Project.

To insert an object, go to Insert, Object. Microsoft Project 2007 will open the Insert Object dialog box, as shown in Figure 27.14. Your default option button is Create New, which allows you to create a new, embedded object using one of the listed applications in the Object Type box. If the data has already been created and saved, select Create from File to insert a linked or embedded copy of the source data.

List of available server options

Figure 27.14
You have the option of creating an object from scratch within Microsoft Project 2007, using the Insert Object dialog box.

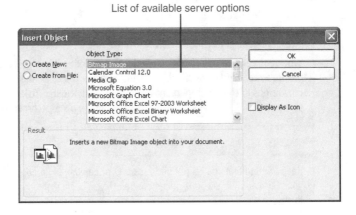

You could, for instance, embed in a new Excel object in the Gantt Chart view—a worksheet that shows budgeted (baseline) and current gross margin data for a project. You would follow these steps to create a new worksheet object:

1. Activate the Gantt Chart view in the top pane of the combination view.

2. Go to the Insert, Object command to open the Insert Object dialog box. It might take some time for this dialog box to appear, since Microsoft Project 2007 needs to prepare a list of all server applications on your system that support OLE 2.0 or higher.

3. Select Create New, which is the default.

4. Select which server application you want to use from the list in the Object Type list. In this case, you would select Microsoft Excel Worksheet.

5. Select the Display as Icon box if you want to see only an icon, instead of the worksheet object in the Gantt Chart view. Once the object is inserted, you can double-click the icon to show the object's contents. This is a good choice if you have little room for objects in the graphical area of your Gantt Chart view. In this case, use the check box.

> **TIP**
>
> It is usually a good idea to use Display as Icon when you are first inserting an object. With the Display as Icon option, Microsoft Project 2007 will open Excel into its own window, allowing you to enter and format your Excel data. You will also have full access to Excel's features and toolbars. Once the data has been entered and formatted, it is easy to convert the object to be shown as a mini-worksheet. If you decide not to use the Display as Icon option, the object will appear in a small window within the graphics area of the Gantt Chart view, making editing difficult. Not all of the Excel menu commands will be available either.

6. Click OK to insert your new object. If you selected the Display as Icon box, Microsoft Project 2007 will open an Excel window that you can use to create a worksheet.

7. You can now enter your data and edit and format the spreadsheet so that it will appear as you want in the Gantt Chart view.

8. Once your worksheet is finished, go to File, Close and Return to *filename* (where *filename* is the name of the Microsoft Project 2007 document in which you inserted the object). The icon for your object will now be displayed in the Gantt Chart view, as shown in Figure 27.15.

When you select the Display as Icon box, Microsoft Project 2007 will show you what that icon will look like in the small space directly under the Display as Icon check box. It is not always an icon; it is often a word, such as *Chart* or *Document*. You do, however, have the option of changing what the icon looks like if you do not like it or want it to stand out more. You can click on the Change Icon button, and the Change Icon dialog box will be pulled up. You can pick predesigned icons, or browse for a graphic to use, if you so choose.

27

Figure 27.15
You can display any data you want, such as relevant cost and gross margin data, on the Gantt Chart view. Here, the worksheet object has been shown as an icon.

An Excel chart object displayed as an icon

Once the object is embedded into Microsoft Project 2007, you can double-click it to open or edit the data; plus you can convert the object from an icon to a displayed worksheet instead.

Follow these steps to convert the object from icon to worksheet:

1. Select the object by clicking on it.
2. Go to Edit, Worksheet Object, Convert to open the Convert dialog box, as shown in Figure 27.16.

Figure 27.16
The Convert dialog box can be used to change the display of an object from an icon to a formatted data worksheet.

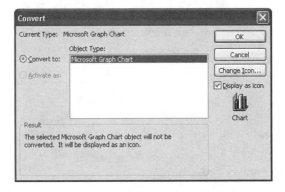

3. Clear the Display as Icon check box, and click OK. Your icon will now appear as a small worksheet, as you can see in Figure 27.17.

In the previous example, you created a new object and inserted it into the Gantt chart, using the Insert, Object command. If you have a preexisting file that you want to place into the Gantt Chart, simply follow these steps:

1. Activate the Gantt Chart view in the top pane of a combination window.
2. Go to Insert, Object to open the Insert Object dialog box.
3. Select the Create from File option. This will open a File text box and a Browse button, as shown in Figure 27.18.

Figure 27.17
Your icon from Figure 27.15 is now converted into a worksheet object, which now displays the relevant cost and gross margin data.

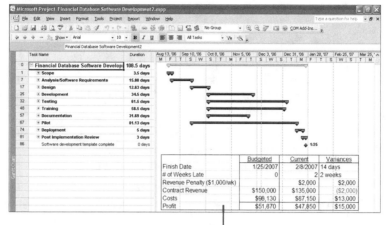

Excel workbook object displayed as a small worksheet

Figure 27.18
You can insert external document files as objects into Microsoft Project 2007 using the Insert Object dialog box.

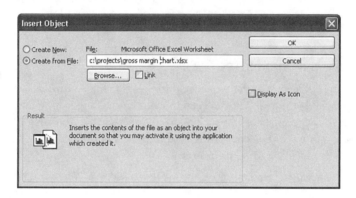

4. You can either enter the file's path name manually or use the Browse button to find and open the file.

5. Select the Link check box to insert a linked copy of the file's data. If you want to embed a copy that will not update, do not use the Link check box.

6. Choose the Display as Icon check box for the file to appear as an icon, instead of as a worksheet.

7. Click OK to create the object.

If you want to open or edit the object, first click on it. You will now find at the bottom of the Edit menu a submenu named for the object type. For instance, the submenu for an object that was originally a worksheet could be titled Worksheet Object, whereas a sound file might be Wave Sound Object. There will be one or more commands in the submenu, depending on the format of the object:

27

- **Edit**—With this command, you can open the server application to edit your object. Once you are finished, close the server application, and you will be returned to Microsoft Project 2007.

- **Open**—With this command, you can open text-based formats, such as worksheets or documents, for editing. If you have media object, this command will show a picture of the object in the sever application, or play a sound or video file, and so on. Most media objects cannot be opened for editing.

- **Play**—This command will only appear for some media objects, such as sound and video files. It will play the media data and then close the file. For most media objects, this will be the default action when double-clicking the icon.

- **Convert**—This command will only appear for some objects. You can use it to change the Display as Icon choice for the object, or change the format of the object itself.

NOTE

> Use the Edit, Links command to manage linked objects, as described earlier in this chapter, in the "Refreshing Linked Data in Microsoft Project 2007" section.

PLACING OBJECTS IN THE NOTES FIELD

You can place objects into the Notes field for assignments, individual tasks, or resources. The Notes field is a great place to keep track of links to supporting documents stored elsewhere on your computer or in your organization's network. You could, for instance, insert into a note a group of objects, shown as icons, that link to documents defining authorization, budget, and scope for your project.

→ For more information on placing objects into the Notes field, **see** "Inserting Object in Notes," **p. 181**.

PLACING OBJECTS IN THE TASK OR RESOURCE OBJECTS BOX

There are three standard task form views (the Task Form, the Task Details Form, and the Task Name Form) you can use to display an Objects box. An Objects box is a spot where you can place a data object you want to associate with a task—a specific place for objects. Likewise, there are two standard resource form views (the Resource Form and the Resource Name Form) that can also be used to display an Object box that you can associate with a resource. To access the Object box, right-click on a blank area of the Task Form and select it from the context menu.

→ For additional information about custom reports, **see** Chapter 20, "Creating and Customizing the Basic Reports," **p. 657**.

You can use either the Paste or Paste Special command to paste objects into an Object box. Unlike pasting notes, you can also paste links to objects by using the Paste Special command. In addition, you can use the Insert Object command to place linked or embedded objects into an Objects box.

As another option, Microsoft Project 2007 offers a task Objects field and a resource Objects field. When you display an Objects field in a table, it shows the number of objects stored in the Objects box for that task or resource. The Objects field's main use is in filters; you use it to identify tasks or resources that have objects in their Objects boxes. You can use the standard filters of Tasks with Attachments and Resources with Attachments when choosing which tasks or resources have an Objects field with a value of greater than zero, or a Notes field that contains text. You can also build a custom filter to show records that have objects stored in their Objects boxes.

→ For additional information about custom filters, **see** "Creating and Customizing Filters," **p. 785**.

In Figure 27.19, a Task Form view has been set up under the Gantt Chart view, with the Objects box shown in the details area. The previous example of the gross margin worksheet has been used as the display in the Objects box.

The Gantt Chart view table has been modified to show the Objects field. You can see that two objects are attached to this resource. To see the next object, you will need to use the scroll bar to scroll down.

Follow these steps to paste an object into the Objects field:

1. Go to the server application and select the object, and copy it into the Clipboard.
2. Activate Microsoft Project 2007, then open one of the task or resource form views, depending on what kind of record you are pasting your object into.
3. Go to Format, Details, Objects, or you can right-click anywhere outside a field box on the form, and select Objects from the shortcut menu.
4. Select the Objects field in the bottom of the form by clicking on it. A thick black border will appear around the field, letting you know it has been selected. You can see an example of that in Figure 27.20.
5. Go to Edit, Paste Special to open the Paste Special dialog box.
6. Select either Paste or Paste Link, depending on if you want to embed the item or link it.
7. Select the format option from the As list box.
8. Click OK to finish pasting the object.

If you wish to insert an object into the Objects box, choose the Objects box and go to Insert, Object to open the Insert Object dialog box. You can now use the dialog box options as mentioned previously for inserting an object into notes and in the Gantt Chart view.

You can also place multiple objects into the Objects box. The first object you paste or insert will appear first and is automatically selected. When you insert additional objects, Microsoft Project 2007 will place them below whichever one is selected, usually the first. Once a new object has been inserted, it is not automatically displayed or selected; you must scroll down to see the newly placed object. If you insert a second object, and do not scroll down and select it, when you insert a third it will be placed between the first and second. This will continue until you change which object is selected.

27

Number of objects in this Objects window

Figure 27.19
Microsoft Project 2007 presents objects that are attached to an individual task or resource in the Objects field.

Excel worksheet option displayed in Task Form view, with Objects details applied

Scroll to next object in the window

Black border indicates that the Objects pane is selected for pasting or inserting objects

Figure 27.20
Select the Objects field of the Task Form view, before pasting or inserting objects into it.

TIP

If you have an Objects box with multiple objects in it and would like to change the order in which they appear, use the Cut and Paste tools to move the objects around. Select which object you would like moved, and use the Edit, Cut (Ctrl+X) command. Next, choose which object you want your recently cut object to appear after, and use Edit, Paste or Paste Special. If the object you are moving is not formatted as a simple picture object, you must use the Paste Special command to retain its format.

TIP

The Objects box scroll bar does not scroll through a single object; instead, it jumps from object to object. So, if you have an item that is too large for the area it is displayed in, you will have to try another option to see it. You can increase the size of the form, or open it in the server application. You cannot, however, resize any objects that are pasted into the Objects box. If your object has been pasted as a picture, and you cannot see all of it, you will need to resize the picture with the object's server application, if possible.

To delete an object from the Objects box, simply select said object and press the Delete key, removing the object from your document.

PLACING OBJECTS IN HEADERS, FOOTERS, AND LEGENDS

You can customize your printed views and reports by placing graphics into the print header, footer, or legend area, such as your organization's logo or a symbol for the project. A Sailboat logo has been inserted into the left header in the Gantt Chart Page Setup dialog box, as shown in Figure 27.21. You can paste a picture or insert a graphic file to create the object in this context, but you can only embed it. It cannot be linked.

Inserted graphic

Figure 27.21
Objects such as company or project logos can be placed in headers, footers, and legends.

Inserted Object button

In order to place a graphic object into a view, or a report's header, footer or legend, you must first open the Page Setup dialog box for the view or report. If you want the object in the view, simply open the view and use the View, Header and Footer command. You can also go to the File, Page Setup command and click on the Header or Footer tab. Follow these steps, however, if you want to place a graphic object into a report:

1. Open the Reports dialog box by selecting Report, Reports.

2. Choose the Custom box, and click Select to open the Custom Reports dialog box, in which all of the reports are listed.

3. Choose which report you want to use in the Reports list, and click Setup.

NOTE
> You cannot define a legend for any report, and you cannot create a header or footer in the Project summary.

Once the Page Setup dialog box is active, you can embed pictures using these steps:

1. If you are copying a picture, choose your picture in its source application and use the Copy command to place it into the Clipboard.

   If you want to insert a graphic file, you should make sure to create a copy of the graphic sized appropriately for the report. Resizing pictures in the Page Setup dialog box can be difficult.

2. Choose the Header, Footer, or Legend tab, depending on where you want to place your graphic.

3. Choose the Left, Center, or Right tab to position your picture on the page, depending on your preference.

   On a legend, you can only customize the left portion area. Using the position tabs will determine the location of the graphic within that area.

4. When pasting a picture, right-click in the text box, below the alignment table, and use the Paste command from the shortcut menu (or Ctrl+V).

   If you are inserting a picture file, select the Insert Picture tool and find your file. Once that file is selected, click the Insert button to place your image on the tab.

TIP
> Although the Paste Special command might be available on the shortcut menu, and it might offer to paste an object in the server application's format, be cautious about using this option. Server-formatting objects can be unstable and can make the project file unstable as well. Your best bet is to only use the Paste command, and only use simple pictures, when pasting objects into headers, footers, and legends.

5. If you want to resize the object, select it to display the sizing handles and use them to change the object's size.

6. Once the picture has been embedded, you can click the OK button, or you can proceed with printing by clicking either the Print Preview or Print button.

PLACING OBJECTS INTO OTHER APPLICATIONS

Microsoft Project 2007 uses several different and distinctive graphic views that can be very effective when pasted into other applications. You can copy any of the following views:

- All of the Gantt Chart views
- The Network Diagram and Detailed Network Diagram views
- The Calendar view
- The Task Usage and Resource Usage views
- The Resource Graph view
- The Calendar view
- Any of the sheet views, such as the Task Sheet or Resource Sheet view

NOTE

> You cannot use Microsoft Project 2007 to copy the Relationship Diagram view or any of the form views. If you want a copy of these views, you must use either the Windows Print Screen command or a third-party screen capture program.

Most of these views can be copied by using the Edit, Copy command or Copy Picture button in the Standard toolbar. In the case of the Gantt Chart view, you will need to select the rows of tasks you want to copy and then use the Edit, Copy Task command. If you wish to paste a linked object into another application, or embed a Microsoft Project 2007 object that can be edited, you have to use the Copy command. The Copy Picture command will only let you paste an unlinked picture. You can see from the following descriptions which results you will get when using the different commands:

- To paste a static, unlinked picture object or to create a GIF file to include on a web page, use the Copy Picture command. This allows you to precisely control the date range to include timescale views, and you can resize easily without seriously distorting the fonts.

- To paste an object that is linked to the source document in Microsoft Project 2007, use the Copy (or Copy Task for the Gantt chart) command. You can paste the object as a linked picture object, or a linked Microsoft Project 2007 object. There is little difference between these two options. You can update both to show changes in the timescale data for any tasks included in the original picture, and you can double-click either type of object to open the Microsoft Project 2007 document that is the source of the link. There are, however, limitations to this object type:

27

- You cannot change the tasks or resources that have been included in the original picture without deleting the object and starting over.

- You have limited control over the date range included, if the view contains a timescale. The Gantt Chart view, in particular, uses graphic elements that extend before and after the start and finish dates for tasks, such as summary task bars, linking lines, and bar text. These items often appear truncated in the final object.

- To have total control over what is being displayed in the object, you should capture the view using the Copy command, and paste it as an unlinked Microsoft Project 2007 object. Your data cannot be updated, and the entire project is embedded into the other application, which will increase the file size dramatically. However, you will have total control over what is displayed in the object image. You can even change the view, change the formats, and use the filters.

USING THE COPY PICTURE COMMAND TO COPY A VIEW

The Copy Picture command is the best way to prepare a static picture object for inserting into other applications. It is also the only way to create a GIF format for use with web browsers. You can find the Copy Picture button on the Standard toolbar. If you cannot find it on the Standard toolbar, you might need to click on the Toolbar Options button at the end of the Standard toolbar to either expand the toolbar into two rows or select the Copy Picture icon from one of the hidden icons. There is no corresponding menu command for the Copy Picture button.

→ For additional information about modifying toolbars, **see** "Customizing Toolbars," **p. 817**.

When preparing the view in Microsoft Project 2007 before making a copy, you have several options in the Copy Picture dialog box that offer control over what will be included in the image. Use these guidelines when you are arranging to copy a view:

- It is best to set up whatever view you plan to copy so that it is contained in one screen. Microsoft Project 2007 allows you to capture larger areas, but it becomes more difficult to get the results you want as the image gets larger.

- If your view includes a table, you should prepare the columns that are displayed and the rows that need to be selected. You can use any of these techniques to prepare a table:

  - Only completely visible columns are included in the picture. You should, therefore, arrange the display of columns as you want them to appear in the picture. Also, be sure that the vertical split bar is not covering up any part of the rightmost column you want included in the picture.

  - You have the option with the Copy Picture dialog box to include the rows that are visible on the screen, or only the rows you have previously selected. To include selected rows, click at least one cell in each row you want included. If you choose nonadjacent rows, your image will only contain the rows you have selected.

  - If you choose a summary task row, its subtasks will not be included in the image. They have to be selected separately as well.

- If your view has a timescale, you will get your best results by compressing the date range you want to include in the picture onto no more than two or three screens. You can create a picture that includes more screens of the timescale if you want. However, the printed image can be no wider than 22 inches. You will need to zoom out the timescale if you want to get a very large date range into the image successfully.

- When copying the Task Usage or Resource Usage view, make sure your cells in the grid are at least 100% of their normal size. If not, you may see many cells filled with pound symbols (#), indicating the data cannot be displayed, even though you can see the values on the screen. If you need to fix the cell size, go to Format, Timescale, and you can set the value in the Size box to 100% or greater.

- When you are copying the Calendar view, one of the Network Diagram views, or the Resource Graph view, Microsoft Project 2007 will include only the current screen in the picture. You will need to prepare the display to fit onto one screen before you capture your picture.

The Copy Picture dialog box, as shown in Figure 27.22, offers options that vary depending on the view you are copying. With all views, you have choices about the format in which the picture is rendered, including the following:

Figure 27.22
The Copy Picture dialog box can be used to tailor the image you copy, allowing you to set up what it includes and how it is rendered.

- Select the For Screen option if you want to paste the picture into another application, to simply be viewed onscreen.

- Select the For Printer option if you want to paste your picture into an application for printing. The format will be determined by the printer you have selected in Microsoft Project 2007 at the time you save the picture. If you change printers before you print, you should recopy the picture.

- Select the To GIF Image File option if you want to use the picture in a web page. Your image will be saved in a GIF-format file that most web browsers can display. You will need to enter the path and filename for the file being created. You can use the Browse button to search the directory structure or search for a filename you might be replacing.

If the view you are copying included a table, such as a Gantt Chart view or a Task or Resource Sheet view, you have the choice to include the following:

- **Rows on Screen**—Only the rows that are visible when you actually take the picture
- **Selected Rows**—Only the rows you have selected at least one or more cells in, before using the Copy Picture command

If your view contains a timescale, such as the Gantt Chart view or the Task or Resource Usage view, you have a choice of the following:

- You can use the dates shown on screen, meaning that you must arrange the timescale onscreen as you want it to appear in the picture, and then capture only that range of dates in your picture.
- You can use a range of dates you specify in the From and To date boxes.

TIP

> If you are selecting a date range with the Gantt Chart view, you should include at least one time unit before the From data, and several after the To date. Many task bars have graphic elements that extend beyond the start and finish dates of the task. This is especially true for bar text, such as resource names, that are displayed to the right of the task bar. If you do not add these extra time units to the date range, the data in your picture might appear to be cut off.

Use these steps to copy a view to the Clipboard:

1. Use the guidelines listed earlier in this section to set up the view you want to copy.
2. Use the Copy Picture button on the Standard toolbar to open the Copy Picture dialog box, as shown in Figure 27.22.
3. Select either For Screen, For Printer, or To GIF Image File. If you use To GIF Image File, you will need to supply the path and filename for the GIF file in the text box.
4. If you are taking a picture of a table display, select either Rows on Screen or Selected Rows.
5. If there is a timescale in the display, either choose As Shown on Screen or fill in the From and To dates. You should add an appropriate number of time units before the From and after the To selections to prevent your image from being incorrectly cropped.
6. Click OK to save your picture.

The maximum size for a picture is 22 inches by 22 inches when using the For Screen or For Printer option. If the number of tasks you have selected or the date range specified for the timescale cause the picture to be greater than 22 inches in either direction, Microsoft Project 2007 will alert you with the Copy Picture Options dialog box, as shown in Figure 27.23. If, however, you are using the To GIF image file option, you can create a GIF image up to 100 inches by 100 inches. A GIF image, however, is static, and best used for a website. When copying and pasting images to be placed in other applications, use the For screen option.

Figure 27.23
If your picture exceeds 22 inches in either dimension, you must decide what you wish to do with it using the Copy Picture Options dialog box.

You have the following options with the Copy Picture Options dialog box:

- Select the Keep the Selected Range option if you want to use the picture anyway, although you might experience some distortion.

- Select the Zoom Out the Timescale So the Picture Can Fit option to have Microsoft Project 2007 automatically change the timescale units, allowing the date range to fit within the maximum dimensions.

- Select the Scale the Picture to 22 Inches in Width option, and Microsoft Project 2007 will compress the date range to fit within 22 inches, without changing the timescale units. You can also choose the Lock Aspect Ratio check box if you want to keep the proportions intact during the scaling.

- Select the Truncate the Picture to 22 Inches in Width option if you want Project to use only the date range and rows in the table that fit.

- Select Cancel if you want to begin the Copy Picture command over.

You will get the best picture, in most cases, if you select Cancel and go back and manually adjust the timescale so the picture will fit. You might save a little time by selecting the Zoom Out the Timescale So the Picture Can Fit option and then pasting the picture to see what timescale unit is needed. You can manually zoom out the actual timescale when you capture the picture again.

When you open the application where you plan to paste your picture, select the location of the picture and use the Edit, Paste command (or Ctrl+V). You will have the Paste Special command available, but it will produce the same end result—pasting the picture as a picture object.

The object will now appear with a border and resizing handles. You can change the height and width proportionally by using the corner handles.

USING THE COPY PICTURE TO OFFICE WIZARD

Another option for copying a picture of your project data into an Office document is using the Copy Picture to Office Wizard. You can open the wizard from the Analysis toolbar; go to View, Toolbars, Analysis. You can see the wizard's welcome page and the Analysis toolbar in Figure 27.24.

27

If you go to open the Analysis toolbar and find that it is not there, you will probably need to reset Project to turn the Analysis toolbar on. Follow these steps to turn the toolbar back on so you can access the Copy Picture to Office Wizard:

1. Open the Customize dialog box by selecting View, Toolbars, Customize.
2. Select the Commands tab.
3. Select All Commands in the Categories box.
4. In the Commands box, click on the ComAddInsDialog command. You will need to drag it to a toolbar currently on display, such as the Standard toolbar.
5. Close the Customize dialog box.
6. Click the COM Add-Ins button you added. This will open the COM Add-Ins dialog box.
7. Clear the check boxes in the COM Add-Ins dialog box (Adjust Dates, Compare Project Versions Utility, Copy Picture to Office, PERT Analysis). Click OK to close the dialog box.
8. Click on the COM Add-Ins button again to reopen the COM Add-Ins dialog box.
9. Select all of the check boxes again, thus reactivating them. Click OK to close the dialog box.

You can now go to the View, Toolbars and select the Analysis toolbar.

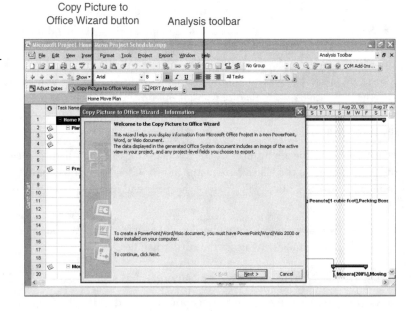

Figure 27.24
You can present project data very easily using the Copy Picture to Office Wizard.

The wizard allows you to copy a picture of the Gantt Chart view into another Microsoft
Office application, such as Word, Excel, or PowerPoint. In the wizard, specify the outline
level you want to detail your project at, as shown in Figure 27.25. Keeping your original
outline level will use the current view to decide if each summary task is collapsed or
expanded.

Figure 27.25
You can select which
outline level you want
to use with the Copy
Picture to Office
Wizard.

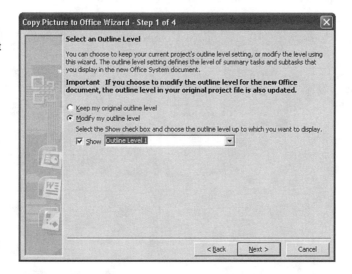

The second screen of the wizard allows you to specify the rows and timescale limits of your
image, as shown in Figure 27.26. You can either base your image on Rows on Screen,
Selected Rows in View, or All Rows in View. As with the Copy Picture command, discussed
earlier in this chapter, the image is limited to a height and width of 22 inches.

Figure 27.26
You can use the Copy
Picture to Office
Wizard to set your
dimensional parame-
ters.

27

The third step of the Copy Picture to Office Wizard lets you choose your target Office application—PowerPoint, Word, or Visio—as shown in Figure 27.27. Your client application must be Office 2000 or later compatible. If you are sending your picture to Word or Visio, you can choose a portrait or landscape orientation. The Preview button opens a GIF image in Internet Explorer, allowing you to see how your picture will turn out. You can save this GIF by right-clicking on it and selecting Save Picture As.

Figure 27.27
The Copy Picture to Office Wizard gives you a couple options when you are ready to save your picture.

In the last step, you can export project-level data into a table that will be embedded into the same document as your picture, as shown in Figure 27.28. Some of the fields have been pre-selected, such as Copy, Current Date, and Title. Project will use the current view to select which task-level fields to include in the picture. It will only include full columns, as with a printout or with the Copy Picture command.

Figure 27.28
You can select the project-level fields to include in the new document with the Copy Picture to Office Wizard.

Figure 27.29 displays the results of using the Copy Picture to Office Wizard, after importing the picture into PowerPoint. You can see the project-level information that has been included with the table made up of individual data cells, and you can modify the contents. The Microsoft Project 2007 picture placed in PowerPoint is a graphic, and you can modify it the same way you would with any other graphic, including cropping, resizing, rotating, and modifying brightness and contrast.

Figure 27.29
This is the result of using the Copy Picture to Office Wizard to copy a picture into PowerPoint.

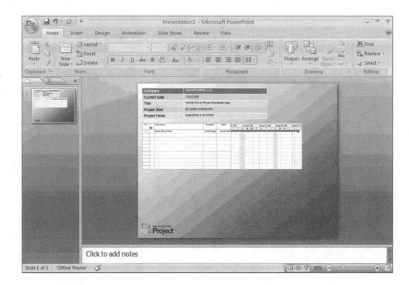

CONSULTANTS' TIPS

This chapter has discussed some excellent Copy/Paste functionality for dealing with data, objects, and so on, in Microsoft Project 2007 and other applications; however, a word of caution is in order. As was previously mentioned, copying and pasting all of this information from one application to another can result in the creation of very large files. Imagine a Microsoft Project 2007 file that has an embedded logo in each of its reports, an Excel chart embedded in the Gantt view, and several Word documents embedded into the Notes field of one or more tasks. Depending on the choices made when creating these embedded objects and the size of the original files, a .mpp's file size could easily grow very large, very quickly.

Creating the objects as links can be a viable alternative that results in a smaller-sized file, with the caveat that you need to be diligent about maintaining the links. For instance, what happens if you decide to reorganize your computer's Windows folder structure and inadvertently move a document that you created a link to in a .mpp file?

These techniques do work effectively and you should use them, but just make sure to exercise caution and be aware of the potential consequences with this great functionality.

27

INDEX

How can we make this index more useful? Email us at indexes@quepublishing.com

BOOKS ONLINE
ENABLED

THIS BOOK IS SAFARI ENABLED

INCLUDES FREE 45-DAY ACCESS TO THE ONLINE EDITION

The Safari® Enabled icon on the cover of your favorite technology book means the book is available through Safari Bookshelf. When you buy this book, you get free access to the online edition for 45 days.

Safari Bookshelf is an electronic reference library that lets you easily search thousands of technical books, find code samples, download chapters, and access technical information whenever and wherever you need it.

TO GAIN 45-DAY SAFARI ENABLED ACCESS TO THIS BOOK:

- Go to **http://www.quepublishing.com/safarienabled**
- Complete the brief registration form
- Enter the coupon code found in the front of this book on the "Copyright" page

If you have difficulty registering on Safari Bookshelf or accessing the online edition, please e-mail customer-service@safaribooksonline.com.

QuantumPM
It's the way you work

Thank You for buying our book! We have shared project management and planning expertise gained from hundreds of customer engagements in this book. We hope you enjoy it.

ENTER:
QPMBOOK as the promotion code when you purchase **WBS *Director***
online and receive a **DISCOUNT** on your purchase (discounted licenses are limited).
Visit QuantumPM book community page
www.quantumpm.com/QPMBooks.aspx
for updates on best practice guidance and
additional material.

Visit QuantumPM, LLC website at **www.quantumpm.com** for information about our line of products and solutions that support the way you work!

Microsoft Office Project Desktop add-ins:

QPM Schedule *Auditor* - Check your project schedule in minutes instead of hours with 17 out-of-the-box checks.
Expand them with your own standards.

WBS *Director* - Plan your project scope before you schedule. Guard your project scope during execution. A unique merging of two best practices into one!

Earned Value *Manager* - S-curves, control accounts, financial integration, and CPR reports! A robust extension of WBS Director, supporting EVM novices and practitioners alike.

303.699.2334
9085 E. Mineral Circle Suite 235
Centennial, CO 80112

info@quantumpm.com